Britain in the Twentieth Century

Britain in the Twentieth Century is a new approach to teaching and learning twentieth-century British history at A level. It meets the needs of teachers and students studying for today's revised AS and A2-level exams.

In a unique style, *Britain in the Twentieth Century* focuses on the key topics within the period. Each topic is then comprehensively explored to provide background, essay writing advice and examples, source work and historical skills.

From 1900 to the new millennium, the key topics featured include:

*   Britain in a New Century, 1900–1914
*   The First World War and its Impact
*   Inter-war Domestic Problems
*   British Foreign Policy, 1919–1939
*   Britain and the Second World War
*   Social and Economic Change, 1945–1979

Using essay styles and source exercises from each of the exam boards, AQA, Edexcel and OCR, this book is an essential text for students and teachers.

Ian Cawood is Senior Lecturer in History at Newman College of Higher Education, Birmingham and author, with David McKinnon-Bell, of *The First World War*.

Spotlight History

Ian Cawood

Britain in the Twentieth Century

Routledge
Taylor & Francis Group

LONDON AND NEW YORK

First published 2004 by Routledge
11 New Fetter Lane, London EC4P 4EE

Simultaneously published in the USA and Canada
by Routledge
29 West 35th Street, New York, NY 10001

Routledge is an imprint of the Taylor and Francis Group

© 2004 Ian Cawood

Typeset in Minion and Helvetica Neue Light by
Florence Production Ltd, Stoodleigh, Devon
Printed and bound in Great Britain by
St Edmundsbury Press, Bury St Edmunds, Suffolk

British Library Cataloguing in Publication Data
A catalogue record for this book is available from the British Library

Library of Congress Cataloging in Publication Data
Cawood, Ian.
    Britain in the twentieth century / Ian Cawood
        p. cm. – (Spotlight history)
    Includes bibliographical references and index.
    Contents: Introduction to Britain in the twentieth century – Britain in
    a new century, 1900–1914 – The impact of the First World War,
    1914–1918 – Inter-war domestic problems, 1918–1939 – British foreign
    policy between the wars, 1918–1939 – Britain and the Second World
    War, 1939–1945 – The age of consensus: domestic affairs, 1945–1979 –
    The wind of change: foreign and colonial policy, 1945–1979 – Social
    and economic change, 1945–1979 – Towards the millennium
    1979–2000 – Conclusion: end of the period survey.
    (alk paper)
        1. Great Britain – History – 20th century [1. Great Britain – History
    – 20th century.]   I. Title: Britain in the 20th century.
    II. Title.   III. Series
        DA566.C39   2003
    941.082–dc21   2003007321

ISBN 0–415–25456–6 (hbk)
ISBN 0–415–25457–4 (pbk)

Contents

Illustrations

Figures

Tables

Abbreviations

ABCA	Army Bureau of Current Affairs
ANZAC	Australia and New Zealand Army Corps
BCP	British Communist Party
BEF	British Expeditionary Force
BOAC	British Overseas Air Corporation
BUF	British Union of Fascists
CAP	Common Agricultural Policy
CIGS	Chief of the Imperial General Staff
ECSC	European Coal and Steel Community
EEA	European Economic Area
EEC	European Economic Community
EFTA	European Free Trade Association
EMU	European Monetary Union
ERM	Economic Exchange Rate Mechanism
GDP	Gross Domestic Product
GNP	Gross National Product
ILP	Independent Labour Party
IMF	International Monetary Fund
INLA	Irish National Liberation Army
IRA	Irish Republican Army
IRB	Irish Republican Brotherhood
LEA	Local Education Authority
LRC	Labour Representation Committee
NATO	North Atlantic Treaty Organisation
NEC	National Executive Committee
NCB	National Coal Board
NICRA	Northern Ireland Civil Rights Association
NTW	National Transport Workers
NUR	National Union of Railway Workers
NUWSS	National Union of Women's Suffrage Societies
OMOV	One Man One Vote
RAF	Royal Air Force
RPI	Retail Price Index
RUC	Royal Ulster Constabulary
SDI	Strategic Defence Initiative
SDP	Social Democratic Party
TGWU	Transport and General Workers Union
TUC	Trade Union Congress
UDC	Ulster Defence Constabulary
UDI	Unilateral Declaration of Independence
WEU	West European Union
WLA	Women's Land Army
WSPU	Women's Social and Political Union
WVS	Women's Volunteer Service

Acknowledgements

The author and publishers would like to thank the following for permission to reproduce material:

Mary Evans Picture Library (illustrations 1.1, 1.2a, 1.2b, 1.3, 2.1, 3.3, 3.4, 3.5, 3.6, 3.7, 3.8, 5.2a, 5.2b); Atlantic Syndication/Centre for the Study of Cartoons, University of Kent (illustrations 4.1, 5.1); *British Political History, 1867–2001*, Malcolm Pearce and Geoffrey Stewart, 1992, Routledge (illustrations 2.2, 6.4); *Dent Atlas of British History*, Martin Gilbert, 1993 (illustration 2.4); *The Routledge Atlas of the First World War*, Martin Gilbert, 2002, Routledge (illustration 3.1 and 3.2); *A Social History of England, 1851–1990*, François Bedarida, 1991, Routledge (illustration 4.2); Christopher Thorne, *The Approach of War 1938–39*, 1968, Macmillan, reproduced with permission of Palgrave Macmillan (illustration 5.3); Imperial War Museum, London (illustration 6.2); Punch, Ltd (illustration 7.1); Express Newspapers/The Centre for the Study of Cartoons, University of Kent (illustration 8.2); Bettmann/CORBIS (illustration 9.2); HMSO Labour Force Surveys 1987–9, OPCS 1991, Crown copyright material is reproduced with the permission of the Controller of HMSO and the Queen's Printer for Scotland (illustration 9.1); J. Brown and W.R. Louis, 1999, *The Oxford History of the British Empire, Vol. IV: The Twentieth Century*, map 30.1 'The Commonwealth in 1998', reprinted by permission of Oxford University Press (illustration 10.1). Neville Elder/CORBIS SYGMA (illustration 10.2); TBWA/London for The Labour Party (illustration 10.3); Tim Page/CORBIS (illustration 10.4); The Sun/NI Syndication (illustration 10.5).

While every effort has been made to trace and acknowledge ownership of copyright material used in this volume, the publishers will be glad to make suitable arrangements with any copyright holders whom it has not been possible to contact.

Series Introduction

This aim of this book is to help prepare you for the papers in AS History. It is written very much with the AS specifications in mind, although it is clearly desirable to use other books as well. It is also hoped that the advice given in this book will be valuable to students preparing for courses other than AS.

Each chapter is divided into standard parts, the purpose of which is to combine essential knowledge and the various skills necessary to achieve the highest grade in line with the AS specifications.

Part of the chapter	Purpose	Method
Part 1: Historical background	To provide the basic, factual background and issues related to each topic. This may also be relevant to some questions of the simpler format.	The factual narrative is structured to include all the key themes. A chronological summary is also provided to give perspective at a glance.
Part 2: Essays	To provide worked answers to the major aspects of each topic. These provide examples of interpretation and factual support.	The wording of the question varies to allow for different types of examination response. Further questions are provided for term-work and examination practice; these can be prepared through the further reading recommended.
Part 3: Source analysis	To provide a selection of some of the key sources – primary and secondary – for each topic and to examine the different types of questions which can be asked about these.	Each set of sources has two sets of questions: one with worked examples and one without. The worked examples are accompanied by a brief explanation of the approach used. The questions without worked examples allow for class discussion or for individual practice.
Part 4: Historical skills	To provide some suggestions about how the topic can be used as a focus for selected skills not already covered in Parts 2 and 3.	The types of skills covered vary from chapter to chapter: they include discussion and presentation.

The rest of this general introduction deals with essays, source analysis, and key skills as general concepts and briefly explains the essential meaning of each. The explanations are developed in each chapter by the use of specific examples.

Part 1: Historical background

A good understanding of the topic in each chapter is essential before any meaningful analysis can be done. This involves three main approaches.

Type of approach:	Reason for this:	How it is accomplished:
1. Outline perspective	An ability to visualise the structure of the topic covered in the chapter and the way in which components of the topic fit together.	Through the chronological summary, the headings and sub-headings, and the introductory paragraphs of each section.
2. Knowledge in depth	An ability to focus on parts of the topic in depth.	Through careful and systematic development of details. These are grouped within an overall structure.
3. Integrating perspective and depth	An ability to combine the overall perspective with a focus on specific selected details.	By relating the details to the interpretations in the essays.

Part 2: Essays

What is an essay?

An essay is a formal attempt to answer a question or to provide a solution to a problem; the term derives from the French '*essayer*' and the Latin '*exigere*', the latter meaning 'to weigh'. The better the attempt, the higher the mark will be. There is usually no right or wrong solution. But there can be a solution which is presented well or badly, or which makes good or poor use of supporting material.

An essay should always be written in full sentences and paragraphs and should not normally include notes or bullet points. Appropriate lengths vary considerably, but some idea can be gained by the worked answers in Part 2 of each chapter. Relevance is vital throughout. This means keeping exactly to the confines of the question asked. The answer should be direct and should start within the first sentence or two. You should also keep the question in mind throughout the essay, answer all parts of it and include nothing which is not relevant to it. Think in terms of '*The question, the whole question and nothing but the question*'.

Instruction	Meaning of instruction	Examples
Outline . . . Describe . . .	Provide a coherent summary of the topic or issue in the question. It is important to include at least some specific factual references. ('Outline', does not mean 'be vague about'.) This type of instruction is less common than the others and, if it does appear, is more likely as a short question.	pages 33, 35, 38, 70, 164, 166, 221, 259, 390, 395
Examine . . . Why. . .? Explain why . . .	The, emphasis switches from 'describing' to 'providing reasons for'. This means looking at the question as a problem to be solved by a direct answer based on an argument which selects relevant factual information to support it.	pages 25, 27, 30, 33, 35, 38, 40, 80, 110, 115, 119, 164, 166, 170, 172, 174, 176, 221, 258, 261, 298, 336, 339, 340, 390, 394, 398
Identify . . . and explain TWO . . .	In addition to the previous instruction, this involves choosing two areas to 'explain'. Make sure that they are relevant to the question and that they can both act as a base for argument. This is common as a second question in a two-part structure.	pages 256, 398
Assess . . . To what event . . . ? How far . . . ? How far do you agree . . . ? How valid is the view that . . . ? How successful was . . . ? How serious were . . . ? How important was . . . ? With what justification . . . ?	This group of instructions involves more directly the notion of 'weighing'. It is therefore essential to have a clear idea of the 'extent' to which you 'agree' with the proposition put in the rest of the question. The extremes are 'entirely' or 'not at all'. If you adopt one of these, you need to explain why the alternative is not acceptable. More likely are 'to a very limited extent' or 'to a large extent, but not entirely.' In 'weighing' two arguments you need to explain: why one is 'heavier' or 'lighter' than the other. In terms of style, it is better to avoid using 'I' in the answer even if there is a 'you' in the question.	pages 24, 27, 40, 68, 76, 80, 117, 162, 168, 177, 213, 216, 223, 224, 252, 259, 332, 334, 336, 388
Compare . . . Compare and contrast . . . Compare the importance of three reasons . . . Assess the relative	The approach will involve the process of 'weighing', as with the previous set of questions. There are, however, two or more specific items to 'weigh'. These may be policies, or they may be arguments	pages 42, 115, 174, 256, 336, 340, 392

importance of . . .
How similar were . . .?
How different were . . . ?

about policies. They may be named in the question, or you may be asked to select your own. Whatever the case, you need to consider the two against each other; at all costs avoid a description of the two separately. 'Compare and contrast' (or 'compare' by itself) involves finding similarities and differences between items, as do 'how similar were' and and 'how different were'.

Argument and support

Since most essays involve an attempt to solve a problem, the solution should be clearly presented and well supported. The structure should be argument backed up by factual examples. This is much more effective than factual narrative followed by deduction. For most types of question you should argue then support; do not *narrate then deduce*.

Appropriate essay technique

Argument
Factual detail supporting the argument

Inappropriate essay technique

Narrative
Argument deducted from narrative

To become accustomed to writing in this way it can be helpful to outline or highlight *argument* in red and *factual detail supporting the argument* in blue; there will, of course, be some overlapping between the two. For each issue covered in the essay the red should come *before* the blue.

Stages in the essay

Stages	Appropriate development
Introduction	Mostly argument: considering the meaning of the question and offering an outline answer without detail.
Each subsequent paragraph	A part of or stage in the argument. The first sentence of each paragraph is based on argument. The rest consists of argument supported by factual detail. It should not normally be factual detail followed by deduction.
Conclusion	Need not repeat the arguments already provided, but may pull together any threads. The final sentence should be a generalisation. Never write 'unfinished'.

The introductory paragraph is vital since it will usually provide the direction for the rest of the essay; it will also provide the initial impression for the person reading or marking it. It should be a single paragraph and of immediate relevance to the question rather than leading gradually to the point. It should be largely argument, attempting to consider *all* the key words and concepts in the question and to provide a brief outline answer to it. This can then be developed in the rest of the essay. All this means that the introductory paragraph can and should be quite short.

The main section of the essay (about 90 per cent) will consist of several paragraphs that will develop the issues raised in the introduction. Ideally, each paragraph should start with a stage in the argument, with the rest of the paragraph comprising a combination of the argument in more detail and relevant factual support. Paragraphs therefore need to be seen as units within the answer. The reason for starting another paragraph is usually to move on to another unit. A sequence of very short paragraphs usually shows a disjointed argument, and a complete absence of paragraphs makes it difficult to follow the stages in the argument at all.

It is important to have some sort of conclusion and not to stop suddenly. This should round the essay off by pulling threads together and giving a final assessment in any 'to what extent?' essays. It might also be a fitting place for a quotation, especially one which complements or contradicts any quotation included in the question. Never write 'unfinished'; in the event of mistiming, use a rounding off sentence rather than a full conclusion.

The different styles of essay question

The examining boards provide differing essay styles, which are reflected in the various chapters.

Board	Style of essay question, choice and time allowed	Example of style of essay question
OCR	One-part essay question in 45-minutes, testing all essay skills. (90)	How serious was the impact of the Second World War on the British Empire? (90)
AQA	Brief quotation, followed by three-part essay question in 60 minutes, testing: (a) Contextual knowledge (3) (b) Background knowledge (7) (c) Interpretation, discussion (15)	'The great social revolution of the past fifteen years may not be the one which redivided wealth amongst adults in the Welfare State, but the one that has given teenagers economic power' (Colin MacInnes, 1958) (a) Explain the reference to the Welfare State. (3) (b) Why had teenagers gained economic power by the late 1950s? (7) (c) Did the discovery of the teenager amount to a 'great social revolution'? (15)
Edexcel	Two-part essay in 60 minutes, testing: (a) Knowledge of issues. (30) (b) Causation. (30)	(a) Explain why Britain did not join the EEC in 1957. (30) (b) Why was Britain unable to become a member of the EEC until 1973? (30)

📖 Part 3: Source analysis

Questions are set on primary sources, secondary sources or both. There are different styles of source-based questions (see p. xix). Despite contrasts in wording, however, they do have certain common features (see below).

Type of question	Examples of question structure	General advice on the answer
The source used for information and inference	• What can you learn from this Source about . . .? • What evidence is there in Source 1 to suggest that . . .?	Identify implications as well as information. This means inferring, not describing.
The source used as a stimulus for further knowledge. Usually this means explaining a particular sentence or phrase in the source: this will involve further material outside the source.	• Using Source A and your own knowledge, explain the meaning of '. . .' [a phrase in quotation marks]. • Using your own knowledge, explain briefly, why '. . .' [an event or development in quotation marks].	Identify precisely what is required and confine the use of 'your own knowledge' to explain the words in the quotation marks. This will, however, need accurate detail rather than vague generalisation.
Questions on a source's 'usefulness' and 'reliability'.	• How useful is Source A about . . . ? • How reliable is Source A about . . .? • How useful are these Sources to the historian studying . . . ?	For usefulness distinguish between internal criteria (i.e. content) and external criteria (i.e. the type of source). Reliability can also be assessed by referring to whether the content is accurate and the circumstances in which the source was produced. A source may be unreliable but still useful.
Questions asking for comparisons between sources. These may concern similarities, or differences, or both. They may involve an explanation of the reasons for similarities or differences.	• Compare . . . according to Sources A and B. • How would you explain the differences? • What evidence in Source 1 supports the view in Source 5 that . . . ? • Explain how the judgement in Source A challenges the judgement in Source C that . . .	'Compare' or 'compare and contrast' mean finding similarities and differences. These may involve details or general arguments. In either case precise references are needed, using brief quotations from the sources. Reasons for differences in the content of sources usually involve a comment on the differences in the type of source.

Questions which provide a viewpoint that needs to be tested against the sources and against additional knowledge beyond the sources.

- Use Sources A to D, and your own knowledge, to explain whether the view that '. . .' is accurate.
- Study Sources A, B and C and use your own knowledge. How important . . .
- Refer to Sources A, B and C and use your own knowledge. Explain . . .
- Do you agree that '. . .' Explain your answer, using the sources and your own knowledge.

The answer needs two dimensions.

- The content and your own knowledge of the sources should be 'used' to test the viewpoint in the question. At the same time, the reliability of this content should be briefly assessed: does the source apparently support . . . and does it really support . . .?
- 'Own knowledge' should have the same amount of time and space as the 'use of sources' and should include material beyond the sources.

As with the essays, the Boards have different styles of questions on sources, even though they are testing very much the same skills.

Board	Style of source-based questions and time allowed	Example of style of source-based question
OCR	4 primary sources, 3 questions in 60 minutes (a) Explanation of context of an issue mentioned in a source. (20) (b) Comparison between sources. (40) (c) Testing a viewpoint against all the sources and own knowledge.(60)	(a) Study Source A. From this source, and from your own knowledge, explain . . . (20) (b) Study Sources B and C. Compare . . . according to Sources B and C and explain the difference. (40) (c) Use all the Sources. Use all the sources and your knowledge to explain . . . (60) Total (120)
AQA	1 primary source, 2 secondary sources; 3 questions in 45 minutes. (a) Explanation of context of an issue mentioned in a source. (3) (b) Comparison between sources. (7) (c) Explanation of importance of issue 'in the relation to other matters'; use of sources and own knowledge. (15)	(a) Study Source A. Using your own knowledge, explain briefly . . . (3) (b) Study sources B and C. With reference to your own knowledge, explain how the judgement on . . . expressed in Source C, challenges the judgement put forward in Source B. (7) (c) Refer to Sources A, B and C and use your own knowledge. Explain the importance, in relation to other factors, of . . . (15) Total (25)

Edexcel 4 primary sources, 1 secondary source; 5 questions in 90 minutes

(a) Explanation of context of an issue in the source. (3)

(b) Use of own knowledge to describe or explain an issue related to the sources. (5)

(c) Comments on usefulness of sources for the historian studying . . . (5)

(d) Comparison between sources. (5)

(e) Comments on a viewpoint, using 2 specified sources and own knowledge. (12)

(a) Study Source 1. What does this source reveal about . . .? (3)

(b) Use your own knowledge. Use your own knowledge to explain . (5)

(c) Study Sources 2 and 3. How far does Source 3 support the statement in Source 2 that . . . (5)

(d) Study Sources 4 and 5. Compare the value of these two sources to the historian studying . . . (5)

(e) Study Sources 1 and 5 and use your own knowledge. Do you agree that . . .? Explain your answer, using these two sources and your own knowledge. (12)

Total (30)

Combined essay and source-based questions

Two Boards have a combination of essay questions and one source. Here the source is intended as a stimulus for the essays.

Board	Style of essay and source question, and time allowed	Example of style of essay and source question
AQA	Brief quotation from a secondary source followed by three-part essay question in 60 minutes, testing: (a) Contextual knowledge. (3) (b) Background knowledge. (7) (c) Interpretation, discussion. (15)	'The great social revolution of the past fifteen years may not be the one which redivided wealth amongst adults in the Welfare State, but the one that has given teenagers economic power' (Colin MacInnes, 1958) (a) Explain the reference to the Welfare State (3) (b) Why had teenagers gained economic power by the late 1950s? (7) (c) Did the discovery of the teenager amount to a 'great social revolution'? (15) Total (25)
Edexcel	1 or 2 primary sources, followed by three-part essay question in 60 minutes, testing: (a) Contextual knowledge. (5) (b) Background knowledge. (7) (c) Interpretation discussion (18)	(a) What does this source suggest about the impact of the Depression in Britain in the 1930s? (5) (b) How did the government limit expenditure between 1931 and 1939? (7) (c) Was the whole of Britain equally affected by the Depression? (18) Total (30)

How does this book combine the different approaches of the Boards to essays and source questions?

The use by the Boards of different styles is an opportunity to see common objectives from slightly different angles. It is very likely that an approach used by a Board you are not following will clarify at least one approach used by the Board that you are. At the very least, you will learn a great deal about what essay and source skills mean by comparing the ways in which they are approached. This is because you will be doing the most important thing you can do: you will be thinking about what the skills actually *mean*.

This book attempts to use all the approaches of the Boards in a way in which they relate to each other and reinforce each other. At the same time, it intends to give precise examples of how the questions of specific Boards can best be approached.

The basic principles behind the essays in this book are as follows:

(a) The single-essay approach of OCR is used as the basis, since this is similar in terms of length (45 minutes) to the second essay in the Edexcel questions (30 minutes) and the third essay in the AQA questions (36 minutes). The material covered relates to the whole of the OCR period specifications, but overlaps substantially into the period specifications for Edexcel and AQA; in this case, the answers provided should cover all the topics and skills needed and require little adjustment to meet the different style of question.

(b) Each chapter also contains a proportion of essay styles which relate specifically to Edexcel (in two parts) and AQA (in three parts). There is much in common between the length and style of the first Edexcel essay (30 minutes) and the second AQA essay (18 minutes). Where the subject specifications overlap, they would therefore be interchangeable. Any subject area which is not represented in a Board's specifications contains no essays in that Board's question style.

(c) In this way it is intended that all the topics are covered for all the subject specifications in a way which develops the skills required by each Board. Good essay-writing is a skill which crosses all the boundaries and an awareness of the variety of skills expected can only help to sharpen them in practice.

The differences in the source-based questions are more in terms of style than of skills. The main principles in covering the sources are as follows:

(a) The styles of AQA and Edexcel are used as the basis. AQA features in Chapters 2, 3, 4, 5, 6 and 7; Edexcel in Chapters 3 and 5; and OCR in 3, 4 and 8.

(b) Edexcel has an additional essay-source combination in certain topics. Examples of these feature in the Sources sections of Chapters 4 and 8.

Question styles of the Boards and where they are located in this book

Board	Styles of answers	Where located in chapters								
		1	2	3	4	5	6	7	8	9
OCR	Essay (one-part)	✓	✓	✓	✓	✓	✓	✓	✓	✓
	Sources (3 questions)	✓	✓	✓	✓	✓	✓	✓	✓	✓
AQA	Essay (three-part)	✓	✓	✓	✓	✓	✓	✓	✓	✓
	Sources (3 questions)	✓		✓		✓		✓	✓	
Edexcel	Essay (two-part)	✓	✓	✓	✓	✓	✓	✓	✓	✓
	Sources (5 questions)		✓		✓		✓			✓
	Essay/Source combination (3 questions)			✓	✓					

Part 4: Historical Skills

History is a diverse subject with wide-ranging skills. There is also much more emphasis on academic skills within the context of the sixth form. The two can be closely connected and the purpose of Part 4 of each chapter is to suggest how specific skills can be developed both within the History course and with a close connection to more general sixth-form courses. The intention is to enhance techniques already developed in essay-writing and source-analysis – but also to go beyond them in anticipating the needs of students of higher education. The focus of Part 4 of the various chapters is summarised below. These overlap – but are not intended to duplicate – the various patterns of key skills.

Each chapter considers the development of a different skill. The historical context may not be directly relevant to what you are studying, but the skill will be transferable to the area that is. This has the added benefit of making you think about the process of transferring ideas from one context to another and, in the process, changing and refining them. This, as much as anything else, is what History is about.

Type of skill	What is covered	Where it is covered
1. Essay-writing	• Purpose of essays. • Preparation and structure; analysis and factual support. • Precise coverage of the requirements of different styles of question.	Chapters 2–10, Part 2.
2. Source-analysis	• Types of sources and techniques of analysis. • Different types of question. • Contextual knowledge. • Comparison between sources. • Usefulness and reliability of sources. • Use of sources and own knowledge in an overall assessment.	Chapter 2–10, Part 3.

3. Problem solving	• Relating the factual knowledge in the text to a particular historical circumstance. • Explain the behaviour of differing groups in a diverse society.	Chapter 1, Part 4 (pages 55–56).
4. Effective communication	• Developing an awareness of how to use carefully chosen language to deliver a complex message by supporting a visual image. • Contribute to a group discussion on a complex subject. • Being aware of the ways in which propaganda operates in a modern society. • The ability to set aside modern techniques of communication and to empathise with the attitudes and values of a different age.	Chapter 2, Part 4 (pages 95–98).
5. Application of number (statistics)	• Different types of data used in History and how to interpret them. • Effective ways of using ICT to convert statistics to charts. • Questions relating to numerical data.	Chapter 3, Part 4 (pages 134–42).
6. Working with others (role play)	• Effective communication to a group. • Planning an activity with others. • Using a historical simulation to arrive at collective decisions. • Working towards agreed objectives. • Reviewing the success of the collaboration.	Chapter 4, Part 4 (pages 194–98).
7. Research methods and approaches	• Advice on how to identify an issue • Techniques on finding material and reading. • Advice on preparation, note-taking, planning, writing. • Explanation of the purpose of Coursework.	Chapter 5, Part 4 (pages 237–41).
8. Understanding interpretation (Anticipating the skills required for A2)	• Historiography and the study of different interpretations. • Developing some of the techniques necessary to achieve a successful transition to A2.	Chapter 6, Part 4 (pages 277–79).

9. Working with others (research)	• Dividing a complex task into manageable sections. • Preparing for a presentation to the class. • Revision for examination.	Chapter 7, Part 4 (pages 312–13).
10. Information Technology	• Present information from different sources using appropriate information technology. • Use information technology to help to draw historical conclusions from statistical data.	Chapter 8, Part 4 (pages 353–56).
11. Presentation of material	• Use a range of given historical source material to produce a whole-class presentation. • Carry out research to enable a presentation to be given confidently and effectively. • Choose an appropriate method of presentation of information.	Chapter 9, Part 4 (pages 412–14)

Connection with the specifications

Board	Specifications	Chapter
EDEXCEL	Welfare and the Constitution: The Liberal Governments, 1905–15 *(Unit 2/9a)*	(1), (2)
	Votes for Women *(Unit 1/4a)*	(1), (2)
	Conflict, Depression and Opportunity: British Society between the wars, 1919–1939 *(Unit 3/10a)*	(3)
AQA	Britain 1895–1918 *(Module 2/Alt R)*	(1), (2)
	Aspects of British History, 1895–1921; a: The Nature and Impact of New Liberalism 1906–1915 *(Module 2/Alt R)*	(1), (2)
	Aspects of British History, 1895–1921; b: Unionism and Nationalism in Ireland, 1895–1921 *(Module 2/Alt R)*	(1), (2) (1), (2), (3)
	Britain 1929–1951 *(Module 2/Alt U)*	(3), (4), (5), (6), (7)
OCR	England in a new century *(Module 1/Comp 3)*	(1)
	Britain 1899–1964 *(Module 2/ comp 2)*	(1), (2), (3), (4), (5), (6), (7)
	Europe 1890–1917 *(Module 3/Comp 2)*	(2)

Chapter 1

Introduction

This introductory chapter is concerned with presenting a picture of British social and economic life in 1900. It has sections on: The British economy in 1900; British social structure in 1900; Poverty; Religion; Gender relations; Race; The media; The British Empire.

Introduction: Britain in 1900

Perhaps the most familiar picture of social structure in Edwardian Britain comes from the story of the *Titanic*, the largest ship in the world in 1912, which sank on its maiden voyage to New York. The vast difference in conditions on board the ship, between the emigrants packed in steerage and the plutocrats in the luxury of first class, was in many ways a floating version of the country it left. The difference in treatment of the classes when the ship struck an iceberg in the Atlantic is equally revealing, for, as a socialist newspaper pointed out, 'fifty-eight 'men' of the first-class were saved; one hundred and thirty four steerage women and children were lost'. Though to be fair to the crew, most believed the ship to be 'unsinkable' and were not to be held accountable for the ship's design which had placed the lifeboats on the first-class only promenade deck.

As with every society in the modern industrial period, Britain in 1900 was undergoing profound change. First, in terms of technology, Marconi was on the point of revolutionising communications by sending the first wireless message to America and the Wright Brothers were about to achieve the world's first powered flight. Automobiles were still rare, but were beginning to affect the construction of roads in towns and the very layout of communities. Second, new forms of entertainment, such as cinema and popular newspapers (most notably the *Daily Mail* and the *Daily Express*) and popular periodicals were beginning to supplement music-halls and the traditional press.

Britain in 1900 was the still the richest and most powerful country in the world. Much of her wealth was based on the British Empire which made up roughly a quarter of the earth's surface.

Figure 1.1 **The SS Titanic** *leaving Southampton, 1912*

Table 1.1 **Population of the United Kingdom in millions, 1871–1901**

	1871	**1881**	**1891**	**1901**
England and Wales	22.7	26.0	29.0	32.5
Total	31.5	34.7	37.7	41.5

The nineteenth century had seen more people living in towns than in the countryside for the first time, and most population growth had taken place in the provincial cities. By 1900, London had a population of 6.5 million, while Glasgow, Liverpool, Manchester and Birmingham all had a population over 500,000.

The British economy in 1900

Britain had been the first industrial nation and had been able to exploit this advantage by becoming the 'workshop of the world' with an economy which dominated world trade with its exports of cotton, coal, iron, steel and machinery and its dominance of the shipbuilding industry. By the beginning of the new century she was facing fierce competition from other suppliers of her products and services. This had led to a questioning of **free-trade**, the free exchange of goods between countries, which had been a key element of Victorian economic policy. Other nations, in particular Germany and the United States, were successfully expanding their shares of world trade, while tax-barriers (**tariffs**) kept their domestic markets free from competition.

Demands for protectionist tariffs in Britain had been made since the late 1870s by manufacturers in West Yorkshire and the Midlands, but the campaigns lacked widespread political support until Joseph Chamberlain launched his campaign in 1903.

Britain, or rather London, was also the financial centre through which most trade was conducted. The use of British banking, insurance and other financial services by the world's businesses helped to ensure that Britain maintained a healthy **balance of payments** even though the value of visible imports exceeded visible exports by this period. Even the imports benefited Britain in one way as the majority of freight was transported in British ships.

Table 1.2 **Percentage distribution of world manufacturing production, 1870, 1913**

Year	United Kingdom	United States	Germany
1870	31.8	23.3	13.2
1913	14.0	35.8	15.7

Table 1.3 **Employment patterns in Britain (in millions), 1851, 1901**

	1851	**1901**
Agriculture	2.17	0.87
Industry	4.29	4.63
Commerce	1.58	2.14
Domestic service	1.01	0.95
Armed Forces	0.14	0.11
Public and other services	0.81	1.30

As Table 1.3 shows, while the number of people employed in agriculture was in rapid decline in the second half of the nineteenth century, industry, commerce and the service industries continued to expand as they would continue to do for the first half of the twentieth century. It is important to remember that for women, the most common form of employment remained domestic service.

British social structure in 1900

Table 1.4 *Income distribution in 1905*

Class	% of population	% of national wealth	Income per year (in £)
1	1	55	1,000 or more
2	2	25	400–1,000
3	8	11	160–400
4	56	8	60–160
5	33	1	under 60

1 – rich; 2 – upper middle class; 3 – lower middle class; 4 – skilled working class;
5 – casual and agricultural labour

In terms of land ownership, it was estimated that 4,000 people owned half of the land of Britain, while, as Table 1.4 shows, one tenth of the population (classes 1, 2, 3) owned nine-tenths of the country's wealth.

This economic power was also translated into political power. As the following table makes clear, despite the increase in the electorate during the nineteenth century, aristocrats continued to make up a significant proportion of Cabinets, even in the Liberal governments

Table 1.5 *Political divisions of Cabinets, 1895–1914*

Date	Party	PM	Cabinet size	Aristocrats	Middle class	Working class
1895	Con/LU	Salisbury	19	8	11	0
1902	Con/LU	Balfour	19	9	10	0
1905	Lib	Campbell-Bannerman	19	7	11	1
1914	Lib	Asquith	19	6	12	1

The contrast of earnings and life style can be observed from the following extracts. First, the lifestyle of the very rich, described from *Queen Magazine* in 1909:

To the average man, the Season comprises courts, state dinners and balls, royal garden parties and a few other events of the hardy annual class. But in reality these are merely the cream of the Season's features. The balls, for example, include private and semi-private dances and balls for charity. The list of dinners, again, comprises innumerable regimental banquets, Empire Day banquets, political dinners, Derby Day dinners, such as that at which the Duchess of Devonshire entertained Her Majesty and thirty other guests in 1907 and afterwards received a thousand favoured friends; country dinners and private dinners without number . . .

The operas, the theatres and concerts, sales of work, musical receptions at Mansion House and elsewhere, picture shows, lectures, exhibitions, cricket, croquet, lawn tennis and other sporting events, bring together great crowds of people. The Henley Regatta, Ascot, Speech Day at Harrow, ballooning at Hurlingham are also important items . . . that assist to fully occupy the time of those who pursue the giddy round of pleasure.

Society (with a capital 'S'), although still small, was changing as men of business were welcomed in the houses of the traditional élite, perhaps most typified by the political alliance between the middle-class Joseph Chamberlain and the aristocrat, Lord Salisbury. Land-values were declining, forcing titled families to exploit their contacts in commerce or industry if they were to maintain their comfortable standards of living. These were the privileged few and there was a huge gap between them and the majority of the population.

By this period the 'middle classes' (meaning those salaried non-manual workers) had increased in numbers as commerce and services had developed over the previous century. The term 'middle class' is, in many ways, rather unhelpful, as it covers the factory owner as well as the lowliest clerk in his employ, yet it was this class that was to prove to be the most influential in its style of life in the century ahead.

The richest 'middle class' kept servants and enjoyed a life-style comparable to that of the landed gentry, albeit more focused on town-life. Poorer white-collar workers, such as primary school teachers and shop assistants sometimes earned less than skilled craftsmen, and, although they often had money to spare for a sewing-machine or a bicycle, they, like the working class, had to rely on good fortune to avoid redundancy, illness or the loss of the wage-earner and the accompanying descent into poverty.

Poverty

The gap between rich and poor was not a new fact for Edwardians. As early as 1883, there had been published anonymously a penny pamphlet which described the full horror of life in the slums of Bermondsey in London. Its title was 'The Bitter Cry of Outcast London'. In twenty pages, its author Reverend Andrew Mearns, in charge of a non-conformist mission, exposed the problem of abject poverty. Its tone was uncompromising:

Every room in these rotten and reeking tenements houses a family, often two. In one cellar lives a father, mother, three children and four pigs! In another room a man ill with smallpox, his wife just recovering from her eighth confinement, and the children running around half naked and covered with dirt . . . seven people living in one underground kitchen and a little dead child lying in the same room . . . That people condemned to exist under such conditions take to drink and fall into sin is surely a matter for little surprise.

Who can wonder that every evil flourishes in such hotbeds of vice and disease? Who can wonder that little children taken from these hovels to the hospital, cry when they are well, through dread of being sent back to their former misery? Who can wonder that young girls wander off into a life of immorality, which promises release from such conditions?

As the work of the newly founded Salvation Army and the social surveys of investigators such as Charles Booth and Seebohm Rowntree were to reveal, such abject poverty was all too common in Edwardian Britain.

Figure 1.2(a) **A middle-class Edwardian afternoon tea-party, c.1905**

Figure 1.2(b) **The family and home of an unemployed workman, c. 1908**

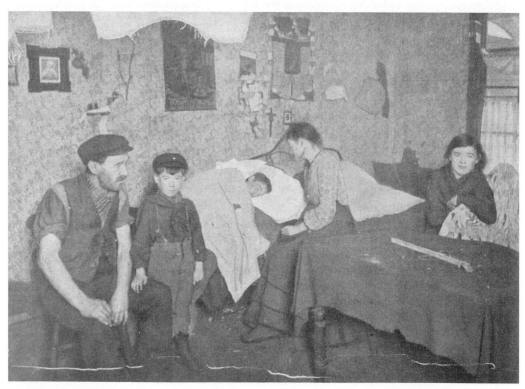

The seriousness of the problem was officially recognised when almost half the volunteers for service in the Boer War were found to be medically unfit for the army. Balfour set up a Royal Commission on the Poor Law in 1905 to investigate. When it reported in 1909 the Commission called for the system of Boards of Guardians running the Poor Laws to be abolished. A majority of the Commission wanted the duties of the Guardians to pass to local councils, but a minority, led by Beatrice Webb, wanted 'the break-up of the Poor Law' to create a system of assistance rather than punishment for the poor. It was this minority report which had the greater impact.

Religion

Judging from the scale of public debate, religion seems to have been the most important social activity of the nineteenth century. For every pamphlet published on the question of poverty, it has been estimated that there were around 50 published on religion. Organised religion played a role in the lives of all but the committed atheists (of whom there were very few), as baptisms, marriages and funerals were almost all carried out in church or chapel. For example, in 1901, of 259,400 marriages in England and Wales, 66.6 per cent were carried out at Anglican churches and 17.6 per cent at other places of worship, with only 15.8 per cent as civil (non-religious) ceremonies. The clergy comprised the largest profession in the country and the numbers of clergymen reached a peak in 1901, by which time there were over 25,000 ministers of the Anglican church. The Anglican church included almost all the British 'establishment'. Almost all the British Cabinet in 1900, almost all the House of Lords, most professors, judges, generals, admirals and senior civil servants were Anglicans.

What all these figures signify, of course, is that most men and women in 1901 genuinely believed in the truth of Christian religion, even if the practice of their faith varied considerably. The Bible was regarded as the true word of God and was in many poor families the only book in the home, often used as a family record or account ledger. With sudden, unexpected death from disease a common experience, the message that one's behaviour in this world decided one's fate in the after-life was a very powerful influence on daily behaviour. An all-knowing and all-seeing God, who sent his only Son to save sinful man, was widely accepted and the Church was seen as Christ's instrument, and therefore essential to salvation.

As a consequence of this, antagonism between the various types of churches was understandable. The bitterness of argument between Anglicans, non-conformist Protestants (such as Baptists, Methodists and Congregationalists) and Catholics over the nature of religious education to be given by elementary schools following the 1870 Education Act, eventually drove the government to take the management of schools into the hands of local councils in 1902. The religious diversity of Britain always produced tensions which could erupt into riots and often bred prejudice, but by the standards of the rest of Europe, Britain by 1900 was a relatively tolerant society in which the right to practise one's faith freely, even among the small Jewish, Hindu and Muslim communities, was generally protected. It has been argued that popular apathy towards organised religion, may have had a part to play in this. But certainly, before 1914, regular church attendance was the norm rather than the exception. One

Table 1.6 **Membership of main religious denominations in 1900 (in millions)**

Church of England	2.90
Church of Scotland	1.15
Methodists	0.77
Congregationalists	0.29
Baptists	0.25
Catholics	1.8

can conclude that after the bitterness of religious conflict in Britain's history, most religious ministers were keen to emphasise the tolerance and compassion of the Christian faith and to encourage their followers to extend this, in public at least, to their neighbours. It was therefore the First World War, and in particular the behaviour of senior clerics, which forced many people to seriously question the dominance of the Christian doctrine in public life and their own beliefs.

Gender relations

To talk about the 'position of women' has been shown to be almost meaningless, as the lives of middle class and working class women were hugely different. Both certainly benefited from the expansion of education in the nineteenth century, but working class girls tended to receive schooling to prepare them for a life of domesticity, studying subjects such as cookery and needle-work, with only some middle class girls able to study mathematics and science and to go onto the new higher education institutions. Similarly, in the world of work, working class women could only find low paid and unskilled employment, most of them becoming domestic servants, although secretarial opportunities in banking and business were expanding as the new century opened. Middle class women were still expected to tend the home as their first priority, but new 'professions' such nursing and school teaching, were offering more opportunity.

The inferior position of women as a whole in 1900 is usually indicated by the exclusion of all women from the franchise (the right to vote). In fact, the political rights of women had made considerable progress during the nineteenth century. Unmarried women and widows were allowed to vote for municipal councils after 1869 and both married and unmarried women could vote for the county councils set up in 1888. In 1894 urban and rural district councils were established and women ratepayers could vote and stand for election for these.

Women's legal rights had been advanced by the Married Women's Property Acts (1870 and 1882) which allowed a woman to continue to own her property when she married, and by the Guardianship of Children Act (1886) which allowed a mother to claim custody of her children after separation from her husband. Josephine Butler's national campaign against the Contagious Diseases Act, which allowed for the compulsory inspection of women declared 'common prosti-tutes' by the police, resulted in the repeal of the act in 1886.

Both the Liberals and Conservatives had formed organisations to involve women voluntary workers, who were essential to electoral success. Neither party had any firm plans to grant women the right to vote, however, and most campaigning took place outside them. In particular, the emer-gence of the **Independent Labour Party**, allowed many working class women, such as Esther Roper, to have a voice, which they used to demand the granting of a full democracy, which would include votes for women in contrast to the middle class demand for 'equal suffrage'.

In 1897 the National Union of Women's Suffrage Societies (NUWSS) was organised by Millicent Fawcett to unite the '**suffragists**' as they were known. The principal argument of the NUWSS was that if women could vote for local councils, why could they not vote for the national assembly in Westminster?

Race

In 1900, the vast majority of the population was by far white, British born, but that is not to say that Britain can be described as homogenous or mono-ethnic at the start of the new century. There were of course, increasingly important attempts by non-English Britons to define themselves as a separate ethnic group by the promotion of non-English languages, customs and sports. In the case of Wales and Scotland, these were not especially aimed towards the creation of a separate nation, but in Ireland, the activities of the Gaelic Sports Association, in particular, were designed to spread the sense of a distinct Irish identity as the prelude to Irish independence. One of the main factors behind this desire for independence was the continued poverty of the largely agrarian Irish economy, which drove many Irish to emigrate to Britain as well as to the United States. The Irish made up the largest immigrant group on the British mainland, numbering nearly half a million in 1901. They tended to concentrate in London, Glasgow and Lancashire, the traditional areas of settlement since the Irish famine of 1845–49. They were largely employed in menial occupations and faced hostility and violence for their Catholic faith, especially in Scotland. Non-Britons were easy to find as well. Immigrants from Europe included a large German population and significant Polish and Russian communities. Most of these latter two groups were Jews, fleeing anti-Semitic persecution from Tsarist Russia. Settling in almost all the major cities of Britain, this group was the target of much fear and resentment as they tended to have to settle in the poorest parts of the cities where their white neighbours feared they were threatening their job security by working for lower wages as well as contributing to overcrowding and crime. Non-white groups were quite rare, mainly concentrated around the docks like the Chinese of London. In the case of the Black population, this had actually declined during the nineteenth century, but despite this a permanent community had established itself in London and Liverpool.

Bills to control immigration had been introduced as early as 1894, but none had been passed. By 1901, though, a militant anti-Jewish organisation called the British Brothers League had been set up by a Conservative MP, which organised demonstrations and mass meetings in the East End. In response to its activities, Balfour's government set up a Royal Commission into alien immigration and found that the numbers of immigrants was very small and that they were no less healthy, law-abiding or capable of educating their children than the host population. The Commission did, nevertheless, agree to recommend that limits should be placed on the continued free entry of 'aliens' to the British Isles. The first restriction on immigration to Britain was passed as the Aliens Act of 1905 and it allowed the Home Secretary to refuse entry to anyone who could not support him or herself. The principle of stopping 'economic migrants' was therefore embedded in law very early in the century.

Table 1.7 **Foreign-born population of England and Wales, 1901**

Birthplace	
Ireland	426,565
France	20,797
Greece	997
Italy	9,909
Germany	50,599
Russia	23,626
Poland	21,448
China	767
United States	19,740
Total immigrants	619,678

The media

Due to the existence of a large urban population, concentrated in cities in Britain in 1900, with rising real earnings and increased leisure time, 'mass entertainment' was emerging rapidly as an important part of the media.

The nineteenth century had seen two very important innovations in the press industry, which had a huge impact on the newspaper industry in the next century. First, advertising became a major part of the industry, providing content and revenue and generating huge profits for newspapers. Second, Harmsworth copied US papers by selling a newspaper much cheaper than all his rivals when he launched the *Daily Mail* in 1896. He succeeded in covering his costs by a huge circulation (200,000 copies a day) and advertising. This newspaper, the first tabloid, was completely unlike any other newspaper yet printed in Britain, as it served up lurid stories of crime and scandal and largely ignored the high politics of Westminster. The years between 1900 and 1914 saw a huge expansion of this sector of the newspaper industry and they began and remained, for the whole century, the most popular form of print journalism.

The first showing of a film is generally accepted to have been at the London Polytechnic, Regent Street in February 1896, using the new technology of the Lumière brothers. By the end of the year, moving picture shows were part of many music hall performances around Britain. By 1900, films were being shown in vacant shops, known as 'penny gaffes' and by 1906, 'picture palaces' were being constructed to comply with new safety regulations. At first, the bulk of the films shown were French and American. By 1910, there were 1,600 cinemas, by 1914, there were 4,000. The British cinema industry was beginning, belatedly, to respond to the new demand, but by then the Hollywood industry dominated film production and from then until the end of the twentieth century, it was the myths, values and attitudes of America that most Britons came to experience when they went to the cinema.

The British Empire

The British Empire was the product of the sea-borne expansion of trade which Britain had enjoyed since the sixteenth century, but it was scattered across the globe having been assembled in piecemeal fashion as Britain's needs had dictated. As a result the Empire lacked any geographical or strategic unity and necessitated the provision of a large and powerful Navy. The Royal Navy, which Britain also relied on to protect her communications and trade route, cost £29 million pounds a year to maintain. Britain's policy of deliberate aloofness, known as **splendid isolation**' was increasingly questioned, especially when Britain's tactics in the later years of the Boer War exposed her unpopularity in Europe.

The last years of the nineteenth century had seen the considerable enlargement of the British Empire. Benjamin Disraeli had championed a new purpose for the Empire, not merely one of

Table 1.8 **Colonial possessions of Great Britain in comparison to France and Germany, 1876, 1914**

Country	Colonial Possessions				
	1876			**1914**	
	Area*	**Pop.****		**Area**	**Pop.**
Great Britain	22.5	251.9		33.5	393.5
France	0.9	6.0		10.6	55.5
Germany	–	–		2.9	12.3

* Area in millions of km^2
** Population in millions

Figure 1.3 **A map of the world showing British Empire possessions in 1897**

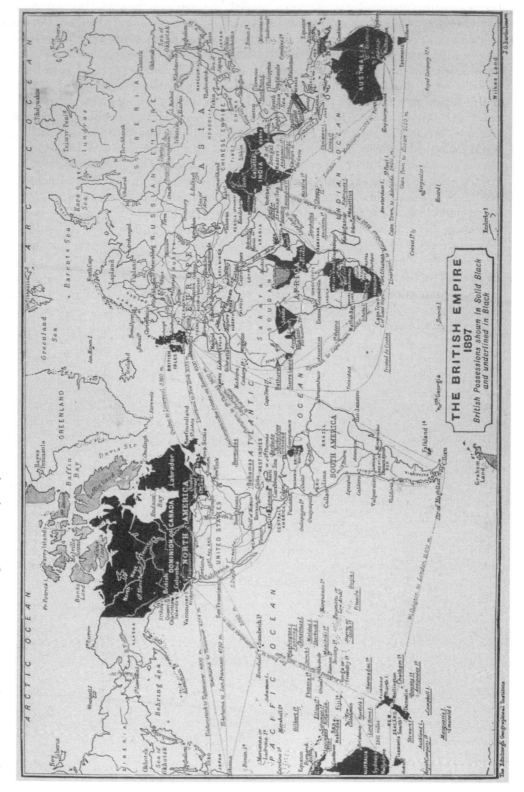

THE BRITISH EMPIRE
1897
*British Possessions shown in Solid Black
and underlined in Black*

exploitation, but one of 'courage, discipline, patience, reverence for the public law and respect for national rights' – in other words, sharing the benefits of British civilisation with those regarded as primitive. Whatever the true motivation, successive British governments had participated in the so-called 'Scramble for Africa' in competition with the other great powers and taken control of Egypt, Somaliland, Sudan, Bechuanaland, Rhodesia, Uganda and Kenya. Finally, in 1899, the British High Commissioner for South Africa had provoked the independent Boer republics of Transvaal and the Orange Free State into attacking, thus starting the Boer War, which was to last until 1902. British influence had also been extended in China, with the British taking a leading role in suppressing the nationalist Chinese 'Boxer Rising' of 1900. The older possessions of Canada, New Zealand and Australia, by now self-governing (and renamed 'Dominions' at the 1907 Colonial Conference), were still the most valuable in terms of trade, and as destinations for emigrants seeking a better life than was available in British cities. However, by the end of the century, Britain was finding the dual role of protecting her Empire and maintaining her influence in Europe increasingly difficult without a reliable ally among the Great Powers.

Chapter 2

Britain in a New Century, 1900–1914

This chapter is concerned with the period that is usually referred to as 'The Edwardian Age' despite the fact that Edward VII only reigned between 1901 and 1910. It is a period often remembered as a 'golden age of peace and harmony' before the disruptions brought by the First World War, but it was in fact a period of great turmoil. The last Conservative government before the war broke up in disarray and the Liberal government which replaced it attempted to radically alter the entire political approach to social welfare. The means to pay for this brought the government into conflict with the House of Lords and for a time the two chambers of Parliament were in a state of open hostility. The government also faced demands for women's rights to vote from militant campaigners, and a wave of industrial unrest. Outside the British mainland, Ireland appeared to be descending into a civil war, while Europe was rapidly aiming for a decisive conflict between the rival Great Power blocs.

 ## Historical background

Political parties

a) The Conservatives and **Liberal Unionists**
b) The Liberals
c) The Labour Party

Constitutional problems
Challenges to the State
Britain's foreign policy

a) 'Splendid isolation'
b) The search for allies
c) Rivalry with Germany
d) The coming of war

 ## Essays

1. The decline of the Unionists
2. The 1906 general election

3. The formation of the Labour Party
4. Liberal social reforms
5. The constitutional crisis
6. Ireland
7. Women's rights and the suffrage movement
8. Industrial unrest 1908–14
9. British foreign policy 1900–14

 ## Sources

1. National insurance proposals
2. Britain and the origins of the First World War

Historical skills

1. Analysis of the possible voting behaviour of a number of key social and professional groups in the 1906 election

Chronology

1899	Declaration of War against Boer republics
1900	Relief of Mafeking, Kimberley and Ladysmith
	General election victory for Conservatives
	Formation of Labour Representation Committee (LRC)
	Boxer Rebellion in China
	Lord Lansdowne becomes Foreign Secretary
1901	Death of Queen Victoria, Edward VIII becomes King
1902	Anglo-Japanese Alliance
	Balfour becomes PM
	End of Boer War
1903	Formation of Women's Social and Political Union (WSPU)
	Joseph Chamberlain resigns as Colonial Secretary
1904	**Entente Cordiale** agreed with France
1905	First Moroccan Crisis
	Resignation of Balfour's Unionist Government
	Formation of Campbell-Bannerman's Liberal Government
1906	Liberal general election landslide
	LRC renamed Labour Party
1908	Asquith becomes PM
	Old Age Pensions Act
1909	Lloyd George's Budget rejected by House of Lords
1910	Two general elections
1911	Parliament Act
	National Insurance Act
1912	Introduction of 3rd Irish Home Rule Bill
	Formation of Ulster Volunteers and signing of 'Solemn Oath and Covenant'
1913	Formation of Irish Volunteers
	'Triple Alliance' of trade unions agreed
	Emily Davison killed at the Derby
1914	Curragh 'mutiny', Larne and Howth gunrunning 'incidents'
	4 August – Declaration of war against Central Powers

Part 1: Historical background

Political parties

Table 2.1 *General elections 1895–1910*

Year	Conservative/ Liberal Unionist		Liberal		Labour		Irish Nationalist	
	% vote	No. of seats	% vote	No. of seats	% vote	No. of seats	% vote	No. of seats
1895	49.1	411	45.7	177	1.0	0	4.0	82
1900	51.5	402	44.6	184	1.8	2	2.5	82
1906	43.6	157	49.0	401	5.9	29	0.6	83
1910 (Jan.)	46.9	273	43.2	275	7.7	40	1.0	82
1910 (Dec.)	46.3	272	43.8	272	7.2	42	2.5	84

The two main political parties in 1900 were the Conservatives (also referred to as the Unionists) and the Liberals (also referred to as the Radicals).

a) THE CONSERVATIVES AND LIBERAL UNIONISTS

The Conservatives had dominated British politics for the last 15 years, and were the party in power in 1900 under the Prime Ministry of Lord Salisbury. They were also known as the Unionists because of their strong attachment to continued union with Ireland. The proposal of **Home Rule** for Ireland, put forward by a previous Liberal PM, William Gladstone, had led some in his party to split off and form the **Liberal Unionists**, who had virtually united with the Conservatives in 1895, when the two most important **Liberal Unionists**, Joseph Chamberlain and the Duke of Devonshire had joined the Conservative cabinet.

Arthur Balfour became leader of the Conservative Party and Prime Minister in 1902 on the resignation of his uncle, Lord Salisbury. He had been a leading member of the party since 1885, but he was not temperamentally fitted to lead. He was an aloof figure, happiest engaged in academic study or on the golf course. His interest in philosophy led him to see both sides of an argument which often caused him to be indecisive and to appear weak as a leader, especially when confronted by Joseph Chamberlain – a man, who Lord Salisbury had accurately described as unable to 'believe in the earnestness of the other side'. When Chamberlain challenged Britain's (and thereby Balfour's) economic policy of **free trade**, the Conservative Party was thrown into turmoil. In the public's eyes, **free trade** remained the reason for Britain's nineteenth-century prosperity and many, especially the working classes, wondered what tariffs would mean for the price of their food, much of which was produced outside Britain. Perhaps most seriously of all, Balfour's party was inevitably seen as divided and his leadership as weak. It is difficult to see how Balfour could have contained Chamberlain once the tariff reform campaign was launched, without entirely alienating one side or the other, but as leader he ought to have been more alert to Chamberlain's schemes at an earlier stage. Having said that, such was Chamberlain's egotism and belief in his own popularity, it is unlikely Balfour could have done much to stop him, short of blackmail or murder. Lord Salisbury, a much more adept political manipulator, had constantly struggled to keep Chamberlain on a firm leash and had relied on the then party agent, Middleton to remind Chamberlain that he wasn't indispensable. By 1903, Salisbury and Middleton had retired and Chamberlain took his chance with his usual arrogant disregard of the consequences. One can almost regard his intervention as a type of natural disaster for the Conservatives, one which they might have made some preparation for had it not been quite so unexpectedly catastrophic as to render all their defences useless.

After a series of poorly judged attempts to win favour by appealing to traditional Tory voters such as Anglicans though the Education Act of 1902 and publicans and the brewing industry through a new Licensing Act in 1904, Balfour's government appeared increasingly short of ideas as the enthusiasm for Empire waned after the revelations of Britain's tactics in the Boer War and the 'Chinese Slavery' scandal. Social investigators such as Booth and Rowntree had exposed the depth of poverty in Britain, yet the Conservatives had not introduced any major social reforms for 20 years. Balfour fell back on the only weapon he had, he resigned as Prime Minister in 1905, in the forlorn hope that the Liberals would prove as disunited as the Tories once they got into office. Sadly for him, the Liberals called his bluff and called a general election that reduced the Conservatives and **Liberal Unionists** to a rump of 157 MPs. Even Balfour lost his seat, though he managed to retain the leadership of the Conservatives until 1912, when, having failed to win a further two elections and having sacrificed the power of the House of Lords to veto bills in a confrontation with the Liberal government, the Conservatives finally got rid of him. His replacement was a staunch opponent of **Home Rule** and a supporter of **Tariff Reform**, the Canadian born Andrew Bonar-Law, who was determined to see the Conservatives return to power and who oversaw the immediate amalgamation of the Conservatives with the **Liberal Unionists**. Joseph Chamberlain had suffered a stroke in 1906 and was no longer able to take an active role in politics until he died in 1914.

b) THE LIBERALS

The Liberal Party, was by 1900, still in a fairly weak position, divided over their response to the Boer war. Given the war's initial popularity, many Liberals such as Herbert Asquith, Edward Grey and R.B. Haldane felt that war should be supported largely to prevent accusations of a lack of patriotism. These 'Liberal Imperialists' (or 'limps') were challenged by those such as David Lloyd George who saw the war as morally wrong and who were branded 'pro-Boers' by the jingoistic press. As the war dragged on and lost its appeal, they were beginning to re-group under the leadership of Henry Campbell-Bannerman. The increased concerns over Britain's status and the health of its inhabitants that the Boer War generated, encouraged some Liberals to reassess their priorities and support limited state intervention to secure a minimum standard of living for all. This 'New Liberalism' reunited the party and gave the party renewed appeal to the working classes, many of whom had been tempted by the socialist ideas of the various 'labour' organisations. Faced with the prospect of minority government, when Balfour resigned in 1905, Campbell-Bannerman chose to call an election instead to contrast the Conservatives' in-fighting over **Tariff Reform** with his party's firm commitment to **free trade**, which the Liberals cleverly exploited by accusing the Conservatives of wishing to introduce 'food taxes' that would hurt the poor. His gamble paid off and the Liberals won 400 seats, guaranteeing them power for the foreseeable future. Campbell-Bannerman was frustrated by the Conservative rearguard action in the House of Lords, though, and although by the time of his death in 1908 he had successfully settled the South African issue, he had been unable to make much progress towards the social reforms that were the centrepiece of 'New Liberalism'.

It was left to Campbell-Bannerman's Chancellor, Herbert Asquith to confront the Lords and to use the skills of David Lloyd George and a Conservative rebel, Winston Churchill, to carry out the government's social reforms. Asquith was a skilled debater and a fearsome political strategist, successfully negotiating the Liberal Party through a series of challenges in the years before 1914. He was the longest serving Prime Minister in the first half of the century, winning two elections in 1910, and it is unfortunate that his reputation was tarnished by his failure to adequately respond to the unprecedented crisis of government, caused by the First World War.

c) THE LABOUR PARTY

Separate working class political organisations had existed since the days of the Chartists, but these had tended to be small and relatively unimportant compared to the trade unions. In 1900 however, with the backing of the Trade Union Congress, the Labour Representation Committee (LRC) had been formed. The LRC lacked funds and had only managed to contest 15 seats in the 1900 election and had only won two of these. Therefore their secretary, Ramsay MacDonald, chose to form an electoral pact with the Liberals in 1903, which would allow 31 LRC candidates to fight the Conservatives alone, in return for LRC support for Liberals. By then over 150 unions had affiliated to Labour, largely as a result of the Taff Vale case which made unions liable for damages and losses incurred during a strike and this brought a secure financial basis for the party. When 29 LRC MPs were returned in 1906, the party was renamed the Labour Party.

The Party continued to co-operate with the Liberals and in 1906, the Trade Disputes Act reversed the Taff Vale decision. Even more unions now began to affiliate to Labour, including the National Union of Mineworkers who switched their support from the Liberals in 1909. The electoral pact still held, however, and Labour increased their seats to 42 in December 1910. By the time the First World War broke out, the pact was under pressure though. The pace of social reform had slowed and many Labour members believed that, now they had the bulk of unions behind the party, they could win even more seats if they stood against Liberal candidates.

Constitutional problems

The House of Lords was still very important in 1900 as it retained the power to block legislation even if it had been passed by a large majority in the House of Commons. In 1900 this was not a serious problem as the House of Lords was dominated by Conservatives, but a previous Liberal government had threatened to reduce this power of 'veto', if the Lords blocked any important legislation during a future Liberal government. When the Liberals came to power with a huge majority in 1906 they found that the Lords were quite prepared to block some of the legislative programme on which they were elected. A serious constitutional struggle between the Liberal government in the House of Commons and the Conservative opposition in the House of Lords then ensued, which led to two general elections in 1910. The Liberal majority from 1906 was wiped out in these, but with the support of Labour and the Irish nationalists, the Liberals were finally able to reduce the powers of the Lords in the 1911 Parliament Act, but only at the cost of continued delay of important legislation until 1914.

A general election had to be held every seven years until 1911, and, although the right to vote (the 'franchise') had been extended during the nineteenth century, in 1900 only 6.7 million men had the right to vote (approximately 58 per cent of the male population). Unmarried women had the

Figure 2.2 **The constitution of the United Kingdom in 1900**

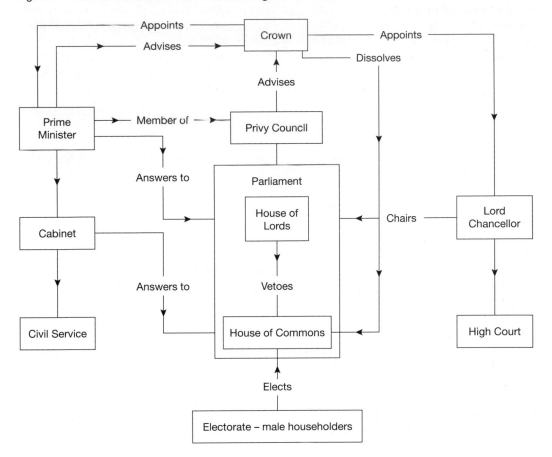

right to vote in local elections, but not in general elections. Daily life for Cabinet ministers and many members of the public was disrupted by the inventive and well disciplined tactics of the suffragettes, whose campaign for women's rights had divided the country between opponents, unequivocal supporters and those who agreed with the cause whilst eschewing their growing militancy.

THE BIRTH OF SOCIAL SERVICES

The Liberals' first social reforms addressed the problem of child poverty. Local authorities were given the discretionary power to provide free school meals for children in 1906. This was not compulsory, but when it was found that less than half of Local Education Authorities (LEAs) were providing free meals in 1914, it became compulsory to do so. Compulsory medical inspections in schools were introduced and education authorities were given the power to provide free medical treatment in 1907, but again LEAs were slow to act until 1912, when the government made grants available to set up school clinics. While primary education was free and compulsory, secondary education was costly, so in 1907 the government ordered schools to set aside 25 per cent of their places, free of charge for deserving children.

Figure 2.1 *Lloyd George's budget scare in the House of Commons, 1909*

PUNCH, OR THE LONDON CHARIVARI—July 28, 1909.

THE ALL-NIGHTMARE.

"STILL IT CRIED 'SLEEP NO MORE!' TO ALL THE HOUSE."—*Macbeth*, Act II., Scene 2.

Old age pensions were introduced in 1908 at the rate of five shillings (25p) a week for single people over 70 and a lower joint rate for married couples. No contributions had to be made, but one could not receive the pension if a person's income from other sources was more than £21 a year.

Labour Exchanges were set up in 1909 by Winston Churchill and William Beveridge at the Board of Trade. As unemployment had grown in 1908–9, Churchill told employers with vacancies to inform the Labour Exchanges so that unemployed workers could find out what jobs were available. Although there were 430 exchanges by 1913, the system was still voluntary for employers, but compulsory for the unemployed who only received benefits if they 'proved their readiness to work'.

The Trades Board Act of 1909 was another achievement by Churchill. It dealt with the problem of low-paid and ill-treated workers in the 'sweated industries'. These usually employed female and child labour often working excessively long hours in their own homes for very little pay. They had no trade unions, so Churchill set up Boards to fix minimum wages in four occupations, tailoring, box-making, lace-making and chain-making. In 1913 this was extended to cover 6 more 'sweated' trades, so that almost four million were protected and were ensured a reasonable wage.

The National Insurance Act of 1911 was Lloyd George's greatest achievement before 1914. Health Insurance was provided by a fund into which the worker paid 4d (pence), the employer paid 3d and the state paid 2d. If he/she fell ill, the worker would receive 10s a week sick pay, and was entitled to free medical attention, medicines and an allowance towards rest care in case of tuber-culosis. Benefits did not apply to wives and children apart from a maternity grant of 30s nor to those who earned £160 a year. It caused huge controversy, and the Conservatives argued that the government had no right to force workers to pay money from their wages. There was also fierce opposition from the doctors' representatives, the British Medical Association, who feared that they would lose their independence and from insurance companies who feared for their business. In this scheme the worker paid 2½d, the employer paid 2½d and the state paid 2d. Unemployment benefit was 7 shillings a week up to a maximum of 15 weeks in any 12-month period.

 ## Challenges to the state

The government had faced a serious wave of industrial disorder, focused in South Wales, the North of England and Clydeside, which had required the Home Secretary, Winston Churchill, to use police and to send in troops to keep order on several occasions. Most seriously of all, the Liberals' reliance on the Irish Nationalists to keep them in power after the general election of December 1910 had re-ignited the issue of **Home Rule** for Ireland, which the Irish demanded in return for their compliance. After the defeat of the Lords, the Protestant Ulstermen had resorted to force to defend their cause of continued Union with Britain, smuggling in guns with the tacit approval of many senior figures in the British army in Ireland. They had been encouraged by an increasingly office-hungry Conservative party, whose leader, Andrew Bonar Law, had declared

Figure 2.3 **The Protestant and Catholic divide in Northern Ireland, 1911**

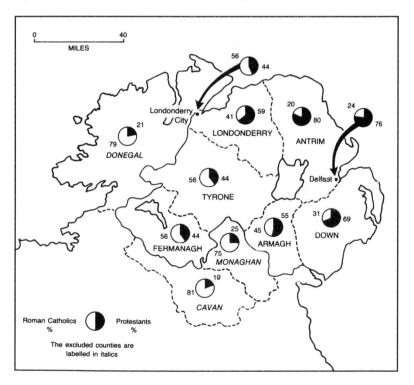

Figure 2.4 **The location of industrial unrest, 1910–12**

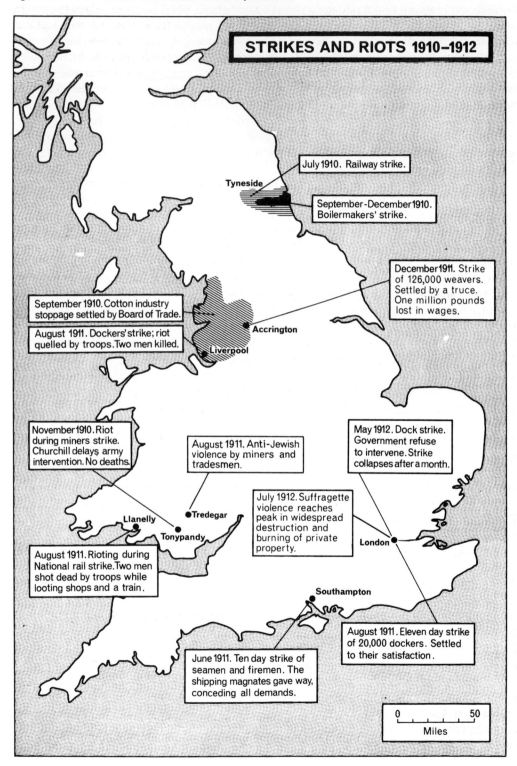

STRIKES AND RIOTS 1910–1912

July 1910. Railway strike.

September–December 1910. Boilermakers' strike.

December 1911. Strike of 126,000 weavers. Settled by a truce. One million pounds lost in wages.

September 1910. Cotton industry stoppage settled by Board of Trade.

August 1911. Dockers' strike; riot quelled by troops. Two men killed.

November 1910. Riot during miners strike. Churchill delays army intervention. No deaths.

August 1911. Anti-Jewish violence by miners and tradesmen.

May 1912. Dock strike. Government refuse to intervene. Strike collapses after a month.

July 1912. Suffragette violence reaches peak in widespread destruction and burning of private property.

August 1911. Rioting during National rail strike. Two men shot dead by troops while looting shops and a train.

June 1911. Ten day strike of seamen and firemen. The shipping magnates gave way, conceding all demands.

August 1911. Eleven day strike of 20,000 dockers. Settled to their satisfaction.

Tyneside

Accrington

Liverpool

Llanelly

Tredegar

Tonypandy

London

Southampton

0   50
Miles

'I can imagine no length to which **Ulster** will go which I shall not be ready to support', thereby giving political respectability to paramilitary action on behalf of the Ulstermen. When the government had tried to send reinforcements to the North of Ireland, officers had resigned in protest, in the so-called 'Curragh mutiny'. Finally, having failed to stop Unionist gunrunning, the army attempted unsuccessfully to prevent Nationalists landing guns at Howth, near Dublin, on 26 July 1914. This demonstration of supposed British favouritism was compounded by the troops, who then opened fire on an unarmed crowd in Dublin, killing three people. It seemed Ireland was on the verge of Civil War.

 ## Britain's foreign policy

After the difficulties Britain had faced in winning the Boer War of 1899–1902, she had begun to realise how isolated she was in attempting to defend her vast Empire against a host of unfriendly powers. When Lord Salisbury resigned as Foreign Secretary in 1900, his successor, Lord Lansdowne, decided on a new approach. He managed to check Russian ambitions in China by signing an alliance with Japan in 1902, which led to a war between Japan and Russia in 1904–5. Britain stayed neutral, as agreed, but the Japanese victory and annihilation of the Russian fleet at Tsushima calmed her nerves and made Russia less of a threat to her interests in the Far East. Fear of foreign aggression, which had been trumpeted by various right wing leagues, had forced Britain, somewhat unwillingly, into increasingly close alliance with other continental powers as well. The chief danger was perceived as the German Reich, headed by the ever more unpredictable Kaiser. It was widely believed that Wilhelm II wished to challenge Britain's global power and to that end had begun to build a naval fleet to rival Britain's. Britain, and in particular, the Liberal Foreign Secretary after 1905, Sir Edward Grey, was finding it increasingly difficult to resist demands for closer military ties with her closest European ally, France, and for an escalation of Britain's arms programme, despite the costs to the Liberals' ambitious programme of domestic reform.

In 1904 the Anglo-French Entente had been signed, putting an end to years of colonial rivalry, but as the Germans regarded this as a threat to her colonial ambitions, it actually provoked the Kaiser into a series of rash moves, to try to separate them by challenging French control of Morocco. It had the opposite effect, however, and Britain and France began to engage in military discussions to determine strategy in the face of a German attack. There was no written military alliance, but Grey felt that Britain was now bound by honour to come to France's aid. In 1907 he even signed an agreement with Britain's traditional enemy Russia, to prevent their respective colonial ambitions from forcing France to choose between them.

This of course further inflamed the Kaiser and in retaliation he became increasingly unwilling to restrain his own, much weaker ally, Austria-Hungary in its attempt to challenge Russian influence among the newly independent Balkan nations. In particular, the Kaiser encouraged Austria-Hungary to confront the Russian backed government of Serbia by promising that he would give Germany's full assistance in the event of a war. After a series of crises that Grey did well to defuse, the heir to the Austro-Hungarian throne was assassinated by Serbian terrorists in June 1914 and Austria-Hungary declared war on Serbia. Russia came to Serbia's aid, Germany supported Austria-Hungary, France supported Germany, and finally, after a day's delay, Britain declared war on Germany on 4 August 1914, using Germany's violation of Belgian neutrality as their reason. Ironically, relations between Britain and Germany had been improving over the previous months, but now the two countries were thrown into conflict for the first time, as a result of their obligations to their allies.

Part 2: Essays

1. The decline of the Unionists (OCR)

Assess the problems facing the Unionist Government of 1902–5.

(90 marks)

The political scene was changing when Balfour took over as PM. While the Boer War had lasted, public interest had been deflected from domestic policies. When the war ended in 1902, interest in home affairs revived. In order to try to maintain electoral support, Balfour introduced a series of domestic reforms, many of which proved controversial, and which ultimately helped to bring about the defeat of the Conservative government.

The Education Act of 1902 showed that Balfour could put together very constructive legislation, but at the same time, could be blind to possible public opposition. The act established Local Education Authorities (LEAs) to supervise secondary and elementary education and allowed church schools to receive funding from LEAs as long as they maintained their own buildings. State schools meanwhile were required to teach without bias towards any religious denomination. As a result many new secondary schools were built and LEAs proved very successful in their role, but Nonconformists (such as Methodists and Baptists) objected to church schools being funded from their rates (especially Catholic schools – the nonconformist slogan was 'No Rome on the rates!'). This factor was decisive in causing many middle-class Nonconformists to vote Liberal in 1906.

Throughout the nineteenth century there was constant agitation to reduce the number of public houses and beer sellers, championed by the hugely popular National Temperance Union. The 1902 Licensing Act did this, but the question remained whether landlords who lost their licenses were entitled to compensation. The test case of Sharpe vs Wakefield in 1891 had decided against compensation. The 1904 Licensing Act established that compensation should be paid, not by the government, but from a fund levied on the licensing trade itself. The **temperance movement** was incensed by this move and led a campaign to have the act repealed.

The working classes were becoming increasingly disillusioned with the Unionists well before 1902. Since 1895 most of the government's attention had been on the Empire and little social reform had been passed, despite the attempts of Joseph Chamberlain, who had unsuccessfully tried to get the Conservatives to accept a number of proposals, including old age pensions, before he became colonial secretary in 1895. Trade Unions, many of which had been quite supportive of Conservatism were offended by the refusal of Balfour's government to overturn the Taff Vale judgement of 1901 which had forced a railway union to pay £42,000 in damages and costs to the Taff Vale Railway Company following a strike.

Lord Milner, the British High Commissioner in South Africa, suggested that to meet the shortage of native labour in the gold and diamond mines of the newly captured Boer states, Chinese men should be brought in as cheap labour. Balfour gave his approval, and, by 1905, 47,000 Chinese had been imported. Middle class humanitarians were outraged when news reached England of the terrible conditions they worked in, living in segregated compounds. Working class trade unionists were horrified that cheap **'sweated' labour** was being brought in to keep costs down, and feared that similar action might follow in Britain, with consequent reduction in wages.

Balfour's most difficult problem arose when the colonial secretary, Joseph Chamberlain, worried by the party's increasing unpopularity and ambitious for political success at the end of a long and controversial career, launched a crusade to revitalise trade by advocating tariffs on imports from Britain's competitors. This campaign, known as '**Tariff Reform**', meant abandoning Britain's long-standing policy of **free trade**, but, as Chamberlain argued, USA and Germany had already done so and were prospering. Chamberlain went further, arguing that Britain could promote trade within the Empire by setting tariffs at lower rates on goods from the colonies, which was known as 'imperial preference'. Unfortunately for Balfour, the issue split the Conservatives, with many like the Chancellor, Ritchie, believing that **free trade** was vital to Britain's future economic prosperity. In spring 1903, when Balfour failed to overrule Ritchie, Chamberlain resigned. Balfour desperately tried to find some compromise, suggesting just retaliatory tariffs against those who had taxed British imports, but the situation was hopeless. Those Conservatives in favour of Chamberlain's full programme of imperial preference, the 'whole hoggers', formed the **Tariff Reform** League and those against, the 'free fooders' formed a Free Food League, while the 'Balfourites' continued to pretend that the party was still united. Some in favour of **free trade**, most notably Winston Churchill, even left the party and joined the Liberals, who remained united in defence of **free trade**.

Britain's poor showing in the Boer War had made Balfour appoint himself as Chairman of the Committee of Imperial Defence, with the intention of auditing the military requirements of the huge (and still growing) British Empire. It was partly the fears of weakness in the army that led Lord Lansdowne, the Foreign Secretary to seek an understanding with France to counter the threat of the powerful German army. When the Entente Cordiale was signed with France in 1904, it may not yet have been a military alliance, but it provided the grounds for one in the future. Britain also had to respond to the increasing size of the German navy. The newly appointed First Sea Lord, Fisher, and Lord Cawdor, the first Lord of the Admiralty decided to make all existing warships obsolete by commissioning a faster more powerful series of ships, which became known as Dreadnoughts after the first of the series. They also created an Atlantic fleet to bolster the existing Mediterranean and Channel fleets. Although this prompted a 'naval race' between the super powers, Britain had at least responded swiftly enough to avoid any risk of having her superiority overtaken, as subsequent events in the Great War were to prove.

 ## 2. The 1906 general election (OCR)

Why did the Liberals win the general election of 1906?

(90 marks)

Balfour had resigned in December 1905 in order to force open a split between Liberal Imperialists and Radicals, but he miscalculated and the Liberals were able to form a united Cabinet. In January 1906, Campbell-Bannerman, the Liberal leader, chose to take advantage of the opportunity of the Conservative's perceived unpopularity and divisions over tariff reform, and called an election. The Conservatives were reduced from the 402 seats they won in 1900 to a mere 157 and the Liberals increased from 184 to 400. Even Balfour lost his seat in Manchester.

The dominant issue of the election was clearly tariff reform. The tariff reformers, preoccupied with the struggle for the leadership of the Conservative Party clearly failed to convince the general public to abandon **free trade**. Although many right-wing politicians feared for the continued prosperity of the British economy in the face of foreign competition and the unity of the empire after the Boer War, the public did not share this sense of impending crisis. The threat of the 'little loaf' and the 'dear breakfast table' as a possible result of food taxes, gave the Liberals an opportunity to fight as a united party after their divisions over the Boer War and their propaganda played unceasingly on the issue. Chamberlain did attempt to allay this fear by promising that the revenue raised by tariffs would be spent on social reforms such as old age pensions, but the Conservatives' record on alleviating poverty had been fairly unimpressive over the previous ten years and the working classes in particular were never converted to the cause.

The Conservatives' record over the previous five years also damaged their chances of winning the election. The triumph after the capture of Johannesburg during the Boer War had swiftly worn off and the war had dragged on for a further two years as the Boers carried out a guerrilla campaign. The British army under Kitchener had resorted to herding Boer families into 'concentration camps' to prevent supplies reaching their enemies, but they had proved unequal to the task of maintaining adequate sanitation and between 20,000 and 40,000 men, women and children had died. When the pioneering journalist, Emily Hobhouse, revealed the truth about the conditions in the camps, the cause was taken up by the Liberals and their leader, Campbell-Bannerman accused the government of employing 'methods of barbarism'. Britain's difficulties in defeating a nation of farmers and the brutality employed in doing so clearly took the sheen off the glittering façade of Empire, a cause which had served the Conservative party very well in general elections since Disraeli's success in 1874. Attention shifted to the question of 'national efficiency' and the poor state of the nation's youth revealed by the report of the Inter-Departmental Committee on Physical Deterioration in 1904 seemed to finally condemn the Conservatives' failures over their long period of administration.

South Africa returned to haunt the Conservatives again in 1903 when the British High Commissioner attempted to rebuild the economy by importing Chinese labourers into the gold mines of the country. Chamberlain had vetoed this plan previously, but it went ahead once he was out of the Cabinet. The use of labour camps revived memories of Kitchener's methods, much to middle-class nonconformist disgust in Britain. Working-class reaction was less humanitarian, but no less hostile. Unions feared that the government would similarly use cheap foreign labour to keep wages down in Britain and there was much racist hostility in their anger. Combined with the failure to overturn the 'Taff Vale' decision which made trade unions liable for damages caused during a strike, Conservative working-class support, so vital in the two previous electoral success, was lost, even in strong Tory areas such as Lancashire and the south-east.

The Conservative party, bitterly divided over tariff reform, failed to maintain its organisational superiority over its rivals after the retirement of the party agent, Richard Middleton in 1903. Internal struggle between the Free Food League and the Tariff Reform League meant that the grass roots organisers of Tory victory in the past, such as the Primrose League were starved of funds and volunteers. Yet in 1906, only four Conservative candidates were unopposed, compared with 163 in 1900. 100 Conservative MPs also retired at the election, taking with them the personal links with voters they had built up over the years. It seems very unlikely that Middleton and Salisbury would have allowed such a situation to occur.

The Liberals by contrast, re-united under their traditional cause of **free trade** were much better organised. **Home Rule**, their greatest potential vote-loser in England, had been successfully shelved by Campbell-Bannerman, and the promises of no food taxes, repeal of the Licensing Act of 1904, the Education Act of 1902 and reversal of the Taff Vale decision revitalised the traditional Liberal alliance of workers, temperance campaigners, non-conformists and trade unions. The programme of social reform which dominated the subsequent Liberal governments was kept deliberately vague, as Campbell-Bannerman feared that the middle classes would baulk at the prospect of tax increases.

The Liberals also gained a crucial electoral advantage when Herbert Gladstone, the Liberal Chief Whip formed an electoral pact with the Labour Representation Committee secretary, Ramsay MacDonald in 1903. Under the terms of this deal, the danger of splitting the anti-Conservative vote between LRC and Liberal candidates was averted, as the Liberals agreed to stand aside in certain constituencies in order to give the LRC a free run. In return, the LRC would support Liberal candidates elsewhere and would support the Liberals at Westminster. In 1906, 29 LRC MPs were returned and the Labour vote certainly proved decisive in a number of Liberal gains.

It is frequently said that governments lose elections, oppositions do not win them. This certainly appears to have been the case in 1906. Divided, associated with unpopular policies and perceived as having been in power too long, the Conservatives handed the Liberals a golden opportunity. The Liberals simply had to keep their battle with the Conservatives largely clear of LRC interference and not to make too many promises which might backfire and the election was theirs. Although he is much underestimated by historians, Campbell-Bannerman had done a remarkable job in keeping the Liberal party together and he maintained their discipline throughout the campaign and judged the moment for the election to perfection. Although the blame for the scale of the Conservatives' defeat must lie with Balfour and especially with Chamberlain, the Liberals had effectively exploited public fears and had organised themselves effectively enough to guarantee that their victory was finally achieved after years in the political wilderness.

3. The formation of the Labour Party (AQA)

Read the following source and then answer the questions which follow.

As soon as the 1906 Parliament assembled, the LRC assumed the name of 'Labour Party' and its twenty-nine MPs elected officers and whips ... The Labour Party was a federation of independent organisations and it was natural that the differences existing between the bodies sponsoring the MPs, and particularly those between the socialist societies and the trade unions, should appear on the parliamentary scene.

From *A Short History of the Labour Party* by Henry Pelling
and Alistair J. Reid, 1996

a)   **Explain the reference to 'the differences existing between the bodies sponsoring the [Labour] MPs'.**   **(3 marks)**

b)   **Explain why a separate Labour Party was formed by 1906.**   **(7 marks)**

c)   **How successfully did the Labour Party achieve its aims between 1906 and 1914?**   **(15 marks)**

a)   The trade unions who provided the means for the Labour Party to fight elections and support MPs at Westminster through a 'political levy' were in favour of supporting any party that looked willing and capable of improving the conditions of working men and protecting the rights of unions. As a result, the majority of these had continued to support the Liberal Party in the days of the Labour Representation Committee (LRC), though by 1906 increasingly large numbers of unions were switching their support to Labour. By contrast, the socialist organisations such as the **Fabian Society** and the **Independent Labour Party** (ILP) favoured more overtly collectivist policies such as **nationalisation** of industry and increases in direct taxation to fund social reform. There was even a group committed, in theory at least, to violent marxist revolution, the Social Democratic Federation.

b)   The Labour Party (until 1906 called the Labour Representation Committee) was formally created in 1900 from a number of political groups, the Fabians, the Social Democratic Federation and the **Independent Labour Party**. Although the three groups had somewhat different aims, they all agreed that, in order to improve life for working people in Britain, they could not rely on the other parties and that they had to seek election to Parliament themselves. However, in order to form a national political party they needed the financial and administrative help of the trade unions.

The trade unions themselves had undergone a recent transformation, with the formation of unions among the unskilled and casual labour force for the first time. This 'New Unionism' had had its first success in the London dock strike of 1889, when a minimum wage had been achieved. Although subsequent achievements were minimal, the new unions' call for working class solidarity affected the traditional unions as well. This growth of class politics in the 1890s was also driven by the repeated failure of working-class men to be selected as Liberal candidates. This had been the impetus behind Keir Hardie's successful campaign as an independent 'Labour' candidate in 1892. Instead of working with the Liberals, the new unions and some older unions began to demand immediate social improvements and supported independent labour candidates. For example, the **Independent Labour Party** was set up largely as a trade union response to an unsuccessful textile workers' strike in Bradford which had been vigorously opposed by local Liberals. The defeat of the most powerful engineering union in a six-month lock-out in 1898, seemed to signal the failure of traditional union approaches and union leaders were now willing to support the formation of a body which could influence Parliament directly. These leaders pushed the unions' central body, the Trade Unions Conference (TUC), to support the setting up of the LRC, but only ten unions were actually willing to give it financial support. As a result, the LRC only ran 15 candidates in the 1900 election and only two were successful.

In 1901, the decision of the House of Lords to award damages against the Amalgamated Society of Railway Servants after the Taff Vale strike meant that unions could no longer afford to strike, and deprived the union of two thirds of its annual income. Even conservative union leaders could now see the need for a separate political organisation and the number of unions affiliated to the LRC rose to 165 by 1904.

The LRC had no prospect of electoral success on its own, so the party chose to co-operate with the Liberals for the forthcoming election, on the grounds that the Liberals were more willing to reform the law than the hostile Tories. The resulting '**Lib–Lab**' **pact** of 1903, signed between Herbert Gladstone and Ramsay MacDonald arranged that Liberals would not contest the seats that LRC candidates stood for and that LRC would not challenge Liberal candidates in return. As a result, 30 LRC MPs were elected in 1906, helped by working-class distrust of Joseph Chamberlain's **Tariff Reform** campaign. As the group of MPs was large enough to no longer be considered a committee, the LRC was renamed the Labour Party after the election.

While the action of individuals such as Keir Hardie was important in promoting the Labour cause, the crucial factors explaining the creation of the Labour Party are the change in attitude of the trade unions in the face of legal and establishment obstruction, and the willingness of the Liberal Party to allow the LRC candidates a free run against unpopular Conservative representatives in 1906, despite the feeling of some Liberals that Labour was 'a serpent that would sting their party to death.'

c) The Labour Party had great success in increasing its support between 1906 and December 1910, as far as can be measured by general election results. Mainly as a result of the **Lib–Lab pact** of 1903, 29 LRC MPs were returned in the general election of 1906, allowing the LRC to reconstitute itself as the Labour Party. The affiliation of the miners' union in 1909 increased this number to 40, and the same number of MPs were successfully returned in January 1910, with an additional two being added in December 1910. It is important to note however, that the party had little success in winning or holding seats without Liberal support.

Although no election took place between 1911 and 1914, it is likely that support for the Labour Party did not increase any further and may well have decreased in Labour strongholds, as a result of the chaos and disruption caused by the wave of industrial unrest that swept the country between 1910 and 1912. Fears of militant trade unions holding the democratically elected government to ransom may well have caused some potential Labour supporters to reconsider their voting behaviour, especially among the middle classes. In all the by-elections held between 1912 and 1914 in which all three parties competed, Labour finished last in the poll.

When the Labour Party won 30 seats in 1906, it had a clear agenda of pushing the Liberal Party to improve working and living conditions for the working classes, but most urgently, it wanted the Liberal Party to reverse a number of recent legal decisions which had jeopardised the position of trade unions and the consequent funding for the Labour Party. In addition, the Labour Party had the long-term aim of increasing the number of its MPs and becoming less dependent on the support of other parties. It is important to recognise that although it contained many socialists, the Labour Party did not believe in a revolutionary overthrow of capitalism by the workers, and in many ways simply wished to improve working-class conditions within the current capitalist, **free trade** economy.

In 1906, the Liberals passed the Trades Disputes Act which reversed the decision in the Taff Vale case to force unions to pay costs for damage caused during a strike, thus giving unions complete immunity from legal action. In the same year, the Workmen's Compensation Act prevented employers from offering less comprehensive protection than the national scheme, and this was shortly followed by the granting of an eight-hour limit on the working day for miners, which had been demanded for 20 years.

There was also considerable Labour support for the provision of social welfare, especially for free school meals for children in need and compulsory medical inspection in schools which were granted by Campbell-Bannerman's government. Labour also put pressure on the government to swiftly introduce old age pensions, which many members of the Liberal cabinet were quite happy to grant. The pensions were non-contributory, but the health and unemployment aspects of National Insurance were only received by workers who had paid sufficient funds. When the Act was introduced the benefits in the scheme were not immediately forthcoming for the workers, but the costs of contribution still had to be borne. Therefore, many Labour figures, such as George Lansbury, publicly opposed a scheme which they felt ought to be paid for by a tax on the rich. That said, some Labour leaders felt that the principle of contribution did continue to encourage thrift among workers and helped them to maintain self-respect in an age when receiving state aid was still regarded as a social stigma.

In 1909, W.V. Osborne a Liberal, challenged the right of his union to demand the political levy (the small weekly payment on top of their usual union subscription, used to pay Labour MPs' salaries). The House of Lords ruled it was illegal for unions to demand such a payment for the purpose of helping a political party. As the Labour Party depended upon trade union funds to pay MPs and fight elections, this seriously challenged its ability to operate as a credible political force.

The problem was initially overcome by the introduction of a salary for MPs in 1911, but by 1913 the government was facing a series of strikes, and, to reduce pressure and keep Labour's support, they reversed the 'Osborne Judgement'. Any individual who objected to contributing to Labour, could 'contract out', but unsurprisingly, few workers bothered to do so. This was not quite as complete a victory as MacDonald had wanted, but for the sake of continued good relations, he accepted the partial compromise.

Considering the party's size and its increasingly poor relations with the Liberal Party after 1910, as the grassroots of the Labour movement became more militant and less patient in both its demands and its methods, it has to be said that the party was very successful in achieving its aims. The legal position of trade unions and their ability to fund the Labour Party were protected, and a number of crucial social reforms were passed which formed the basis for future welfare legislation by Labour governments. Although the party did not grow further after 1910, it had been able to resist absorption by the Liberal Party and yet to continue to benefit from the electoral compact of 1903. Labour's future achievements after the First World War were only possible once the party was able to point to its prior successes before 1914.

4. Liberal social reforms (OCR)

Why did the Liberal Government introduce a series of social reforms between 1906 and 1914 and how effective were these in tackling poverty in Britain?

(90 marks)

The policies of the Liberal Party had been dominated by the personality of the party leader from 1867 to 1893, William Gladstone. His priorities had been maximising opportunity for all and eliminating privilege, the granting of **Home Rule** for Ireland, but, most of all, cheap, efficient administration and minimal state intervention (a policy often referred to as *laissez faire*). The investigations of Charles Booth and Seebohm Rowntree carried out between 1889 and 1903 highlighted the issue of poverty in Britain. Booth showed that over 30 per cent of the population of London lived in serious poverty. Rowntree discovered that the proportion was almost as high in York. Both denied that poverty was the fault of the poor themselves, as many had believed in the nineteenth century. Booth explained that in a depression, a worker might be unable to find a job, Rowntree found that in York wages were so low that men in full-time employment lived close to the poverty line. He recommended a minimum wage of 21s 8d a week to keep a couple with three children in 'Spartan physical efficiency'.

Liberal motives for introducing the reforms were mixed. There was a genuine sense of compassion, a belief in social justice which claimed it was morally wrong for 30 per cent of the population of such a rich country to live in such miserable conditions. However, despite this outcry, the new government had not drawn up a programme of reform and it took time for one to develop.

There was, of course, the need for a healthy working class for military and economic reasons. If Britain was involved in a major war, an efficient army was needed to defend the Empire and the weaknesses of the current armed forces had been thrown into sharp relief by the failures in the Boer War. The Birmingham Chamber of Commerce called for health insurance and old age pensions on the grounds that a healthy workforce would work harder and be more profitable. Reform was therefore needed to improve 'national efficiency'. 'New Liberalism', championed by writers such as J.A. Hobson and L.T. Hobhouse, called on the state to take a greater role in social reform, to prevent the development of a disaffected underclass. They believed that traditional liberal concerns over legal, political and religious liberties had been successfully addressed by the party in the nineteenth century, but that now the chief limitation on individual liberty was economic and social deprivation which had to be alleviated. These ideas particularly influenced the Liberal Chancellor, David Lloyd George, but equally did much to convince the Prime Minister, Asquith, that welfare reform, financed by redistributive taxes, was necessary.

The Liberal Party was also under pressure from the new Labour Party with its 29 MPs and from trade unions (24 Liberals had been supported by the miners' union in 1906). It was hoped that a limited amount of social reform would satisfy the people and prevent working-class voters from supporting radical socialist ideas, and thus voting Labour. Lloyd George had visited Germany in 1908 where Bismarck had introduced social reforms for precisely these reasons and adopted the principle of social insurance he saw in operation there. There could not be too much reform either, otherwise traditional middle-class Liberals would resent the extra taxes needed and the increased role of the state and begin to support the Conservatives. Equally, the Conservatives claimed that they would finance similar reforms by imposing tariffs on imports to Britain and the Liberals needed to prove that social reform could be funded within a **free trade** economy as they had claimed in 1906.

More immediate political needs also played a part. After the frustrations of the Lords' opposition to many of their earlier measures, the government had been losing by-elections, and, as Lloyd George put it, 'It is time that we did something that appealed straight to the people – It will, I think, help to stop this electoral rot and that is most necessary'. The old age pension was duly introduced and proved enormously popular. The Liberals were swift to point out that although Joseph Chamberlain had been promising pensions for years, it had taken a Liberal government to actually implement them. In much the same way, the Liberals were able to use the 'People's Budget' and the promise of further social reforms such as National Insurance to help defeat their opponents in the struggle with the Lords and the two elections of 1910.

Finally, one should not ignore the ambitions of individuals, eager to make a name for themselves and gain public popularity in their pursuit of promotion. The two young Liberal Ministers who used the reforms most to further their careers towards the post of Prime Minister were Lloyd George and Churchill, who tried to out-do one another with speeches and newspaper articles. But even civil servants, such as William Beveridge at the Board of Trade had ambitions for a long career in social administration, which dramatic early achievements could launch.

Between 1906 and 1914, the Liberal government passed a series of social reforms which were implemented alongside existing Poor Law legislation, often contradicting it. As the reforms were introduced in a piecemeal fashion without an overall plan, it is extremely difficult to analyse the effectiveness of the legislation as a whole. Instead, each individual measure needs to be considered before an assessment can be reached.

Certainly, the Children's Charter, in particular the provision of free school meals and free medical treatment in schools can be seen as a major breakthrough in the elimination of the abject levels of child poverty that existed before 1906. On the other hand, neither of these measures was compulsory at first, and the government failed to provide funds meaning that the effects of both were not widely felt before the First World War.

When Lloyd George introduced old age pensions in 1908, there was criticism from the Labour Party that five shillings was a very small amount, only a quarter of a labourer's wage, and that the pension should begin at 65 not 70, as few people in their late sixties were able to continue to earn a living. One also had to be deemed 'deserving' in order to receive the pension: anyone who had been in prison in the last ten years, had claimed poor relief in the last two years, or was a known drunk or had failed to find work was excluded from the scheme. As a consequence the numbers claiming the pension in 1909 was not much different from those receiving Poor Law relief in their own homes beforehand. On the other hand, as the pension was non-contributory all could claim it, and as it could be collected from post offices, it did not have the stigma of the Poor Law attached to it and became hugely popular and helped to eradicate the worst cases of poverty among the elderly, the other group together with children, most exposed to dire poverty.

Many Labour activists also claimed that once it had been introduced in Churchill's Trade Boards Act, the principle of a minimum wage should be applied to all trades, but Liberalism had its limits. The government did introduce a Minimum Wages Act for miners in 1912 as a result of a damaging strike, but this only fixed minimum wages in particularly difficult seams, and wasn't the national agreement that the miners wanted.

When the National Insurance Act was finally passed in 1911, Labour moderates accepted the principle of contributory health and unemployment relief, but convinced socialists like Keir Hardie denounced it bitterly. They wanted benefits to be paid from heavier taxes on the rich. Unemployment Insurance applied only to workers in certain trades where casual labour was commonly employed, such as building, shipbuilding and iron-founding, which both Booth and Rowntree had identified as one of the chief causes of urban poverty in their surveys of city life. Two and a quarter million men and women were protected by the scheme, but the workhouse was still the only option if the worker was still unemployed after 15 weeks. Lloyd George had intended to extend the provisions of unemployment insurance as soon as possible, but the First World War prevented this. Under the Health Insurance scheme, only the worker was covered, not his wife or children, and as many Labour supporters pointed out, the worker was still having to pay for his own medical treatment.

Although individual reforms had varying degrees of success, taken together they must have done a lot to relieve the worst effects of poverty especially among children, the elderly and workers. But the recommendations of the Poor Law Commission had not been fully carried out and there were some areas which the Liberals had not touched. Nothing had been done to help agricultural workers and domestic servants who remained the worst paid and worst treated of all workers, although the Liberals had launched a Land Campaign to address rural poverty, which was interrupted by the Great War. Poor housing had not been tackled effectively. Poverty and its consequences, especially poor health among non-working women and the disabled remained acute. For such groups, the workhouse still remained the only source of support if they were prepared to bear the social stigma of entering it. Even for workers, wages rose very little between 1905 and 1914 and trade unions showed their disappointment with the Liberals in the series of strikes which broke out in 1910–14. In 1914, the number of army volunteers rejected as physically unfit was almost as high as it had been in 1900, in the Boer War – in a way, this was to be expected, as it would take time to feel the effects of the new state aid.

The important point to remember is that the Liberals took the first crucial steps towards establishing minimum standards of wealth and health in Britain. They did so in the face of bitter Conservative opposition, and on these minimum standards, reformers, such as Lloyd George and Churchill, both intended to build further, as soon as the opportunity presented itself. However, most of the Liberal Party felt that they had violated individualism and self-help, the historic principles of Victorian Liberalism as far as they ought and regarded the programme of reforms as complete and final.

5. The constitutional crisis (EDEXCEL)

a) **In what ways did the House of Lords challenge the Liberal government in 1909?** (30 marks)

b) **Why did the attempt to reform the constitution in 1910–11 succeed?** (30 marks)

(Total: 60 marks)

a) The House of Lords, with its large Conservative majority, was continually rejecting Liberal bills, although during the previous ten years of Conservative rule, it had not once interfered with a Conservative bill. The Liberal government, therefore, in spite of having been elected with a huge majority, was being prevented from carrying out its social policies, by a House of Lords which was not elected. If the Lords persisted, a constitutional crisis was inevitable.

Gladstone's second Irish Home Rule Bill of 1893 had passed in the House of Commons, but had been rejected by the Lords. The Lords had also defeated the majority of the measures introduced by Gladstone's successor, Lord Rosebery. The Lords had justified this by pointing to the Liberals' tiny majority at the time. After the 1906 Liberal landslide, however, there could be no excuse of a flimsy Liberal majority that did not reflect the wishes of the entire nation. The Conservative leaders, Balfour and Lord Lansdowne, were using the Lords to protect their party's interests. As Balfour quite blatantly declared, the Conservatives 'should still control, whether in power or opposition, the destinies of this great Empire'. He discounted the 1906 result as a freak, and encouraged the Lords to reject several key Liberal measures, including several Education Bills, a Plural Voting Bill, a Licensing Bill and four land bills, though not the Trades Disputes Bill, which as Lansdowne noted 'had the approval of working men'. Lloyd George derided the Lords as simply 'Mr Balfour's poodle' rather than the 'watchdog of the constitution'. Campbell-Bannerman, the new Liberal Prime Minister, then warned that if this continued, an attempt would be made to restrict their powers.

When Asquith succeeded Campbell-Bannerman in 1908, the Liberal party were still undecided on how to resolve this stalemate. It fell to the new Chancellor, Lloyd George, to suggest a solution. The Liberal social welfare programme of old age pensions and national insurance, combined with the costs of the 'naval race' which was developing with Germany left the government facing a potential budgetary deficit of £16 million. To raise the revenue, Lloyd George's budget of 1909 proposed a major increase in levels of taxation with income tax going up from 1s to 1s 2d in the pound on incomes over £3,000 and a 'supertax' of an extra 6d in the pound to incomes over £5,000. Higher taxes on tobacco and spirits were charged and higher charges were made for liquor licences. Taxes on petrol and cars were introduced and taxes were also introduced on the royalties accrued from mining. Most controversially, a 20 per cent tax was to be placed on the increased value of land when it was resold. The Lords, landowners to a man, feared that the introduction of any land tax would be the first step towards the abolition of private land ownership. However, it had become accepted that the Lords would never veto a 'money bill', so it seemed that Lloyd George had solved the difficulty.

Unfortunately, the Conservatives were not willing to back down and they encouraged the Lords to reject the budget by 350 votes to 75, ignoring a plea from the King not to do so. Asquith was horrified, calling their action 'an usurpation of the rights of the Commons', but Lloyd George was jubilant. 'We have got them at last!' he said, as a general election was called to determine the future of the budget. By this stage the details of the budget and the social purposes in passing it were subsumed in the wider question of 'peers versus people'

b) In the campaign for the January 1910 election, Lloyd George and Winston Churchill continued to provoke the Lords, accusing them of being 'a class that declined to do the duty which it was called upon to perform', whose sole function was 'the stately consumption of wealth produced by others.' The Labour Party fully supported the Liberal campaign against the Lords, seeing in them the obstacle to the further reforms that they desired.

The result of the election was disappointing for Asquith as the Liberals lost more than 100 seats. The Liberals' radical approach scared off many of their middle class supporters from 1906. The Liberals had 275 seats and the Conservatives and unionists had 273. The Liberals could, however, rely on the support of Labour, who had 40 seats and the Irish Nationalists who had 82. It was clear, though, that the price of the Irish Nationalists' co-operation would be a third Home Rule Bill, and the Lords would never agree to that, so their veto would have to be removed, not just their opposition to the budget.

Asquith now had to push a Parliament Bill which would restrict the Lords' powers through the upper house. He consulted with Edward VII on the possibility of creating about 250 new Liberal peers, enough to defeat the Conservatives in the Lords. Before the issue was settled Edward died suddenly in May and the new King, George V, called a Constitutional Conference to try to resolve the matter. The conference broke down over the problem of Ireland, because the Conservatives wanted to retain veto of a Home Rule Bill, but Asquith would not agree.

In November 1910, Asquith set the battle in motion again by sending the Parliament Bill to the Lords; when they refused to pass it, he met the King and asked him to create the necessary Liberal peers if the Liberals won another election. George agreed 'most reluctantly' (as he put it in his diary). Armed with this promise, Asquith called an election in December 1910. The result was very similar to the January election, with the Liberals with 272 seats, the Conservatives and Unionists with 272 as well, Labour now with 42 and the Irish Nationalists with 84. The Liberals and their allies could claim to have won the issue in two elections and so the Parliament Bill again passed the Commons with a clear majority in May 1911 despite Conservative attempts to construct a compromise.

In July 1911 Asquith announced to the Commons that the King had promised to create as many as 500 Liberal Peers if necessary to get the bill through the Lords. Although furious, when faced with such a prospect, just enough moderate Conservative Lords abstained, allowing the *Parliament Act* of 1911 to become law. Under its terms the Lords could no longer amend or reject a finance bill, but they could still amend or reject other bills. However, if a bill was passed by the Commons in three successive parliamentary sessions, and rejected three times by the Lords, it would become law on the occasion of its third rejection. In other words, the Lords could no longer control the country's finances; they could delay other legislation for two years, but could not prevent it becoming law eventually, provided the government stayed in power long enough. On the other hand, the Lords still had the power, if they felt like using it, to paralyse a government for the last two years of its five-year term.

The attempt to reform the constitution succeeded for a number of reasons. First, in two general elections, parties supporting reform won clear majorities of seats. Second, the Conservatives' blunder in opposing the 'people's budget' gave the Liberals the political ammunition they needed to discredit the Lords. Finally, Asquith handled the situation very effectively, exploiting the new King's inexperience and the Conservatives' stubbornness over Ireland to secure the Lords' approval for a measure which reduced their own power. That the success did his party no favours in the next three years reveals much of the bitterness of the dispute, but does not reduce the importance of the result for the future of British democracy.

6. Ireland (EDEXCEL)

a) **In what ways did the Liberal Governments attempt to solve the problems of Ireland in the years 1905 to 1912?** (30 marks)
b) **Why were they unable to establish Home Rule by 1914?** (30 marks)

(Total: 60 marks)

a) The Irish problem had existed even before the Act of Union in 1800 which had made Ireland part of the United Kingdom. During the nineteenth century, a largely Catholic Irish nationalism emerged, demanding a greater degree of autonomy (usually expressed as '**Home Rule**'), which divided the country even more sharply on the largely religious lines that had had fractured Ireland since the sixteenth century.

Since the rejection of Gladstone's Second Home Rule Bill by the House of Lords in 1893, the question had been pushed into the background by Imperial and social issues. However, the commitment to some form of Irish **Home Rule** was still very much part of the Liberal programme, and the Irish Nationalists, led by John Redmond, expected much from Campbell-Bannerman and the Liberals after 1906, especially after he gave self-government to the Boers of South Africa. All that the Liberal government were initially prepared to do was to set up an Irish Executive Council to deal with various internal policies such as education. Redmond was not prepared to accept this and the scheme foundered. Redmond was increasingly coming under pressure from **nationalists** to make some real progress towards **Home Rule**, especially Sinn Fein ('Ourselves Alone') led by Arthur Griffith. They were tired of waiting for Britain to allow **Home Rule**, they wanted to go ahead and set up their own parliament in Dublin which would gradually take over the function of governing the whole of Ireland. Redmond needed some concrete achievement to keep control of Irish nationalism and therefore he had to become increasingly urgent in his demands for action from the Liberals.

The matter came to the fore after the election of December 1910 when the Liberals won 272 seats as did the Conservatives and Unionists. The Liberals now had to rely on the support of the Irish Nationalists who had 84 seats. Asquith found that to make certain of Irish support for Lloyd George's budget, he had to promise a third Home Rule Bill which meant passing a measure to remove the Lords' power of veto. When the resulting Parliament Act passed in August 1911, the way was open for the Third Irish Home Rule Bill. Asquith himself was worried about the rise of extremism in nationalist circles and feared that Redmond's nationalists would be eclipsed unless **Home Rule** was achieved. As he put it, 'an ungovernable Ireland is a much more serious problem than rioting in four counties'.

The Bill was introduced in April 1912 and provided for an Irish Parliament with the power to pass some limited laws, with foreign affairs, defence and finance still controlled by Westminster, to which Ireland would send 42 MPs. This bill passed the Commons in 1912, but was immediately rejected by the Lords, who, under the Parliament Act still had the power to block legislation for up to two years.

b)   One of the chief difficulties of the Irish Nationalists' cause was the failure of all parties to agree on what **Home Rule** actually meant. While most Liberals agreed with Gladstone's definition of 1886 that it meant limited self-government and a separate Irish Parliament, more extreme nationalists demanded complete independence, which roused the fears of the Protestant minority concentrated in the North of Ireland.

Since the First Home Rule Bill in 1886, the **Ulster** Protestants had feared that they would be swamped by Catholics in a separate Ireland. By 1912 **Ulster** had developed industrially, particularly shipbuilding at Belfast, while the rest of Ireland remained agricultural and backward, emphasising this lack of national identity. Ulstermen felt themselves to be a separate community both economically and in religious matters. Four Counties – Antrim, Armagh, Derry and Down were overwhelmingly Protestant and they emphatically did not want to be part of an independent Ireland in which they would be dominated by and perhaps discriminated against by the Catholic South. Ulster Unionists had begun to organise themselves to resist **Home Rule** before the Home Rule Bill was introduced into the Commons and had as their spokesman Sir Edward Carson, a prominent barrister and Liberal Unionist MP. They held a massive demonstration and threatened to set up a provisional government if the bill passed. Hundreds of thousands of Ulstermen publicly signed a Solemn Oath and Covenant (some signing in blood) swearing to fight any government which tried to thrust **Home Rule** on them.

The Conservatives intensified the crisis by encouraging the Ulster Unionists. Having lost three consecutive elections, they had ousted Balfour as their leader and replaced him with Andrew Bonar Law, who had grown up in **Ulster**. He saw the **Ulster** situation as the perfect weapon with which to embarrass Asquith and perhaps bring down the government. When Carson openly organised a military force, the Ulster Volunteers and held drills and parades, Bonar Law went to Ireland and actually took the salute of the force. He told a Conservative Party rally at Blenheim Palace in July 1912, 'I can imagine no length to which **Ulster** will go, which I shall not be ready to support'. In their eagerness to destabilise the government, the leader of the British Conservative Party was encouraging armed rebellion against a law about to be passed by the legally elected British government. Asquith refused to have Carson and Law arrested, however, as he wished to demonstrate Liberal tolerance in the face of Conservative extremism.

In purely practical terms however, the Home Rule bill was prevented from becoming law by the actions of the Conservatives in the House of Lords. As many Conservatives resented the Liberals' recent treatment of the Lords, and as many of the Lords had estates in Ireland, such as Lord Lansdowne, they chose to do their utmost to block the bill.

Probably because he realised that the Conservatives were only using the Irish situation as a lever to get the government out, Asquith decided to let events take their course, or, as he put it, to 'wait and see'. He could have eased the situation from the beginning by discussing the possibility of a partition, allowing at least the four counties of **Ulster** to remain under British rule. There would have been opposition from the Nationalists, but it was not out of the question for them to accept such a compromise and it would have avoided the formation of the Ulster Volunteers. Not until early in 1914 did Asquith show that he was prepared to exclude **Ulster** from **Home Rule**. By this time, the Nationalists had already organised their private army, the **Nationalist** Volunteers. Here was another fatal omission by Asquith; he should have taken prompt action to ban all private armies and the import of arms. Nothing was done, and both the Ulster and **Nationalist** Volunteers began to import arms and built up their troops. Only in March 1914 did Asquith decide to send troops into **Ulster** to guard strategic points and arms depots and the Royal Navy to post destroyers off the coast.

When the government's intention became known, about 60 army officers stationed at the Curragh in Dublin threatened to resign if they were ordered to force **Ulster** to accept **Home Rule**. The War Secretary, J.E.B. Seeley (an ex-Conservative), caved in at this 'mutiny'. The plan to send troops into **Ulster** had to be abandoned and Seeley assured the army that they would not be used to force **Home Rule** on Ulster. Furious at this loss of nerve, Asquith demanded Seeley's resignation and took over the War Office himself, but he failed to dispel the impression, that in the event of **Ulster** resisting **Home Rule**, the government might not be able to rely on the loyalty of the army; this now encouraged the Ulster Unionists to step up their preparations to fight. The Ulster Volunteers were allowed to smuggle in 35,000 rifles and ammunition at Larne without interference from the police. The situation had clearly moved beyond the government's ability to control it.

The Home Rule Bill passed the Commons for the third time in May 1914, but it still contained no provision for a separate **Ulster**. At first Asquith proposed an Amending Bill which would allow the counties of **Ulster** to vote to remove themselves from **Home Rule** for up to six years, but this did not satisfy the Unionists and the Lords changed it to permanently exclude **Ulster** from **Home Rule**. Frantic negotiations followed, culminating in an all-party conference in July at Buckingham Palace. At one point Redmond apparently agreed to the exclusion of the four Protestant counties from **Home Rule** rather than risk civil war. But the Unionists stepped up their demands and insisted that **Ulster** should contain Fermanagh and Tyrone, whose population was at least 50 per cent Roman Catholic. Redmond could not agree to this, given the growth of nationalist militancy and so the conference collapsed. The Amending Bill had to be scrapped.

On 26 July **Nationalist** Volunteers brought in 1,500 guns to Howth, just outside Dublin, and troops were sent to stop them. A hostile crowd gathered, angry that the Nationalists should be treated with differently to the Ulster Unionists. Stones were thrown at the troops who opened fire, killing three people and wounding 38. Tension was high and Ireland seemed on the brink of civil war. Only a few days later the First World War broke out, and the government suspended the Home Rule Bill until at least a year after the war was over. No solution had been found, but it was generally hoped that the Irish would remain quiet and support the war effort, which most did, at least until Easter 1916.

7. Women's rights and the Suffrage Movement (EDEXCEL)

a) **Describe how the Suffragette Movement challenged the state between 1903 and 1914** (30 marks)

b) **Why had women failed to gain the vote by 1914?** (30 marks)

(Total: 60 marks)

a) Women had achieved considerable social and political progress throughout the nineteenth century. By 1900 middle-class women had been accepted as teachers and office workers, as well as in the medical professions. Unmarried women and widows were allowed to vote for new county and borough councils and both married and unmarried women could vote for the new urban and rural district councils and could stand for election for these. Women's legal rights had been advanced by the Married Women's Property Act (1882) which allowed a woman to continue to own her property when she married, and by the Guardianship of Children Act (1886) which allowed a mother to claim custody of her children after separation from her husband.

Movements demanding that women should have the right to vote for MPs had been organised since the 1860s, but in 1897 the National Union of Women's Suffrage Societies (NUWSS) was organised to unite the 'suffragists' as they were known. The principal argument of the NUWSS was that if women could vote for local councils, why could they not vote for the national assembly in Westminster? However, in 1903, Emmeline Pankhurst, irritated by what she saw as the NUWSS's cautious approach, founded the Women's Social and Political Union (WSPU). To differentiate between the groups, the *Daily Mail* nicknamed this group '**suffragettes**'.

Mrs Pankhurst, the widow of a Manchester barrister, believed that only when women had the vote, could sufficient pressure be put on governments to improve social conditions. She hoped for satisfaction from the new Liberal Government, as it was well known that Campbell-Bannerman, Lloyd George and Grey were sympathetic. Their hopes were raised further by the Qualification of Women Act (1907) which allowed women to become members of county and borough councils and even mayors.

When a private member's bill to give women the vote was heavily defeated in 1907, however, it became clear that, however logical the women's cause was, the Liberal government was not sufficiently impressed by it. One of their excuses for lack of action was the problem of whether to give the vote to all women or just to unmarried women and widows, since married women were not considered to be householders. The real reason was that Asquith was against it, fearing that women would be politically ignorant and easily swayed by the crude appeals of conservatism. Women were to be excluded from the Liberals' public meetings, the government refused to meet suffrage deputations and harassed the WSPU press. Two Conciliation Bills granting women the vote were carried by the Commons, but the government refused to carry them further.

Faced with the government's refusal to listen to peaceful protest, illegal methods were employed by both suffragists and suffragettes, most notably tax evasion and resistance to the census of 1911. Inspired by the relative success of trade union militancy and the behaviour of the Ulster Unionists the suffragettes gradually became more militant. Since 1905, they had been disrupting meetings addressed by Liberal politicians; Christabel Pankhurst and Annie Kenney, a Lancashire cotton worker, spent a week in gaol after being ejected from the Manchester Free Trade Hall, where they had heckled Sir Edward Grey. Now rank and file WSPU members turned to smashing windows of shops and government buildings, attacking paintings and chaining themselves to the railings of Buckingham Palace and Downing Street. When these actions led to arrest and imprisonment, the suffragettes went on hunger strike to protest against what they saw as unfair protest and to gain publicity. The government was faced with the danger of the women dying in prison and so chose to order the force feeding of the women.

b) The principle of votes for women had probably been accepted by the majority of the MPs in the new Parliament of 1906, but actual legislation was delayed by a number of factors. The government had a full programme of reforms to implement in the face of opposition to some measures from the House of Lords and were unwilling to give parliamentary time to a measure which many Liberals feared would benefit the Conservatives more. The Conservatives themselves were divided on the issue, with the leadership seeing the tactical advantages in the suffragist cause, but the bulk of Tory backbenchers leading the opposition to votes for women. There was also still no agreement on which women should receive the vote. Not all men had the vote, so should the same restrictions be placed on female suffrage? Should married women qualify, although they were not legally regarded as householders?

By 1912, Asquith and the cabinet had accepted the principle of female suffrage and to save time, made a late amendment to the Plural Voting Bill which was already under discussion. The amendments gave the vote to certain categories of women. However, in January 1913, the Speaker ruled that the additions could not be allowed as they changed the nature of the Bill. As a result of this political incompetence, a handful of the suffragettes stepped up their militant campaign. They began setting fire to post boxes, churches and railway stations, and physically attacking cabinet ministers, particularly Asquith. Lloyd George's new country house in Surrey was badly damaged by a bomb explosion, for which Mrs Pankhurst received a three-year gaol sentence. Then, most famously of all, Emily Davison was killed as she threw herself in front of the King's horse at the 1913 Derby.

Since the Liberals had accepted the principle of votes for women in the Plural Voting Bill amendment, it was more likely that they would have tried again in 1913, and that the Commons would have approved it by 1914. But the violence discredited the suffragettes and divided the women's rights movement. The NUWSS had, at first been sympathetic to some of the more militant tactics of the WSPU, but after 1909, it began to voice public disapproval of suffragette tactics. Even within the WSPU itself, the Pankhursts were losing support because of their dictatorial approach.

As the suffragettes became more militant, the government response became more unpleasant and insensitive. When suffragettes went on hunger strike in prison, the government authorised that they should be forcibly fed. When this provoked more criticism, the government responded with the farcical Prisoners' Temporary Discharge for Ill-Health Bill (known as the 'Cat and Mouse Act' in 1913), which allowed the release from prison of women who were weak from hunger striking, and then for them to be re-imprisoned once they had recovered their strength. This did gain the movement some sympathy, particularly from nonconformist groups, but many people regarded the treatment as self-inflicted.

Ultimately, the campaigners for the suffrage failed to achieve their objectives by 1914 for two fundamental reasons. First, they had failed to allay the fears of the Liberal government, and had hardened their resistance by their increasingly militant tactics and second, they seemed to have failed to convince the majority of voters, in other words British men. The press remained almost unanimously hostile, trade unions were largely indifferent and of the other political parties, only the small Labour party actually included votes for women in their manifesto (and then only in 1914). Although the government was seriously considering the introduction of some form of franchise reform in 1914, it still remains unclear whether this would have included votes for women, and whether the issue would have been approved by either the Commons or the Lords.

8. Industrial unrest 1908–14 (OCR)

Why was there so much industrial unrest between 1908 and 1914 and how successfully did the government deal with it?

(90 marks)

The years before the First World War were a period of unprecedented industrial unrest. Between 1900 and 1907 there had been few major strikes, the average number of days lost had been about 2.75 million per year. In 1908 this figure jumped to almost 11 million, and in 1912 it reached a massive 41 million. A strike by shipbuilders in the North East in 1908 was followed by a series of strikes in Yorkshire, South Wales and Durham over pay in summer 1910. There were dockers' strikes in Liverpool, Southampton and Cardiff, a national rail strike in 1911, and finally a strike by the whole Miners' Federation, involving a million miners in 1912. One historian has written that 'frightened police going berserk with batons were almost a commonplace' in the five years before the war.

'Syndicalists', such as Tom Mann, the founder of the National Transport Workers' Federation in 1910, believed that trade unions should join together in massive strikes to bring down unsympathetic governments and even the capitalist system itself. Although 'sympathetic strikes' did take place between 1908 and 1914, and the impressive sounding 'Triple Alliance' of transport workers, miners and railwaymen was formed in 1914, in reality, most union leaders were interested in the negotiation of improved wages and conditions, not revolutionary socialism. Mann's attempts to elicit support for a dock strike in 1912 met with little response, and after 1912 the number of days lost to strikes fell back to 10 million, with no significant change in 1914. Syndicalist ideas were only held by a minority of trade unionists and most unions had to have a ballot before they went on strike.

The union militancy may also have been due to disappointment with the Labour Party. Many activists at the time felt that the **Lib–Lab pact** of 1903 was benefiting the Liberals far more than Labour and that Labour lacked a distinctive radical programme with which to challenge 'New' Liberalism. After the 'Osborne Judgement' of 1909 declared unions' political levy illegal, the Liberal government failed to act until 1913. Similarly, Labour was unable until 1911 to persuade the Liberals to introduce payment for MPs without which most working men could not afford to stand for Parliament. On the other hand, the Labour Party was attracting the affiliation of many more trade unions in the period, including the miners in 1909, and was scoring a number of successes in local council elections, especially in the cities. In 1914, 60 out of 63 unions which were balloted agreed to set up a political fund for the Labour Party

Although these factors did make some contribution towards this industrial unrest, clearly the most important was economic. Wage levels, although rising, were not keeping pace with the increase in the cost of living. The worst years for inflation were 1911 and 1912, the worst years for strikes. The hardest hit were manual workers, most especially the unskilled or semi-skilled, and it was these workers' unions, which were the most militant. Meanwhile, employers, concerned at the increasing competition from countries overseas such as Germany, USA and Japan, were attempting to keep costs down, and were thus minimising pay increases. This left many unions with little alternative but to first threaten and then, somewhat reluctantly, to initiate strike actions. When a trade boom in 1913 reduced unemployment to 3 per cent, despite the decreased threat of blackleg labour and the increase in size and power of the unions, the number of strikes declined, demonstrating that the strikes were fundamentally economic rather than political. It must also be noted, that it was not an overall improvement of industrial relations which finally ended the industrial unrest, but, as with the suffragettes and Ireland, it was the outbreak of war. Industrial issues were to re-emerge once the war was over.

The Liberals did not demonstrate a consistent policy towards the various strikes which occurred in this period, responding to some with a conciliatory approach, but preferring to use force in other cases.

In 1907 the new era of labour militancy began when the Railway Servants' Union called for a national strike. On this occasion the government intervened and prevented the strike by setting up conciliation boards, where the railway companies agreed to meet with workers' representatives to discuss wages and hours.

During the wave of strikes in 1910, the Home Secretary, Winston Churchill, sent in the army to reinforce the police at Tonypandy in South Wales, and although the troops were never used, three miners were killed during confrontations with the police and the strike dragged on for ten months. During the sailor's and firemen's strike, there were two more deaths in Liverpool when troops were sent in to keep order and the government consented to the Mayor of Liverpool's request that warships should be moored in the Mersey with their guns trained on the city. In the 1911 national railway strike, Asquith's insistence that the strikers must not disrupt essential services led to the use of troops for a third time and there were two further deaths in Llanelly during a riot. At this point it seemed that the government's actions were merely exacerbating the situation.

At this point Asquith demonstrated his willingness to compromise to deal with the strike and appointed a Royal Commission to investigate the railway union's claims. This didn't improve matters. He then allowed negotiations to take place under the guidance of Lloyd George, whose first step was to secure the co-operation of Ramsay MacDonald. The strike ended after four days with the railwaymen gaining some wage increases. In a similar fashion, when faced with the miners' strike in 1912, the government rushed through the Coal Mines Minimum Wages Act. This did not grant a minimum wage, but each district could and did set their own minimum. This satisfied the miners who returned to work in April.

At a time when there were no established systems of collective bargaining and when unions were growing in power and size, the government had to abandon its traditional 'laissez faire' approach to solve particularly entrenched industrial unrest by using its powers to help employers meet some of the demands of the unions. Confrontation had clearly not been successful, and the government, and Asquith in particular, had to adapt the role of government to new circumstances, which they did effectively, if the relative industrial calm of 1914 is a reliable indicator of success.

9. British foreign policy 1900–14 (OCR)

Did improved diplomatic relations between France and Britain lead to Britain's declaration of war in 1914?

(90 marks)

In November 1900, Prime Minister Salisbury resigned as Foreign Secretary and handed the position to Lord Lansdowne, although Lansdowne did continue to ask Salisbury's advice and frequently waited for his approval before taking action. After the difficulties in defeating the Boers, Lord Lansdowne was aware that Britain's lack of firm allies anywhere in the world could prove disastrous in the event of a war, especially in the Far East, where the presence of the Royal Navy was quite small. Lord Lansdowne, like Chamberlain, favoured a European alliance to secure Britain from attack from Europe. Chamberlain had twice sought an alliance with Germany and Lansdowne tried again following an Anglo-German agreement over China, but the Germans refused to be drawn. As hostility towards Russian expansion still defined Britain's eastern policy, she entered into negotiations with Russia's main opponent, the newly emergent Japan, who, like Britain was a naval power and wished to exploit trade with China.

The Anglo-Japanese treaty which was signed in 1902 was, principally, defensive. Japan, however, interpreted the treaty as an opportunity to attack Russia, as they now had an ally in the unlikely event that the Russian ally, France intervened in the eastern conflict.

Although the French press had been extremely anti-British during the Fashoda incident, when they had quarrelled with the French over the area of the Nile, and the Boer War, the French government were anxious to come to an agreement with Britain, as they still feared the power of Germany and had little faith in their ally, Russia. When the Anglo-Japanese alliance was signed they were worried that they could find themselves in a war against Britain if a Russo-Japanese war broke out.

The French Foreign Minister, Delcassé and the British Colonial Secretary, Chamberlain, worked hard to come to good terms. A visit by King Edward VII to Paris in May 1903 was used to demonstrate Britain's readiness to work with France, and the outbreak of the Russo-Japanese war in the following year pushed the two sides into finally settling an agreement.

Under its terms Britain recognised French supremacy in Morocco, while she accepted Britain's role in Egypt and Sudan. Disputes over territory in Canada, Africa and the Far East were also settled. It is important to see the entente in the tradition of Britain's long term aim of limiting Britain's liabilities abroad. By securing agreements over colonies, Britain was attempting to prevent colonial disputes causing her to become embroiled in conflicts with her European neighbours that might drag her into a European war. This was not a military alliance, either offensive or defensive. As a result of the entente, the Russo-Japanese war remained contained, and it became a useful channel for settling disagreements between Britain, France and their allies.

Germany, however, interpreted the entente as the prelude to a full military alliance aimed against them and decided to drive a wedge between Britain and France by asserting her own interests in Morocco and demanding an international conference. Sadly for Germany, this had precisely the opposite effect and actually caused the entente to become closer. The new Liberal Foreign Secretary,

Grey, was determined to support the French against what he saw as German sabre-rattling. At the conference on Morocco's future at Algeciras in January 1906, he supported French demands for control of the Moroccan police and bank. If he did not, Grey feared, France would move closer to Germany. He also managed to secure Russian, Spanish and Italian support, thus humiliating Germany. Now clearly committed to France, Britain entered into 'military conversations' regarding their future co-operation (which were clearly aimed against Germany). This did not amount to a commitment to come to France's aid if she was attacked by Germany, but when the details of the conversations were made clear to the Cabinet in 1911, there was great uncertainty as to what they did imply.

After a rebellion in Morocco, the French occupied Fez, the capital, and seemed likely to annex the country. To try to gain some compensation, the German government sent a gunboat, the Panther to the Moroccan port of Agadir. Worried about Germany being granted a Mediterranean base which might threaten the trade route to India, Grey allowed Lloyd George to make a speech at the Lord Mayor's banquet at the Mansion House, warning the Germans to keep their noses out. The Germans retreated, in return for the promise of two strips of land in the French Congo. This second defeat roused German public opinion against the British, but drove the entente allies still closer together. In 1912, a joint naval strategy was agreed, whereby the French would concentrate on defending the Mediterranean, while the British protected the Atlantic and the Channel. However, Grey resisted French demands for a formal treaty against Germany, fully aware that the Cabinet and his Party would not support him. His middle way between supporting France and avoiding over-commitment was only abandoned in 1914, when the violation of Belgian neutrality unified the Cabinet in agreeing to go to war with Germany.

After the Balkan League's victory in the war against Turkey in 1912, Grey decided to try to build some bridges with the Germans by organising a peace treaty in London to decide which territories the Balkan states should be granted from Turkey. In supporting the Austrians and Germans in their demand for an independent Albania, to check Serbian aggression, Grey did much to reassure the Germans. When the Balkan League fought among themselves over the spoils in 1913, the British and Germans co-operated again to restrain Austria, who was eager to attack the Serbs. Unfortunately, the Germans misread Grey's policy as an indication that Britain was not really committed to the entente, and so believed that, in the likely future war between Austria and Serbia, Britain would remain neutral if the war escalated across Europe.

When Franz Ferdinand was assassinated in Sarajevo in June 1914, most British attention was on the crisis in Ireland. The Balkan crisis became more acute for Britain when on 23 July, Austria sent an ultimatum to Serbia which she could not possibly agree to. The Germans, in light of the improved relations with Britain, clearly did not believe that the British would fight for France, and therefore implemented their Schlieffen Plan which involved the immediate invasion of France. Grey tried desperately to arrange negotiations, and then warned Germany that Britain might not stay neutral, but the central powers appear to have swiftly convinced themselves that the Bosnian crisis could only be solved by war, even one against the French and the Russians. In any case, Grey could not promise British intervention, as he had not got the backing of the Cabinet for this yet and Britain had no formal commitment to France. But the Cabinet was too concerned about a dominant Germany to allow France to fall, and she had a moral obligation to her as a result of the entente, especially since the 1912 naval agreement had left the whole of France's Atlantic coast unprotected. The Cabinet's indecision was only finally resolved on 3 August when the Germans requested that their troops be given free passage through Belgium in their invasion of France.

Britain had guaranteed Belgian neutrality since 1839, so this was sufficient to finally persuade the Cabinet that action against Germany was necessary. Parliament was finally convinced by Grey's speech of 3 August when he told the house that Britain 'could not stand aside and see this [the invasion of Belgium and France] . . . with our arms folded . . . doing nothing'. An ultimatum was issued to the Germans to withdraw from Belgium. When that was ignored, the Cabinet declared war on Germany and Austria on 4 August, with two members resigning in protest.

Britain clearly had much reluctance in going to war over a crisis which had its origins in the Balkans. Improving relations with Germany over colonies and the slowing of the recent 'naval race' made many, including Lloyd George, reluctant to become involved in the July crisis. The Cabinet was aware, however, that although no military alliance existed with France, the entente did oblige Britain to offer some assistance to her. The question of what sort of assistance Britain should offer was only finally resolved the day before Britain's declaration of war, when Germany threatened Belgium and seemed to confirm fears of a brutal militaristic regime unwilling to observe international law. Such a nation had to be stopped and Britain's reservations were swiftly put aside and she entered the war with near unanimous support for a cause seen as just. However, Grey was devastated by his inability to prevent war, as he revealed to the US ambassador, 'thus the efforts of a lifetime go for nothing. I feel like a man who has wasted his life'.

Additional essay questions

Although these questions are similar to those which have been answered on pages 24–44, it is assumed that some additional reading will be done for each one; it is never a good idea to rely on any one source. It is also necessary to adjust your approach to fit each question. Assume that examination conditions allow for about one hour for each group of two questions, but under normal conditions much longer will be available and necessary.

1. The decline of the Unionists (OCR)

Why did Joseph Chamberlain launch his campaign for tariff reform in 1903 and how seriously did his campaign weaken the Conservative Party?

(90 marks)

Essay plan

The economic need for protection:

- *The condition of British industry.*
- *Competition from Germany and USA in iron, steel, textiles and coal.*
- *Outdated machinery and techniques.*
- *The condition of British agriculture.*
- *Competition from USA especially in wheat and meat.*

The Imperial Opportunity:

- *The need to unite the Empire following the Boer War.*
- *The untapped potential of the Empire as market and source of raw materials.*

Joseph Chamberlain's ambition:

- *His desire for extra funding to pay for social reforms such as pensions to which he had given public commitment.*
- *His hopes to lead the Conservatives as well as the **Liberal Unionists** following the resignation of Lord Salisbury.*

Conservative 'crisis':

- *Growing unpopularity of the party since the end of the Boer War.*
- *Need to respond to the formation of the LRC and introduce social reforms without having to raise taxes – tariffs as a source of revenue.*

Serious nature of the tariff splits within the party:

- *Division between the Chancellor, and Joseph Chamberlain reflected by party split between the 'free fooders' and the 'tariff reformers'.*
- *Setting up of rival 'leagues' – Conservative structures such as Primrose League undermined by this.*
- *Balfour's unwillingness to take sides – both groups dissatisfied – Balfour's leadership appeared weak to the electorate.*
- *Effective exploitation of the divisions within the party by the Liberals.*

Importance of other factors in weakening the Conservative government:

- *Unpopularity of issues such as the Licensing Act, the Education Act and the Taff Vale judgement with particular interest groups.*
- *The revelations of the conditions in concentration camps in South Africa during the Boer War and the scandal over 'Chinese slavery' in the region.*
- *The demands to tackle the problem of poverty from 'New' Liberals such as Lloyd George and Hobson, the newly founded Labour Representation Committee and social investigators such Booth and Rowntree – how to resolve this issue also divided the party.*
- *The effect of the **Lib–Lab pact** in effectively organising the anti-Conservative vote.*

*Conclusion – Although the actions of the Conservative Party in passing reforms and its policies abroad alienated certain interest groups, the open divisions over **Tariff Reform** within the party conveyed a more general image of a government that had been in office for too long and which was no longer able to operate effectively. To this can be added the failure of the **Tariff Reform** campaigners to persuade the working classes of the benefits of imperial protection – the Liberals very effectively played on fears of 'food taxes'. In other words, the Conservatives suffered all the problems of a major policy shift, without reaping any of the rewards.*

2. The formation of the Labour Party (EDEXCEL)

a) **What legal obstacles did trade unions face between 1900 and 1914 and how successfully did they overcome them?** (30 marks)

b) **Why and with what consequences was the Lib–Lab pact of 1903 agreed by Ramsay MacDonald and Herbert Gladstone?** (30 marks)

(Total: 60 marks)

3. Liberal social reforms (AQA)

Read the following source and then answer the questions which follow:

In 1906, as in 1908, the Liberals had still to formulate a policy of social reform that would move the party away from nineteenth-century political Liberalism – the mixture of the freedom of the individual, the absolute necessity of **free trade**, an acceptance of capitalist economics – on which the party was still living. The Liberals had yet to find the policies to tackle the grave social problems in the country that had been highlighted by Charles Booth's study of London and Seebohm Rowntree's survey of York. It was against this background that the 'New Liberalism' was born.

From *A Short History of the Liberal Party* by Chris Cook, 1993

a) **What social problems had Booth and Rowntree highlighted?** (3 marks)

b) **What was 'New Liberalism'?** (7 marks)

c) **Did the Liberals abandon 'nineteenth century political Liberalism after 1906?** (15 marks)

(Total: 25 marks)

4. The constitutional crisis (EDEXCEL)

a) **In what ways did the Liberal Government's attempts to implement social and welfare reforms between 1906 and 1911 bring about conflict with the House of Lords?** (30 marks)

b) **Were the Lords unwise to oppose the 1909 budget?** (30 marks)

(Total: 60 marks)

5. Ireland (OCR)

Why were both Ulster Unionists and Irish Nationalists turning to violence to achieve their ends by 1914?

(90 marks)

6. Women's rights and the Suffrage Movement (OCR)

How significant is the division between the WSPU and the NUWSS in explaining why the Liberal government had failed to grant the right to vote to women by 1914?

(90 marks)

7. Industrial unrest 1908–14 (EDEXCEL)

a) **Describe the extent of the industrial unrest of 1909–13.**   **(30 marks)**
b) **How successful were the strikes of 1909–13?**   **(30 marks)**

(Total: 60 marks)

8. British foreign policy 1900–14 (OCR)

To what extent did Lord Lansdowne change the aims and the methods of British foreign policy between 1900 and 1905?   **(90 marks)**

9. General questions (OCR)

'The Liberal Government of 1906–14 owed its success chiefly to the influence of David Lloyd George'. Do you agree?

(Total: 90 marks)

Was the Liberal Party in crisis by 1914?

(Total: 90 marks)

Essay plan

Introduction – The idea, first expressed by George Dangerfield, that the Liberalism could no longer cope with the social, economic and political problems of the early twentieth century.

Crises of 1911–14 – describe their seriousness and analyse the success of the Liberal response:

*   *The demand for the vote: The growing criticism of the Liberal tactics, such as the 'Cat and Mouse Act', but the cross-party rejection of militancy.*
*   *The Ulster crisis: The threat of civil war following the Howth incident, but the extremism of the Conservative position and the continued possibility of excluding Ulster from Home Rule.*
*   *The confrontation with Germany: The expense of the dreadnought programme and the commitment to intervention in Europe, but Germany and Austria remained contained both in Europe and Africa.*

- *The conflict with the House of Lords: The continued use of the veto to block **Home Rule**, but the restrictions on this authority and the established supremacy of the House of Commons.*
- *The challenge of Labour: The wave of dangerous strikes of 1911–13, but these seemed to be decreasing by 1914 and the unions accepted the use of government-led arbitration.*

*Conclusion – Extremely difficult problems faced the Liberals after 1911, not least because they were also introducing a series of wide-reaching social reforms. However, with the exception of the **Ulster** crisis, the Liberals had had some success in tackling the other four crises and much credit for their social reforms.*

The Liberal Cabinet remained united with no minister resigning before the outbreak of war.

*While the Conservatives had recovered from their own crisis of 1903–11, the Labour Party was still an ally of the Liberals within the **Lib–Lab pact** and as a result the Liberal vote in their industrial and working class strongholds held up after 1906.*

*There is sufficient evidence to say that the crises of 1911–14, with the threats from extremists from both left and right actually strengthened the authority of the centrist Liberals and that it was the impact of the Great War, with its need for greater **collectivism**, that undermined the strong position of the Liberals.*

Part 3: Sources

1. National insurance proposals (OCR)

Source A: Lloyd George introduces his National Insurance proposals

It would improve the self-respect of the British worker that he should gain benefit from a scheme to which he himself was a major contributor. This Bill is setting up a great scheme which will be woven into the fabric of this country, and will be regarded by all working men with gratitude as something which has given them a vital guarantee in their daily lives. It is a Bill which the employers will accept as something which improves the efficiency of their labour and which gives stability to the existing order of things.

Lloyd George, speaking in the House of Commons on the National Insurance Bill, 6 December 1911

Source B: Lord Robert Cecil, an aristocratic Conservative MP, opposes Lloyd George's proposal

People bitterly (and rightly) resent in this country being made to contribute their own money for benefits in a way they do not approve. Individual freedom is the foundation upon which our prosperity and our existence are built and, for my part, I believe that the qualities of self-control, self-reliance, and self-respect depend upon individual liberty and the freedom and independence of the people of this country.

Lord Robert Cecil, speaking in the same debate, 6 December 1911

Source C: George Lansbury, a socialist founder member of the Labour Party, expresses doubts about Lloyd George's proposal

Instead of Parliament voting to take away money from ordinary people it ought either to be voting to give them money or, much better, it ought to pass reforms which will enable these men and women to earn living wages. I am perfectly certain that when you attempt to collect the money, you will have a revolt. I do not understand MPs who have three or four square meals a day thinking that a man can keep his family on just 7 shillings a week, and then tell him that the new scheme is some great gift you are offering him. I believe this Bill does not touch any root cause of poverty at all, either through sickness or unemployment.

George Lansbury, speaking in the same debate, 6 December 1911

Source D: A letter to the *British Medical Journal* expresses concern about the health aspects of Lloyd George's proposal

It is a step in the downward path towards socialism. It will destroy individual effort and increase the spirit of dependency which is always found in the degenerate races. This spoon-fed race will look to a fatherly government to feed and clothe it, and not to require it to work more than a few hours daily. They will be encouraged to multiply their breed at the expense of the healthy and intellectual members of the community. Every source of money is being tapped for the benefit of our least worthy citizens. Now, doctors are to be sweated in order to provide free medical advice for the least worthy of the wage-earning population in this country.

From a letter in the British Medical Journal, 30 December 1911

QUESTIONS WITH WORKED ANSWERS

a) **Study source A. In light of your own knowledge, what does this Source tell us of official attitudes towards the working classes?** (10)

b) **Study source D. From your own knowledge, how typical of contemporary medical opinion is this source?** (25)

c) **Study sources B and C. Explain the difference in attitude between these two sources to Lloyd George's proposals for National Insurance.** (25)

d) **Study all the sources and use your own knowledge 'Lloyd George's proposals met with opposition because his aims went beyond improving labour efficiency and stabilising the existing order'. Do you agree?** (60)

(Total: 120 marks)

ANSWERS

a) In the early nineteenth century, government legislation and established opinion had emphasised the view that the working classes should practise 'self-help', a view echoed by Lloyd George's emphasis on the contributory nature of National Insurance, which would 'improve the self-respect of the British worker'. However, social investigations at the end of the century had revealed the lack of control the working classes had over their levels of employment, and so Lloyd George, in line with 'New Liberal' thinking, is offering the workers 'a . . . guarantee'.

The National Insurance scheme that Lloyd George is defending here, was designed to improve the 'efficiency' of the working classes, in the face of economic competition from the USA and Germany in particular, and so is to be 'woven into the fabric of this country' by compulsory contributions by employer, employee and the state. It was only one aspect of the drive for efficiency that also involved acts protecting the well-being of children and the provision of Labour Exchanges to improve the opportunities available to the unemployed.

Lloyd George's speech is deliberately designed to appeal to both the workers and the employers, at a time when the Liberal Government was facing criticism for its proposals from both the Conservative majority in the House of Lords, who believed they went too far in the redistribution of wealth, and from the Labour movement, who believed that they didn't go far enough. Having said that, it is important to note that Lloyd George, as a politician keen to make his name as a popular reformer, may not be the most typical of 'official attitudes', and the controversy that this proposal and the means of financing it evoked, clearly demonstrated this.

b) This letter was published in a journal associated with the British Medical Association (BMA) and it expresses many of the views of that institution, that is, strongly opposed to state intervention in the provision of health care, and determined to protect the interests of private doctors, which appeared to be threatened by the health aspects of the National Insurance Bill. The letter was probably written by a private doctor, who resented that his profession was about to become a 'sweated' industry, for the benefit of 'the least worthy' in society. In this respect it may well reflect a genuine concern among many such medical practitioners. However, as a single letter to a journal, rather than an editorial from that journal, or a statement by a leading member of the BMA, one cannot say with any certainty whether or not it was printed because it was a typical view or because it was unusual and printed to provoke a reaction among the readership.

The views expressed in source D expressing contemporary concern over the fitness of the English race and the need to encourage 'individual effort' amongst the population and to discourage 'dependency', cannot be said to provide evidence of medical opinion, however. Such a belief in 'eugenics' may have been typical of many doctors, but it is essentially a political opinion, rejecting the philosophy of socialism, rather than a medical one. It is certainly interesting to know that at least one doctor held such views, but without corroborating material it is unwise to draw too many conclusions from it.

c) Cecil, in source B, opposes the compulsory nature of the National Insurance legislation and warns of popular resentment as a consequence. Lansbury, in source C, also opposes the element of compulsory contribution, and he too warns of a 'revolt', if it is enforced. In this sense, the sources do not differ.

However, Cecil opposes the Bill because of its threat to 'individual liberty' and is ideologically opposed to any intervention by the state. Lansbury, by contrast, does support state intervention, as he believes that Parliament should 'give them [ordinary people] money' and resents the lack of more radical action by rich MPs. By this he clearly means the use of direct redistributive taxation.

As a leading Conservative, it is ironic that Cecil is expressing views that had been associated with Gladstonian liberalism in the nineteenth century – those of self-help and limited interference by the state. Such views, however, had been shared by Cecil's father, Lord Salisbury, who as Prime Minister and leader of the Conservatives, had sought to avoid any excessive expansion of the role of the state in alleviating poverty, preferring instead to concentrate on the expansion of Britain's colonial possessions. It is, however, indicative of the radicalism of Lloyd George's proposals that such a traditionally liberal argument is being used against a Liberal Chancellor. Lansbury, as a socialist, is, from his personal experience in local government in the East End of London, ideologically committed to removing the 'root cause[s] of poverty' rather than offering families 'just 7 shillings a week', and making them pay for it themselves. His attitude reflects the increased disenchantment that the Labour Party felt with the Liberals and helps to explain the wave of industrial unrest that was sweeping the country at the time.

d) Lloyd George, in source A, states that the objective of the bill is to improve 'the efficiency of . . . labour' and that it will benefit both worker and employer and will no doubt encourage social stability. By contrast, Cecil, in source B, believes that it challenges the very nature of 'individual liberty' and will cause popular resentment. Similarly, Lansbury, predicts 'a revolt', but he regards the scheme as insignificant in raising the standard of living of the working class. The author of source D, believes that efficiency will be discouraged as only 'the least worthy' will benefit. He clearly implies that a move 'towards socialism', such as this, will cause divisions to emerge in society between 'the healthy and intellectual members of the community' and 'our least worthy citizens'.

From my own knowledge, I can add, that Lloyd George and the Liberal Party were acting from political motives which did go beyond those laid out in source A. The Liberals were facing competition from the newly formed Labour Party and so sought to offer the working population an incentive to continue to support Liberalism, as well as offering an alternative approach to full-blooded socialism which the Liberal Party opposed. Lloyd George's policies were those of 'New Liberalism' which emphasised an increased role for the state to alleviate the worst suffering of the 'deserving poor' (the elderly, the sick, those unable to find work, and the poorly paid). The plight of these groups had been made clear by the social investigations of Charles Booth in London and Seebohm Rowntree in York, which had revealed that approximately a third of the population lived in poverty. Such revelations did cause genuine humanitarian outrage, which also influenced the Liberals' social reforms after 1906. 'New Liberal' policies did still require an element of self-help by the poor, however, in the compulsory contribution element of National Insurance, which the Labour Party was opposed to, as Lansbury makes clear in source C. On the other hand, in 1911, many workers still lacked the vote, so it is possible to regard Lloyd George's defence as a valid one, rather than judging National Insurance as just a cynical attempt to win votes from Labour. It is far more realistic to regard Cecil's defence of 'individual freedom' in source B as a cynical attempt to appeal to traditional Liberal voters who were worried about the more interventionist aspects of the policy. After all, the Conservative Party had been more concerned with defending the interests of Church, Land, Crown and Empire during the nineteenth century.

Equally, the way in which the health aspects of National Insurance were implemented was designed to have a limited impact on doctors, who remained self-employed with their services hired by the state when required. In this way, the attacks made in source D, seem to be extreme and motivated more by a passionate support for the concepts of racial fitness, than concern for the position of the individual doctor.

Therefore it is possible to regard the opposition that Lloyd George faced as largely political rather than social and economic, prompted by genuine Labour and Conservative fears as to the success of the National Insurance scheme, which required them to mount a vigorous defence of their positions. Unlike the author of source D, the parties did not oppose the principle of health care for workers, rather the system of funding that National Insurance entailed. If it was Lloyd George's aim that other forms of social provision were to be funded in this fashion, then the statement may well be valid, but as the old age pensions of 1908 had proved, National Insurance was not the only funding principle that the Liberals were prepared to employ, and as the years after 1911 demonstrated, there were clear limits to the Liberal social reform programme.

PARALLEL QUESTIONS WITHOUT WORKED ANSWERS

a) Study Source A and use your own knowledge. Explain Lloyd George's reference to 'a scheme to which he himself [the British Worker] was a major contributor'. **(10)**

b) Study sources A and D. What do these sources reveal about the significance of 'national efficiency' in early twentieth century British history? **(25)**

c) Study sources B and C and use your own knowledge. How useful are Sources B and C as indicators of the attitude of the Conservative and Labour Party towards National Insurance? **(25)**

d) Use all the sources and your own knowledge. 'There was widespread hostility to measures which entailed greater control over, and intrusion upon, the lives of the working classes by those of other classes'. Explain the opposition to Lloyd George's proposals. **(60)**

---

2. Britain and the origins of the First World War (AQA)

Study the following source material and then answer the questions which follow.

Source A: Sir Edward Grey, in a letter to the French ambassador, defines the extent of Britain's commitment to France, November 1912

I agree that, if either Government had grave reason to expect an unprovoked attack by a third Power, or something that threatened the general peace, it should immediately discuss with the other, whether both governments should act together to prevent aggression and to preserve peace. If these measures involved action, the plans of the General Staffs would at once be taken into consideration, and the Governments would then decide what effect should be given to them.

Source B: David Lloyd George reflects on the lack of openness in Cabinet on foreign affairs, 1938

There was a reticence* and secrecy which practically ruled out three-quarters of the Cabinet from the chance of making any genuine contribution to the momentous questions then fermenting on the continent of Europe, which ultimately ended in an explosion that almost shattered the civilisation of the world. During the whole of those eight years, when I was a member of the Cabinet, I can recall no review of the European situation being given to us . . . There is no more

---

* 'reticence' – unwillingness to speak openly

conspicuous example of this kind of suppression of vital information than the way in which the military arrangements we entered into with France were kept from the Cabinet for six years . . . When in 1912 . . . Sir Edward Grey communicated these negotiations and arrangements to the Cabinet the majority of its Members were aghast. Hostility scarcely represents the strength of the sentiment which the revelations aroused: it was more akin to consternation*.

Source C: From *Splendid Isolation? Britain and the Balance of Power 1874–1914*, by John Charmley, 1999

In 1912 Churchill had pointed out the danger that the naval agreement with France would oblige Britain to go to her rescue; now it had; or rather, Grey's insistence that he would break up the government rather than leave France in the lurch had done so. In 1906, he had thought that deserting France would lead Britain into dangerous isolation, and he had learnt and forgotten nothing since then.

QUESTIONS WITH WORKED ANSWERS

a) **Study source C. With reference to source C and using your own knowledge, explain what is meant by the reference to 'the naval agreement with France', which is underlined in the source.** (3 marks)

b) **Study source A. With reference to your own knowledge, explain how useful source A is as evidence of Britain's commitment before 1914.** (7 marks)

c) **Refer to sources A, B and C and use your own knowledge. To what extent did the 1904 entente and subsequent agreements make British intervention inevitable in the event of a German attack on France?** (15 marks)

ANSWERS

a) In 1912 a secret Anglo-French naval agreement was signed following the **Agadir crisis** of 1911. Under its terms, the French Navy was to concentrate on the defence of the Mediterranean, with Britain obliged to defend the North Sea and Atlantic Ocean, which would, naturally, include the French coast. The British Cabinet, including Churchill, made it clear that this did not mean that the Entente Cordiale of 1904 had become a formal military alliance, but in reality it was to prove a commitment that would contribute to Britain's declaration of war in August 1914.

b) In source A, Sir Edward Grey was attempting to satisfy the demands of the French for a more secure alliance with Britain than the Entente Cordiale of 1904, following German aggression in the **Agadir Crisis** over Morocco in 1911. With the outbreak of war between the Balkan States and Turkey in October 1912 which threatened a war between Germany's ally, Austria-Hungary and France's ally Russia, France became concerned that Britain was not obliged by their previous agreement to come to her aid in the event of a German attack. Grey therefore assured the French ambassador that there would be immediate consultation between the governments of France and Britain even if they merely 'expect an unprovoked attack by a third Power', which could lead to

---

* 'consternation' – dismay caused by surprise

the involvement of 'the General Staffs', that is the British and French military commanders. This clearly implied that British military aid against any country that attacked France was certainly possible in any future dispute. On the other hand, Grey does not openly commit Britain, as military aid is only a possibility, not a certainty, as the two governments should, as he put it, 'act together to prevent aggression and to preserve peace'. In other words, Britain's first priority would be to avoid war, rather than send aid to France immediately.

Grey's careful diplomatic language, was of course, open to different interpretations and coming on the heels of the secret Naval Agreement, was more likely to encourage the French to believe that they could rely on Britain in any future conflict with Germany. It did, at the same time, give the British government the freedom to decide for themselves whether a particular crisis amounted to the circumstances requiring intervention as was evident from the Cabinet discussions between 1 and 4 August 1914.

c) Given the secrecy of Grey's diplomacy and the obvious surprise that the revelation of his negotiations caused in Cabinet in 1912 according to Lloyd George in source B, it is perhaps unsurprising that, when Germany declared war on Russia on 1 August, there was a protracted and bitter debate in the Liberal Cabinet over Britain's course of action. The Liberal Party, under Gladstone, Campbell-Bannerman and Asquith had always opposed unnecessary foreign intervention, and was therefore reluctant to go to war to protect Tsarist Russia's interests in the Balkans. It was only with Belgium's refusal to give passage to the German Army that the majority of the Cabinet swung behind Grey's call for an ultimatum to Germany and backed Britain's entry into the war on 4 August. The Belgian cause also served to unite the country behind Asquith's decision.

Source A, Grey's letter to the French ambassador, effectively binds Britain to consult with France if there was a threat of attack by Germany. However, the circumstances that required British military assistance were left undefined and at the discretion of the British government. The letter, the Entente Cordiale itself and the Anglo-French naval agreement, referred to in source C were, therefore, merely attempts by Sir Edward Grey to reassure the French and to dissuade the Germans from attempting to upset the status quo in Europe, despite the instability caused by the break-up of the Turkish Empire in the Balkans. They did not amount to a formal commitment, merely to a moral obligation, unlike the 1839 treaty with Belgium. This explains why the British government took until 4 August to declare war on Germany, and why the German invasion of Belgium was cited as the main cause of British intervention, as the commitment to France remained so unclear.

What was far more important than this commitment or the Treaty with Belgium, however, was the behaviour of the German government after the mobilisation of the Russian army on 30 August 1914. Once this took place, the government of Bethmann-Hollweg effectively handed foreign policy to the German Army High Command, who immediately began to implement the Schlieffen Plan which required an immediate attack on France through Belgium. Thus the Germans were to launch an attack on France, who had had virtually no involvement in the July crisis, which would cross Belgian territory, whose neutrality Britain had guaranteed since 1839. In such circumstances, Britain had little choice but to intervene, as German success would seriously threaten Britain's interests in Europe. In addition, failure to aid a democratic ally against such a display of aggression would cause public outrage. Third, Britain's international reputation would be in tatters as she would have failed to aid three countries with whom she had some form of agreement: Russia (since 1907); France (since 1904); and Belgium (since 1839). As Grey put it in his memoirs, had Britain failed to intervene in August 1914, 'we should have been isolated, discredited and hated;

and there would be before us nothing but a miserable and ignoble future', as 'Germany would wield the whole power of the Continent.' Despite his later attempts to distance himself from the decision to go to war, as in source B, Lloyd George had stated in 1911 that if Britain stood aside in any future European war, 'peace at that price would be a humiliation intolerable for a great country like ours to endure'. Therefore, British intervention on the side of France in a war with Germany was likely, following the agreements of 1904 and 1912, but only inevitable in circumstances that could command the support of the Liberal Cabinet, and, more importantly, the British public. These circumstances were created by the uncompromising approach of Germany once authority was passed from the civilians to von Moltke's military and the disastrous Schlieffen Plan was launched.

PARALLEL QUESTIONS WITHOUT WORKED ANSWERS

a) Study Source B. With reference to source B, and using your own knowledge, explain what had caused Sir Edward Grey to communicate the 'negotiations and arrangements' of the Anglo-French Entente to the Cabinet in 1912?   **(3 marks)**

b) Study sources B and C. To what extent does the evidence in source B justify the criticism of Grey in source C?   **(7 marks)**

c) Refer to sources A, B and C and use your own knowledge. 'Edward Grey is one of the two men primarily responsible for the war' (Lloyd George). Do you agree with this judgement?   **(15 marks)**

Part 4: Historical skills

Logical reasoning

The exercise below requires students to apply their knowledge to a structured analysis of voting intentions. For each named individual (representative of a particular group or interest), the student must determine electoral behaviour through motivation from complex historical data.

1. 1906 – Analysis of voting intentions of social/occupation groups

Any exercise such as this is very imprecise as regional factors, religious affiliation, peer influence, security of income and type of work could easily affect individuals who might otherwise be expected to vote differently. However, it does allow students to realise that a wide range of different groups had reasons to vote against the Conservatives in 1906, although they may not have been altogether clear what they were voting *for*.

Read the section on the Liberal victory of 1906 in this chapter, and then attempt to complete the table below. For each representative of a group, consider which political issues were most likely to influence voting decisions and from that basis, judge which political party they were most likely to support in the 1906 general election. If you are unsure of any section, consult Martin

Pugh, *The Making of Modern British Politics*, 2nd edn (Blackwell, 1993). Henry Pelling, *Social geography of British elections, 1885–1910* (Macmillan, 1967) will also be very useful here.

Social/occupation group	Issues of concern	Party likely to vote for
Wealthy land-owner	1. Fear of Liberal land tax 2. Concern over Trade Union power	
Factory owner	1. Increased competition from USA and Europe 2.	
Teacher in Anglican school	1. 2.	
Pub landlord	1. 2.	
Shopkeeper	1. 2.	
Nonconformist bank clerk	1. 2.	
Temperance campaigner	1. 2.	
Trade Union official	1. 2.	
Welsh nationalist	1. 2.	
Steel-mill worker	1. 2.	
Lancashire cotton worker	1. 2.	
Unemployed ex-soldier (served in South Africa)	1. 2.	
Farm labourer		

Chapter 3

The Impact of the First World War, 1914–1918

This chapter is concerned with the impact of the Great War on Britain, rather than the actual military events of the conflict. It examines how well prepared Britain was for war in 1914 and the economic, social and political consequences of the decision to declare war on Germany. Historians have argued fiercely over how disruptive the war really was. Some believe that the war finally destroyed Victorian British society and ushered Britain into a modern age of democracy and egalitarianism. Others identify many of the 'effects' of the war as having begun long before 1914. It is possible to agree with both views, though, for some changes such as the move towards democracy had been prepared by the events of the nineteenth century, while others, such as the fall of the Liberals (who would never form a government again after 1918), were caused by the war itself.

 ## Historical background

The opening phase
'Total war'
Women at war
Ireland
The fall of Asquith
Lloyd George as war leader
The war at sea
The 1918 Representation of the People
    Act
Victory

3. Wartime politics
4. Women's wartime role
5. Opposition to the war
6. Overall assessment

Sources

1. Votes for women
2. The impact of the war on
    labour

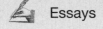 ## Essays

1. Preparation for war
2. The British economy in wartime

Historical skills

1. Discussion of propaganda posters
    issued during the war

Chronology

1914	—	4 August – Declaration of War against Germany and Austria-Hungary
	—	German advance stopped at Ypres
	—	First Defence of the Realm Act
1915	—	'Treasury Agreements' signed with trade unions
	—	Second battle of Ypres
	—	Allied landings at Gallipoli
	—	'Shell scandal' – Lloyd George made Minister of Munitions
	—	Asquith forms first coalition government
	—	Chancellor McKenna introduces protective tariffs
1916	—	Conscription introduced (apart from Ireland)
	—	Dublin Rising, Easter Monday
	—	Battle of Somme, 620,000 Allied casualties
	—	Asquith resigns, Lloyd George forms second coalition government
1917	—	Russian Revolution
	—	USA declares war on Central Powers
	—	Resignation of Arthur Henderson from War Cabinet
	—	Third Battle of Ypres (Passchendaele)
	—	Convoy system established
1918	—	Introduction of rationing
	—	Maurice Debate
	—	German Spring Offensive
	—	New Labour Party Constitution agreed
	—	Representation of the People Act
	—	Allied Counter-Offensive
	—	Fisher's Education Act
	—	Armistice signed with Germany
	—	Coalition government wins 'coupon' election

Part 1: Historical background

The opening phase

Despite the undoubted threat posed by the German Imperial Army, the British population were confident that the Allies would win the war in a matter of weeks. There had been demonstrations and appeals against Britain's involvement in the war, right up until 4 August, but the crowds gathered in Trafalgar Square greeted the news of war with cheering and flag waving. The government decided on a policy of 'business as usual' to prevent a run on savings. When the conflict began, a meeting of the Army Council on 5 August, with ministers present, decided, for the first time, to send the whole of the British Expeditionary Force (BEF) abroad, and leave the territorials at home to guard against invasion. Sir Henry Wilson, director of military operations, suggested that the BEF be sent to Maubeuge to protect the left flank of the French army. In this way the BEF, comprising only four divisions 'became an auxiliary to the French army' of 70 divisions and found

Figure 3.1 **Key areas of combat during the First World War**

Table 3.1 **The nations at war**

The Allied Powers	The Central Powers
Britain and the British Empire	Germany
France	Austria-Hungary
Russia (until December 1917)	Turkey (from November 1914)
Japan	Bulgaria (from October 1915)
Italy (from May 1915)	
Serbia	
Belgium	
Rumania (from August 1916)	
USA (from April 1917)	

itself facing the full force of the German invasion. In the battles of 1914, first at Mons and then at the First Battle of Ypres in Autumn 1914, this professional army suffered one tenth of its forces killed and one third injured. Such a high level of casualties meant that a mass recruitment of British men was required. But, considering its size, the BEF had played a major role in helping to stop the German advance towards Paris.

The longer that the First World War dragged on, the more the new-found political unity, the 'spirit of August 1914', gradually came under pressure, as the government was unable to achieve a swift success despite the confident picture maintained by the press. They recruited military and civilian personnel on a huge scale, from sections of the population never previously involved, even indirectly, in combat, and flung men and ordnance against the enemy in huge battles which left Britain close to bankruptcy. Lord Kitchener, the newly appointed Secretary for War, decided that Britain needed an army of 70 divisions herself and launched a recruitment campaign that had brought in over 1.3 million men by January 1915. The government increasingly, albeit reluctantly, intervened in the economy and assumed vast powers over their population in order to ensure the redoubling of the war effort. The British government had, through the Defence of the Realm Act (D.O.R.A.), granted itself enormous directive powers which laid the basis for extensive government interference. The first act, of August 1914, gave the Cabinet the power to 'issue regulations as to the powers and duties of the Admiralty and Army Council, and other persons acting on their behalf, for securing the public safety and defence of the realm'.

 'Total War'

In the spring of 1915, the Western Allies undertook huge offensives at Neuve Chapelle, Champagne and Artois. These failed to achieve the expected breakthrough, at a cost of more than a million British, French and German casualties. As a result, newspaper headlines in Britain screamed 'Need For Shells: British Attacks Checked: Limited Supply The Cause'. Despite the powers available through D.O.R.A., the economic demands of war were at first met through a market economy, with the government as customer dispensing lucrative contracts to private industry. Most military experts, however, had anticipated a war of movement and had thus not prioritised the role of heavy artillery. When trench warfare developed, the need for large calibre, high explosive shells became pressing. The army had few such guns and therefore few such shells and the existing munitions factories, with their ill-trained workers and ill-organised processes were not capable of such an extremely dangerous, highly skilled enterprise. By spring 1915, Britain was producing only 700 shells per day, whilst Germany produced 250,000! The 'shell scandal' brought matters to a head, provoking demands for greater central direction of labour and industry.

Figure 3.2 **The war on the Home Front**

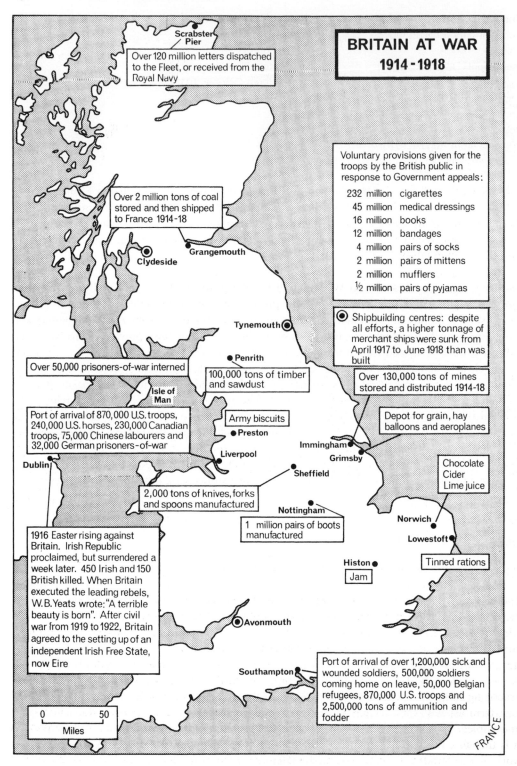

BRITAIN AT WAR
1914 - 1918

Over 120 million letters dispatched to the Fleet, or received from the Royal Navy

Voluntary provisions given for the troops by the British public in response to Government appeals:

232 million cigarettes
45 million medical dressings
16 million books
12 million bandages
4 million pairs of socks
2 million pairs of mittens
2 million mufflers
½ million pairs of pyjamas

Over 2 million tons of coal stored and then shipped to France 1914-18

⊙ Shipbuilding centres: despite all efforts, a higher tonnage of merchant ships were sunk from April 1917 to June 1918 than was built

Over 50,000 prisoners-of-war interned

100,000 tons of timber and sawdust

Over 130,000 tons of mines stored and distributed 1914-18

Port of arrival of 870,000 U.S. troops, 240,000 U.S. horses, 230,000 Canadian troops, 75,000 Chinese labourers and 32,000 German prisoners-of-war

Army biscuits

Depot for grain, hay balloons and aeroplanes

Chocolate
Cider
Lime juice

2,000 tons of knives, forks and spoons manufactured

1 million pairs of boots manufactured

Tinned rations

Jam

1916 Easter rising against Britain. Irish Republic proclaimed, but surrendered a week later. 450 Irish and 150 British killed. When Britain executed the leading rebels, W.B.Yeats wrote:"A terrible beauty is born". After civil war from 1919 to 1922, Britain agreed to the setting up of an independent Irish Free State, now Eire

Port of arrival of over 1,200,000 sick and wounded soldiers, 500,000 soldiers coming home on leave, 50,000 Belgian refugees, 870,000 U.S. troops and 2,500,000 tons of ammunition and fodder

Scrabster Pier
Clydeside
Grangemouth
Tynemouth
Penrith
Isle of Man
Preston
Liverpool
Immingham
Grimsby
Sheffield
Dublin
Nottingham
Norwich
Lowestoft
Histon
Avonmouth
Southampton
FRANCE

0   50
Miles

Table 3.2 **Fleet sizes, 1914**

	Britain		Germany	
	(sea-worthy)	(under construction)	(sea-worthy)	(under construction)
Dreadnoughts	20	–	13	–
Battleships	55	11	33	7
Battlecruisers	7	3	3	3
Cruisers	51	–	9	–
Light cruisers	77	9	45	4
Destroyers	191	38	123	9
Torpedo boats	137	1	80	–
Submarines	64	22	23	15

Table 3.3 **Size of armed forces**

	Britain		Germany	
	Army	Navy	Army	Navy
1911	247,000	128,000	622,500	33,500
1914	247,000	146,000	791,000	73,000

In May 1915, the Chancellor of the Exchequer, Lloyd George, was appointed Minister of Munitions, with responsibility for delivering adequate military supplies for the front. He brought energy and determination to his post, setting in place a series of organisations to centrally direct war production. The Munitions of War Act, which became law two months later, was 'a considerable extension of the Government's powers of economic control' as it not only provided subsidies to allow private firms to increase production, but also gave the ministry power to establish state-owned munitions factories and shipyards with state of the art equipment and production techniques. However, no equipment of any kind produced by the Ministry of Munitions became available until October 1915, and none in any quantity until the spring of 1916. The impact of the reorganisation of supplies was only felt in 1917, and only became decisive in 1918.

 Women at war

The demands for soldiers and sailors meant that there were immediate shortages of workers in Britain, and contemporary commentators were right in pointing to the fact that the British war effort required the mobilisation of women in the labour force. Women became factory workers, farm labourers, clerks, nurses and even policewomen. But journalists, amazed by this demonstration of female prowess, both understated the level of women's industrial work in the pre-war period and overstated the change caused by the war, partly because the dangerous, yet vital work producing munitions dominated the attention of observers and obscured the continuities and long-term aspects of the changes elsewhere. Women were recruited not from those previously unoccupied, but rather from those who had already been paid labour elsewhere in the economy. It is therefore inaccurate to describe the war as having had a 'revolutionary' effect on women's work. Rather, women's work, on buses, in factories or in hospitals, became more visible than it

Table 3.4 *Percentage of women in employment*

	Industry	Transport	Agriculture	Commerce	All workers
July 1914	26	2	9	27	24
July 1918	35	12	14	53	37
July 1920	27	4	10	40	28

had been prior to 1914. The basic relationship between men and women did not change, and women continued to be expected to act as child-bearer, carer and -rearer. While millions of women were in work, the vast majority stayed at home during the Great War.

Despite press stories about the classes mixing on the factory floor, most female munitions workers were working-class. Any middle-class women employed in factories appear to have usually acted as supervisors. Outside munitions, most of industry remained unenthusiastic about employing women workers, arguing that they were unwilling to take responsibility, unreliable and difficult to train. In mining and shipbuilding, employers and unions conspired to keep women out of the workforce, while in transport, where 55 per cent more women were employed, train-driving remained an exclusively male occupation. In this way, it is inaccurate to write of women 'taking over' from men. Attitudes that they were a cheap, temporary and unskilled workforce appear not to have altered in the war, and the lower pay rates for women reflected this attitude. Furthermore, the lack of adequate childcare arrangements meant that many of these new workers were single women.

Lack of adequate training and the failure to alter the relationships between the male trade unions and the employers meant that women were not able to keep the jobs specifically labelled 'war work' and the attitude of the press changed dramatically once the war ended. Women were urged to go back to the home, to domestic service and the laundry trade and to release their jobs to the returning soldiers. Those women who refused to accept domestic service jobs from labour exchanges found their benefits stopped. The Restoration of Pre-War Practices Act took jobs away from working-class women while middle-class women benefited from the Sex Discrimination Removals Acts, which applied to the professions.

The British trade union leader, Mary Macarthur, led the campaign to protect the women forced to work in the munitions industry. She pointed out that women in the industry received on average less that half of what the men were paid. After much discussion it was agreed to increase women's wage-rates in the munitions industry. However, by 1918, whereas the average male wage in the munitions industry was £4 6s. 6d. for women it was only £2 2s. 4d. As a result, women became much more active in union matters, with 383 trade unions with women members and thirty-six women-only unions by 1918. In August 1918, women transport workers in London went on strike over 'equal pay' and their right, like their male colleagues, to a 'war bonus'. The employers conceded the latter but not the principle of 'equal pay'.

It is difficult to be precise about what war work meant to these women. Many upper- and middle-class women remember the social aspects of escaping the home and the pleasure in learning new skills. Others remember long hours and the burden of combining paid work, unpaid housework and child-minding, which included queuing for scarce supplies either before or after working hours. Undoubtedly, working in new situations and taking an active role in supporting the national war effort did raise the consciousness of many women and made them more aware of their own potential and more willing to speak out for their rights. But in many ways, the war reinforced women's position in the home, for, as mothers, they had responsibilities which became more demanding as the war went on. Many households had to produce food rather than simply buying it. 'Making do' with whatever resources were available, naturally placed a heavier burden on women than before the war, and this experience, unpaid, and often unappreciated, was a more common shared experience of women's war work than the 'liberating' experience of labour.

 ## Ireland

The Third Irish Home Rule Bill had, under the terms of the Parliament Act, become law in 1914, but the government decided that, to keep Ireland quiet during the war, there would be no attempt to implement it until peace was restored. Both Irish Nationalists (partly motivated by fighting for the rights of a small sovereign country, Belgium, oppressed by a powerful neighbour, Germany) and Ulster Unionists flocked to volunteer and to prove their fitness for self-government. A group of revolutionary Irish radicals, the Irish Republican Brotherhood (IRB), ignored Redmond's call to volunteer and began to plot a rising against British rule, with the support of Germany. A former British diplomat, Sir Roger Casement attempted to persuade the Kaiser's government to land troops in Ireland to aid an uprising, but all he received was the promise of arms, which never reached the rebels. The IRB leadership split on whether to go ahead with the insurrection, and so when they seized the General Post Office and other buildings in Dublin on Easter Monday, 1916, there were only 1,600 of them and they were given little support from the people of Dublin. The British sent in troops with howitzers and took a week to defeat the uprising. 132 soldiers and police died and 450 Irish men and women. The British, determined to stamp out any threat of a further rising, decided to make an example of the ring leaders and executed 15 of them by firing squad. Casement, who was also captured, was hanged as a traitor. Martial law was imposed and mass arrests followed. Although the people of Ireland had had little sympathy with the rising, especially while Irish men were fighting and dying in Flanders, this wave of repression horrified even moderate Irish opinion.

In three months that followed Irish opinion hardened. The threat of conscription being imposed on Ireland drove even more people to desert Redmond's **Nationalist** party and to support Arthur Griffith's Sinn Fein group, who called for complete independence, rather than merely **Home Rule**. Sinn Fein won four by-elections in 1917, and, as many of the surviving leaders of the Easter Rising were released from internment by an increasingly desperate British government, they were boosted by the prestige that these returning 'heroes' gave the movement. The only surviving commander of the Rising, Eamonn de Valera became the leading figure in Sinn Fein's 1918 election campaign, which saw them winning 73 out of the 105 Irish seats and reducing the Nationalists to 6.

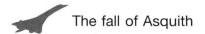 ## The fall of Asquith

Asquith's Liberal government, in office since the general election of December 1910, remained in power for only nine months after the outbreak of war. The cause of the 'shell scandal' was placed at the door of the government by Sir John French and the Unionist Business Committee was quick to exploit this, putting down a motion on the issue in the House of Commons. The pressure on Asquith increased in May 1915 when Sir John Fisher, the First Sea Lord, resigned in protest at the decision to send more ships after the failure of the initial attack on the Dardenelles to capture Constantinople and eliminate Turkey from the war. The Conservative leader, Andrew Bonar Law, had not intended to bring the Liberal government down, but he saw no way to resolve this crisis without a change of personnel. Lloyd George agreed, saying: 'Of course we must have a coalition, for the alternative is impossible' – referring to the impossibility of organising a general election during wartime. Asquith accepted a deal with the Conservatives, hoping that they would bear the responsibility for sacking the popular Kitchener, who was blamed for the shell shortage. Asquith was perfectly willing to demote Churchill, however, who was blamed for the Gallipoli disaster, when a landing of Australian and New Zealand troops on Turkish soil had been blocked by fierce Turkish resistance. Kitchener actually survived, but lost his powers over supply to Lloyd George's new Ministry of Munitions. The Conservatives received little reward for their support (Law became Colonial Secretary and Balfour replaced Churchill at the Admiralty), which angered Conservative backbenchers, who believed that Asquith had deceived them, especially when Labour received their first ministerial post in the coalition.

However, government continued to function much as before, presiding over more military disasters, such as the defeat of Serbia and the retreat from Gallipoli, culminating in the long-drawn-out agony of the Somme in 1916, when a huge assault launched partly to relieve the pressure on the French at Verdun, led to horrific casualties on the first day (20,000 killed). By November 1916, the British had advanced 10 miles at the cost of 400,000 casualties. The government was also hampered by Liberal opposition to increased state control in areas such as conscription, which Asquith himself opposed. The press, especially *The Times*, continued to castigate Asquith for his short-comings as a war leader. Eventually, Bonar Law, aware of rumblings of discontent from within his party, demanded that a small War Cabinet should be empowered to make all vital decisions. He was supported in this by Lloyd George, who had become War Minister in July 1916 following Kitchener's death, and who felt frustrated by his lack of control over the military establishment. Asquith, hoping to outmanoeuvre his critics, resigned in December 1916, but found himself replaced when Lloyd George patched together a deal which saw him, a Liberal, become Prime Minister of a predominantly Conservative coalition when the rest of the Liberal ministers resigned. The War Cabinet comprised Lloyd George, Bonar Law, Lord Curzon, Alfred Milner and the Labour leader, Arthur Henderson. The ambition of the Conservatives in general and Lloyd George in particular, combined with the popular perception of Asquith as an unsuitable war-leader put out by anti-Liberal elements of the press, thus radically altered the complexion of British politics and would fatally divide the Liberals.

Lloyd George as war leader

Lloyd George's priority, however, was to win the war, with, as he phrased it, 'a knock-out blow', and he immediately began to bring experts in to run new ministries such as Food, Shipping, Labour and Reconstruction, created solely for that purpose. Merchant shipping was brought under government control, farmers were ordered to bring more land under cultivation, and factories received instructions as to what to produce. By 1918 the Ministry of Munitions owned more than 250 factories, administering a further 20,000, and the government employed five million workers. A huge experiment in 'state capitalism' was underway, and the significance of this was not lost on workers, employers, unions and Labour politicians. Lloyd George also introduced the Cabinet Secretariat under Maurice Hankey to co-ordinate government policy, which became a permanent feature of British politics.

In order to secure his coalition with the Tories though, Lloyd George had been forced to promise not to dismiss the British Commander in Chief, Douglas Haig, in whom he had little confidence, especially when the much vaunted 1917 Flanders campaign stalled in the mud and squalor of Passchendaele. As a result, Lloyd George set up the Supreme War Council to afford himself more control over the war effort on land, but he was still plotting the removal of Haig when the German offensive of 1918 forced him to postpone his plans. Despite serious shortages, the Germans launched a final desperate offensive on 21 March 1918 at the junction of the British and French armies on the Somme. Using new 'stormtrooper' tactics, the Germans advanced up to 50 miles in four consecutive assaults, threatening Paris as they had in 1914. A political storm broke at Westminster where Lloyd George was accused of having withheld troops from the army to prevent Haig launching any more offensives. Although there was some truth in the accusation, Lloyd George managed to bluff his way out and rushed troops to France. With the influx of American troops as well, the allies reinforced their lines and the impetus of the German advances was slowed and the Germans found themselves in exposed positions, having lost 500,000 of their best men without achieving a decisive breakthrough.

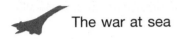

The war at sea

Despite expectations of a monumental naval confrontation, the German High Seas Fleet only once ventured into the open seas to inflict a number of losses on the British Grand Fleet at the battle of Jutland in Spring 1916, before swiftly retreating back to the safety of their harbours for the remainder of the war. A much more serious threat was posed by German and Austrian submarines which launched a campaign of unrestricted warfare in the waters around Britain in response to the Allied **blockade** of German ports. By April 1917, the Germans were sinking 430 ships a month and Britain was down to only six weeks' supply of corn. Lloyd George overruled Admiralty misgivings and ordered the use of convoys of merchant ships protected by warships, which dramatically reduced the losses of shipping. The German attacks also backfired when American ships and ships carrying American passengers were sunk, as they contributed to President Wilson's decision to declare war on the Central Powers in April 1917. The British were therefore able to keep themselves supplied, with only a brief resort to rationing, to supply the front in France with Allied troops and equipment, and to successfully maintain a rigorous **blockade** against Germany, that contributed markedly to the weakening of the German war machine.

The 1918 *Representation of the People Act*

There was much feeling in Westminster, that, after the huge sacrifices made by the British people in the war, it was unfair that 40 per cent of adult males still did not have a right to vote and that, by joining the army, many thousands had actually lost that right. It was also considered unfair that women should be excluded from the franchise, but there was little agreement over which women should be allowed to become electors. Following the meetings of an all-party committee called by the government, known as the Speaker's Conference, it was agreed that the occupational basis of the franchise should be replaced by a simple residential qualification (six months in the same dwelling), and that women would be allowed to vote on equal terms with men, but only when they reached 'a specified age' – most likely thirty, when a woman was likely to be married and influenced by her husband's views. Lloyd George fully supported these proposals and even Asquith spoke in favour of women's suffrage from the opposition benches, claiming that 'my eyes . . . have at last been opened to the truth'.

The government introduced a bill which gave the vote to all adult males and women over thirty in June 1917 and passed both Houses of Parliament with little opposition. Even Lord Curzon, who had been one of the suffragettes' bitterest opponents called on his supporters to abstain from voting against the bill. It became law in February 1918. In October, a law was hurried through

Parliament that allowed women to become MPs. This was followed in December by the passage of the Sex Disqualification Act, which allowed women to become magistrates, barristers, Q.C.s, senior civil servants and to serve on juries.

 Victory

Exhausted and demoralised, the Germans fell back in summer 1918 in the face of furious French attacks along the Marne which combined pinpoint artillery barrages, tank assaults, air support and infantry attacks. When the British joined the operation near Amiens on 8 August, the true state of the German army's morale was laid bare, as 30,000 troops surrendered in two days. The allies were only able to advance slowly over the war-torn terrain, and the Germans managed to stage a coherent retreat, but the result of the war was no longer in question. On the other fronts, Germany's allies began to collapse. At the end of September, when the allies finally broke out of Macedonia and into Serbia, the Bulgarians sued for peace. Following a major defeat at the hands of the British, the Turks surrendered on 30 October. Earlier in October, the Italians with allied reinforcements, broke through the Austrian lines near Vittorio Veneto. Austria-Hungary formally surrendered on 3 November.

Table 3.5 **The cost of the war**

	Cost in dollars in 1914–18
United States	22,625,253,000
Great Britain	35,334,012,000
France	24,265,583,000
Russia	22,293,950,000
Canada	1,665,576,000
Australia	1,423,208,000
New Zealand	378,750,000
India	601,279,000
South Africa	300,000,000
British Colonies	125,000,000
Germany	37,775,000,000
Austria-Hungary	20,622,960,000

The German High Command finally admitted that the war was lost on 29 September 1918 and a new, more representative government sought terms for an **armistice** from President Wilson of USA. Wilson insisted on the withdrawal of all German forces from occupied territory before terms would be agreed – in effect he demanded a surrender rather than an **armistice**. Faced with social revolution, starvation as a result of the Allied **blockade**, the disintegration of the army and navy and the threat of invasion, the German government had no choice but to accept. Germany agreed to evacuate all occupied territory on the Western Front and surrendered her surface and U-boat fleets. The news led to riots across Germany, and to save the country from revolution, the Kaiser was forced to abdicate on 9 November. At 11.00 a.m. on 11 November 1918 hostilities ceased, rather to the surprise of the Allies who had been busy preparing their military and civilian forces for another war winter.

Essays

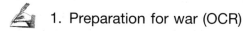 ## 1. Preparation for war (OCR)

Did Britain's preparations for war in 1914 prove adequate?

(90 marks)

Great Britain, after her economic heyday in the mid-nineteenth century, had found her primacy challenged since 1873. Britain's share of the world's manufacturing output had declined from

nearly 20 per cent in 1860 to 14 per cent by 1914. While her rate of growth in exports of manufactured goods continued to grow by 2.72 per cent, Britain's industrial base was worryingly narrow,
based on the same staple industries of textiles, coal, iron, shipbuilding and engineering, which had
been so profitable in the previous century, yet which were now increasingly outdated in their technology. New industries such as electrical manufactures, rayon production and chemicals only
contributed 6.5 per cent of all output in contrast to USA and Germany. For many vital industrial
components, such as ball-bearings, optical glass, magnetos, dyes and drugs, Britain relied on
Germany herself.

As an island with a vast overseas Empire, Britain had, historically, depended on her Navy for
protection and expansion. The army's role was to subdue those parts of the Empire which gunboats
could not reach. Inevitably, the commitment to intervene on France's side on the occasion of a
German attack had rendered this position redundant, but Britain's traditional dislike of large
peacetime armies prevented expansion being in any way adequate. R.B. Haldane, Secretary of State
for War from 1905 to 1912 had established an army general staff and a Territorial Force and
prepared a British Expeditionary Force for immediate deployment on the continent, but the army
in 1914 comprised less than 250,000 men, scattered across the world, with reserves of 213,000.
Only £29 million a year was spent on the army, compared to £51.5 million on the navy. In some
ways this was understandable, as Britain imported 50 per cent of the meat, 80 per cent of the
wheat and 65 per cent of the dairy products that she needed for her population of 45 million, and
the navy could guarantee that Britain would be fed in the event of a global war, and it did so until
the German submarines improved in range and daring.

In Britain, despite the challenge of the German attack and the limited size of the BEF, Parliament
ruled out conscription. The army was given permission to increase in size by 500,000, but these
would be volunteers. Therefore, in Britain, unlike the rest of Europe, a recruitment drive was
begun, with 100,000 young men volunteering in September, as the news of the retreat from Mons
began to filter through. Although, by January 1915, there were 1,342,647 recruits, the numbers of
new volunteers had dwindled to less than 22,000 per week. With the battles of 1915 killing and
maiming troops at a horrendous rate, the Parliamentary Recruiting Committee began to try new
tactics, shaming potential recruits into joining up by aiming posters at women inciting them to
send their men to the front.

The Conservative Party, many of whose members also belonged to the National Service League,
which called for conscription long before the war, began to demand that voluntarism be replaced
by compulsion. The Times claimed on 6 May 1915 that 'The voluntary system has its limits and
we are fast approaching them'. It was clear that not only was the number of recruits decreasing,
but that the propaganda campaigns were recruiting men from essential wartime production, thus
inhibiting the potential size of the army by reducing the supplies that were needed to sustain it.
Conscription would not only guarantee the supply of men to the front, but it could, if managed
effectively, guarantee the supply of equipment to enable the British army to outlast the blockaded
Germans. When Conservative ministers in Asquith's new coalition government threatened resignation, the Prime Minister produced a compromise, first introducing a National Register, which
obliged every British subject aged between 16 and 65 to register for national service, and second,
allowing Lord Derby's scheme to encourage men between 18 and 41 to 'attest' a willingness to
serve when called upon, thus avoiding conscription. While 1.35 million married men attested, on
the understanding that the unmarried should be called up first, as Asquith had promised, only
840,000 unmarried men out of a possible 2.2 million of military age did so.

Asquith therefore could say that he had tried to prevent conscription, but that he had been faced with no alternative and thus avoided the mass resignation of Liberal anti-conscriptionists that had been threatened. In the event, when Asquith introduced the Military Service Act of January 1916, which imposed conscription on single men aged between 18 and 41, with exemptions for ministers of religion, the medically unfit, Irish and conscientious objectors, only the Home Secretary, Sir John Simon resigned from the government in protest. It was left to local tribunals to decide which workers were carrying out 'essential' work and were also exempt, which caused a lack of consistency from one area to another and a shortage of men which was only remedied in April 1916, when conscription was extended to married men. The army and the War Office continued to complain of manpower shortages, however, even after conscription, and a War Priorities Committee was only set up late in 1917, to co-ordinate manpower needs. Yet the British army was able to help to keep the Germans at bay for four years and to act as the decisive force in bringing victory in 1918.

2. The British economy in wartime (EDEXCEL)

a) **Describe how Britain restructured its economy to meet the demands of the war**   (30 marks)

b) **What impact did the war have on living standards in Britain?**   (30 marks)

(Total: 60 marks)

a) In August 1914, a Railway Executive Committee, comprising the ten general managers of the larger companies, assumed control of the railway network. Alongside this, all shipping in home waters was requisitioned, and by 1918, the government controlled all maritime and canal transport. Other immediate controls included the suspension of stock-exchange dealing, restrictions on the printing of paper money and an export ban on explosives. Profits in government-controlled industries were fixed at 1913 levels. For the sake of public unity, the Munitions of War Act limited excess war profits of private companies to 20 per cent of pre-war profits which, although difficult to enforce because so many new firms were established during the war, created an impression of equality of sacrifice.

After 1915, Lloyd George's Ministry of Munitions encouraged co-operation between workers and employers. Business leaders such as Sir Eric Geddes, chief manager of the North Eastern Railway, were recruited as senior administrators. Private firms were pushed to amalgamate and carry out research and development on a scale impossible under the normal competitive conditions of a peacetime economy. Trade union leaders were consulted and accepted the suspension of the right to strike and restrictive trade union rules in the munitions industry for the duration of the war, in return for restrictions on wartime profits; the so-called 'Treasury Agreement'. This permitted semi-skilled workers to carry out jobs previously reserved for certain skilled craftsmen, and complex tasks could be broken down into smaller simpler operations ('**dilution**'), thus opening the way for a rapid recruitment of munitions workers, especially women. However, the ministry was unable to extend its powers into every sector of the economy, for example in shipbuilding, where the dangerous nature of the industry precluded the wholesale employment of women and the employers and trade unionists resisted **dilution**. Despite this, the achievement of the ministry remains impressive. From August 1914 to June 1915, the army received 110 artillery pieces, but in the first year of the ministry's existence, 5006 were produced. Similarly, grenade production increased in the same period from 68,000 to 27 million.

The government was less inclined to intervene in the food supply, and until late 1916 there was little need. During 1917, however, the government was forced, by strikes and demonstrations, to subsidise bread and potato prices and to create Divisional Food Commissions with the authority to introduce local rationing. In 1918, butter, margarine, lard, meat and sugar were all nationally rationed, and by the end of the war the government controlled 85 per cent of food sales, thereby restraining prices and preventing shortages. These restrictions were rigorously enforced with 65,000 prosecutions for breaches of the food control orders.

From August 1914 to April 1917, Britain acted as principal banker and loan-raiser for the allies, raising loans for France, Italy and Russia as well as financing her own war effort. In order to pay for this, War Savings Certificates and Bonds were sold, and taxation was dramatically increased. During the first year of the war, three war budgets raised income tax by nearly 150 per cent, and by the end of the war it stood at six shillings in the pound, an 800 per cent increase on the rate in August 1914. Tax thresholds were lowered, and as wages rose, more people paid. The supposedly ineffective excess profits duty raised £200–300 million a year. Indirect taxes were raised or introduced on a range of consumer goods. Despite all this, the government was forced to sell 25 per cent of overseas investments to meet the spiralling costs of the war (£7 million a day by 1917) and still fell short. Borrowing, particularly from the United States, was the only answer.

b) Britain witnessed perhaps the least disruption to civilian society during the war. Living standards were maintained and the centralised distribution of food supplies and rationing ensured that diet and nutrition, notably amongst the poorest in society, improved dramatically.

British workers gained by the war, using their role in war production to force improved pay and conditions, as well as greater participation in government. Employers were encouraged to pay war bonuses by the Ministry of Munitions, which wanted industrial peace so as to maximise production. Collective pay bargaining was actively encouraged by the ministry, and National Pay Awards were introduced for the first time. After 1915, arbitration tribunals were set up to resolve disputes, thereby ensuring negotiated wage rises and uninterrupted production. Even so, workers became aggrieved over the rising cost of living, the increasing '**dilution**' of skilled work, through the introduction of unskilled (often female) labour and new, mechanised processes, and the high cost of housing and rents. The wave of strikes on the Clyde during 1915 led Lloyd George to promote the Rent Restrictions Act at the end of the year, pegging rents at 1914 levels. In 1915, after a period of unchecked price inflation, the state introduced fixed prices for essential foods, so as to maintain morale, and in February 1918, the Minister of Food Lord Rhondda introduced rationing.

For all the government's sincere efforts to mitigate the worst effects of the war, living conditions suffered. Wages did rise, during 1914–18, by 75 per cent, but prices increased generally by 105 per cent and food prices by 110 per cent in the same period. However, for many households, the absence of father or sons at the front meant that the family income actually went further and resulted in better diet and nutrition. And for many poorer working class families, work in munitions factories and plentiful overtime gave them an unprecedented purchasing power, which they were keen to protect once the war was over. Even so, government initiatives designed to make food stretch further (such as 'meatless days'), were often regarded as derisory by the workers (who regularly went meatless). There was resentment at the apparent prosperity of the wealthy amidst the privations of war, and this concern was shared by members of the government. 'Profiteering is rife in every commodity – bread, meat, tea, butter – and the masses are being exploited right and left', observed Lord Devonport.

On the other hand, whilst German children seem to have suffered from declining nutrition and health during the war, British children's diet seemed to have improved. But why was this? The principal difference between the western democracies and the other belligerents appears to have been the establishment of an effective system of centrally-directed rent controls, subsidies, separation allowances and efficient rationing and food distribution, enabling the preservation of the health and welfare of the population. This was in turn only really possible because the state was prepared, at least partially, to put the needs of state before the interests of business. Britain's tax on excess profits, for example, prevented industrialists from profiteering on the grand scale that some German firms did.

As the war progressed, Britain evolved a system which sustained their large armies and the populations from which they were recruited and equipped, while Germany and Russia failed to do so, resulting in the collapse of civilian and Front Line morale. Ultimately, this may explain why the Western Allies were able, during 1918, to rally their exhausted people for one last effort, whereas efforts by the Central Powers to do so met with sullen compliance, but with little active enthusiasm and support.

 ## 3. Wartime politics (OCR)

In what ways did the First World War transform the position of the political parties in Britain?

(Total: 90 marks)

When the first coalition government was formed in May 1915, it soon became clear that neither Liberals nor Conservatives were happy with the arrangement. The Liberals felt that the Conservatives had deliberately undermined the government in order to gain political advantage, and they resented the way in which Asquith and Lloyd George had agreed on the move without consulting anyone else in the Cabinet. Bonar Law had not consulted his party and the Conservatives were not satisfied with the very slim pickings of ministerial office which they received. As the war continued to go badly for Britain in 1916 with the failures at the Somme and Kut, the escalating U-boat campaign and the Dublin Easter Rising, it was clear that further change would be necessary to prosecute the war more effectively. In the first instance, the supply of manpower had to be maintained and at this point the incompatibility between a traditional liberal, 'laissez-faire' approach and the need for central state intervention became manifest. When conscription was introduced, the Liberal Party split and 27 Liberal MPs voted against their own leader and the Home Secretary, Sir John Simon, resigned. However, state intervention needed to go further to overcome Britain's problems, and Asquith, attempting to keep his party together was perceived as the obstacle to this. To steer around the obstacle, Lloyd George proposed a small War Committee, consisting of himself, Bonar Law, Edward Carson, Arthur Henderson and later Jan Smuts. Asquith initially agreed to this, but changed his mind after an article critical of his leadership appeared in *The Times* which he believed was organised by Lloyd George. Lloyd George and the Conservatives resigned in protest to this sudden about-face, and then managed to hammer out a deal to form a government with Lloyd George as Prime Minister and Bonar Law as Chancellor of the Exchequer. Lloyd George's supporters in the Party backed him, but all the Liberal Cabinet ministers followed Asquith into opposition. Asquith's supporters accused Lloyd George of betraying Asquith and the Party for personal advancement and the bitterness of their feeling became clear in the Maurice Debate of 1918 when the party spilt 98 to 71 in favour of Asquith. In the election of December 1918, Lloyd George and Bonar Law used the vote in the Maurice Debate as the means to decide which Liberals to endorse with the 'Coupon' and the Asquithian Liberals suffered major defeats as a consequence. This made the split last beyond the duration of the war and the resentment between the two groups even more intense. The Liberals would never regain their pre-war parliamentary strength and the pattern of Edwardian politics was shattered.

The Labour party had been keen to demonstrate its patriotism in August 1914 and had supported the government and forced Ramsay MacDonald to resign for his anti-war stance. The new leader, Arthur Henderson became the first Labour cabinet minister in the coalition of 1915 with responsibility for labour relations and became a member of the War Cabinet in December 1916 with the firm backing of the party conference. This gave the party credibility as a potential governing party in its own right and gave it valuable political experience. He was forced to resign in 1917 after supporting Labour attendance at a socialist peace conference in Stockholm which German socialists also attended. This effectively ended the **Lib–Lab pact** which had existed since 1903 and so Henderson began to reorganise Labour as a fully independent political party. The increase in trade-union membership from 4.1 to 6.5 million, caused by the war, boosted Labour's funds and the increase in the working class electorate in 1918 made this practically possible, and so Henderson sought to increase the membership and fight more constituencies. The Party established its own National Executive Committee and adopted a socialist programme, 'Labour and the New Social Order'. This included the famous 'Clause Four' pledging the party to 'the common ownership of the means of production'. This gave the Labour movement a much clearer sense of purpose and a greater coherence than it had previously and the complete enfranchisement of the male working classes gave it the opportunity of competing for a majority of seats. In 1918 it fielded 388 candidates, and, although it only won 63, it survived the pressures of the 'coupon' more effectively than Asquith's Liberals and became the largest party outside the coalition – one which it could exploit when the coalition collapsed.

The Conservatives helped to bring Asquith down, then hesitated over whether to join Lloyd George's coalition in 1916, but in contrast with the Liberals the majority of senior figures followed their leader Bonar Law into the coalition. This time they were rewarded far more handsomely, as they formed the bulk of the government's supporters. Bonar Law became Chancellor and Leader of the House of Commons and Lords Curzon and Milner were admitted to the War Cabinet. This coalition gave the Conservatives the opportunity to appeal to a wider social group than they had traditionally. Lord Milner set up the British Workers' League to appeal to the patriotic working class and it succeeded in returning ten MPs of its own in 1918. The party also agreed to the Representation of the People Act in 1918 which increased the electorate from 8 to 21 million, but the party leadership knew that they needed the continued assistance of a popular figurehead such as Lloyd George in order to guarantee support from the new younger male voters. Therefore, the election of December 1918 served Conservative purposes rather than Lloyd George's by giving Lloyd George's approval to 374 Conservative candidates but to only 159 'Lloyd George-ites'. The Conservatives had to swallow Lloyd George's radical promises of reconstruction and social reform (even though they were later able to scupper many of them), but as Baldwin later demonstrated, the party came to accept some state intervention as the price to be paid for electoral success. Labour's decision to fight the election completely independently additionally benefited the Conservatives as the end of the **Lib–Lab pact** divided the anti-Conservative vote and improved Conservative chances of success at elections.

The war also ended the Liberal-Irish alliance. John Redmond, leader of the Nationalists, refused a Cabinet position in 1915 as he felt, quite rightly, that his position, already weakened by the suspension of the Home Rule Act for the duration of the war, would be undermined if he shared office with Unionists. To keep the Conservatives happy, Asquith appointed the Ulster Unionist leader, Carson, as Attorney-General, but he did at least refrain from introducing conscription to

Ireland, which would have been fatal for **Nationalist** support there. The crucial event, however, took place in Dublin, rather than Westminster, when a Rising by the radical Irish Republican Brotherhood on Easter Monday, 1916, was brutally put down by the army. The execution of the leaders turned them into martyrs and the clumsy threat to extend conscription to Ireland turned the Irish people away from the constitutional Nationalists to support the radical Sinn Fein. In the election of 1918, Sinn Fein won the seats previously controlled by the Nationalists, and they promptly refused to attend Parliament, setting up their own assembly, the Dail, in Dublin.

In brief, therefore, the split in the Liberal Party was the crucial event in the politics of the war. The Liberals were never able to form or dominate a government again and the animosity between the leaders caused by the split helped to swiftly reduce the party to a position of near insignificance after the war. The Conservatives were the chief beneficiary of this, although they were careful to remain in Lloyd George's coalition after the war, until the behaviour of the new electorate could be established. Labour's fortunes improved too as they inherited the mantle of progressive radicalism. This was largely due to subsequent Liberal blunders, as Asquith failed to fulfil this role, and the actions of Henderson in revitalising the party and keeping it united. In addition, the south of Ireland chose to reject the authority of Westminster completely and to establish its own, as yet illegal, parliamentary structure. Of course nothing in history is inevitable and it took the subsequent six years of political realignment to confirm that the effects of war would not be swiftly reversed.

How much control over the armed forces did politicians manage to exert during the war?

(Total: 90 marks)

At the beginning of the war, control of the campaigns was largely handed to Lord Kitchener, a hugely popular veteran commander of the Sudan and South African campaigns who was made War Minister. He immediately announced that the war was likely to last at least three years and that a huge army of volunteers should be created to prepare for this. He himself supported an 'eastern' approach, but after the failure at Gallipoli, he was largely discredited. The 'Shell Scandal' of spring 1915 effectively ended his total control of the conflict as the government reacted to the crisis of confidence by removing control of the supply of munitions from the War Office and created the Ministry of Munitions under the civilian leadership of David Lloyd George (formerly Chancellor of the Exchequer). Asquith also forced the replacement of the commander of the British Expeditionary Force (BEF), Sir John French. Kitchener, in turn, handed immediate control of the war to the Chief of the Imperial General Staff (CIGS), William Robertson and the new commander in France, Douglas Haig. Robertson, in particular resented the 'interference' of civilians and excluded the Secretary of State and the Cabinet from his strategic planning. Both men were determined to avoid another 'sideshow' such as Gallipoli, believing that the war had to be won on the western front. Kitchener himself was increasingly kept out of cabinet discussions on the war effort and was eventually sent on a mission to Russia, where his ship, the HMS Hampshire was sunk en route and Kitchener was lost.

Lloyd George then became War Minister and his attempts to affect the direction of the war brought the enmity of Haig and Robertson. They tried to keep Lloyd George out of decision making, believing that he would compromise the effectiveness of the army in his attempts to maintain his personal popularity. Lloyd George responded by trying to gain a greater say in military policy, but he failed to get Asquith's support, despite threatening to resign. He therefore had to accept Haig's decision for a summer offensive on the Somme. After he became Prime Minister in 1916, Lloyd George also faced the difficulty that a majority of the Conservatives who supported him in the Commons still believed that the war was best left to the generals.

The new Prime Minister found his plans for an offensive in Italy blocked, but Lloyd George managed to undermine Haig, however, when in 1917 the French commander Nivelle was appointed above Haig. Nivelle's promise of a victorious offensive turned out to be hollow and Lloyd George was forced to allow Haig to attempt an attack of his own – the disastrous Passchendaele offensive (also known as the third battle of Ypres). After the loss of 400,000 men in this campaign, Lloyd George refused to allow another offensive and limited the supply of reinforcements to Haig with the full backing of his War Cabinet. Lloyd George then managed to appoint Sir Henry Wilson, a general prepared to listen to politicians, as British representative to the Executive War Board set up by all the allies to control reserves. Robertson resigned in protest at being undermined in this way, but that suited Lloyd George even more and made it easier for him to confront Haig, especially as he then appointed Wilson as CIGS. By working more closely with his foreign allies, Lloyd George had finally found the means to overrule his recalcitrant generals. The generals attempted to fight back when the former Director of Military Operations, General Maurice, claimed that the government had deliberately withheld troops which had led to the German breakthrough in the spring offensive of 1918, but Lloyd George refused to accept this. Believing Haig to be behind this attempt to sabotage his premiership, when the German offensive finally wore itself out, Lloyd George persuaded the allies to agree to unify command under the French general Foch in order to marshal their forces most effectively. For Lloyd George, of course this meant the removal of Haig from overall command, and thus the battle for control of the army was eventually won by the politicians, but only by handing overall command to a foreign 'generalissimo'.

In a similar fashion, the government faced a battle for control over the navy. The instigation of the Dardenelles campaign had been opposed by Admiral Fisher in 1915 and he had publicly criticised the First Lord, Winston Churchill, one of the principal supporters of the strategy, and been forced to resign. Churchill had angered the Conservatives by this clash and he himself did not survive the formation of the coalition, being unacceptable to the Conservatives after this clash. Eventually, Carson, the Ulster Unionist leader, became First Lord in 1916 and effectively abdicated his responsibility and allowed the admirals to run the navy as they saw fit. The major confrontation took place over the escalation of submarine warfare in 1917 and the consequent threat to Britain's supplies (especially her food). By March 1917, the Admiralty had still failed to issue clear instructions to the merchant fleets, as it did not regard such private activity as part of its business. In other words, merchant ships were still travelling unescorted and U-boats were being hunted separately. In the first half of 1917 the British lost 2.5 million tons of shipping, a rate which would leave Britain facing starvation by the winter. Lloyd George managed to persuade the Admiralty to allow the government to organise some merchant fleets into convoys protected by Royal Navy vessels and the clear success of these made the Admiralty give way. In April 1917 a naval general staff was created and the direction of the Navy's resources passed into the hands of the War Cabinet. Carson was replaced by Eric Geddes and the course of the war at sea showed swift improvement. Here, the victory of the politicians was unconditional.

4. Women's wartime role (AQA)

Read the following Source and then answer the questions which follow

From the outset [of the war] women of all social classes were absorbed into the war effort and played a crucial part on the Home Front during the war, entering occupations that would have been deemed unsuitable in peacetime . . .

Unlike most of their upper- and middle-class colleagues, working-class women did not go out to work because of the war. They had to work anyway. However, war did change the nature of their occupation

From *Votes for Women, 1860–1928* by Paula Bartley, 1998

a) **Why were so many women needed to work on the Home Front?**   **(3 marks)**
b) **How did the First World War change the nature of women's**
    occupations?   **(7 marks)**
c) **To what extent did the war transform the cause of women's suffrage?** **(15 marks)**

a) As men volunteered to join the army and navy in the opening months of the war, women were first encouraged, then compelled, to fill the vacancies left by men. In Britain, the number of women employed increased from 3,224,600 in July, 1914 to 4,814,600 in January 1918. Had it not been for the huge demand for men in the armed forces caused by the appalling casualty rates on the Western Front, it seems unlikely that 'upper-class and middle-class women' would have had to take jobs such as nurses, clerks, and teachers and that working-class women would have had to enter such physical occupations as blacksmiths, quarry workers and foundry workers.

b) Nearly 200,000 women were employed in government departments, with half a million becoming clerical workers in private offices and a quarter of a million working on the land. The greatest increase of women workers was in engineering. Over 700,000 of these women worked in the highly dangerous munitions industry. Whereas in 1914 there were 212,000 women working in the munitions industry, by the end of the war it had increased to 950,000. Christopher Addison, who succeeded David Lloyd George as Minister of Munitions, estimated in June 1917, that about 80 per cent of all weapons and shells were being produced by 'munitionettes'. The work was extremely dangerous and accidents at munitions factories resulted in over 200 deaths in Britain alone. Some women suffered health problems such as TNT poisoning because of the dangerous chemicals they were using.

The British government decided that more women would have to become more involved in producing food and goods to support their war effort. This included the establishment of the Women's Land Army in 1917, which despite popular myth, was a relatively unpopular form of war work, only employing 16,000 women in the 1918 harvest. Farmers failed to accept women as acceptable alternative workers to men and most working-class women realised that money could be made (and spent) more easily in towns and cities. A disproportionate number of middle-class women joined the WLA, and found the work exhausting and dangerous, with low pay and poor accommodation. In Britain, 4,808,000 women were in employment by the end of the war, an increase of over one and a half million. The exclusion of women from heavy industry and skilled work, such as shipbuilding and iron and steel and from professions such as dentistry, accountancy and architecture remained essentially unchanged in 1918. However, women did enter the civil service, transport areas, munitions factories, the post office and banking. In commerce and civil service, women achieved lasting gains. However, no more than 5 per cent of new women workers were in these areas.

c) It was until quite recently accepted that the Great War acted as a significant breakthrough in the campaign for female suffrage as women in Britain were granted the right to vote during the war. However, certain points need to be borne in mind before such a simple analysis is accepted. Male political leaders assented to the granting of the vote for women on their own terms, to suit their purposes, not those of the feminists, at this particular time. In addition, the campaign for women's suffrage had a long history before 1914, and women had equal voting rights to men in local elections. One must therefore recognise that the granting of the vote during the Great War must be seen as part of a long-term movement towards equalising the suffrage, as well as part of a wider campaign to widen the right to vote to include more men as well.

Two days after England declared war on Germany and after it participated in the great Peace Meeting in London, the National Union of Women's Suffrage Societies (NUWSS) announced that it was suspending all political activity until the war was over. On 7 August 1914 the Home Secretary announced that all suffragettes would be released from prison. In return, the Women's Social and Political Union (WSPU) agreed to end their militant activities and help the war effort. Some leaders of the WSPU such as Emmeline Pankhurst and her daughter, Christabel, played an important role as speakers at meetings to recruit young men into the army and the WSPU journal, the *Suffragette* was replaced by *Britannia*, which zealously hounded alleged traitors and called for the internment of enemy aliens and conscientious objectors. Encouraged by Lloyd George, anxious to recruit women munitions workers, Mrs Pankhurst encouraged a mass march of 20,000 women demanding the 'right to serve' on 7 July 1915. While the outbreak of hostilities in 1914 led to splits within the various suffrage organisations, it cannot be said that the campaign for women's suffrage came to a halt. The NUWSS continued to hold meetings, draft petitions and stage demonstrations in support of female suffrage. Most effectively of all, they responded to the government's public praise for women workers by enquiring if the government would reward such patriotism as soon as possible.

The women's suffrage clause in the Representation of the People Act of 1918 reflected significant compromises worked out between the Conservative-dominated coalition government and the NUWSS during the war years. The legislation did not extend the franchise to women on equal terms with men: women had to be aged thirty or above and local government electors or the wives of such electors; men only had to be aged twenty-one or above or military veterans aged nineteen or above. Women who had served their country as munitions workers and who were typically under thirty and unmarried were not enfranchised by the measure. Thus, there is little evidence that the suffrage was conceded as a reward for women's contribution to the war effort. The 8.4 million women who gained the vote in 1918 were more likely to be married, to have children, and to have no interest in a career which brought with it further demands for equality. Conservatives and right-wing Liberals felt there would be little threat to the existing political order from such mature, stable new voters, and in light of political behaviour after the war, they seem to have made quite a shrewd judgement.

5. Opposition to the war (EDEXCEL)

a) In what ways was opposition to the war organised in Britain? **(30 marks)**

b) How effectively did the British government respond to pacifism and
opposition to the war? **(30 marks)**

(Total: 60 marks)

a) In Britain, the absence of anti-war sentiment was striking. Despite the passage of the Defence of the Realm Act in August 1914, by which the government obtained extensive powers to control public opinion and opposition, the state rarely felt the need to deploy its powers against the ranks of the dissenters and pacifists.

This was because there were very few of them. On the political left, groups like the Herald League and the Workers' Socialist Foundation campaigned against the war from the outset, but gained very little public support, garnering dozens rather than hundreds of members. The Union of Democratic Control (UDC), founded by Charles Trevelyan on 5 August 1914 was larger, but it campaigned for a peaceful post-war world rather than an immediate end to the war. The No Conscription Fellowship, formed by Clifford Allen in response to the Military Service Act in 1916, had only a limited impact. Primarily supported by religious dissenters (especially Quakers), socialists and radical feminists, and numbering amongst its energetic and dedicated supporters such luminaries as Bertrand Russell, Fenner Brockway and Sylvia Pankhurst, it provided moral and legal assistance to men who refused to serve. However, in the event, only 16,100 men 'objected'. Furthermore, objectors received very little support or sympathy from the public as a whole. Disappointingly for these (mostly) socialist campaigners, the working classes rejected utterly conscientious objection, pacifism and even moderation in British war aims. The repetition of 'atrocity' stories in British propaganda had convinced the majority of the population that they were fighting for the survival of civilisation which required nothing less than total victory. The Labour Party itself remained deeply divided over demands for peace, with principle jostling with the achievement of power in Lloyd George's Cabinet. The press lambasted and ridiculed campaigners, and their meetings were disrupted. Indeed, the state seems judiciously to have left the task of discrediting and disrupting the activities of 'pacifists' to the people themselves.

There was, however, growing industrial unrest as the war continued. Workers were aggrieved over 'shaking-out', rising prices for coal and food, stagnant wages, the increasing **dilution** of skilled work through the introduction of unskilled (often female) labour and new, mechanised processes, the high cost of housing and rents, and the perceived failure of the government to honour its promises regarding reserved occupations. Despite Lloyd George's efforts to recruit the support of the union movement, huge strikes during 1915 immobilised the Welsh mining areas and Clydeside. A further wave of strikes affected Britain during 1917, but the government's policy of meeting strikers' demands, establishing rent controls and granting war bonuses and concessions to workers, minimised the disruption. It is noticeable, however, that the German offensive of March 1918 was marked by a lull in industrial action, suggesting that British workers were prepared to put the need to win the war before their own demands.

The only notable armed opposition came from Ireland, where a collection of Republican extremists, who had rejected Redmond's call to serve in the Army, decided that 'England's difficulty is Ireland's opportunity' and contacted the German authorities to supply guns for an uprising.

The Easter Rising of 1916 may have marked the first declaration of an Irish Republic, but to most Dubliners and to the British army who crushed it in a week, with the loss of 116 men, such rebels were traitors, who discredited the Irish cause by their actions. It was the British response to the rising that shifted sympathy towards the republicans.

It is evident that Britain experienced less discontent than elsewhere during 1915–17. Britain's smaller commitment of manpower, and therefore fewer casualties, than France, Germany or Russia may partially explain the relative quiet on the Home Front. Certainly the economic strain was less keenly felt in Britain, as imports were maintained, serious bread shortages never really affected the public, and rationing was only introduced during the final year of the war. It appears that, by paying greater attention to the subsistence needs of their people on the Home Front, Britain and France prevented the emergence of significant anti-war opposition. Second, the British army, at least, was made up of the most highly disciplined industrial labour force in the world and it seemed quite prepared to continue to obey orders. Collective behaviour like the 'mutiny' at Etaples or individual behaviour like that of Lieutenant Siegfried Sassoon, who published a condemnation of the war, was significant only because of its rarity.

b)   In Britain, the Defence of the Realm Act (DORA), passed in the first days of the war, considerably restricted personal liberty, with the government assuming the power to court martial anyone 'jeopardising the success of the operations of His Majesty's forces or assisting the enemy'. This was later extended to cover 'spreading disaffection'. Remarkably, however, the state used its extensive powers sparingly. Rather than deploy DORA against the strikers in South Wales and Clydeside in 1915, Lloyd George chose instead to pacify them with concessions, war bonuses and reforms. 'Joint Industrial Councils' were initiated to draw the unions into partnership with the government, and Lloyd George continued this approach when he became Prime Minister, appointing Henderson to his inner 'War Cabinet' and two other Labour MPs as ministers of state. For the most part the state relied on the patriotic enthusiasm of the people and of the press in particular, to squash expressions of dissent and limit the effectiveness of 'anti-war' campaigns.

The same approach was taken towards 'conchies' with, it may be argued, considerable success. The 'No Conscription Fellowship' never posed the government a realistic challenge regarding the morality of conscription or on the wider issue of the war itself. Only 16,100 men 'objected' and these, when brought before the conscientious objection tribunals, often received surprisingly lenient treatment. Four fifths received some form of exemption, and the remainder by and large were allocated non-combatant duties. Even so, in the end many served prison sentences, and 71 died in prison, some after torture, such as mock firing squads, force-feeding and being suspended off the ground with a 20lb weight tied to their feet for 28 hours, which reflected badly on Britain's claim to be defending civilisation against 'German barbarism'.

In general, however, the government's handling of opposition and conscientious objection was distinguished by its skill and lightness of touch. Lloyd George seems to have appreciated that the population as a whole had little sympathy with 'shirkers', and he showed an acute awareness of the value of meeting the welfare needs of the working people during the conflict. By ensuring that labour was won over through the approval of arbitration tribunals, rent controls, price fixing and eventually rationing, the government ensured that the public at large, for all their weariness, remained supportive of the war and therefore unreceptive to the arguments of the peace lobby. Given this, the government felt able (largely) to ignore these voices, although prominent campaigners, like the U.D.C.'s Morel, did serve jail sentences. In Ireland, however, a different approach was taken and 15 of the leaders of the Easter Rising were executed by firing squad. This caused such a storm of protest that the shootings were stopped and Lloyd George, as War Minister, was dispatched to try to calm the country. As Prime Minister, he continued to try to mollify the Irish, until manpower shortages on the Western Front drove him to threaten to extend conscription to Ireland (it had been exempted in 1916, for fear of provoking riots). The reaction of the nationalist community was so strong that Lloyd George was forced to withdraw the threat, but not before Sinn Fein had become the most influential political movement in the south. Lloyd George's attempts to untangle the Irish problem would see him continuing to veer from violent coercion to friendly co-operation after the war.

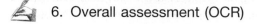 ## 6. Overall assessment (OCR)

Why did Britain win the Great War? **(Total: 90 marks)**

The First World War was ultimately a war of attrition, and the countries best able to sustain the terrible human, financial and economic costs were the ones which would prevail. Therefore any analysis explaining the outcome of the war must explain why the Germans and their allies failed to overcome the test of war before describing those strengths which enabled France and Britain to emerge victorious in 1918.

The defeat of Germany and her allies was not inevitable until August 1918, but following the early failure of the Schlieffen Plan, it was always the most likely outcome. Germany, for all her tremendous efforts, possessed neither the financial nor the material resources to defeat such a large coalition of enemies, and the addition of the USA to that coalition in 1917 more than offset the loss of Russia, with the result that, in 1918, the balance tipped decisively against the Central Powers and defeat became unavoidable.

Yet, at the outset of the conflict, Germany had seemed better equipped to wage a large modern war than her enemies. Her army and navy were the most modern and efficient in the world, and her economy was, in many respects, better suited to the production of military materiel even than that of Great Britain, out-producing Britain in steel for example. In the early days of the conflict then, Germany possessed the advantages of greater preparedness (although even she was not really ready for 'total war') and superior quality of arms and soldiery. These advantages were however only good for the short term, and the Schlieffen Plan indicates that the more thoughtful military minds in pre-war Germany appreciated the importance of a quick victory. Once the Schlieffen Plan had failed and the initial offensives of 1914 had ground to a halt, Germany's isolation and her inability to guarantee supplies of crucial raw materials and food hamstrung her war effort.

All the long term advantages were possessed by Great Britain: the World's most powerful navy, her extensive overseas empire, enormous financial power and (vitally) open trade routes to Japan, the USA and the Commonwealth. The problem for Great Britain was that she was wholly unready in 1914 for total war, in material, ideological and psychological terms. Britain's early contributions to the Entente's war effort were unimpressive – she never had more than 1 million men under arms at any one time – and indeed the French and Russians were quick to notice this. British lassitude was a common theme of French and Russian complaints during 1915. It was 1916 before the introduction of conscription and the establishment of Lloyd George's coalition government enabled Britain to begin to mobilise her superior resources effectively, and more or less throughout the war Germany managed to squeeze more out of her economy and society than Britain did, although it may be argued that the lengths to which the German regime went to achieve this partly explain the war weariness and discontent within Germany which culminated in revolution in 1918.

The eventual triumph of the Western Allies is most effectively explained in terms of their greater success in balancing the needs of these two sectors, and a brief examination of the way in which the response of the belligerent states evolved as the war progressed exemplifies this. Initially, in 1914, mobilisation in every European power was largely spontaneous, a product of 'national culture', expressing itself as popular support for a war in defence of the homeland. The State did acquire new powers, but generally hesitated to deploy them at first, relying on propaganda to mobilise the nation (even here, the press, intellectuals, educationalists, churches and voluntary organisations did the lion's share of the work). In economic matters the State worked in partnership with industry to produce the necessary munitions.

Gradually, the need for total effort by state and society in order to win the war, the 'totalising logic of the conflict', became clear. The national myths mobilised in 1914 began to create divisions and social solidarity was strained by evidently contrasting experiences of war. Consequently self-mobilisation had lost all its momentum by 1916. Thereafter, the state in most countries sought to assume a more central, directing role in the war effort. Conscription in Great Britain, the Hindenburg Programme in Germany, and Clemenceau's remobilisation of French society after his appointment in France in 1917, all bear witness to the state adopting a more dominant role in the organisation of the war, 're-mobilising' the nation.

However, in their response to the crises of 1916–17, the wartime regimes revealed the essence of their state systems, and this determined their ultimate fate. In Russia, the tsarist regime was simply unable to cope with criticism in any way other than with repression. However, repression deepened the gulf between state and society, and ultimately led to the February Revolution. In Germany, the nature of the German Constitution allowed those in power to rule autocratically but it was not possible to coerce greater commitment from the German people when their elected representatives in the Reichstag had been alienated from the regime. Wages, consumption and nutrition declined and the German non-combatant death rate during the war climbed to six times that of France. Although the German people did not starve, the episodic hunger and the demoralising lengths to which ordinary citizens were forced to go in order to obtain food inexorably ground down their will to continue.

By the end of 1917, the elements which would result in victory for the Western Allies and defeat for the Central Powers were in place. Germany was running short of money, materiel and men and the enormous needs of the war machine could not be met. By 1918 the Western Allies possessed huge advantages in terms of aeroplanes, tanks and trucks, and these would prove crucial during the final campaigns of the war. Germany began 1918 heavily outnumbered, and by the time Ludendorff's suicidal Spring offensive had ground to a halt, Germany had sustained almost 500,000 casualties. She lost a further one million men due to sickness, desertion and self-inflicted wounds by August, leaving only 2,500,000 active front line troops left. The war was lost.

Contrast this with developments in the Western democracies. In both countries, power was wrested away from the generals and enshrined in coalition governments headed by populist civilian politicians, Lloyd George and Clemenceau. The British regime promised democratic reform at the end of the struggle. The French anyway were fighting to liberate their homeland from the occupying Germans, and for all their exhaustion and disaffection, they would not rest until they had done so. As the war progressed, both governments stepped up their efforts and assumed greater powers over industry and the people. The resulting experiment in 'State Capitalism' from 1915 onwards succeeded in sustaining the civilian population's standards of living, via subsidies, rent controls, separation allowances and active intervention by the state in worker–employer relations. Britain was the only country where profiteering by industrialists was even vaguely reined in by the state, through the taxation of war profits. The state emphasised the limited nature of the nation's war aims. As a result of this intelligent and inclusive approach, Britain and France balanced civilian and military needs more effectively. Therefore, when Britain and France asked for one last effort in 1918, they got it, unlike the German government, later the same year. In the crisis of the war, democratic regimes proved more capable of demanding further sacrifices than autocratic ones.

To conclude, therefore, the military defeat suffered by Germany is only partly explicable in military terms. The German army performed remarkably well during the First World War, but the sheer enormity of the demands placed upon German society and the economy in order to meet the challenge of total war were ultimately too great to be overcome. This was true almost from the very beginning of the conflict, and it was only the extraordinary efforts of the German people and soldiery that staved off the inevitable for four years and brought their nation to what appeared to be the brink of victory during 1917. However, by this stage Germany was exhausted and whereas Britain and France had access to overseas sources of grain and materiel, Germany, bankrupt and blockaded, was unable to draw upon such a reserve. American intervention merely reinforced this situation and hastened the end.

Did the First World War have any long term effects on Britain?

(Total: 90 marks)

The most obvious effect of the war, it might seem, was the annihilation of an entire 'lost generation' of young men, which, as one would expect, caused the marriage and therefore the birth rate to drop, depriving the country of the leaders, managers and workforce of the future. However, Britain's birth rate was declining before 1914, and the reduction in this rate attributable to the war was almost made up by the post-war baby boom. After that, the birth rate continued the gradual downward spiral it had demonstrated before the war. Therefore the impact of the war on the birth rate was disruptive but not revolutionary. As for the 'lost generation', Britain had, before 1914, suffered a net loss of 200,000 people per year through emigration either to the colonies or, as with the majority of European emigrants, to the United States. The advent of war curtailed such emigration, and it is arguable that had war not intervened Britain may have lost more of its young men to emigration than death in military conflict. The post-war imposition by the United States of restrictions on immigration, and the growth of independence movements in some of Britain's colonies, ensured that emigration remained at a much lower rate during the post-war years, and therefore the 'lost generation' was quickly replaced. This is not to argue that imbalances were not felt for many years. In 1911, there were 100 men to every 101 women. By 1925, there were 100 men to every 113 women. Unmarried women of this generation and the next generation put their position down to the effects of the war. The upper classes suffered a disproportionately large number of losses, as the young men from these groups tended to become front-line officers, whose survival rate, as they led their men over the top, was the worst for any rank in the armed forces.

Although Britain did not suffer as much structural damage as France, her economy was equally adversely affected by the war. The 'staple industries' of textiles, coal, iron, steel and shipbuilding, on which the British economy was dangerously reliant, lost vital overseas markets, either to domestic production or US and Japanese firms. In Brazil, an important customer of the British cotton industry before the war, domestic production replaced British imports, and the Japanese cotton industry gobbled up British markets in south-east Asia. Only one third of wartime expenditure was covered by increased taxation, which had forced Britain to liquidate many of her foreign investments and to borrow heavily, especially from the USA. As a result Britain was to emerge from the war a debtor nation, when before it had been a creditor. Servicing these debts, especially those to the US, severely limited the government's ability to satisfy demands for more and better services. The City of London had been the hub of global financial services such as banking and insurance before the war, but with its assets depleted, New York displaced it as the world's premier financial centre. On the other hand, the loss of German imports encouraged Britain to develop newer industries such as chemicals, electrical goods, radio, motor vehicles, and aircraft. New industrial techniques, such as standardisation, mass production and more efficient management were introduced widely. Heavy industry enjoyed a boom, which makes one wonder, if, had their profits been more wisely spent on modernising and diversifying, whether these industries would have been better able to withstand the industrial recessions of the 1920s and 1930s.

In general, Europe's historical, economic and political world dominance was terminated by the First World War. Her share of world manufacturing production fell from 43 per cent (1913) to 34 per cent (1923), with the main beneficiary being North America, although Asia (particularly Japan) gained ground too. Europe's share of world trade showed a similar trend.

Workers (at least those who survived) made significant gains during the war as real wages increased and both the trade unions and the socialist parties emerged stronger in 1918 than they had been in 1914. The Ministry of Labour survived the 'Geddes Axe', unemployment insurance was extended to cover nearly all workers in 1920 and a Ministry of Health was established in 1919. These and other wartime gains, which marked a distinct break from pre-war attitudes towards welfare provision, led to further demands for more improvements such as better pay and conditions, improved education and more housing. The state's capacity to direct, intervene and improve had been confirmed by the war, and many believed that this power could continue to be used to remedy social injustices after the war. However, it is equally true to say that the middle classes, who had suffered disproportionately high death rates and, for those on fixed incomes especially, a decline in their standard of living, now became more determined to resist these demands. They believed, quite correctly, that they would have to fund such improvements through higher taxes. Thus the political legacy of the war was heightened inter-class antagonism, rather than the mythical cross-class camaraderie that was supposedly encouraged in the trenches. This led to the inter-war dominance of the Conservatives, the return of industry to private control, the formation of the Middle Class Union, and organised opposition to the general strike.

At the end of the war, both the British and French Empires were at their zenith in terms of their size, as the German and Turkish colonies were dismembered and transferred (under the fig leaf of League of Nations mandates) to Britain and France, despite the promise of 'self-determination'. However, given the cost of the war, neither could now afford to control and defend this enormous portion of the earth, especially as the war had caused many rural peoples in the colonies to move into cities where they became increasingly conscious of nationalist movements, such as those of Gandhi in India and the Wafd party in Egypt. Britain also had responsibility for two of the most bitterly divided areas of the world – Palestine and Ireland, and her decision to grant autonomy to the South of Ireland in 1922, demonstrated the 'imperial overstretch' that she was suffering. That move made the situation worse in some ways, however, as nationalists elsewhere attempted to follow the Irish Free State's example, and Britain and France oscillated between repression and reform in order to contain the problem. Furthermore, they both had to defend these troublesome areas from external threat as well, which may well go some way to explain their reluctance to confront the aggression of Mussolini and Hitler during the inter-war years, as the difficulties of defending their Far East possessions from militant Japan were felt to be more pressing than the problems in central and eastern Europe.

British politicians failed to understand this geo-political development and attempted to return to a pre-war 'golden age' of imperial and economic domination. Too late, they discovered that the war had rendered them incapable of fulfilling such a role, and it took a second war and prolonged economic decline to convince the British that European co-operation was the only means for small nation states to prosper in an age of super-power confrontation.

Additional essay questions

Preparation for war (EDEXCEL)

a) **How politically and socially united were the British people in 1914?**   **(30 marks)**
b) **What contribution did propaganda make in the maintenance of civilian morale during the First World War?**   **(30 marks)**

(Total: 60 marks)

Essay plan

a)   Britain seen as internally united, but had in fact seen an unusual number of political crises in the years before 1914 which revealed social divisions in Britain:

- *Constitutional struggle over the House of Lords revealed lower class resentment of the privileged position of the aristocracy in Britain.*
- *Militant campaign of the suffragettes and the peaceful protests of the suffragists demonstrated that many women no longer accepted an inferior social position.*
- *The **Ulster** crisis polarised British society with many anti-Catholic prejudices being revealed among those who opposed the Liberals' attempts to introduce **Home Rule**.*
- *Wave of industrial unrest in South Wales, Clydeside and the North of England revealed deep divisions between workers and employers, which reflected huge divisions in wealth in Britain – the Lib–Lab **pact** which united the progressive forces of Britain was becoming increasingly strained.*

However, the British government's careful handling of the declaration of war concentrating on the treatment of Belgium united the nation on the issue of resistance to German aggression on which there had been near unanimous pre-war agreement. The overwhelming majority of workers, loyalists, nationalists, suffragettes immediately rallied to the war effort. The only serious exception to this were the militant Irish Nationalists who plotted with Germany and staged an uprising in Dublin in 1916.

b)   Nature of propaganda in First World War – largely voluntary – produced by the media without the interference of government. Ministry of Information only set up in 1917 and had only limited success.

Reason for propaganda – need to maintain confidence in victory and belief in the British cause in face of unprecedentedly long and costly conflict.

Types of propaganda:

- *Soldiers' disdain for the enemy and personal bravery – rarely challenged by soldiers.*
- *Atrocity stories – following the German army's treatment of Belgian civilians and the sinking of the Lusitania, these were believed despite the lack of evidence in many cases.*
- *Suppression of bad news, such as the Gallipoli campaign, and lists of casualties.*
- *Exaggeration of successes, such as the Battle of Jutland in 1916 and exaggeration of the 'equality of sacrifice' by all classes in the domestic hardships caused by deaths, shortages and inconvenience.*

Propaganda proved less successful as the war continued – the use of advertising by the National Service Scheme failed to enrol half the expected numbers. Audiences became increasingly cautious of accepting stories, especially by 1917 when there was still no sight of ultimate victory, soldiers' versions of the war seemed to contradict the media and atrocity stories were becoming less convincing.

Ultimately, the British people were sufficiently convinced of the rightness of the cause for which they were fighting, and propaganda served merely to remind people of this, especially as the war dragged on. But propaganda was useless without substantial existing support for the war, as was evident from the example of Russia in 1917.

2. The British economy in wartime (OCR)

How important was the First World War in the decline of the British economy?

(90 marks)

3. Politics (EDEXCEL)

a) **What impact did the First World War have on the Liberal Party?**   **(30 marks)**
b) **Did the First World War 'transform' the Labour Party from a narrow interest group to a national political party?**   **(30 marks)**

(Total: 60 marks)

(OCR)

Why, and with what consequences, did Asquith agree to form a coalition government in 1915?

(Total: 90 marks)

4. Women's wartime role (EDEXCEL)

a) **Describe the contribution of British women to their country's war effort between 1914 and 1918.** (30 marks)

b) **Why did some women get the parliamentary vote in 1918, but not all?** (30 marks)

(Total: 60 marks)

5. Opposition to the war (OCR)

How effectively did the government control the media and limit opposition during the First World War? (90 marks)

6. Overall assessment (OCR)

Was the eventual loss of Empire the cost of British success in the First World War? (Total: 90 marks)

Essay plan

Introduction – the victory in the war was achieved partly because of the unity of the British Empire, with colonial troops contributing significantly to the defence of the Western Front and the decisive attacks of Autumn 1918. However, Britain ended the war having lost the economic superiority which made such a vast Empire sustainable.

Costs to Britain – financial, manpower, strategic:

1. *British control weakened during war – led to challenge to imperial authority in Ireland – the wartime and post-war achievement of independence for Southern Ireland acted as an example to other nationalist groups.*

2. *Need to defend a vast, geographically dispersed area – need for large navy, increasingly difficult to afford in the face of demands for social reform at home. Empire strategically difficult to defend, especially when Britain faced competition from outside Europe from countries such as Japan and USA.*

Impact on colonies:

- *Experiences of imperial troops – witnessing white troops fighting one another.*
- *Experiences of colonies – demand for war materials had led to the mass movement of population to urban areas, especially in India and Egypt. Here they became more susceptible to nationalist propaganda.*
- *Colonies saw little reward for their contribution to the war, despite promises of improvements in return for their involvement in the war. Wave of protests – Amritsar 1919, 1921 riots in Egypt.*

British response:

- *Granting of dominion status to the Irish Free State in 1922.*
- *Gradual loosening of direct control over Egypt (protectorate ended in 1922) and India – most significantly seen in the 1935 Government of India Act.*
- *No consideration of a similar approach to African and other Asian colonies – the intention was to exploit the as yet untapped economic potential of the Empire.*

Conclusion – As a result of victory, Britain's empire expanded to its largest size, with the addition of former German and Turkish colonies as 'mandates' administered on behalf of the League of Nations. However the costs of the war as well as the experiences of colonial troops served to reduce the long-term capacity of Britain to sustain such a huge Empire. The effect on foreign policy was for Britain to attempt to sustain her Empire through moderate reform and long-term promises of independence and to avoid a further war which might expose Britain's 'imperial overstretch'. It was only the failure of that policy and the costs of that second war which made the granting of immediate independence to India unavoidable.

Was British society or British politics more seriously affected by the First World War?

(Total: 90 marks)

Part 3: Sources

1. Votes for women *c.*1880–1918 (EDEXCEL)

Study sources 1–5 below and then answer questions (a) to (e) which follow.

Source 1: From *Factories and Workshops Report for 1916*

'If they stick this, they will stick anything' a manager is reported as saying of the grit and pluck of the women in a gas works in the recent severe weather.

It is permissible to wonder whether some of the surprise and admiration freely expressed in many quarters over new proofs of women's physical capacity and endurance is not in part attributable to lack of knowledge or appreciation of the very heavy and strenuous nature of much of normal pre-war work for women, domestic and industrial.

Source 2: From an article written by J.L. Garvin, editor of *The Observer*, 1916

Time was, when I thought that men alone maintained the state. Now I know that men alone could never have maintained it, and that henceforth the modern state must be dependent on men and women alike for progressive strength and vitality of its whole organisation.

Source 3: From a letter written by Millicent Fawcett to the Prime Minister, Herbert Asquith, in May 1916

When the government deals with the franchise, an opportunity will present itself of dealing with it on wider lines than by the simple removal of what may be called the accidental disqualification of a large body of the best men in the country, and we trust that you would include in your Bill, clauses which would remove the disability under which women now labour.

An agreed Bill on these lines would, we are confident, receive a very wide measure of support throughout the country. Our movement has received very great increases of strength during recent months, former opponents now declaring themselves on our side, or at any rate, withdrawing their opposition. The change in the press is most marked. The view has been widely expressed in a great variety of organs of public opinion that the continued exclusion of women from representation will be an impossibility after the war.

Source 4: From the autobiography of the suffragette, Evelyn Sharp, *Unfinished Adventure*, 1933

When militants and non-militants alike hastened to offer war service to the Government, no doubt many of them felt, if they thought about it at all, that this was the best way of helping their own cause. Certainly, by their four years' war work, they did prove the fallacy of the anti-suffragists' favourite argument, that women had no right to a voice in questions of peace and war because they took no part in it.

Personally, holding as I do that the enfranchisement of women involved greater issues than could be involved in any war, even supposing that the objects of the Great War were those alleged, I cannot help regretting that any justification was given for the popular error which still sometimes ascribes the victory of the suffrage cause, in 1918, to women's war service. This assumption is true only in so far as gratitude to women offered an excuse to the anti-suffragists in the Cabinet and elsewhere to climb down with some dignity from a position that had become untenable before the war.

Source 5: From Arthur Marwick, *Women at War, 1914–1918*, 1977

To say that war brought votes for women is to make a very crude generalisation, yet one which contains an essential truth. One must see the question of women's rights not in isolation, but as part of a wider context of social relationships and political change. A broad liberal-democratic movement starting in the late nineteenth century had come near to achieving votes for women before 1914. Yet the political advance of women in 1914 was still blocked by the vigorous hostility of men, and the often fearful reluctance and opposition of many women. [The war] brought a new confidence to women, removed apathy, silenced the female anti-suffragists. Asquith was only the most prominent of the converts among men. Undoubtedly the replacement of militant suffragette activity by frantic patriotic endeavour played its part as well.

QUESTIONS WITH WORKED ANSWERS

a) **Study Source 1. What evidence in this Source suggests that the traditional role of women was being challenged by the war?** (6)

b) **Use your own knowledge to explain why the government agreed to use women workers during the war.** (10)

c) **Study Sources 2 and 3. How far does the evidence provided by source 2 support the opinion of Mrs Fawcett in Source 3?** (10)

> d) Study Sources 1 and 3. Assess the value of these two sources to an historian studying the history of the women's suffrage campaign in the years 1914–18. (10)
>
> e) Study Sources 4 and 5 and use your own knowledge. To what extent do you agree that the work of women in the war led to the achievement of the franchise in 1918? (24)

ANSWERS

a) Source 1, written by a factory inspector at the time of the war, mentions, anecdotally, the respect with which women workers are treated as a result of their endurance of poor working conditions. More importantly, as an official report, it is bringing to government and public attention the work that women have performed during and before the war. The report appears to be obliquely criticising media and government propaganda surrounding women's war work, suggesting that women were not taking on tasks in the war which were particularly more taxing than their pre-war work, it was simply that the nature of their pre-war work had largely gone unrecognised.

b) As a result of the enthusiastic response to Kitchener's call for volunteers in 1914, many workers in essential trades, such as transport, metal work and mining left their jobs to join the army. The government did their best to prevent this, but until a National Register was established in 1915, it was difficult to measure the numbers of workers in any profession and to thus make long-term plans for the future needs of industry. With the realisation of the need for more industrial workers, in particular in the munitions industry, following the 'Shell Scandal' of Spring 1915, business and government began to regard women as substitutes for male workers. When the National Register was created, it therefore included a Register of Women for War Service, and Mrs Pankhurst joined with Lloyd George in calling for women to enter the factories.

c) In source 3, Mrs Fawcett writes that the campaign for women's suffrage has, as a result of the war, gained much greater support than previously, even from 'former opponents'. In particular she notes 'the change in the Press'. In source 2, the editor of *The Observer* newspaper comments that he had previously dismissed the contribution of women to British society, thus suggesting that he may have been, one of Mrs Fawcett's 'opponents'. He has, as a result of the war, changed his opinion and realises that his previous opinion was wrong and that Britain is dependent on 'men and women alike'.

As the editor of an influential newspaper which supported the Liberal Party, one can assume that Garvin's public declaration may well influence the opinion of leading members of that Party, but it is noticeable that Garvin does not go on to give public support to the cause of female suffrage in particular. He may well imply that some social change is necessary and that a larger political role is needed for women in Britain, but he fails to specify what action the government should take in order to recognise the contribution that women can make.

d) Source 1 is significant in that it demonstrates the point at which the government made clear its admiration for the work done by women. An official government inspector, not only notes the achievements of women, but also records the unacknowledged work done by women before 1914. It clearly does not confirm any change in attitude towards the suffrage itself, but it does make clear that conventional attitudes towards the nature and value of women in the workforce were being challenged.

Source 3, written by the NUWSS leader, Millicent Fawcett, clearly demonstrates that the campaign for women's suffrage is, by 1916, increasingly confident of achieving its aim. The 'great increases of strength during recent months', especially 'the change in the Press' resulting from the reports praising the patriotism of women workers allows Mrs Fawcett to confidently expect that to resist the demands for the vote would be 'an impossibility after the war'. As it was known that Asquith, himself once so opposed to women's suffrage, had been convinced of the need to extend the suffrage to them as a consequence of their war work and the support for the war effort from the suffrage campaign leaders, Mrs Fawcett goes so far as to 'trust' that women's right to vote will be included in the expected alteration to the franchise. Perhaps this source, in contrast to the celebratory tone of source 1, is of the greatest utility to the historian, clearly showing an improvement in the relationship between the Prime Minister and the suffrage campaigners during the early years of the First World War.

e) Both the suffragette, Sharp and the historian, Marwick, are clearly aware that the war in itself did not directly cause the enfranchisement of women. Sharp writes that the opinion that 'the victory of the suffrage cause in 1918 [being due] to women's war service' is a 'popular error' which tallies with Marwick's evaluation that the 'wider context of social relationships', most particularly in the First World War, altered to benefit the suffrage cause.

Similarly Marwick cites the contribution of 'frantic patriotic endeavour' and Sharp agrees that this 'prove[d] the fallacy of the anti suffragettes' favourite argument'. Both also see the crucial factor as being the removal of male opposition, as women's war work gave opponents 'an excuse' to change their public view (source 4) and 'silenced the female anti-suffragettes' and converted many men, including Asquith (source 5).

Marwick stresses the importance of political change in its own right, especially the development of the 'broad liberal-democratic movement', but Sharp only sees political change as being due (by implication) to the pre-war arguments of the suffrage campaigners, which the war work of women only confirmed. From my own knowledge, it is clear that war work alone was not the decisive factor in the decision to grant women the vote. The legislation did not extend the franchise to women on equal terms with men: women had to be aged thirty or above and local government electors or the wives of such electors; men only had to be aged twenty-one or above or military veterans aged nineteen or above. Women who had been employed as munitions workers were typically under thirty and unmarried were not enfranchised by the measure. Thus, there is little evidence that the suffrage was conceded as a reward for women's contribution to the war effort.

The women's suffrage clause in the Representation of the People Act of 1918 was a compromise worked out between Lloyd George's government and the suffragists during the war years. It is therefore clear that the concerns of party leaders were paramount in the nature of the franchise that was granted, but certainly there is little doubt that the wartime efforts of all women played a significant role in changing the hardened pre-war attitudes that had prevented granting of the vote to any women before 1914.

2. The impact of the war on labour (OCR)

Source A: *Table 3.6 **Annual earnings of skilled and unskilled workers***

	1914	1919
Skilled workers		
Bricklayer	42s 10d	79s 2d
Shipyard riveter	37s 9d	74s 9d
Compositor	36s 0d	72s 0d
Unskilled workers		
Bricklayer's labourer	29s 1d	65s 2d
Engineering labourer	22s 10d	58s 3d
Fireman	26s 0d	66s 0d

Source B: From a speech given by Lloyd George to the Clyde ship workers, 15 December, 1915

Let me put this to you, friends: whilst we are comfortable at home on a Christmas day – (interruption – 'No sentiment; we're here for business') – there are hundreds of thousands of our fellow countrymen, some of them our own sons, some of them our brothers, in the trenches facing death. ('You're here to talk about the **dilution** of labour.') It's on their behalf and at their written request, that I come here to put before the workmen of Glasgow their appeal for help.

We need a very large number of heavy guns and projectiles, and I am going to put before you a business proposition. ('For the exploiters'.) Do you think these men in the trenches are exploiters? ('Don't hedge'.) ('The shipowners are doing their bit'.) Do let me state the facts. ('We know them'.) ... What steps have we taken? We have started great National Factories, state-owned and state-controlled; every timber and nail in them belonging to the state. My friends, these are great Socialist factories. (Violent interruption.) Believe me, the whole of them owned by the State, erected by the State; no profit made by any Capitalist, because they don't belong to the Capitalist.

Source C: *Table 3.7* ***Trade-union membership during the war, 1914–19***

1914	1,572,391
1915	2,053,735
1916	2,170,782
1917	2,415,383
1918	2,960,409
1919	3,464,020

Source D: From the diary of John Glasier, Labour journalist, May, 1915

This is the first instance of a member of the Labour Party joining the government. Henderson is a clever, adroit*, rather limited-minded man – domineering and a bit quarrelsome – vain and ambitious. He will prove a fairly capable official front-bench man, but will hardly command the support of organised Labour.

> ## QUESTIONS WITH WORKED ANSWERS
>
> a) **Study source A. From this source and from your own knowledge, explain what can be learnt about the impact of the war on the standard of living of the working classes from these figures.** (10)
> b) **Study source C. Assess the value of this source as evidence of working class dissatisfaction with the Government's economic policy.** (25)
> c) **Study sources C and D. In what ways do these sources suggest that organised labour became more powerful during the First World War?** (25)
> d) **Study all the sources. Using all the sources and your own knowledge, explain how far you agree with the view that 'labour, especially unskilled labour, benefited considerably during the war'?** (60)

a) From the figures in source A, it is clear that the annual earnings of both skilled and unskilled workers increased dramatically during the First World War. Although all the figures show an increase, the unskilled workers all have increases of over 50 per cent, whereas the skilled workers' wages all increase by no more than 50 per cent. This was partly due to the '**dilution**' of skilled labour, and it meant that craftsmen could no longer force employers to pay excessively high wages for their work. On the other hand, the shortage of all workers led to higher wages for the unskilled and the government's need for high war production allowed the unskilled to force employers to increase wages. Prices, especially for some food stuffs, increased even quicker than wages, however, and would have caused the standard of living to fall for most workers, had it not been for the opportunities for plenty of well-paid overtime that the war demanded, so one should not read too much into these seemingly massive increases.

---

* 'adroit' – skilful

b) Although source B is only the transcript of a single meeting that Lloyd George held, it does demonstrate that some workers in the shipbuilding industry distrusted the government, as they were prepared to openly heckle even Lloyd George, the Liberal minister who was seen as being the most sympathetic to working class interests. In particular, the audience shows their dissatisfaction with '**dilution**', the process of breaking complex industrial tasks into simpler smaller stages that less skilled (and therefore cheaper) workers could perform. In addition, the government's call for extra efforts in wartime is not appreciated by the workers as they see their employers as 'exploiters' and Lloyd George has to go so far as to describe the government control of wartime production as 'socialist' in order to win their support. The very fact that Lloyd George, the second most important member of the coalition government after the Prime Minister himself, should actually travel to the Clyde during the war, gives an indication of just how seriously the government took the possibility of major industrial unrest.

Beyond this, it is impossible to say from this one source, how far the views of this audience of Clyde shipbuilders reflected those of the working classes as a whole. The Clyde was a notorious area of working class radicalism, as it had demonstrated in pre-war industrial disturbances and it was perhaps untypical in the violence of its hostility towards employers and the government in general and, on this occasion, Lloyd George in particular.

c) According to source C, membership of Trade Unions more than doubled between 1914 and 1919. As all members paid a subscription to their union's Trade Union, funds significantly increased. This made unions more able to take forceful action against unfair treatment by employers and to even afford to organise short strike actions in extreme cases. With the overturning of the 'Osborne judgement' Trade Unions could raise funds for the Labour Party through an optional political contribution and with the payment of MPs since 1911 they could use these funds for electioneering and thus bring their message to many more than before the war.

The appointment of Arthur Henderson as President of the Board of Education in Asquith's coalition, described in source D, may be seen as a breakthrough for organised labour, as Henderson was chairman of the Labour Party and his appointment was the first time that a member of the Labour Party had gained a place in a government Cabinet. Therefore the Labour Party had a voice in the most powerful decision making body in the country. On the other hand, as Glasier comments, he was not popular with the trade unions, and therefore, one should not see the appointment of such a pragmatic, unideological figure as particularly significant.

d) As can be seen in source A, wages for all workers did increase dramatically. Although price rises probably cancelled out the bulk of the skilled workers' increases in real terms, the unskilled workers' family wages certainly increased significantly more than inflation, especially with the opportunities for overtime and for younger members of families to fill the jobs left by their elder brothers, now at the front. Many workers left domestic service or agricultural labour during the war, such were the demands and rewards for unskilled industrial work. As source B demonstrates, skilled workers were nervous of losing their advantages and were prepared to use their membership of Trade Unions in order to protect their status. They were only partly successful in this, managing to restore pre-war conditions after 1918, but having to give up their exclusive control of the Trade Union movement as unskilled and semi-skilled workers were able to afford Union subscriptions and the TUC recognised the advantages of a mass membership as shown in source C.

These new unionists, as well as the traditional skilled members all benefited from the political impact of the war, as the government acknowledged the role of labour in contributing to victory, first, by allowing Unions a role in deciding economic policy in the Treasury Agreement of 1915, and second, by bringing Arthur Henderson, the Chairman of the Labour Party into the Cabinet in 1915, as described in source D, and then into Lloyd George's five-man War Cabinet. Although Henderson, and the Labour figure who replaced him in the War Cabinet in 1917, George Barnes, were not closely linked to the trade union movement, their roles in contributing to Britain's eventual victory in the war allowed Labour to prove their 'fitness to govern' and, with the increased funding from the unions and a new and attractive manifesto, to mount an effective challenge to the other two parties after 1918, eventually forming a minority government in 1924. Labour also benefited in that it was the unskilled labour force that received the vote, along with women over 30 in the Representation of the People Act of 1918 which forced even the Conservatives to take a greater account of the needs of the working man, both skilled and unskilled, especially as Labour threatened their new-found monopoly of political power if they failed to do so.

Among the workers, however, those who had volunteered or had been called up saw few of these advantages, and the families dependent on a private's or NCO's salary, suffered severe hardship as a result of rising prices and shortages. For them, the promise of better conditions after the war proved to be illusory, as the 'Geddes Axe' reduced 'homes fit for heroes' into 'homes that only heroes would live in'.

For those workers who were not in uniform therefore, there were genuine political benefits for both skilled and unskilled workers, which heralded further social improvements to come. For the unskilled workers, the First World War offered a temporary escape from the grinding poverty of pre-war years, if not from physically exhausting work. Skilled workers, although achieving guarantees of a post-war return to restrictive practice, saw little substantial improvements in their standards of living, and, even in their political and industrial representation, they saw their unique position being encroached upon by the mass of the unskilled.

QUESTIONS WITHOUT WORKED ANSWERS (AQA)

a) **Study source D. With reference to your own knowledge, explain briefly who was 'Henderson'.** (3 marks)

b) **Study source C. With reference to your own knowledge, explain how useful source C is as evidence of the impact of the First Word War on industrial relations in Britain.** (7 marks)

c) **Refer to sources A, B, C and D and use your own knowledge. 'The war has brought a transformation of the social and administrative structure of the state.' Explain whether you agree or disagree with this view from the official War Cabinet report for 1918.** (15 marks)

Part 4; Historical skills

1. Group work – analysis of visual sources

As a group examine the following British propaganda posters from the First World War. As you will see, the captions have been removed from these.

Figure 3.3
First World War recruitment poster

Figure 3.4
First World War propaganda poster

Figure 3.5
First World War recruitment poster

Figure 3.6 **First World War propaganda poster**

Figure 3.7
**First World War
propaganda poster**

Figure 3.8
**British poster
issued after the
sinking of the
Lusitania,** *in the*
First World War

1. Organise your group to investigate the needs of the country during the First World War in the following areas:

    a) Army recruitment
    b) Maintenance of civilian morale
    c) Maintenance of army morale
    d) Raising of war loans
    e) Appeals for support to non-combatant countries

2. Allocate at least one poster to each of these causes.

3. Write a caption for each poster suitable for an early twentieth-century British audience. Try to avoid modern slang and disrespect for authority. Stress instead duty, patriotism, sacrifice and heroism and contrast these 'British' virtues with the uncivilised conduct of Germany and her allies.

4. Use the internet to find the actual captions for the posters – how similar were your efforts?

Chapter 4

Inter-war Domestic Problems, 1918–1939

This chapter is concerned with a period in which the political landscape of Britain was dramatically altered. The Liberal Party, already suffering from the impact of the First World War on their unity and ideology, continued to decline, despite Lloyd George's best efforts. The Conservatives by contrast, carefully exploited their wartime links with Lloyd George and the public demands for tranquility, to emerge as the chief party of government in the inter-war years, holding office either independently, or as part of a coalition for all but 30 months of the 21 years between the wars. They managed this, despite the creation of a full democracy in Britain in 1928, despite bitter industrial disputes which culminated in a general strike in 1926, and despite the apparent failure of capitalism in the depression which followed the Wall Street Crash of 1929. It was the rise of the Labour Party that seems most striking, however. Although they only held 63 seats in 1918, within six years they had formed their first government, and their leader, Ramsay MacDonald was chosen to head the 'National Government' that was formed by members of all three parties to resolve the financial crisis that confronted Britain in summer 1931. Labour, however, split with MacDonald over his action and never held office again in the 1930s.

Historical background

The decline of the Liberals 1918–24
Baldwin's second government and the
    general strike
Labour and the 1931 crisis
The 'Great Depression'
The National Governments 1931–39
Labour in opposition 1931–39

Essays

1. The inter-war economy
2. The Lloyd George coalition 1918–22
3. The general strike
4. The rise of Labour
5. The decline of the Liberals and the dominance of the Conservatives

6. The 1931 crisis and Ramsay MacDonald
7. The National Governments and opposition

Sources

1. The decline of the Liberal Party
2. The press and the general strike
3. British society between the wars

Historical skills

1. Analysis of statistical evidence in order to create a picture of the impact of the depression on the lives of the people of Britain.

Chronology

1919	Housing and Town Planning Act (Addison Act)
	Ministry of Health set up
1920	Unemployment Insurance extended to all manual workers, except in railways, agriculture, and domestic service
1921	Economic recession
	Miners' strike – failure of the 'Triple Alliance' on 'Black Friday'
1922	'Geddes Axe'
	Carlton Club meeting – Conservatives leave Lloyd George coalition, Lloyd George resigns as Prime Minister
	Conservatives under Bonar Law win general election
	British Broadcasting Company (radio) is formed
1923	Bonar Law retires, Baldwin becomes Prime Minister
	Reunification of Liberal Party
	General election produces hung Parliament
1924	First Labour government
	Wheatley's Housing Act
	Conservatives win general election
1925	Britain returns the pound to the **gold standard**
	Baldwin grants nine month subsidy to the miners – 'Red Friday'
1926	General strike
1927	Trades Disputes Act
1928	Voting age for women reduced from 30 to 21
1929	Labour becomes largest party in general election
	Formation of second Labour government
1931	Financial crisis
	Fall of Labour government
	Formation of National Government (coalition) led by Ramsay MacDonald
	Britain leaves the **gold standard**, unemployment benefit cut by 10%, introduction of means test
	National Government wins landslide in general election
	George Lansbury becomes leader of Labour Party
1932	Chancellor, Neville Chamberlain introduces protective tariffs
	Ottawa Conference
1933	'Samuelite' Liberals leave the government
1934	Restoration of 1931 level of unemployment benefits
1935	Clement Attlee becomes leader of the Labour Party
	Stanley Baldwin becomes Prime Minister
	National Government wins general election
1936	**Abdication crisis**
	Jarrow March
	BBC television begins broadcasting
1937	Baldwin retires, Neville Chamberlain becomes Prime Minister
1939	Declaration of war with Germany

Part 1: Historical background

The decline of the Liberals 1918–24

After the war, politics did not return to the pre-war norm of a struggle between the Liberals and Conservatives. The Representation of the People Act had enfranchised five million more men and eight million women. The coalition government appealed to this mass electorate through Lloyd George's personal popularity as the 'man who won the war', by promises of creating 'a fit country for heroes to live in' and to 'make Germany pay'. Lloyd George won an overwhelming majority in the coupon election of December 1918 as the head of the wartime coalition between his group of Liberals and the Conservatives. This coalition continued to govern Britain for the next four years. However, a post-war economic depression, the conflict with Irish nationalists, and the growing doubts about Lloyd George's honesty quickly caused the government's popularity to wane. In 1922, the Conservatives met at the Carlton Club and dramatically voted to withdraw from the coalition and fight the forthcoming election as an independent party. Fatally, the personal antagonism between Lloyd George and Asquith prevented the Liberals from immediately re-uniting and the Labour Party came second to the Conservatives in the election.

Despite gaining a large majority in 1922, the Conservatives were still divided over the need for a coalition, so their new leader, Stanley Baldwin decided to re-adopt the traditional Tory cause of **Tariff Reform**, in order to find a common cause in the election he called in 1923. It did indeed serve to unite the Conservatives (as well as the Liberals) but proved sufficiently unpopular with the electorate to win the Labour party enough seats to form a minority government with Liberal

Table 4.1 *General elections, 1918–39*

	Conservative		Liberal		Labour	
	% vote	No. of seats	% vote	No. of seats	% vote	No. of seats
			(Lloyd George)			
1918	32.6	335	13.5	133	22.2	63
			(Asquith)			
			12.1	28		
			(Lloyd George)			
1922	38.2	345	17.5	54	29.5	142
			(Asquith)			
			11.6	62		
1923	38.1	258	29.6	159	30.5	191
1924	48.3	419	17.6	40	33.0	151
1929	38.2	260	23.4	59	37.1	288
			(pro-National)		(pro-National)	
1931	55.2	473	10.2	68	1.6	13
			(independent)		(independent)	
			0.5	4	30.6	52
1935	53.7	432	6.4	20	37.9	154

support. This administration, under the moderate leadership of Ramsay MacDonald, only managed to last for a few months, but it dispelled many fears about the nature of a Labour government. Many middle-class Liberals, however, were disillusioned by Asquith's support for Labour and turned decisively towards the Conservatives in the next election in 1924. As a result, the Conservatives won a decisive majority and were able to hold office for a full five years.

 ### Baldwin's second government and the general strike

Between 1924 and 1929, Baldwin kept his party united and avoided controversial issues such as protection and class conflict. The only significant crisis was the general strike. When the strike began on 4 May 1926, there was an overwhelming response from the workers. Four million workers went on strike including the Durham miners who had just been on strike for eight months. The railway system was immobilised, trams failed to run, docks and ships stood idle, most newspapers failed to appear, power stations closed down, iron and steel works damped their furnaces, and building workers downed tools. In every town, a strike committee was organised which co-ordinated strike pay and picketing, ran meetings, printed bulletins and distributed *The Daily Worker*. Food and essential supplies were allowed passage. There was little violence at first.

For many managerial and office staff, the chief preoccupation was getting to work. Baldwin dropped his previously conciliatory tone and claimed that the trade unions were not entitled to attack the whole community. He claimed that the general strike was an attempt to usurp the power

Figure 4.1 **Front page of the** British Worker *showing the response to the call to a general strike*

of Parliament and undermine the constitution. He refused to be bullied into restoring the subsidy to the miners and allowed Winston Churchill, the Chancellor of the Exchequer, to print the *British Gazette*, which accused the Trade Union Congress (TUC) of 'playing the game of the Kremlin' In the opinion of the government, the TUC had outlawed itself, and there should be no negotiation until the strike was called off. There was widespread support for the government, with thousands volunteering to man the services or to serve as special constables or simply to offer lifts or carry goods. The volunteers seem mainly to have been professional men of all ages, retired army officers, young men from the Stock Exchange and City finance houses, office workers or university students. Very few unemployed manual workers volunteered. Some were forced by employers, but most were pleased for the chance to put the workers in their place.

There was a body of middle-class support led by the Archbishop of Canterbury that called on the government to compromise, but the hard-liners in the Cabinet, Churchill, Joynson-Hicks (Home Secretary), Neville Chamberlain, Balfour and Douglas Hogg insisted on the TUC's unconditional surrender. As one said, 'As soon as the strike began, Baldwin was a passenger'.

As the strike went on, violence began to spread. Overeager police raided Communist Party offices and charged demonstrators in Glasgow, London and Doncaster, while strikers attacked strike-breakers and pulled up railway lines. Only 3,000 were arrested in the strike, however, and the only deaths were caused by the incompetence of volunteers driving trains unsupervised.

The TUC, terrified of being thought of as revolutionary tried its best to minimise confrontation. J.H. Thomas (railways), J.R. Clynes (general workers) and Arthur Pugh (iron and steel) all urged caution and looked for a solution, before the TUC was bankrupted and violence spread.

On 6 May, Herbert Samuel returned from holiday in Italy and offered his services as a negotiator. The government refused, but Samuel met some TUC leaders and suggested that the miners ought to be willing to accept some temporary wage cuts if the mining industry was reorganised. He made it clear he had no understanding with the owners or the government, but would urge the government to renew the subsidy and reopen negotiations *only if* the strike was called off. This was accepted by the General Council on 11 May, but the miners refused to call off the strike without firm guarantees. The TUC ignored the miners' protests and at noon, 12 May, the strike was called off without any commitment on the government's part and without even the customary assurance that there would be no victimisation of returning strikers.

Baldwin then offered a modified version of the 1925 Samuel Commission Report with an extra subsidy. Both miners and owners refused. Baldwin then tried to win the owners over by passing an Eight-hour Act which extended the working day. The owners refused to compromise and the strike continued. Miners' families began to go hungry, and a national relief fund was set up and raised £300,000. Starving, with disease spreading, the miners held out until November when the federation was forced to give in. The miners returned with local wages, wage cuts and an eight-hour day and no reorganisation – a total defeat.

For Baldwin as well, the strike damaged his prestige. When the TUC called off the strike, he was seen as the pilot who had safely steered Britain through the rocks. When he was unable to persuade the owners to back down, he began to be seen as weak, ineffective and deceitful, and having misled the TUC as to his intentions in his speech of 8 May: 'A solution is within the grasp of the nation the instant that the Trade Union leaders are willing to abandon the general strike. I am a man of peace . . . Cannot you trust me to ensure a square deal, to secure even justice between man and

*Figure 4.2 **Industrial unrest, 1920–39***

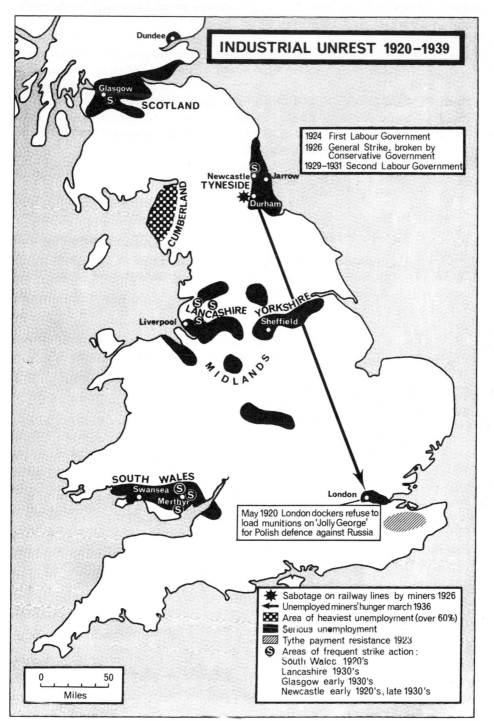

INDUSTRIAL UNREST 1920–1939

1924 First Labour Government
1926 General Strike, broken by
     Conservative Government
1929–1931 Second Labour Government

May 1920 London dockers refuse to
load munitions on 'Jolly George'
for Polish defence against Russia

✸ Sabotage on railway lines by miners 1926
← Unemployed miners' hunger march 1936
▦ Area of heaviest unemployment (over 60%)
▮ Serious unemployment
▨ Tythe payment resistance 1923
Ⓢ Areas of frequent strike action:
  South Wales 1920's
  Lancashire 1930's
  Glasgow early 1930's
  Newcastle early 1920's, late 1930's

0   50
Miles

man?' The Trades Disputes Act of 1927 seemed to be the government's revenge against the unions, as it made general strikes illegal and made the collections of the 'political levy' to the Labour Party more difficult.

Alarmed by the class conflict created by the strike, Baldwin continued to attempt to incorporate Labour into the mainstream of politics to avoid it developing into a mass, militant, socialist party and sought to introduce cautious and inexpensive reform where it was genuinely wanted and needed. Although it is now generally recognised that Churchill's tenure at the Exchequer was ineffective and, in the case of the return to the **gold standard**, unwise, the government, in particular, Neville Chamberlain as Health Minister, passed a series of significant reforms. The party became increasingly fractious, however, and seemed incapable of reducing the high unemployment levels. Faced with the energy of Lloyd George and the dignity of Ramsay MacDonald, Baldwin's government seemed to have exhausted much of the public's patience by 1929.

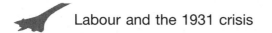 ## Labour and the 1931 crisis

The election of 1929 was significant for a number of factors. It was the first fully democratic election as the female franchise had been equalised to that of the male in 1928. Furthermore, it was perhaps the first truly three-cornered fight as the Liberals, using Lloyd George's infamous 'electoral fund' as he was now leader, were able to put up candidates in most seats. Although the Liberals did relatively well, the nature of the British electoral system prevented them translating their share of the vote into an equivalent number of seats, though they did hold the balance between the other two parties. Lloyd George's antipathy towards Baldwin, however, prevented any real choice of action and the Liberals again paved the way to their own obsolescence, by putting the Labour Party back into power.

This time however, Labour was in a stronger position than in 1924, having won the largest number of seats in the Commons for the first time in its history. After the experience of 1924, MacDonald was more confident and he planned to be in office for two years. He announced that the government would deal with the two most important issues: unemployment and international disputes, but they were immediately faced with the most serious economic crisis of the decade when the Wall Street Crash occurred in October 1929. By December 1930, unemployment had reached 2.5 million and unemployment benefit was now costing £125 million a year.

A special team led by J.H. Thomas, including the ex-Conservative, Sir Oswald Mosley and George Lansbury was set up to investigate ways of reducing unemployment. The group was hampered by Chancellor Snowden's insistence on financial orthodoxy and balancing of budget, so Mosley presented his own plans influenced by Keynes, Lloyd George and Tory protectionists. In it he called for government direction of industry, increased pensions and allowances to boost consumption, early retirement, public control of banks, protective tariffs for home market and public works schemes. Thomas was alienated by this as he was not consulted and tried to get rid of Mosley. In May 1930 the Cabinet rejected the scheme as MacDonald supported Thomas and moderation. Mosley attempted to use the Labour Party Conference to promote his ideas, but he was defeated. As a consequence he resigned and left Labour to form the New Party.

Snowden put his faith in a balanced budget as a symbol of confidence and stable economy. Keynesian ideas of 'reflation' using deficit financing and large scale public works were rejected. Instead 'deflation' was adopted, cutting in government spending and hoping for improvement in future. Balancing the budget was increasingly difficult with the contraction in the economy however, as tax income was reduced but expenses of unemployment benefits went up.

In his 1930 budget Snowden raised income tax to 4s 6d but by 1931 tax yield had still gone down. Sir George May (former chairman of Prudential Insurance) was appointed chairman of an economy committee set up to prepare for economies (as Geddes had done in 1921).

MacDonald himself favoured introducing tariff barriers but felt isolated and unsure. He wanted to get rid of Snowden, who he felt was far too timid in his approach but wasn't confident enough to challenge him on economics and was worried that Labour's economic competence would be questioned if they abandoned orthodox economics.

The subsequent financial crisis of 1931 exposed the weaknesses of Labour as an avowedly socialist party governing in a capitalist economic system. The party split over the need for government expenditure cuts and was forced to resign. Unexpectedly, the king managed to persuade MacDonald to form a 'National Government' of all the parties to solve the crisis, and MacDonald agreed without consulting his party. Although the **gold standard** had to be abandoned, the crisis passed, but Labour refused to support MacDonald, branding his actions a 'betrayal' and expelling him and the other Labour supporters of the National Government.

The formation of the National Government the following day, came as a surprise to most of the Labour Party and it found itself opposing a broad coalition headed by its former leader, approved by the King and with the claim that it had secured the necessary loan to stop the run on the pound. Inevitably in these febrile circumstances, Labour suffered a massive election defeat, and even Henderson, the new leader, lost his seat.

 ### The 'Great Depression'

Britain's experience of the Depression was made worse by the poor state of the British manufacturing industry after the First World War. Textile production was cut by two-thirds. Coal dropped by a fifth. Shipbuilding fell to 7 percent of its pre-war figure. Steel production fell by 45 per cent between 1929 and 1932, with iron production falling by 53 per cent in the same period. Britain's share of global commerce fell from 10.75 per cent in 1929 to 9.8 per cent in 1937. Invisible earnings from services such as shipping, insurance and investment overseas dramatically declined as global trade contracted. By 1932 unemployment had reached 22.5 per cent in Great Britain. Those areas dependent on the old 'staple' industries were worst hit. Scotland, dominated by shipbuilding, coal-mining and heavy engineering saw a rate of 27.7 per cent unemployment. Wales, dependent on coal-mining and iron-smelting, had an even worse experience, with unemployment of 36.5 per cent, and nearly 50 per cent in some towns such as Merthyr Tydfil.

On the other hand, by 1934, the economy as a whole was beginning to recover. New industries such as chemicals, electrical goods, cars, processed foods and aircraft were growing in the South

Table 4.2 **Distribution of world's manufacturing trade, 1913–38 (in percentages)**

Year	UK	US	Japan	Germany	France	Russia
1913	14.1	35.8	1.2	14.3	7.0	4.4
1926–9	9.4	42.2	2.5	11.6	6.6	4.3
1936–8	9.2	32.2	3.5	10.7	4.5	18.5

of England to replace the trade lost by the old industries of the North. First the global recovery and then the need for heightened production as war threatened at the end of the decade meant that even the staple industries began to show significant signs of recovery, although these were still working below their full capacity as late as 1939. As a result of the low interest rates maintained by the national government, the building industry in particular grew spectacularly. Unemployment fell from its peak of three million in 1932–33 to 1.5 million by 1937. It was not until 1940 that it finally fell below one million.

The economic record of the 1930s is therefore a paradoxical one with a major downturn in one part of the economy but as fast a rate of growth in the new industries as had ever been seen.

The National Governments 1931–39

After the October 1931 election the National Government had 554 seats and the Opposition (Labour and Independent Liberal) 52 seats.

It seemed as if conventional politics had ended. The coalition, perhaps remembering the experience of the Lloyd George coalition of 1918–22 was not expected to last long, as it was formed to solve the immediate crisis in 1931. However it remained in office until September 1939.

The Government became increasingly dominated by the Conservatives under Baldwin (they had 473 seats). The original cabinet of August 1931 was 4 Labour, 4 Tory, 2 Liberals, but after November 1931 there were 4 Labour, 11 Tories, 3 Liberals. The Prime Minister Ramsay MacDonald was, like Lloyd George, 'a hostage of the Conservatives', especially after Snowdon went to the House of Lords in November 1931 and Neville Chamberlain became Chancellor. As before, MacDonald mainly concerned himself with Foreign Policy, particularly at Lausanne where he reduced, then ended Germany's reparation payments in 1932. He was, however, physically and mentally exhausted and his position became 'more and more degrading' as the Tories blamed him for the government's problems and Labour continued to attack the 'traitor of '31'. Baldwin propped him up, to maintain the illusion of a government of national unity until June 1935 when he was persuaded to accept the nominal post of Lord President and Baldwin 'at last accepted the responsibility for the power he had previously wielded from behind the scenes' (A.J.P. Taylor). MacDonald lost his seat in the 1935 election, but managed to get back in a by-election. He finally resigned in 1937 and died at sea later that year. The National Labour group gradually dwindled, though Ramsay's son Malcolm was Dominions and Colonial Minister in Chamberlain's government.

After 1931 Lloyd George refused to support the National Government and when the government introduced Protective Tariffs in 1932, the National Liberals split between the 'Simonites' (35 MPs led by Sir John Simon, the Foreign Secretary) who supported the government and the 'Samuelites' (32 MPs led by Sir Herbert Samuel) who stuck with **free trade**. Eventually in 1933 the Samuelites 'crossed the floor' and joined the opposition, leaving the Conservatives more in charge than ever.

Baldwin had agreed to join the National Government to avoid the attacks on him that had followed the 1929 election defeat. He occupied 11 Downing Street and used his closeness to dominate MacDonald. He did believe in the benefits of a National Government, as it gave him a chance to practise moderate Conservatism without alienating the far-right of his party – this is probably the reason he allowed MacDonald to totter on for so long. In terms of policies and ideas, though,

Neville Chamberlain was the government's motor. He was recognised as Baldwin's successor and was prepared to wait, not to 'play Lloyd George to his Asquith'. He was not very interested in consensus government and made no secret of his contempt for Labour: (he once said 'intellectually, they are dirt'). When he finally became PM in 1937, he was 68 and keen to carry on a policy of moderate domestic reform. It was his misfortune that he had to deal with an international situation he was not suited for and a man, Adolf Hitler, whom he completely misjudged.

 ## Labour in opposition 1931–39

The events of 1931 shattered Labour and made them fear that the march towards Socialist victory had been halted. The largest party in 1929 now only had 52 MPs. The new leader, George Lansbury, faced a financial crisis and the party was unable to put forward any candidates in the 1932 by-elections.

Labour did not follow the Liberals into decline, but re-organised to ensure recovery, retaining its separate identity and its position as an alternative to the National Government. Labour agreed never to form a minority government again and promised to introduce 'definite socialist legislation immediately in office' particularly **nationalisation** of railways and mines. Instead of a swing to radicalism, the party remained dominated by pragmatic men such as Clement Attlee, Ernest Bevin and Hugh Dalton. A by-election fund was started in 1933 and a recruitment drive led to 140,000 new members. The party won ten by-elections before 1935 and gained control of London County Council in 1934.

The party's continued need for moderation and respectability was demonstrated when the leadership was forced to change as Lansbury's pacifist policy was defeated at conference in 1935 and he resigned. His replacement was the modest, public school and Oxbridge-educated, hard-working, Clement Attlee, who proposed democratic socialism and did not associate the party with communism, revolution or pacifism. Those who argued in favour of affiliation with the Communist Party, such as the Socialist League were expelled. It was his belief that socialism could only be attained if the party had a clear parliamentary majority and that all efforts should directed to this end. The gain of 94 seats in the 1935 election in which Labour won the highest percentage of the vote it had ever had (37.9 per cent), demonstrated that the Labour Party had regained the confidence of many and was rebuilding its strength to challenge for government again. By 1939, Labour had managed to regain much of the confidence they had lost in 1931, and it was clear that Chamberlain's foreign policy failures reflected well on Attlee and Labour. The party rejected MacDonald's bankrupt approach of 'regulated capitalism' and began to consider more radical Keynesian approaches to managing the economy, which would include some degree of **nationalisation**. This policy would form the basis for Labour's manifesto in 1945 when the experience of war had shattered popular acceptance of 'orthodox politics' and Labour had the chance to atone for their failure in 1931.

Part 2: Essays

1. The inter-war economy (EDEXCEL)

a) **Explain why the Conservative government of 1925 sought to return the pound to the gold standard** (30 marks)

b) **Why did Britain undergo a period of sustained unemployment between the wars?** (30 marks)

(Total: 60 marks)

a) During the War, the government had been forced to abandon the **gold standard** and to issue paper money for the first time. Since 1918, financial experts had recommended returning the pound to the **gold standard** at the pre-war rate, in order to stimulate Britain's staple industries, such as iron, coal, shipbuilding and textiles which had slumped since the fall in demand at the end of the war. These industries depended upon exports and it was felt that once the pound was restored as the leading currency in the world market, British goods would once again be in demand. It was also hoped that a return to the **gold standard** would encourage investment in Britain and thus help the economy to return to its strong pre-1913 state by lowering unemployment and stimulating internal demand for British goods as well.

The Conservative Chancellor at the time was Winston Churchill who lacked expertise and relied on the advice of Montagu Norman, the governor of the Bank of England. As an ex-liberal he had ensured that the 1923 election promise of tariff reform was not honoured or even mentioned. Instead he pursued a thoroughly orthodox **free trade** financial policy and returned the pound to its pre-war **gold standard** in 1925. The pound was now worth $4.86 – which was mainly of benefit to the City of London as debts to the USA were now less expensive and currency trading boomed. John Maynard Keynes, the economist, wrote a leaflet, 'The Economic Consequences of Mr Churchill' in which he claimed that the pound was over-valued by 10 per cent. Churchill could never claim to have been the architect of the policy as he was no financial expert and once commented that his advisers 'might as well be speaking in Persian'.

The result for industry was that British exports were now over-priced and uncompetitive, which forced employers to cut costs in areas such as wages. In this way, the policy directly caused industrial unrest, most importantly the general strike, when British coal became uncompetitive on the world market and mine-owners chose to reduce wages to solve the problem. The policy also failed to solve the problem of relatively high unemployment. The home market did indeed grow, and between 1924 and 1929 British manufacturing production increased by 14 per cent, but this was significantly lower than in other industrial countries given the smallness of the British market. The staple industries continued to decline without secure export markets and long-term unemployment became the lot of many manual workers in these trades.

Churchill's economic policy was ultimately incoherent as interest rates were kept high to protect the **gold standard**, which discouraged entrepreneurs from borrowing, yet income tax was reduced to 4s in the £ to offset the impact of wage reductions. As a result the unemployment fund was allowed to get into debt and funding had to be diverted from other areas to pay for this. The Conservative government's refusal to accept a lower currency level ruined Britain's chances of economic revival and left the Labour government to face the consequences when the global downturn after the Wall Street Crash exacerbated Britain's poor economic position.

b) The average level of unemployment between 1921 and 1939 was 14 per cent per annum, a considerable increase on the pre-war figure. In that period, unemployment had largely been caused by downturns in the global trade cycle, which always affected Britain due to its reliance on overseas trade. Such 'cyclical unemployment' was generally temporary, but in the inter-war period it was made more serious by the increasingly permanent 'structural unemployment' caused by the long-term decline of Britain's staple industries. It was this combination of factors which led to the depression of the early 1930s and condemned around a quarter of the unemployed to a long, agonising period without work.

Britain depended on five trades for most of its exports – iron, steel, coal, textiles and shipbuilding. These trades had been diverted from export to providing for Britain's war effort between 1914 and 1918 and in that period, many of Britain's trading partners had either bought such products from other countries (most notably USA and Japan) or become more self-sufficient. In the post-war years, after a brief domestic boom, the long-term decline in these British staple industries became apparent, exacerbated by the increasing poverty of African, Asian and Latin American economies whose primary products were falling in value. Coal production was protected by tariffs in some of Britain's rivals and was becoming less important with the development of new power sources such as oil and gas. Textile production (which in Britain was chiefly cotton and wool) was facing competition from native Indian producers as well as the Japanese and was facing the advent of more sophisticated man-made fibres. Iron, steel and shipbuilding all suffered as trading partners became more industrialised, and all were deeply affected by the global decline in trade which followed the Wall Street Crash in USA in 1929. For these reasons, even when the trade cycle was at its height in 1929 and 1937, unemployment was above 10 per cent.

When the Crash occurred, the USA's ability to import manufactured goods declined and the consequent lack of trading hit the primary producing countries, Britain's greatest potential markets, the hardest. By 1932, 35 per cent of British coal-miners were unemployed. The staple industries responded to the decline in demand by reorganising and reducing capacity – thus fuelling the increase in unemployment further. The staple industries were largely located in areas rich in coal and minerals – the North and the West. New industries, such as car production, chemicals and electrical engineering which could absorb unemployment were largely located close to the largest concentration of population – the Midlands and the South and East. Older skilled workers, with family responsibilities were not able to move location as easily and pockets of intractable long-term unemployment developed in areas dependent on a single-industry such as the Rhondda Valley, Barrow-in-Furness and Burnley.

The dominant images of poverty in the inter-war years, dole queues, slum housing, infant mortality and **hunger marches** were largely confined to areas of the country where the downward cycle of trade devastated an already struggling economy and caused long-term unemployment which successive governments could not resolve, relying as they did on the eventual upturn in the trade cycle which was not enough in itself to solve Britain's more long-term economic problems. Unemployment remained at over one million until 1940 and would have remained at that level for a considerable period had not the Second World War altered both the short and long term approach to state intervention in the economy.

2. The Lloyd George coalition 1918–22 (OCR)

Account for the downfall of Lloyd George's coalition government in 1922.

(90 marks)

As Lloyd George was widely regarded as 'the man who won the war' in 1918, the Conservatives were keen to be associated with him as they had not won an election since 1900 and were afraid of the consequences of fully emancipating the male working class in 1918. They reaped the benefits of maintaining the coalition in the 1918 general election, when they won 335 seats under the protection of the 'coupon' and became the majority party in the Commons. 'Lloyd George thinks he's won the election,' said one commentator at the time. 'Well, he hasn't. It was the Tories that won the election and he will soon begin to find that out'. In effect, Lloyd George could only remain Prime Minister as long as the Tories tolerated him. The Conservatives remained deeply distrustful of Lloyd George, however, given the class antagonism he had stirred up during the confrontation with the Lords between 1909 and 1911 and his perceived lack of integrity in affairs like the pre-war 'Marconi scandal'. Most of all, the Conservative backbenchers feared that Lloyd George, without a party of his own to return to, would seek to 'fuse' the Conservatives with his Liberal supporters to create a 'centre party' and thus destroy the distinctive identity of Conservatism. In more immediate terms, the Conservatives resented the fact that the Liberals held half of the Cabinet positions, despite only representing 30 per cent of the government's majority.

The problems of peacetime Britain proved to be as awkward to deal with as the problems of the war, however, and Lloyd George was unable to find permanent solutions for the economic depression and the chronic difficulties faced by the coal industry.

Difficulties arose with demobilisation when the government began to release holders of key civilian jobs first, leaving the ordinary rank and file until last, in order to prevent post-war unemployment. Lloyd George and the new War Minister, Winston Churchill, couldn't ignore demands for quick demobilisation when they led to riots among troops in France and those posted to Russia, and demonstration by soldiers in Whitehall. Sir Eric Geddes was appointed Minister for Reconstruction and initiated a policy of 'first-in, first-out'. By 1920 over four million troops had been demobbed (78 per cent of soldiers and 55 per cent of officers) and most had found jobs, due to the post-war boom. The army became, once more, a force of long-term volunteers.

There was a sudden period of inflation at the end of the war partly caused by the removal of government wartime controls on prices, profits and wage levels. Prices and profits rose, but not wages. Trade unions, encouraged by their role in the war, were determined to protect their members and in 1919–20 there were over 2,000 strikes. These were also partly caused by the perception that it had been the working classes suffering in the trenches, while capitalists and 'privateers' had done well from the war. The Russian Revolution gave the workers an example of a worker-controlled state to emulate and the government was constantly afraid of revolutionary sentiments in Britain. In February 1919, while Germany underwent an attempted Bolshevik revolution, Clydeside engineers and shipbuilders went on strike demanding a 40-hour week. Huge demonstrations took place and Glasgow Town Hall was stormed and the Red Flag raised. The government over-reacted, sending in troops and tanks and arresting two of the leaders, Willy Gallacher and Manny Shinwell.

An economic depression began in early 1921, throwing two million people out of work. There was a domestic post-war drop in the demand for goods such as heavy industrial products, textiles and raw materials, once the military need dissipated, but more seriously, Britain had lost valuable export markets during the war. Many countries, previously dependent on British products, had had their supplies interrupted by the war and had turned to alternative suppliers, such as Japan and USA, or had begun to develop their own manufacturing industries.

Unfortunately, to maintain good industrial relations, Lloyd George had extended the 1911 National Insurance Act to make unemployment benefit available to all earning less than £250 p.a., except agricultural labourers, domestic servants and the civil service. This meant that an additional nine million workers were now protected, but when unemployment rose, the insurance fund was quickly depleted. The Treasury therefore stepped in and paid the money directly but the government soon found itself short of funds for the proposed reconstruction. Labour criticised the policy as it attacked the symptoms of unemployment rather than the root causes.

The coal industry had been taken over by the government during the war, but miners feared that it would soon be returned to private hands, with no long-term gains for them achieved. In 1919, the Miners' Federation threatened a strike if demands for a six-hour day, a 30 per cent wage increase and full **nationalisation** of the mines were not met. Having used violence on the Clyde, Lloyd George chose to be more conciliatory, offering a seven-hour day, temporary continuation of government control and a Royal Commission headed by Lord Sankey to investigate the miners' conditions. The miners agreed. The Commission failed to agree a solution, and the whole industry came out on strike on 1 April 1921 when the government announced that they would return the mines to private control and, for their part, the mine-owners promised an immediate pay cut. Lloyd George lost patience with the miners and decided to risk a confrontation. Under the terms of the pre-war 'Triple Alliance', the miners could have expected support from the railway and transport unions, but on 15 April, the railwaymen's negotiator, J.H. Thomas refused to order his union on strike. The miners named this day 'Black Friday' as they believed they had been betrayed and they stayed out on strike alone for three months until they were forced to return and accept wage cuts and private control. Workers in other trades had to accept wage cuts and Lloyd George's position as hero of the workers was destroyed as he was forced to pursue the policies of his Tory supporters.

Due to the expense of unemployment benefits and the falling off of business revenue, the government had to agree to wide-ranging expenditure cuts under intense pressure from the media and Conservative back-benchers. An anti-waste committee was set up under Geddes and suggested reducing expenditure on the army and navy, education, health services and council house building. The 'Geddes Axe' saved £64 million, but was viewed as a class measure by Labour. Reconstruction suffered, especially housing. The Liberal Minister of Health, Christopher Addison had estimated that 400,000 homes were unfit and in 1919 he provided subsidies to local authorities to build more homes. By 1921 100,000 had been built, but then subsidies were limited (at which point Addison resigned in protest) and then Geddes stopped them altogether. Housing was at least established as a social service, even though many homes were 'houses only heroes would agree to live in'.

As he faced successive crises, Lloyd George became far more isolated within the coalition. He was forced to abandon most of his reconstruction policies in the face of the economic slump and the Conservative support for 'anti-waste'. The growing Liberal disillusion was confirmed when Lloyd George was forced into a confrontation with the trade unions after the majority findings of the Sankey Commission were ignored. The Conservatives themselves bitterly resented the Anglo-Irish treaty and were perturbed by Lloyd George's diplomatic overtures to the Soviet Union. His personal behaviour didn't help either. Once, during the Irish negotiations he held a Cabinet meeting in Inverness Town Hall so as not to interrupt his holiday. To secure his position as leader he bought up the *Daily Chronicle* and gave peerages to seven newspaper editors and proprietors. He also drew up a formal price list for the sale of honours and invested money raised in this way into the Lloyd George political fund, to use as he pleased. This money could, he thought, be used to finance a new political party. He even invented a new honour, the Order of the British Empire as an additional way of raising money. When fraudsters, tax-dodgers and convicted criminals received honours there was pressure from the Tories, especially the back-bench spokesman, Stanley Baldwin who referred to the 'morally disintegrating effect of Lloyd George'. Lloyd George had to agree to set up a Royal Commission to investigate the honours system.

The Conservatives themselves had split in 1916 over whether to co-operate with Lloyd George. Then, and again in 1918, they had followed the advice of their leaders, Bonar Law and Austen Chamberlain, to join a coalition with Lloyd George, but to reject all ideas of fusing the Conservatives and the Lloyd George Liberals to form a new Centre Party. Lloyd George's failures over the following years gradually convinced the ordinary Tory MPs that the coalition wasn't working. Labour had achieved major by-election and local election successes and in 1922 an Independent Conservative, Reginald Clarry, pushed a coalition Liberal into third place, behind Labour in the Newport by-election. The coupon system now acted in reverse – it was political suicide to be associated with Lloyd George.

When Bonar Law was forced to retire due to ill health in 1921, his replacement, Austen Chamberlain was felt to be too cold and aloof to command loyalty (although this may have had more to do with his short-sightedness than his personal nature). After the deal with Irish Republicans in 1921 and Lloyd George's poor handling of the Chanak Crisis, when the Foreign Secretary, Lord Curzon resigned in protest at Lloyd George's behaviour, the Conservative back-benchers had had enough. When Lloyd George announced a general election, the party held a meeting at the Carlton Club on 19 October 1922. At the meeting, Baldwin spoke of Lloyd George as 'a dynamic force' but adding that such a force could be 'a terrible thing'. Most importantly of all, Baldwin persuaded Bonar Law to attend the meeting, Bonar Law, alarmed that the possibility of 'fusion' between the two branches of the party would hand political advantage to Labour, spoke against Lloyd George and the backbenchers refused to obey Chamberlain's instructions to remain in the coalition and voted 187 to 87 to fight the election as an independent party. Lloyd George resigned at once and Andrew Bonar Law was re-elected leader of the Conservative party and thereby, Prime Minister.

3. The general strike (AQA)

Read the following source and then answer the questions which follow:

The mine-owners rejected any reorganization: they demanded not only lower wages, but also longer hours . . . The miners answered: 'Not a penny off the pay, not a minute on the day'. Herbert Smith, when asked what the miners could offer to help the industry, replied: 'Nowt. We've nowt to offer'. Both Stanley Baldwin and the TUC general council tried to lure the miners into accepting some reduction of wages, in the vague hope that they might then lure the owners into some concession also. The miners would not give way until the owners had done so – and perhaps not even then.

From *English History 1914–1945* by A.J.P. Taylor, 1965

a) **Explain why the coal industry was in crisis in 1926.**   **(3 marks)**

b) **Why was a strike in the coal industry in 1926 likely to lead to a
    general strike?**   **(7 marks)**

c) **How far was the general strike caused by lack of flexibility on the part
    of both mine-workers and mine-owners?**   **(15 marks)**

(Total: 25 marks)

a) The British coal industry had lost a number of their most important export markets during the First World War. Faced with cheaper foreign competitors, a sluggish domestic market, and an overvalued pound as a consequence of the government's return to the **gold standard**, the mine-owners felt that they had little alternative but to cut the wages of their employees to make their industry more competitive. The miners had been able to resist this as long as the German coal industry remained on strike in retaliation against the French occupation of the Ruhr, but when this came to an end and German coal, in form of reparations, began to flow once again, the mine-owners were no longer willing to contemplate any further delay to their plans. It was only the government's willingness to grant a nine-month subsidy that had prevented a lock-out and a strike, and that subsidy was due to expire at the end of April 1926.

b) The mines had been taken into government hands during the First World War, and in 1919, Lloyd George's coalition government had set up a Royal Commission under Lord Sankey to consider whether to return them to their pre-war owners. The majority report of the Sankey Commission had favoured keeping the mines under national control, but, under pressure from his Conservative colleagues, Lloyd George had been forced to ignore the report and had ordered the return of the mines to the private owners. When this happened in March 1921, the owners insisted on reducing pay and locked out those who refused to agree. The miners threatened to strike and called on their allies in the railway and transport workers unions to strike in sympathy. On 'Black Friday', 15 April 1921, the NUR and the NTW refused to do so and the miners were left to strike alone. After being forced to accept lower wages, the miners were keen to force the TUC into a definite agreement to prevent a repeat of this defeat. The TUC itself, although led by moderate figures, feared the consequence of a second failure of the movement to stand together and organised a General Council to organise mass action in the event of another major industrial crisis.

In June 1925, the mine-owners announced another reduction of wages and the General Council prepared to organise an embargo on the movement of coal. At the last minute, Baldwin's government intervened and announced that it would pay a nine-month subsidy to the mining industry to maintain wages at their current levels. This seeming capitulation by the government, known as 'Red Friday' seemed to indicate that the unions only had to threaten a mass strike for the government to cave in, and it made the General Council far more willing to organise a general strike. In fact, the government had felt ill-prepared for a confrontation with the unions and, in Churchill's words, 'decided to postpone the crisis'. The government chose to spend the nine-month breathing space stockpiling resources and establishing systems to cope with the mass strike that most of the government felt was now unavoidable.

c) The traditional view of the causes of the general strike tends to lay the blame at the feet of the intransigent mine-owners and the stubborn mine union leaders who dragged an unwilling TUC into a general strike, which the latter took the first available opportunity to end. However, the role of both the TUC and the government need to be examined in order to fully explore why a dispute in one industry led to arguably the most serious industrial dispute in Britain's history.

The owners of the mines of Britain must certainly bear a considerable share of responsibility for the dispute as they reneged on the wage and hours conditions that had been conceded during and after the war. In their defence, they did so to keep labour costs down in order to compete with cheap foreign imports, but their lack of flexibility and their tactics only served to provoke the miners' federation. In 1921, the owners insisted on an immediate cut in wages once the mines were handed back to private hands and enforced a lock-out – the bitterness caused by the defeat of the miners did much to harden attitudes in other unions in 1926. With the fall in the demand for British coal in the aftermath of the Ruhr Crisis, the owners insisted on wage cuts again, although they knew the likely consequences of such an action. Again they enforced a lock-out and left the miners with little alternative to striking.

The miners themselves had faced a series of disappointments since the end of the First World War, most notably the rejection of the recommendations of the Sankey Commission and the subsequent re-privatisation of their industry in 1921. On that occasion the other members of the so-called 'Triple Alliance' – the transport and railway workers, had failed to support the miners' strike on 'Black Friday'. The miners had been forced back to work on the owners' terms, and both they and the TUC were keen to avoid such a 'betrayal' again. The miners' leaders, Arthur Cook and Herbert Smith were so determined to improve the lot of their men, that they pursued an intransigent policy of 'not a penny off the pay, not a minute on the day', or as Smith put it when faced with negotiation, 'nowt doing'.

It was the TUC's responsibility to cajole the miners into a position where negotiation could take place, but they proved incapable of doing this. There was much guilt over the debacle in 1921, and they were determined to stand firm this time. On the other hand, the Industrial Committee of the General Council of the TUC was made up of moderates, who feared that the intransigence of the miners was driving the TUC into a strike which it could not win and which might very well be unconstitutional. They therefore made little attempt to prepare for a long strike and attempted to continue negotiating with the government for as long as possible and created an impression of unwillingness which the government was quick to notice.

The Conservative government must carry some blame for the strike, however. Although it is clear that Baldwin was essentially a man of peace, who hoped to build industrial reconciliation to benefit owners and workers. In 1925 he spoke out against a right-wing Conservative attempt to repeal the 1912 Trade Union Act, his speech included the memorable phrase, 'give peace in our time, oh Lord'. He had been left a crisis in the mining industry by Lloyd George after the rejection of the Sankey Report, the reprivatisation of the mines and the strike of 1921. He did set up the MacMillan enquiry to attempt to resolve the crisis, but was undermined by the actions of the owners, who he failed to control and by the Chancellor, Winston Churchill's, decision to restore the **gold standard** which made British coal even less competitive with European producers.

In order to prevent a crisis in July 1925, the government issued a nine-month subsidy, which temporarily maintained their current wage levels. A Royal Commission under Herbert Samuel was set up, but in case it failed to resolve the impasse, the government used this period of industrial truce to stockpile coal and to prepare essential services for a general strike. Regional commissioners were appointed and preparations made to use volunteers to man transport and distribution services. Although understandable, the trade unions and the Labour Party denounced such action as provocative.

Finally in the short term, Baldwin became a lot less willing to negotiate, once he had been persuaded by more hard line colleagues that confrontation was inevitable. Although a deal was possible on the basis of the Samuel Report, Baldwin refused to negotiate until the TUC threat of a general strike was lifted. On 3 May the government announced that it would not meet a delegation from TUC as the strike had already begun. In fact, a the compositors at the *Daily Mail* had refused to print an editorial attacking the idea of a general strike which may have been written on the instructions of Churchill. In this way the government certainly must be blamed for failing to prevent a dispute turning into a general strike.

 ## 4. The rise of Labour (EDEXCEL)

a) **Explain the rise of the Labour party from the third largest party
    in Parliament in 1918 to the largest one by 1929.**   **(30 marks)**
b) **Did the Labour government of 1924 prove that the party was
    'fit to govern'?**   **(30 marks)**

                                                                          (Total: 60 marks)

a) In 1918, it seemed that the Labour Party would not form a government for a long time to come. They had gained valuable experience in Lloyd George's coalition government, but Arthur Henderson's decision to leave the War Cabinet over the Stockholm conference had been unpopular and he had lost his seat in 1918, along with Ramsay MacDonald, who had opposed Britain's entry into the war in 1914. In the face of the coalition government's 'coupon' tactics, the party only won 63 seats. But this unimpressive showing hid the important fact that, with the Asquithian Liberals only winning 28 seats, they were now the main opposition to the Conservative-dominated government.

As a party they not only emerged from the war still united, but they also had a clear programme, stated in the party's new constitution, and a potential reservoir of support in the newly enfranchised working classes. Over the next few years, as well as benefiting financially from the increase in trade union membership which continued its upward trend from the war, the party took care to recruit individual members from the middle classes, especially former Liberals who were disenchanted with the Liberals' fractured and compromised nature and who were forced to look to Labour for progressive policies. Men such as Christopher Addison, R.B. Haldane and Charles Trevelyan defected from the Liberals, as did some prominent conservatives such as Oswald Mosley and Lord Chelmsford, a former Viceroy of India. Consequently, the Labour party was able to pose as a national party with wide-class support in contrast to the predominantly English middle-class Conservatives. Party branches were set up in every constituency giving the party the basis for mounting a national campaign in forthcoming elections. The 1918 constitution gave the party the unity it needed as it put central power in the hands of the trade unions by giving them a block vote at the annual conference that was big enough to decide the membership of the National Executive Committee. In this way the 'extremism' of smaller socialist groups and the **Independent Labour Party** was avoided and moderate middle- and working-class voters were not alienated. The party began its rise to power by vigorously contesting the municipal elections of 1919 and it had much success, especially in London.

Ramsay MacDonald, who became leader of the party in 1922 was careful to appeal to all classes. His anti-war stance began to benefit the party as public opinion became less tolerant of aggressive foreign policy in the aftermath of the Great War, as reaction to the Chanak incident demonstrated. Once disarmament and international co-operation became accepted as desirable policies, the Labour Party had a good case for arguing that only they had demonstrated commitment to these principles in the past.

The Party did have its share of good luck, as well. There was no pressing need for Baldwin to have called the 1923 election, but in doing so at a time when the Liberals had only just reunified and the two branches of the party still did not trust one another, and on a policy as unpopular as Protection, gave Labour an opportunity they would have had to wait much longer for in other circumstances.

Similarly, the Liberals' inability to put their differences behind them and Asquith's refusal to give up the leadership until 1926 allowed Labour to portray themselves as the best alternative to the Conservatives while the Liberals who appeared wedded to old-fashioned ideas such as temperance and non-conformity had lost their appeal.

When the party came to power, it was keen to prove its moderation and its lack of partisan bias in its economic policy. Snowden, as Chancellor, was as orthodox as his Conservative predecessors in his insistence on a balanced budget, and failed to act on the commitment to **nationalisation** of industry which was promised in **Clause IV** of the party's constitution. Of course, as a minority government dependent on Liberal support in both periods in office, one might argue that such attempts would only have served to bring the governments down more prematurely.

b)   The government took office with the express purpose of proving that, contrary to Winston Churchill, the Labour Party was 'fit to govern' and that it had a broad base of support rather than merely representing a small section of the working class. As the government was a minority government, dependent on the support of the Liberals under Asquith, there was no opportunity for the introduction of radical policies. In fact, MacDonald was quite pleased as he had no radical programme and was concerned that any attempt to introduce one would offend many of the party's new middle-class supporters. Instead he filled his Cabinet with former Conservatives and Liberals such as Lord Chelmsford and Robert Haldane and moderate trade unionists such as J.H. Thomas. The Chancellor of the Exchequer, Edward Snowden, introduced an orthodox budget which reduced indirect taxes but failed to introduce any substantial redistribution of wealth. Ramsay MacDonald took the position of Foreign Secretary himself and continued a vigorous defence of the Empire, as well as a positive approach towards the League of Nations, both of which proved popular in the country. The Parliamentary Labour Party were not even in regular contact with the trade unions and left wing radical groups, unlike the Annual Conference and the Executive Committee. Trade union militancy continued, despite the Labour government, with Ernest Bevin's Transport and General Workers Union (TGWU) launching a dock strike in February which spread to London tram drivers and busmen in March. Bevin then threatened to call out the London underground drivers, but MacDonald retaliated by threatening the use of emergency powers. The strike was called off, but only on the TGWU's terms.

The only real domestic success of the government's brief period in office was Wheatley's *Housing Act* which gave subsidies to local authorities worth £9 million p.a. for the building of council houses for rent. Some half a million houses were built under the scheme over the next ten years. Further innovative reform was impossible, given Snowden's insistence on a strictly balanced budget, but increases in both old age pensions and unemployment benefit were funded, as well as the commissioning of five new cruisers in the naval race with Japan and the USA.

MacDonald's only concession to socialist sympathies was the recognition of the Soviet Union as the government of Russia for the first time and a subsequent trade agreement between the two countries. This allowed some right-wing conservatives such as Churchill to claim that Labour was actually promoting the recently formed Communist Party of Great Britain. Two events served to confirm this. In September, Macdonald, exhausted by the pressure of holding two senior Cabinet positions, intervened to prevent the trial for sedition of Campbell, the editor of the *Communist Workers' Weekly*. The newspaper had printed a notice calling on soldiers not to fire on their fellow workers, but Campbell had not been editor at the time, so the trial could not have succeeded. However, it looked to the Opposition that MacDonald had interfered for political reasons. The Conservatives called for a vote of censure and the Liberals demanded an inquiry. The government lost the vote on the issue of the enquiry and MacDonald promptly resigned.

The subsequent general election was dominated by the issue of the 'Zinoviev letter' which was leaked from the Foreign Office four days before the election. It was addressed to the Communist Party of Great Britain and actually criticised the Labour Party for having resisted the affiliation of the communists at the 1924 election, but claimed that the recent trade agreement would allow communist agents to infiltrate Britain. The subsequent scandal clearly alarmed many middle-class voters who might previously have supported the Liberals and enabled the Tories to gain a comfortable victory, but in fact the Labour Party actually increased its share of the vote.

Labour certainly succeeded in reassuring many voters that it did not intend to introduce revolutionary policies, and those alarmed by relations with the Soviet Union and the 'Zinoviev letter' were not likely to have been Labour voters anyway. On the other hand, the lack of substantial achievement by the government may have dissatisfied many. MacDonald's caution had prevented him from introducing policies such as widow's pensions and an equalisation of the franchise for women, both of which would have had Liberal support. The party had done little to address the continuing problem of unemployment and had demonstrated lack of experience in its poor handling of the Campbell case. It has been suggested that MacDonald deliberately orchestrated the government's collapse.

5. The decline of the Liberals and the dominance of the Conservatives (OCR)

Account for the decline of the Liberals and the Conservatives' dominance in the inter-war years.

(90 marks)

Since the 1930s there has been a debate among historians as to the causes of the decline of the Liberal Party. George Dangerfield in his study, 'The Strange Death of Liberal England' suggested that this decline began before the First World War with the party facing a number of challenges from groups it had previously relied on for support. In particular, Dangerfield drew attention to the period of industrial unrest after 1909, when trade unions, angry at the continuing legal challenges to their position, took their financial backing away from the Liberals and chose instead to support the nascent Labour Party. Despite this theory, the most convincing explanation for the Liberal decline is in the party's fortunes during the First World War. As well as the acrimonious split that took place between Asquith and Lloyd George in 1916, the party was still believed to have put party principle before the nation's needs in its reluctance to intervene in the economy and in particular to introduce conscription.

Unlike the Labour and Conservative parties which had also suffered splits as a result of the war, the divisions within the Liberal Party were perpetuated by the positions of the leaders which became established in 1918. First, during the Maurice debate of March 1918, Asquith did his best to bring down Lloyd George's government. Then, in the election in December, Lloyd George took his revenge, issuing a letter of support to Coalition Conservatives standing against Asquith's Liberals, which resulted in Asquith's being reduced to only 28 MPs. Neither of these events was forgiven by the other side even after Lloyd George's coalition collapsed and the two wings of the party were reunited although Lloyd George refused to spend his controversial 'political fund' on the party as long as it was headed by Asquith, despite the party being very short of funds.

Asquith had allowed the party to drift since 1916, failing to mount a convincing opposition to the wartime coalition and allowing Labour to take over the leadership of the radical left after the **armistice**. His main action after 1922 was to remain as leader of the party, even after losing his seat in 1924, simply to prevent Lloyd George gaining the leadership. When he finally did retire in 1926, too many radicals had been lost to Labour to permit even Lloyd George to restore the party's old strength.

The 1923 election demonstrated the failure of the Liberals to seize their opportunities. After the Conservatives lost their majority in the 1923 election, if the Liberals had refused to support MacDonald, the King would have been obliged to ask Asquith to form a government. It seems likely that many Conservatives would have preferred to have kept Asquith in office for a brief period, to prevent a Labour administration, while they regrouped. It would have been difficult to achieve much, but it was the last chance to restore Liberalism as an independent governing party. It did not happen because Lloyd George was not prepared to return so quickly after losing office, and not as Asquith's junior, and Asquith was not keen to preside over a ministry that contained the mistrusted 'Welsh wizard'. Asquith did not have any formal agreement with Labour when he allowed them to form a government and could not claim any credit for their achievements, but he did drive many Liberal middle-class supporters into the arms of the Conservatives who resented Asquith for having done so. In addition, the party was so short of funds by 1924 that it failed to contest 275 seats, leaving anti-socialists little alternative but to vote Conservative.

After becoming Liberal leader, however, Lloyd George did his best to revitalise the party, organising an inquiry on British industry and producing a report, *Britain's Industrial Future*, to which Keynes and Beveridge contributed. The Liberal programme which emerged from this included a commitment to large scale public works schemes in order to stimulate the economy and reduce unemployment by half a million and was published in 1929 under the title *We Can Conquer Unemployment*. The subsequent campaign benefited from the use of Lloyd George's political fund, but was unable to overcome the difficulties that a third party always faces in the British electoral system and failed to break the class-based support for the other two parties. Although the party's vote increased, it only managed to win 59 seats. It was hoped that this would be the basis for further recovery, especially when the second Labour government again proved to be incapable of radical action to solve the economic crisis of 1931, but the creation of the National Government removed this possibility. The party split again over whether to join the coalition, with Lloyd George remaining outside. The National Government's decision to abandon **free trade** in 1932 split the Liberals again and in the face of the Labour recovery the party became increasingly irrelevant during the 1930s.

Between 1918 and 1939 the Conservative Party was the largest parliamentary party except for a brief period between 1929 and 1931. It was in power either alone or as part of a coalition for all but 36 months of the inter-war period. The leaders of the Conservative Party between 1918 and 1939 except Austen Chamberlain all became Prime Minister and he was only leader for 18 months.

At a time when British politics became increasingly democratic, it might have been expected that the largely middle-class Conservative Party would be at a disadvantage compared to a party which stood for the working class majority. The situation in 1918 gives some clues as to why this was not to be the case. First, the electoral system in Britain, especially in a period of genuine three-party politics, allowed a party without an overall majority of votes to win a majority of seats. For example in 1922 the Conservatives won 345 seats with a share of the poll 5 per cent *less* than they received in 1906, when they had only won 157. Second, with its strong financial backing, the party was able to contest almost all political constituencies, even when there were three elections in three years between 1922 and 1924, unlike the Liberals and Labour. Finally, once Sinn Fein refused to take its seats at Westminster in 1918 and then the Irish Free State was created in 1922, the handicap of around 65 seats that Irish MPs had caused the Conservatives was removed. As a result, the non-Conservative forces found it far more difficult than before to muster a majority.

One explanation of the Conservative inter-war predominance therefore lies in the weakness of the other parties. The split within the Liberals was perpetuated for long enough by the obstinacy of their leaders for the Conservatives to pose as the best available bulwark against socialism at the time of Labour's electoral breakthrough. Many right-wing Liberals despaired of their party's ineffectiveness and were sufficiently reassured by Baldwin's moderation and effective publicity to turn to the Conservatives as the best (often the only) alternative to Labour.

Labour ironically helped the Tories by refusing to support any moves towards proportional representation as they feared that it would allow the Liberals to challenge them at a time when a Labour majority government still seemed very possible. Without such a move the Tories retained an unfair electoral advantage, but it was a price that Ramsay MacDonald seemed happy to tolerate until the Liberals ceased to be a credible political force. Labour's lack of unity also favoured the Conservatives, as, in 1931, the party was divided between those who were committed to continuing orthodox economic policies and those who favoured radical alternatives. Obviously it was Baldwin's great fortune that he did not have to face the consequences of his unsuccessful economic policy, but Labour's failure to agree on a policy, allowed the Conservatives to claim that they, unlike Labour, put country before party in the time of national crisis.

It is of course impossible to ignore the fact that the Conservatives had a large base of popular support, which they were able to marshall effectively at elections. This support was concentrated in southern and midland England, but included many seats where the middle classes were less than 20 per cent of the population. The party had therefore been able to convince many of the newly enfranchised voters who had no traditional loyalty towards parties. The explanation for this lies in the success of the party organisation in responding to a larger, less committed electorate. The Conservatives recruited and trained 352 new party agents between 1924 and 1937 who proved very efficient at organising the new absent voting system. The party also began organising a fund-raising drive in order to recruit less wealthy, but more able candidates. The traditional tactics of local party branches, recruiting women and concentrating on social functions, continued to succeed in appealing to the less-politically committed.

The party's record between 1922–39 also served to appeal to the generally apolitical. Baldwin was keen to emphasise his moderate, inclusive approach to politics and his lack of ideology, apart from patriotism, attracted those alienated by socialist rhetoric. The party's moderation was proved by the adoption of collectivist policies such as the creation of the British Broadcasting Corporation, the National Grid and the British Overseas Air Corporation and the work of Neville Chamberlain at the Ministry of Health in Baldwin's second government. This seemed confirmed after 1931, when the Conservative-dominated National Government was able to share power with a large proportion of the Liberal Party and some significant Labour leaders.

The leadership of the party must be given some credit for the Conservative successes as well. Bonar Law had managed to associate his party with Lloyd George in order to secure a majority of seats for his party in the 1918 'coupon' election, and he came out of retirement to end the coalition when he realised that Austen Chamberlain's policy would split the party and lose the forthcoming election in 1922 Despite his reputation as a moderate, Baldwin was however capable of determined leadership in moments of crisis such as during the General Strike and the **Abdication crisis** of 1936 and he faced down the challenge to his leadership by the Empire Free Traders and the Press Barons following the Conservative defeat in 1929, with courage and good judgement. Even his greatest blunder, the 1923 election can be seen as laying the foundation for future Conservative success for the very issue that lost Baldwin the election – protection – served to reunite the party after the split at the Carlton Club in 1922. Neville Chamberlain, too, deserves credit for his reforming work at the ministry of health in Baldwin's second administration and his careful handling of the economy as Chancellor from 1931–1937.

The Liberal split and the Conservative contribution to the victorious wartime government had clearly handed the Conservatives an opportunity, which they were eager to exploit following the years in opposition before the war. They displayed ruthlessness in dropping Lloyd George when he was no longer useful to them and a wise approach to mass democracy, carrying out reforms and resisting the extremism of the General Strike in the 1920s and the British Union of Fascists in the 1930s. Perhaps most of all, the party was lucky that the inter-war economic crisis which Churchill's decision to return to gold exacerbated, reached its peak when Labour was in power and the Liberals no longer a serious challenger. The formation of the National Government in 1931 allowed the Conservatives to introduce their preferred methods of dealing with the depression without facing the blame for the social consequences alone, at least not until 1945.

6. The 1931 crisis (AQA)

Read the following source and then answer the questions which follow:

MacDonald had always believed that party loyalty could conflict with higher national or international loyalties and that it should come second if it did. That was why he had gone against his party in 1914; as he saw it, 1931 was 1914 all over again. He has often been accused of betraying his party, but if he had acted differently he would have betrayed his whole approach to politics.

From *Ramsay MacDonald* by David Marquand, 1977

a) **What is meant by the reference to MacDonald's behaviour in 1914?** **(3 marks)**
b) **Why was the Labour government unable to overcome the financial crisis of 1931?** **(7 marks)**
c) **Did Ramsay Macdonald betray his party?** **(15 marks)**

(Total: 25 marks)

a) In August 1914, Ramsay MacDonald opposed Britain's declaration of war against Germany. He resigned as Chairman of the Labour Party, as the bulk of the Party supported the actions of the government.

b) In the face of the deepening economic crisis caused by the end of US investment and recall of loans and the continued reduction in British exports, Chancellor of the Exchequer Snowden introduced a balanced budget in April 1931 with a view to major cuts in welfare in Autumn 1931 which could be justified as a result of the May committee's report on possible economies. In the meantime, a treasury committee under Lord MacMillan compiled a report on Finance and Industry which discussed broad issues of the crisis, but although it gave Keynes a platform for his 'reflationary' ideas, it failed to convince MacDonald that this was the solution to the crisis and he chose to increase expenditure on public works instead.

The May Report was published on 31 July and it forecasted a £120 million deficit in the government's accounts. The committee proposed economies of £96 million in salary cuts and 20 per cent cuts in unemployment benefit. Keynes called it 'the most foolish document I ever had the misfortune to read'. The TUC were hostile to the report and proposed a levy on industrial profits and called for 'equality of sacrifice'.

The cabinet still believed there was no great urgency and left for their holidays, but in the next few days a 'run' on the Bank of England began as foreign investors withdrew their funds as a consequence of the May Committee's report and the collapse of banks in Austria and Germany in which the Bank had invested. The Bank of England now required a loan to maintain the **gold standard** after the European banks had defaulted on their loans from Britain.

American and French sources were willing to lend but insisted on the economies of the May Report as they would only lend money to Britain if the budget balanced. Snowden was thus convinced of the need for immediate cuts in expenditure.

The Cabinet clearly had to act quickly to stop the run on the Bank. MacDonald was recalled to London to be told 'we are on the edge of a precipice'. Montagu Norman, governor of the Bank of England called for the printing of ration books. On 19 August, the Cabinet sat from 11 a.m. to 10.30 p.m. arguing over the extent of the cuts. Henderson and others did not wish to persecute the unemployed and they had support from the TUC delegation. MacDonald decided to support Snowden's wish for cuts in order to act in the interests of the whole country. By 21 August, cuts of £56 million were accepted by the Cabinet but no cut in unemployment benefit. Snowden and MacDonald however, insisted on reductions of £78 million. On 22 August, when Snowden again proposed cuts of £78 million with 10 per cent cut in unemployment benefit, the Cabinet split 11–9 in favour. The government couldn't survive the resignation of nine of its members, especially as it was a minority administration, and so, on the following day, MacDonald was authorised to go to Buckingham Palace and tender his resignation.

c) After the collapse of the Labour government and the surprise formation of the National Government with Ramsay MacDonald at its head in 1931, the Labour Party claimed MacDonald had plotted together with the King, the other party leaders and the bankers, to throw out Labour and take power themselves.

Although it is true that George V did implore MacDonald to stay on as Prime Minister after the collapse of the Labour government, he did so in accordance with his constitutional duty to appoint the head of the strongest government available. And, with Labour holding the largest number of seats in a hung Parliament, and the Conservatives unwilling to take over, he had little alternative. He had certainly suggested that MacDonald should form a coalition before, but he had compared the crisis of 1931, with three million people unemployed, to the wartime crisis of 1916 and persuaded MacDonald that it was his duty to stay on. Therefore he encouraged MacDonald to place national concerns above those of the party, but in many ways, that is the monarch's task at such a time.

The opposition leaders such as Herbert Samuel (Lloyd George was ill at the time) also urged MacDonald to lead a coalition. The Liberals couldn't afford another election and they saw it as their only route back into power. Neville Chamberlain, for the Conservatives, saw that the necessary benefit cuts had split Labour and recognised that a coalition would prevent the Conservatives being solely blamed for this. Baldwin, however, was unenthusiastic towards the coalition, but as long as Lloyd George was not included, he was prepared to agree.

MacDonald's own motives are consequently questionable. Consideration of a coalition was an entirely valid move given the depth of the crisis, the paralysis of the Cabinet and the lack of a majority for any party. MacDonald, however, failed to discuss this possibility with his Cabinet or any of his senior colleagues and the presence of Samuel and Baldwin at Buckingham Palace lends credence to those who claim that he mislead his party as to his intentions on 24 August. When presented with the opportunity to be a national hero, MacDonald agreed, motivated by patriotism and vanity. He hoped to be able to return to the Labour Party after the crisis, or even to retire, seeing the coalition as temporary. Official statements made it clear that the newly formed National Government was 'to deal with the national emergency that now exists' and 'when that purpose is achieved the political parties will resume their respective positions'.

This was, however, an extremely unlikely occurrence, as MacDonald, Snowden and Thomas all now supported a policy of benefit cuts and retrenchment which was the complete opposite of the policy they were elected on in 1929. They failed to meet with the Parliamentary Labour Party to explain themselves and all three were expelled from the Labour Party at the end of September.

In the sense that he abandoned Labour's policies, Ramsay MacDonald did indeed betray the Labour Party and he acknowledged this when he spoke to his National Government colleagues for the first time and explained that 'he was absolutely satisfied that it was necessary, in the national interest'. However, Labour's policy of 'regulated capitalism' had clearly failed and ten of his Labour ministers had agreed with him when they supported the cuts in cabinet in August. To MacDonald, only a genuine all-party coalition could command the cross-class support needed to implement the expenditure cuts, and he therefore felt it his duty to support it in whatever way the King advised.

To say that he betrayed the Labour Party by forcing it out of office in a conspiracy is, however, quite inaccurate. He may have been unwise in not informing his colleagues of the possibility of a coalition, but he may not have wished to allow the party to avoid its responsibilities until the cabinet split made a coalition unavoidable. The Labour government had already collapsed by the time MacDonald went to the Palace and the failure of eight of the ministers who had supported the cuts to follow MacDonald, disguised the true nature of the party by August 1931.

7. The National Governments and opposition (EDEXCEL)

a) **What measures did the National Governments of 1931 to 1939 take to aid Britain's recovery from the Depression?**   **(30 marks)**

b) **Explain the failure of fascism as a political force in Britain in the 1930s.**   **(30 marks)**

(Total: 60 marks)

a) The National Government was formed to keep the pound on the **gold standard**. Snowden, who remained Chancellor, introduced an emergency budget on 10 September 1931 and cut unemployment benefit by 10 per cent. Taxes were increased, with income tax increasing to 25 per cent. In addition, government expenditure was cut, pay was cut by 10 per cent for government employees and civil servants, and by 15 per cent for teachers. In this way £70 million was saved. Many commentators have criticised this policy of deflation, however. By imposing the cuts the government was reducing demand among millions of consumers and actually worsening the depression.

Ironically it was not this policy, but the forced reverse of the National Government's aim to save the pound that actually did the most to alleviate the effects of the Depression. In protest against the cuts, sailors at Invergordon refused to obey orders. When news of the 'Invergordon Mutiny' was announced, another run on the pound took place as investments were cashed in before the value of the currency dropped. Montagu Norman, the Governor of the Bank of England suddenly changed his previous policy and announced that the **gold standard** should be abandoned. On 21 September the pound was taken off gold and the exchange rate fell to $3.40 to the pound by December. This proved to be largely beneficial for Britain's export trade as it was a far more realistic rate and it served to boost Britain's internal trade. The run on the pound halted immediately, but the pound had been sacrificed.

The National Government had thus lost its purpose within a month of being formed and the subsequent election became a vote of confidence in the National Government who called for a 'Doctor's mandate' to address Britain's difficulties. They had clearly gained the trust of the nation as the National Government was returned with 67 per cent of the vote, with the bulk of their seats belonging to the Conservatives.

After Neville Chamberlain became Chancellor, the policy of cautious reform continued. Freed from the **gold standard**, the Bank of England was able to cut the interest rate from 6 per cent to 2 per cent in 1932, which allowed cheap loans for business, in particular the building industry, which began a period of substantial expansion, with one million houses constructed between 1931 and 1935. In 1934, the cuts in unemployment benefit were restored and income tax relief was introduced in the following year.

Apart from this, most of the governments' actions had little effect. **Free trade** was finally abandoned with the Abnormal Importation Act of 1931 and the Import Duties Act of 1932, but apart from a stimulus to the domestic vacuum cleaner trade this had little effect. If the Ottawa Conference had managed to create an Imperial trading zone, the policy may have had a greater effect, but neither the **Dominions** nor India were willing to drop their tax barriers for the mother country.

The aid offered by the government to the depressed regions of Britain was even less effective. The *Special Areas Acts* of 1934/7 were laudable in their intention of improving the infrastructure of such areas, but the £2 million budget for the scheme was derisory. The government was unwilling to embark on a costly programme of state intervention as some such as Keynes and Lloyd George advocated.

Perhaps the true reason for British economic recovery was the general world recovery after 1934, from which Britain, with her valuable monopoly of primary goods from the Empire, as well as her industrial products, was able to benefit. By 1939, the economy had clearly recovered despite a further slow-down in 1938, but unemployment remained at nearly 11 per cent. Most new industrial development had taken place in the South East and the Midlands and many workers in depressed areas could not afford to move to areas of expensive housing and relatively low wages. It is ironic that the measures that did the most to benefit the British economy's chances of recovery were not entirely the intention of the National Government. Coming off gold had been the policy that the National Government had been created to avoid, while the reduction in interest rates was done mainly to reduce the National Debt costs and thus balance the budget, rather than to stimulate cheap loans to business. The Acts designed to solve the problems of recovery, were by contrast largely ineffective and in the case of expenditure cuts and tax increases, actually harmful. Therefore it is perhaps wisest to conclude that the National Government did in fact both help and hinder the recovery from the Depression, but managed to do both somewhat unintentionally.

b) The British Union of Fascists (BUF), led by Sir Oswald Mosley, reached a peak of membership in the early 1930s. It is not clear how many members the party had, but it claimed to have 500 branches across the country. It had the support of influential figures such as Lord Rothermere who used his newspapers to promote the cause. The *Daily Mail*, one of his most popular papers carried an article entitled 'Hurrah for the **Blackshirts**' in 1934. Many disillusioned young Conservatives felt that that their party had failed to deal adequately with the depression, and Mosley's programme of tariff barriers and public works seemed an attractive alternative to the National Government's largely passive approach. They also agreed with Mosley's vigorous anti-communist stance which on occasion involved the use of force to ensure that meetings were not disrupted by right-wing groups. This robust stance, admired by many, backfired in 1934, when the BUF held a rally at Olympia in London. To ensure order, the blackshirt stewards dealt with hecklers with open violence that was widely reported and condemned.

Mosley had expressed admiration of the economic achievements of the Fascist government of Italy and the Nazis, and he had increasingly adopted anti-semitic policies. He could claim that as in Germany in 1933, a British fascist government would only seek to exclude those of non-British blood or of socialist sympathies from power and would not challenge the rule of law. The 'Night of the Long Knives' in June 1934, although it was favourably reported by the *Daily Mail*, appalled many British observers as the methods of organised crime were used to settle an internal Nazi Party feud. As disturbing reports about the nature of the treatment of those held in German concentration camps were circulated, many more respectable politicians in Britain became unwilling to publicly support a party that appeared, at Olympia, to advocate, albeit on a somewhat milder level, the use of political violence.

After 1934, the economy displayed clear signs of recovery. By 1935, the National Government felt strong enough to risk a general election. As the BUF had not been organised as a parliamentary force, rather as a revolutionary, paramilitary group, Mosley was unable to reorganise his party in time and therefore chose to boycott the election. This meant that the party remained without any parliamentary voice to defend its position when Parliament debated measures which would harm the BUF following the violence of the 'Battle of Cable Street' in 1936.

Government action must be said to have played a part in the decline of all paramilitary groups, most significantly the BUF, when it issued the Public Order Act which banned the wearing of uniforms by political groups and military displays such as marches and drilling. On the other hand, the Act did not come into force until 1937, by which time the BUF was already in decline. The BUF did remain politically important especially when the popular mood towards Hitler became more positive after the Munich agreement, but with the horrors of 'Kristallnacht' and finally the declaration of war with Germany, the BUF became seen as a potentially destabilising force in Britain, possibly even a Nazi-controlled one, and Mosley and his supporters were interned early in the Second World War.

The Depression in Britain was not as socially devastating as it was in Germany. The middle class, whose support was crucial in any fascist victory, were largely unaffected by it and the working class who retained their jobs actually saw their standard of living rise. The fascist message in both Italy and Germany had appealed to those threatened by a seemingly unstoppable communist movement. In Britain, the Communist Party was never a serious enough threat to make respectable voters support an extreme group such as the fascists. With the added benefit of victory in the First World War, the institutions of Britain were never sufficiently weakened to make the fascist threat a serious possibility. Mosley made a crucial series of miscalculations, most significantly to fail to contest the 1935 election and to model his party on the Nazi pattern, which ultimately undermined his key message of nationalism as Britain found itself confronting Germany in the second half of the decade.

Additional essay questions

1. Lloyd George and the Coalition (OCR)

Is it accurate to describe Lloyd George as 'the prisoner of the Conservatives' between 1918 and 1922?   **(Total: 90 marks)**

Why did Lloyd George's political influence decline after 1922?   **(Total: 90 marks)**

Essay plan

Lloyd George lost office in 1922 having been Prime Minister for six years and a senior government minister for 16 years. Yet he never held political office again – why?

Associated with the failures of the 1918–22 government – especially his personal corruption ('Lloyd George knew my father'), his personal immorality (known as 'the goat') and personal conceit (his presidential style).

Lack of party base – he had split the Liberals and made the split worse in the 1918 'coupon election'. He failed to become Liberal leader until 1926, by which time the Liberals only had

40 seats. Liberal Party did not fully trust him – as witnessed by arguments over 1929 electoral strategy and the behaviour of Samuel and Simon in 1931.

Lack of political judgement – refusal to use his political fund in crucial 1923 election when the Liberals might have prevented the first Labour government. Unsuitability of 1929 Keynesian programme at a time of international economic instability. Decision to visit and publicly praise Nazi Germany at a time of growing confrontation and discovery of inhuman treatment. Hence not seriously considered for premiership in 1940, despite his success in First World War and his role in bringing down Neville Chamberlain – fear that he might prove a 'British Pétain'.

Poor fortune – Asquith's refusal to give up the leadership until 1926. Illness at the time of the 1931 crisis – may have been seen as an alternative to MacDonald.

Conclusion – polarisation of politics into class lines following First World War as seen by the general strike – Lloyd George's political approach seen as increasingly irrelevant. Memories of his personal failings between 1918–22 constantly reinforced between the wars by those he had offended during his long years in office (which included most influential politicians and media figures).

2. The general strike (OCR)

Lord Grey, writing in the *British Gazette* in May 1926, said of the general strike that 'It is an attempted revolution'. How far do the events of the summer of 1926, and subsequent actions of the government and unions support this view? (90 marks)

3. The rise of Labour (OCR)

How far did the lack of parliamentary majority inhibit the Labour governments of 1924 and 1929–31? (Total: 90 marks)

Had the Labour Party recovered from the disaster of 1931 by the end of the decade? (Total: 90 marks)

4. National Government (EDEXCEL)

a) **Explain why a National Government was formed in 1931.** (30 marks)
b) **Why did the Communist Party fail to achieve a significant level of popular support during the 1930s?** (30 marks)

(Total: 60 marks)

Essay plan

a)   *Economic Crisis of 1929–31, dramatic increase in unemployment, business failure – Labour unwilling to attempt radical economic solutions as demonstrated by the rejection of the Mosley memorandum.*

1931 financial crisis caused by collapse of German and Austrian banks. Britain needed to secure a loan to end a run on its financial reserves – May Committee recommended severe reductions in government expenditure.

Political crisis as Labour government failed to agree on cuts in unemployment benefit. Labour forced to resign – need for a 'National Government' to resolve the crisis and reassure the international finance markets.

MacDonald's motives:

- *patriotism, having been asked by the King to head the National Government.*
- *Resentment of his Labour colleagues for refusing to put the country's needs first (as he saw it).*
- *Genuine belief in his own abilities to bring working class support to the National Government.*

Baldwin's motives for joining the National Government:

- *Willingness to let MacDonald lead a government forced to take unpopular economic decisions.*
- *As Conservatives would form bulk of the National Government, they could benefit electorally for their patriotic gesture.*
- *Baldwin much criticised recently by press, the National Government could offer a way of uniting the Conservatives around his leadership.*

Liberal motives for joining the National Government:
- *Desire for office following nine years in political wilderness.*
- *Little future as a separate party following the party's declining funding and the failure of the 1929 campaign to make a breakthrough.*
- *Lloyd George ill and unable to prevent the bulk of the party joining the National Government.*

b)   *Communist Party never achieved more than a single MP in the 1920s and 1930s despite worst economic crisis in Britain's industrial history. In 1932 only had 6,000 members.*

- *Traditional British dislike of extremist parties – as seen by the failure of the British Union of Fascists.*
- *Failure of the communists to infiltrate the Labour Party – return of a Communist Party donation during the General Strike, rejection of the Socialist League's offer of a Popular Front in 1939.*
- *National Unemployed Workers' Movement was more successful, in winning support, but this tended to be towards the unemployed generally rather than the Communist Party in particular.*

- *Although the depression was very badly felt in some areas of the country, in these areas traditional support for Labour was preserved as Labour was, after 1931, the chief form of opposition to the National Government and effectively fulfilled this role.*
- *Ultimately, communism was most closely associated with the Soviet Union and the experience of the Civil War, the suppression of opposition in Russia and the Stalinist purges led most voters to reject any form of communism. This anti-communist position was a feature of almost all the influential inter-war media.*

*The fear of communism that had begun with Russia signing an **armistice** with Germany in 1918 and repudiating all her debts and had continued with the 'Zinoviev letter' of 1924 and the Arcos affair in 1928, proved so deeply embedded that Britain refused to turn her back on traditional political approaches. May also be due to the relative lack of severity of the Depression, compared with the experience of Germany and France.*

Part 3: Sources

1. The decline of the Liberal Party (AQA)

Source A: From a letter by L.T. Hobhouse, 1924

My difficulty about the Liberal Party lies further back than yours. I doubt if it any longer stands for anything distinctive. My reasons are on the one side that moderate Labour – Labour in office – has on the whole represented essential liberalism, not without mistakes and defects, but better than the organised party since Campbell-Bannerman's death . . . Of the present fragment, part leans to the Tories, part to Labour, part has nothing distinctive, but is a kind of **Free Trade** Tory group.

Source B: *Table 4.3 The liberal vote, 1918–35*

Election	Candidates	MPs elected	Total votes
1918	421	163	2,785,374
1922	477	115	4,080,915
1923	457	158	4,301,481
1924	340	40	2,931,380
1929	513	59	5,308,738
1931	118	37	1,506,630
1935	161	21	1,443,093

Source C: From *History of the Liberal Party, 1895–1970* by Roy Douglas, 1971, writing about the Liberal Party's poor results in the 1929 general election

The personal record of Lloyd George was a very dubious asset. Liberals could, and did, argue that in the war he 'got things done'. But could men who had written in 1926 of Lloyd George that, 'confidential relations are impossible with one whose instability destroys confidence' expect to carry much conviction three years later when they declared that he was the best possible leader for the nation? And when Lloyd George made sweeping promises about conquering unemployment, even though those promises were upheld by serious professional economists and others, men were all too inclined to recall the disappointments and the real – or alleged – broken promises of the Coalition. For all his genius, and for all his genuine concern for the poor and down-trodden, a vast number of people, both inside and outside the Liberal Party, utterly mistrusted him as a man.

QUESTIONS WITH WORKED ANSWERS

a) Study source C. With reference to source C and your own knowledge, explain the reference to 'broken promises of the Coalition' in the context of Lloyd George's career. (3 marks)

b) Study source A. With reference to your own knowledge explain how useful Source A is as evidence for the decline of the Liberals after 1918. (7 marks)

c) Study sources A, B and C and use your own knowledge. What were the major difficulties facing the Liberal Party after 1918? (15 marks)

ANSWERS

a) In the war years and the election campaign of December 1918, Lloyd George and his coalition government attempted to use their wartime record of social innovation to appeal to the new mass-electorate created by the Representation of the People Act. A ministry of health had been established and a hospital building programme was unveiled. There was to be full-time compulsory education for all up to 14 and more nursery and 14–16 places. In particular, the need to improve the poor state of Britain's housing was recognised by Lloyd George himself, who spoke of 'homes fit for heroes'. With the economic depression of 1920–21, however, many of these schemes were significantly reduced in scale, in the so-called 'Geddes Axe' which cut £64 million of government expenditure, prompting the resignation of his Liberal Minister of Health, Christopher Addison. Although these measures were largely forced on Lloyd George, as Prime Minister, he had to bear ultimate responsibility for an episode which damaged his pre-war reputation as a radical social reformer.

b) Source A was written by L.T. Hobhouse, a journalist and sociologist, who had been one of the chief advocates of what became known as '**New Liberalism**' in the first decade of the twentieth century. He had argued, prior to the 1906 general election, that improving the conditions of the working classes was a priority for the Liberals, if they wished to benefit the country as a whole. He criticised the traditional Liberal support for uncontrolled free enterprise and called for some form of state intervention by the government, as the only effective way of eliminating the worst examples of poverty. He and his fellow Liberal thinker, J.H. Hobson, were credited with inspiring the Liberals to introduce a far more interventionist social policy between 1906 and 1914, with measures such as the introduction of old age pensions and free school meals and medical inspections for the children of the poor.

In source A, Hobhouse demonstrates his exasperation with the Liberals, complaining that they no longer stand for anything distinctive and that the parliamentary Labour party more accurately reflect the priorities of what he describes as 'essential liberalism', that is, one can assume, the desire to see the worst social ills of Britain effectively addressed through state intervention. Surprisingly, he claims that Labour has represented such opinion since the death of Campbell-Bannerman in 1908, but he does demonstrate the frustration that many liberal supporters felt after the limited achievements of the Lloyd George coalition of 1981–22 and failure to adopt a coherent policy by the Liberals since then. He also cites the problem of divisions within the Liberals since the split between Asquith and Lloyd George in 1916. He correctly sees a division between those sympathetic towards the Labour Party's programme and those opposed to it and those pre-occupied with the Liberals' great cause of the nineteenth century – **free trade**. He does not mention the ongoing division between the reunited Liberal leaders, Asquith and Lloyd George, but the whole tone of the source describes a party no longer capable of unity and therefore of little use in the cause of social improvement to which Hobhouse was committed.

c) Source A suggests that the Liberals themselves were to blame for their decline due to their divisions during the First World War which were perpetuated by the leaders for too long afterwards and due to the perceived personal and political failings of Lloyd George. The source therefore largely refutes the assertion in the statement.

Source B on the other hand highlights the increasing moderation of the Labour position, as well as that of the Conservative Party, which led voters to regarding the Liberal Party as largely superfluous in the battle between Labour and the Conservatives. The source does suggest that the moderation of the Conservative Party under Baldwin had as much to do with the obsolescence of the Liberals as that of the Labour Party under Henderson.

In addition to the evidence contained in the sources, the Labour Party did succeed in replacing the Liberals as an 'alternative' to the Conservatives in many ways between 1918 and 1939. The Labour Party emerged from the First World War unified and with some experience of government, in contrast to the divided Liberals and were therefore able to act as the main opposition to the coalition government with 63 seats compared to Asquith's 28. They sought to capitalise on the full enfranchisement of the male working class by offering a distinctive and clearly defined political programme which included commitments to avowedly socialist policies such as **nationalisation**. Many workers had been politicised by their experiences during the war and membership of trade unions had more than doubled, thus providing the Labour Party with the funds necessary to mount a national challenge for government. Furthermore, when the Labour Party succeeded in forming governments in 1924 and 1929, Ramsay MacDonald was careful to follow a moderate course, which was designed to attract as wide electoral support as possible. Even after the electoral disaster of 1931 the party was keen to avoid extremism, even changing leaders in 1935 when George Lansbury advocated adopting a pacifist approach. It seems clear that Labour was keen to offer itself as an alternative to Conservatism rather than as a radical pressure group.

It is also clear that at a number of crucial moments, the Liberal leadership made tactical errors which allowed the Labour Party to gain valuable political experience. Most crucially in 1923, when Baldwin's party lost their majority, Asquith could have formed a minority Liberal government if he had been prepared to work with Lloyd George. Instead he chose to use his party's support to allow Labour to form their first minority government and thus demonstrate their fitness to govern. As a consequence, many of the middle-class Liberal supporters were outraged by Asquith's act and deserted to support the Conservatives in the 1924 election. By 1931 the party had become so demoralised that most Liberals leapt at the chance of joining the National Government despite clear dominance of the Conservatives, which led to the adoption of policies which caused the Liberals to split again. By 1935, the party was reduced to 20 MPs and continued to decline until 1939.

In conclusion, therefore, the decline of the Liberals was partly caused by the previous failings of the party and its leaders and the moderation of both the Conservatives and Labour, but chiefly by the emergence of the Labour Party which was aided by the miscalculations and maladroitness of the Liberal leaders in the crucial years of three-party politics.

QUESTIONS WITHOUT WORKED ANSWERS (AQA)

a) **Study source A. Explain what is meant by the reference in the source to 'the election of 1924, [which] had encouraged those voters who 'vote for a Government' to turn away from the Liberals'.** (3 marks)

b) **Study sources A and C. Compare the sources' judgement of the leadership of the Liberal Party in causing the decline of the party.** (7 marks)

c) **Refer to all the sources and use your own knowledge. Was the decline of the Liberal Party unavoidable after 1918?** (15 marks)

---

2. The press and the General Strike (OCR)

Source A: The *Daily Mail* article that caused the printers to strike prematurely, 3 May 1926.

A General Strike is not an industrial dispute. It is a revolutionary movement intended to inflict suffering upon the great mass of innocent persons in the community and thereby to put forcible constraint upon the Government. It is a movement which can only succeed by destroying the Government and subverting the rights and liberties of the people.

Source B: *The British Worker* responds to this accusation, 8 May 1926.

There is as far as the trade union movement is concerned, no 'attack upon the community'. There is no 'challenge to the Constitution'. The workers have exercised their legal and long-established right of withholding their labour, in order to protect the miners against a degradation of their standard of life, which is a menace to the whole world of labour.

Source C: From *The British Gazette*, 5 May 1926.

The general strike is in operation, expressing in no uncertain terms a direct challenge to ordered government . . . an effort to force upon some 42,000,000 British citizens the will of less than 4,000,000 others engaged in the vital services of the country.

Nearly all the newspapers have been silenced by violent concerted action . . . The Government have, therefore, decided not only to use broadcasting for spreading information, but to bring out a paper of their own on a sufficient scale to carry full and timely news throughout all parts of the country.

The *British Gazette* is run without profit on the authority and if necessary, at the expense of the Government. It begins necessarily on a small scale, and its first issue cannot exceed 700,000 copies. It is proposed, however, to use the unlimited resources of the State, with the assistance of all loyal persons, to raise the circulation day after day until it provides sure and sufficient means of information and a guide for action for all British citizens.

Source D: The parliamentary secretary at the Admiralty, J.C.C. Davidson on Winston Churchill's role during the General Strike.

Winston is really a most remarkable creature. His energy is boundless and he ran entirely on his own lines. Whether it was right or wrong he desired to produce a newspaper rather than a news-sheet. He, in fact, conceived that the *British Gazette* should be a better newspaper than any of the great journals whose operations had been temporarily suspended. I, on the other hand, had laid it down as rule absolute and unchangeable that no official news should appear which was not true, and that propaganda as such should be no part of the activities of His Majesty's Government. Winston, after a great fight, agreed to be blue-pencilled* and the blue pencil was seldom idle.

QUESTIONS WITH WORKED ANSWERS

a) **Study Source A. From this source and your own knowledge, explain why this article triggered the general strike in 1926.** **(10 marks)**

b) **Study source C. Assess the value of this source as evidence of the Government's attitude towards the general strike.** **(25 marks)**

c) **Study sources A and B. How effectively does source B refute the allegations in Source A regarding the legality of the general strike?** **(25 marks)**

d) **Study all the sources. Using all these sources and your own knowledge, explain how far you agree with the view that 'the voice of the government predominated and thus presented the strike as a challenge to the constitution'.** **(60 marks)**

(Total: 120 marks)

ANSWERS

a)   The source, an editorial article from the *Daily Mail*, portrays a general strike as an attack on the Government and 'the rights and liberties of the people', rather than merely an economic weapon to force the mine-owners to withdraw their proposed wage cuts. Such an attack was bound to offend the strongly unionised printers, even at the notoriously right-wing *Daily Mail*, and they refused to print the edition of the paper containing it. When the government heard that this had happened they assumed the general strike had begun and broke off negotiations with the TUC,

*blue-pencilled – censored

who knew nothing of the incident. It has been suggested that the paper's editor was encouraged by a member of the cabinet, possibly Winston Churchill, to prepare the editorial, knowing that it would provoke such a reaction and thus force the Prime Minister, Stanley Baldwin, into a confrontation with the unions which he, unlike the right-wingers like Churchill in the cabinet, was keen to avoid.

b) The publication of the *British Gazette* during the nine days of the General Strike in 1926 demonstrated how seriously the Conservative government regarded the strike as a threat to their position. Once a General Strike had been declared, Baldwin's government had no intention of negotiating with either the miners or the TUC and concentrated instead on maintaining its control over the nation. As the bulk of the newspapers in Britain were severely affected by the strike of their printers and distributors' drivers, there was a danger of panic, due to the lack of news. Baldwin therefore allowed the Chancellor, Winston Churchill, who had much earlier experience in journalism, to set up and edit a government newspaper to encourage those who were opposed to the TUC's tactics. The TUC was forced to respond with the *British Worker*.

The *British Gazette* proclaimed itself the official government broadsheet, but, in fact, under Churchill, it was far more aggressive in its attitude towards the General Strike, denouncing the strikers as 'the enemy' and calling for 'unconditional surrender' which contrasted sharply with the more measured and moderate broadcasts of Stanley Baldwin during the crisis, in particular his broadcast of 8 May when he promised to 'secure even justice'. Therefore one should not read too much of the attitude of the government as a whole into the paper's reports.

c) Source A from the *Daily Mail*, regards the proposed General Strike as an illegal attempt at revolution as it attempted to force the government and the British people to accept a change in industrial policy. Source B replies to this directly by simply denying that there is any intention to challenge the political system in Britain, merely that workers were practising a 'legal and long-standing right' and were protecting the 'whole world of labour'. Whilst this is quite an effective counter argument, the *British Worker* does appear to claim that they are acting in the interest of the trade union cause, and the miners in particular, rather than the community as a whole. In this way, it could be said that the description of the General Strike as a 'movement' aimed against he 'great mass of innocent persons' is not fully refuted. Second, and more importantly, the statement in source B that the General Strike is the exercise of a 'legal' right, is open to question, as the right of workers directly involved in an industrial dispute to withdraw their labour was certainly recognised, but the position of those in other industries who struck in sympathy was much less clear and there was considerable debate during the nine days over the legal position of the TUC. In both these ways therefore, the willingness of the *British Worker* to debate the legal nature of the strike allowed the government to exploit a very effective weakness in the TUC's position and to allow the government to garner sympathy for their resolute action in resisting the strikers' demands.

d) The view of the strike as a challenge to the constitution was already endorsed by newspapers such as the *Daily Mail*, as seen in source A. The majority of white-collar workers and a significant proportion of blue-collar workers were opposed to the idea of a General Strike and they were receptive to the views put out by the *British Gazette* such as those in source C. The *British Gazette*, published using the full resources of the government, including the involvement of the civil service, as shown in Source D, was a much fuller newspaper than any other available during the nine days of the strike. The *British Worker* by contrast was constrained by the limited funds of the TUC and by the government's insistence that it was barred from giving ordinary news or making propaganda. If a member of the public, uncommitted to either side of the dispute wished to see a weather forecast for example, he or she would have to buy the *British Gazette* and thus to read the government's interpretation of the strike. Similarly, the government was able to use its influence over the BBC to suppress news it did not wish to be broadcast, although it did not go so far as to dictate to the company how the rest of the news was presented.

The government therefore had a number of advantages compared to the TUC. First, they could portray their position as that of the democratically elected representatives of the whole country and the TUC as a selfishly interested minority attempting to 'hold the country to ransom'. Second, it had an effective monopoly of the chief broadcasting organs, which it used to ensure that its voice did prevail, apart from among the strikers themselves, with whom it used other methods to coerce. It is certainly true that it used these advantages to good effect, with Davidson careful to ensure that Churchill's presentation of the official news did not too blatantly appear as a government propaganda sheet, and the Cabinet using Parliament to ensure its views were associated with the seat of British democracy, where it found allies on the Liberal benches. In this way, the TUC were not able to effectively counter the government's description of the strike, either in scale of distribution, range of support or strength of argument and the government view of the strike prevailed among those not strongly committed to the trade union cause.

QUESTIONS WITHOUT WORKED ANSWERS (OCR)

a) Study Source A. From this source and from your own knowledge, explain why the TUC began a General Strike on 4 May 1926. **(10 marks)**

b) Study source D. How reliable is this source in describing the behaviour of Winston Churchill during the General Strike? **(25 marks)**

c) Study sources B and C. Explain the reasons why source B and C differ in their views of the legality of the General Strike? **(25 marks)**

d) Study all the sources. Using all these sources and your own knowledge, explain why the General Strike divided Britain during the 'nine days' of 1926. **(60)**

(Total: 120 marks)

3. British society between the wars, 1919–39 (EDEXCEL)

Source 1: From *The Road to Wigan Pier*, by George Orwell published in 1937.

A Labour Exchange Officer told me that to get at the real number of people *living on* (not drawing) the dole, you have got to multiply the official figures by something over three. This alone brings the number of unemployed to round about six millions. But in addition, there are numbers of people who are in work, but who, from a financial point of view, might equally well be unemployed, because they are not drawing anything that can be described as a living wage. Allow for these and for their dependants, throw in as before the old-age pensioners, the destitute and other nondescripts, and you get an *underfed* population of well over ten millions.

QUESTIONS WITH WORKED ANSWERS

Study Source 1 and answer questions (a) to (c) which follow:

a) What does this source suggest about the impact of the Depression
    in Britain in the 1930s?   (10 marks)
b) How did the government limit expenditure between 1931 and 1939? (14 marks)
c) Was the whole of Britain equally affected by the Depression?   (36 marks)

(Total: 60 marks)

a) Source 1 certainly seems to suggest that the Depression was more widely felt by the people of Britain than the unemployment figures alone can indicate. Orwell takes the unemployment figures and then attempts to roughly calculate the numbers of those dependent on the dole, that is, wives, dependent children and older family members. He thus arrives at a figure of those living on the dole of six million. As the threat of unemployment caused many wages to be forced down, the number of those living on a wage equivalent to the dole and their dependents, plus those who cannot or will not work adds up to a further four million, leaving a figure of ten million underfed directly or indirectly as a result of the Depression in Britain. As the population of the country at the time of the Depression was approximately 50 million, this meant that over a fifth of the population was suffering acute destitution during this period.

b) Faced with the run on the pound in summer 1931, the Labour leadership had proposed expenditure cuts of £78.5 million, to satisfy the conditions set by financiers in order to secure a loan. The Cabinet had split on this question and the Labour leader, Ramsay MacDonald, had been persuaded by the king to establish a National Government made up of Labour, Liberal and Conservative ministers. This new government had pushed through expenditure cuts, which saw a 10 per cent reduction in the level of unemployment benefit and cuts in the pay of the civil service, teachers, the police and the armed services between 5 and 15 per cent. In the next few years expenditure was further restricted as housing, school and road building schemes were practically halted, and the government put pressure (although not always successfully) on local authorities to do the same.

In 1931, the unemployed received 26 weeks benefit, after which time they received 'transitional payments' set by the Public Assistance Committee (PAC) of the local authority, which were set after a Means Test which measured a family's sources of income. In 1934, the government established a national Unemployed Assistance Board (UAB) which set a uniform rate of transitional payment and operated a standardised Means Test. As a result of this, some long-term unemployed received a lower payment from the UAB than they had from their PAC. The government did raise the level of payment in 1937 however, once the Depression was clearly over.

In the subsequent years of peace, the government refused to follow the examples of Roosevelt's USA and Hitler's Germany and embark on large scale public works schemes to tackle unemployment, preferring to maintain a balanced budget to prevent any further financial crises. The Special Areas Act of 1934 demonstrated this reluctance to spend as the newly appointed (and unpaid) Commissioners only had £2 million at their disposal. The government chose instead to introduce protective tariffs and to keep interest rates down to 2 per cent and to await the eventual improvement of the trade cycle which was evident as early as 1934.

c)   Certainly there was great hardship in some parts of British society as recorded by writers such as George Orwell, J.B. Priestley and Walter Greenwood. The physical effects of living on the dole, with the need to rely on cheap foodstuffs and avoid all luxuries were bad enough, but added to this were the mental effects of enforced idleness. The urban communities of South Wales, the North and the Clyde were strongly influenced by non-conformist traditions which spoke of the nobility of labour and the need to maintain personal respectability. Once the individual was unemployed, an entire family would face mild, but persistent social humiliation as a consequence. Furthermore, there is startling evidence as to the consequences of poor diets on the families of the unemployed. Infant mortality, measured as the number of deaths before the age of one per thousand live births, was significantly higher in areas of high unemployment. The average figure for England and Wales in 1935 was 57, but in affluent Surrey it was as low as 41. By contrast in the north of England it was 68, and 92 in Sunderland. The highest figure recorded that year was in that symbol of the depressed areas, Jarrow, famous as 'the town that was murdered', where the figure was an appalling 114, twice the national average.

On the other hand, the effect of the Depression was to drive prices down, and for the majority who kept their jobs, this was an age of increasing affluence. As a whole, British society in the 1930s was more prosperous and healthier than ever before. Consumer products were more widely available, and as interest rates were low, credit was cheap. These products improved the lifestyle of many, especially women, as they required the housewife to spend less time carrying out housework. The 1930s also saw a housing boom, as cheap mortgages, due to low interest rates and cheap building costs allowed many to own their own homes for the first time, or to afford to move to more agreeable surroundings in the newly expanding suburbs.

Certainly most communities faced some level of hardship, with government employees undergoing pay cuts as a result of the emergency budget of 1931, wages being forced down and imported goods increasing in price after the value of the pound fell. However, compared to those suffering the personal agonies of long-term unemployment, the operation of the Means Test and the 'help' of the Public Assistance Committees or the Unemployed Assistance Board, this can hardly be described as serious hardship. That term must, with any degree of justice, be applied to communities such as South Wales and the North-East where the daily struggle for survival left such a legacy that its images dominated British social policy for decades to come. Meanwhile, the lower prices meant that those in stable jobs or employed by the newer industries such as electrical goods, chemicals or the motor industry found that they could afford a standard of living much better than that enjoyed by their parents and they supported those political groups who promised to protect this new prosperity, even at the cost of harsher standards for the unemployed. In this way, Britain became a more divided nation politically as well as socially during and immediately after the Depression.

QUESTIONS WITHOUT WORKED ANSWERS

Study Source 1

a)   Why, according to source 1, does the official unemployment figure not reveal the true extent of the impact of the Depression?   **(10 marks)**

b)   What, in the years 1931–39, did the National Government do to attempt to alleviate the impact of the depression?   **(14 marks)**

c)   Why was there no significant challenge to the National Government between 1931 and 1939, despite the experience of the Depression?   **(36 marks)**

(Total: 60 marks)

Part 4: Historical skills

👑 1. Statistical analysis

Statistics are notoriously easy to distort, and many exam questions, text books and contemporary politicians will often select a statistic in order to force us into agreeing with a particular interpretation. The only solution to this crude manipulation is to recognise that statistics in general, and economic statistics in particular, can be confusing, contradictory and unclear. This exercise, therefore, asks you to analyse a series of statistical tables on a range of issues relating to life in the 1930s. There are some questions for each table, to help you understand the table, and others at the end to encourage you to compare the tables to draw conclusions.

1. What were the effects of these price and wage fluctuations on (see Table 4.4):

    a) The employed?
    b) The unemployed?

2. How do Tables 4.5 and 4.6 challenge traditional views of life during the depression?

3. In which years did the proportion of unemployed exceed the inter-war average? (See Table 4.7.)

4. Which areas suffered the greatest increases in unemployment between 1929 and 1932?

5. Which areas had recovered the quickest from the depression?

Table 4.4 *Indices of wages, prices and earnings, 1920–38 (1930 = 100)*

	Weekly wages	Prices	Annual real wages
1920	143.7	157.6	92.2
1921	134.6	143.0	94.1
1922	107.9	115.8	93.2
1923	100.0	110.1	90.8
1924	101.5	110.8	91.6
1925	102.2	111.4	91.7
1926	99.3	108.9	91.2
1927	101.5	106.0	95.8
1928	101.1	105.1	95.2
1929	100.4	103.8	96.7
1930	100.0	100.0	100.0
1931	98.2	93.4	105.1
1932	96.3	91.1	105.7
1933	95.3	88.6	107.6
1934	96.4	89.2	108.1
1935	98.0	90.5	108.3
1936	100.2	93.0	107.7
1937	102.8	97.5	105.4
1938	106.3	98.7	107.7

Table 4.5 **Percentages of domestic electric usage, 1932–38**

	Homes connected to electricity supply	Cookers	Irons	Water heaters	Wash boilers	Fridges
1932	31.8	4.9	–	–	–	–
1933	49.2	6.1	56.4	1.2	0.9	–
1934	49.3	9.3	–	1.9	1.4	–
1935	54.5	11.3	–	3.1	2.0	–
1936	57.8	13.4	70.9	3.8	2.4	2.3
1937	61.77	15.4	–	4.8	2.9	–
1938	65.39	16.9	–	5.6	3.5	2.4

Table 4.6 **Measures of domestic consumption, 1930–38**

	Radio licences per 1,000 families	Private motor cars	Telephone rentals
1930	37.1	1,177,900	514,000
1931	44.5	1,192,900	551,000
1932	50.0	1,236,000	580,000
1933	56.1	1,313,300	609,000
1934	60.7	1,420,500	667,000
1935	64.4	1,592,400	757,000
1936	68.3	1,726,000	882,000
1937	–	1,890,400	1,024,000
1938	–	2,045,400	1,143,000

Table 4.7 **British unemployment figures, 1921–38**

	Employed (1,000s)	Unemployed (1,000s)	Unemployed (%)
1921	15,879	2,212	12.2
1922	15,847	1,909	10.8
1923	16,068	1,567	8.9
1924	16,332	1,404	7.9
1925	16,531	1,559	8.6
1926	16,529	1,759	9.6
1927	17,060	1,373	7.4
1928	17,123	1,536	8.2
1929	17,392	1,503	8.0
1930	17,016	2,379	12.3
1931	16,554	3,252	16.4
1932	16,644	3,400	17.0
1933	17,018	3,087	15.4
1934	17,550	2,609	12.9
1935	17,890	2,437	12.0
1936	18,513	2,100	10.2
1937	19,196	1,776	8.5
1938	19,243	2,164	10.1

Table 4.8 **Regional unemployment of insured workers, 1929–37 (in percentages)**

	1929	1932	1937
London and South-East England	5.6	13.7	6.4
South-West England	8.1	17.1	7.8
Midlands	9.3	20.1	7.2
North England	13.5	27.1	13.8
Wales	19.3	36.5	22.3
Scotland	12.1	27.7	15.9
Northern Ireland	15.1	27.2	23.6
Great Britain	**10.5**	**22.5**	**10.8**

Table 4.9 **Population movement, 1931–38**

	1931	1938	Increase/ decrease (%)
Great Britain	44,795,000	46,208,000	3.2
Greater London	8,204,000	8,700,000	6
Rest of South-East	5,274,000	5,790,000	9.8
Northumberland/Durham	2,243,000	2,204,000	−1.7
West Midlands	4,534,000	4,751,000	4.8
South Wales	1,898,000	1,783,000	−6.1
Rest of Wales	696,000	683,000	−1.9
Scotland	4,843,000	4,993,000	3.1

Table 4.10 **Unemployment in the West Midlands, 1931–38**

Labour exchange areas	Unemployment rate (%)								
	1931	1932	1933	1934	1935	1936	1937	1938	8 year average
Dudley	38.8	34.6	21.7	21.2	18.2	13.8	9.3	14.8	21.6
West Bromwich	28.6	27.1	21.6	12.3	11.3	7.9	5.2	9.4	15.4
Sutton Coldfield	27.7	23.3	22.9	12.3	10.4	7.3	6.2	7.1	14.6
Wolverhampton	27.0	25.0	21.8	16.1	14.8	11.2	7.2	10.6	16.7
Stourbridge	27.2	26.5	24.3	17.4	15.4	12.4	11.0	14.7	18.6
Birmingham	17.7	15.3	12.1	8.1	6.6	5.2	4.3	7.7	9.6

6. How far does Table 4.8 explain the population movement described in Table 4.9?

7. Do the statistics in Table 4.10 demonstrate that unemployment was evenly spread across each region?

8. Research to find similar statistics for the distribution of unemployment in your local area in this period.

9. Suggest why such great regional variation as in Table 4.10 occurred.

10. To what extent can the figures in Table 4.11 be explained by the regional impact of the depression?

Table 4.11 **Infant mortality by regions (number of infants under one year dying per 1,000 live births)**

	1935
England and Wales	57
Scotland	76.8
Surrey	41
Greater London	51
Midlands	59
North England	68
Wales	63
County Durham	72
Sunderland	92
Jarrow	114

General questions on the tables

1. Using only the statistics contained in these tables, assess the relative impact of the Depression on the population, looking at the following categories:

   a) Employed
   b) Unemployed
   c) Regions of Britain

2. Research further to find similar statistics for:

   d) Men and women
   e) Different age groups
   f) Insured and uninsured workers

3. What conclusions can you draw on the impact of the Depression from these?

4. Research to find comparative statistics for the impact of the Depression on:

   g) France
   h) Germany
   i) USA
   j) Japan
   k) USSR

5. How serious does the Depression in Britain seem when compared to the other major industrialised countries of the world?

Chapter 5

British Foreign Policy
Between the Wars,
1918–1939

This chapter is concerned with Britain's relations with other powers in the period between the wars. It was a period in which fear of another terrible world war weighed heavily on the minds of every statesman, yet which ended with Britain declaring war once again on Germany. Britain also faced problems from her colonies, who were increasingly impatient for greater autonomy, and even from parts of the United Kingdom, as the southern Irish effectively set up their own government and went to war with Britain. That Britain had to face these challenges at a time of industrial depression and social hardship, may explain why she was reluctant to confront aggression even when it threatened her interests.

 ## Historical background

Britain's world position in 1919
The Versailles Treaty
The principles of Britain's foreign
    policy after 1919
The Empire
Foreign policy in the 1920s
Foreign policy after 1930

a) Japan
b) Germany
c) Italy and the Abyssinian crisis

The reoccupation of the Rhineland,
    1936
The Spanish Civil War 1936–39
Neville Chamberlain's foreign
    policy
The Anschluss with Austria, 1938
Czechoslovakia and the Munich
    crisis
The uneasy peace – September
    1938–March 1939
The end of Czechoslovakia
The Polish crisis
Anglo-Soviet relations
The outbreak of war

Essays

1. The Treaty of Versailles
2. Ireland
3. British foreign policy in the 1920s
4. British imperial policy
5. British responses to aggression in the
    1930s
6. Relations with Germany after 1933
7. Chamberlain and the Munich
    Agreement
8. The outbreak of war
9. British foreign policy in the 1930s

Sources

1. Anglo-Russian relations in the 1920s
2. Neville Chamberlain and
    appeasement
3. Imperial defence in the inter-war
    years

Historical skills

1. Investigation of the foreign policy
    options available to the British
    government through a role play

Chronology

1918	November – Armistice Day
1919	The Peace Treaties with the Central Powers signed in Paris
	League of Nations established
	Amritsar Massacre
	Government of India Act
1922	Washington Naval Accord
	Chanak crisis
	Mussolini becomes Italian Prime Minister
1923	France occupies Ruhr
1924	Diplomatic relations established with Soviet Union
	Dawes Plan
1925	Treaty of Locarno
1929	Young Plan
	Wall Street Crash
1930	Statute of Westminster
1931	Japan invades Manchuria
1932	Imperial Conference, Ottawa
1933	Hitler appointed Chancellor of Germany
	Germany leaves League of Nations
1935	Government of India Act
	Stresa front agreed
	Anglo-German Naval Agreement
	Italy invades Abyssinia
	Hoare–Laval Pact exposed by British Press
1936	Germany re-occupies the Rhineland
	Military rebellion leads to Spanish Civil War
	Arab rebellion in Palestine
1937	Neville Chamberlain becomes British Prime Minister
1938	Germany occupies Austria
	Chamberlain visits Germany to negotiate the Czech crisis
	Munich Agreement signed
	'Kristallnacht' in Germany
1939	Germany occupies Bohemia and Moravia
	Britain and France give guarantees to Poland
	Nazi–Soviet non-aggression pact signed
	Germany invades Poland, Britain and France declare war

Part 1: Historical background

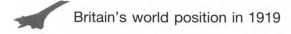 Britain's world position in 1919

Britain's world position appeared secure in 1919:

- Germany had been defeated
- The Imperial German Navy had been dismantled
- The German Army was limited to 100,000 men
- With the acquisition of German East Africa, the Cameroons and Palestine, Jordan and Iraq, the British Empire had reached its greatest size
- France had been weakened by her huge losses and remained an ally
- Russia was distracted by civil war and revolution
- The USA had retreated into isolation
- Britain was still on good terms with Japan

But the scale of Britain's victory was limited by:

1. The financial cost of the war (the National Debt had increased elevenfold) and the huge debts to the USA.
2. With such financial difficulties, the British government were reluctant to support French demands on Germany, but were keen to regain the $2,472 million owed to the British by Russia.
3. As Japan become more aggressive towards USA, Britain was unable to maintain her naval rivalry.

Figure 5.1: *'History retold'*

HISTORY RETOLD.

Table 5.1 **Prime Ministers and Foreign Secretaries, 1918–39**

Date	Government	Prime Minister	Foreign Secretary
1918–22	Coalition	David Lloyd George	Marquess Curzon
1922–23	Conservative	Andrew Bonar Law/ Stanley Baldwin	Marquess Curzon
1924	Labour	Ramsay MacDonald	Ramsay MacDonald
1924–29	Conservative	Stanley Baldwin	Austen Chamberlain
1929–31	Labour	Ramsay MacDonald	Arthur Henderson
1931–35	National	Ramsay MacDonald	John Simon
1935	National		Samuel Hoare
1935–38	National	Stanley Baldwin/ Neville Chamberlain	Anthony Eden
1938–40	National	Neville Chamberlain	Earl of Halifax

4. The British Empire began to show signs of strain as the Dominions called for self-government and India and Ireland were swept by nationalist discontent.
5. The British public were exhausted by four years of war, and increasingly blamed traditional diplomacy for what was increasingly seen as a waste of young lives. In such an atmosphere calls for disarmament and even pacifism grew stronger. With more effective media and a wider electorate, their views mattered as well.

 ## The Versailles Treaty

The peace conference in Paris held from 18 January 1919 to 20 January 1920 was dominated by three individuals:

Woodrow Wilson (President of the United States and author of the '14 points')
Georges Clemenceau (Prime Minister of France)
David Lloyd George (newly re-elected Prime Minister of the United Kingdom)

Peace Treaties were eventually signed between the allies and all the defeated central powers:

The Treaty of Versailles was signed with Germany
The Treaty of St Germain was signed with Austria
The Treaty of Trianon was signed with Hungary
The Treaty of Neuilly was signed with Bulgaria
The Treaty of Sèvres was signed with Turkey

Lloyd George's main concern was to achieve a lasting peace which would allow Europe to recover from the economic and emotional damage of what was then, the bloodiest war in history. Britain wanted to punish Germany, but not so harshly that it hindered her recovery or encouraged her people to turn to Communism, which was at the time, posing a very real threat to democracy in Europe. Lloyd George therefore found himself at odds with Clemenceau who wanted Germany reduced in strength so that she could never invade France again. The resulting Treaty of Versailles was a compromise:

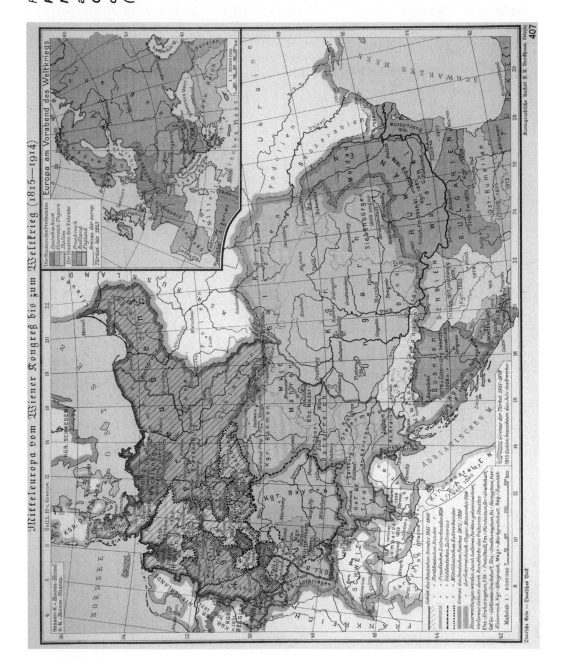

Figure 5.2a

**Pre-Versailles Europe:
Map of middle Europe
after the Vienna
Congress until the start
of the First World War
(1815–1914)**

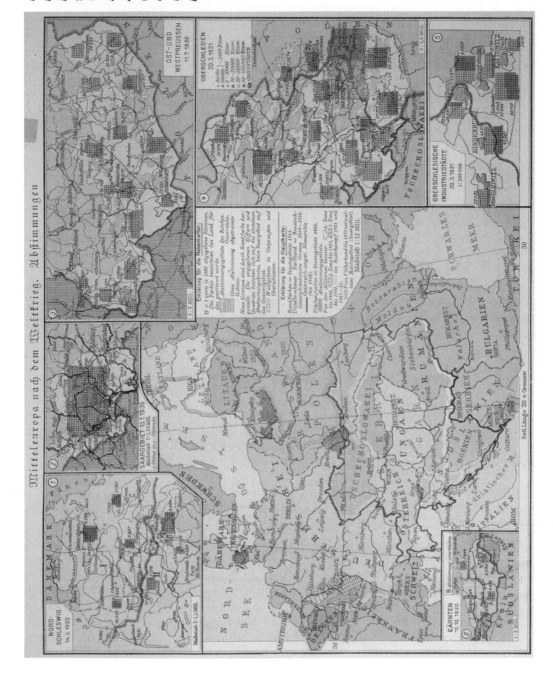

Figure 5.2b
Post-Versailles Europe: Europe at the end of the First World War. Shaded areas show Abstimmungsgebiete (those areas to be decided upon by a referendum of the population)

Main Terms of the Treaty of Versailles

A League of Nations was set up to solve future international disputes.

Germany accepted responsibility for having started the war deliberately.

Germany had to pay damages for the war ('reparations') which were eventually fixed at £6,600,000,000 (plus interest).

Germany was forbidden from unifying with Austria.

Germany was deprived of all her overseas colonial possessions.

The following German territory was lost:

Alsace and Lorraine (annexed in 1871)	to France
Eupen and Malmedy	to Belgium
Memel	to Lithuania
Northern Schleswig	to Denmark
Poznan and parts of East Prussia	to Poland
Danzig	became a 'free city', administered by the League of Nations

The area of Germany west of the Rhine was placed under Allied occupation for 15 years and Germany agreed not to station troops there.

The Saar coal field area was to be controlled by the League of Nations.

Despite Britain's efforts, Germany resented the treaty hugely. The loss of four million people from the German state, in particular incensed them. One of the guiding principles of the treaty had been that of 'self-determination' for the peoples of Europe, yet it seemed that this was ignored in Germany's case. As Lloyd George warned himself, nothing was more likely to cause a future war 'than that the German people should be surrounded by a number of smaller states, each of them containing large numbers of Germans, all clamouring for reunion'. It was to be a constant stumbling block in the search for peace after 1919 and one which Hitler was able to effectively exploit to destroy the Versailles settlement.

 ## The principles of Britain's foreign policy after 1919

Following the Treaty of Versailles, Britain's chief priority was to maintain the peace which had allowed it to prosper for most of the nineteenth century. The huge loss of life, the extent of injury and social dislocation endured by Britain and her Empire in the First World War was to be avoided at all costs. Therefore, British foreign policy was based on the following principles:

a) To maintain peace if at all possible, as long as British interests were not jeopardised.

b) Preserving the current settlement in Europe, which although unsatisfactory in many ways, did serve the traditional British interest of preventing one country from dominating the continent.

c) Avoiding commitments, such as military alliances with other European countries. It was widely felt Britain had been dragged into the First World War by her entente with France and that Britain would avoid involvement in future wars and would have the freedom to pursue her interests without such arrangements in the future. Britain was, however, not averse to France and the smaller countries of Europe establishing and maintaining alliances. In fact, Britain often encouraged this, as such alliances would obviate the need for Britain to have to protect these countries, as she had done with Belgium in 1914.

d) Although America never ratified the Paris peace treaties and remained outside the League of Nations, Britain was determined to maintain good relations with the USA. Her financial and industrial aid had been essential in achieving final victory and Britain knew that trade with the USA would be paramount while the shattered economies of Europe rebuilt themselves. Britain was also aware that she was now heavily in debt to the USA and would need to achieve a settlement which would not be too crippling to her finances especially when the expected post-war boom proved so short-lived. Britain was also aware of just how exposed her Far Eastern possessions were and needed US co-operation to maintain these. Although the USA was certainly not keen to prop up the British Empire, she was far more concerned by the rise of an aggressive Japan and was, therefore prepared, albeit reluctantly, to support Britain as a bulwark against Japanese expansion.

e) Britain now had a large scattered Empire to defend and she needed to limit expenditure on home defence in order to protect and police it. The relative decline of the British economy also meant that funds for defence were short, especially as the state continued to take more responsibility for the alleviation of poverty during this period.

f) As a consequence, Britain was keen to promote global disarmament after the war. This would reduce expenditure, whilst promoting stability in Europe. Disarmament was popular with the voters as well, as the arms race before 1914 was felt to have contributed to the outbreak of the war. Britain abolished conscription in 1920 and military expenditure dropped from £692 million in 1919–20 to £115 million in 1921–22.

Given these priorities, it was therefore unsurprising that Britain chose to follow a policy of **appeasement** towards the other Great Powers between the wars. This meant that Britain would seek to find a compromise in disputes with other powers, in order to avoid the expense of war. The first most significant example of this was in Britain's handling of Turkey. The Turks, in the Treaty of Sèvres had been forced to accept Greek control of Smyrna on the Turkish mainland. Turkish anger had led to the downfall of the last Sultan and his replacement by the Nationalist general, Mustafa Kemal. When the Turks expelled the Greeks, Britain sought a settlement rather than fighting to maintain the Sèvres settlement. The Treaty of Lausanne of 1923 accepted the Turkish achievement, while maintaining that element of Sèvres that suited Britain, the freedom of passage through the Straits of Constantinople.

If **appeasement** meant altering the Versailles settlement, Britain was clearly prepared to do so, as long as her interests were not challenged, nor her strategic position weakened. The shadow of the First World War with its unprecedented loss of young life constantly influenced public opinion though and thereby politicians between the wars took a much a narrower view of British interests than before 1914. This ultimately and tragically led Britain to make a series of tactical blunders in her handling of the resurgent Germany and Italy which contributed to the outbreak of the Second World War.

 The Empire

As a result of the Versailles settlement, the British Empire dramatically expanded in size. Britain was, however, no longer in a position to be able to maintain it as she had done before the war. Strategically, the British Empire remained very difficult to defend, especially in the face of a threat of a war from more than one European country or from an Asian country. Many of Britain's possessions were distant and dependent on the Royal Navy's ability to defend these. For that reason, bases such as Singapore and Hong Kong were vital as were the passages through the Straits of Gibraltar and the Suez Canal. Once Britain found herself facing two potential aggressors in Europe and one in Asia, it soon became clear that defending all the Empire would be almost impossible in these circumstances.

Perhaps most seriously of all, however, in an age of democracy, the British public were becoming, not disillusioned, but rather disinterested in the British Empire. During the 1920s and the 1930s, national politics appeared to revolve around social questions, most especially poverty and unemployment. The public were becoming increasingly impatient with the cost of maintaining an Empire that no longer seemed to appreciate the benefits of colonial rule, while there were pressing demands for government action in the United Kingdom. To reflect that, by 1933 only 10.5 per cent of public funds were being spent on defence, while 46.6 per cent was being spent on the social services.

Foreign policy in the 1920s

After the peace conferences, France continued to call for a formal alliance with Britain to guarantee its frontiers as established at Versailles, but without US involvement, and with its Imperial commitments, Britain was reluctant to agree, and vetoed a treaty of mutual assistance in 1923, leaving France to invade the German industrial Ruhr alone in a dispute over the payment of German war reparations. Ramsay MacDonald worked hard to achieve a settlement of this dispute, the most dangerous of the 1920s, but having done so he lost office and the incoming Conservatives dropped McDonald's idea of compulsory arbitration for international disputes known as the 'Geneva Protocol'.

It was left to the British Foreign Secretary after the 1924 general election, Austen Chamberlain, to work directly with Briand and Stresemann, the French and German foreign ministers, to achieve a settlement. In December 1925, the Locarno Treaty was signed in which the French, Germans and Belgians pledged to respect one another's borders, with guarantees supplied by Britain and Italy.

The years 1925–29 are often referred to as 'The Locarno Honeymoon' and culminated in the removal of British and French troops from the demilitarised Rhineland area of Germany, but:

1. The Locarno Treaty gave no guarantees to Germany's eastern neighbours and Chamberlain's comments that the Polish corridor was territory 'for which no British government ever will or ever can risk the bones of a British Grenadier' implied that Germany could be allowed to revise the Versailles borders there.
2. The League of Nations was not involved in the Locarno and post-Locarno agreements at all – demonstrating the revival of traditional diplomacy and the helplessness of the League without the willing co-operation of its leading members.
3. The financial stability of Europe was, as a consequence of allied borrowing during the First World War and the Dawes and Young Plans, dependent on the stability of the US economy. If that economy should suffer a setback, as it did in October 1929, the recovery of Europe would be severely retarded, with the consequent threat of social unrest and political extremism.

 Foreign policy after 1930

a) JAPAN

Although the Anglo–Japanese alliance remained intact after the first World War, Japan had emerged in a much strengthened position. It was apparently secure in its domination of northern China and hence a potential threat to Britain's interests in the rest of the country. Most worrying, however, was the extent of Japanese naval power. Very quickly, Japan came to represent a threat to Britain's Far Eastern position.

Table 5.2 **Defence expenditure among the Great Powers (in millions of dollars)**

	UK	Germany	France	USSR	Italy	USA	Japan
1930	512	162	498	722	266	699	218
1933	333	452	524	707	351	570	183
1934	540	709	707	3,479	455	803	292
1935	646	1,607	867	5,517	966	806	300
1936	892	2,332	995	2,933	1,149	932	313
1937	1,245	3,298	890	3,446	1,235	1,032	940
1938	1,863	7,415	919	5,429	746	1,131	1,740

Under pressure from the USA, who wanted to counter Japan's rise in the Pacific, Britain finally relinquished her position of naval supremacy in 1922. The Washington Naval Agreement fixed the proportion of capital ships of the naval powers as: USA – 5; GB – 5; Japan – 3; Italy – 1.75; France – 1.75. No new capital ships were to be constructed for ten years.

In 1931, the Japanese army embarked upon an expansionist policy on the mainland of China against the wishes of the government in Tokyo. In September 1931, Japanese forces in Manchuria (there because Japan had acquired Russia's leasehold rights over parts of Manchuria in 1905), used a minor attack on the Japanese controlled railway at Mukden as an excuse for the immediate occupation of the city. By the end of the year, they had military control over the whole of Manchuria. Japan, as a member of the Council of the League of Nations, had violated a number of clauses in the Covenant. Britain, with a number of strategically exposed possessions in the Far East, was keen to avoid a confrontation with Japan and so sought to limit her response to formal diplomatic protests, while she began to build up her defences in the region, in particular, re-equipping the vital military base at Singapore. Japan continued in an aggressive fashion, invading anther Chinese province in 1933 and withdrawing from the League of Nations. The 'ten year rule', by which the British Cabinet assumed that 'the British Empire will not be engaged in any great war during the next ten years' was abandoned in 1932, partly as a result of the Manchurian Crisis and partly due to the growing strength of Hitler's Nazi Party in Germany.

b) GERMANY

The rise of Hitler in Germany shortly after the Manchurian crisis, forced Britain to re-evaluate her position in Europe. Hitler withdrew from the League of Nations and the Geneva Disarmament Conference in October 1933, on the indisputable grounds that, after 14 years of peace, none of the wartime allies had made any concrete moves towards disarmament and that Germany should merely seek a position of parity. This was his first pubic violation of the Versailles Treaty and instantly caused alarm in Britain and France. After all, Hitler's book, *Mein Kampf* did not hide his intention of overthrowing most of the terms of Versailles, in particular, reuniting East Prussia with the rest of Germany and expanding into the east, where, he claimed, Germans needed 'lebensraum' for their growing population. If the policies enunciated in *Mein Kampf* and Hitler's untitled *Second Book* were to be believed, Britain would have to confront Hitler at an early stage, to prevent Germany once again dominating Europe.

The government of Ramsay MacDonald, preoccupied with the consequences of the Depression at home, chose to ignore Hitler's earlier writings, believing that, once in office, wiser heads would persuade him to moderate his policy. This hope seemed to be borne out as Hitler stressed his desire for a peaceful understanding with Britain. Britain had not been wholly content with the harsh treatment of Germany in 1919, and so many British politicians and commentators, especially those on the right of the Conservative Party, saw Hitler as merely attempting to correct the excesses of Clemenceau's punitive approach. In particular, the Paris Peace Treaties had attempted to establish national boundaries on the basis of Woodrow Wilson's call for 'self-determination'. This had clearly not been applied in Germany's case, as German majorities in areas of Poland and Czechoslovakia demonstrated. It was also felt that if Britain began to rearm now, this would only provoke Germany into an arms race, such as had taken place before 1914. Britain could not afford such a race, given her parlous financial condition. Therefore, despite Germany's withdrawal and her aggression towards Austria, Britain encouraged the disarmament conference to continue until 1934 and did not begin to rearm until after it had collapsed.

Germany's rearmament was finally made public in 1935, when Hitler introduced conscription and unveiled his airforce, the Luftwaffe. This spurred Britain into calling a meeting with Italy and France at Stresa, where a declaration was drawn up that they would defend each other against 'any unilateral repudiation of treaties'. Within two months however, Britain had gone behind her partners' backs and signed a Naval Agreement with Germany, acknowledging and accepting a German fleet, 35 per cent the size of the Royal Navy, in breach of the Versailles Treaty. The Stresa front was therefore almost immediately worthless, and Italy decided to take the opportunity to expand their African Empire by attacking Abyssinia, having gained the approval of the French. Britain, worried about the naval threat of Japan and the cost of another naval race, had chosen to put her own interests before collective security.

c) ITALY AND THE ABYSSINIAN CRISIS

When the Italian attack on Abyssinia did take place in October 1935, Britons were divided between sympathy for the Abyssinians and a reluctance to risk war over the issue. The government, mindful of their weak response to Japan and Germany, decided to support a call by the League of Nations for collective action against Italy, largely because of a forthcoming general election. Economic sanctions were imposed on Italy, and this helped Stanley Baldwin win the election with another huge majority for his National Government. The government was very concerned however, that a strong response to Italy might provoke them into forming an alliance with Germany, so, behind the scenes, they sought a peaceful resolution which would satisfy Italian ambitions. The resultant deal, the Hoare–Laval Pact, agreed by the British and French foreign secretaries, actually gave Mussolini two thirds of Abyssinia. Unfortunately, news of the deal reached the press and the public reacted angrily to what seemed to be a cynical betrayal of the government's election promises. The deal was hastily dropped, Hoare was replaced as Foreign Secretary by Anthony Eden, one of Mussolini's strongest critics and the sanctions remained, infuriating Italy, who went on to conquer the whole of Abyssinia by 1936 and to declare the Rome–Berlin axis in November. Britain thus failed either to protect Abyssinia or prevent Mussolini moving closer to Nazi Germany.

 ## The re-occupation of the Rhineland, 1936

With international attention thus distracted, on 7 March 1936, Hitler sent troops into the demilitarised Rhineland. France was seriously alarmed by this build up of German forces on her border, but her political instability meant that she could not act alone. Therefore she contacted the British for help. Britain's government decided that there was nothing to gain from confronting Hitler over what was, after all, a part of his own country, and that the public would not support an aggressive response to an action that had been greeted with jubilation by the Rhineland Germans. In his memoirs, Lord Halifax, who was a member of the Cabinet, noted:

I have little doubt that if we had then told Hitler bluntly to go back [in 1936], his power for future and larger mischief would have been broken. But, leaving entirely aside the French, there was no section of British public opinion that would not have been directly opposed to such action in 1936. To go to war with Germany for walking into their own backyard, which was how the British people saw it, at a time moreover when you were actually discussing with them the dates and conditions of their right to resume occupation, was not the sort of thing people could understand. So that moment which, I would guess, offered the last effective chance of securing peace without war, went by.

 ## The Spanish Civil War 1936–39

In 1936, a military revolt against the left-wing government in Spain, grew into a full-blown civil war and caused a fresh Mediterranean crisis almost as soon as the Abyssinian one ended. 20,000 communist and socialist volunteers from Britain went to fight to defend the Republic against fascism in international brigades and the war was followed with alarm by the press and intellectuals, especially when the German 'Condor Brigade' bombed an undefended civil town called Guernica and caused huge civilian casualties. The government of Stanley Baldwin had little sympathy for either side, and was most concerned to prevent the conflict involving any more European countries. A non-intervention agreement was made among the main European powers, including Italy and Germany but it soon became clear that Mussolini in particular, and Hitler, were assisting the right-wing rebels under General Franco. Britain and France banned the export of arms and materials to Spain, thus denying the legitimate Republican government its right to trade freely. The only active protest to the supply of German and Italian tanks, planes and men came from the USSR, which gave active support to the Republic. The British government then proceeded to blame the USSR for the continuation of the war, rather than the Italians and Germans who pretended to uphold the agreement. Baldwin wanted to re-establish better relations with Italy, so the government pretended that the Italian intervention didn't exist (even when an Italian submarine fired on a British warship) and continued to blame the war, which Franco finally won in 1939, on the USSR.

Neville Chamberlain's foreign policy

British foreign policy was transformed in 1937, however, by the accession to the premiership of Neville Chamberlain, whose priority was domestic policy, but who threw himself into using his personal influence to resolving the growing international tension of the late 1930s, despite the warning of his brother, the former Foreign Secretary Austen Chamberlain, 'Neville, you must remember you don't know anything about foreign affairs.' Chamberlain and his chief advisor, Sir Horace Wilson, largely dispensed with collective cabinet policy and ran foreign policy alone, eventually forcing the resignation of his Foreign Secretary, Anthony Eden and replacing him with the loyal Lord Halifax.

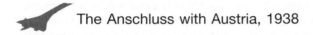

The Anschluss with Austria, 1938

In February 1938, Austrian Chancellor, von Schuschnigg, visited Hitler at Berchtesgaden to ask him to restrain Austrian Nazis who were creating disturbances. Hitler demanded the subordination of the Austrian economy, and foreign policy to Germany, and the appointment of the Austrian Nazi leader, Seyss-Inquart as minister of interior (who had control of police). Italy's support was vital for Britain to prevent Germany taking over Austria, but after the imposition of sanctions in the Abyssinian crisis, this was not forthcoming, despite Mussolini's own reservations about Hitler's actions. Schuschnigg, angered by Hitler, announced a plebiscite to maintain Austrian independence for 13 March. Incensed, Hitler immediately sent troops into Austria, breaching the Versailles Treaty again, which had forbade the union or *Anschluss* between Germany and Austria and facing Chamberlain with his first major crisis. Chamberlain, aware of Britain's military weaknesses, did little but protest, but began to plan for British policy in Czechoslovakia, which would surely be Hitler's next target and to review Britain's defence programmes.

Czechoslovakia and the Munich crisis

The *Anschluss* with Austria focused attention on Czechoslovakia, much of which was now surrounded by German territory. Of the country's population of 15 million, only about half were Czechs. The country contained Slovaks, Hungarians, Ruthenians, Poles and Germans. In the Sudetenland, three and a quarter million Germans resided, and they claimed to be victimised by the Czechs and wanted either '**Home Rule**' or union with Germany. President Benes and Prime Minister Hodza realised that Sudeten German autonomy would be 'tantamount to suicide'.

Most politicians had some sympathy with Czechoslovakia, because, despite its problems, Czechoslovakia had preserved a democratic constitution more successfully than most other European states like Hungary or Poland. Some, like Churchill, thought Czechoslovakia was worth fighting for. Chamberlain had some sympathy for the Sudeten Germans, and was quite willing to see the Sudetenland handed over to Germany, provided this could be done by negotiation rather than by force. He thus put pressure on the Czechs to make concessions before the quarrel developed into a confrontation. In March 1938, Chamberlain told the Commons that vital British interests were not involved in Czechoslovakia. Britain had no treaty obligation to defend her and was in no position to offer serious military aid. The French had given a guarantee to Czechoslovakia through the Locarno treaties of 1925, but Chamberlain refused to make a military alliance with the French to help the Czechs in March, and the French submitted to the British position.

The main aim of Chamberlain's policy was to extract concessions from the Czech government, which would satisfy the Sudeten Germans before Hitler used force to impose a settlement. The only flaw in Chamberlain's argument was that the Czech government was not prepared to make concessions.

In May, German troops were reported to have moved to the Czech frontier. The Czechs mobilised some of their reserves and prepared for war. Britain and France did not want to have to fight for Czechoslovakia, and so pressed for a settlement. Chamberlain's argument was, that if Germany now had control over Austria, the Czech defences in the Sudeten region were no longer so important. If Germany wanted to invade Czechoslovakia, she could now do so through Austria.

As the summer wore on, tension increased. Chamberlain has been criticised for ignoring the position of talks with the USSR. Russia, like France, had an alliance with the Czechs and might have been prepared to support the western powers against Hitler. However, Chamberlain distrusted Stalin, and military experts had assured Chamberlain that the Russian army was not prepared for an offensive war.

In August, Lord Runciman, a Liberal politician with little diplomatic experience, was sent to Prague to try and mediate between the various parties. His mission achieved little as no one was prepared to compromise. By September, Chamberlain was increasingly anxious. In Britain, there was suddenly awareness that there was a crisis brewing. The country was divided, and this would not make a formidable fighting force. This was not helped by the fact that the Dominions were predominantly hostile to the idea of fighting for Czechoslovakia. Tension between the Sudeten Germans and Czechs grew until the Sudeten German leaders, instructed by Hitler, tried to bring about a general rising. It was swiftly crushed by the Czechs and thousands of Sudeten Germans fled across the border to Germany. It seemed that war between Germany and Czechoslovakia was imminent.

Chamberlain now took the initiative and asked Hitler to meet him to mediate over Czechoslovakia. This was to be the first of three meetings in two weeks.

BERCHTESGADEN – 15 SEPTEMBER 1938

Chamberlain flew (for the first time in his life) to Germany and had a three hour meeting with Hitler. Hitler demanded that all areas in Czechoslovakia in which Germans comprised over 50 per cent of population, should be handed over to Germany.

He gave Chamberlain the assurance that he had no greater designs on Czechoslovakia and agreed not to attack Czechoslovakia until Chamberlain had consulted the French and the Czechs.

Chamberlain returned to London and persuaded the Cabinet, the French, and finally the Czechs, that this was the only solution: to preserve European peace by weakening Czechoslovakia. He did it by assuring them it would lead to a lasting peace and agreeing to guarantee the new, weakened state of Czechoslovakia, in the event of it being threatened in future by Germany.

BAD GODESBERG – 22 SEPTEMBER 1938

Chamberlain flew back to Germany expecting that 'I had only to discuss quietly with him, the proposals that I had brought with me'. But Hitler raised his demands:

- The claims of Poland and Hungary to Czech territory had to be met.
- The areas to be ceded to Germany must be evacuated by the 1 October 1938 by the Czechs, without a plebiscite. There was to be no compensation for loss of property.
- German troops would occupy the Sudetenland on 1 October 1938.

Chamberlain was astounded and returned to London without reaching an agreement. Flying back to London, Chamberlain is supposed to have looked down on London and feared for the lives of its citizens if a war broke out. Perhaps this accounts for his desire to still find a settlement, even if it meant accepting Hitler's outrageous demands. But, many of the Cabinet rejected the Bad Godesberg proposals; the Czechs refused and ordered a general mobilisation of forces, and the French called up 500,000 men.

On 25 September 1938, Chamberlain promised Daladier that if France were to go to war, Britain would support her. On the 27 September, the fleet mobilised, trenches for air-raid precautions were dug in London, 38 million gas masks were distributed and instructions were issued for the evacuation of schoolchildren. War seemed imminent.

Chamberlain, however, still hoped for an international conference, with the assistance of Mussolini, to settle the problem. On 28 September, news came through, during a Commons debate, that Hitler had accepted Mussolini's suggestion of a four-power conference, to be held at Munich. The Commons erupted in relief, as it seemed that war had been avoided.

THE MUNICH CONFERENCE – 29–30 SEPTEMBER 1938

On 29 September, Chamberlain, Daladier, Hitler and Mussolini, but not Stalin or Benes, met to discuss the fate of Czechoslovakia. Agreement was finally reached in the early hours of 30 September.

There were only slight modifications to the Bad Godesberg demands:

*   The evacuation of the Sudetenland was to take place in five stages over a ten-day period, from 1 October.
*   Doubtful areas were to be settled by a plebiscite.
*   Czechs wishing to move out were allowed to take their possessions.
*   The precise borders of the new Czechoslovakia would be determined by a conference of the four powers.

Benes had to choose whether to accept the Munich terms or to fight alone. He chose to surrender. Before returning to London, a separate document was signed between Hitler and Chamberlain, re-affirming the Anglo-German naval agreement of 1935 and promising that any future difficulties would be settled by further conferences.

Chamberlain returned to Britain exultant that he had avoided a war: 'This is the second time in our history there has come back from Germany to Downing Street peace with honour. I believe it is peace for our time'.

Churchill may have described the agreement as 'an unmitigated defeat' and the first Lord of Admiralty, Duff Cooper, may have resigned in protest, but public opinion strongly supported the Prime Minister. On his return, Chamberlain was greeted at London airport by cheering crowds. He was cheered all night outside Downing Street.

Some Labour MPs claimed that Britain should have asked for better terms and some Conservatives said it proved that Hitler's bullying tactics could succeed, but the majority of MPs strongly supported Chamberlain's actions.

The uneasy peace: September 1938 – March 1939

The French government was anxious to obtain firmer pledges of British support. In particular, it wanted Britain to commit itself to sending a large army to defend France. In February, Chamberlain accepted that in the event of war, Britain would have to help France, and agreed to open detailed staff talks. This was a radical change in Britain's defence policy.

Chamberlain favoured rearmament and the pace increased after Munich. 'We should hope for the best, but be prepared for the worst'. British rearmament had been geared to reach a peak in 1939–40, but it was vastly increased after Munich. In 1938, 240 aircraft per month were produced. This increased to 660 by September 1939. In September 1938, only the Thames Estuary had radar. By September 1939, a radar chain ran from the Orkneys to the Isle of Wight. By 1939, therefore, Chamberlain was much more confident of Britain's capacity to fight, and, in particular, to resist an air attack. As a result, he may have been prepared to take a firmer line with Hitler, but he still hoped for, and talked of, peace.

The end of Czechoslovakia

The Munich agreement was welcomed by most people in England. Hitler's actions, however, in the following months, led to a dramatic change in British foreign policy.

The fears that the Czech president had expressed about national minorities seeking independence became realities after Munich. The Slovaks, in particular, showed their resentment of the Czech dominated state, and Hitler encouraged them. Hacha, the new president, introduced martial law. Hungary demanded Ruthenia. With his country falling apart, Hacha appealed to Hitler. Hitler's response was not what Hacha expected, and he was told Germany intended to occupy the rest of Czechoslovakia, either by force or negotiation. Hacha broke down, and on 15 March 1939 German troops entered Czechoslovakia under the pretext of preventing civil war.

Munich had been overturned and **appeasement** was in ruins. Chamberlain had been shown as naive in his trust of Hitler. British opinion was outraged and there was a marked shift in the views of the Conservative Party and the press. Something now had to be done to stop Hitler before he controlled the whole of Europe.

On 18 March 1939 the British and French governments delivered sharp protests to Germany. Chamberlain told the Cabinet that his hopes of working with Germany were over. 'No reliance could be placed on any of the assurances given by the Nazi leaders.' On April 26 conscription was introduced.

Mussolini had not been informed by Hitler of his intention to occupy Czechoslovakia, and this was a blow to his pride. Determined not to be outdone by Hitler, Mussolini embarked on his own policy by invading Albania in April. He also announced that the Balkans and the eastern Mediterranean should be regarded as being in the Italian sphere of influence.

This was a breach of the Anglo-Italian agreement of 1938, and although Britain did not wish to drive Mussolini into complete co-operation with Hitler, it was these actions which led them to give guarantees to Greece and Rumania, in April 1939.

 ## The Polish crisis

After the fall of Czechoslovakia in March, Hitler's next target was Poland. At the end of March he demanded Memel from Lithuania, which was returned. But Poland was different. There were some 800,000 Germans in Poland and Danzig was 96 per cent German. German-Polish relations had been remarkably good since signing a non-aggression treaty in 1934, but the Poles were not prepared to accept being a German satellite state. Germany increased her demands for not only Danzig, but the return of the 'Polish Corridor', which divided East Prussia from the rest of Germany. The Poles were determined to resist.

At this stage, Chamberlain probably still hoped for a negotiated settlement. After Munich, however, public opinion and a large number of MPs would no longer allow this approach. Consequently, on 29 March, Anglo-French staff talks were held, planning the dispatch of British troops to France in the event of war. On 31 March, Chamberlain announced that Britain would come to the aid of Poland if she were attacked. The French government offered a similar guarantee. This agreement was freely given by Britain, not asked for by Poland.

Hitler remained unimpressed by the British and French guarantees. On 28 April he denounced the Anglo-German naval treaty and the German-Polish pact. On 7 May he concluded the 'Pact of Steel' with Italy. This said each country would help the other unconditionally in the event of war.

Anglo-Soviet relations

Chamberlain realised that the guarantees given to Poland were less effective without the Soviet Union's involvement. However, he had no desire to ally with the USSR. He distrusted Stalin and feared and hated the Soviet state. He also believed that a policy of 'encirclement' of Germany, as in 1914, could be counter-productive. It might lead to, rather than prevent, war. Intelligence reported that Russia's army was of little military value. 80 per cent of all the USSR's senior army officers had been killed or imprisoned in Stalin's recent purges. Even so, he did suggest a pact in March, but the Poles rejected this, believing, probably quite correctly, that the USSR would use such a situation to benefit herself.

In 1939, Stalin had a far worse record of terror and mass-murder than Hitler, but this was concealed. So Chamberlain found himself at odds with public opinion which supported some kind of deal with the USSR.

Throughout the Summer of 1939 there were a series of Anglo-French delegations to Moscow, but these came to nothing. The Russians were suspicious of the West who had rejected their offers in the previous year. The Poles would not contemplate Russian troops on their soil and Chamberlain sympathised with this view. As later became clear, these suspicions were well founded. Finally it was obvious that Stalin was pursuing his own policy with Hitler.

In May, the pro-Western foreign minister, Litvinov, was replaced by Molotov. While British and French negotiators were in Moscow, Stalin was putting out feelers to Berlin. This resulted in the Nazi–Soviet (Molotov–Ribbentrop) pact, of August. This gave spheres of influence to each country in Europe and divided Poland between them.

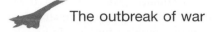

The outbreak of war

Hitler believed the pact with the USSR would stop the West going to war over Poland. However, Chamberlain had no intention of abandoning Poland. He believed that Britain, France and Poland were strong enough to deter Hitler. He made his intentions clear by sending a letter to Hitler on 22 August 1939. On 25 August an Anglo-Polish pact was signed in London.

Hitler had planned for the invasion of Poland on the 26 August. Mussolini warned Hitler that he wasn't ready for war. Hitler may have been surprised by the reactions of Britain and France, but it made little difference to his actions. He delayed the invasion for a few days, but on 1 September 1939, he launched his surprise attack on Poland.

There was no immediate action from Britain or France as France wanted to delay the declaration of war as long as possible to complete her mobilisation. Throughout 1 and 2 September, there was a frantic exchange of notes and telephone calls asking the Germans to withdraw their troops from Poland as a preliminary to further negotiations.

Figure 5.3 **The approach of war, 1938–39**

Chamberlain still appeared reluctant to declare war, despite the assurances given to Poland. It was the House of Commons that forced the issue. On 2 September, angered that no ultimatum had been sent to Hitler, Arthur Greenwood, the Labour spokesman (speaking for the House who scented **appeasement** once more), demanded immediate action.

France was informed that there could be no more delay. At 9.00 a.m. an ultimatum was sent. Germany made no reply and at 11.00 a.m. on the morning of Sunday 3 September 1939 Britain declared war on Germany once more. France followed suit and within one week, Australia, New Zealand, South Africa and Canada had all declared war on Germany.

Chamberlain commented after declaring a state of war with Germany:

This is a sad day for all of us, and to none is it sadder than to me. Everything that I have worked for, everything that I have believed in during my public life has crashed in ruins. There is only one thing left for me to do; that is to devote what strength and powers I have to forwarding the victory of the cause for which we have to sacrifice so much. I cannot tell what part I may be allowed to play myself; I trust I may live to see the day when Hitlerism has been destroyed and a liberated Europe had been re-established.

Chamberlain had been forced into a war which he and the British public had always tried to avoid. However in September 1939 most people accepted the necessity for war. A Gallup poll showed 89 per cent of the British people in favour of 'fighting until Hitlerism is done away with.'

Part 2: Essays

1. The Treaty of Versailles (OCR)

**'The Versailles Peace Settlement failed to secure British foreign policy interests.'
How far do you agree with this statement?**

(90 marks)

At the peace negotiations at the Versailles palace, the Prime Minister, Lloyd George, led the British delegation himself. Having achieved victory after four years of unprecedentedly costly and bloody struggle, he was determined that Britain should gain the maximum from the peace settlement. This did not mean that Lloyd George supported calls to put the ex-Kaiser, now living in Holland, on trial as a war criminal, or attempt to 'squeeze Germany until the pips squeak' as some had called for in the general election in the previous year. Lloyd George realised that such punitive policies would only serve to perpetuate the conflict between Germany and the allies.

In fact, many of Britain's main objectives had been achieved before the powers met in Paris. The German colonies were already under allied control, the German Navy had been captured and then scuttled by its own crews at Scapa Flow and the German army had been defeated and driven back within its own borders.

Lloyd George's first priority was therefore to have these facts confirmed – for the colonies to be divided as it suited the allies and for the German navy and army to remain limited in size. Further than this, Lloyd George was less concerned than the French to punish Germany. Britain had no territorial claims in Europe and was more concerned about the damage that an aggrieved Germany would do in the years to come.

On the other hand, Lloyd George had to remember the wishes of the British public and the call to 'make Germany pay' was one that he was willing to accommodate. Britain had spent heavily and amassed huge debts in the war and should, he felt, receive her fair share of the reparations. Always the practical politician, Lloyd George decided that Germany should pay what could be reasonably expected of her. Indeed, if Germany's economy was too severely damaged, Britain would lose a valuable trading partner and her own economy would suffer. Worse, Germany might undergo a communist revolution, as seemed possible at the time, and ally with the feared Bolsheviks in Russia, thus facing Europe with a far more serious threat to its own security.

Finally, although Lloyd George was happy to support the concept of the League of Nations, he did so mainly to retain the support of the USA. The scheme for the League as envisaged by the British, drafted by Jan Smuts the South African minister of defence, was actually adopted as the model for the new organisation. It would be accurate to say that the British governments never used the League for the purposes for which it was established and preferred to employ traditional diplomatic channels instead.

At the time, it seemed that the Versailles settlement gave Britain everything she could wish for. The Germans were strictly limited in the size and type of fleet they could have. The German and Turkish Empires were divided among the allies under the guise of '**mandated territories** of the League of Nations'. The Germans had agreed to pay reparations to offset the cost of the war and the debts cancelled by the Bolshevik government in Russia. Finally, the German army was reduced in scale and penned within the east bank of the Rhine where, it was felt, it could not threaten the peace of Western Europe again.

The position of Germany, however, was not necessarily to Britain's liking. Germany had been an important trading partner before the First World War, and Britain worried that unlimited, or at least, very high reparations would severely hamper Germany's recovery, just at the time when the British economy needed all the export markets it could find. Second, the principle of self-determination, although not one of Britain's original war aims, proved very popular with the British public, but was clearly not applied in Germany's case. German minorities in France, Poland and Czechoslovakia would prove to be a major stumbling block in the attempt to find a permanent settlement in Europe and British resolution to defend Versailles was undermined by a degree of sympathy for the German position.

The treaty also created large numbers of small nations, especially in the east where they filled the vacuum left by the collapse of the Hapsburg and Tsarist Empire. These small countries, just like the Balkans before 1914, faced an uncertain future surrounded by larger, dissatisfied powers, who sought influence in the region. Britain like France, would have to decide how far she intended to defend the autonomy of these countries and what she would do if they were threatened. Their existence brought a degree of constant instability into Britain's continued attempts to prevent one country dominating Europe.

Britain's role in arbitrating the future of Europe was particularly crucial given the position of the two great powers who failed to agree to the Versailles Treaty. Both the USA and Russia had vast potential influence, both military and economic, in the European theatre, but neither was in a position to exert this. The USA, horrified by the loss of life in her brief involvement in the Great

War, retreated into a deep isolationism, failing to ratify the Versailles Treaty, despite President Wilson's crucial role in its drafting, and raising tariff barriers and immigration controls to isolate itself. Only in the Pacific did the USA continue to take an active role, and there it frequently acted as much as a threat to British interests as a former wartime ally. For its part, Russia had been convulsed by the Civil War which followed the Bolshevik revolution, and as a communist state intent on fomenting revolution abroad, even at rifle point if necessary, as it demonstrated in its war with Poland in 1920, it became a pariah nation in Europe. Its intentions were always distrusted by Britain in the inter-war years.

The former German and Turkish territories that Britain came to administer proved to be something of a poisoned chalice. The Near East in particular gave Britain no peace as she was forced to resolve the consequences of conflicting wartime promises to both Jews and Arabs. The Balfour declaration had promised a Jewish homeland, but land had also been promised to the Arabs by Sir Henry MacMahon. The reality turned out to be a division of land between the French and the British (the Sykes–Picot pact), with Britain controlling the most disputed area of all, Palestine. There she would be caught between the obligations of defending Jewish rights, which had strong American backing, and protecting the interests of the Arabs, who controlled important oil fields, vital for any future war. Apart from this particular problem, Britain found herself responsible for a huge, scattered Empire, which was expensive to maintain and militarily difficult to defend. Add to this the rise of nationalist movements, especially in India, and Britain found her foreign policy being constrained by the need to avoid conflict on more than one imperial front which her scant resources would not allow.

2. Ireland (EDEXCEL)

a) **Describe the events which led to the Anglo-Irish treaty of 1921.** (30 marks)

b) **Why was the British government unable to prevent the partition of Ireland?** (30 marks)

(Total: 60 marks)

a) Before the First World War, the Catholic majority of the population in the south of Ireland supported the Irish **Nationalist** party which wanted some degree of independence for Ireland. The Liberal Party under Gladstone had committed itself to satisfying this cause, but the first two attempts to introduce it had been stopped by their political opponents who could claim that they represented majority opinion in England which opposed **Home Rule**. When the Liberal government of Asquith had introduced a third Home Rule bill, the Protestant minority in the North of Ireland had, with the approval of the Conservative party and some officers in the British army, begun to arm themselves. It seems likely that only the intervention of the First World War prevented a civil war.

During the war, Protestants and Catholics had both joined the army to prove the legitimacy of their cause, but some extreme nationalists refused to do so, believing that 'England's difficulty is Ireland's opportunity'. Instead they contacted the German authorities and organised a rising against British rule in Dublin on Easter Monday, 1916. This was swiftly crushed, but, unwisely, the military authorities in Dublin ordered the execution of the ring-leaders. Irish sympathy immediately began to swing towards political groups such as Sinn Fein who had supported the rising. When the British government toyed with the idea of introducing conscription to Ireland in 1918, the idea horrified the Irish people and Sinn Fein won 73 Irish seats at the general election in 1918.

Their MPs rejected the authority of the Westminster Parliament, and set their own in Dublin, which they named the Dail Eirann, and declared an Irish republic.

The new British government, immediately attempted to restore the authority of the British authorities. But such was popular support for the Dail and their military wing, the Irish Republican Army (IRA), that the police were hampered by intimidation, informers and public non-co-operation. In desperation, reinforcements were sent from Britain, the notorious '**Black and Tans**' and the 'Auxis' who attempted to counter the IRA with terror methods. Although, in military terms, these paramilitary forces were successful, they hardened opposition to British rule in Ireland and caused outrage in Britain. The British government took the opportunity of the IRA's weakness in 1921 to sign a truce with the Dail and to negotiate a settlement. Lloyd George threatened the IRA and Sinn Fein negotiators that he would send the full force of the British army against them if they did not agree to the terms he offered. They were thus forced to accept a permanent partition between the protestant north and the rest of Ireland, in return for giving the south **Dominion** status, which meant virtual independence.

b)   Ireland had always lacked political and cultural unity and the resistance of Protestant dominated **Ulster** to the three Home Rule bills demonstrated how difficult it would be to find a solution which would satisfy the whole of the Irish people. The tense years which followed the introduction of the Third Home Rule Bill had seen the two sides arming and civil war had seemed close in summer 1914, with the British army unwilling to play a role. On the other hand, most nationalists still supported the parliamentary approach favoured by the Irish **Nationalist** Party led by John Redmond.

The Easter Rising of 1916 had certainly not been supported by the mass of Irish people, but the execution of the 15 ring-leaders and the threat of conscription in 1918 had certainly damaged relations with the British government. In the end the government had chosen to exclude Ireland from the Conscription Act, and released many of the prisoners taken after the rising, but the damage had already been done. By the time of the 1918 election, with Redmond dead and his Nationalist party in disarray, Sinn Fein, which advocated armed resistance to British rule, had managed to replace the old **Nationalist** Party as the largest political force in the South. When the alternative Parliament, the Dail was set up in Dublin, Ireland was, in effect, partitioned already.

The Anglo-Irish War seemed to confirm this fact. The Royal Irish Constabulary was unable, and in many cases unwilling, to resist the authority of the Dail, and so the troops sent in to restore British rule were non-Irish and unsurprisingly brutal in their handling of a delicate political situation. The violent acts carried out by the troops hardened Southern Irish feelings against British rule and served to discredit the government when news of their activities reached England, with Asquith referring to 'things being done in Ireland which would disgrace the lowest despotism in Europe'. The government, dominated by the Conservative party, desperately searched for a solution which would at least preserve the union with the Protestant dominated counties of the north. The Government of Ireland Act of 1920, did attempt to maintain the superiority of the Parliament at Westminster, but only by creating two subordinate Parliaments, one in Belfast and one in Dublin. In this way, the British authorities accepted the principle of partition, as did the unionists in the north, who thus escaped the threat of being ruled from Dublin. When the Sinn Fein clearly rejected this approach the government was forced to offer partition, with **Dominion** status for the south. At the meetings at Downing Street, Lloyd George used a threat of an almost immediate return to conflict to make the nationalists accept this, as they had wanted a united Ireland and a republic. He deceived the nationalists, by assuring them that the Boundary Commission set up by the treaty would make Northern Ireland economically unviable, whereas it actually led to nationalist areas being included. A civil war was immediately fought over the treaty once the Irish Free State was created in 1922. The British government was quick to offer military support to the new Free State army to ensure that the anti-Treaty forces were defeated and that partition became institutionalised.

3. British foreign policy in the 1920s (EDEXCEL)

a) **Describe Britain's relations with Russia between 1919 and 1929.**   (30 marks)

b) **Why did British relations with Germany improve between 1919
    and 1930?**   (30 marks)

(Total: 60 marks)

a) Like Germany, Russia emerged from the war as a pariah state and was given no role in the 1919 peace conference. Unsuccessful attempts to intervene during the Civil War on the side of the Whites left a legacy of deep mutual suspicion, reinforced in the West by the new regime's repudiation of all Tsarist War Debts and its policy of nationalising foreign assets without compensation.

In the early 1920s, Russia was preoccupied with internal problems of civil war and reconstruction. Partly because of its need to re-establish export markets, Britain was deeply interested in developments in Bolshevik Russia in the 1920s. However, the problem of war debts, especially after the highly unfavourable debt settlement with the United States that Baldwin forced on the Cabinet in 1923, continued to sour relations.

The British government had initially been divided in its response to the new regime in Russia. On the one hand, Churchill strongly advocated military force to bring down the 'foul baboonery of Bolshevism' and had sent the White Russians financial support and a detachment of British troops in the Civil War of 1918–21. On the other hand, Lloyd George saw this as counter-productive and sought instead to rebuild the West's economic links with Russia, signing an Anglo-Soviet trade agreement in 1921, in which the Russians accepted that it must pay for goods received during the war.

Against a background of industrial unrest in Britain in the early 1920s, the creation of the Communist Party and the Communist International (Comintern) in 1920 reinforced fears in official circles of Soviet subversion as communist risings took place in Germany and Hungary. As a result, Anglo-Soviet relations failed to improve further for several years, with the Soviet Union remaining unrecognised by the British government. Lloyd George's attempt to involve the Russians at the Genoa Reconstruction Conference in 1922, failed, partly due to the Russians and Germans signing their own treaty at Rapallo, which allowed the German army to train on Russian soil in violation of the Versailles treaty. Such a move hardly improved British attitudes towards the Soviet Union, and the Anglo-Soviet trade agreement barely survived.

Despite fears of being regarded as 'fellow-travellers', or at least, naïve idealists, Ramsay MacDonald's minority Labour government gave official diplomatic recognition of the USSR in 1924 and an Anglo-Soviet Agreement was signed, which promised to settle the issue of war debts in exchange for a British loan of £30 million. This policy of conciliating the Soviet Union backfired however, when the Liberals withdrew their support for the government and the Conservatives exploited the widespread unease with the Bolshevik regime in using the so-called 'Zinoviev letter';

to undermine Labour during the 1924 election campaign. The left subsequently learned to treat relations with the USSR very carefully, for fear of confirming middle-class fears, as in 1926 when a donation to the miners' federation was rejected.

Baldwin's Conservative government refused to ratify the Anglo-Soviet agreement, and, after the defeat of the general strike which many thought to be communist-inspired, the right wing of the Conservative Party was determined to reverse Labour's policy towards the USSR. In 1927 the Soviet Arcos trading company had their headquarters raided by the police. Although no incriminating evidence was found, Britain broke off diplomatic relations later that year, believing that strikes in China and India which damaged British trade had been organised by the Comintern. With the Conservative defeat in 1929, however, Labour believed that public opinion was ready to accept a more constructive policy towards Russia and diplomatic contacts were restored, although the issue of debts and loans was not raised again.

b)   Germany's defeat and the humiliating 'Diktat' of Versailles did not permanently cripple Germany, but it did make future conflict more likely, by inflaming mass opinion against the Treaty and fuelling demands for revision of the treaty, if not repudiation. Most British diplomats thought that Germany's eastern frontiers were unsatisfactory, especially the creation of the 'Polish corridor', and the treaty was widely perceived as harsh, especially as the policy of 'self-determination' had clearly not been applied to areas dominated by German peoples. Politicians, nervous as to the robustness of the British economy in light of the post-war depression, believed that to weaken the German economy was to punish Britain's trade. On the whole, Britain recognised that concessions to Germany were both desirable and necessary.

France however, wanted guarantees of security from German aggression, and the resulting hesitancy of British policy towards Germany worried the French (now Britain's only major ally), but failed to prevent them acting aggressively towards Germany – thus making the Germans more aggressive in return.

In 1921, Germany had finally been presented with a bill of 50 billion Gold Marks, but Britain and France soon argued over the implementation of these 'reparations'. The French wanted maximum payment from Germany on schedule, but Britain was willing to accept a suspension of payments to prevent a collapse of the Germany economy.

In January 1923, contrary to British advice, France occupied the Ruhr (Germany's industrial heartland) with the intention of forcing Germany to meet her obligations. The invasion caused a general strike which prevented France receiving any reparations of any kind and caused hyper-inflation in Germany which came close to destabilising international currency markets. This forced Britain and the USA to guarantee a new reparations scheme – the Dawes Plan, which restructured the German finances with a US loan of 800 million Marks to Germany. At the London conference of 1924, the then Labour government persuaded France and Germany to accept the deal, while France withdrew from the Ruhr and Germany resumed payments. Britain managed to persuade the French not to intervene in this fashion again and to build a defensive barrier on the border with Germany instead. Britain also acted as a guarantor for the Locarno Treaty signed in 1925 in which the Germans, French and Belgians promised to accept Germany's western borders as established at Versailles.

Relations continued to improve as Germany became a member of the League of Nations in 1926 and in the following year Allied military controls (the only effective means of verifying German disarmament) were lifted. Finally, in 1929 the Young Plan reduced Germany's reparations to a third of the original sum, and the former allies agreed to evacuate their troops from Germany by 1930, five years ahead of schedule. Britain had chosen to conciliate Germany, largely by abandoning France, and for the governments at least, relations between Britain and Germany were perhaps at their best since the turn of the century. But there were still plenty of people in Germany who felt that the revision of Versailles had not gone far enough and began to support more extreme nationalist groups who promised to do so.

4. British imperial policy (AQA)

Read the following extract from *the Rise and Fall of the Great Powers* by P. Kennedy and answer the questions which follow.

As soon as the First World War was over, the self-governing dominions had pressed for a redefinition of their status. . . . More important still, in strictly military terms, were the 'imperial policing' activities in which the British army, and also the RAF were engaged in India, Iraq, Palestine and elsewhere.

a) **Explain what is meant by the term 'self-governing Dominions'.** (3 marks)
b) **Why did Britain agree to give the Dominions independence in 1926?** (7 marks)
c) **How successfully did Britain manage to maintain the unity of the Empire in the inter-war years?** (15 marks)

a) 'Self-governing Dominions' were those member countries of the British Empire that had been granted increased control over their internal affairs before 1914, largely because their populations were dominated by English-speaking settlers.

b) The Dominions, although ruled by recent British settlers, were demanding greater autonomy from the mother-country. Together, they had contributed over a million men to Britain's struggles against the Central Powers during the First World War and 140,000 of them had died. Canada, Australia, New Zealand and South Africa (and the Irish Free State since 1922) already controlled their internal affairs, but increasingly wanted to control their foreign affairs as they feared being dragged into another 'British' war. The war had seriously weakened the willingness of the south of Ireland to remain a part of the United Kingdom. Canada wished to draw closer to her neighbour, USA, and in South Africa, the defeat of General Smuts by the **Nationalist** Party in 1924 implied the rise of an anti-British foreign policy. Australia was developing her own manufacturing sector and no longer saw a need to act as a source of raw material for the metropolitan country. Only New Zealand seemed fairly willing to continue close relations with Britain, but even she, as well as Canada, refused to help Britain over Chanak and didn't sign the Locarno Treaty. Eventually Balfour organised the Imperial Conference of 1926 at which he defined the dominions as free countries equal to Britain and in complete control of internal and foreign policy, but with a common monarchy.

They were to be 'freely associated as members of the British Commonwealth of Nations' which satisfied the Dominions and was passed through Parliament as the Statute of Westminster in 1931. Under its terms, a declaration of war by the Empire had to be approved by the parliaments of the dominions, and in 1938, it certainly seemed that Britain might have gone to war over the Czech crisis without the support of the Dominions. On the other hand, when war did come in 1939, despite reservations, the Dominions, with the exception of **Eire**, did join in the struggle and demonstrated the vast reserves of imperial loyalty and commitment in the subsequent war effort.

c) To encourage India's assistance in the First World War, the Indians had been promised 'the progressive realisation of responsible [self-] government in India' and in 1919, the Government of India Act created a national parliament with two houses and five million Indians were given the vote. The Indian Congress Party was disappointed as Britain still had control of central government and the Indian people were suffering the consequence of wartime taxes and conscription. After the **Amritsar Massacre** when troops opened fire on an unarmed crowd, killing 122 people, Mahatma Gandhi emerged as the leader of peaceful resistance to British rule. By sheer force of personality he encouraged Indians to co-operate in 'civil disobedience' – refusing to work, staging sit-down strikes, not paying taxes and boycotting elections. Britain oscillated between a harsh approach, putting Gandhi in jail in 1924, and a more lenient one, appointing the Simon Commission (with no Indian members) in 1928 to investigate India's future. When it reported in 1930, it proposed self-government for the provinces, but by now Congress was demanding immediate **Dominion** status. To satisfy as many opinions as possible, the government eventually introduced the 1935 Government of India Act. This granted elective self-government and gave the local vote to 35 million Indians.

This provoked the anger of both the hard-line imperialist critics led by Winston Churchill and the nationalist advocates of independence such as Gandhi and Nehru who believed that the Act was a fraud as central government was still under the control of the Viceroy. It did at least give the British a breathing space, and kept India relatively peaceful until the outbreak of the Second World War. But the long-term future of the **Raj** looked extremely unsure, especially when Congress dominated the first provincial elections in 1937.

In Egypt, demands for more independence were easier to settle, at least temporarily. The establishment of a British protectorate in 1914 had frustrated the professional Egyptian elite and the war inflation had impoverished the peasantry. As a result, riots, looting and assaults on Europeans spread across upper Egypt. Britain was reluctant to commit her troops and sparse resources to another unwilling colony, if her interests could be secured by compromise, so Lord Allenby negotiated the Anglo-Egyptian settlement of 1922, which dismantled the Protectorate but left Britain in charge of the Suez Canal and Egypt's foreign policy. The upper class nationalist Wafd party was largely satisfied by this and the region remained calm for the next 20 years.

By contrast, British rule was never seriously challenged in Africa south of Egypt. The white settlers of Southern Rhodesia rejected incorporation into the increasingly anti-British South Africa. In other areas, 'indirect rule' as pioneered by Lord Lugard in Nigeria was practised, which put power in the hands of native chiefs, bolstered by local courts and treasuries. There were tensions between white settlers, educated Africans and Indian merchants, but little of this was, as yet, directed against the British authority. In fact, most regarded Britain as a protector against a feared racial confrontation, such as was developing in South Africa at the time.

In the **Mandated territories**, Britain had mixed success, perhaps unsurprisingly, given the lack of a previous relationship between Britain and these territories. In Iraq, Britain won the support of the Arab peoples when they set up an Iraqi government with Amir Feisal, the Arab leader, as King. An elected government was set up in 1924, industry and agriculture were re-organised and the oil producing area of Mosul was won from Turkey. Eventually in 1932, Iraq became fully independent, but with permanent British bases. By contrast, Palestine proved a serious burden as Jewish settlement in the area caused conflict with the Arab population. By 1928 150,000 Jews had settled, buying land from Arabs and setting up industries. The Arabs rebelled in protest against this process and many Jews were killed. By 1930, Labour decided to limit Jewish immigration, but this caused protest from the Jews. Arab/Jewish tension increased as refugees flooded into Palestine fleeing from Nazi persecution in the 1930s. The Arabs finally revolted against Jewish settlement in 1937 and declared an *intifada,* which British troops had to put down. To prevent a repeat of the situation, the government placed severe restrictions on Jewish immigration in May 1939. This won vital Arab support which guaranteed oil supplies throughout the Second World War, but condemned tens of thousands of Jews to remain in Nazi occupied Europe.

In the Empire, therefore, as in her dealings with the Dominions, Britain chose to attempt to cooperate with local interests to preserve her rule as long as possible. This had varying degrees of success given the differences in nationalism across the Empire, but with the exception of India and Palestine, the British Empire was by no means moribund by 1939.

5. British responses to aggression in the 1930s (OCR)

Why and with what consequences did Britain fail to react more strongly towards Japanese and Italian aggression in the 1930s?

(90 marks)

After the First World War, Britain had moved away from the alliance with Japan, preferring instead a four power alliance to maintain the status quo in the Far East between herself, USA Japan and France. As part of this approach, the powers agreed an open-door policy of trade with China and British business began to build up trade in the area.

After the attack on Manchuria and the subsequent Japanese advance towards Shanghai, British commercial interests were under threat, but Britain was not in a position to do much to militarily stop Japan. The British government was undergoing a financial crisis at the time and was not politically or economically stable enough to intervene successfully in a conflict on the other side of the world. If she had done so, she would have relied on her base at Singapore, but given the state of the fortifications there it was very unlikely that the British fleet could reach Singapore before the Japanese overran it. Britain was also worried that to drive the Japanese out of Manchuria would leave the area open to the Russians. In the debates at Geneva, Sir John Simon, the British Foreign Secretary, distinguished himself by expounding the arguments on the side of Japan so fully, that he earned the public thanks of the Japanese delegate at the League of Nations.

China appealed to the League, and an enquiry was set up under Lord Lytton. The report, issued in 1932, claimed the Japanese attack was unjustified, and stated that Manchuria was now a Japanese province. On the other hand, it suggested creating a self-governing Manchuria which recognised Japanese economic interests. The League also passed a motion condemning Japan for using aggression whereupon Japan gave notice to leave the League.

Britain certainly bears some blame for the lack of actions against Japan. Although military action was certainly inadvisable, Simon's actions in defending Japan and Lytton's willingness to accept Japan's interests in Manchuria did much to undermine the resolve of the Great Powers. Neither Britain nor the League took any direct action when Japan finally invaded China in 1937. Certainly France did little more than join in diplomatic protests, but she, like Britain, was more concerned with the state of her economy and the rise of extremism in Germany. As the two most powerful members of the League of Nations, they were equally responsible for the failure of the League to take a more robust approach and impose economic sanctions on Japan. At a time of global depression, however, no member was keen to damage the fragile state of world trade. As the other member of the four power alliance, and the one with the strongest concentration of military force in proximity to the area, the United States should bear equal blame for the lack of effective action. Outside the League of Nations and pre-occupied with the after-effects of the Wall Street Crash, America continued her dangerous policy of ignoring events outside her immediate vicinity – one which would have dire consequences in the next decade.

Finally, the political situation in Japan played a part in the failure of the international community. As the Japanese military, rather than the civilian government were in charge of Japan's military campaign, unanimous world condemnation of aggression made little impression on those actually conducting the aggression. The Japanese government might respond positively to calls for moderation, but as they could no longer restrain the military and saw the popularity of the conquest in Japan, they could do little to affect the situation on the ground as the other powers may have believed.

After Britain had signed the Anglo-German Naval Treaty in June 1935 in contravention of the outcome of the Stresa Conference, the French Foreign Secretary Laval, wanted to keep on good terms with Italy as he now mistrusted Britain. Mussolini, however, was preparing for a full-scale war in Abyssinia, to take advantage of the allies' disunity and to restore his regime's popularity at home. The British government, however, was still afraid of the resurgent Germany and feared driving Mussolini towards Hitler if they reacted strongly.

To prevent a war, Anthony Eden, as minister for the League of Nations offered Mussolini a strip of Abyssinian territory, in exchange for which Britain would give Abyssinia an outlet to the sea in British Somaliland. Mussolini rejected this, but the British were clearly happy to see Abyssinia lose territory.

In August, Mussolini announced: 'We shall go forward until we achieve the Fascist Empire'. This so incensed the TUC that they said they would give their full support to any government action to restrain Italy. So the government could not claim a lack of home support for sanctions. In September, the British Foreign Secretary, Samuel Hoare declared at Geneva that Britain would stand by the maintenance of the Covenant to resist unprovoked aggression. Mussolini took no notice and began the full scale invasion of Abyssinia in October. Haile Selassie, Emperor of Abyssinia, appealed to the League who condemned the invasion. A scheme was drafted by a committee of 18 members for the application of economic sanctions. To the French, Britain were threatening their security when they proposed economic sanctions as Italy might leave the League and ally with Germany against them.

By November, however, all the League had done was to recommend a limited economic embargo. The question of oil supplies was to be left until later. Stanley Baldwin, the British Prime Minister, wouldn't act independently, even though the British public favoured sanctions. He therefore refused to close the Suez canal to Italian ships. There was a general election in Britain that month and so, despite his weak stance, Baldwin promised that the government wouldn't waver in its support of collective security. The Conservative-dominated National Government won a landslide victory.

With the election safely won, Hoare visited Paris in December for negotiations with Laval. The subsequent 'Hoare–Laval Pact' offered Mussolini two-thirds of Abyssinia, in return Abyssinia got access to the Red Sea by cession of a small strip of Italian Somaliland. The object was to restore the Stresa front against Hitler by sacrificing Abyssinia, but news of the deal leaked out and there was a public outcry in Britain. The government were seen to be rewarding the aggressor by giving him more territory than they had been able to gain by force and going back on their electoral promises and violating the League's Covenant. As a result, Hoare was forced to resign and was replaced by Eden, who supported the escalation of economic sanctions. Mussolini was furious at this about-face and pulled Italy out of the League, allying her with Hitler instead in the 1936 Rome–Berlin axis.

Despite the British and French efforts, the imposition of sanctions had destroyed the Stresa front and the Hoare–Laval pact had destroyed the idea of collective security and ended the effective life of the League of Nations. The war in Abyssinia ended in May 1936 with a complete Italian victory and proclamation of the King of Italy as Emperor of Abyssinia. In July 1936, the feeble sanctions were called off.

All that Britain appeared to have achieved in her dealings with Italy were failures. The Stresa front had been broken and Italy was firmly in Hitler's camp. The aggression of Mussolini had gone unpunished, leading the dictators to believe that the British would not go to war to protect the status quo. The credibility of the League appeared to have collapsed and perhaps most seriously of all for Britain's future, serious differences over policy had arisen with the French. It was therefore unsurprising that, when he became Prime Minister, Neville Chamberlain should attempt to introduce a new, more dynamic approach to foreign affairs.

6. Relations with Germany after 1933 (AQA)

Read the following source and then answer the questions which follow.

The spirit of the British nation and of the Parliament they had elected in 1935 gradually rose as consciousness of the German, and soon of the German-Italian, menace slowly and fitfully dawned upon them. They became willing, and even eager for all kinds of steps, which, taken two or three years earlier, would have prevented their troubles. But as their mood improved, the power of their opponents and also the difficulty of their task increased. Many say that nothing except war could have stopped Hitler after we had submitted to the seizure of the Rhineland. This may indeed be the verdict of future generations. Much however, could have been done to make us better prepared and thus lessen our hazards.

From *The Second World War Vol I: The Gathering Storm*
by Winston Churchill, 1948

a) **Explain the reference to the seizure of the Rhineland.**   (3 marks)
b) **Why did Britain become aware of the menace of Germany after 1935?**   (7 marks)
c) **Explain how British foreign policy towards Germany between 1933 and 1937 can be criticised.**   (15 marks)

a) In 1936, the German government sent troops to occupy the Rhineland, which had been declared a demilitarised zone in the Versailles Treaty and which the Locarno Treaty of 1925 had confirmed. Britain and France chose not to react to this act of aggression by Hitler and decided to negotiate with Hitler rather than to confront him.

b) Britain had been wary of Germany's declared intentions to overturn the treaties of Versailles and Locarno and had begun, slowly, to rearm, but they had also attempted to negotiate with Hitler, seeking to satisfy German demands. In particular, despite having signed the anti-German Stresa agreement, Britain had signed the Anglo-German Naval Agreement in 1935 which allowed the Germans to build a naval and submarine fleet, in disregard of the Versailles Treaty.

This conciliatory gesture did not lead to any improvement in Germany's approach. First, the Rhineland was re-occupied and military fortifications were developed on the border with France. In response, the government produced a major defence review and accelerated rearmament, especially in air fighter and naval provision. Then, in 1938, the Germans put pressure on the Austrian government to be invited to occupy Austria, which they duly did, and the Nazis declared the *Anschluss* or union between the two countries. Many policy makers still regarded this as a legitimate revision of the Versailles Treaty, but most were alarmed by the belligerent and uncompromising approach of the Germans. Then the Nazis demanded that the Sudetenland, which contained a majority of Germans should be handed to them, despite belonging to the independent democratic state of Czechoslovakia. Although Neville Chamberlain worked tirelessly to avoid war, the government's defence committee recognised that German aggression was making war increasingly likely and local authorities were ordered to draw up evacuation and emergency plans to cope with future German aerial attack.

c) In 1932 the Joint Chiefs failed to approve the 'ten year rule' due to the political instability in Germany as well as the situation in Manchuria. Fears of Hitler's intentions seemed to be confirmed in October 1933, when Germany withdrew from the Disarmament Conference at Geneva, and then from the League of Nations. This effectively destroyed the disarmament conference, so, from 1934 onwards, Britain began to gradually rearm, but Germany was already doing so and at a faster rate than Britain.

In 1934, there was an attempted coup by the Austrian Nazi party which resulted in the murder of the Chancellor, Dolfuss and then, in March 1935, Hitler renounced the Treaty of Versailles and introduced conscription, creating an army of 500,000. In response to these actions, Ramsay MacDonald called a conference with Mussolini and the Foreign Secretary, Laval, at the Italian resort of Stresa. The three countries agreed to combine together against the unilateral repudiation of treaties. At last it appeared there would be some collective action against Germany, and the French strengthened this idea by signing a pact of mutual assistance with the Soviet Union in May 1935.

Hopes were dashed, however, when the Anglo-German Naval Agreement was signed in London in June. This destroyed the Stresa agreement since it meant that almost immediately after adhering to France and Italy against Germany, Britain now had a contradictory treaty encouraging Hitler to repudiate Versailles. Britain was there not in any position to condemn when Italy broke the front by invading Abyssinia in October.

When Hitler invaded the Rhineland in 1936, therefore, there were severe strains in the Anglo-French alliance. German forces were in fact not strong enough to resist joint action from Britain and France. But Britain persuaded France not to react because they did not regard the Rhineland as a vital interest to Britain. The Foreign Secretary, Eden, wanted to build up a new working relationship between Britain, France and Germany, and therefore was not prepared to take positive action against Germany. It is now widely believed that If France and Britain had mobilised their forces and entered the Rhineland, Germany would almost certainly have withdrawn. Many historians have claimed this was 'the last chance' to stop Hitler without war. However, although French action may well have stopped Germany in 1936, it wouldn't have solved the 'German problem'.

Hitler showed that he would break any treaty and should never have been trusted again. However, it is important to remember that British actions were influenced by public opinion that largely wished to avoid another war. Equally the British were both short of troops tied up in colonial police duties outside Europe and they also lacked reliable intelligence as to the precise strength of Germany's armed forces, which Goebbels' propaganda did so much to exaggerate. After the Rome–Berlin axis and the Anti-Comintern Pact, Britain was confronted by Japan in the Far East, Germany in Central Europe and Italy in the Mediterranean. With the USSR engaged on a self-destructive series of purges and the USA refusing to become involved, Britain was left with little room for manoeuvre.

7. Chamberlain and the Munich Agreement (EDEXCEL)

a) **What impact on British Foreign Policy did the accession of Neville Chamberlain as Prime Minister in 1937 have?** (30 marks)

b) **Why did Chamberlain sign the Munich Agreement in 1938?** (30 marks)

(Total: 60 marks)

a) Neville Chamberlain became Prime Minister in 1937 at the age of 68, having effectively acted as Stanley Baldwin's deputy for six years. He was determined to stop the drift and disarray of British foreign policy. He was dictatorial, caring little for the press or the advice of experts, and took a firmer line of policy than Baldwin had done. He regarded war as detestable and was certain all disputes could be settled peacefully with his arranging. He had little faith in the League and felt rearmament was vital to be able to negotiate from a position of strength. He also felt that the USA, USSR and France were unreliable allies and that it would be better if Britain took the lead in negotiating with Hitler to avoid a war.

From May 1937 to March 1939 he had a consistent and coherent policy. He had no liking for the Axis powers, but believed that the formation of a bloc against them would only make matters worse. Given his feelings for the other powers, this was unlikely anyway as he didn't trust them or had no faith in their ability to fight against the Axis powers. He rejected absolutely the traditional device of a grand alliance against aggressors. Alliances, he believed, caused wars. He saw himself as a one man device for the settlement of international disputes without recourse to war. He therefore introduced a policy of 'positive **appeasement**'. Rearmament continued, although not until September 1938 with any great urgency. As a very last resort he was prepared to contemplate war. But he thought it unlikely that military intervention by Britain and Germany could save Eastern Europe from Germany.

Chamberlain was determined to try for better relations with Italy and worked closely with the Italian ambassador in London, Count Grandi. This caused a rift between Chamberlain and the Foreign Secretary, Eden. Both agreed that a rapprochement with Italy was needed and a good bargaining point would be recognition of Italian possession of Abyssinia. Eden, though, mistrusted Mussolini and said there should be no talks until Italy withdrew troops from Spain. Chamberlain did not agree. Eden was also angry at Chamberlain's rejection of an American proposal in January 1938 for an international conference to relax tension, without consulting Eden. The Cabinet supported Chamberlain and Eden resigned in February 1938. In March, Hitler sent troops into Austria, but no action was taken by Britain and France. Chamberlain felt Italian co-operation was vital to stop further advancement of Hitler so Eden's replacement, Lord Halifax, concluded the Anglo-Italian Agreement in April 1938, in which Britain recognised Italy's conquest of Abyssinia, and Italy promised to observe a policy of non-intervention in Spain.

b)   When Neville Chamberlain signed the Munich Agreement in September 1938, which handed the Sudetenland to Germany, resistance seemed hopeless. Chamberlain was unconvinced of Russian proposals to support the West, and ignored Russia's claims to be consulted as a member of the Council of the League of Nations. He knew the USA would stay neutral and that the Dominions had refused to commit themselves to a war for Czechoslovakia's sake. He was aware that Britain was facing an aggressive and expansionist Japan in the Far East as evidenced by the invasion of China in 1937. Given the need to defend the scattered imperial possessions there the British army and airforce were relatively unprepared. In September 1938, he had written, 'you should never menace unless you are in a position to carry out your threats, and although, if we were to fight, I should hope we should be able to give a good account of ourselves, we are certainly not in a position in which our military advisers would feel happy to fight'. As Chancellor of the Exchequer he had worked hard to help Britain recover from the Depression of the early 1930s and he was reluctant to risk that recovery by embarking on an accelerated rearmament programme or by embroiling Britain in another financially disastrous war. Finally, on personal moral grounds, Chamberlain was totally opposed to war and believed that it should always be the last resort in foreign policy.

The Munich Agreement, only reached after war had seemed a strong possibility, has since been condemned as a painful surrender to threats, and a catastrophic failure of British foreign policy. To Churchill, **appeasement** at other people's expense was morally reprehensible, especially as the Czechs were well fortified and the Germans not prepared for a full scale war.

One counter argument to this is that Munich successfully 'bought time'. Britain certainly felt that its defences were insufficient against the perceived might of the German armed forces. Given the fragile state of the British economy in the 1930s the Treasury advised the government that the necessary rearmament would be difficult to achieve and that on 22 September 1938, the day Chamberlain was meeting Hitler at Bad Godesberg, General Ismay, Secretary to the Chiefs of Staff of Imperial Defence, had drawn up a balance sheet of advantages and disadvantages of fighting Germany immediately and postponing possible conflict for a year or more. He concluded that the balance favoured postponement. His clinching argument was that delay would enable Britain to improve their air defences. The earlier plans had yet to come to maturity; Spitfires were not available; only a third of anti-aircraft defences were ready and the power of British bomber retaliation was estimated to be a sixth of German capacity. Ismay and his colleagues were not to know that there were in fact no clear plans for the Luftwaffe to attack Britain if a continental war broke out in 1938.

The Munich Agreement was based on one serious misconception, however. Chamberlain signed the agreement in the belief that Hitler would keep his word that he had no more territorial ambitions. The declaration of friendship given to Hitler to sign by Chamberlain demonstrates this clearly. Unfortunately, Hitler had no intention of keeping to any agreement. He believed that Chamberlain had signed away the Sudetenland, because Britain was not prepared to fight for Eastern Europe and therefore continued to pursue an opportunistic policy of expansion that led to occupation of Prague in March 1939 which destroyed the Munich agreement and led to the confrontation between Britain and Germany over Poland in September 1939.

8. The outbreak of war (OCR)

**Why did Neville Chamberlain abandon appeasement in 1939 but not form
an alliance with the Soviet Union?**

(90 marks)

Chamberlain, was not convinced that Munich made peace more secure. After the Bad Godesberg meeting, he had few illusions left about Hitler, and regretted using the term 'peace with honour' to describe the settlement he reached with Hitler at the Munich conference. However, he remained confident that he alone could handle the difficult problems that undoubtedly lay ahead. In public, Chamberlain continued to talk hopefully of Hitler and Mussolini's peaceful intentions, in order to avoid any increase in tension. However, the actions of Hitler in particular gave little cause for optimism. He gave a number of anti-British speeches, and showed no signs that his ambitions had been finally satisfied at Munich. Any goodwill of the British people towards the German government was finally destroyed when news came in November of 'Kristallnacht', when the Nazis openly set out to destroy the Jewish community in Germany, smashing shops, burning synagogues and sending Jews to concentration camps. In two by-elections in November, the government candidates were both defeated and Chamberlain was forced to recognise that public support for the government's foreign policy was faltering.

The Cabinet began to prepare for a possible war in Europe. This gradual change in attitude was accelerated in March 1939, when Hitler sent his troops into the Czech provinces of Bohemia and Moravia, ostensibly to protect them against Polish and Hungarian aggression, but in direct violation of the Munich agreement. It was now clear to Chamberlain that Hitler's promises were valueless and that the policy of **appeasement** had, in Germany's case at least, to be abandoned.

Now, when Hitler made demands of a small European neighbour, the British government would publicly guarantee to support them against Hitler. Military consultations began with France, the pace of rearmament was stepped up and a Ministry of Supply was established in July, to organise munitions production. Britain had had to adopt a different policy to stop Hitler, otherwise he would become so dominant in Europe that Britain's interests would be threatened.

There were limits to Chamberlain's change of heart, however, as he still refused to appoint Winston Churchill as Minister of Supply, despite the demands of the press, for fear that this would unduly provoke Hitler. He believed that the guarantee to Poland would lead to negotiation, albeit based on threat, rather than compromise. As he wrote to his sister in July 1939, during the Polish crisis 'I can imagine a way could be found of meeting Germany's claims while safeguarding Poland's independence and economic security'. It would not be until September that Chamberlain would finally be prepared to go to war to resist Hitler, and even then, only very reluctantly.

After the occupation of Bohemia and Moravia, the USSR repeatedly attempted to reach an agreement with Britain and France on how to resist Hitler. Its overtures were supported in Britain by a diverse selection of politicians, Lloyd George, Churchill and the Labour Party leadership. In March 1939, Stalin proposed a conference to organise an anti-German alliance. Britain and France chose to ignore this, as they had chosen to ignore the USSR's demands for a place at the Munich conference the previous September. When Stalin then proposed a military alliance between France, Britain and the Soviet Union, Britain gave an unenthusiastic response, refusing an invitation for Lord Halifax, the Foreign Secretary, to go to Moscow for negotiations. The only contact between

Britain and the Soviet Union was through the British Ambassador in Moscow, Sir William Seeds, who was told by Halifax that 'the time is not yet ripe for the comprehensive counter-proposal which the Soviet Government have put to us'. When joint military talks were proposed, the British and French delegates were sent by boat and train, rather than by plane. Unsurprisingly, after all this, Stalin concluded that Britain was not seriously interested in any form of alliance or joint action against Hitler, and began, instead, to negotiate with the Germans. The Jewish, pro-Western Russian foreign minister, Litvinov, was replaced in May 1939 by Molotov, who would be more easily able to reach an understanding with the Nazis.

Stalin had distrusted Chamberlain since the Munich agreement and was worried that it had fore-shadowed an anti-communist alliance between Germany and Britain. The British and French guarantee to Poland also irked him, as he wished to regain the Polish territories held by the Tsars. He had made the negotiations with Britain difficult by demanding a free hand in the Baltic states, but refusing to offer help if Germany attacked Holland, Switzerland or Luxemburg. Worst of all, he insisted on the right to send Russian troops across Poland and Rumania to attack Germany, which those countries would not agree to. Clearly, Stalin was primarily interested in gaining as much as he could from any agreement with the West.

Chamberlain, himself did not want an alliance with the USSR and he had the support of the service chiefs in this. Principally, he and Halifax detested communism and they did not relish having to allow Soviet troops into Eastern Europe. The Soviets were regarded as untrustworthy, and their attitude towards Poland, Rumania and the Baltic States seemed to confirm this. British intelligence had also discovered that Stalin was negotiating with the Germans as early as July. Third, the effectiveness of the Russian troops, following the army purges in which 80 per cent of the senior command had been 'liquidated', was also highly questionable. Finally, the Poles refused to allow Russian troops to cross their territory to take up positions on the German-Polish border as they would have to do in order to make any alliance meaningful. Chamberlain believed that negotiation with Hitler was still possible, but that an agreement between the British government and Stalin would only make conflict unavoidable. The steps towards military co-operation with Russia were therefore half-hearted at best, and, although the Molotov–Ribbentrop non-aggression pact of 24 August came as a shock, it was met, at least in some quarters of Westminster, with some sense of relief.

9. British foreign policy in the 1930s (OCR)

How far were Britain's leaders responsible for the outbreak of war in 1939?

(Total: 90 marks)

No one suggests that Britain's leaders actively sought war. Both Baldwin and Chamberlain and their Foreign Secretaries put a huge effort into avoiding conflict if at all possible. There is certainly no doubt that war was extremely likely in 1938 and that the actions of Neville Chamberlain were crucial in avoiding it that year. What the British leaders were accused of, both by Winston Churchill and by a group of left wing writers in their book *Guilty Men* (1940) was incompetence. It is claimed that the wrong message was sent to the German leadership at crucial moments, which encouraged the Nazis to believe that their aggressive foreign policy would be rewarded and that Britain would fail to fight to protect the Versailles settlement. As a result, Britain found itself in a weak position in 1939 and was unable to prevent the fall of France in the following year and the subsequent near-defeat of Britain itself.

Given the economic problems of the Depression of the early 1930s and the consequent need for Britain to keep government spending to a minimum, it is perhaps understandable that Britain, like France, cut its defence spending in the early 1930s. There was a widespread public belief that the stockpiling of weapons had helped to cause the First World War, and the Labour Party was, under George Lansbury, in favour of more cuts than the government, an attitude that Labour retained until 1937. However, it does seem folly to keep British defence spending quite so low, once the economy had begun to recover and Japanese, German and Italian aggression had been made plain. Conversely, one could argue, that faced with this combination of aggressors, Britain did not have much chance of defending her interests with only France as a sure ally.

The USSR had not only been militarily weakened by the Stalinist purges of 1938 as British secret service reports emphasised, but, as a communist state, she was deeply suspicious of the western democracies. Britain, in her turn, had no desire to allow Russia any more influence in Eastern Europe than she already had, especially as she had already demonstrated in Spain that her assistance came only with the promotion of communist control.

The USA had not only failed to ratify the Treaty of Versailles and never joined the League of Nations, but she refused to allow Britain to use her financial assistance to either buy off or arm herself against the aggressive states. As for France, she remained weakened, not only by economic weakness and colonial police duties, but also by bitter political division.

Given the strategic weakness and the overwhelming public antipathy towards war, both in Britain and the Empire, it is perhaps not surprising that Britain resorted to a policy of compromise and diplomacy, rather than one of confrontation in the late 1930s. The military experts who advised the government, took great pleasure in reminding the politicians of the threat of multiple attacks on the exposed Empire, and of the likelihood of mass civilian casualties in any future war, given the apparent strength of the Luftwaffe and the impossibility of defence against the 'bomber-threat'.

But, there were other military experts, such as Churchill, whose voices were ignored. These opponents of **appeasement** pointed out the potential value of countries such as the USSR and Czechoslovakia as military allies and questioned the true strength of the German and Italian forces (especially in light of the endurance of the Spanish republican forces). The Soviet Union, certainly, was viewed with complete hostility in Whitehall and Britain's refusal to form an alliance with her drove Stalin into Hitler's non-aggression pact in 1939.

Perhaps most seriously, Britain's leaders showed a breathtaking willingness to invest trust in the Nazi regime that was already notorious for its complete refusal to observe any diplomatic niceties in its dealings with other countries. The signing of the Anglo-German Naval Agreement ruined the first attempt to form an anti-Nazi pact, the Stresa front, and Chamberlain's repeated statements of public trust, culminating in the notorious 'piece of paper', were political folly of the highest order. Perhaps crucially, having handed over Czechoslovakia without a fight, and facing Germany and Russia, Britain then chose to issue an ultimatum over the fate of Poland, a country which Britain had neither the ability or the motive to defend. Having forced Britain's capitulation over the Rhineland, Austria and Czechoslovakia, Hitler, was quite astonished that she should go to war over Poland, yet at the same time, not much perturbed about Britain's commitment to the war effort.

Additional essay questions

 1. The Treaty of Versailles (AQA)

Read the following source and then answer the questions which follow.

Lloyd George had judged public opinion shrewdly when he told Clemenceau that the only question on which he was likely to be seriously attacked was reparations. The treaty was ratified by the Commons without serious criticism.

From *England 1914–1974* by W.N. Medlicott, 1976

a) **What is meant by 'reparations' in the context of the Versailles Treaty?**   **(3 marks)**
b) **Explain the ways in which Lloyd George was able to satisfy most British demands at Versailles.**   **(7 marks)**
c) **'British appeasement of Germany began at Versailles'. Explain why you agree or disagree with this statement.**   **(15 marks)**

 2. British foreign policy in the 1920s (OCR)

Explain why Britain signed the Locarno Treaty in December 1925 and assess the achievements of Austen Chamberlain as Foreign Secretary.

(90 marks)

Essay plan

The Locarno Treaty – its principal agreement – to accept the Western borders of Germany established by the Treaty of Versailles.

- *Britain acted as guarantor of the treaty.*
- *Britain wished to reward France for abandoning her aggressive policy which had led to the occupation of the Rhineland in 1923.*
- *Britain wished to encourage the Germans to seek revisions to the Treaty of Versailles through peaceful methods and the Locarno Treaty was a bargaining piece in that policy as it led to reduction in the allied forces based in the Rhineland.*
- *The treaty gave France the security she had craved since 1918 by protecting the east bank of the Rhine as a demilitarised zone.*
- *Britain was not guaranteeing Germany's eastern borders – left France to sign the 'little entente' with Poland and Czechoslovakia.*
- *The guarantee was to both Germany and France – Britain had to make no military commitment. This, together with the increased stability in Europe, allowed Britain to direct her limited military resources to the policing of the restive parts of the Empire such as India, Palestine and Egypt and the defence of areas vulnerable to attack, especially from the increasingly aggressive Japan.*

Chamberlain – longest serving British Foreign Secretary of the 1920s. Often seen as isolationist and too pro-French, but a study of his actions reveals a more complex policy aimed at freeing Britain from commitments to Europe and the Dominions, in order to concentrate on the restive and strategically exposed Empire.

- *Locarno – problem of Franco-German border largely solved. Mutual trust and co-operation reintroduced after the Ruhr crisis. Did not force Britain to become the policeman of the world, unlike the 'Geneva Protocol' favoured by his predecessor, Ramsay MacDonald. France rewarded for more diplomatic approach.*
- *Inter-Allied Military Commission of Control, supervising German disarmament replaced by occasional League of Nations inspections – to reward German acceptance of Locarno.*
- *Other German grievances, such as position of German minorities in Poland and Czechoslovakia were discussed to achieve a positive revision of Versailles.*
- *1928 Kellogg–Briand Pact demonstrated a world-wide commitment to peace, which suited Britain.*
- *1929 Young Plan reduced German reparations payments.*
- *1929, allies agreed to withdraw all troops from Rhineland, five years ahead of schedule.*
- *Dominions given greater control over their foreign affairs, following the Imperial Conference of 1926.*

There were failures, however:

- *The failure to make progress on allied disarmament – which caused much anger in Germany which had been forced to disarm – a factor which helped Hitler to power and to reject the Locarno approach.*
- *The failure to effectively engage in a similarly positive dialogue with the Soviet Union and, to some extent Japan – both of whom threatened the security of the Empire.*
- *The failure to satisfy Indian demands for Dominion status which led to Britain continuing to have to police the region with troops and to defend a strategically difficult supply line to the area.*
- *The ongoing problems of Palestine, Egypt and Kenya were not effectively resolved.*

Conclusion – Chamberlain's success largely short-term. Based on political stability in Europe, which came to an end with the economic depression of 1929–33 (although it is unfair to blame Chamberlain for not foreseeing such an unprecedented collapse). It was also largely based on satisfying German demands for revision of the Versailles Treaty, and in many ways Stresemann's foreign policy was a forerunner of Hitler's – albeit with very different methods. The point of the policy was to allow Britain to concentrate on her Empire and its defence, but by 1929, the Empire, especially India, was even more unsettled than before and the strategic threats of Japan and Russia were not contained. As the 1930s showed, Chamberlain's policy could quickly unravel and leave Britain facing a multiplicity of powerful enemies across the world with few reliable or powerful allies.

3. The Empire (EDEXCEL)

a) **How did Britain respond to demands for independence from India in the inter-war years?** (30 marks)

b) **Why were the Dominions able to achieve self-government by 1931?** (30 marks)

(Total: 60 marks)

Essay plan

a)   Demands for independence in India before the First World War had led to the Morley–Minto reforms of 1909 which increased Indian representation in the administration of India and gave more power to the legislative councils. But demands for independence were not satisfied, especially with India's contribution to the war effort between 1914 and 1918. During the war, India had been promised eventual self-government within the Empire, but Britain wished to ensure that inter-caste and inter-faith rivalry did not lead to a break down of order and a divided India after this was granted – hence the initial slowness of reform.

- *In 1919 the Government of India Act (Based on the Montagu-Chelmsford reforms), gave autonomy to eleven provinces and gave Indian ministers control of public health, education and agriculture – Indian nationalists still felt that too much power was left in the Viceroy's hands and the situation was inflamed by the **Amritsar massacre**. The multi-faith Indian National Congress (Congress Party), led by Gandhi and Nehru became increasingly popular and his calls for non-cooperation with the British authorities made the task of controlling India increasingly difficult.*

- *In 1927, Baldwin's government sent a Royal Commission under Sir John Simon to investigate the need for further reform, but refused to meet Indian representatives, leading to Congress boycotting the Commission. While it was investigating, the **viceroy** announced that India would be granted **Dominion** status, but Congress demanded full independence. Three round-table conferences were held on the future of India, but despite including Indian representatives, these were boycotted by many others.*

- *As a result of the conferences and the Simon Commission's report, the 1935 Government of India Act gave control of provincial government to the Indians and in the subsequent elections, Congress agreed to participate and won 8 of the 11 provinces. The **viceroy** remained in charge of central government however as the relationship between the Hindu majority and the Muslim minority was still not resolved.*

*By 1939, the reforms of 1935 had managed to engage the Congress Party in the process of reform by granting local self-government. It had taken a long period of confrontation and violence to persuade Britain that the pace of reform had to be quickened after the First World War. However, the nationalists regarded this as merely a stepping stone to the ultimate goal of independence, although Britain had only promised **Dominion** status at a time of Britain's choosing.*

b)   Like India, the Dominions (South Africa, Canada, Australia and New Zealand) wanted complete independence from Britain, especially as they had contributed two and a half million men and resources to the First World War and did not wish to be dragged into another war on Britain's behalf. At the 1917 Imperial War Conference, the Dominions demanded a post-war conference to redefine their position within the Empire.

- *At the 1921 conference, Lloyd George failed to address these demands as he was pre-occupied by the violent crises in Ireland, India and Egypt. As a result, the Dominions failed to offer support to Britain in the 1922 Chanak crisis and refused to sign the 1925 Locarno Pact. In 1924, the anti-British, pro-Boer National Party of General Hertzog won power in South Africa and began the policy of race segregation known as 'apartheid'.*
- *A second conference held in 1926 was more successful. Here, the colonies minister, Balfour, moved to address the Dominions' concerns and offered a definition of them as 'autonomous communities within the British Empire'. This allowed the British to maintain the appearance of imperial unity to potential aggressors, while allowing the Dominions the greater autonomy they sought, especially in the exercise of foreign affairs.*
- *Finally, in 1930, a third conference considered the issue of the application of British law to the Dominions. As a result, the 1931 Statute of Westminster allowed the Dominions to become completely self-governing if they wished to do so, with the Parliament at Westminster no longer able to overrule the legislatures of the Dominions. The British monarch remained head of state, represented by a High Commissioner.*

Britain had learnt from the non-cooperation of the Dominions in the early 1920s and realised that, in order to maintain any military, strategic or economic benefit from the Dominions, she had to accede to their demands for complete autonomy. Although she gained little economic benefit from them in the subsequent Depression, despite the 1932 Ottawa conference, the Dominions all supported Britain in the Second World War and played an invaluable role when Britain had no other allies between May 1940 and June 1941.

4. British foreign policy in the 1930s (OCR)

Compare the importance of at least three reasons why Britain declared war on Germany on 3 September 1939.

(90 marks)

Part 3: Sources

1. Anglo-Soviet relations in the 1920s (EDEXCEL)

Study sources 1–5 below and then answer questions (a) to (e) which follow:

Source 1: Stanley Baldwin, the Prime Minister, speaking in 1926

If you look at a doctrine which is being preached today in certain parts of the Continent, and even here, the teaching of communism, you will find that, whatever else may be said about it, it is a system in which there can be no freedom as we understand that word in England. It is a system that can only be ordered by an iron discipline, and no system that requires an iron discipline is adapted to our people.

Source 2: From the minutes of a discussion on the diplomatic recognition of Russia by the Liberal and Conservative Cabinet, 1922

The Home Secretary had circulated a paper recording an interview with a Russian trader, who represented a very important Corporation. According to this trader, Lenin was personally largely responsible for the . . . recent economic laws, which amount to an abandonment of Communism. If the Russian Delegation came to Genoa having practically surrendered their Communistic principles and willing to enter into negotiation with Capitalistic communities, we ought to give all necessary support to the anti-Communistic elements in Russia, and declare that if Communistic principles are abandoned we are ready to assist in the economic development of Russia.

Source 3: From a *Daily Mail* report on the 'Zinoviev letter', October 1924

The publication of the 'very secret' Moscow letter of instruction to Communists in Britain (who are the Socialist Government's masters) to take steps to paralyse our Army and Navy and to plunge England into civil war has profoundly shocked the whole country . . .

Throughout the weekend a storm of criticism has been directed against Mr MacDonald and his ministers, because it was they who signed the treaty to 'lend' British money to these Moscow murderers. These criminals sent their civil war orders over here, despite their solemn undertaking in the treaty to cease all such poison plots . . .

Source 4: An account from *The Times* of a police raid on the offices of a Russian trading company in London, 1927

A raid on the offices of Arcos Ltd in Moorgate was carried out by a strong force of police yesterday. The numerous staff engaged there were surprised at 4.30 p.m. by the entry of about 150 police, who at once ordered the cessation of work, and began a systematic search of the papers in every department, which lasted until 11 o'clock and will be resumed today. The raid took place in consequence of search warrant granted by a City magistrate on information which was laid before him . . . The search was conducted by about 50 members of the Special Branch, who were assisted by Foreign Office interpreters.

Source 5: From *Britain: Foreign and Imperial Affairs 1919–1939* by A. Farmer, 2000

Most Conservative and Liberal MPs were implacably opposed to Lenin and agreed with Winston Churchill when he spoke of 'the foul baboonery of Bolshevism'. Churchill was all for sending British forces into Russia to destroy the Bolsheviks before they could sow the seeds of revolution elsewhere in the world, possibly even in Britain . . .

To a considerable extent, after 1920 Anglo-Soviet relations depended on which party was in power in Britain, with Conservative governments far less willing to do business with the USSR than Labour. However, policy also shifted in response to changes in Soviet objectives.

QUESTIONS WITH WORKED ANSWERS

a) Study source 1. What does Source 1 reveal about Stanley Baldwin's attitude towards the Soviet Union? **(6 marks)**

b) Study source 2 and use your own knowledge. Explain why Britain's relations with Russia were so poor in the four years after the cessation of the First World War. **(10 marks)**

c) Study sources 2 and 5. How far does the evidence provided by source 2 support the views of Farmer in Source 5? **(10 marks)**

d) Study sources 3 and 4. How useful are these two sources to an historian enquiring into Anglo-Soviet relations between the wars? **(10 marks)**

e) Study source 5 and use your own knowledge. Do you agree with the view that 'Anglo-Soviet relations depended on which party was in power in Britain' with reference to the 1920s? **(24 marks)**

(Total: 60 marks)

ANSWERS

a) Stanley Baldwin clearly regarded communism as a political system based on compulsion, as he stated in source 1 that 'it is a system in which there can be no freedom as we understand that word in England'. He does not necessarily see it as wicked or evil, merely unsuited to use in Britain, for as he comments, it is a system based on authoritarian rule and 'no system that requires an iron discipline is adapted to our people [the British]'. Of course, in the use of a pejorative term such as 'iron discipline', it is reasonable to assume that Baldwin does not approve of the methods employed by the Soviet government. It is important to point out, however, that this was his opinion of communism as a political system, not of the Soviet Union. One may infer from what Baldwin says that while the Soviet Union remains strictly communist, he will remain suspicious of its intentions, but if it demonstrates a more open economic and political structure, he would be willing to open normal international relations with the country.

b) As a result of the Bolshevik revolution of October 1917, Russia had signed an armistice with Germany, which allowed the Germans to concentrate their forces on the western front. Desperate to reverse this, the allies gave support to the anti-Bolshevik 'white' forces in the subsequent Russian Civil War. The British also sent troops to support the 'whites' which were not withdrawn until 1920. Relations between the two governments were not likely to be good in these circumstances.

Second, the British government feared the spread of the ideas of the Bolsheviks to Britain. There had been much sympathy for the Bolshevik revolution from trade unionists and Labour politicians, and although that became more muted during the civil war, Lloyd George's government still feared the development of British revolutionaries, especially among the radical areas of Clydeside and the Welsh mines. Lenin's establishment of the Comintern, committed to promote communist revolutions in other countries, did much to fuel this fear. The government therefore continued to support Russia's enemies and allowed the Polish government to buy arms when she fought the communists in 1920. In principle she sought to construct a cordon sanitaire around the rogue Soviet state.

Finally, the behaviour of the communist government, seizing British assets and repudiating the Tsarist government's substantial debts to Britain, caused many influential businessmen and financiers to urge the government to continue to refuse to recognise the Soviet government until the debts were settled. The assassination of the former Tsar and his entire family at the hands of local communists, as well as causing widespread revulsion in largely royalist British, also ensured that the British royal family would have nothing to do with a regime responsible, as they saw it, for the murder of a fellow monarch and cousin of the king.

c) In source 5, Farmer writes that 'Anglo-Soviet relations depended on which party was in power in Britain, with Conservative governments far less willing to do business with the USSR'. However, Lloyd George's Conservative dominated Cabinet was willing to engage in a rapprochement with the Soviet government, although this was clearly motivated by the rather over-optimistic belief that the Soviets had, in 1922, 'practically surrendered their Communistic principles and [were] willing to enter into negotiation with Capitalistic communities'. It is of course difficult to assess whether these Cabinet minutes reflect the views of the Liberal Prime Minister, or of the Cabinet as a whole.

As Farmer goes on to write, however, British 'policy also shifted in response to changes in Soviet objectives'. As is reported in source 2, however, the recent announcement of the New Economic Policy, are read by the Cabinet to 'amount to an abandonment of Communism'. If this is proved to be the case by the behaviour of the Soviet delegates at the forthcoming Genoa economic conference, the British government is willing 'to assist in the economic development of Russia', and therefore was shifting policy in response to the Soviet's behaviour. Clearly there are limits to how achievable this policy shift actually was, as the Cabinet are only willing to offer aid 'if Communistic principles are abandoned', which is perhaps an example of a more hard-line stance on the part of the Conservative members of the Cabinet.

d) Source 3, from the *Daily Mail*, reveals, how the right-wing press was determined to portray the Soviet government as a threat to British democracy. Terms such as 'Moscow murderers' attempting to send 'civil war orders over here', reveal an absolute contempt for the Soviet regime from the popular Conservative media. Furthermore, the source shows that the press were convinced of a connection between the Russian communists and Britain's Labour party, which had recently formed a minority government and signed a trade agreement with the USSR. In revealing the 'Zinoviev letter', they hoped to support this argument with evidence, showing that the British Communist Party was 'the Socialist Government's masters'.

Source 4 from *The Times*, less openly partisan than the article in the *Daily Mail*, simply reports the events at the Arcos offices. The article reveals the extent to which distrust of the Soviet government's intentions still continued in the Conservative government after 1924. Following the General

Strike and the rise of the Indian National Congress Party in India, there was fear that Arcos, the Soviet trading organisation established after the 1924 trade agreement was acting as a cover for communist infiltration. Such was public hostility to the Soviet system, that there is no element of criticism of the government's action, despite the clear implication in the article that no evidence was found despite the scale and the surprise of the raid. The government subsequently broke off relations with the Soviet Union once again, to hide their embarrassment.

e) Sources 1, 3 and 4 clearly indicate a hostility towards the Soviet Union on the part of the Conservative party, through its leader in the 1920s, its supporters in the press and its actions. The actions of the Bolshevik regime in seizing power through a coup and then making peace with Germany, dissolving the constituent assembly and ruling through force, did much to disgust British politicians of all the major parties. The subsequent civil war, the use of secret police and the murder of the Romanovs, all contributed to making all members of the British establishment reluctant to remove the Soviet Union's post-war status as a pariah nation. When the British Communist Party (BCP) was established in 1920, the Labour Party refused its offer of affiliation, especially as Lenin had made clear his attitude towards Labour when he wrote 'we shall support Henderson as a rope supports a man who is hanged'.

For the Conservative Party in particular, though, the Soviet repudiation of all debts incurred by the previous governments proved a very significant obstacle to future relations, as many Conservative members had had commercial interests in Russia, and the British government, now in serious debt to the USA, had lent a significant amount themselves. Added to this was the commitment of the communists to spread the revolution to capitalist countries using criminal methods and political infiltration.

In light of this, the surprisingly conciliatory attitude of the Conservative dominated Cabinet towards future economic and diplomatic relations with the USSR, evident in source 2, becomes more understandable. With the announcement of the New Economic Policy, the British government believed that the Soviet government was formally renouncing communism and was therefore hopeful, that, once ideological conflict was ended, the disputes of the past could be forgotten and normal relations resumed. Although the Soviet–German pact at Rapallo revealed that the ideological position had not altered, the position of the Conservatives did not significantly alter until the formation of the first Labour government in 1924. Although Baldwin was keen for Labour to be given 'their chance' as he put it, many middle-class Conservatives feared the growth in state power and punitive taxation that a Labour government might bring, and used the trade agreement with Russia, as a good opportunity to discredit their opponents. The Campbell case and the arrival of the 'Zinoviev letter', whether genuine or forgery, at the offices of the *Daily Mail*, days before the election, gave the Conservatives a political opportunity that even Baldwin could not resist exploiting. The Conservatives therefore became established as a national anti-socialist party and their actions immediately before and during the general strike are explicable as an attempt to fulfil this role. Anglo-Soviet relations were thus part of the Conservatives' appeal to their domestic audience, and the Arcos raid of 1927 was another attempt to remind the electorate of their determination to root out communist infiltrators (even if they were fictitious in this case).

For their part, the leadership of the Labour Party recognised that many activists, if not rank-and-file trade unionists, had sympathy with Soviet Russia. The diplomatic recognition of the Soviet Union in 1924 and the limited trade agreement were therefore, in part a token gesture to please their supporters.

However, after the 'Zinoviev letter', the Labour Party was determined to avoid being accused of being 'fellow travellers' of the communists again, and carefully avoided any future associations, continuing to refuse affiliation to the BCP and refusing an offer of financial support for the TUC from the Soviet Union during the General Strike.

It is therefore, more plausible to conclude that, while the attitude of the British towards Russia did alter according to the party in power, it is equally true to say that the attitude was affected by both domestic and foreign policy concerns, and that neither party acted from purely ideological motives in their attitude to the Soviet Union, being mostly concerned to strike a posture most likely to reassure their core voters, whilst not alienating potential allies.

QUESTIONS WITHOUT WORKED ANSWERS (EDEXCEL)

a) **Study source 2. What does this source reveal about British attitudes towards the Soviet Union?** (6 marks)

b) **Use your own knowledge. Explain why the British government was more willing to formally recognise the Communist regime in Russia in 1922.** (10 marks)

c) **Study sources 1 and 4. How far were the actions described in source 4 made more likely by the attitude demonstrated by Baldwin in source 1?** (10 marks)

d) **Study sources 1 and 3. How useful are these two sources to a historian studying the importance of Anglo-Soviet relations to Conservative dominance in the late 1920s in Britain?** (10 marks)

e) **Study source 5 and use your own knowledge. Explain why Britain and Russia still regarded one another with suspicion by 1929.** (24 marks)

(Total: 60 marks)

2. Neville Chamberlain and appeasement (OCR)

Source A: Neville Chamberlain, in a letter to his sister, March 20, 1938

You only have to look at the map to see that nothing that France or we could do could possibly save Czechoslovakia from being overrun by the Germans, if they wanted to do it . . . I have therefore, abandoned any idea of giving guarantees to Czechoslovakia, or to the French in connection with her obligations to that country

Source B: Neville Chamberlain, in a letter to his sister after his first meeting with Hitler at Berchtesgaden, 17 September, 1938

I had established a certain confidence [with Hitler], which was my aim, and on my side, in spite of the hardness and ruthlessness I thought I saw in his face, I got the impression that here was a man who could be relied on when he had given his word.

Source C: From the diary of Sir Alexander Cadogan, undersecretary at the Foreign Office, 24 September 1938

Hitler memo now in. It's awful . . . Hitler says he must march into the whole area [the Sudetenland] at once (to keep order!) and the safeguards – and plebiscites! Can be held after! This is throwing away every safeguard we had. PM is transmitting this 'proposal' to Prague. Thank God he hasn't yet recommended it for acceptance . . .

Meeting of 'Inner Cabinet' at 3.30 and PM made his report to us. I was completely horrified – he was quite calmly for total surrender. More horrified still to find that Hitler has evidently hypnotised him to a point . . . I'd rather be beat than dishonoured. How can we look any foreigner in the face after this? How can we hold Egypt, India and the rest?

Source D: Chamberlain's broadcast to the nation, 27 September

How horrible, fantastic, incredible, it is that we should be digging trenches and trying on gas-masks here because of a quarrel in a far-away country between people of whom we know nothing . . .

I would not hesitate to pay even a third visit to Germany, if I thought it would do any good . . . I am myself a man of peace to the depths of my soul . . . war is a fearful thing, and we must be very clear, before we embark on it, that it is really the great issues that are at stake.

Source E: Duff Cooper, who resigned as First Lord of the Admiralty over the Munich Agreement, on Neville Chamberlain

He [Chamberlain] himself hated the idea of war. So, he believed, did all sensible men. Mussolini and Hitler must surely be sensible men too or they would never have risen to the great positions they occupied. Therefore they would not want war. There were certain things they did want, and there were certain things that we could give them. If he were in control of foreign policy he could meet these men round a table and come to terms with them. The danger of war would be removed and we could all get on with social reform. Chamberlain had many good qualities but he lacked experience of the world, and he lacked also the imagination which can fill the gaps of inexperience . . . He had been a successful Lord Mayor of Birmingham, and for him the Dictators of Germany and Italy were like Lord Mayors of Liverpool and Manchester, who might belong to different political parties and have different interests, but who must desire the welfare of humanity, and be fundamentally reasonable, decent men like himself. This profound misconception lay at the root of his policy and explains his mistakes.

QUESTIONS WITH WORKED ANSWERS

a) **Study source A. From this source and your own knowledge, explain why Czechoslovakia was such an important issue in Britain's foreign policy in 1938.** (10 marks)

b) **Study Source B. How useful is this source in explaining Chamberlain's actions during the Czechoslovakian crisis?** (25 marks)

> c) Study Sources C and D. Explain why these sources differ in their attitude towards Czechoslovakia. **(25 marks)**
>
> d) Study *all* the sources. Using all the sources and your own knowledge, do you agree that Chamberlain had little realistic alternative to appeasing Hitler in 1938? **(60 marks)**
>
> **(Total: 120 marks)**

ANSWERS

a) By 1938, Hitler had annexed Austria and turned his attention next to Czechoslovakia, with its significant German minority population, concentrated in the Sudeten border area near Austria. Many British politicians had sympathy with the Czechs who refused to cede authority over the Sudetenland to Germany, as Czechoslovakia was a democracy. For the Prime Minister, Neville Chamberlain, the most important issue was how to solve the crisis as amicably as possible, as his overriding priority was to prevent the issue creating a war which Britain might be dragged into.

b) Source B is a letter by Neville Chamberlain to his sister, so, as a private letter, it can be relied on to give Chamberlain's genuine opinion on his first meeting with Hitler. On the other hand, Chamberlain may well want to justify his actions to his family, just as much as he might to his Cabinet colleagues, to Parliament or the public.

It is clear from source B that Chamberlain believes that he can trust Hitler, for he writes that 'I got the impression that here was a man who could be relied on when he had given his word'. In light of Chamberlain's actions at the Munich conference, in which he gave the Germans control over the Sudetenland and effectively neutralised the Czech's natural defensive barriers, he continued to trust that Hitler would keep his word and not take the opportunity to occupy the whole of Czechoslovakia. Furthermore, the infamous 'piece of paper' on which Hitler and Chamberlain signed a pledge never to go to war again, demonstrates that Chamberlain did not lose his trust in Hitler's good intentions until after the Munich conference.

On the other hand, Hitler's behaviour at the second meeting at Bad Godesberg did much to shake Chamberlain's belief that he 'had established a certain confidence (with Hitler)' as Hitler increased his demands from the initial meeting between the two leaders at Berchtesgaden. Chamberlain's initial positive feelings about Hitler were undermined by this, and it perhaps too simplistic to assume that it was merely Chamberlain's initial sense of trust that caused him to sign the Munich agreement.

c) In source C, Sir Alex Cadogan is alarmed by Chamberlain's passive response to Hitler's telegram and incensed by his willingness to recommend that the Cabinet agree to Hitler's proposals. As he puts it, 'how can we look any foreigner in the face after this?' meaning that such an action would reflect very badly on Britain's international standing as she would be seen to be allowing an act of aggression by a dictatorship against a democracy to not only go unpunished but to be condoned by Britain. In particular he wonders at the impact of such behaviour on the colonies which were already restive under British rule by 1938, as he asks, 'how can we hold Egypt, India and the rest?' It is his concern for Britain's future world role that makes his reaction so vehement.

Chamberlain, by contrast, in source D, refers to Czechoslovakia as 'a far-away country' occupied by people 'of whom we know nothing'. For Chamberlain, the crucial element of the crisis was to avoid a war which Britain would be dragged into. Although Czechoslovakia was a democracy facing an aggressive dictatorship, Chamberlain felt that the Sudeten Germans did have genuine grievances and he was determined to put pressure on the Czech government to agree to concessions. By this stage Chamberlain was aware that war seemed likely as Hitler had increased his demands and the Czechs were unlikely to agree, and he was keen not to provoke the British people into rash demands for the defence of Czechoslovakia. If one is generous, one might assume that he is deliberately denying British interest in the conflict, so he can act as an effective mediator in his proposed summit conference with Hitler. If one is critical, one might accuse him of deliberately misleading the British people into thinking that Czechoslovakia was not worth fighting for, to prepare the public opinion for the impending British surrender at Munich.

d)   Chamberlain did have alternative policies at Munich to that of accepting Germany's demands, and trusting the German Chancellor to not exceed these in future, but the important question to ask is whether they could be considered realistic.

The main alternative was, of course, to refuse to accept Hitler's increased demands at Bad Godesberg, refuse to accept the terms of the Munich agreement and to threaten to come to Czechoslovakia's aid if Germany attacked her. From accounts of Hitler's behaviour in 1938, it seems likely that, as in September 1939, Hitler would not have taken any ultimatum seriously, at least if it was only issued by Britain and France, and would have invaded Czechoslovakia regardless. Britain would therefore have gone to war over the Sudeten crisis. Although she would undoubtedly have had the support of the French, as they were an ally of the Czechs, it was doubtful whether the Dominions would have supported Britain, at least in the opening campaign. As Chamberlain put it in source D, for many people in Britain and the Commonwealth, the Sudeten crisis was between 'people of whom we know nothing'. Second, there would be the difficulty of how to effectively help the Czechs, as British military rearmament had been pursued slowly by the government since 1933, and she was in no position to attack Germany or to attempt to airlift military aid to Czechoslovakia. As Chamberlain says in the letter to his sister (source A) 'you only have to look at the map to see that nothing that France or we could do could possibly save Czechoslovakia from being overrun by the Germans, if they wanted to do it'. The British chiefs of staff were equally pessimistic, advising Chamberlain that Britain could do nothing to prevent a German victory in Bohemia. Finally, the state of Britain's own defences was relatively poor in 1938, with British arms and equipment still relatively obsolescent, particularly the defences against bomber attack. British military strength was spread across the world, defending and policing British colonial possessions, and this could not be significantly changed in 1938 without seriously exposing the Empire to attack, particularly from the Japanese.

There was of course, a second alternative of seeking an alliance to resist Hitler's assault on Czechoslovakia by the only power in the area capable of putting sufficient troops in the field, namely, the Soviet Union. This may have had some greater possibility of success, but this would not have been welcomed by the Czechs, as they would have distrusted Stalin's motives, as his aid to the Republicans in Spain had led to the purging of left-wing groups that the Soviets disapproved of. In addition, Russian troops would have needed passage through either Hungary or Poland, and neither of these powers was friendly with Czechoslovakia or willing to allow the Soviets such freedom. The British government, in particular Halifax and Chamberlain, hated communism, regarding it as a more serious threat to democracy and Britain's interests than Germany and they were very reluctant to become reliant on a state they only grudgingly had diplomatic contacts with. Finally, although the British government would not be fully aware of this at the time, the Soviet army was not in a strong position to fight Germany, having had the majority of its officers purged in the months before the Czech crisis. On the other hand, the threat of a war against the USSR, France and Britain combined, must have made Hitler seriously reconsider his policies, with his experience of fighting a war on two fronts in the First World War, even if the threat had been largely based on bluff. Hitler was aware that his army was by no means fully rearmed and that important elements of the air force were still fighting for Franco in Spain, making a war on two fronts very difficult to undertake.

One might therefore assume that Chamberlain did have realistic alternative policies, particularly the potential alliance with the USSR but such was his desire to secure peace and to believe in Hitler's good faith, that he refused to consider these. As he said in source B, 'here was a man [Hitler] who could be relied on when he had given his word'. Whether these alternative policies would have had much more success than Britain's pitiful attempts to aid Poland in September 1939 seems unlikely, however, and the British armed forces would certainly have performed as poorly in spring 1939 as they did in spring 1940. Perhaps the crucial question should be not whether Chamberlain had any realistic alternatives, but whether, having accepted the German occupation of the Sudetenland, he did enough to secure the defence of the British Isles by 1939. After all, he chose to go to war on a more confident footing over another question of principle in 1939, Poland, to which he was just as unable to offer realistic aid as Czechoslovakia, yet he had refused to do in 1938.

QUESTIONS WITHOUT WORKED ANSWERS

a) **Study source B. Explain why Neville Chamberlain was so confident of success following his initial meeting with Hitler in September 1939.** (10 marks)

b) **Study source A. How far does this source explain Chamberlain's behaviour at the Munich conference?** (25 marks)

c) **Study sources C and E. To what extent do these two sources agree in their criticisms of Chamberlain's actions?** (25 marks)

d) **Study *all* the sources. Using all the sources and your own knowledge, do you believe that Chamberlain's policy at Munich is defensible?** (60 marks)

(Total: 120 marks)

3. Imperial defence in the inter-war years (EDEXCEL)

Study Source 1 below and then answer the questions which follow.

Source 1: From a memorandum by the Chief of Imperial Staff on Britain's Imperial Commitments, 1927

I would now turn to the consideration of the adequacy of our general reserve, i.e. the Expeditionary Force, to meet our more extended liabilities. Apart from the somewhat indefinite liability which we have assumed under the Locarno Pact, the chief military liability of the British Empire appears to be the defence of India against Russian aggression. A recent study of this question by a Sub-Committee has enabled us to arrive at the strength of the force which we, so far as can be calculated beforehand, shall have to send out to India during the first twelve months of such a war. This force would amount to the equivalent of 11 divisions, which is more than twice the strength of force which can to-day be organized out of the regular units in England.

QUESTIONS WITH WORKED ANSWERS

Study source 1.
a) **Why according to the Chief of the Imperial General Staff had the Locarno Treaty made defence of the Empire more difficult?** (10 marks)
b) **Why was the defence of India dependent on troops sent from England by 1927?** (14 marks)
c) **How far did the pre-occupation with India between the wars blind British leaders to other threats in the East?** (36 marks)

(Total: 60 marks)

ANSWERS

a) Under the terms of the Locarno Treaty signed by Britain, Germany and France, Britain acted as guarantor of Germany's western borders as agreed at Versailles in 1919. Although not committed to defending Germany's eastern neighbours, this did commit Britain to coming to the defence of France, Belgium, Luxembourg or Holland, even if there was no direct threat against Britain. As the French army was not especially strong, and those of the Benelux countries too small to be of much importance, this meant British troops would have to be committed to guarding the border with Germany, thus limiting the number of troops that could be posted elsewhere for imperial defence.

b) Traditionally the defence of India and the rest of Britain's Empire in Asia had been in the hands of the largely Indian-manned British Indian army. By 1927, however, the success of the Indian National Congress (Congress Party) in publicising its demands for independence had seriously weakened the reliability of the Indian army. In particular, many senior British military and political figures believed that the campaign for independence was being encouraged by the Communist government of the USSR, and that, in the case of conflict with Russia, the loyalty of Indian forces would be doubly suspect.

Second, the northern border of India was so large, covering a distance of several hundred miles, that it was also unlikely that the Indian army would be able to defend this area alone. There was the possibility of having to defend India's border with China, as well as that with Afghanistan, as the rise of the Chinese Communist Party was taken by British generals to be an attempt by Russia to create a base in that country from which to attack India. Finally, the potential size of any Soviet army was vast, given the enormous population of the area, so the CIGS is, most likely, anticipating an enormous threat from the north and is ensuring that he has sufficient forces available to cope with the worst possible situation. Therefore, the Chief of the Imperial Staff recommends the deployment of British troops to assist the British Indian army.

c) Britain's concerns about the security of India, especially at a time when a significant proportion of the Indian people appeared so reluctant to continue as members of the Empire, meant that she tended to regard those powers on India's borders as the greatest threat to her imperial status. In particular, the threat of communism as an ideology might appeal to the Indian people and might encourage them to revolt against British rule and ally with the Soviet Union. It was widely believed in Westminster that the Congress Party in India and even Gandhi himself received financial assistance from the Comintern in Moscow. In particular, the Congress links with peasant communities and their hostility to the pro-British landlord parties, made many assume that Congress supported communist policies. The series of rural revolts across India from 1931 to 1935, and in particular the terrorism in Bengal, seemed to a credulous British government to confirm the relationship between peasant, Congress and the Kremlin. As a result, the British administration repressed Congress and built up problems that were to erupt in the 'Quit India' campaign of 1942, just when Britain had a major war to fight in the region. In addition, the growing influence and power of the Chinese Communist Party, which manifested itself in the attempted takeover of Shanghai in February 1927, was seen by Britain to be a direct attempt by Moscow to expand into an area of huge economic and strategic importance to the West, possibly as a step towards threatening India. In fact, the Russian advisers in China had actually advised against the rising and were expelled when it was crushed in March by Chiang Kai-Shek's Nationalist government. Britain remained preoccupied with the Russian threat to China and India, even when, in 1931, it became obvious that there was a far more serious threat to her imperial status in the Far East.

Japan, the country which actually invaded British controlled Burma 15 years after this memorandum was written was not seriously regarded as a threat by British leaders until the Manchurian invasion of 1931. Japan had become Britain's first ally in 1902 and she had fought on the side of the Allies in the First World War, but the alliance was abandoned with the signing of the Washington agreement in 1922, when it was replaced by a three-power naval standard with the USA which left Japan in an inferior position. Despite her large military forces, in particular her fleet, which was, by 1927, the third largest in the world, Britain's military experts were largely contemptuous of her military ability when facing British and colonial troops. Certainly, before 1931, she had been embroiled in her attempts to control territory on the Chinese mainland, with little clear signs of success, despite the weaknesses of the Chinese Nationalist Government forces that she faced. Although Britain abandoned the 'ten year rule', which anticipated at least a further ten years' peace, in 1932, it was felt by most British military and political leaders that the arrival of a large Royal Navy fleet at Singapore would suffice to make the Japanese think twice about attacking British colonies. Despite the Lytton Report's condemnation of the Japanese actions in Manchuria, the possibility of economic sanctions was not raised by the British government at the League of Nations. Britain took no action against further Japanese expansion, even when she invaded China itself in 1937 and took control of the Nationalist capital, Nanking, in an orgy of violence. It was only in 1938, that the British completed the reinforcement of her exposed base at Singapore, and even then only the seaward defences were adequately reinforced, which would prove disastrous in February 1942. Britain's preoccupation with defending the Northern borders of India and labelling both peaceful and violent Indian nationalists as communist-backed, prevented her from taking more seriously the threat from Japan, until it was too late. Perhaps it was only with the sinking of the *Repulse* and the *Prince of Wales* in 1942 that she finally realised how inadequate her preparations had been. As it was, the USSR became Britain's ally and India's northern defences became unnecessary, whereas the border between Burma and Thailand offered little resistance to the advancing Japanese Imperial Army.

QUESTIONS WITHOUT WORKED ANSWERS (EDEXCEL)

a) Why did Britain anticipate a war against Russia over India, when
they had been wartime allies only ten years earlier? (10 marks)

b) To what extent had the Locarno Treaty eased British fears of a war
in Europe by 1927? (14 marks)

c) To what extent did British armed forces suffer from 'imperial overstretch' between the wars? (36 marks)

(Total: 60 marks)

Part 4: Historical skills

1. Role play: The remilitarisation of the Rhineland, 1936

INTRODUCTION

This role play can with be played by one whole class, with class members acting as advisers to the ministers, or by a series of different groups, with the conclusions that each group reaches compared at the end.

The aim of the role-play is to consider the alternative courses of action available to the British Government in 1936 and to understand why Britain took such a restrained approach to the Rhine crisis. Some contemporaries, such as Churchill and Halifax, have suggested that this was the best opportunity to stop Hitler before the Sudeten crisis in 1938. It is possible that you consider Baldwin's government simply to have been 'weak', without really understanding the factors which limited their freedom to respond. After completing this role play, you should be more able to answer the following questions:

1. Why did Britain fail to act when Hitler reoccupied the Rhineland in 1936?
2. Account for Britain's policy towards Germany between 1933 and 1938.

THE SITUATION

News has just arrived in Downing Street that German troops have entered the Rhineland, the western-most part of Germany, bordering on France, Belgium and the Netherlands, which was declared a de-militarised zone in the Versailles peace treaty of 1919.

In May 1935, France signed a treaty of friendship and mutual support with the USSR. In response, Hitler claimed this treaty was hostile to Germany and used this as his reason for ordering German troops into the Rhineland in March 1936, contrary to the terms of the treaties of Versailles and Locarno. It is 11 March 1936. The Cabinet is meeting in emergency session to discuss what action should be taken.

The following is a list of those present at the meeting, in order of seniority, with a summary of their priorities in the forthcoming debate:

1. Prime Minister

You are chiefly concerned with the Italian invasion of Abyssinia. In the general election last year, you promised to support the League of Nations in standing up to aggressors, but in reality you want to avoid a conflict as you know that the electorate wants peace and is not prepared to go to war for Abyssinia or the Rhineland. Although you are worried about Germany's intentions, you do not wish to provoke a war when Britain's rearmament programme has barely started, the area concerned is part of Germany anyway and the German action has been welcomed enthusiastically by the inhabitants.

2. Chancellor of the Exchequer

The British economy has, in the last three years shown dramatic signs of recovery, but there are still some severely depressed areas of Britain where unemployment is very high. You are therefore very reluctant to support any military action over the Rhineland as the cost would damage Britain's recovery. There is a fear that a war could ensue, for which Britain is not economically prepared and which, even if it were won, would permanently weaken Britain's financial independence.

3. Foreign Secretary

You are keen that Britain should be seen to act, but you are very concerned about the reliability of your chief ally, France. The French have recently signed a pact with the Soviet Union, of which you disapprove, as you do not wish Stalin's influence to spread into Eastern Europe. The French want to send troops into the Rhineland, but the last time this happened in 1923, a general strike crippled the German economy and violence broke out. Most of all, political and economic instability in France convinces you that the government has no popular support for its plans and that if Britain supports them, it will find itself taking the brunt of the effort.

Second, you are conscious that Japan's continued aggression in the Far East poses a threat to British interests in that area. An unnecessary war with Germany, might give Japan the opportunity they want to strike at the lightly defended British bases at Singapore and Hong Kong.

4. Dominions Secretary

If the crisis escalated, Britain, allied to a weak France and, indirectly to an unreliable Soviet Union, would find it needed help from the Dominions, such as Canada, Australia and South Africa. The recent **Dominion** conference has demonstrated that these countries do not wish to become involved in another European war if they can help it and wish to concentrate on internal development. Then, there are the ongoing problems of policing restive colonial possessions, such as Palestine and Egypt, but most of all India. There is no guarantee that nationalist forces in the colonies will not take the opportunity of a European crisis to organise challenges to British rule which could be difficult to contain.

5. First Lord of the Admiralty

Although the British fleet patrols the North Sea, there is little it can do to assist an action in Germany. It could certainly **blockade** the German ports, but this will not have an immediate effect and would provoke counter action from the Germans, who are known to have been building submarines and aircraft, both of which could cause considerable damage to Britain's largely obsolete navy.

6. Secretary for War

You are well aware of the poor status of the British armed forces, in particular the lack of tanks and modern military aircraft. You therefore doubt how effectively Britain will be able to fight against the rearmed Germans. You also doubt whether the French army has much appetite for combat that does not involve defending French soil. On the other hand, France will follow Britain's lead on this issue.

7. Secretary for Air

You know that Britain lacks adequate defences to stop German bombers from attacking targets in Britain at will and, like most British people, you believe that Germany has a large number of bombers which will devastate British cities, killing thousands of civilians. You also know that Britain's offensive capabilities in the air are quite limited as well.

8. Minister for League of Nations Affairs

You are conscious that Britain has supported economic sanctions against Italy, with much popular support from the British public. Although you are aware that Germany's action has not breached the Covenant of the League, you are keen that the League be involved in any settlement of the issue. On the other hand, Germany withdrew from the League in 1933 and so the League's ability to enforce a settlement is limited. Also, you are only a junior member of the Cabinet and any future promotion depends on the attitude of the Prime Minister.

9. Minister of Health

Considering the impact of the Depression on the health of the working-class population, you are very concerned that many men of fighting age may be unfit to serve, or at least will not perform well on the battlefield. As minister responsible for housing and hospital provision, you also fear that a war will continue to delay the desperate housing and health shortages, especially among the poor.

10. Minister of Labour

Although you know that many unemployed men would welcome the new jobs that a war would bring, you are concerned by the disruption that a war would bring to the gradually improving employment situation. If a war came, that recovery would be jeopardised by the dislocation of industry caused by the need for war production. You are also worried that, once the unemployed are back at work, there might be a return to serious industrial unrest and even another general strike as workers seek to exploit their new employment and secure their positions.

PROCEDURES

It is intended that roles should be allocated before the simulation begins and that all the participants are aware of their ministerial priorities and of the procedure to be followed.

1. Preparation (5 minutes)

The following statement should be read out by the Prime Minister. It is a transcript of the opening minutes of the actual Cabinet meeting of 11 March 1936.

The Secretary of State for Foreign Affairs gave the Cabinet an account of the conversation he and the Lord Privy Seal had held with representatives of the French, Belgian and Italian governments in Paris on the previous day. Both ministers were impressed by the complexity and gravity of the situation which confronted Europe, and more especially our own country as one of the guarantors of Europe. On the outcome of the present situation depended the course of events in Europe over the next ten years, and it had to be remembered that our influence was greater than that of any other nation.

Each minister or ministerial team then draws up a statement of his/her position on the German reoccupation. In it s/he should clearly state whether s/he is in favour of a British military response and why.

2. Initial Cabinet discussion (15 minutes)
This meeting is chaired by the Prime Minister. In it s/he invites statements from the Cabinet and suggestions for future action.

3. Consideration of action (10 minutes)
Each minister is then to arrange a list of priorities from the following possible courses of action (these could be read out by the Prime Minister or Foreign Secretary at the conclusion of the initial Cabinet discussion).

a) No action
b) Formal diplomatic complaint to the German ambassador.
c) Motion condemning the German action to be discussed at the next meeting of the Council of the League of Nations, with the intention of calling for economic sanctions against Germany.
d) Military preparations to convince the Germans to back down – introduction of conscription, call up of reserves, mobilisation of fleet and sending of a British Expeditionary Force to the Franco-German border.
e) Immediate military co-operation with France – British troops to be placed under French command to act as French government sees fit.
f) Immediate signing of Anglo-French defence treaty, to include the Soviet Union in the near future.
g) Immediate deployment of British troops to the Rhineland to drive the Germans forces out. Assistance to be called for from other signatories of the Treaty of Versailles.
h) Declaration of war against Germany.

4. Cabinet discussion and decision (15 minutes)
The Prime Minister invites her/his colleagues to give their recommendations for action from the given list. As the options include possible military action, it is recommended that s/he asks the Ministers for War, Air and the Admiralty to give their preferences first, and then asks his/her other colleagues to consider their views again in light of this military advice. If the Prime Minister has, by this stage, already decided on what action *not* to take, s/he can, of course, choose not to ask a member of Cabinet for his/her opinion, if s/he prefers.

At the end of this meeting, the Prime Minister must make a decision on what policy to take. Once that has been decided, any ministers are welcome to comment, even to offer their resignations if they disagree strongly enough with the Prime Minister's decision.

POINTS TO NOTE

It is recommended that minutes are taken during the meeting for the Prime Minister to consult at any stage.

If a member of the Cabinet feels badly treated by the way in which the discussions are going, s/he can threaten to resign. The Prime Minister is more likely to take this threat seriously and change his/her views depending on how senior the rebellious Cabinet Minister is.

DEBRIEF

To compare the outcomes and decisions of this Cabinet meeting, it is recommended that students visit the Public Record Office website on the Cabinet meeting of 11 March 1936. It contains numerous actual transcripts of the Cabinet meeting and encourages students to consider a number of issues:

http://learningcurve.pro.gov.uk/snapshots/snapshot30/snapshot30.htm

Chapter 6

Britain and the Second World War, 1939–1945

This chapter is concerned with a short period, but the Second World War is seen by most historians as the defining moment in Britain's twentieth century history and therefore needs quite a lot of serious scrutiny. Of course, the fact that Britain very nearly lost the war, yet managed to emerge victorious in 1945 deserves some detailed analysis. Yet, in many ways, the fact of survival was not the most important impact of the war, at least not in the longer term. The changes in attitude created by the war, attitudes towards society, towards the economy, towards politics itself and to some extent towards Britain's role in the world, were the most profound that Britain had encountered for centuries. British life was affected by memories of Britain's wartime experiences for the rest of the twentieth century, and, as the huge celebrations to mark the 50th anniversary of VE Day in 1995 demonstrated, even those born long after the end of the war, grew up with the sense that this was an event of huge and lasting significance.

Historical background

The coming of war
Evacuation and immediate wartime
    restrictions
The events of 1940
The Battle of Britain and the **Blitz**
Relief organisations and wartime welfare
The war at sea and self-sufficiency
The **Beveridge Report**
The war in the Far East
North Africa and the liberation of
    Europe
The media
Wartime strikes
The end of the war and the 1945 election

3. The British economy in wartime
4. The impact of the war on society
5. Domestic politics
6. Overall assessment

Sources

1. The social impact of the **Blitz**
2. The political impact of the Second
   World War
3. The War Economy
4. The fall of Neville Chamberlain

Historical skills

1. Research methods and approaches
   towards an AS-level piece of
   coursework on the impact of the
   Second World War on Britain.

Essays

1. Preparation for war
2. The conduct of the war

Chronology

1939	Conscription introduced
	3 September – Declaration of war with Germany
	September – Evacuation of children
1940	Chamberlain resigns, Churchill becomes Prime Minister
	Germany defeats France, troops evacuated from Dunkirk
	Battle of Britain
	Bombing of British cities begins
1941	Reconstruction Committee established
	Lend-lease agreement signed with USA
	Germany invades Soviet Union
	Japan attacks Pearl Harbour and attacks British colonies
	Germany and Italy declare war on USA
1942	Fall of Malaya, Singapore and Thailand
	Publication of the Beveridge Report
	Battle of El Alamein
1943	German army surrenders at Stalingrad
	Allied invasion of Italy
	Tehran Conference
1944	June – D-Day – the Allied invasion of occupied France
	V-1 and V-2 attacks in Britain
	White Paper on health promises a National Health Service
	White Paper on employment advocates policy of full employment
	Butler's Education Act
1945	Churchill, Roosevelt and Stalin meet at Yalta
	May – VE (Victory in Europe) Day
	Potsdam Conference
	July – Labour win first majority in general election
	August – VJ (Victory in Japan) Day

Part 1: Historical background

Table 6.1 *General election results for 1935 and 1945*

	Conservative		Liberal		Labour	
	% vote	No. of seats	% vote	No. of seats	% vote	No. of seats
1935	53.7	432	6.4	20	37.9	154
1945	39.8	213	9.0	12	47.8	393

 ## The coming of war

In 1938 there was much support for Neville Chamberlain's **appeasement** policy from the middle classes. They had not really suffered from the Depression and they expected any future war to be a devastating bomber war in which poison gas would be used. Many small evacuations of children from London had already taken place during the Munich summer both to the countryside and abroad.

Many of the working classes were, of course, bitterly hostile to Chamberlain, who, as a former Chancellor was forever associated with the brutal Means Test for unemployment benefit. This class relied on the limited medical provision available from the National Insurance schemes, lived in some appalling slum housing, such as those in the East End of London, and felt their interests had been neglected by the Conservative dominated National Government.

War in September 1939 was not greeted with cheers as in 1914. Chamberlain himself viewed it a personal and national disaster. Most people were only too aware of the losses of 1914–18 and viewed the struggle ahead with worry. As one, fairly representative woman wrote later:

Now the thing was actually upon us and I had no heart to meet it. In 1914 we had had no idea of what we were in for and we all felt excited. There is not much glamour and excitement for us about the war. I feared that I was going to lose all the pleasures and activities that I had found so dear.

Conscription had already been introduced in April. The regulars and the territorials were called up first and a national register of occupations set up. Within minutes of the declaration of war, the air raid sirens went into operation and people went into the new public shelters calmly. It was the first of many false alarms that year.

After the collapse of Poland, and no sign of further German aggression, the Allies prepared a defensive position similar to that which had seemed to bring victory in 1918. Chamberlain, under pressure from his own party, reluctantly brought Churchill back as First Lord of the Admiralty and a **blockade** of German ports was imposed. Troops were sent to France in an expeditionary force and the French Maginot line (a line of forts and tunnels on the Franco-German border) was strengthened. This period, until Spring 1940 was nicknamed the 'phoney war' and many believed that Hitler would begin negotiations to end the war.

Evacuation and immediate restrictions

Evacuation began on the weekend of 2/3 September and one and a half million people moved from evacuation areas to reception areas. The public were presented with a view of evacuation as well organised with the children looking forward to an adventure. In truth the children were mostly scared, ill-dressed and often auctioned off at reception centres.

A girl of 12 presented such a dirty, unkempt appearance that the woman refused to have her. At the end of the day the child was presented again. Nobody would take her in. The woman had compassion on her and gave her shelter. The child was nervous, dirty and badly clad. She wet the bed the first night and was terrified of the consequences.

Mass Observation reporters listed the problems of evacuations under the following headings: Bad health; vermin; dirt; odd and rude behaviour; clothing; food problems; trouble with evacuees' mothers; money difficulties.

Most of the problems were caused by the mixing of the social classes and the mixing of town children with country households. In many ways, though, evacuation failed as London wasn't bombed until August 1940 and over half the evacuees returned home despite the government's attempts to stop this.

Figure 6.1 **'Smiling Through' – country billeting cartoon**

Due to the fear of bombing, blackout was imposed immediately, but before the necessary adjustments such as painting white lines on pavement edges and masking headlights and streetlights had been made. The result was a doubling in road deaths before action was taken. Cinemas and theatres were closed and spectator sports were all stopped, but quickly resumed as no bombs fell. Schools reopened after the evacuation crisis and these stayed open, with, in many cases, no school holidays.

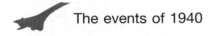 ## The events of 1940

In 1940, when Germany invaded Scandinavia and Britain failed to defend Norway effectively, the mood changed and discontent with the government even affected Tory MPs. Chamberlain had his secure majority dramatically reduced and was forced to ask Labour to join a coalition government. Attlee agreed, but only if Chamberlain resigned. Chamberlain tried to persuade Halifax to take over, but in the end he had to accept the popular demand to make Winston Churchill Prime Minister (although Chamberlain remained as Lord President until his death in September). Churchill immediately called a political truce and formed a coalition government, with Attlee as deputy Prime Minister, Eden as Foreign Secretary, Lord Beaverbrook as Minister of Aircraft Production and Ernest Bevin as Minister of Labour. Censorship and the power to intern were granted by Parliament, mostly with popular approval (Mosley was locked up) and civil liberties were held in abeyance until the war was won.

The shock defeat of France between May and June 1940 was alleviated by the 'miracle' of Dunkirk when 350,000 troops were rescued by an armada of private ships from French beaches, Churchill having taken the decision to turn and run rather than defend France to the end. Although the men were rescued, almost all the heavy equipment such as large guns and tanks were lost. Despite the advice from Halifax and Chamberlain to negotiate through Mussolini, Churchill decided to fight on and was backed by the Cabinet:

I am convinced that every man would rise up and tear me from my place if I were for one moment to contemplate surrender. If this long island story of ours is to end at last, let it end only when each of us lies choking in his own blood on the ground.

Most people supported this attitude of fighting on alone and accepted the new restrictions. Sign posts and place names were removed. Defences were installed along the coast. All aliens of German or Austrian origin were interned. All holidays were suspended. Late coming and absenteeism virtually vanished and long hours were worked voluntarily and productivity soared. Leaflets were distributed advising civilians to 'stand firm' and 'stay where you are' in the event of an invasion, to stop refugees clogging the roads as they had done in France. Coastal defences were swiftly installed and lines of defence were built across southern England, using concrete pillboxes, gun emplacements, anti-tank obstacles, trench systems, minefields and barbed wire. A 'stay-behind' army of guerrilla fighters was even organised, to disrupt the German army once it had occupied parts of Britain, giving some indication of just how seriously the government took the possibility of invasion.

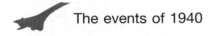 ## The Battle of Britain and the Blitz

The invasion never took place, due to the British victory in the Battle of Britain which the people of South East England witnessed over their heads and they eagerly followed the (deliberately inaccurate) scores as if it were a test match with both sides accumulating a series of runs.

Figure 6.2 **The German threat to Britain, 1939–41**

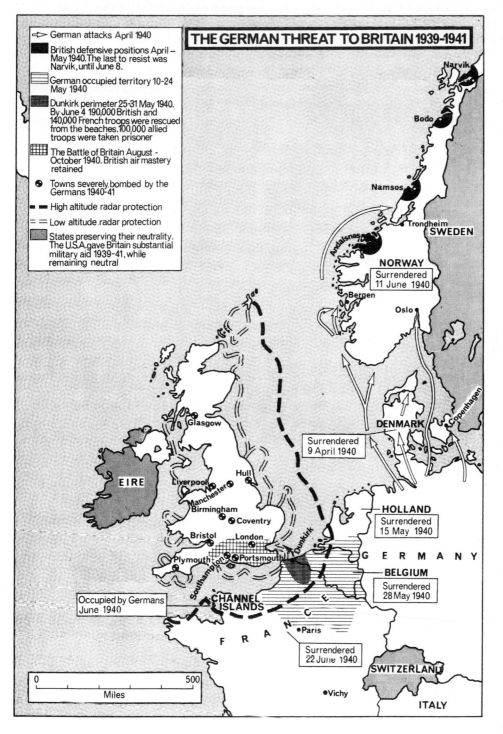

The nature of the battle changed, however, when Hitler ordered bombing campaigns against British civilian cities in August 1940. The authorities were not prepared for the scale of these attacks, especially those on Liverpool and the East End of London where nearly 1,000 people died in two days. The newspapers spoke of endurance and determination, but the reality was somewhat harsher:

Of course the press versions of life going on normally in the East End were grotesque. There was no bread, no electricity, no milk, no gas, no telephones. There was no understanding in the huge buildings of Central London for the tiny overcrowded streets of dusty, massed population. Here the people wanted to be brave, but found bravery was something purely negative, cheerless and without encouragement or prospect of success.

Many people saw the inadequacies of poor housing as they were destroyed without receiving a direct hit. Raids hit Birmingham, Coventry (where 600 troops were needed to keep order), Southampton, Manchester, Sheffield, Portsmouth, Leicester, Belfast and Clydeside. Many 'trekkers' fled every night to the surrounding countryside, to return the next day. Reports of direct hits on shelters and the deaths of several hundred when a bomb severed water pipes at Balham were suppressed. Many people complained of the insanitary nature of the shelters and many richer people preferred their own cellars, but for most, shelter life became a matter of routine. Some also complained that the army was kept safe away from the dangers experienced by civilians in the cities. The experience of common suffering drew people together: as the Queen said when Buckingham Palace was hit: 'At last, I can look the East End in the face'. The first wave of attacks ended in 1941 when Hitler turned his attention on the Soviet Union, but Britain suffered later raids on historic cities (the 'Baedeker raids') and the South-East underwent the V-1 and V-2 rocket bomb attacks in 1944 and 1945, which were only stopped when the launch sites were overrun in the liberation of Europe. All in all, some 60,000 people were killed in the bombing and 100,000 seriously injured. Britain responded to all these attacks with her own costly and militarily largely ineffective bomber raids on German cities which increased in scale once American bombers were based in Britain. These culminated in the attack on Dresden in February 1945 when 135,000 civilians (mostly refugees) were killed in one night. After this, the bomber campaign was swiftly scaled down.

Relief organisations and wartime welfare

In 1940, the Womens' Voluntary Service (WVS) was set up by a group of upper-class women to help on the Home Front, providing food and clothing after bomb attacks. Gradually the WVS developed, becoming involved in salvage, make-do-and-mend campaigns and welfare activities such as visiting the elderly and play centre provision. Many middle- and upper-class volunteers experienced at first hand the squalor and deprivation of the urban poor:

The room was littered with household things. Laundry, clean and dirty covered the floor; the few bits of furniture were buried deep under heaps of stuff and the impression of disorder was bewildering and produced a feeling of hopelessness.

The government also took direct action – setting up a unified Emergency Hospital Scheme, providing free treatment for victims of air raids and making an effort to provide cheap travel facilities for relatives to visit evacuees.

Education was, of course, severely disrupted, as air raids destroyed one fifth of the country's schools. The planned raising of the school-leaving age to 15 had been due to commence from 3 September

1939, and consequently was delayed until long after the war. The social work of schools in ensuring the health of pupils and their diets was also interrupted by the war, although the introduction of free school milk and free school meals would pay dividends after 1945. On the other hand, the war increased demands for a more egalitarian system of education, and caused education to be one of the first areas of society to be targeted for action, while the war still continued, when Butler's 1944 *Education Act* introduced the '11-plus' and the three tier system of education which lasted until the 1960s.

Hundreds of thousands of people had been left homeless by the bombing. Over 200,000 houses were destroyed and a quarter of a million more rendered uninhabitable. In response the government set up the Uthwatt Committee which recommended that the state should have the power of compulsory purchase over properties needing redevelopment in built-up areas.

The war at sea and self-sufficiency

Almost as soon as the war began, Hitler sent his U-boat submarines to harass Allied shipping in the Atlantic. With the fall of France, the Germans gained valuable Atlantic coastal bases from which they launched a naval campaign to try to starve Britain of supplies. This 'Battle of the Atlantic' cost the lives of thousands of merchant seamen and reduced Britain's food and material supplies to a minimum, forcing the government to concentrate on shipping the most needed supplies only. Eventually, with the breaking of the German Enigma Code, German naval movements were anticipated and gradually defeated.

Faced with the U-boat campaign, the government tried to make Britain as self-sufficient as possible. Farmers were encouraged to plough up pasture land and cultivate marginal land, which led to an increased demand for tractors which the government helped to supply. 'Dig for victory' became a great wartime slogan as householders dug up lawns and used flower beds to produce vegetables. Salvage campaigns began with railings around public and private gardens removed in 1940 and Beaverbrook asking for aluminium pots and pans for aircraft (despite the fact that they were useless for this purpose). Later, people salvaged metals, bones, paper and wastes for animal feed, with children encouraged to search for salvage. People were encouraged to reuse old clothes to avoid using coupons and to do-it-yourself.

The Beveridge Report

Under direct pressure from the TUC, an inter-departmental committee of civil servants under Sir William Beveridge was appointed to 'undertake a survey of the existing national schemes of social insurances and make recommendations' and soon he had included the issue of health reform into his survey as well.

Freedom from want cannot be forced on a democracy or given to a democracy. It must be won by them. Winning it needs courage and a sense of national unity: courage to face facts and difficulties and overcome them; faith in our culture and in the ideals of fair-play and freedom for which century after century our forefathers were prepared to die; a sense of national unity overriding the interests of any class or section. The Plan for Social Security in this report is submitted by one who believes that in this supreme crisis the British people will not be found wanting.

The Report, published in 1942, recommended an insurance scheme to cover all classes in society, to cover all contingencies and to provide uniform benefits. There should also be attacks on ill-health, inadequate education, bad housing and unemployment. The successful implementation of his social security proposals depended on three assumptions:

- children's allowances
- a comprehensive health service
- the avoidance of mass unemployment.

The scheme was attacked by those who thought that the war had nothing to do with social change – insurance and medical professionals, industrialists and the *Daily Telegraph*, which wrote: 'if this scheme were to come to pass, truly might not Ribbentrop allege that the Anglo-Saxon race was decadent.'

With its Cromwellian language and messianic tone, published just after Britain's first victory at El Alamein, the **Beveridge Report** captured the spirit of the time, though. Such was the popularity of Beveridge's report that it sold 100,000 copies in the space of a month – unprecedented for a government report. By 1943, a poll found that 19 out of 20 people had heard of the report. The principle of 'universality' that the report advocated, the idea that the whole nation should be covered by the new social provisions, became and still is the most important feature of what we call the modern **Welfare State**.

The war in the Far East

Driven out of mainland Europe and fighting for Egypt and control of the Mediterranean, Britain was in no position to resist the Japanese assault on her Far Eastern colonies in December 1941. On the same day as the surprise attack on the US fleet at Pearl Harbour, Japan invaded Malaya, which soon fell. Britain immediately sent two battleships, *HMS Repulse* and *HMS Prince of Wales* to defend the base at Singapore. Without air cover they were sunk by Japanese torpedo-bombers almost as soon as they arrived, and the Japanese reached Singapore from the land, something the British had considered impossible and therefore had not defended Singapore against. Unlike Dunkirk, there was no 'miraculous' evacuation at Singapore and 100,000 British, Australian, New Zealand and Indian troops were captured when it fell on 15 February 1942, Britain's blackest day of the war.

The Japanese drove on, capturing British territory in Borneo, Papua New Guinea and Hong Kong and invading Burma. Britain was hard pressed to resist the Japanese attacks, but determined defending and effective guerrilla operations by General Wingate's 'Chindits' stopped the Japanese early in 1943. The bulk of offensives against the Japanese were then taken by the Americans in the Pacific and it was not until May 1945 that Rangoon, the capital of Burma, was recaptured by General Slim. Most military experts expected the liberation of the rest of South East Asia to take until 1946, but with the entry of the USSR into the war in the Far East, America was keen to force Japan to surrender quickly, and so carried out the atom-bomb raids on Hiroshima and Nagasaki in August 1945. Japan surrendered within a week and Empire troops re-entered the colonies, but the myth of British imperial might in the Far East now lay in tatters.

Figure 6.3 *War in the Pacific*

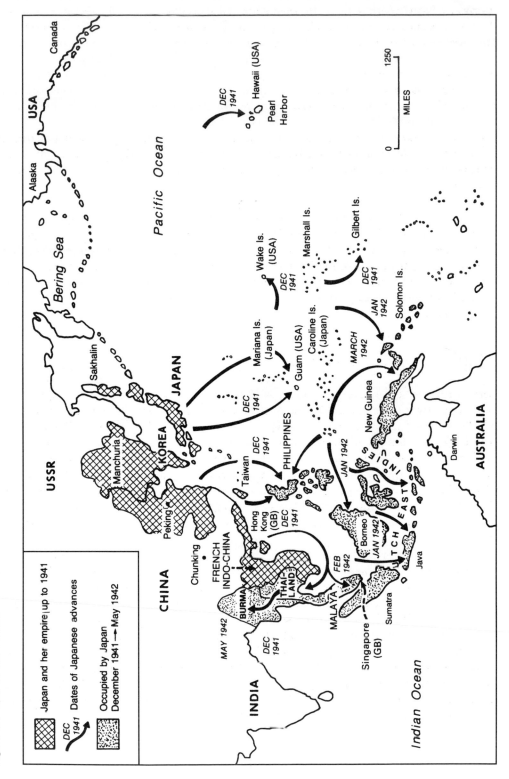

North Africa and the liberation of Europe

Mussolini had declared war on the allies as soon as France seemed on the point of capitulating. He was keen to match Hitler's achievements in Europe by capturing British possessions in and around the Mediterranean. In September 1940, at the height of the Battle of Britain, Italy invaded Egypt in an attempt to capture the Suez Canal. As the British swiftly drove the Italians back, Hitler sent the Afrika Korps to keep pressure on the British. After a number of setbacks, including the loss of Tobruk, the British Eighth Army eventually defeated the Germans at the battle of El Alamein in November 1942. The Germans and Italians were gradually driven out of North Africa and then, to satisfy Stalin's demands for the Western Allies to relieve pressure on the Eastern Front, an invasion, first of Sicily, then of mainland Italy was launched. When Italy surrendered and Mussolini was overthrown, the Germans took up the war effort in Italy and slowed Allied progress to a crawl up the Italian peninsula.

On D-Day June 1944 the Allies made a series of successful landings in Normandy in Northern France and drove inland, albeit with very heavy losses. By August, the Allies had captured Paris and landed in the South of France. As the Russians neared the German borders in the east, however,

Figure 6.4 **Allied advances, 1944–45**

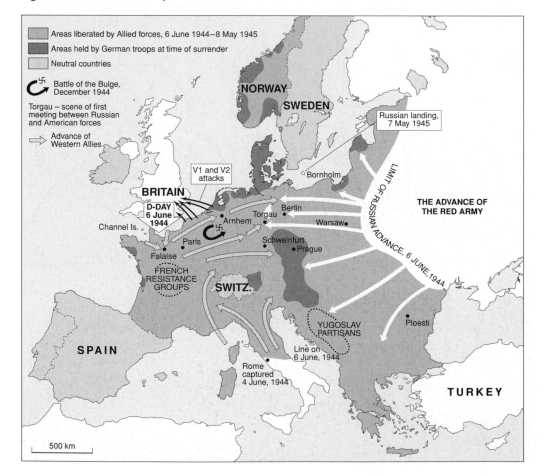

the Allies attempted an ambitious British paratroop assault on the bridges of the Rhine which ended disastrously. From this point onwards the war in the West continued cautiously, leaving the Russians to reach Berlin (and take the consequent heavy casualties) first. The greatest successes from the British point of view were, arguably, the destruction of the V-1 and V-2 launch sites and the discovery of the German concentration camps, such as that at Belsen, which gave Britain, the only nation to have fought Germany for the full duration of the war, an appalling reminder of the rightness of her struggle.

 ## The media

In cinemas showing films such as *Millions Like Us*, *In Which We Serve* and *A Canterbury Tale* emphasised national unity and a common cultural heritage. Despite Churchill's best efforts to stop it, the film *The Life and Death of Colonel Blimp* poked fun at the military. On the radio, J.B. Priestley's *Postscripts* broadcast after the 9 o'clock news on Sundays often talked of a better life after the war, and *It's That Man Again* (ITMA) lampooned the Ministry of Information. The *Daily Mirror* became the most popular newspaper and *Picture Post* combined photography with radical journalism. Even *The Times* carried articles calling for social justice, causing one Tory MP to mock it as 'the 3d edition of the *Daily Worker*'. Government posters, often well-designed, kept up the spirit of national co-operation and exhorted, guided and advised the public. Occasionally they backfired, however, as with the slogan, '*your* courage, *your* cheerfulness, *your* resolution will bring *us* victory'.

It soon became clear from public opinion surveys and Mass Observation that people wanted a better world after the war than the one they had known in the 1930s. Penguin Books, the Workers

Figure 6.5 *'Your Britain – Fight for it now!' Propaganda poster for the Second World War*

Educational Association and the Army Bureau of Current Affairs (ABCA) all helped to foster an interest in social and political issues. Churchill found these trends disturbing, however, writing 'I hope you will wind up the ABCA as quickly and decently as possible and set the people concerned to useful work'. Many Conservatives and Industrialists agreed with this social concern. William Temple, the Archbishop of Canterbury, used his position to speak out in favour of social reform in his widely read book, *Christianity and the Social Order*.

Wartime strikes

Irritation with the government and war-weariness did start to manifest itself by 1942 in a series of strikes which rose throughout the war, reaching a peak with nearly four million working days lost through strikes in 1944. Most were settled with employees gaining higher wages as they knew they were in a strong bargaining position and employers didn't want to risk their profits in long industrial unrest.

Table 6.2 **Wartime strikes**

Year	Number of strikes	Number of workers on strike	Working days lost due to strikes
1939	940	337,000	1,356,000
1940	972	299,000	940,000
1941	1,252	360,000	1,079,000
1942	1,303	456,000	1,527,000
1943	1,785	557,000	1,808,000
1944	2,194	821,000	3,714,000
1945	2,293	531,000	2,835,000

 The end of the war and the 1945 election

Table 6.3 **Opinion polls, 1943: 'If there was a general election tomorrow, how would you vote?'**

Political party	% of electorate that would vote for parties indicated	
	In June 1943	In August 1943
Conservative	25	23
Labour	38	39
Liberal	9	9
Communist	3	3
Common Wealth	2	1

At the defeat of Germany and the victory celebrations of 8 May 1945 Churchill emphasised the mood of unity: 'This is your victory. It is the victory of the cause of freedom in every land. In all our long history we have never seen a greater day than this. Everyone, man or woman has done their best'. The Labour Party, however, was keen to return to peacetime politics and capitalise on the positive attitude towards the **Beveridge Report**.

Table 6.4 **General election result, 1945**

Political party	% of votes	Seats
Labour	48	393
Conservatives	40	213
Liberals	9	12
ILP	2	3
Communists	1	2

Churchill threatened an election if they left the government, so Attlee called his bluff. Churchill resigned and the King reappointed him as Prime Minister of a caretaker government until the vote among the overseas troops could be organised. As Table 6.4 shows, Labour achieved a land-slide majority.

As Attlee noted, in typical fashion, in his diary, 'it had been quite an exciting day'.

Labour won because of the mood for radical change among the middle as well as the working class voters. One third of the middle class voted Labour, providing the key to victory. When Churchill heard the news, he was shocked but he accepted it: 'This is democracy. This is what we have fought for. The people have made their choice'. President Truman of the USA telephoned King George VI and commented, 'You've had a revolution', to which the King replied, 'Oh no! We don't have those here'.

Part 2: Essays

Preparation for war (OCR)

How successfully did Britain mobilise her population, and did Britain's preparations for war in 1939 prove adequate?

(90 marks)

Following the difficulties in providing sufficient manpower in the First World War, Chamberlain's government had introduced conscription as early as April 1939 for men. In 1941 conscription was extended to unmarried women in the auxiliary services and the factories. Under the terms of the Emergency Powers (Defence) Act of May 1940 'all persons could be required to place themselves, their services and their property' at the service of the state, thus giving the government an unprecedented ability to control and direct every area of life and labour to aid the war economy.

Ernest Bevin, the Minister of Labour and National Service, appointed by Churchill in May 1940, had the power to direct workers where they were needed under the 1940 Emergency Powers Act and he did his job with such tact and sensitivity, that there were very few exemptions. For example, one in ten of those conscripted were sent down the coal-mines as 'Bevin Boys' regardless of which class they came from.

At first, there was competition between employers for skilled workers as in 1914–18, but the Restriction on Engagement (Engineering) order of June 1940 led to the recruitment of all key workers via their Trade Unions or labour exchanges. By 1941, labour mobility was restricted by the government. To make up for skills shortages, training programmes were established. In contrast to Germany, women workers were recruited and trained to replace men in commerce and industry as well as in the auxiliary services. By 1943, there were 2,250,000 women employed in Britain, including half a million in the forces.

In May 1940, a call for volunteers led to the creation of a number of vital defence organisations. Most fears centred on the threat of German parachutists who had been used against the Dutch. Eden organised the Local Defence Volunteers (later known as the Home Guard) of a quarter of a million men for civil protection. Gradually the Home Guard received weapons, uniforms and a military structure. Although never called on to deal with an invasion and viewed as something of a joke by many, it performed valuable services such as aircraft spotting, guarding bomb sites and routine identity checks. Like the Air Raid Warden and the Fire Watcher, these part-time posts gave civilians the feeling of complete involvement in the war effort. Even those not formally employed in war work were encouraged to help the government. Housewives were constantly exhorted to save food, 'dig for victory' and 'make-do-and-mend'. Children were encouraged to collect salvage materials, while the better off bought war bonds and raised money for tanks and spitfires.

By 1943, however, the services and arms production needed another million workers, but the size of the workforce was shrinking as the older men had to stop working and there were not enough young men to replace them. The Ministry of Labour was actually forced to run down civil defence in order to solve the problem, but it soon became clear that in shell production at least, supply had exceeded demand. Men were moved from munitions to the front line, but still there were not enough. Bevin and Churchill were therefore forced to take the decision to reduce the production of guns, tanks and aircraft in order to supply the services. It meant that Britain, self-sufficient in munitions apart from aircraft earlier in the war, now had to lend-lease war supplies from the USA, increasing her post-war debts, but it was an indication of just how well the British had mobilised for war – there were now simply not enough people to satisfy all the needs of such a mechanised type of combat, fought on such a global scale.

The mobilisation of the entire nation was a remarkable achievement by Churchill's government and demonstrated the power of the state in co-ordinating the nation's economic and military efforts. It was to be a lesson not lost on either the public or the political establishment in the post-war years, when Labour and Conservative alike faced the problem of reconstructing the British economy.

Although the policy of the government before 1939 appeared to be to avoid war at all costs, this did not imply that the government had done nothing to prepare for conflict. As soon as the war broke out, new ministries were created for Home Security, Economic Warfare and Food and Shipping. However, very few ministers with valuable wartime experience, apart from Winston Churchill, were appointed and the effectiveness of the new ministries varied considerably.

The effect of the Depression of the early 1930s had been to force Britain to develop newer industries, such as chemicals, vehicle production and electrical engineering, but her economy had not modernised sufficiently for her to be able to be fully self sufficient in either food or manufactured goods. Of course, she did have a large supply of skilled workers in coal, iron and textiles production and shipbuilding, many of whom had been unemployed since the Depression and who found that they were now a vital part of Britain's war effort.

The nature of the British Empire with its long supply lines crossing seas close to potential enemies, meant that Britain was still as exposed to the threat of U-boat **blockade** as it had been during the First World War. Given the increased range of submarines and aircraft and the threat of both the Italian and Japanese fleets and airforces, in some ways, Britain's import trade was even more vulnerable than it had been in 1914. The government did not introduce food rationing until January 1940, despite the fact that ration books had been ready since 1938. It half-heartedly attempted to promote the growing of food, and was reluctant to intervene to increase food production on privately owned farms. As a result, Britain was desperately short of food when France fell.

Due to public fears of the consequences of rearmament, the National Governments had been slow to build up Britain's military capacity, despite the perceived threats from Japan and Hitler's Germany. The priority at all times was to maintain defensive safety and to avoid damage to Britain's economy, which was still fragile after the experience of the Depression. The army's size was limited by the assumption that it would serve only to repel an invasion in Europe and would not need to have the resources necessary to mount offensives. Wars would be won, it was believed, by bombing the enemy into submission and therefore priority had been given to bomber production. The Commons had recommended the creation of 25 new fighter squadrons for the RAF, but the Cabinet had been slow to act. As Baldwin had stated in 1932, most military experts believed that the bomber could always get through and therefore to spend too much on defensive air forces was merely to waste money. The government chose instead to pursue a policy of appeasing the dictators of Europe and to build up the bomber forces instead, to act as a deterrent. In the Far East, after Manchuria, the threat of Japan was recognised and rebuilding of the base at Singapore was resumed in 1932, but gradually, as the situation in Europe deteriorated during the 1930s, less priority was given to the area, and British commitment to defending the area was quietly abandoned, with disastrous consequences in 1942.

Although Churchill campaigned tirelessly to improve Britain's military preparedness, it was only with Neville Chamberlain as Prime Minister that a more urgent approach was taken. He increased income tax to pay for expansion of the Royal Air Force, especially for the development of high-speed fighters and for the development of aircraft carriers for the Royal Navy and for improvements to imperial defences in Egypt. The Army was still relatively neglected as it was felt a large build up of arms would make negotiations with Germany more difficult. A Ministry of Supply, to co-ordinate munitions production was only established in 1939, after the German occupation of Prague, and it was clear that armaments production had not reached full potential when the war broke out. Therefore, when war in Western Europe broke out in 1940, the British army had few tanks and inadequate training to deal with German '**Blitzkrieg**' tactics that had first been suggested, ironically, by a British writer, Liddell Hart. Most of all, Britain had little faith in the fighting ability of her ally, France. It was only in February 1939 that the government decided that an expeditionary force should be sent to France. On the other hand, Chamberlain had been astute enough to authorise the construction of a chain of radar stations around Britain's coast, which would prove invaluable in the second stage of Britain's war, when Germany attempted to win superiority in the sky over Britain. However, the relative lack of fighters forced Churchill to take the drastic step of appointing Lord Beaverbrook as minister in charge of Air Production in May 1940, telling him to abandon all previous plans for methodical expansion of the air force and to galvanise fighter production, by any means necessary, to prepare for the forthcoming Luftwaffe attack. That Britain had just enough fighters to sustain the Battle of Britain, did owe something to the pre-war preparations and Beaverbrook's last-ditch effort, but the eventual victory owed as much to Hitler and Goering's tactical mistakes as it did to Britain's achievements in production.

2. The conduct of the war (EDEXCEL)

a) **What were Britain's war aims?** (30 marks)
b) **How far did Britain achieve these by 1945?** (30 marks)

(Total: 60 marks)

a) Britain and France went to war against Germany to defend Poland against German attack. She had no great love of the Polish government, and no plan to send troops, rather her motivation was to stop German territorial expansion by the threat of war. Hitler himself detected a lack of clarity in British thinking after Chamberlain's government rejected a German peace offer after the defeat of Poland: 'Why do they fight? They have no definite objective'.

Despite this, given the British policy before the war, as well as traditional British foreign policy, it is possible to see Britain fighting, as they had done against Napoleon, to prevent one country becoming dominant in Europe and thus threatening British trading and strategic interests. The government was aware of how ill-prepared for war it was, but such was the need to maintain Britain's status as a global power that they felt they had little choice.

Once Churchill became Prime Minister, Britain's specific war aims became more closely defined. In December 1941, following Pearl Harbour, Britain and America agreed to concentrate on defeating Germany before defeating Japan. By the Casablanca conference of 1943, Churchill and Roosevelt agreed that Germany and Japan could not ask for terms and that the allies should fight until the Axis powers surrendered unconditionally. When the Italian government that replaced Mussolini later that year sought terms for an **armistice**, they too were told that only unconditional surrender would be accepted.

Although this policy was largely agreed to ensure that Stalin would not seek an **armistice** once the Germans were driven out of Russia, it soon became morally justified as evidence of German atrocities towards Jews, gypsies and Russian prisoners was revealed by allied advances. A Gallup poll in September 1939 had showed that 89 per cent of the British people were in favour of 'fighting until Hitlerism is done away with' and this was, in effect, British policy throughout the war. Once the war drew to an end, other much more problematic issues, such as the future of the British Empire, the nature of government in Eastern and Central Europe and the need for American help in reconstruction, were thrown up and it proved impossible to find a consensus of allied opinion on these.

b) For Churchill, as for the majority of the British nation, the one overriding priority had been victory against the Axis powers. With the surrender of Japan in August 1945, all three of Britain's primary enemies had been defeated. Hitler and Mussolini were both dead and the military establishment of Japan was overthrown. If, as was often said, the war was one of democracy versus dictatorship, the victory of democracy in 1945 was undeniable, at least in Western Europe.

Britain had gone to war to protect her status as a Great Power, but by 1945, Britain was effectively bankrupt, losing a quarter of her national wealth and two thirds of her export trade. The war had cost £28,000 million which Britain had only managed to raise by borrowing heavily, chiefly from the USA and by selling much of its remaining overseas assets. Britain had a debt of £3,000 million, and when the USA unexpectedly halted lend-lease in 1945, Britain was left facing what some termed 'a financial Dunkirk'. As a consequence, Britain became financially dependent on the USA, as well as militarily dependent on her armed forces to defend Western Europe against the perceived threat from the Soviet Union after 1945. Given her remaining colonial possessions and the physical state of the rest of Europe, Britain was undeniably still a Great Power, but not a superpower in the league of the USSR and the USA.

Britain's global importance had rested on her control of the Empire, but the war had actually done serious, possibly even fatal damage to that institution. Although African, West Indian, Canadian, Indian and Australian and New Zealand Army Corps (ANZAC) forces had made an immense contribution to Britain's ultimate victory, popular support for the Empire was dwindling among the colonies themselves. In India, in particular, the war had increased calls for Britain to 'quit India' and the colonial government found itself facing mass non-co-operation from the people. This attitude was best expressed in the violent opposition to the trial of Bose, leader of the pro-Japanese Indian National Army. In 1942, Stafford Cripps had offered India **Dominion** status once the war was won, on behalf of the whole Cabinet, and Britain was no longer in any position to delay. In some ways, however, the decision to leave may have contributed to Britain's mainte-nance of Great Power status, as she did not become involved in a lengthy and unwinnable fight to keep India, unlike the French in Vietnam or Algeria, and she retained favourable economic relations with India as a member of the Commonwealth.

Finally, it is worth remembering that, Britain actually went to war to defend Poland. Not only had Poland been split between Germany and the Soviet Union in 1939, the Russian area had then been captured by the Germans, and then the whole area invaded and occupied by the Red Army. The Soviets, despite the attempts of Britain and the USA at Yalta and Potsdam, were to impose a pro-Stalinist regime and pursue policies which led to an eventual Polish uprising in 1956. It could hardly be said to have been a successful achievement of Britain's initial war aim.

3. The British economy in wartime (OCR)

How effectively did Britain restructure its economy to meet the demands of the war and what effects did this have on living standards in Britain?

(90 marks)

Under the terms of the Emergency Powers Act the government gained almost dictatorial powers to control and direct the economy as it saw fit. This was accompanied by a new approach in fiscal policy, as John Maynard Keynes was brought in to oversee a new approach which concentrated on limiting demand and seeking international trade and currency agreements, such as that signed at Bretton Woods in 1944. Taxation was substantially increased as part of this policy as well as paying for the war effort. Income tax went up from 25 pence in the pound in 1939 to 42.5 pence in 1940 and eventually to 50 pence by 1945. All in all the British paid 55 per cent of their incomes to the war effort: a much higher rate than in the First World War.

The war economy produced full employment for the first time since 1918, and the poorer working class groups probably benefited from this. The government tried to keep prices under control to avoid inflation, and, although it did not succeed completely, wages rose faster than prices.

The government directed the economy towards victory, regardless of the long-term consequences for the nation. Good labour relations were put ahead of financial restraint, as the swift settlement (and occasional popularity) of strikes demonstrated. The government invested in new technology and improved production techniques, most notably in agriculture, where tractors almost completely replaced horse-power. The government borrowed heavily to pay for all this, most notably through the lend-lease agreement with the USA. Under the terms of this arrangement, agreed in 1941, while the USA was still neutral, Britain could import war materials from America without paying for them until the war ended. In 1943, as the services began to run out of men, the government was forced to run down arms production and use lend-lease to supply the British forces with American equipment, in order to free sufficient manpower for the frontline. By 1945, Britain had almost ceased to be an exporter of goods and consequently, her **balance of payments** deficit was £875 million. In total she owed around £3 billion pounds, £30 million of it under the lend-lease scheme. The move from creditor to debtor nation, begun in the First World War, was now complete. But as 1945 demonstrated, she had at least emerged a debtor free from Nazi tyranny.

Britain's main problem after the Battle of Britain was in getting supplies through in the face of German U-boat attacks. In the First World War, rationing had only been introduced in 1918, but by 1941 rationing was quite severe, with only 8 oz. of meat and 2 oz. of tea allowed per week. The Ministry of Food provided recipes for substitute dishes such as Woolton Pie (named after the Minister of Food, Lord Woolton), lentil roast and carrot tart. Some could afford restaurant meals or the black market, but for most, eating habits were levelled out and institutionalised at the level of the skilled worker, which actually meant an improvement in diet for many. The government intervened further to make emergency welfare provision for children, such as milk for babies and concentrated orange juice and cod-liver oil for children (although only half of those eligible for this free provision actually took it). This helped to continue the pre-war trend in the decline in infant mortality rates across Britain.

There were lengthy queues for anything scarce or subject to irregular supply, but food subsidies and price control meant that the cost of living was kept relative to wage increases. Clothing was also rationed on a points system, which limited people to one complete outfit a year. A utility scheme was devised whereby clothing and furnishings were made to certain restricted specifications which saved on raw materials. It may not have been as ornate or plentiful as in the pre-war years, but supplies for the home were still available. Personal spending on food, clothing and household goods consequently fell, but, perhaps not surprisingly, in a war, spending on beer, tobacco and the cinema actually increased.

As a result of the **Blitz**, 200,000 houses were destroyed and another 250,000 made uninhabitable. With manpower called away to war, only 200,000 new houses were built, adding to the pre-war housing shortage. The increase in homelessness and the fall in quality of the housing stock, was in many ways, the worst aspect of the war on the Home Front for the British people. The result was a determination to improve matters as soon as the war ended.

At the beginning of the war, average weekly earnings were around £2.65, while at the end they were £3.80. It is estimated that the cost of living rose by an average of 30 per cent in total, but only 20 per cent for food alone, meaning that most saw their standard of living slightly improving. Some groups, such as manual workers, however, saw increases of their salaries of anything up to 75 or 80 per cent, and for them, the war saw the greatest leap forward in living standards since the Industrial Revolution, especially as it brought full employment to those staple industries that had been suffering since the end of the previous war. Those on military pay and those on separation allowances were far less fortunate.

4. The impact of the war on society (AQA)

Read the following source and then answer the questions which follow.

By the time peace came, war had affected every avenue of life, every channel of activity in Britain. New assumptions gleamed, where old certainties had been whisked away under the pressure and motion uniquely applied by total war. Everything – the parameters of politics, the organisation of industry, the place of labour, the status of women, the philosophy of economics, the power and reach of the state – had altered visibly. It was as if all the historical processes at work in Britain had been speeded up when one man, Adolf Hitler, pressed the button for the invasion of Poland in September 1939.

From *Never Again: Britain 1945–51* by Peter Hennessy

a) **What is meant by the phrase 'total war'?**   (3 marks)
b) **How did the war affect the 'status of women'?**   (7 marks)
c) **In what ways was British society changed by the impact of the war?**   (15 marks)

(Total: 25 marks)

a)   The phrase 'total war' means the involvement of the whole of a nation in a conflict. All the resources, finances and the manpower of that nation are to be put into the single effort to win the war, and every effort is made to impede and destroy the enemy.

b)   Women had played a crucial role in the First World War and in 1940 the Women's Land Army was formed employing 65,000 women. The civil service expansion provided 225,000 jobs for women making them 48 per cent of the total civil service. As before, they took over as bus and train conductresses. Women also took up manual labour and skilled engineering especially in aircraft factories.

Conscription of women was introduced in December 1941, with married women exempt. They had to choose between serving in the auxiliary services, civil defence or civilian employment. Most women in the services ended up doing domestic or clerical services, but some had military roles such as manning anti-aircraft batteries.

Despite the persistence of sexist attitudes among trade unions and employers, women did begin to view their roles differently. They demanded 'equal pay for equal work' and some employers accepted married women and the government provided nurseries for their children. The majority of women remained at home, looking after their families for the duration. On the whole, the war gave economic and social freedom to women and allowed them new opportunities even if the majority of women still built their hopes on marriage and raising a family. This was demonstrated by the fact that within a few months of the war's end, 75 per cent of women war workers had left their jobs and returned to their domestic pre-war roles.

c)   The war affected British society in a way in which no other event since the Civil War of the seventeenth century had done. Although overall the number of casualties was much lower than in the Great War, 60,000 civilians died on the Home Front as a result of German air raids. The effect of these raids, which popular mythology says brought Britons together, was actually to highlight the gross inequalities of life in Britain. The protection against bombing varied enormously according to one's wealth and status. While the upper classes could flee abroad or at least to the

Dorchester Hotel's steel reinforced basement and the middle classes could shelter in their cellars or in the 'Anderson shelters' built in the garden, the working classes were left to manage in surface shelters, with poor ventilation, little sanitation and no protection against a direct hit. Although the government tried to prevent it, workers took direct action and began to occupy the Underground Tube stations in London and large, strong factories. It was only when Herbert Morrison, the Labour MP, became Home Secretary that the indoor 'Morrison shelter', which any home could accommodate, was introduced. Even so, it was soon noticed that in poorer, working-class areas, a bomb might destroy a whole street of houses, whereas only one or two houses in a middle-class street might be left uninhabitable. As the workers tended to live closer to the factory areas and the communications points in Britain's cities, they also suffered a disproportionately high number of attacks and, consequently, casualties.

In many ways, evacuation too revealed the great gulf between rich and poor and brought it home to all. The schoolchildren moved from London, Birmingham, Liverpool and other major cities to the rural areas of Britain revealed in stark physical fashion, the consequences of the policies employed before the war. The food and medical provision for these children led to a dramatic improvement in their health and caused many to consider whether such wartime innovations could not be retained after the defeat of Germany.

Perhaps the best indication of how far the war had changed social attitudes was given by the reception of the **Beveridge Report** into social insurance, published in December 1942. Its message of higher taxes to pay for a scheme of social security that would last 'from the cradle to the grave' was hugely popular, selling 250,000 copies and winning virtually unanimous support of those asked about the scheme. Approximately 88 per cent of those polled said they thought it should be implemented in full.

The call up of manpower, too, had a levelling effect on the classes of Britain. Far more talented working-class soldiers were promoted into the ranks of officer than in the First World War and the experience of upper- or middle-class people being commanded by working-class leaders also occurred in administration, in the volunteer services and in local government. Rationing, treating everyone equally, demonstrated that living standards could be increased for all if the upper classes accepted some sacrifice of luxury. The war produced full employment for the first time since 1918, benefiting the poorer classes in particular.

Perhaps most importantly of all, though, the propaganda issued by the government and the media, often penned by left-wing writers such as J.B. Priestley, Humphrey Jennings and George Orwell, which stressed the need for common effort from all the people, had a self-fulfilling nature. Appeals to the 'Dunkirk Spirit', recognition of the contribution of factory workers, firemen and ARP wardens and the achievements of a 'people's army' created an impression of comradeship and community so strong, that it entered the national consciousness and became accepted fact, as Angus Calder has described in *The Myth of the Blitz*. This sense of the interdependence of the different sectors of society and the success of wartime **collectivism**, created a nation more united than ever before and more determined to create a better and more egalitarian society after the war. The governments and classes of society that had maintained the pre-war status quo had to admit that the poor had, through their sacrifice and effort, earned the right to a better standard of living, better education and welfare services. As one Home Guard told another in the wartime film *Dawn Patrol*, 'we found out in this war how we're all neighbours, and we aren't going to forget it when it's all over'.

5. Domestic politics (EDEXCEL)

a) **Describe the impact of the Second World War on the position of the political parties in Britain** (30 marks)

b) **Why did the Labour Party win the 1945 election?** (30 marks)

(Total: 60 marks)

a) Although enjoying a considerable majority in the Commons, Chamberlain's government fell in May 1940, when sufficient members of the Conservative Party voted against their leader in a vote of no confidence after the debate on the Norwegian campaign. Chamberlain immediately attempted to restructure his government, much as Asquith had done in 1915, by inviting the Liberals and Labour to form a coalition government with him. Labour, who had always been the object of Chamberlain's scorn, refused to do so and Chamberlain was forced to resign on 10 May.

Churchill was then asked to form a government and he succeeded in bringing Labour and the Liberals into his government and agreeing a by-election truce between the political parties. The new Cabinet gave important positions to the Labour leader, Clement Attlee, the trade union leader, Ernest Bevin and later to Herbert Morrison. With one or two exceptions, the Labour members of the coalition government performed their duties with outstanding success. In this way, the old insult of Churchill's that Labour wasn't 'fit to govern' was refuted by his own government. Equally, memories of the hesitant and economically disastrous Labour minority government of 1929–31 were quickly left behind.

The Conservatives, on the other hand, were slow to support Churchill's leadership, even after Chamberlain's fall from power and his death in November 1940. Churchill had his core of loyal Conservatives, but it was clear as the war went on that the party was fragmenting between Churchill's supporters, Chamberlain's old supporters and those on the left of the party, such as Harold Macmillan and the Education Minister, R.A. Butler, who founded the Conservative Post-War Problems Committee and later introduced the 1944 Education Act which finally made secondary education compulsory.

As Labour were part of the government however, any political opposition had to come from other organisations. There was, if anything, a strong anti-party spirit in the country as a result of failures of 1940. Groups who offered themselves as outsiders in the political world, as representatives of the ordinary people who suffered most in the war found that they had a willing audience. The Christian socialist Common Wealth party, whose message was one of better welfare provision for all, won four by-elections during the war and the left-wing **Independent Labour Party** (ILP) and Scottish Nationalists managed to rally significant support. Often these groups won votes at by-elections as they were the only means to protest at the government's behaviour, given the electoral truce. On one occasion, the ILP nearly defeated Sir James Grigg, Under-Secretary at the War Office in Cardiff.

After the popular reception of the **Beveridge Report** on social security in 1942, cracks began to appear in the coalition. Attlee and the Labour Party felt that the war had lead to popular support for state control of the economy and more intervention to solve social problems and reduce class differences. They were alarmed by the rise of the ILP and Common Wealth however and so put pressure on a reluctant Churchill to issue White Papers committing the government to a National

Health Service, a comprehensive Social Insurance scheme and an economic policy designed to avoid mass unemployment.

Not surprisingly, there were now grave doubts as to Churchill's position as a potential post-war leader. Most still approved of him as wartime Prime Minister, but in 1944, 62 per cent of those polled thought he would be a bad peacetime leader.

Therefore, although the Labour Party was almost unarguably helped by the social climate of the war and the governmental experience they gained, the Conservatives became more fragmented. Even in 1945, although they coalesced around Churchill's leadership, the looseness of the alliance made it impossible for the party to match the clear, positive message of the socialists. Churchill's leadership itself, given his poor peacetime record and unwillingness to consider far-reaching reform, proved to be a very mixed blessing for the Tories and the party found themselves out of office for the first time for 14 years.

b)   As soon as the war against Germany was won, the Labour party left the wartime coalition government and chose to fight the election which Winston Churchill then called, as an independent party, much as they had done in 1918. By 1945, however, the experience of six years of war had dramatically altered the political outlook of many in the British electorate.

According to the mass observation movement of social reporters, the issues the electorate were most concerned about were housing, full employment, and social security. The wartime **Beveridge Report** had revealed the popular support for welfare reform and Labour had been keen to advocate 'Beveridge in full' at the time and in their manifesto, 'Let Us Face the Future', they carefully adumbrated their proposals for reform. It was well known that the Health White Paper of 1944, proposing a National Health Service had been opposed by the Conservatives and that Churchill was reluctant to commit himself to increasing expenditure on welfare.

Rather than simply hoping for full employment as the Conservatives seemed to, Labour appeared to have a policy, **nationalisation** of industry, which assured a high level of employment. Traditional dislike of state of control had been overturned by the war, when government direction of industry, both in Britain and the Soviet Union, had achieved victory. Memories were still strong of the economic depression which followed the First World War, when the Conservatives had dominated the post-war coalition government.

The Labour leader, Attlee seemed to be alert and optimistic, sure that the effort which had been put into winning the war could be used to build a better society. By contrast, Churchill had, during his years as Prime Minister, failed to build support within the Conservative Party and constituency work had been neglected. The lack of a clear policy to counter the Labour manifesto was a telling indictment of the once formidable Conservative party machine, and the attempt to use Churchill's status as wartime leader failed to convince those, especially soldiers facing demobilisation, who were more concerned about their peacetime future. This distinction was reinforced in the election campaign, when Churchill spoke of his wartime Labour colleagues having 'to fall back on some form of Gestapo' if they came to power. Attlee replied to this electoral gift by thanking Churchill for having reminded voters of the difference between 'Winston Churchill the great leader in war of a united nation and Mr Churchill, the party leader of the Conservatives'. Churchill's exaggerated rhetoric looked out of place in an election and his fear of socialism seemed bizarre from a man who had organised the most collectivist state that Britain had seen.

Labour also benefited from the inequalities in seat distribution, which meant that most urban Labour constituencies contained fewer voters than rural Conservative ones. In this way, although they gained only 8 per cent more votes than the Conservatives, they actually won 170 more seats. In truth, many people, including vital middle-class voters turned against the Conservatives not because of Churchill's howler, but because they saw the Conservatives as the Party of the 1930s, the Party of unemployment, the Party of the Means Test and the Party of **appeasement**. As Harold Macmillan complained, 'it was not Churchill who lost the 1945 election, it was the ghost of Neville Chamberlain'.

6. Overall assessment (OCR)

How serious was the impact of the Second World War on the British Empire?

(90 marks)

Britain's Empire undoubtedly contributed significantly to the successful war effort, most particularly with brave and skilled servicemen. But the Empire was also faced with a rising tide of anti-colonial sentiment during the war, which it had to contain in order to win the war, but often at a cost for the long-term survival of the colonial system. For example, in Egypt, when the King appointed an anti-British Prime Minister in 1942, the British Ambassador surrounded the royal palace with tanks and forced a change of premier. This may have guaranteed continued commitment in the war, but it seriously damaged the monarchy and led to the rise of an anti-British clique in the Egyptian army that eventually toppled the King in 1952.

In Asia, the humiliating defeats at the hands of the Japanese, such as the capture of Singapore in February 1942 and the fall of Burma later that year, meant that the image of British superiority was permanently shattered. The British were defeated by an Asian enemy, who took great pains in the early years of the conflict to appeal to nationalists who opposed British rule. 'Nationalist', pro-Japanese armies such as the Indian National Army led by Subhas Chandra Bose were formed to fight the British. The Japanese also promised to create a 'Greater East Asia Co-prosperity Sphere'. It may have been a front for Japanese economic exploitation, but the support for the concept, especially among non-Christian religious groups, demonstrated deeply held anti-British attitudes. After the Battle of Midway in 1942, the Japanese knew they could not win the war in Asia, so they took care to encourage anti-British groups, such as in the occupied colonies, to hamper any attempts to reimpose imperial rule. In 1945, Japanese commanders effectively allowed these groups to seize control after their surrender, which left Britain with the awkward task of re-imposing British rule by force.

In India itself, war had been declared by the Viceroy, Lord Linlithgow without consulting the Indian nationalist parties. Both Gandhi and the leader of Congress, Nehru, refused to assist the government, complaining that the war to defend democracy in Europe was preventing it in India. The autonomous governments of the Indian provinces also resigned in protest, leaving Britain to rule by decree. In order to keep popular support, the British government offered India **Dominion** status after the war and sent Stafford Cripps to negotiate a settlement in 1942. None was forthcoming, however and so the Congress party launched a policy of non-co-operation calling for Britain to 'Quit India'. The Indian army stayed loyal however and the Congress leadership, including Gandhi, were interned until the end of the war. Churchill refused to commit himself to a policy of British withdrawal, but the control of India became increasingly difficult to sustain.

On the other hand, the Muslim League chose to support the British government, in the hope of winning concessions for the Muslim minority of India, once the war was over, but their price was a separate Muslim state of Pakistan. At the Simla Conference of 1945, following Gandhi's release, insistence by the nationalists on British withdrawal was clear, but the divisions between Congress and the League meant that the British could at least dictate the pace and nature of that withdrawal. The election of 1945 and the coming to power of the Labour Party, which had always supported self-government for India, meant that in India at least, the demands of the nationalists would not be strongly resisted.

In Africa, where the influence of the war was perhaps least felt, the British Empire seemed the most secure. When the Asian colonies had been lost, production of vital crops such as rubber had been developed in Africa instead.

Even so, the war did have a major social effect on Africa. Inflation, shortages and the need to move labour to the cities for war production led to a growth in the politicisation of African societies. In West Africa, the Head of the Africa Division of the Colonial Office, Andrew Cohen, recognised the importance of the 'new' African, educated, urbanised and detribalised, in the development towards eventual self-government. In East Africa, the government even considered leaving the government to the white settlers, who had become more influential during the war. But for the time being, Africa remained a useful and relatively compliant part of the Empire, which could potentially develop into as useful a part of the British economy as India had been in the nineteenth century, and Britain was in no mood to consider more than African or white settler involvement in local government.

The mass celebrations for VE Day, which took place while many of Britain's Asian colonies were still under Japanese rule, compared to the much more muted VJ Day, were a stark comment on the public's general apathy about the Empire, and their desire to concentrate on those issues which affected their personal lives, as was made even more clear by the election of the Labour government in July 1945.

How successful was Churchill as Britain's war leader?

(90 marks)

It is a testament to Churchill's achievement as leader in 1940, that even A.J.P. Taylor, one of his harshest critics otherwise, described him as 'the saviour of his country'. Most historians agree that without his inspired rhetoric and faith in ultimate victory, Britain would have sought peace terms with Germany after the fall of France. His decision to withdraw the British Expeditionary Force (BEF) from France at Dunkirk and to keep the Royal Air Force (RAF) from fighting on the continent certainly contributed much to the country's survival and its subsequent contribution to the allied campaigns in North Africa, Italy and Normandy.

Churchill did clearly make mistakes. Arguably his most serious one was at Mers-el-Kebir in 1940 when he ordered the sinking of the French fleet against the advice of the War Cabinet and the Chiefs of Staff. Vichy France instantly regarded Britain as an enemy and handed her air and naval bases in the Gulf of Siam to the Japanese from where they were able to launch their successful attack on Malaya and Singapore. Luckily, in North Africa, when the Allies landed on French territory in 1942, Churchill chose to negotiate with the Vichy leader there, Admiral Darlan and thus avoid any further resistance. Churchill also blundered when he sent troops to defend Greece in

1941, but at least this time, he did so with the full support of the War Cabinet. Equally, Churchill should shoulder some of the blame for the fall of Singapore. After the German invasion of Russia, Churchill had eagerly sent planes and tanks to Stalin to secure him as an ally and neglected the defence of the exposed areas of the Empire in the Far East. When Japan attacked, Britain could only send warships, and these were easy prey for the Japanese torpedo-bombers. After the fall of Singapore in February 1942, Churchill's popularity sank and some considered replacing him with Eden as Minister of Defence, but Churchill threatened to resign as Prime Minister if that happened, and all those in government knew what an aid to morale he was. As it was, Montgomery's successes in North Africa bolstered Churchill's position, and with Germany's disaster at Stalingrad and the arrival of American troops in Europe, confidence in final victory was restored.

When the time came to launch the main assault on fortress Europe, Churchill insisted on Montgomery to command the ground forces, which proved an inspired choice, despite American misgivings. Despite the failure to capture a bridge across the Rhine at Arnhem, Montgomery came very close to succeeding and nearly shortened the war by several months.

Churchill has been criticised for his lenient attitude towards Stalin, especially when he signed the notorious 'percentages agreement' in Moscow in 1944, when he effectively gave Stalin a free hand in the future government of Eastern Europe. On the other hand, Britain was in no position to try to impose their preferred model of government there when it was being overrun by the Red Army. At the 1945 Yalta conference, under pressure from Roosevelt, Churchill joined in American demands for 'free and democratic elections' in 'liberated Europe' and insisted on a change in the composition of the Moscow-imposed Polish government. As the next months showed, there was very little way to force Stalin to carry this out, especially when they still needed Russian help against Japan. When Truman became President, it was clear that Britain would have a struggle to retain American economic and military assistance, let alone force Stalin to behave as she wished. It was largely due to the close relationship that Churchill had built up with the USA during the war that future governments were able to secure some degree of 'special relationship' with America and thus, some say, in the new age of superpower confrontation.

Additional essay questions

 1. Preparation for war (AQA)

Read the following source and then answer the questions which follow.

The various disruptions of normal domestic life during the period of the 'phoney' or 'invisible' war arose from a preconception of what the war would be like, rather than from the war when it actually materialised.

Britain in the Century of Total War by Arthur Marwick, 1968

a) **What is meant by the 'phoney' or 'invisible war' in the context of 1939?** **(3 marks)**
b) **Explain the consequences of the government restrictions of the first months of the war.** **(7 marks)**
c) **'The war machine resembled an expensive motor car, beautifully polished, complete in every detail, except there was no petrol in the tank.' Do you agree or disagree with this assessment of Chamberlain's wartime leadership?** **(15 marks)**

2. The conduct of the war (EDEXCEL)

a) **In what ways did the leadership of Winston Churchill ensure Britain's survival in 1940?** (30 marks)

b) **Explain why the British government was able to maintain the support of its people for the whole of the Second World War.** (30 marks)

(Total: 60 marks)

Essay plan

a) Historical consensus on the decisive nature of Churchill's role in 1940.

- *Previous figures such as Chamberlain and Halifax abhorred war and would rather come to terms with Hitler after the fall of France.*
- *He created a genuine coalition government comprising of Labour, Conservative and Liberal MPs, which united the country behind it, after a decade of bitter division.*
- *Churchill's role was crucial in continuing the fight: he persuaded a divided cabinet to support him and used his oratorical skills to persuade the Houses of Parliament and the public through his radio broadcasts.*
- *Churchill's decision to evacuate the BEF from Dunkirk, rather than continuing to support the French war effort provided Britain with 340,000 troops with which to defend British soil.*
- *Churchill's decision to also withdraw the RAF to Britain during the battle of France allowed Britain to win the Battle of Britain – Britain had only just enough fighters to defeat the Luftwaffe, had she lost any more planes in France in the spring, it may have been decisive.*
- *Churchill forged a personal friendship with President Roosevelt of the USA, obtaining vital lend-lease agreements which enabled Britain to maintain the war at sea in particular.*
- *He also used his personal prestige to maintain morale by touring bombed areas of the country and ordering retaliation attacks on Berlin and other German cities.*

Important also to remember the contribution of the RAF in the Battle of Britain, the contribution of British workers to keep the war machine supplied and the role of the British public in supporting Churchill unquestioningly despite the ordeal of the **Blitz** *– Churchill's defiance would have been insignificant without the whole-hearted support of the British people.*

b) Crucial nature of the wartime leadership – at the moment of crisis, Neville Chamberlain was fortunately replaced by Churchill, who created a coalition government containing other popular flamboyant figures such as Eden, Bevin, Morrison and Beaverbrook as well as able administrators such as Attlee and Woolton. The nation rallied behind a government that seemed to be a cross-section of British society.

- *Before the battle of France, the government assured the public of the efficacy of the naval* **blockade**, *which had proved so decisive in the First World War.*

- On the fall of France, British attention was focussed on the 'miracle of Dunkirk' – in fact a major retreat, but one very effectively turned into a success by Churchill and broadcasters such as J.B. Priestley.

- By use of effective propaganda, the government was able to maintain morale during the months of the **Blitz** when Britain stood alone. There was virtually no serious criticism of the government from the press until 1942 – bad news, such as shipping losses, was suppressed, instead the country was encouraged to take communal action in reducing food waste, growing one's own, saving, salvaging and 'making do'. This made the whole nation feel involved in the war effort.

- The military support of the Empire and provisional governments of occupied Europe and the financial support of the USA, even during 1940, provided the public with hope that Britain would not be overwhelmed. When the USSR and USA entered the war in 1941, Britain was convinced that with two such powerful allies, victory would be forth-coming.

- After 1942, with the Japanese stopped at Midway and Burma, the Germans halted at Stalingrad and the British victory at El Alemein, the tide of victory had shifted in the Allies's favour and all the allies were committed to the unconditional surrender of the Axis countries.

- Despite some reluctance on Churchill's part, the coalition government accepted the find-ings of the **Beveridge Report** and had begun reforming the education system in 1944 as well as issuing White Papers on a National Health System, full employment and social insurance. It seemed to many that there would be a significant increase in the standard of living for all, once victory was achieved.

Ultimately, the British public were convinced of the rightness of their cause, as they had been in the First World War. They were fighting for democracy, freedom, the right to a better life in the post-war world. The barbaric nature of the regimes against which they were fighting were so anti-thetical to all these aims, that the belief in the war was never seriously questioned.

 3. The British economy in wartime (OCR)

Why and to what extent did the Second World War led to an increase in the power of the state in Britain?

(90 marks)

4. The impact of the war on society (EDEXCEL)

a) **Describe the ways in which the German bombing campaigns affected British social attitudes.** (30 marks)

b) **Why was the Beveridge Report so popular when it was published in December 1942?** (30 marks)

(Total: 60 marks)

Essay plan

*a)   The **Blitz** – the sustained night-bombing of British cities between September 1940 and May 1941. 44,000 people died and hundreds of thousands were injured or made homeless. The Germans' aim was to destroy civilian morale and cause the British to sue for peace. Although morale largely survived, there were instances of panic and confusion and the reality of the immediate reaction, judging from mass observation reports, was more complex than the 'Britain can take it' attitude promoted by the government and the media.*

- *Official evacuation of children from danger areas had taken place before the bombing started, but a further wave took place as the **Blitz** began. The mixing of the classes, as urban working-class mothers and children were sheltered by the rural middle classes, caused a greater understanding of the nature of poverty and deprivation in the cities on the part of the middle class and the media. The work of groups like the Women's Voluntary Service (WVS) in providing relief services.*
- *The 'shelter controversy'. The difference between the safety of the surface public shelters in which working class families had to shelter and the cellars and gardens of the richer classes in which 'Anderson shelters' could be erected. The London public occupied the Underground stations as a response, despite government opposition. It took a Labour Home Secretary to design a shelter for all classes – the indoor 'Morrison shelter'.*
- *The differential impact of the bombing. Working-class housing, closer to the factories and docks was more frequently damaged than middle-class housing in the suburbs. The damage caused by bombs was greater in working-class areas as the quality of housing here was poorer. The issue of housing became a major priority – central government action was seen as the best solution, with a need for public, not private, house building.*
- *The encouragement of communal responsibility – air raid patrols, fire-watching, growing of food, collection of salvage. Created a sense of common struggle and national endeavour that transcended class boundaries – reinforced by the media and government's message of undaunted national resistance. The bombs did not discriminate on the basis of wealth, so why should the government?*

*Overall, the **Blitz** caused the British to accept the need for greater government intervention to eradicate the inequalities of wealth that the social upheaval of the **Blitz** had revealed. Best practical example – the success of the centrally administered emergency hospital scheme helped to pave the way for the creation of a National Health System paid through taxes and free for the use of all.*

b)   Difficulties and hardships of war encouraged hope for reductions in social inequalities afterwards. Memories of the pre-war Depression and its divisive effects on Britain compared to the relatively cohesive society needed to win a war – a mood of 'never again' had emerged by 1941.

- *War had also obliged the government to take a collectivist approach – this led to a wider acceptance of state intervention after introduction of rationing, evacuation of children, emergency hospital, nursery and housing provision and the provision of free school meals for children.*

- *Pre-war welfare provision exposed as inadequate, especially in health care and housing – need to abandon Means Test demonstrated by case of the Family Allowance as early as 1941.*
- *Principle of centrally-planned welfare provision made more acceptable by the use of economic and industrial planning during the war. Principle of increased personal taxation for the public good also made acceptable.*
- ***Beveridge report** deliberately written to capitalise on the opportunity that war provided. Cromwellian language of eliminating the 'five giants on the road to recovery'.*
- *Media attention – publicity given to the **Beveridge Report** in all the popular newspapers, on radio discussions, through the Army Bureau of Current Affairs (ABCA). Influential left-wing publications such as the Daily Mirror and Picture Post championed the Report.*
- *Political support – suited the policies of the Labour Party and appealed to the sense of social justice and national benefit of left-wing Liberals and Conservatives. Labour did not allow Churchill to 'bury' the Report.*
- *Principle of universality of benefits, regardless of need, in the place of selectivity – chimed with wartime mood of universality of sacrifice for universality of benefit.*

*The **Beveridge Report** was the product of an able self-publicist determined to take the opportunity presented by the war to reorganise the provision of welfare and who found many allies in all political parties, the media and even in the Church. In many ways, the **Beveridge Report** was a relatively conservative document, as demands for social change had been even more radical before 1942. It served to coalesce general demands for improved social services in a way that seemed both practical and desirable in the context of a total war fought in the name of democracy.*

5. Domestic politics (OCR)

Assess the impact of the publication of the Beveridge Report on the British political parties and plans for post-war reconstruction.

(90 marks)

6. Overall assessment (AQA)

Read the following source and then answer the questions which follow.

The war had proved that Great Britain still had the political flair, the personal authority, the industrial know-how and the military capacity for a major role in world affairs.

Contemporary England 1914–1964 by W.N. Medlicott, 1976

a) **Comment on the 'military capacity' that Britain demonstrated in the Second World War.** **(3 marks)**

b) **Explain how Britain had organised its 'industrial know-how' to maintain 6 years of fighting.** **(7 marks)**

c) 'The British empire declined; the condition of the people improved'. To what extent do you agree with A.J.P. Taylor's assessment of the impact of the war on Britain? **(15 marks)**

(Total: 25 marks)

Part 3: Sources

1. The social impact of the Blitz (AQA)

Read the sources below and then answer the questions which follow.

Source A: From the *Wimbledon Borough News*, March 1941

Time has gone by when a man could say he has lived all his life in one house without so much as knowing his neighbours' name. Almost every week people living in the same street meet and discuss fire fighting and fix up rotas of duty. But this neighbourly business has a lot more to it. The man who is doing his bit is keen on seeing that the other man is doing it, or wants to know the reason why. So, in the long run, these fire parties are starting points which will ensure that everyone is doing something to help the war effort. They will also break down an age old tradition of isolation and class consciousness.

Source B: From a Mass Observation report on Southampton, December, 1940

Many people did not believe the official [casualty] figures [of 370 killed]; they said that there must be many more still in shelters under wrecked buildings, one man (aged 45) said, '3,700 is far more like the right figure.' There was a fairly general feeling that Southampton was done for. More than one person expressed the opinion that the Germans would not come back again because there was nothing left for them to come back to. One man (aged 55) said, 'We'll have to abandon the whole damn town and build it up again'.

Source C: From *Blitz, Women and Work* by D.W. Thomas, 1998

The early period of war, including the retreat from Dunkirk and the air raids on Britain's industrial cities and coastal regions, placed an immense strain on civilian morale. Investigations by Mass Observation and other social enquirers suggest there were local problems of a serious nature. In national terms, however, there is no evidence that the country came close to breaking point – though had the full force of the **blitz** continued beyond June 1941, the problem may have become more serious.

QUESTIONS WITH WORKED ANSWERS

a) Study source C. With reference to source C and using your own knowledge, explain the reference to 'the retreat from Dunkirk'. **(3 marks)**

b) Study source B. What are the strengths and weaknesses of this source as evidence of public morale during the Blitz? **(7 marks)**

c) Refer to sources A, B and C and use your own knowledge. 'The image of a people standing together in communal defiance of the German bombs seems to be, in part, a myth'. Do you agree with this view? Give reasons for your answer.   (15 marks)

ANSWERS

a) After the invasion of Belgium, France and Holland by the German Forces in May 1940, the British Expeditionary Force was cut off from the bulk of the French forces when the Germans reached the sea at Abbeville. The British government therefore decided that France could not be saved and that they must evacuate the British and French troops they could reach. 'Operation Dynamo' which lasted for six days managed to bring nearly 350,000 troops from the beaches at Dunkirk. Although this was a considerable achievement, and was celebrated as a 'miracle' by the press, the French campaign was, none the less, a humiliating defeat for Britain.

b) 'Mass Observation' was a sociological experiment, set up before the Second World War, in which unpaid volunteers would keep records of their everyday lives to allow a picture of real life in Britain to be collected. The government commissioned the organisation to monitor public opinion during the war. This report is, therefore, a first hand account of the aftermath of the **Blitz** on Southampton, drawn up by an individual observer, attempting to be as impartial as he or she can. As it was not intended for public broadcast, it therefore is largely free from any form of censorship, either from the observer or from outside authorities. It can therefore be relied upon to give a number of genuine reactions to the experience of bombing, at least in the immediate aftermath. It is also useful, because it gives the ages and the sex of those commenting on the German attack, allowing one to measure the extent to which the feelings of the ordinary people of Southampton varied.

One must, however, be cautious in reading too much into this report. One does not know how many people the observer spoke to, and whether he or she chose to only include those views which gave one particular reaction. Many of those involved in mass observation held strong left-wing views and were unhappy with the ways in which the **Blitz** was reported by the press under government censorship. This observer may well have exaggerated the views of those he or she spoke to or may have omitted contrasting views, in order to deliberately create an impression of a public reaction very much at odds with the official view of strong, unflinching public morale in the face of the bombing.

c) The 'myth' of the **Blitz**, that the classes found a new camaraderie and co-operated as never before is supported by source A, which suggests the organisation of 'fire parties' were serving to 'break down an age old tradition of isolation and class consciousness' in many communities. The reliability of this piece of journalism could be questioned though, as it predicts the creation of a new community rather than reporting it, and admits that organising fire parties is only a 'starting point'. Second, the article is from a newspaper covering the new suburbs of Wimbledon, where the middle classes lived and where the organisation of housing discouraged the development of community spirit. It might be argued that in such areas the need for co-operation that the war engendered was much more revolutionary in its effects, whereas in more working-class or more mixed areas, the impact of the **Blitz** was far less noticeable, at least in this respect.

Source B by contrast, suggests that the picture of the British, unflinching in the face of brutal attack, may well be simplistic. As the source notes, 'there was a fairly general feeling that Southampton was done for'. Although one cannot be absolutely sure that this was indeed the 'general feeling', given the techniques employed by mass observers, one can assume that it reflects a fairly genuine attitude among survivors in the immediate aftermath of the attack. Source C, written by a historian, corroborates this, writing that 'investigations by Mass Observation and other social enquirers suggest there were local problems of a serious nature'. The source suggests, however, that nationally the mood of resistance was not broken, although it questions how long British morale would have remained high, had not Hitler turned the Luftwaffe to the USSR in summer 1941.

Clearly, popular reaction to the **Blitz** was varied, as any study of the sources demonstrates, and it will always be possible to find individual sources that seem to contradict one another as to personal reactions to the **Blitz**. It is possible to say that the British people genuinely supported Churchill in his defiance in the face of the German attacks, but that those who had direct experience of bombing were much less likely to be optimistic of Britain's chances of survival, as source B shows, if the raids continued with the ferocity that they did between September 1940 and May 1941. Morale was certainly shaken by the attacks, as the controversy over the lack of adequate shelter provision and the mass evacuation of cities demonstrated, but with the army rescued from Dunkirk and the media united in presenting a picture of a nation capable of ultimate victory, the British showed no signs of seriously supporting any other leader than Churchill, at least in the immediate future. And Churchill refused to accept any course of action other than 'victory'. As it is put by the historian in source C, 'in national terms . . . there is no evidence that the country came close to breaking point'.

As for the creation of a new form of community, that, at least, does appear to have been largely the creation of the media, building on individual experiences, as in source A. There is very little reliable evidence, from government or mass observation records of the genuine mixing of the classes. The very rich continued to live separately from the rest of British society. The middle classes tended to avoid communal shelters and were disgusted by the squalor of the tube shelters and the Tilbury 'shelter'. Evacuation of working-class families caused as much inter-class friction as it did new appreciation of different life styles. The middle and upper classes were willing to accept the myth of commonality of sacrifice and to see the workers receiving the social protection it was felt they now deserved, but very few examples exist of middle- and upper-class families sharing their private homes or private shelters willingly with those of the lower classes. The myth of the **Blitz** therefore became hugely important not only in maintaining morale but also in altering political priorities and allegiances (at least in the short term). But it did remain, in part, a myth.

2. The political impact of the Second World War (OCR)

Read the sources below and then answer the question which follows:

Source A: From *Postscripts*, a BBC broadcast by J.B. Priestley, July 1940

Now the war, because it demands a huge collective effort, is compelling us to change not only our ordinary, social and economic habits, but also our habits of thought. We're actually changing over from the property view to the sense of community, which simply means that we realise that we're all in the same boat. But, and this is the point, the boat can serve not only as our defence against Nazi aggression, but as an ark in which we can finally land in a better world.

Source B: From *The Beveridge Report on Social Welfare*, November 1942

Want could have been abolished before the present war by a redistribution of income among the wage-earning classes, without touching any of the wealthier classes. This is said not to suggest that redistribution of income should be confined to the wage-earning classes; still less is it said to suggest that men should be content with avoidance of want, with subsistence incomes. It is said simply as the most convincing demonstration that abolition of want just before this war was easily within the economic resources of the community; want was a needless scandal due to not taking the trouble to prevent it.

Source C: From the Conservative Party Beveridge Report secret committee, January 1943

There is no doubt that the great publicity which the Report has received in the Press, on the platform and over the wireless has unfortunately led many people to assume that it represents Government policy and is likely to be carried into speedy effect as soon as the war is over. This does not make an approach to the problem any easier, since many hopes have been raised which it may not be possible to satisfy.

... It must be realised that a great part of the money required for putting his scheme into effect is not devoted to curing want. Provision by the State of complete social security can only be achieved at the expense of personal freedom and by sacrificing the right of an individual to choose what life he wishes to lead and what occupation he should follow.

Source D: From *Let Us Face the Future: A Declaration of Labour Policy for the Consideration of the Nation*, 1945

The nation wants food, work and homes. It wants more than that – it wants good food in plenty, useful work for all, and comfortable, labour-saving homes that take full advantage of the resource of modern science and productive industry. It wants a high and rising standard of living, security for all against a rainy day, an educational system that will give every boy and girl a chance to develop the best that is in them . . .

All parties say so – the Labour party means it. For the Labour party is prepared to achieve it by drastic policies of re-planning and by keeping a firm hand on our whole productive machinery; the Labour Party will put the community first and the sectional interests of private business after.

QUESTIONS WITH WORKED ANSWERS

a) Study source C. From this Source and from your own knowledge, explain why the Conservative Party believed that 'it may not be possible to satisfy' hopes for social welfare reform. (10 marks)

b) Study source A. Assess the value of this source as evidence of the changing political mood in Britain in 1940. (25 marks)

c) Study sources C and D. Compare the attitudes of the Conservative and Labour Party towards welfare reform as shown in these sources and explain the differences. (25 marks)

d) Study all the sources. Use the sources and your own knowledge to explain how the Labour Party was able to take advantage of the political mood created by the war. (60 marks)

(Total: 120 marks)

a) The Conservative Party were extremely divided on whether to attempt to implement the **Beveridge Report**, despite the popular support it had clearly gained since its publication. Some Conservatives such as Harold Macmillan and the Tory Reform Group supported the Report, but the majority of the party believed that not only were the policies suggested by Beveridge counter to their interests, but also completely impractical, given the state of the country's finances, once the war was won.

b) The famous 'postscripts' given by the author J.B. Priestley from the retreat from Dunkirk in June 1940 until the beginning of the **Blitz** in October were a very effective measure of changing public mood in the summer of 1940. The Ministry of Information undertook a survey which found that the majority of the population who heard his talks, agreed with him, and that his broadcasts were heard, on average, by 31 per cent of the population. His message, effectively summarised in this source, was that the war had demonstrated what could be done by a society united in its efforts and not divided by class, or as he put it, 'the property view'. Instead this new 'sense of community' would enable Britain to build a fairer and more egalitarian society once the war had been concluded. That this view, in marked contrast to the attitude towards the unemployed and the 'distressed regions' of the 1930s depression, could be so positively received by the same electorate that had voted for the National Government of Baldwin and Neville Chamberlain, demonstrated very clearly that the events of May, June and July had clearly shaken many people into reassessing their political and social beliefs. When his broadcasts ended in October 1940, there was a press campaign for him to resume and a widespread belief that he had been taken off the air because his views were disliked by many Conservative members of the Cabinet.

c) While the Conservative committee met in secret to discuss the **Beveridge Report** and to conclude that while popular, state-controlled welfare was not an approach favoured by themselves, Labour, openly stated in their 1945 electoral manifesto that they were 'prepared to achieve it by drastic policies of re-planning and by keeping a firm hand on our whole productive machinery'. For Labour, the implementation of a state-run welfare system on the scale proposed by Beveridge, based on the principle of maintaining a high and stable level of employment was relatively easy to reconcile with their socialist principles. The Labour ministers in the wartime Cabinet had pressed for the introduction of reform proposals which had resulted in the so-called 'White Paper chase' between 1944 and 1945. By contrast, the Conservatives, their confidence shattered by the party split over Chamberlain's resignation, were unsure what approach to take when faced with the popular acclaim that greeted Beveridge's Report. As source C indicates, the party's leadership were unconvinced that such **collectivism** was either desirable or practical and they attempted to resist the radical demands of the Labour Party, hoping that the return to the normality of peacetime, and the expected victory of a Churchill-led Conservative party in the post-war election would allow them effectively to water down any of the proposals they were forced to introduce while in coalition.

d) The wartime mood of unity and equality of sacrifice, caused many, middle- and lower-class, to ask serious questions about the direction of social policy in Britain. Those in the armed forces especially, were worried that the sacrifices being made by themselves on the battlefields, would only be rewarded by a return to mass unemployment and very limited welfare, as had happened after 1918. The media, particularly the *Picture Post*, the *Daily Mirror* and the broadcasts of J.B. Priestley on the BBC, questioned the wisdom of pre-1939 policy and promoted the radical ideas of reformers such as William Beveridge. Even 'establishment' figures such as William Temple, the Archbishop of Canterbury, advocated a more collectivist approach. As Priestley put it in source A, the war had taught the need for 'changing over from the property view to the sense of community'. In these circumstances, support for the socialist policies of the Labour Party were perhaps unsurprising. Public ownership of the means of production was **Clause IV** of the party's constitution, and they had always been committed to a policy of high and stable employment and generous welfare benefits, for the workers, whom Ernest Bevin used to refer to as 'my people'. In their election manifesto in 1945, the party strove to emphasise the difference between themselves and the other parties. As source D states, 'the Labour party is prepared to achieve it [better social services] by drastic policies of re-planning and by keeping a firm hand on our whole productive machinery'. In a near paraphrase of the quote from J.B. Priestley, it went on, 'the Labour Party will put the community first and the sectional interests of private business after'. Given that a Gallup poll in June 1945 put 'housing', 'full employment' and 'social security' as the issues which most preoccupied voters, it is easy to see how Labour's position was far more attractive to a war-weary public.

Labour also benefited from participation in the wartime coalition government set up by Churchill in 1940. Attlee, the Labour leader, became deputy Prime Minister, and the Trade Union leader, Ernest Bevin became Minister for Labour. The party was thus able to disprove accusations that it was unfit to govern, following its role in the 1931 financial crisis, as its members played a hugely important role in organising Britain's victorious war effort.

The Conservatives, by contrast, could only offer ideological resistance to the demands for great state security, arguing, as in source C, that 'provision by the State of complete social security can only be achieved at the expense of personal freedom'. This argument reached its ludicrous conclusion on the election campaign of 1945, when Churchill was reduced to accusing his erstwhile wartime Labour colleagues of having to rely on 'some form of Gestapo' to keep control over the people. He was forced to do so, as he had no effective counter-proposals to offer in place of Labour's manifesto. As he put it, 'I have no message for them now'. With Beveridge making a clear political point in source B when he said that 'abolition of want just before this war was easily within the economic resources of the community'. To an electorate who had memories of the deprivation of long-term unemployment and the hated Means Test, Beveridge was condemning the Conservative dominated National Government of the 1930s when he wrote that 'want was a needless scandal due to not taking the trouble to prevent it'.

3. The war economy (EDEXCEL)

Study Source 1 and then answer questions a) to c) which follow.

Source 1. From *A survey of British economic performance in the war*

From September 1939 to the end of 1945 the annual deficit averaged about £700 million, and but for lend-lease would have been much more. This wartime deficit resulted from a deliberate policy of cutting exports to a minimum and concentrating our maximum productive effort on war requirements. In the words of Lord Keynes 'we fought this war on the principle of unlimited liability and with more reckless disregard of economic consequences than other more fortunately placed'.

By 1943, our commercial exports had fallen to 29 per cent of their 1938 volume, while by 1945 they had only recovered to 45 per cent. At the same time there was a considerably less drastic reduction in the volume of imports (excluding munitions) which fell in 1942 to 70 per cent of the 1938 level, rose to 80 per cent in 1944, and dropped again to 63 per cent in 1945.

> QUESTIONS WITHOUT WORKED ANSWERS
>
> **Source 1.**
> a) **What does this source suggest were the consequences of the war for Britain's economy?** (10 marks)
> b) **How did 'lend-lease' help Britain's wartime economy?** (14 marks)
> c) **Did the war cause long-term damage to Britain's economy?** (36 marks)
>
> (Total: 60 marks)

4. The fall of Neville Chamberlain (OCR)

Read the sources below and then answer the questions which follow.

Source A: From the *Manchester Guardian*, 4 May 1940

If we look back over these eight months, with problem after problem mismanaged or neglected, with speech after speech revealing the same lack of grasp and imagination, we are driven to the conclusion that we are facing the greatest crisis in our history with a government weaker than any government that has made war since Addington faced Napoleon. A comparison of the Government's trivial handling of such questions as munitions, unemployment, taxation, nutrition, agriculture and evacuation with the scale of the tremendous task on our hands is enough to show that there is something fundamentally wrong with the Government's view of its duty.

Source B: From Leopold Amery's speech to Parliament during the Norway debate, 7 May 1940

This is what Cromwell said to the long Parliament when he thought it was no longer fit to conduct the affairs of the nation: 'You have sat too long here for any good you have been doing. Depart, I say, and let us have done with you. In the name of God, go!'

Source C: From Neville Chamberlain's speech to Parliament, 8 May 1940

I do not seek to evade criticism, but I say this to my friends in the House – and I do have friends in the House ... At least we shall see who is with us and who is against us, and I call on my friends to support us in the lobby tonight.

Source D: From David Lloyd George's speech to Parliament, in reply to Chamberlain, 8 May 1940

It is not a question of who are the Prime Minister's friends. It is a far bigger issue ... He has appealed for sacrifice ... I say solemnly that the Prime Minister should give an example of sacrifice, because there is nothing which can constitute more to victory in this war, than that he should sacrifice the seals of office.

QUESTIONS WITHOUT WORKED ANSWERS

a) **Study source B. From this source and from your own knowledge, explain why a member of his own party exhorted Chamberlain, 'in the name of God, go!' in May 1940.** (10 marks)

b) **Study source A. Assess the value of this source as evidence of the unpopularity of Chamberlain's government by early May 1940.** (25 marks)

c) **Study sources C and D. Compare the attitudes of sources C and D towards Chamberlain's government as shown in these sources and explain the differences.** (25 marks)

d) **Study all the sources. Use the sources and your own knowledge to explain why Chamberlain was forced to resign as Prime Minister on 10 May 1940.** (60 marks)

(Total: 120 marks)

Part 4: Historical skills

Research methods and approaches

The impact of the Second World War

For this exercise, a number of research issues are suggested, and the means of investigating these for yourself outlined. These could be used to devise a personal study of your own, or simply as an example of the correct way in which to begin any research project of depth. As some exam boards use a marking criterion which measures the independence of your approach, it is, therefore, important that this section does not give too much detail, so that you can carry out the exercise to develop your own independent learning skills.

STEP 1: IDENTIFY THE ISSUE

Writing a study on 'The impact of the Second World War' is inadvisable on two counts: First, it is far too broad to be manageable – Angus Calder's ground breaking study, *The People's War*

(Pimlico, 1969) is 656 pages long, and even that doesn't deal with everything! Therefore, you must decide what aspect of the war's impact you would like to investigate. Here are some suggestions:

a) The impact of the war on the British economy.
b) The impact of the war on the British Empire.
   (remember the size of the Empire though – it might be better to consider the impact of the war on Britain's Far Eastern Empire).
c) The impact of the war on British social attitudes.
d) The impact of the war on the powers of the state.
e) The impact of the war on Britain as a world power.
f) The impact of the war on British political groups (plenty of scope here for looking at any of the political parties, including the Scottish and Welsh Nationalists, N. Irish Unionists, and even fringe groups such as League of Nations Union and the Imperial League).
g) The impact of the war on British relations with the USA/USSR/Dominions/Ireland.
h) The impact of the war on the civilian population.

You could even look at the impact of *one* crucial aspect of (h) above:

i) The impact of evacuation.
j) The impact of bombing on Britain.
k) The impact of the **Beveridge Report** of 1942.

You could look at the impact of the war in your local area (and *every* local area has produced at least one book on its role in the war).

Second, you need to write the issue as a question, so that you can clearly show the examiner that you haven't just found out a lot of interesting but fairly random facts, but that you can structure, sustain and justify a sophisticated argument. So the issue might now read: *How important was the impact of the Second World War in extending the powers of the state?*

If you're not sure of how to phrase a suitable question, just ask your teacher or look at some of the more challenging past A-level questions. You'll discover that 'describe . . .', 'explain . . .' and 'what . . .' questions, although popular with some exam boards, won't let you demonstrate your analytical powers much, so ought to be avoided. Try to think of a 'how significant/important . . .', 'why . . .', 'to what extent . . .' question instead. Of course, it's even better if you can find a question that historians have been arguing about for years.

STEP 2: IDENTIFY THE DEBATE

Before going any further, it is most important that you try to find out what various possible arguments and counter arguments might exist to answer your question. Whilst not doubting your ability to think up some for yourself, it is often best, and certainly quickest, to discover what previous historians have written.

You will discover pretty quickly that no two historians ever agree completely on any issue (if they do agree, they tend to keep very quiet about it). You will therefore find that in any study of the impact of the Second World War much time is spent attacking and attempting to disprove the ideas of those who have written on the topic before. This is very useful, as this will help you to identify two rival points of view which you can use to structure your argument into a for and against fashion. Do take care though. Historians tend to argue endlessly over minute details, such as the precise meaning of one document (such as Churchill's 'naughty' percentages agreement with Stalin, signed in Moscow in 1944), so try to keep looking for historians arguing about the bigger issues. A very good example of this is in *'England Arise': the Labour Party and Popular Politics in 1940s Britain* (Manchester University Press, 1995) by Steven Fielding, Peter Thompson and Nick Tiratsoo, which has a chapter on 'Popular attitudes in wartime' which seeks to question the perception of a radical wartime shift in attitude, found in books like Paul Addison's *The Road to 1945* (Pimlico, 1975), and Peter Hennessy's *Never Again, Britain 1945–1951* (Vintage, 1993).

You might even come across a historian who seems to have changed his mind over time. Angus Calder's book, mentioned earlier in this section, suggests a genuine change in opinion caused by the bombing of British cities in 1940, but in his later book, *The Myth of the Blitz* (Pimlico, 1991), seems to suggest that effective propaganda has caused all involved to subsequently exaggerate its significance, to the extent of even distorting their own memories.

It is also vital therefore, that you find as many up-to-date arguments as you can, because while those written long ago (in the study of history that actually means more than 20 years ago) won't mention the latest research, those written recently undoubtedly will, and may well fill you in on the debate in the past as well (as historians love to prove how well informed they are). So you must now try to find these.

STEP 3: FIND THE SOURCES

Most important of all – despite the attraction of running straight to the primary sources, don't! Primary sources in their raw form are often contradictory, hard to put into context, fragmentary, frequently distorted (usually by the author's sense of self-importance) and sometimes just plain wrong (bear in mind the need for confidentiality and propaganda in the Second World War). For most of your study, you need to look at secondary sources – that is the writings of historians. After all, they have done all the searching through archives for you, so why re-invent the wheel? And if there are any really useful primary sources, they'll flag this up by referring to them and usually quoting from the really important ones. As an exercise on Britain in the Second World War – pick up any book on the topic and count the number of references to the **Beveridge Report** in the index.

Or, ask your teacher or pick up the course textbook. They will guide you to some good general reading, preferably written in the last ten years. Once you've got this, use the referencing systems to find more specialist books on your topic – look in the footnotes and in the bibliography. Don't be put off if these books refer to articles in difficult or off-putting journals like *Twentieth Century British History* or *Contemporary Review*. Ask your librarian where you can find a copy of these, they might even be able to get you a copy on inter-library loan. Once you've got five or six books and articles, you've got enough to get started.

Perhaps, most importantly these days, don't just try typing words into an internet search engine. The internet can be useful, mostly for finding transcripts of primary sources, but it will not give you the high quality historical research at the level that you need. It will either be far too simplistic for an A level research piece, or far too advanced and complicated. Bear in mind the two types of historians who tend to use the net – university teachers and school children. As someone who has marked many research pieces, I can guarantee that reliance on the internet for research in history tends to result in very poor studies. I'm afraid books and printed journals are where you will find the information you need.

STEP 4: PUT THE STUDY IN CONTEXT

At this stage it is very tempting, especially if you've already studied the topic, to leap straight into reading the material you've found. Before you do so, it is absolutely crucial to step back and to try to remember the bigger picture and where your study fits in. My advice would be not to try to read the specialist articles and books on our specific topic first, but to read the textbook again or read your lesson notes (or ask for some if you've not covered the topic yet!). If you're writing on Britain's great power status, and you've no idea what the Government of India Act was, you're going to struggle to understand the impact of the war on Britain's Empire. For this topic, I'd suggest reading chapters on the First World War and the inter-war years, so at least 20 years before the events you are looking at. I'd also have a quick glance at the chapters on the years following your topic, after all, you don't want to end up claiming that the war saved the British Empire, only to find out later that most of it had been abandoned by 1965.

STEP 5: RESEARCHING YOUR TOPIC

It is best, of course if you use a word processor when you are researching. That way, you can note down anything you feel is useful and then move the text around and structure your work. If you can start organising your research into chapters, this will speed the process of writing. Do make sure you keep the notes in your own words – copying out a historian's work is very dangerous as you might convince yourself later that you wrote the passage in question yourself. If you put the work of any other writer in any study intended for scrutiny by an examiner, you run the risk of having the whole piece disqualified and all your other A-level work called into question. It is far too dangerous a risk to run, and is another good reason not to use the internet, where the temptation to steal can be even greater.

Do not feel obliged to read a book from cover to cover – you will rarely have the time to do this. Look at the contents page of the book, glance through the introduction and concluding chapter. These will summarise the main points of the book and you can then decide if it will suit your purpose. If the book is relevant to your assignment, select (normally by chapter headings or by using the index) those parts which will help you answer the questions in which you are interested.

When taking notes from books and articles, remember:

- *always* note the precise details of your source material.
- *never* copy another author's material word for word without using quotation marks. This is the single most common way to fall into the practice of plagiarism.
- *do not* hold a pen in your hand while reading. Read a few pages, turn away from the book and then write down *your thoughts*. You can check details afterwards.
- Your notes should reflect *your opinion* on what an author has written. They should not be a copied or a paraphrased version of someone else's thesis.

STEP 6: WRITING YOUR RESEARCH PROJECT

Once you've done the research, how you write the study is really determined by the criteria laid down by the exam board. So, I'm afraid, at this point, it's up to you to find this out. A few words of advice, though:

- Write your argument in a brief form.
- Make a plan based on this.

- Put down both sides of any argument (even if you don't agree with one).
- A clear-cut answer is not necessary.
- Make sure you have always included the evidence to back up what you say (this is where you need those primary sources).
- Leave the introduction and conclusion till the end. The introduction should set out what you will do. The conclusion should summarise and link back to the introduction.
- Draft and redraft at least once (on a word-processor).
- Get someone else (teacher or parent) to read the project to check that it hangs together as an argument and is written in good English (grammar/spelling).

Chapter 7

The Age of Consensus: Domestic Affairs, 1945–1979

This chapter covers the political events within Britain in the 34 years following the end of the Second World War. It is a period that has become known as 'the Age of Consensus', as a result of the reforms carried out by the Labour government that won the election in 1945. These welfare, economic and political reforms were not significantly reversed by the 11 years of Conservative government which followed Labour's defeat in the 1951 election. It is therefore largely agreed that there was a general agreement among the political parties as to what should be the principles of governing Britain, although there were bitter disputes between and within the parties on how best to achieve this. By the mid 1970s however, Britain appeared to be facing a political crisis caused by the economic weaknesses of the country. This led to the emergence of the first party leader to radically challenge the consensus – Margaret Thatcher. Her victory in the 1979 election in many ways marked the end of post-war British history.

Historical background

The Attlee governments 1945–51

a) Introduction
b) 'Slaying the giants' – the welfare reforms
c) The economy
d) Decline and fall – the 1950 and 1951 elections

The Conservatives in power 1951–64
Labour under Wilson 1964–70
Heath's government 1970–74
Wilson and Callaghan 1974–79

Essays

1. Attlee's government 1945–51
2. The dominance of the Conservatives 1951–64

3. Labour in power, 1964–70
4. Britain in the 1970s
5. Northern Ireland 1969–79
6. The rise of Margaret Thatcher

Sources

1. The formation of the National Health Service
2. The IMF loan, 1976
3. The Labour government, 1964–70
4. The winter of discontent, 1979

Historical skills

1. Comparing historical interpretations

Chronology

1945	Labour wins general election – Attlee becomes Prime Minister
	America halts lend-lease deliveries
	Keynes negotiates loan agreement
1947	Nationalisation of coal and cable and wireless
	Sterling made convertible with the dollar
	Nationalisation of railways, electricity, gas and road haulage
	Creation of National Health Service
1949	Devaluation of pound
1950	Labour's majority reduced in general election
1951	Nationalisation of iron and steel
	Resignation of Bevan and Wilson
	Conservatives win general election – Churchill becomes Prime Minister
1952	Death of George VI, accession of Elizabeth II
1953	Re-privatisation of iron and steel and road haulage
1955	Churchill retires, Eden becomes Prime Minister
	Conservatives win general election
	Attlee retires as Labour leader, succeeded by Gaitskell
1956	Suez Crisis
1957	Eden resigns, Macmillan becomes Prime Minister
1959	Conservatives win general election
1962	'Night of the Long Knives' – Macmillan sacks one third of his cabinet
1963	Gaitskell dies, Wilson becomes Labour leader
	Profumo scandal
	Macmillan resigns, succeeded by Douglas-Home
1964	Labour wins general election with tiny majority – Wilson becomes Prime Minister
1965	Douglas-Home resigns as Conservative leader, replaced by Heath
1966	Labour wins general election
	Financial emergency – Labour 'blown off course'
1967	Devaluation of pound
1968	Civil Rights demonstrations in Northern Ireland
1969	British troops sent to quell unrest in Northern Ireland
	Formation of Provisional IRA
	'In Place of Strife' attempts to reform industrial relations
1970	Conservatives win general election – Heath becomes Prime Minister
1972	'Bloody Sunday' in Derry
	Suspension of Northern Irish government – replaced by direct rule from Westminster
1973	Sunningdale Agreement
	Fuel crisis, three-day week
1974	Miners' strike

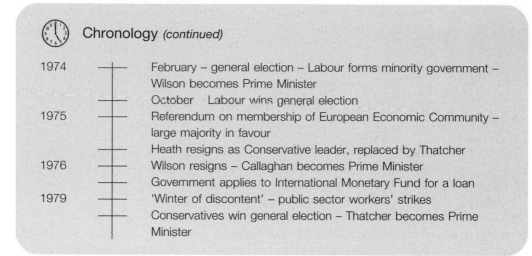

Chronology *(continued)*

1974		February – general election – Labour forms minority government – Wilson becomes Prime Minister
		October Labour wins general election
1975		Referendum on membership of European Economic Community – large majority in favour
		Heath resigns as Conservative leader, replaced by Thatcher
1976		Wilson resigns – Callaghan becomes Prime Minister
		Government applies to International Monetary Fund for a loan
1979		'Winter of discontent' – public sector workers' strikes
		Conservatives win general election – Thatcher becomes Prime Minister

Part 1: Historical background

Table 7.1 **General election results, 1950–79**

	Conservative		Liberal		Labour	
	% vote	No. of seats	% vote	No. of seats	% vote	No. of seats
1950	43.5	298	9.1	9	46.1	315
1951	48.0	321	2.5	6	48.8	295
1955	49.7	344	2.7	6	46.4	277
1959	49.4	365	5.9	6	43.8	258
1964	43.4	304	11.2	9	44.1	317
1966	41.9	253	8.5	12	47.9	363
1970	46.4	330	7.5	6	43.0	287
1974 (Feb)	37.9	297	19.3	14	37.1	301
1974 (Oct)	35.8	277	18.3	13	39.2	319
1979	43.9	339	13.8	11	36.9	269

The Attlee governments 1945–51

a) INTRODUCTION

The 1945–50 Labour government was the first Labour government to enjoy an overall majority, and it would now be able to achieve its most cherished objectives: a **welfare state; nationalisation;** work for everyone; an open foreign policy based on genuine co-operation.

The process of reform has been described as a 'peaceful revolution', but some believe it was more 'evolutionary' as the changes were built on previous welfare achievements.

First of all, however, a new Trades Disputes Act (1946) was passed, which repealed Baldwin's 1927 act. The political levy was now legal again and it was up to individuals to 'contract out' if they did not wish to make a financial contribution to the Labour Party.

Unfortunately the government was hampered by the most appalling economic problems. In the aftermath of the war, the USA had immediately stopped lend-lease, two-thirds of Britain's export trade had been lost, much of her merchant fleet had been lost in the war, and without American aid she lacked the capital to bring the economy back to normal peacetime production, so that she could begin to recover overseas markets.

There were problems in international relations with the start of the **Cold War** and the dilemma of what to do about both the Palestine Mandate and India.

The new Prime Minister, Clement Attlee, came from a privileged middle-class background; educated at public school and Oxford, he had intended to become a barrister, but became interested in social work in the East End of London, following his experiences as a captain during the First World War. He became an MP in 1922 and leader of the Labour Party in 1935. In appearance he was mild and inoffensive, leading Churchill to describe him as 'a sheep in sheep's clothing' and 'a modest little man with plenty to be modest about'. But Churchill was wrong. Attlee was shrewd and determined and an excellent manager of people in the Cabinet.

b) 'SLAYING THE GIANTS' – THE WELFARE REFORMS

The National Health Service, launched on 5 July 1948, entitled everybody, free of charge, to medical care from general practitioners, specialists and dentists, to hospital and ophthalmic treatment, spectacles and false teeth, medicines and drugs, and midwifery, maternity and child welfare services. The scheme was financed mainly from taxation, but some of the revenue came from National Insurance contributions. To make sure that the same standard of health care was provided in all parts of the country, the Health Minister, Aneurin Bevan decided that the hospitals should be nationalised. For health purposes, England and Wales were divided into 14 areas, each under a regional hospital board; Scotland had five. These controlled general policy, while the day-to-day running of the hospitals was looked after by local management committees.

The National Insurance Act extended the original 1911 National Insurance Act to cover all adults. The scheme was compulsory; in return for a weekly contribution from worker, employer and state, the individual was entitled to sickness and unemployment benefit, old age pensions for women at 60, men at 65 (26s per week, 42s for married couples), widows' and orphans' pensions and maternity and death grants.

The National Assistance Act filled in any loopholes not covered by the National Insurance Act, which was supposed to apply to the entire population. However, people joining the insurance scheme were not entitled to full pension rights for ten years, and there were tens of thousands of old people whose only income was the inadequate 10s non-contributory pension of 1908. The Act set up National Assistance Boards where such people could apply for further assistance. This was an innovation, a decisive break with the past, although applicants still had to undergo a Means Test, the money was provided by the government from taxation, and thus it was a move away from the idea that poverty was a matter for local administration. As well as cash benefits the Act also provided personal services, and here the government did make use of local authorities, placing on them the duty to provide homes and other welfare services for the elderly and handicapped.

The government concentrated on carrying out the Butler Education Act of 1944 which had made secondary education until 15 free, and provided meals, milk and medical services at schools. An examination was introduced to select which children were thought to be suitable for a grammar school education (or a secondary technical school in the few areas that one existed) and which would go to secondary modern schools.

Apart from the housing shortage already existing in 1939, a further 700,000 houses had been destroyed in the war. In March 1945 Churchill's government announced that 750,000 new houses would be needed as soon as the war was over. Labour set themselves a target of 200,000 homes a year, but it quickly became apparent that, with labour and building materials in short supply, and the government preoccupied with the foundation of the NHS and **nationalisation**, that it would be years before that level of building would be achieved. In fact, it was only with the creation of entire 'New Towns' such as Basildon and Stevenage that 230,000 houses were built in 1948. During the entire Labour period in office, over a million new homes were built, mainly for rent, a relatively impressive figure, but one which did not end Britain's post-war housing shortage.

c) THE ECONOMY

The idea behind **nationalisation** was that it would give the government control of the country's most important industries. This would permit more efficient planning and co-operation between industries and would ensure fair treatment and better conditions for workers. In particular, greater government control would allow better planning for the allocation of resources, especially manpower, and thus lead to a permanently low level of unemployment, in contrast to the experience of the 1920s and 1930s. The coal-mining industry was a prime example of inefficiency and bad labour relations which could only be improved by government control. Under the general direction of Morrison, the programme of **nationalisation** was carried through:

1946	The Bank of England and civil aviation were nationalised
1947	Coal and telecommunications
1948	Railways, canals, bus companies, electricity and gas
1951	Iron and steel.

Nationalisation aroused considerable opposition from the Conservatives who disapproved of state interference in private industry during peacetime, but also from socialists who disliked the programme because:

- The newly nationalised industries were public.
- Workers had no control of policy and no share in profit-making.
- It was felt that previous owners had been excessively compensated.

The mine-owners received £164 million, and it seemed to the miners that many years' profits would be needed to pay off such a sum. What the government had actually done was to buy out the former owners while keeping the same management.

It is also arguable that Labour missed its chance to implement much greater schemes of industrial democracy in its **nationalisation** programme. The workforce gained no more say in organising British industry than they had before.

d) DECLINE AND FALL – THE 1950 AND 1951 ELECTIONS

Despite the great achievements of the Labour government under Attlee, the country was very frustrated by the continuing rationing and shortages as the economy concentrated on exporting and government expenditure was concentrated on the health system and welfare, while school- and house-building fell behind government targets. The resentment towards the interference of the state was best expressed in the Ealing comedy of 1947, *Passport to Pimlico* in which a London suburb manages to evade government restrictions and becomes a ration-free zone. The feeling was mostly felt by the middle-class who experienced, for them, unprecedented '**austerity**' at the same time as taxes continued to rise. Middle-class pressure groups, most notably, the British Housewives' League demanded an end to restrictions by holding marches and rallies. Labour was forced to back down in 1948, when the President of the Board of Trade, Harold Wilson, announced a 'bonfire of controls', which garnered good publicity, but which ultimately only helped the Conservatives as they promised to 'set the people free' completely.

The government's precarious financial position had led to a severe **balance of payments** crisis in 1949 in which the pound had been devalued after a long period of resistance. This had led to further government spending cuts, and accusations of incompetence in managing the economy. In the general election called in 1950, Labour suffered the loss of 20 seats in the South East as disgruntled middle-class voters reduced Attlee's majority to 5. The **devaluation** did actually improve Britain's export position in North America, but the sudden increase in armaments spending in 1950, caused by the outbreak of the Korean War, led to another crisis, in which Bevan and Wilson resigned when charges were introduced for NHS prescriptions.

The Conservatives took some time to recover from their electoral disaster in 1945, and Churchill did not help by choosing to distance himself from most party political issues, preferring to intervene in matters of international concern. Eventually, a group of Tory reformers, led by R.A. Butler, produced the *Industrial Charter* of 1947, in which they committed the party to acceptance of the new political dogmas of Keynesian economics (including national control of utilities), full employment and the **Welfare State**, which Attlee's government had established. After a recruitment drive and a reorganisation of party structure carried under the new Party Chairman, Lord Woolton, the Conservatives were able to present a fresh face to the voters in the elections of 1950 and 1951. The popular aspects of Labour's reforms were accepted, but promises of a swift end to rationing, increased house-building and more freedom for businesses did just enough to win the Conservatives a small majority of 16 in 1951, despite actually winning fewer votes than Labour.

 ## Conservatives in power 1951–64

Churchill's second period in office was a marked contrast to his wartime administration, being far less dynamic, partly due to his advanced age (he was 77 in 1951) and partly due to his hopes for a period of 'healing and revival' after the burdens of war and reconstruction. His chancellor, Butler, took the opportunity, after an initial period of retrenchment to pay for the Korean War, to end almost all wartime controls, including rationing in 1954. The boom in the economy, which this helped to stimulate was not long-lived however, as Butler was forced to put up interest rates to control inflation as imports flooded into the country to satisfy consumer demand that British manufacturers could not. By contrast, Harold Macmillan, another reformer, continued, and improved on Labour's house-building programme, managing to out-strip his own target of 300,000 new homes every year. Unlike Bevan, though, a substantial number of Macmillan's houses were for private sale, and it was largely the richer workers and the middle classes who benefited from this. As a whole, Churchill's administration demonstrated its commitment to the **Welfare State**, by increasing spending on social services from 39 per cent of total government expenditure in 1951 to 43 per cent by 1955. It was clear that a new social and economic consensus had genuinely developed in British politics.

When Churchill finally, and reluctantly, retired at 80 in April 1955, his successor was not unexpected – Anthony Eden, who had been groomed by Churchill as heir apparent for years. Eden immediately chose to call an election. Despite inflation, personal wealth was clearly increasing and the welfare record of the government was impressive. Perhaps even more importantly, Labour, still led by Attlee, was openly divided between the moderates and the more radical left-wingers led by Bevan. In these circumstances and with his personal charm and 'film-star good looks', Eden increased the Conservative majority to 58 seats and looked comfortably set for at least a full term as Prime Minister. Unfortunately, his handling of foreign affairs proved to be disastrously ill-judged and after the fiasco of the Suez Crisis, he was forced to resign in 1957.

His successor, Harold Macmillan, wisely chose to focus on domestic issues, overseeing a period of sustained improvements in living standards and a substantial consumer boom. In 1957 he famously remarked that 'most of our people have never had it so good' and was depicted by political cartoonists as 'Supermac'. But the consumer boom was mainly generated by cheap imports and he soon found himself facing another serious **balance of payments** crisis. After a series of poor by-election results in 1962, he sacked a third of his cabinet in the so-called 'Night of the Long Knives', but only created an impression of panic. By 1963 the stress of the job and especially the scandal of the **Profumo Affair** drove him to retire due to ill-health. Faced with a choice between R.A. Butler and Quentin Hogg, the Conservatives opted for a compromise candidate and, very unexpectedly, the Foreign Secretary, Alec Douglas-Home, a member of the House of Lords, was appointed Prime Minister after renouncing his peerage and entering the Commons via a by-election. His main energies were devoted to reviving the Conservative Party in time for the forthcoming general election. Considering the deep cynicism that the government provoked after a series of scandals and the opposition of the dynamic new Labour leader, Harold Wilson, Douglas-Home did very well to lose the 1964 election by only four seats.

 ## Labour under Wilson 1964–70

Wilson had become Labour's leader unexpectedly after the untimely death of Hugh Gaitskell, who had skilfully managed to mend the divisions between the **Bevanites** and the party's right wing. Wilson had been seen as sympathetic towards Bevan's ideas, but he attempted to prove himself a unifying figure and threw himself into the job of Prime Minister. Although his government was continually dogged by serious financial problems, caused by Britain's ongoing **balance of payments** difficulties and poor labour relations, it did mange an impressive programme of reform, especially after its election victory in 1966.

The death penalty was finally abolished, male homosexuality was de-criminalised, access to abortion and divorce was made easier and race relations legislation was passed to criminalise racist behaviour. In particular, Wilson's government reformed the education system, abolishing the distinctions between secondary schools and creating 'comprehensive schools', and dramatically expanding the number of higher education institutions, even setting up an 'Open University' which broadcast its lectures via television and radio. Wilson's greatest failure was his inability to reduce the powers of trade unions to call strikes when the TUC forced him to drop 'In Place of Strife', the proposed bill, in 1969. This impression of a weakened government, together with rising unemployment and an unplanned **devaluation** of the pound in 1967, helped to cause Labour to lose the election in 1970.

 ## Heath's government 1970–74

After the election defeat in 1964, Heath had been the first Conservative leader to be chosen by a ballot of MPs and the first Conservative leader not to have attended public school. Although he lost the 1966 election, he had held onto the leadership, despite the scandal surrounding Enoch Powell's 'Rivers of Blood' speech in 1968 and undergone a major policy review, typified by the famous Cabinet meeting at Selsdon Park Hotel, when the party's agenda for government was agreed. He came to office in 1970, promising a limitation of union powers and economic revival, but was almost immediately hit by the death of Iain MacLeod, his Chancellor, who proved difficult to replace. Heath's approach to industrial relations only provoked unrest, most notably in two serious miners' strikes in 1971 and 1972. By 1973, with the miners' enforcing an over-time ban and oil prices rocketing after the Arab-Israeli war, Heath took the drastic step of enforcing a 'three-day week', which limited working hours, as well as limiting speed limits, street lighting and the broadcast of television programmes. This provoked an all-out miners' strike in 1974, so Heath called an election in February on the issue 'who governs Britain – Parliament or unions?'. Although he won more votes than Labour, he lost his majority and was forced to resign. Heath's greatest achievement during his premiership was undoubtedly finally managing to get Britain's application for membership of the European Economic Community accepted and signing up to the Treaty of Rome in 1973. His party clearly regarded his period in office as a failure however, and when Margaret Thatcher, who had become famous as Heath's education minister, challenged him for the leadership in 1975, he actually polled less of the Conservative MPs votes than she did and so immediately resigned as party leader.

 ## Wilson and Callaghan 1974–79

Wilson's government went on to win a narrow victory in a second election in 1974, but the state of the economy showed no signs of improving. Wilson managed to form a 'social contract' with the TUC to limit pay demands, but inflation was at an all-time high and unemployment continued to increase. The Chancellor, Denis Healey, increased income tax to 35 per cent and put up VAT to 25 per cent on luxury items. In these circumstances, some have argued, Wilson should have stayed on, but he chose to resign as Prime Minister in 1976 and left his successor, James Callaghan to face the problems of rising inflation, continuing industrial unrest and a weak **balance of payments**. The situation was so bad that Denis Healey, was forced to apply to the **International Monetary Fund** (IMF) for a loan of $3.9 billion. Callaghan informed the party that 'you can't spend your way out depression' and implemented public spending cuts to comply with the demands of the IMF. By this stage, by-election results meant that Labour had lost its majority and was forced to seek the support of the Liberals in the **'Lib–Lab' pact**, as well as promising the Scottish Nationalist Party and the Welsh nationalists, Plaid Cymru, that Labour would organise referendums on **devolution** for Scotland and Wales. Callaghan also managed to maintain the 'social contract' with the trade unions by getting the TUC to agree to a limit of 5 per cent on pay demands.

By 1979 however, Callaghan's position was crumbling. The Liberal leader, David Steel, ended the 'Lib–Lab' pact in 1978, large numbers of public sector workers defied the 'social contract' and organised crippling strikes, and finally the referendum vote in favour of **devolution** failed to reach the required threshold of 40 per cent of the electorate in both Wales and Scotland, causing the nationalists to desert Labour. Mrs Thatcher forced Callaghan to hold a no-confidence vote in March 1979, which the government lost by one vote.

Callaghan was thus deprived of the usual prime ministerial freedom of calling the election at a time of his own choosing. Some have argued that, had he called the election prior to the **'winter of discontent'** of 1978–79, he would have won, as the economy was improving and there was no enthusiasm for Mrs Thatcher. As it was, in the election on 3 May 1979, the Conservatives gained a 43-seat majority. They had won with only 43.9 per cent of the vote, however, the lowest proportion in modern times for a party winning a clear overall majority.

Part 2: Essays

1. Attlee's government 1945–51 (OCR)

What degree of success did the Labour governments of 1945 to 1951 have in establishing a Welfare State?

(Total: 90 marks)

The **Beveridge Report** had stimulated a debate on what a **Welfare State** should aim to achieve, and Labour had committed itself to a series of wide-ranging reforms at the 1942 Party Conference. In spite of the country's economic difficulties, and despite the opposition of a chorus of vested interests, a mass of legislation reached the statute book.

There was considerable opposition to Bevan's National Health Service scheme from family doctors who disliked the proposal that they should be paid a salary by the government. This, they argued, would reduce them to the status of civil servants, which, they claimed, was beneath their dignity. It would also, in some mysterious way, affect the doctor–patient relationship. In February 1948, 90 per cent of the members of the British Medical Association threatened to boycott the whole scheme. Bevan finally overcame their hostility with a clever device; instead of being paid a salary, doctors received fees based on the number of patients they had on their lists. 'Stuffing the doctors' mouths with gold' made all the difference, and when the scheme was introduced on 5 July, 90 per cent of GPs took part.

The service was expensive, costing more than £400 million in its first year. This led the new Chancellor in 1951, Hugh Gaitskell, to begin charging adults half the cost of false teeth and spectacles. Bevan resigned from the government, furious that his principle of a completely free health service had been violated. It was a sad end, but he will be remembered as the man who brought a striking improvement to the health of the working class, and reduced deaths from diphtheria, TB and pneumonia. The new health service constituted an almost revolutionary social innovation, since it improved the quality of life of most of the British people.

Together with the National Insurance Act, and the increase in pensions, National Assistance Boards provided a whole new social security structure. It was generally welcomed, and the Conservatives did not vote against either bill. The National Insurance Injuries Act was a vast improvement on the old Workmen's Compensation Acts, under which it had been difficult and expensive for a worker to prove that an injury had been caused by his job and even more difficult to win adequate compensation. The new Act made it compulsory for both workers and employers to join the state in making weekly contributions to a fund which would provide compensation to injured workers and pensions for those who were disabled.

Although it did little more than put Butler's 1944 Education Act into operation, in one sense the new system was an outstanding success: it allowed a whole generation of able working-class children to move up the educational ladder, many of them as far as university, this would have been unthinkable before the war. A successful Youth Employment Service was set up and the government embarked on an expansion of university and technical education. However, the education service varied in type and quality from area to area. Some counties, which could afford to provide technical schools as well as grammar schools, could boast that up to 40 per cent of their secondary places were in grammar and technical schools; but in some counties the figure was as low as 15 per cent. The 11-plus exam therefore did not indicate which children were suitable for which type of school; it simply selected the required number of children to fill the places available. In some areas children who were suitable for a grammar school education, had to go to secondary modern schools, because there were insufficient grammar school places.

In addition, the system was divisive; the view rapidly developed that the secondary modern schools were second-class institutions to which the 11-plus failures went; a new type of class distinction was therefore created. If primary education worked successfully without different types of school, then it ought to be possible, critics argued, for secondary education to be conducted in 'comprehensive' schools to which all children went at the age of 11, without selection. It was felt that Labour had missed a wonderful opportunity to introduce a comprehensive system free from class distinction, before the Butler system became established.

Housing came under the control of Bevan's ministry, and although he was preoccupied with the Health Service, he still found time and energy to launch a housing drive. Economic conditions were not helpful: raw materials were in short supply and expensive; nevertheless, Bevan had considerable success. Only 55,400 new houses were completed in 1946, but this rose to 139,690 in 1947 and 284,230 (including pre-fabs) in 1948. There was a slight decline after that, but in 1949–51 Labour still averaged well over 200,000 houses a year (most were council houses) and Bevan had exceeded Churchill's promise. But, because of the 'baby boom' after the war, there was still a serious housing shortage when Labour left office in 1951.

The New Towns Act gave the government the power to decide where new towns should be built and to set up development corporations to carry out the projects. The aim was to create towns which were healthy and pleasant to live in as well as being geared to the needs of the townspeople, unlike the ugly monstrosities which had grown up without any planning during the nineteenth century. The first to be completed was Stevenage, followed by Crawley, Hemel Hempstead and Harlow. Altogether 14 new towns were operational before the end of the Labour government, and these were not just in the south, successful examples elsewhere were East Kilbride, Peterlee and Glenrothes.

The Town and Country Planning Act was another Bevan measure designed to improve the environment. It gave the job of planning to the county authorities, who were all required to produce land development plans for the next 20 years. The planning authorities were given much wider powers of compulsory purchase and the right to control advertisements and to preserve historic buildings. Government grants were available whenever necessary. If there was any increase in land values as a result of profitable development, the government had the power to levy a development charge on the increase.

Labour had managed to construct a universal **Welfare State** system within which citizens were cared for from the 'womb to the tomb'. This in itself was a major achievement, but to build such a system in a time of financial difficulty makes it even more awe-inspiring. Historians argue, however, as to how well the **Welfare State** was put together. Kenneth Morgan sees the construction of the Social Services in terms of a 'mosaic', whereas Arthur Marwick feels that it was more akin to 'crazy-paving'. His opinion is probably the most accurate. The welfare services were not integrated. On the other hand it is difficult to argue with Peter Hennessy who ably summarises that '1951 Britain, certainly compared to the UK of 1931 or any previous decade, was a kinder, gentler and a far, far better place in which to be born, to grow up, to live, love, work and even to die'.

How effectively did Labour tackle Britain's economic problems between 1945 and 1951?

(Total: 90 marks)

The immediate need was to revive the main industries so that Britain could once again begin to export at something like her pre-war level. Only then could the enormous **balance of payments** deficit be removed. With her huge debts and the stoppage of American aid and lend-lease in August 1945, insufficient funds were available; desperate measures were needed.

J.M. Keynes, the famous economist, was sent to Washington to negotiate an interest-loan of $6,000 million. The Americans were unsympathetic and drove a hard bargain – they would lend only $3,750 million at 2 per cent interest, and repayments were to start in 1951 and in 1947 Britain would be required to make the pound freely convertible for the dollar. Britain was not in a position to argue and the loan was made available in July 1946, but within a year it had almost been used up. Industry was recovering and exports had actually reached 17 per cent above the 1939 level, but this was not enough – the **balance of payments** deficit stood at £438 million. However, help was on the way, the American Secretary of State, George Marshall, worried about the poor prospects for American exports and the possible spread of communism in Europe, launched his European Recovery Programme, offering grants to any country in Europe which cared to accept them. In 1948 Britain gratefully took the lead, accepting what amounted to a gift of £1,263 million (known as Marshall Aid). This enabled the recovery to be completed, and by 1950 British exports stood at 75 per cent above 1938 levels.

The government kept a close control on all aspects of the economy, particularly after Sir Stafford Cripps replaced Dalton as Chancellor of the Exchequer in October 1947. Since there was a world shortage of food, wartime rationing was continued. Bread rationing was in operation from 1946–48 and potato rationing was introduced in December 1947; in almost all cases the allowances were lower than the wartime average. As the situation improved, certain commodities were de-rationed, but even in 1951, meat, bacon, butter, tea and sugar were still rationed. However, the government provided subsidies to keep food prices down and gave help to farmers (price guarantees, subsidies for modernisation). This resulted in a 20 per cent increase in agricultural output between 1947 and 1952 and made British agriculture one of the most efficient in the world.

During the disastrously cold winter of 1946–47, demand for coal and electricity was so enormous that all fuels were severely rationed. For several weeks it was illegal to use electricity between 9 a.m. and midday and 2 p.m. and 4 p.m. Many factories had to close through lack of coal, and in March 1947 two million people were out of work.

Building materials were rationed and licences had to be obtained for all new buildings; this was to make sure that resources went into building factories, schools and council houses instead of into frivolous projects like the dance-halls and cinemas. Rents, profits and interest rates were controlled and a tight rein kept on foreign currency so that holidays abroad were out of the question for most people.

Imports were controlled in the struggle to achieve a favourable **balance of payments**. The government bought supplies of raw materials for industry and allocated them to those industries which could contribute towards the export drive: cars, motorcycles, tractors, ships, engineering products, aircraft and chemicals. Cripps' demand to export at all costs certainly worked, but it left a chronic shortage of consumer goods for the home market. Cripps also persuaded the trade unions to accept a policy of wage restraint between 1948 and 1950; at a time of rising prices this was a considerable achievement.

In August 1949, in response to a recession in the USA and a drain of Britain's gold reserves, Cripps devalued the pound so that it was worth $2.80 instead of $4.03. Many people felt that Cripps had gone too far, but **devaluation** made imports more expensive and British exports cheaper, so exports were boosted.

Only about 20 per cent of the nation's industries had been nationalised and most of those taken over were either unprofitable, or in need of investment for modernisation, or both. Profitable industries remained largely in the hands of private enterprise. Yet the government felt unable to afford sufficient investment and consequently the nationalised industries, particularly coal and transport, continued to provide an inefficient service and ran up large deficits. This convinced the public that **nationalisation** automatically implied inefficiency and waste, and Labour failed to point out that the problems were long-standing and that compensation was accounting for most of the profits.

It may well be that the Labour government missed the opportunity to implement a fully-planned economy. The ineffective nature of Labour's planning was highlighted by the 1947 fuel shortage, a situation that could have been avoided.

Due to Marshall Aid and state control, Britain was well on the way to recovery by 1951. Inflation was under control, there was virtual full employment at over 98 per cent and economic recovery was accelerated by a higher rate of industrial investment. The upward trend in both production and exports was continuous. There was, however, a decline in labour productivity, some unchecked inflation, and in 1951 an economic setback with the advent of the Korean War. The USA rearmed, raw material prices shot up, so the cost of imports increased, leaving Britain with a poor **balance of payments** when she started to rearm which meant even more economy and shortage.

2. The dominance of the Conservatives 1951–64 (EDEXCEL)

a) **Assess the success of the Conservative government from 1951 to 1964 in implementing at least three of their domestic policies** (30 marks)

b) **Examine the economic and political factors which explain why the Conservative Party won the election of 1959, but lost power in 1964.** (30 marks)

(Total: 60 marks)

a) The Conservative governments of 1951 to 1964 were led successively by Winston Churchill, Anthony Eden, Harold Macmillan and Alec Douglas-Home. This essay will exam their record in addressing housing, education and management of the economy.

The first Conservative minister for housing was Harold Macmillan and he was faced with an intense housing shortage, which the Labour government's house-building programme before 1951 had alleviated, but certainly not solved. Macmillan gave priority to the building of private housing and achieved an impressive figure of 300,000 new houses built every year after 1953.

On the other hand, for those people unable to get a mortgage, council housing was a much lower priority throughout the 13 years of Conservative rule. Local authorities were forced to use cheap methods to rehouse those who still lived in cramped and insanitary housing. The result was the development of large, high-rise blocks of flats, which were unpopular for breaking up the community of the street and which often suffered from damp.

In many ways, a similar pattern emerged in education. The Conservative governments, like Labour before them, retained the 1944 Education Act as the basis of their policy. In this, the '11-plus' examination sent the more able minority to grammar schools, with the majority forced to attend the inferior secondary modern schools. Children from wealthier backgrounds were able to escape this system by attending fee-paying 'private' or 'independent' schools. It was very rare for a child from a secondary modern school to achieve a place at university as a result. Those attending fee-paying or grammar schools had increased opportunities as colleges of advanced technology were founded for the practically-inclined and the Robbins report, which recommended a doubling of university places in ten years, was approved by the government in 1963.

Although the economy grew steadily during the 1950s and early 1960s, it did so at a rate much slower than other West European countries. The government was keen to avoid industrial unrest and tended to allow trade union demands for higher wages to be met, thus driving up inflation. As a result, the government failed to achieve significant investment in modernising the economy and the higher wages tended to be spent on imported manufactured goods, rather than domestically produced ones. This, in turn, led to a **balance of payments** crisis, which forced the government to increase taxes and put up interests rates, thus slowing any growth in the economy. When elections loomed, as in 1955 and 1959, taxes were cut and interest rates reduced, which put inflation back up again and encouraged more consumer spending. This 'stop-go' approach did not help the British economy to grow, but did keep unemployment levels below one million throughout the Conservative period. It must also be said, that the only serious attempt to reduce inflation by limiting pay rises, in 1961, failed due to the opposition of trade unions, and also, that Labour after 1964 found the problem equally intractable.

In many ways, then, the Conservatives spent their 13 years in power attempting to satisfy the broad bulk of the population, by promoting consumer affluence and by satisfying demands for more private housing and greater access to higher education. The government may be criticised for failing to address the needs of the poorer classes and neglecting Britain's long-term economic prospects, but in a democratic, party political system, it is almost unavoidable that the government should put the short-term demands from the electorate first, unless the social and economic problems become too pressing to ignore.

b)   After the debacle at Suez in 1956, Anthony Eden's leadership had been fatally weakened and after his physical breakdown, Harold Macmillan became leader of the Conservative Party and thus Prime Minister in January 1957. Attention was now put on stimulating consumer spending and the cost of credit was cut and taxation reduced. In the consequent spending boom, Macmillan caught the mood of the time when he said 'let's be frank about it; most of our people have never had it so good'. In contrast to the relaxed and confident Macmillan, Labour still seemed bitterly divided, with their leader, Hugh Gaitskell trying, and failing, to modernise Labour's image by dropping '**Clause IV**' of the party's constitution, which bound it to large-scale **nationalisation**. As a result, the Conservatives achieved a majority of over a hundred seats in 1959, with nearly 5 per cent more of the vote than Labour.

Within a few years, however, the Conservatives seemed a lot less secure. The economic problems caused by the inflationary budget of 1959 led Macmillan to sack one third of his Cabinet, including the Chancellor, in a desperate attempt to revive his Party's fortunes in 1962. As one satirist commented on Macmillan's motives, 'greater love hath no man, but that he lays down his friends for his life'. Macmillan's attempt to find a new course for the economy was not helped when General de Gaulle of France vetoed Britain's application for membership of the European Economic Community in 1963.

Macmillan himself, such an electoral asset in 1959, now became the subject of criticism, especially when he foolishly believed the denials of the Secretary of State for War, John Profumo, over a sexual scandal. When Profumo was shown to have lied to Parliament, Macmillan was seriously weakened. He then fell quite badly ill which forced him to resign at a time when there was no obvious successor. He ultimately nominated the Foreign Secretary, Lord Home, who hurriedly gave up his peerage and became Prime Minister as Sir Alec Douglas-Home, who was little known by the public and undermined, like many leading Tories, by his 'grouse-moor' image in a democratic age.

By contrast, Gaitskell had managed to reunify his party after seeing off a challenge by supporters of nuclear disarmament. He died suddenly in 1963, provoking much sympathy for the party, and was succeeded by the young, charismatic Harold Wilson, who carefully cultivated a more populist image with his pipe and raincoat, and who seemed far more in touch with the needs of the modern world when he spoke of a new Britain 'forged in the white heat of the technological revolution'. Wilson's undoubted economic brilliance and his advocacy of planning for the economy united the party behind the leader as never before. Despite some effective Conservative propaganda stressing the growth in prosperity over the last 13 years and raising doubts about Labour's commitment to the nuclear deterrent, Labour's share of the vote from 1959 increased, while at least a million Conservative voters shifted to the Liberal party. The result was a four-seat majority for Wilson's Labour party.

3. Labour in power, 1964–70 (AQA)

Read the following extract from *A Short History of the Labour Party* by Henry Pelling and Alastair Reid and then answer the questions which follow:

The general election of 1966 had given the Wilson government a good deal more than the ample parliamentary majority that it required for a normal term of office. It also increased the authority of the prime minister . . . In spite of these advantages, it did not take more than a few months for the prime minister and the government to lose all the favour in public opinion that it had won in the preceding eighteen months – and more. By early 1967 the Conservatives had pulled into the lead in the opinion polls and in 1968 they built up so formidable an advantage that it seemed impossible for Labour to recover at any future general election.

a) **Explain the reference to the 1966 general election.** (3 marks)
b) **Why had the government won public favour between 1964 and 1966?** (7 marks)
c) **Explain the dramatic fall for popularity of the Wilson government after 1966.** (15 marks)

a)   In the election of 1966, Harold Wilson appeared to have reversed Labour's slide from electoral respectability that had marked her fortunes in the 1950s, and seemed to have performed the same feat for Labour as Macmillan had for the Conservatives. The figures are almost identical: Labour now had 363 seats, while Macmillan had had 365 in 1959; in 1966 the opposition was reduced to 253, in 1959 it had been 258.

b)   The Labour Party, under Harold Wilson had won a tiny majority of four in the 1964 general election, which meant that it would have great difficulty in passing legislation. On the other hand, the electorate had clearly tired of the Conservatives, who had been in power for the previous 13 years and the Labour Party had the opportunity to demonstrate that they were a viable alternative.

Labour was immediately faced with a financial crisis, but the party leaders responded robustly, using the newly established Department of Economic Affairs. **Devaluation** was to be resisted, so an temporary import duty was imposed, together with loans from foreign banks. With an increase in the bank rate to 7 per cent, the immediate financial crisis was averted. The government then set to work to devise a long-term solution to Britain's economic difficulties. A National Board for Prices and Incomes was set up to limit inflationary demands from both sides of industry, having gained the support of employers and unions. By 1965, it seemed that inflation had been stifled without provoking unemployment.

The government also handled the Rhodesian crisis well and exploited the weakness of the Conservative opposition. Wilson and Labour opposed Ian Smith's **Unilateral Declaration of Independence** and swiftly imposed economic sanctions on the rebel white settlers, taking care to get United Nations support for their actions. The Conservatives meanwhile, with a newly elected leader, were split between support for Wilson's tough stance and support for the white Rhodesians.

It was largely the divided nature of the Conservatives which convinced Wilson to call an election in 1966. In that election, the Labour slogan, 'You know Labour works' seemed justified by the economic situation and Labour increased their majority to 96 seats.

c)   The Labour government quickly became unpopular as it became clear that the economic policies implemented before the election were inadequate in dealing with the scale of the difficulties faced by Britain. Faced with more pressure on the pound in the summer of 1966 and a prolonged strike by seamen, the government abandoned their economic plans and in an emergency budget in July 1966 cut public spending and increased purchase taxes on tobacco, spirits and wine. The trade unions felt angry as this situation persisted and the government was forced to pass the Prices and Incomes Act to ensure that the unions co-operated. The economy continued to stagnate, however, and unemployment rose. When the six-day war in the Middle East weakened Britain's **balance of payments** still further in 1967, the government was forced to abandon its financial policy and devalue the pound. Callaghan was forced to resign as Chancellor. His replacement Roy Jenkins was forced to charge for National Health prescriptions and double the charge for dental service. Cuts were made in the house- and road-building programmes and the raising of the school leaving age had to be deferred from 1971 to 1973. Such measures hit Labour's core voters and their anger was shown in the by-election when the average swing to the Conservatives was measured to be 18 per cent.

The government's attempt to recapture the initiative after **devaluation** was not unsuccessful, but the measures employed damaged their popularity still further. The burden of taxation went up in 1968 and 1969. Wage restraint was strictly enforced causing more trade union rebellions, but when the government introduced a White Paper, 'In Place of Strife' in 1969, which proposed compulsory ballots before strikes, the TUC rejected the idea and forced the government to back down. This gave the impression of a government at the mercy of the unions and weakened Wilson's leadership. The party's lack of clear resolve was also shown when Wilson half-heartedly applied for membership of the EEC in 1968, only to be vetoed by De Gaulle, as Macmillan had been before him. Although the party went into the 1970 election with an improved **balance of payments**, largely due to Jenkins' austerity measures, the disappointment with the government was clear. Faced with a revitalised Conservative party and with some unexpected poor economic figures shortly before polling day, Wilson lost 74 seats and was forced to resign as Prime Minister.

Ultimately, Wilson's government fell because it failed to solve the long-standing problems in the British economy and it was publicly seen to fail in the 1966 crisis, the **devaluation** crisis and the humiliating dropping of 'In Place of Strife'. By 1970 unemployment had increased to over 600,000, and, as Jenkins refused to offer a boom-budget for the long-term good of the economy, Labour had little to offer the public in the general election. Elected with high hopes in 1964, Wilson's Labour government proved to be one of the most disappointing in British history and the public were prepared to give the dynamic Conservative leader, Edward Heath, the opportunity to reverse the perceived decline of Britain's economy.

 4. Britain in the 1970s (EDEXCEL)

a)   **Describe the importance of the trade unions in influencing the success**
or failure of the Conservative and Labour governments between 1970
and 1979.   **(30 marks)**
b)   **To what extent did the Conservative and Labour parties abandon their**
commitment to Keynesian economic policies in the 1970s?   **(30 marks)**

(Total: 60 marks)

a) The Conservative government that came to power in 1970 was determined to control the trade unions more effectively than Wilson's government had done. The policy programme decided at Selsdon before the election seemed to indicate that confrontation would not be long in coming.

Heath unwisely tried to legislate against the unions without consultation, which might have produced a more effective approach and won over moderate unions. The Industrial Relations Act (1971) which imposed secret ballots prior to a strike and established the National Industrial Relations Court was certainly popular, but the unions refused to comply with it, which only revealed the impotence of Heath's administration when faced with concerted union opposition. The miners' strikes in 1971 and 1972, had further reinforced the impression of a government unable to control the state as Heath was forced to instigate power cuts and a three-day week to save energy but then caved in and granted a large pay increase. In 1974 as inflation rocketed, the miners again threatened industrial action for more pay, with the support of many other unions. Heath decided to try to win a popular mandate to crack down on the unions and called an election in February on the issue of 'who governs Britain?' Although the result was inconclusive, the failure to deal more effectively with the unions had clearly been fatal to Heath's government.

After the failure of 'In Place of Strife', few had much hope that Wilson's government would fare any better in his dealings with the unions. However, Wilson chose not to expose his position as he had done in 1969 and wisely appointed Michael Foot, who was popular with the trade union leadership, as Secretary of State for Employment. He managed to agree a wages agreement which lasted for three years.

By 1979, however, the trade unions were tired of wage restraint in a period of high unemployment that saw wages fall, especially in the public sector. When Callaghan proposed a 5 per cent wage increase, he was faced with a trade union revolt that many in his own party supported. Workers at Ford managed to win a 15 per cent pay award and that opened the flood gates. By January 1979, many public sector workers were on strike. Rubbish lay uncollected, the dead were left unburied. In the end most trade union demands for substantial pay rises were met, but the reputation of the government had been seriously damaged, just when it seemed to have begun to have successfully addressed Britain's economic weaknesses.

As can be seen, the trade unions played a hugely significant role in the political events of the 1970s. They may not always have acted in unison and in some cases may have been split internally between a moderate leadership and more militant shop stewards, but their influence over Labour was undeniable. Unfortunately for them as a movement, however, the exercise of their influence in the 1970s, when they were invited to Downing Street for 'beer and sandwiches' proved to be their undoing, as public dissatisfaction with their power led to the election in 1979 of a Prime Minister determined to end their control of policy and severely limit their powers.

b) Following a period of unprecedented social advance between 1945 and 1973, funded by a 65 per cent increase in economic output between 1950 and 1970, the British economy seemed to be in crisis by the early 1970s. British economic growth was slower than the rest of Europe, with Britain falling from ninth place in a league table of GDP per head to fifteenth place in 1971 and to eighteenth by 1976. It seemed by the late 1960s and early 1970s that the economic policies employed by governments were producing the worst possible economic situation: the stagnation of industry, combined with rising prices and a falling pound – a position often described at the time as 'stagflation'. By 1974, inflation was at its highest level since 1945 – at 28 per cent, which harmed those living on their savings, such as pensioners.

The right wing of the Conservative Party, led by Keith Joseph, claimed that these economic problems were the consequence of the Keynesian policies pursued by both Labour and Conservative governments since 1945. They were particularly critical of the powerful role of British trade unions since the war, especially when Labour was in government. They noted sourly, that labour productivity in the USA, where unions were weaker, was 50 per cent higher than in Britain and Germany's productivity was 25 per cent higher. In their place, they called for a tighter control of money supply, limits on the rights of trade unions and reductions in government expenditure, a policy usually referred to as '**monetarism**'. With the fall of Heath and the election of Margaret Thatcher as leader in 1975, one of the two major British political parties now made an ideological commitment to abandoning 'consensus politics' and began drawing up policies to reduce government interference in the economy and to promote free enterprise. The Conservatives were the opposition party after 1974, however, as Labour had a majority of five after October 1974. Labour therefore had to attempt to deal with the economic crisis in Britain.

Most Labour Party leaders had some hopes that, as a party with close links to trade unions, they would be more able to restrain demands for pay increases during this period of economic strain. A 'social contract' was agreed with trade union leaders under which consultation with unions would take place in exchange for limited pay demands. However, a group of influential moderates, including the new Chancellor, Denis Healey and James Callaghan's son-in-law, the journalist, Peter Jay, argued that there was a need to limit the money supply as well, in effect, agreeing to some extent, with the Conservative Party. Healey's first budget in 1975 therefore increased taxes and cut public spending. He found his policy had strong support from Callaghan when he became Prime Minister.

The support of the unions began to weaken however, and the National Union of Seamen called an all-out strike in 1976. Even more seriously, international financiers demonstrated their lack of confidence in the Labour government by a run on the pound which led to a serious depletion of Britain's currency reserves. Caught between the demands of the left wing of their party and the financial crisis in the City of London, Healey and Callaghan chose to apply to the **International Monetary Fund** (IMF) for a loan of $3.9 billion to shore up sterling. They did so, in the certain knowledge that the IMF would insist on even more sweeping government expenditure cuts. With this, the Labour Party, had finally, in effect, renounced **Keynesianism**, but they were still dependent on the support of the unions to prevent damaging strikes from derailing this new policy. The Conservatives meanwhile, argued with some justification that Labour had been forced to follow a monetarist policy and that only they could be trusted to finally conquer inflation by running the economy in a more thoroughly monetarist fashion and reducing the power of the trade unions to derail the fragile economic recovery which began in 1977. With the outbreak of public sector strikes in the '**winter of discontent**' of 1978–9, their warnings seemed vindicated and it was the voters in May 1979 who drove the final nail into the coffin of an already dead economic policy, by electing a committed, if politically cautious, monetarist into No. 10 Downing Street.

 ## 5. Northern Ireland 1969–79 (OCR)

Why did the 'Troubles' break out in Northern Ireland in 1969 and why were British governments unable to achieve a settlement in Northern Ireland between 1969 and 1979?

(90 marks)

Since partition in 1922, the Protestant Unionist majority in Northern Ireland had dominated government in the area. The Catholic **Nationalist** minority was discriminated against in areas such as the allocation of council housing, education and employment. Over 90 per cent of the workers at the huge Harland and Wolff shipyard in Belfast were Protestants, and unemployment among Catholics was three times the level it was among Protestants. The Catholic community also felt harassed by the predominantly Unionist police force, the Royal Ulster Constabulary. Inspired by the successful example of the American Civil Rights movement, the Catholics formed the Northern Ireland Civil Rights Association (NICRA), a non-violent organisation, to protest about their unfair treatment with support from liberal Unionists. Mass marches were organised which led to conflict with the RUC and Unionist groups such as the Apprentice Boys of Derry. The Nationalists responded with riots during the Apprentice Boys' March in August 1969 and support for more violent Republican groups such as the Official Irish Republican Army (IRA) grew. This in turn led to Unionist attacks on Catholic homes and businesses, often carried out by 'B specials', part-time Unionist policemen.

The Ulster Unionist Party leader, Terence O'Neill, had tried to defuse the growing division of Northern Ireland by establishing links with the Republic of Ireland. He was strongly opposed in this by hard-line Unionists, such as Ian Paisley, who did their best to whip up Unionist resentment and fear. As a result O'Neill failed to win a clear majority for his party in the 1969 Northern Irish election and was forced to resign. His successor, James Chichester-Clark was faced with a breakdown in law and order as sectarian battles broke out across the towns and cities of the province and he was forced to ask the Labour Home Secretary, James Callaghan to send troops to reinforce the RUC. Although this helped to protect the Catholics of Northern Ireland from physical attack, the troops quickly became targets for the more extreme Provisional IRA.

The British governments between 1969 and 1979, Labour and Conservative, all genuinely attempted to promote a peaceful settlement in Northern Ireland, but their efforts were hampered by a number of difficult problems. Since 1916, but particularly after the 1969 crisis, violence had become institutionalised in relations between the two communities in the province. This had further hardened the mutual antipathy between the Unionists and Nationalists and between the Northern Irish government at Stormont and the Republic of Ireland's government at Dublin. The presence of British troops, at first welcomed by the Catholic community as protectors against the Unionist paramilitaries, was increasingly resented as the Stormont government remained Unionist-dominated.

A section of the official IRA broke away to form the provisional IRA and began to launch attacks on the British soldiers. This in turn led Heath's government to increase the number of troops in the province and then to introduce internment without trial to stop the terrorists. Internment was used by the Stormont government to arrest large numbers of Catholics and Nationalists, most of whom had little connection with the IRA. As a result, support for the British army dropped and support for the IRA increased among the **Nationalist** community. When an illegal Civil Rights march was organised on Sunday 30 January 1972, the army and the RUC used force to stop it. Believing they had come under attack, the army opened fire on the march and 14 marchers were killed. This led to a complete breakdown in order and the Conservative government was forced to suspend the Stormont government and impose Direct Rule.

The new Secretary of State for Northern Ireland, William Whitelaw, immediately used his powers to open negotiations with all sides, including the provisional IRA, but as they insisted on immediate British withdrawal, the negotiations got nowhere. Whitelaw did manage to get the Ulster Unionist party and the moderate nationalist Social and Democratic Labour Party (SDLP) to sign the Sunningdale Agreement in 1973. Under its terms, Direct Rule was to be replaced by a 'Power-

Sharing' government that would include both Nationalists and Unionists and would create a Council of Ireland to involve the Republic of Ireland in the settlement of Northern Ireland.

Despite its worthy aims, the Power Sharing Executive only lasted four months. Enough Unionists resented sharing power and having to co-operate with the Republic of Ireland for a Ulster Workers' Council to call a general strike which brought Northern Ireland to a standstill for 14 days in May 1974. The new Labour Secretary of State, Merlyn Rees failed to use troops to break the strike and abandoned the Power Sharing Executive. He tried to replace it with a Constitutional Convention, but the Unionist mood had hardened against the Sunningdale Agreement and the Convention failed in turn.

Rees did manage to satisfy the Nationalist demands for an end to internment, but he was hampered in achieving any further breakthrough by the obstinacy of the Unionists and British public anger following the Guildford and Birmingham bombings in 1974. He had to adopt a holding position instead, piloting the Prevention of Terrorism Act through Parliament to try to reduce the violence before attempting more negotiations. His position was reversed by his successor, Roy Mason, who was appointed in 1976. Mason attempted to continue the pressure on terrorists and began to organise counter-insurgency operations using both the RUC and the SAS. This only hardened the provisional IRA's resolve however and they reorganised themselves into cells which were almost impossible to discover and penetrate. By 1979, Britain was no closer to extricating herself from Northern Ireland than she had been in 1969.

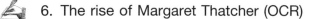 6. The rise of Margaret Thatcher (OCR)

Why did Margaret Thatcher become leader of the Conservative Party in 1975 and go onto win the 1979 general election?

(90 marks)

Edward Heath's government of 1970–74 had attempted to curb the growing power of the trade unions by putting their power to call strikes under the control of the National Industrial Relations Court, but his policy had largely failed. He had attempted to confront the miners in the strikes of 1972–74, but these had resulted in electricity blackouts and an eventual humiliating defeat in the February 1974 election. His attempts to reduce state involvement in the economy were also spectacular failures as his government was forced to intervene to fix prices and wages and to prop up ailing companies such as Rolls Royce and the Upper Clyde Shipbuilders. By 1974, Heath's much trumpeted Selsdon programme was in tatters and many Tories felt that his weak leadership had missed a vital opportunity to reform the country and prevent Wilson's return to power.

Such disappointment among Tory activists was bound to lead to a call for a change in leadership, especially after the second election of 1974, which was the third (out of four) that Heath lost as leader of the Conservatives. Conservative backbenchers and party members were increasingly concerned at the rising levels of industrial unrest and social disorder by the mid 1970s and Heath's refusal to confront these problems in his government, caused many influential right-wing thinkers such as Enoch Powell and Keith Joseph to look for a new leader who would not back down when faced with the consequences of a tougher industrial policy.

Heath was unwilling to resign however, and so he attempted to silence his critics by calling a leadership election in November 1974. To his surprise, his shadow finance minister, Margaret

Thatcher, put herself forward as a candidate. Thatcher felt she had been neglected by Heath, but most of all, she had been convinced by Joseph that the country needed a stronger Conservative leader, who would pursue a monetarist policy. Her leadership challenge, which few regarded as having any chance of success, was carefully presented by Airey Neave as a protest vote against Heath's leadership. Such was back-bench anger with their leader that Thatcher actually won more votes from party MPs than Heath and so, when Heath resigned as leader, she was able to see off challenges from other leading Conservatives, having won prestige as the only shadow cabinet member to dare to actually stand up to Heath.

It was therefore, the failures of Heath's 1970–74 government, combined with the growing fears of Conservatives both within and outside Westminster, about the social and economic condition of Britain, that created a situation where a credible back-bench challenge to Heath could take place. It was Margaret Thatcher's great fortune that no more senior Conservatives challenged Heath, and it was her courage in doing so, and the devious strategy of her campaign that allowed a most unexpected leader of the Conservative Party to emerge.

As is often said, opposition parties do not win elections, but governments lose them. Labour, in power with a small and dwindling majority since 1974, found itself increasingly unable to operate without the consent of minority parties. In the first instance this meant the creation of the **Lib–Lab pact**, but soon it meant attempting to win the support of the nationalist parties in Wales and Scotland. This was achieved by the promise of a vote on **devolution** for both countries, which secured their support, but was unpopular in England, as it was felt that too much time was being spent on the issue at a time of economic emergency. When the **devolution** vote actually took place in 1978, although both countries gave a majority for **devolution**, the majority of 40 per cent of the electorate that Labour had decided was necessary was not achieved and so the two nationalist parties were severely disaffected and eventually turned against Labour. In a vote of no-confidence on 28 March 1979, Labour lost by one vote and Callaghan's government was forced to hold a general election, rather than having the freedom to choose the date of election to suit themselves.

Most importantly of all, Labour suffered from holding office when the effects of the oil crisis of 1973 were finally felt. Britain's North Sea oil did not come on full supply quickly enough for Britain to avoid a serious **balance of payments** crisis and unprecedented levels of inflation. In 1976, the government was forced to negotiate for a loan of £4 billion from the **International Monetary Fund**. Under its terms, Britain had to cut public expenditure, which was unpopular especially at a time of rising prices, but in particular angered the public service unions whose pay was limited. Unemployment rose to a post-war high of 1.2 million. In the winter of 1978–79, there was a rash of strikes, as the previously agreed wage restraint of 5 per cent was rejected by the public service unions. This led to severe disruption to hospitals, schools and council services and created the impression of a government helpless in the face of the unions. The press capitalised on claims that the unions were 'holding the nation to ransom', and caricatured Callaghan's unperturbed reaction to questions about a national crisis, with the headline 'Crisis? What crisis?'.

It was therefore, quite easy for the Conservatives to take advantage of this situation and they shrewdly made promises that would satisfy public, and especially middle-class dissatisfaction with the current policies of the government. Mrs Thatcher promised that a Conservative government would tackle the problem of 'secondary picketing', improve education and health care and strengthen Britain's defence systems. Although it talked of rebuilding the economy by removing restrictive practices and reducing inflation, specific statements about the economy were few and there was no mention of **privatisation**. In many ways, the 1979 manifesto closely resembled that of Edward Heath in 1970.

Aware that she could appear harsh and unfriendly, Mrs Thatcher took lessons in speech delivery and presentation and concentrated on offering a new start in contrast to the apparently failed Labour programme. While Callaghan relied on a personal appeal to the voters, which relied on his calm avuncular charm, the Tories took a far more professional approach and employed the advertising agency Saatchi and Saatchi to attack Labour with the poster 'Labour isn't working' and to produce some extremely effective party political broadcasts.

In the election, Mrs Thatcher won 339 seats to Labour's 269, an overall majority of 43 seats. Although the **'winter of discontent'** (or at least the media's presentation of it) and the unpopularity of trade union power with many middle-class voters was certainly the crucial factor in this relatively narrow victory, it is important to remember that Labour's core support, manual workers, had been declining in number since 1964, when they made up 63 per cent of the population to 1979 when they only comprised 56 per cent. This, along with the over-representation of the mainly Conservative-voting South East of England in Parliament, certainly aided Mrs Thatcher's success. In these circumstances, she needed to do little but keep a relatively low profile and allow her publicists to point to Labour's shortcomings. As Callaghan has said, 'when there is a sea change in political thinking, there is little one can do to stop it'.

Additional essay questions

1. Attlee's government 1945–51 (EDEXCEL)

a) **Describe the developments which led to the establishment of the National Health Service in July 1948.** **(30 marks)**

b) **Why and with what success did the Labour governments of 1945–51 embark on a policy of nationalisation?** **(30 marks)**

(Total: 60 marks)

Essay plan

*a) Before the Second World War, health care had to be paid for by individuals through national or private insurance or by charities. The casualties caused by the **Blitz** had required considerable reorganisation of health provision and a centrally-controlled Emergency Hospital Scheme had been set up to provide free treatment as and when required.*

Proposals for a similar National Health Service had been made by William Beveridge in his second Report into Social and Allied Services. This had resulted in a White Paper on a proposed NHS being issued by Churchill's coalition government in 1944.

After winning the 1945 election, Attlee was committed to creating the NHS as proposed by the 1944 White Paper and appointed Aneurin Bevan as Minister of Health to achieve this.

Bevan used his experiences in South Wales to insist on a nationally run scheme, with salaried doctors, nurses and auxiliary staff. He first took the local and charity hospitals into public ownership.

When he proposed launching a National Health Service to include all voluntary or local authority hospitals, he faced opposition from the doctors who feared losing their independence and valuable private practices. When the British Medical Association threatened to boycott the launch of the NHS, Bevan offered a compromise, in which doctors could continue their private work as well as work in the NHS, and even have private patients in NHS hospitals. As a result, over 90 per cent of doctors registered with the new service and encouraged their patients to do the same.

The NHS that came in to being on 5 July 1948 provided free general practitioner and medical services, free hospital care and free dental and optical services.

b)   Why?

Labour had been committed to the policy of **nationalisation** of public utilities since the drafting of the party's constitution in 1918. The influence of the trade unions in calling for **nationalisation** of industries such as coal-mining, as a solution to the industrial relations which had caused the 1926 general strike, was an important factor in Labour Party policy. Labour's leadership was unsure how far **nationalisation** should progress, though.

The establishment of public corporations such as the BBC and the Central Electricity Board before the war and the government's successful control of all industrial and natural resources during the Second World War, demonstrated that the state could successfully control major economic enterprises.

Labour was committed to **nationalisation** in its 1945 election manifesto, 'Let Us Face the Future' and began a sweeping programme of **nationalisation** in the next six years, which included: The Bank of England (1946); civil aviation (1946); coal mines (1947); electricity (1948); transport (including railways, canals and road haulage) (1948); gas (1949); iron and steel (1951).

Success?

The government was unsure what they wished the nationalised industries to achieve – hence much doubt about whether they were successful or failures. Only the **nationalisation** of iron and steel provoked controversy – the other utilities were accepted and remained in public hands after the Conservative victory of 1951.

In some cases, such as coal-mining and the railways, **nationalisation** prevented a collapse of these industries. Working conditions, especially safety, were improved.

No workers' control, though – public ownership meant a government appointed board, often made up of the old private owners. Most of the nationalised industries were old-fashioned and using out-dated machinery – the government didn't have the money for modernisation. Instead money was spent on compensating the old owners. The nationalised industries were therefore inefficient and badly run. Bureaucracy proved inimical to business success. Nationalised industries did not need to be competitive or effective as they had a guaranteed market.

2. The dominance of the Conservatives 1951–64 (OCR)

Why did the Conservative governments of 1951–64 fail to reverse the reforms of the previous Labour government, yet win three successive general election victories?   **(90 marks)**

Essay plan

*Emergence of a new consensus – Conservatives recognised their lack of enthusiasm for reform in 1945 had cost them the election and hence they accepted the reforms of the Labour Party that were popular, such as the NHS, full employment policy and some **nationalisation**. They reversed some less popular policies such as the **nationalisation** of iron and steel and the policy of **austerity** – ending rationing by 1954. They sought to capitalise on Labour's failures, in particular on housing.*

*The Conservative leadership, such as Macmillan, Eden and Butler persuaded Churchill of the electoral advantages of changing policy to accept the **nationalisation** of other utilities, co-operation with the trade unions and an economic policy which aimed to maintain a high and stable level of employment. New policy stated in The Industrial Charter.*

*Many of the younger leaders agreed with the social policies of Labour and wished to recreate a Disraelian 'one nation' party prepared to consider the interests of all groups in society. The Conservative manifesto of 1950 stressed that the party would protect and develop the **Welfare State**. These Conservatives became the leaders after Churchill's eventual resignation in 1955.*

*Following the end of the Korean War in 1953, favourable economic circumstances allowed the Conservatives to both reduce taxes and increase expenditure on the **Welfare State**. No need to challenge the economic legacy left by the previous government as the country continued to prosper. The full employment policy allowed the whole country to share in the benefits of the nation's prosperity and so support the government in office, hence the Conservative election victory in 1955.*

Despite its impact on the premiership of Anthony Eden, the Suez crisis of 1956 was seen as a strong statement of Britain's determination to maintain a world role. Macmillan, on coming to office, had continued Britain's military campaigns against nationalists in Kenya and Cyprus and against communists in Malaya. Macmillan's strong response to Soviet aggression in Berlin and his good relations with President Eisenhower, enhanced his reputation as a determined defender of Britain's interests. He could also pose as a peacemaker, though, having visited Moscow in 1959 and setting up a conference of Foreign Ministers in Geneva.

By the late 1950s, a new range of cheaper consumer durables, such as cars, fridges, washing machines and televisions became available and the government reduced interest payments to encourage people to buy these items on credit in the so-called 'Barber boom'. 'Most of our people have never had it so good' according to Macmillan.

Macmillan also appealed to the middle-class electorate, frightened by the influence of trade unions. In his defeat of London Bus Strike of 1958. Macmillan himself, already credited with the dramatically successful housing drive of the early 1950s, showed strong leadership in handling the resignation of his Chancellor, Peter Thorneycroft in 1958. He presented a calm and authoritative appearance on the new medium of television, leading one cartoonist to dub him 'Supermac'.

Labour remained divided despite the volte-face of Bevan over unilateral nuclear disarmament, as he failed to carry his supporters behind the Labour leader Gaitskell. Gaitskell was also humiliated when he tried and failed to persuade the party to scrap Clause IV of the constitution in the face of trade union opposition.

Ultimately, the memories of Suez and the resignation of Thorneycroft were insignificant factors compared to the growing affluence. The economic strength of Britain was perhaps over-stated, but as a political tool, the creation of a pre-election boom was a masterstroke and lead to the Conservative majority increasing to 100 seats.

3. Labour in power, 1964–70 (OCR)

Which was more damaging to the Labour government of Harold Wilson: devaluation or the refusal of the trade unions to accept the White Paper on industrial relations, 'In Place of Strife'? (90 marks)

4. Britain in the 1970s (AQA)

Read the following source and then answer the questions which follow:

Labour in 1974 had inherited a poisoned chalice – lame economy and a divided nation – but within a few months appeared to be making some progress.

From *From Blitz to Blair* by Nick Tiratsoo

a) **Using the source and your own knowledge, comment on 'a divided nation' in the context of industrial relations in 1974.** (3 marks)
b) **Explain why Labour was able to govern for five years despite such a tiny majority after October 1974.** (7 marks)
c) **Assess the achievements of the Labour governments of 1974–79.** (15 marks)

5. Northern Ireland 1969–79 (EDEXCEL)

a) **Describe the events which led to the suspension of the Stormont government in March 1972.** (30 marks)

b) **Why did the subsequent Sunningdale agreement fail?** (30 marks)

(Total: 60 marks)

6. The rise of Margaret Thatcher (AQA)

Read the following quote and then answer the questions which follow:

In February 1975, Mrs Thatcher, a surprise candidate, ousted Heath as party leader. Her election should be seen as a reaction against Heath, whom many in the party wanted out at all costs, rather than a victory for the right wing, who were at this point in a minority in the party.

From *The Conservative Party since 1945* by Anthony Seldon

a) **Using the source and your own knowledge, explain what is meant by the 'right wing' of the Conservative Party.** (3 marks)

b) **Explain why 'many in the (Conservative) Party, wanted (Edward Heath) out at all costs'.** (7 marks)

c) **In what ways did Mrs Thatcher alter the policies of the Conservative Party while in opposition between 1975 and 1979?** (15 marks)

Part 3: Sources (OCR)

1. The formation of the National Health Service

Source A: From 'A National Health Service', a White Paper published in 1944 by the wartime coalition government

Every man and woman and child can rely on getting all the advice and treatment and care which they need . . . what they get shall be the best medical and other facilities available . . . their getting these shall not depend on whether they can pay for them, or on any other factor irrelevant to the real need – the real need being to bring the country's full resources to bear upon reducing ill-health and promoting good health in all its citizens.

Source B: From an article by Dr Alfred Cox, in the *British Medical Association Journal*, April 1946

I have examined the [National Health Service] Bill and it looks uncommonly like the first step, and a big one, towards National Socialism as practised in Germany. The medical service there was early put under the dictatorship of a 'medical Führer'. This Bill will establish the Minister of Health in that capacity.

Source C: Anuerin Bevan, the Minister of Health, shown as an unsympathetic nurse force feeding the doctors the unpleasant medicine of the NHS, 1947

Source D: Anuerin Bevan's speech to the Commons, defending the NHS Bill, February 1948

We not only desire in this scheme to relieve patients of financial anxiety; we desire to relieve the doctor of financial anxiety when he approaches his patients. It is one of the most deplorable features of the existing system that young doctors, when they go into practice . . . they have financial burdens put upon them. We consider, therefore, that a salary, only of £300 . . . would be a financial support for the young doctor whilst he is building up his practice . . .

Source E: Anuerin Bevan on his treatment of the BMA

I stuffed their mouths with gold!

Figure 7.1 **Aneurin Bevan force-feeding doctors the unpleasant medicine of the NHS**

DOTHEBOYS HALL
"It still tastes awful."

QUESTIONS WITH WORKED ANSWERS

a) **Study source A. In what ways does this document reveal broad political support for the principles of the National Health System?** (10 marks)

b) **Study sources B and C. To what extent do these two sources agree in their criticism of Bevan's proposals for the NHS?** (25 marks)

c) **Study sources B, C and D. How effectively does Bevan's speech to Parliament refute the accusations in sources 2 and 3?** (25 marks)

d) **Study *all* the sources and use your own knowledge. Why, despite opposition from the BMA, was Bevan successfully able to launch the National Health Service in July 1948?** (60 marks)

(Total: 120 marks)

ANSWERS

a) Source A, a White Paper produced during the Second World War, lays out the universal principles of what was to become the National Health System. Fundamental was the belief that receiving treatment 'shall not depend on whether they can pay'. This proposal of government policy was brought forward by a coalition government made up of Conservatives, Labour and

Liberal MPs while the war was still being waged and demonstrates how a new consensus was emerging between the political parties of the extent and nature of social security that would be introduced after the war.

b) Source B and source C both criticise the power of the Minister of Health, Aneurin Bevan, for the power that he will be able to exercise over the medical profession once the National Health Service has been created. The cartoon, source C, sees him as an authority figure, a Victorian nurse, forcing the doctors to take an unpleasant medicine, while the article from the BMA journal fears that the proposed NHS bill will 'establish the Minister of Health in that capacity . . . of a "medical Führer."'

On the other hand, however, the cartoon does not necessarily condemn Bevan. Unlike source B, which draws an analogy between the NHS bill and the Third Reich which cannot be interpreted as anything other than harshly critical, the cartoon shows Bevan as a nurse. A nurse may be unsympathetic to the wishes of his or her patients, but the medicine they administer is intended to be for the benefit of the patient, whether it tastes unpleasant or not. Therefore, although source B clearly sees the NHS bill as immoral, judging from the comparison that is made, source C seems to find the bill, despite its unpleasant effect on the doctors, ultimately beneficial to the medical needs of the nation.

c) In his speech, Bevan fails to directly respond to the criticism of the growth in his powers (and the consequent limits on the independence of doctors). He chooses instead to concentrate on the position of young doctors, who unlike their richer, more senior elder colleagues, did not have as much to lose from the creation of the NHS. As Bevan points out in source D, 'we desire to relieve the doctor of financial anxiety' and he goes on to specifically refer to 'young doctors' and to condemn the 'financial burdens' they face as 'one of the most deplorable features of the existing system'. Under the existing system doctors would be paid a fee for each patient they treated, which would limit the income of a doctor who had only just established himself in practice. He explains that under the NHS, the young doctor would receive a 'salary' as well, designed principally as a 'financial support for the young doctor whilst he is building up his practice'. He does not, therefore, refute the allegations, perhaps because they hold an element of truth, albeit over-exaggerated. He prefers to outline the benefits that the new organisation will offer doctors as well as patients.

d) Bevan managed to establish the NHS by a number of well judged expedients in the face of much serious institutional opposition. He appealed over the heads of the medical establishment to the most important audience of all, the electorate, who had relied on health insurance to cover the cost of treatment before the war. As had been stated in the 1944 White Paper, in Source A, 'what they get shall be the best medical and other facilities available' and that 'getting these shall not depend on whether they can pay for them'. Similarly Bevan believed that one of the principles of the new health system should be to 'relieve patients of financial anxiety', as he says in source D. He also sought to ensure that doctors were more evenly distributed rather than being concentrated in wealthier areas.

This message, of treating patients according to need, rather than according to ability to pay, did appeal to many idealistic doctors, many of whom had waived their fees from poorer patients in the old system. But Bevan also cleverly split those doctors who opposed him, such as Dr Alfred Cox in source B, by appealing to those outside the senior ranks of the BMA, such as junior doctors, by explaining the advantages of a salary in addition to fees, as a 'financial support', he explains in source D, for those who were not yet established with a private practice. He also offered a compromise in order to get the NHS launched by 1948. If, after three years the doctors were not happy with the 'fee plus salary' scheme they would be given the chance to choose to return to the old 'fee only' system.

Ultimately, however, Bevan had to overcome the opposition of the senior doctors, who objected to their subordination to the state and, as they saw it, the ending of the doctor's primary responsibility to his patient. In 1948, 90 per cent of the BMA had voted not to co-operate with the new scheme. He did so by offering them a deal. Doctors could choose whether or not to continue in private practice exclusively or to retain some private patients in addition to the hours they were expected to fulfil for the NHS, even having private rooms for these patients set aside in NHS hospitals. They were not forced to work for the new health system. As is quoted in source E, he later put it that he had 'stuffed their mouths with gold', in other words, Bevan bought off their opposition, by allowing them to retain their lucrative private work alongside their new duties in the NHS. He had, in fact, also threatened to take away the doctors' 'gold', as he promised to review (that is, seriously reduce) the existing fees if less than 95 per cent of the population signed up as a result of the doctors' obstruction.

For whatever reason, whether through the altruistic nature of many doctors, whether from public pressure, or from a revolt by young doctors, or an acceptance of Bevan's compromises, despite the fact that the BMA continued to call for a boycott of the NHS, when the service was launched on 5 July 1948, 90 per cent of all GPs took part in helping it to operate.

2. The IMF loan, 1976 (EDEXCEL)

Study sources 1–5 below and then answer questions (a) to (e) which follow.

Source 1. Denis Healey on his economic policy as Labour Chancellor, 1974–79

In 1974 the Treasury was the slave of the greatest of all academic scribblers, Maynard Keynes . . . Though he died in 1946, his influence was still dominant . . . I abandoned Keynesianism in 1975

Source 2. Prime Minister James Callaghan speaking at the Labour Party Conference in 1976

We used to think that you could spend your way out of recession and increase employment by cutting taxes and boosting government expenditure. I will tell you in all candour that that option no longer exists, and that in so far as it ever did exist, it only worked on each occasion since the war by injecting a bigger dose of inflation into the economy, followed by a higher level of unemployment as the next stage.

Source 3. Chancellor of the Exchequer, Denis Healey, speaking at the Labour Party Conference in 1976

I'm going to negotiate with the IMF on the basis of existing policies. It means sticking to the very painful cuts in public expenditure on which the government has already decided [jeers from members of the audience]. It means sticking to a pay policy which enables us, as the TUC resolved a week or two ago, to continue the attack on inflation [shouts of 'resign' from members of the audience]. It means seeing that the increase in output which has now begun goes not into public or private spending, but goes into exports and investment. That's what it means and that's what I'm asking for. That's what I'm going to negotiate for and I ask the conference to support me [applause from the audience].

Source 4. Tony Benn on the government expenditure cuts forced by the IMF

Looking back on it now, it was those cuts really which led directly to the 'winter of discontent' and paved the way for the Conservative victory of 1979. And it was all quite unnecessary. For, as Denis Healey very fairly wrote in his book, *A Time of My Life*, 'The Treasury had grossly over-estimated the public sector borrowing requirement which would have fallen within the IMF limit without any of the measures they prescribed'. So it was all a tragic error for which we all paid a terrible price.

Source 5. The historian, Arthur Marwick comments on the IMF crisis

The Left saw the crisis as a capitalist one with right-wing leaders complicit in it. In all sections there was a fear of a 1931-style collapse. In fact Callaghan and Healey, in their negotiations with the IMF, showed great skill and patience: the eventual expenditure cuts of £2 billion were considerably less than the draconian figures put forward at the height of the (somewhat factitious*) panic . . . Certainly, the government was fully in retreat from its policies of subsidizing industry; and actually moved in the direction of privatization, raising £500 million through the sale of shares in British Petroleum.

QUESTIONS WITH WORKED ANSWERS

a) Consult source 1. What does Denis Healey mean by 'Keynesianism'? (6 marks)
b) Consult sources 2 and 3. To what extent do these speeches reveal the same priorities in Callaghan and Healey's economic policy? (10 marks)
c) Consult sources 4 and 5. To what extent does source 4 support the claim in Source 5 that the crisis was 'somewhat factitious'? (10 marks)
d) Consult source 4. Assess the usefulness of this source for a historian studying British politics in the 1970s. (10 marks)
e) Consult all the sources and use your own knowledge. 'The Labour Cabinet . . . prepared the ground for Thatcherism by acceding to IMF monitoring of the British economy' (Roger Middleton). To what extent does the evidence support this statement? (24 marks)

(Total: 60 marks)

a) By 'Keynesianism' Healey is referring in source 1 to the economic principles established by the economist and Treasury official, J.M. Keynes, which became the accepted economic principles of successive Conservative and Labour governments after 1945. In practice, these principles embodied the maintenance of a high and stable level of employment, the provision of welfare for the whole population through services and payments, and the organisation of the economy, all of which would be directly undertaken by the state.

b) Both Callaghan and Healey are announcing to their party that there is a need for a significant shift in the government's economic policy. In source 2, Callaghan was rejecting the Keynesian attitude that one 'could spend your way out of recession', on the grounds that it increased inflation,

---

* factitious = imaginary

which in turn led to 'a higher level of unemployment', which was what the policy was supposed to prevent. In source 3, Healey is responding to the immediate **balance of payments** crisis of 1976 and the consequent run on the pound, by attempting to secure a loan from the **International Monetary Fund** (IMF), rather than increasing public spending to boost the economy, which would have been the Keynesian method. Healey talks of 'the very painful cuts in public expenditure on which the government has already decided', 'a pay policy', and funding going 'not into public or private spending, but . . . into exports and investment', all of which is designed to 'continue the attack on inflation'. In other words, he is supporting a monetarist policy, in keeping with the principles laid out by his Prime Minister at the same conference.

c)　Tony Benn, in source 4, claims that the cuts imposed on public spending to meet the requirements for the IMF to lend money to the Labour government were 'quite unnecessary'. He goes on to quote from the autobiography of the then Chancellor of the Exchequer, Denis Healey, who states that the civil servants at the Treasury seriously miscalculated the costs of government spending and that the conditions for the IMF loan would have been met without the need for any cuts. In this sense, the panicky reaction of the currency dealers and other financiers was certainly 'somewhat factitious'.

On the other hand, the financial crisis itself was certainly not completely imaginary, as Britain did have an adverse **balance of payments** of over a billion pounds in 1976, and a sterling crisis had ensued as financiers took their investments out of Britain and the pound slipped from over $2.00 to $1.56. The government had already admitted the seriousness of the situation when the bank rate had been increased to 15 per cent. The need to prevent the outflow of capital worsening, at least until the revenue from the newly discovered North Sea oil and gas fields became available, meant that the government had to be seen to be acting to restrain public spending. Although the Treasury did overestimate the cost of public spending, almost all economic commentators did likewise, and it was unlikely that the IMF would have been willing to offer sufficient funds in such a heated atmosphere. Although the panic may have turned out to have been 'somewhat factitious' in its causes, it was, nevertheless, a genuine financial crisis, which Healey and Callaghan did well to alleviate, as source 5 states.

d)　Tony Benn, a minister in the Labour governments of 1964–70 and 1974–79 is famous for having kept a daily audio diary of his political activities throughout his ministerial career. He was, in 1976, Minister for Energy, having been moved by Harold Wilson from the Department for Trade and Industry in 1975 as he disagreed with the increasingly monetarist approach of Healey at the Treasury. It is therefore extremely useful for a historian to read his opinion of the 1976 IMF crisis as he has an insight into the event and a knowledge of the participants far more acute than most historians. On the other hand however, as a committed socialist he has very strong views of the events of 1976, which is evident in his comment that the election of Margaret Thatcher in 1979 was 'a terrible price'. This may make one a little more careful in fully relying on the objectivity of his writing.

The source is also written with hindsight as he asserts that the 1976 crisis 'led directly to the **'winter of discontent'**, which he clearly could not have seen at the time of the events. He does quote from Healey's biography in support of his opinion, but nevertheless, his case that the handling of the IMF loan and the government spending cuts that were enforced as part of the loan requirements led to the events of 1979 remains contentious. That the IMF crisis shook confidence in the government's competence and the unity of the Labour Party is certainly true, but most historians would question whether the events of 1979 were 'directly' caused by the IMF crisis or arose out of short-term circumstances that arose during the months preceding the **'winter of discontent'**.

e) In source 4 Tony Benn clearly sees a link between the IMF crisis and the victory of Mrs Thatcher in 1979, although he does not comment on whether the economic policy of the Labour government had now significantly shifted, implying instead that the 1976 crisis led to an inevitable industrial relations dispute over frozen pay rates in winter 1978–79, which contributed to the Conservative victory in May. Source 5, however, goes a stage further than this and sees the government 'fully in retreat from its policies of subsidizing industry'. Marwick goes further than Benn and states that subsequent Labour economic policy 'actually moved in the direction of privatization', by the 'sale of shares in British Petroleum'. Certainly, by accepting the need for control of the monetary supply and abandoning the Keynesian principles, as Callaghan and Healey made clear to the Labour Party Conference in sources 2 and 3, one might very well argue that the monetarist economic policy that was advocated by Margaret Thatcher had already been accepted by the Labour Party. In his autobiography, as quoted in source 1, Healey supports this when he writes that 'I abandoned **Keynesianism** in 1975'.

However, it is also possible to argue that the Labour government was, in many ways, accepting that in the wake of the 1973 oil crisis, the 'party's over', as one Labour minister put it. Although they accepted the need for more rigorous financial management, the Cabinet was clearly unwilling to abandon state management of the nationalised industries altogether and was determined to continue to spend a significant amount of government revenue in subsidising these as well as alleviating poverty and providing the services of the **Welfare State**. The economic outlook in 1976 may have seemed like preparation for Thatcherist **monetarism**, but the prospect of the benefits of North Sea oil, meant that Healey was able to pay the first $2 billion of the IMF loan back by 1977.

In conclusion, therefore, although it is possible to see that Mrs Thatcher, with her outspoken support for monetarist policies, undoubtedly benefitted from what was widely seen as a retreat from **monetarism** by Callaghan and Healey in 1976, to say that 'the ground was prepared for **Thatcherism**', seems a little simplistic. Mrs Thatcher herself was not prepared to confront the centrepiece of Keynesian economics in Britain, the nationalised industries, until her second term of office, when she was protected by a large parliamentary majority. Her first term saw major economic and social difficulties as she tried to control the money supply, and it is doubtful that she would have remained in office after 1984 had it not been for the divisions in the opposition and the 'Falklands factor'. Labour's failure to deal effectively with the industrial relations crisis in 1979, not the 1976 IMF crisis, gave Mrs Thatcher her political opportunity, but it took many years of further struggle before she was able to fully implement her economic agenda. Had circumstances been different, Healey's model of a mixed economy, with trade unions, government and managers co-operating to control the money supply, may well have survived in Britain.

3. The Labour government 1964–70

Study sources 1–5 below and then answer questions (a) to (e) which follow.

Source 1. From Harold Wilson's announcement to the House of Commons on economic measures, 20 July 1966

Sterling has been under pressure for the past two and a half weeks. After improvement in the early weeks of May we were blown off course by the seven-week seamen's strike and when the bill for that strike was presented in terms of the gold and convertible currency figures in June the foreign exchange market reacted adversely. But there were deeper and more fundamental causes . . . abundant market opportunities abroad for British products –which are competitive enough in terms of quality, performance and price – are being lost owing to the shortage of labour . . . Not until we can get this redeployment [of labour for the export trade] . . . can we confidently expect growth in industrial production which is needed to realise our economic and social policies.

Source 2. From an editorial in the *Financial Times* on the devaluation of the pound in 1967

It is an open and humiliating admission that the government's policy has failed.

Source 3. From *Homage to a Government*, a poem by Philip Larkin, 1969

> Next year we are to bring the soldiers home
> For lack of money, and it is all right.
> Places they guarded, or kept orderly
> Must guard themselves, and keep themselves orderly
> We want the money for ourselves at home
> Instead of working. And this is all right.

Source 4. From the authorised biography of Harold Wilson by Philip Ziegler, on trade union reaction to the White Paper, 'In Place of Strife', 1969

On 1 June a group of union leaders dined at Chequers . . . Hugh Scanlon stated flatly that he would never accept any legislation that included penal powers. 'If you say that, Hughie,' replied Wilson, 'then you are claiming to be the Government. I will never consent to preside over a Government that is not allowed to govern. And let us get one thing clear: that means we can't have a Labour government, for I am the only person who can lead a Labour government.' Scanlon accused him of becoming a Ramsay MacDonald. 'I have no intention of being a MacDonald,' retorted Wilson. 'Nor do I intend to be another Dubček. Get your tanks off my lawn, Hughie!'

Source 5. From *The Labour Government 1964–1970. A Personal Record* by Harold Wilson

It was a government which had faced disappointment after disappointment and none greater than the economic restraints on our ability to carry through the social revolution to which we were committed at the speed we would have wished. Yet, despite those restraints and the need to transfer resources from domestic expenditure, private and public, to the needs of our export markets, we carried through an expansion in the social services, health, welfare and housing, education and social security unparalleled in our history.

QUESTIONS WITHOUT WORKED ANSWERS

a) **Consult source 4. Explain Scanlon and Wilson's references to Ramsay MacDonald.** (6 marks)

b) **Consult sources 1 and 2. To what extent do these two sources agree on the causes of Britain's financial difficulties in the mid 1960s?** (10 marks)

c) Consult source 5. Assess the usefulness of this source for a historian studying British politics in the 1960s. **(10 marks)**
d) Consult all the sources and use your own knowledge. Which of the crises described here do you believe was the most damaging for Labour? Use the relevant source(s) to explain your answer. **(10 marks)**
e) Consult source 5. How far do you agree with Wilson's defence of the record of the Labour governments of 1964 –70? **(24 marks)**

(Total: 60 marks)

4. The winter of discontent, 1979 (EDEXCEL)

Read the source below and then answer the questions which follow.

Source 1. Mrs Thatcher, speaking at the 1985 Conservative Party Conference

Do you remember the Labour Britain of 1979? It was a Britain in which union leaders held their members and our country to ransom; a Britain that still went to international conferences but was no longer taken seriously; a Britain that was known as the sick man of Europe and which spoke the language of compassion but which suffered the winter of discontent. Governments had failed to tackle the real problems. They dodged difficult problems rather than faced up to them. The question they asked was not 'will the medicine work?' but 'will it taste all right?'.

QUESTIONS WITHOUT WORKED ANSWERS

a) Study source 1. What does this source suggest were the reasons for the industrial difficulties of the Labour government of 1979? **(10 marks)**
b) Explain why Mrs Thatcher believes that '[trade] union leaders held . . . our country to ransom'. **(14 marks)**
c) Use your own knowledge. Do you agree with Mrs Thatchers's description of 'the Labour Britain of 1979'? **(36 marks)**

(Total: 60 marks)

Part 4: Historical skills

Comparing historical interpretations

The formation of the Welfare State

Read the extracts below, they give a good indication of the differences in interpretation of the creation of the Welfare State between these two authors:

Extract A. From *Never Again: Britain 1945–51* by Peter Hennessy

The Attlee years – had their failures – a refusal to confront the truly harsh reality of diminished world status, a reluctance to modernise the state, a tendency to look back at the problems of the Thirties rather than forward to the needs of the Fifties. Yet Britain had never – and still hasn't – experienced a progressive phase to match 1945–51. It is largely, though not wholly, the achievement of those years – and the wartime experience, the crucial platform on which those advances were built – that 1951 Britain, certainly compared to the UK of 1931 or any previous decade, was a kinder, gentler and a far, far better place in which to be born, to grow up, to live, love, work and even to die.

Extract B. From *The Audit of War* by Corelli Barnett

By the time they took the bunting down from the streets after VE Day and turned from the war to the future, the British in their dreams and illusions and in their flinching from reality had already written the broad scenario for Britain's post war descent to the fifth in the free world as an industrial power, with manufacturing output only two-fifths of West Germany's and the place of fourteenth in the whole non-Communist world in terms of GNP per head. As that descent took its course the illusions and the dreams of 1945 would fade one by one – the imperial and commonwealth role, the world-power role, British industrial genius, and, at last, New Jerusalem itself, a dream turned to a dank reality of a segregated, unskilled, unhealthy and institutionalised proletariat hanging from the nipple of state maternalism.

In his definition of history, *What is History?* E.H. Carr wrote that it is first necessary to 'study the historian', before you begin to study the facts and goes on to warn any reader of history that 'by and large, the historian will get the kind of facts he wants'.

Research the background and views of Barnett and Hennessy:

1. At what type of institution were they educated?
2. At what sort of institutions have the two men worked as historians?
3. Do they have an political affiliations, or has their work been praised by any political party?

This exercise can of course can end up with you having more questions than when you started. If one historian came from a working-class area of London like Walthamstow, does that automatically mean that he will be more sympathetic towards the 1945–51 government's social policies? If the other historian teaches at an institution that may be regarded as 'elitist' such as Oxford or Cambridge University, does that automatically mean that he will be unsympathetic towards the lives of working-class people?

Perhaps, though, it is useful to know something of the educational and career backgrounds of the historians whose judgements you are looking at – especially as you might easily find yourself reading books or information from the internet and you come across views that may well be ideologically motivated by racist or fundamentalist views, which would render their relative objectivity and consequent reliability much more doubtful.

THE HISTORIANS' JUDGEMENT

To what extent do the two historians agree on the achievement of the post-war years?

Look closely at the two passages above. Are the two historians saying completely different things? It may seem so at first sight. But consider the following issues:

1. Had Britain's international importance declined by 1945?
2. Did the post-war governments face up to this immediately?
3. Did the governments of the post-war years change the priorities of the state in significant ways?
4. Did the conditions of people's lives improve in the years after 1945?

Read more fully from the two books from which these extracts come to answer these questions. So what, exactly, do the historians disagree about? Having studied their backgrounds, can you suggest why they might hold the views they do?

YOUR OWN JUDGEMENT

Did the Labour governments of 1945–51 succeed in creating a sustainable Welfare State?

The key word here is 'sustainable'. It is very easy to admire the achievements of the Labour government of 1945–51, as they certainly amounted to a considerable improvement in the standard of living of the ordinary men and women of Britain.

But did this result in the creation of a 'dependency culture'? How much money was being spent on the NHS, schools, housing and Welfare Payments? What else could this money have been spent on?

The relative decline of the British economy after 1950 is difficult to deny, however. But was this decline caused by the Welfare State? Were there any other, more important factors? What was happening in other European countries where welfare spending was also increasing?

Did welfare spending mean that the economy was actually improved?

Having thought about these questions, go back to the original passages. Which sections are based on accurate historical fact? Which ones are based on distorted readings of the evidence? Which historian is the most scrupulous in trying to present a balanced and accurate view of the period? Which parts of the passages do you not agree with?

Hopefully, you will now have your own view of the issue and won't feel obliged to agree with either historian, but will be able to state, defend and prove your own point of view on this topic, which is still central in British political debate today.

Chapter 8

The 'Wind of Change': Foreign and Colonial Policy, 1945–1979

This chapter covers a period of dramatic change in Britain's world role. Faced with three serious problems in the post-war world – the threat of the Soviet Union, the demands for independence from the colonies and economic problems, Britain was forced, not altogether unwillingly, to dramatically reduce her overseas commitments. At first, this took the course of a military alliance with the USA and independence for India and Palestine. In 1956, however, a misguided attempt by Anthony Eden to regain control of the Suez Canal led to Britain having to back down in the face of American disapproval. There is some disagreement over whether the government began to decolonise as a direct consequence of the Suez debacle, but for whatever reason, Britain's historic Empire, which had taken centuries to amass, was discarded with extraordinary haste over the next ten years. Britain was, despite Suez, forced to grow closer to the USA in her need to maintain a nuclear deterrent, which was, by the 1960s, the only feature of Great Power status that really mattered. At the same time, she tried to align her economy closer with that of mainland Europe, but, unsurprisingly, found the other European countries suspicious of her intentions and did not manage to join the European Economic Community (EEC) until 1973.

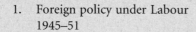 **Historical background**

Britain in 1945
The end of Empire

a) India
b) Palestine
c) Suez
d) Decolonisation 1957–79

The outbreak of the **Cold War**
The Korean War
The 'special relationship'
Britain's defence policy in a nuclear age
Britain and Europe

Essays

1. Foreign policy under Labour 1945–51

2. Britain's defence policy in the 1960s and 1970s
3. Britain and Europe
4. The end of Empire

Sources

1. The Suez crisis
2. Britain and the European Community
3. Decolonisation
4. Britain and the USA 1945–51

Historical skills

1. Group work to study the complex processes that led to the end of the British Empire in this period

Chronology

1945	Surrender of Germany and Japan
	Churchill's 'Iron Curtain' speech – Fulton, Missouri
	British loan from USA negotiated
1946	Truman Doctrine
	Announcement of Marshall Aid
	Partition of India and Pakistan
1947	State of Emergency declared in Malaya
	Road routes to West Berlin cut
1948	North Atlantic Treaty Organisation (NATO) set up
1949	Korean War begins
1950	Anglo-Iranian oil company nationalised
1952	Mau Mau rebellion begins in Kenya
	Britain's first successful atomic bomb test
1953	Shah of Iran restored by Britain and USA
1954	Geneva conference
1955	State of Emergency declared in Cyprus
1956	Suez Crisis
1957	Macmillan and Eisenhower meet in Bermuda
	Gold Coast given independence (Ghana)
	Treaty of Rome creates the European Economic Community
1958	Malaya Emergency ends
1959	Britain helps set up European Free Trade Area as rival to EEC
1960	U-2 crisis
	Nigeria given independence
1961	Berlin crisis
	South Africa leaves the Commonwealth
1962	Cuban missile crisis
1963	Kenya given independence
	General de Gaulle vetoes 1st British application for membership of EEC
1964	S. Rhodesia issues Unilateral Declaration of Independence
1965	General de Gaulle vetoes 2nd British application for membership of EEC
1972	East Pakistan breaks away and forms Bangladesh
1973	Britain joins European Economic Community
1979	Rhodesian civil war ends with Lancaster House Agreement
	Soviet troops invade Afghanistan

Part 1: Historical background

 Britain in 1945

The British Empire was the only major state which had fought throughout the Second World War from beginning to end. Under Churchill's leadership, it had been unquestionably one of the 'Big Three'. Its military performance, at sea, in the air, even on land, had been significantly better than in the First World War. By August 1945, all the possessions of the King-Emperor – including Hong Kong – were back in British hands. British troops were based in North Africa, Italy, Germany and Southeast Asia. The Royal Navy possessed over 1,000 warships, the RAF had the second biggest bomber fleet in the world.

But Britain had overstrained herself, running down her dollar and gold reserves, wearing out domestic industry and becoming increasingly dependent on American munitions, shipping, food-stuffs and other supplies, and the new Labour government had to face a 'financial Dunkirk' when lend-lease was cut off.

On the other hand, Britain became one of the five members of the Security Council of the new United Nations organisation, and she was able to spend the vast sums needed for the country to become a nuclear power, albeit at the cost of abandoning most of her colonial possessions. Britain was undoubtedly still a world power, but it was now a 'bi-polar' world divided between two super-power blocs, and Britain would be forced to choose which side she wished to support in the political, economic and ideological struggle in the '**Cold War**' which would dominate world affairs for the next 45 years.

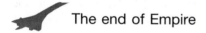 The end of Empire

There was a hope after the war, that if Britain could reduce her responsibilities in troubled parts of the Empire, such as India and Palestine, she would be able to develop more successfully the African and West Indian colonies.

a) INDIA

After the **Amritsar massacre** and the rise of Gandhi, Britain had held onto India only by promising eventual self-government. The failures in the war against Japan (especially the fall of Singapore), made this process gather momentum. Burma, the first colony to be liberated from the Japanese, was the first to gain independence in 1946.

India, however, was deeply divided between the mainly Hindu Congress Party, led by Nehru, who wanted India to remain whole, and the rival Muslim League, led by Jinnah who wanted to create a separate Pakistan in the north. Attlee, an expert on Indian affairs, tried to create a federal state, but the two sides in India could not agree and inter-communal massacres started to break out when Jinnah called a 'day of action' in August 1946. Instead Attlee appointed Earl Mountbatten as Viceroy of India and gave him full powers to make decisions on the spot.

Mountbatten soon realised 'unless I act quickly I may well find the real beginnings of a civil war on my hands' and fixed 15 August 1948 as the date for Indian independence. The nation was

Table 8.1 *British Foreign Secretaries, 1945–67*

Date	Government	Prime Minister	Foreign Secretary
1945–51	Labour	Clement Attlee	Ernest Bevin/Herbert Morrison
1951–55	Conservative	Winston Churchill	Anthony Eden
1955–57	Conservative	Anthony Eden	Harold Macmillan/Selwyn Lloyd
1957–63	Conservative	Harold Macmillan	Selwyn Lloyd/Earl of Home
1963–64	Conservative	Alec Douglas-Home	R.A. Butler
1964–70	Labour	Harold Wilson	Patrick Gordon Walker/ Michael Stewart/George Brown/ Michael Stewart
1970–74	Conservative	Edward Heath	Alec Douglas-Home
1974–76	Labour	Harold Wilson	James Callaghan
1976–79	Labour	James Callaghan	Anthony Crosland/David Owen

partitioned, but Pakistan was divided in two itself and 'moth-eaten' in size, in the hope that it would be forced to rejoin India in the future. In the massive movement of population which followed, around half a million people died.

b) PALESTINE

The mandated territory of Palestine had been difficult to administer before 1945. The Jews' hope for a national home, heightened by the Nazi persecutions after 1933, had clashed with the resentment of Palestinian Arabs displaced by Jewish settlement. Bevin tried to limit Jewish immigration, but USA insisted that the former inmates of the Polish death-camps should be given sanctuary in Palestine. Jewish terrorists blew up the British HQ at the King David Hotel in Jerusalem and launched attacks on British patrols, provoking anti-Semitic riots in London, Liverpool, Manchester, Glasgow and Leeds.

Britain, unable to maintain order, began to withdraw troops and announced that the mandate would revert to UN control. Palestine was to be divided into Jewish Israel and Arab Jordan. The State of Israel was declared on 14 May 1948, the day after the British departure, and the neighbouring Arab states immediately attacked, refusing to recognise it. Unlike India, this was no long-planned withdrawal, Britain was forced out against her will by international pressure and nationalist terrorists and they left behind an area at war.

c) SUEZ

Britain's willingness to go to war to protect her colonial interests was displayed in the Suez crisis of 1956. The nationalist ruler of Egypt, Colonel Nasser, took control of the vital supply route of the Suez Canal following US and British withdrawal of funding for the Aswan High Dam. The Prime Minister, Anthony Eden convinced himself that Nasser could not be 'appeased' and so chose to organise a military seizure of the canal, with French help. To arrange an excuse that would prevent world outrage, Eden persuaded the Israelis to attack Egypt, so that the British and the French forces would have a pretext to land at Suez, posing as 'peacekeepers'. The Israelis attacked on 29 October and over 8,000 British and French troops landed on 5–6 November. The deception fooled no one, least of all the USA, who were horrified that such an incident should occur at a time when the West was condemning the Soviet Union for intervening in Hungary. Under huge financial and diplomatic pressure, Britain had to withdraw her forces and accept a United Nations force as a replacement. US diplomats effectively 'blackballed' Eden, preferring to deal with the Chancellor, Harold Macmillan, who learned the lesson that Britain had always to seek at least tacit approval from America in her foreign policy outside Europe. Eden suffered a breakdown in his health and was persuaded to resign in January 1957 by his colleagues, who had the practical sense to choose Macmillan as the next Prime Minister.

d) DECOLONISATION 1957–79

After Suez, the pace of decolonisation was stepped up, and in 1957, the first African colony, Gold Coast, became independent as Ghana. Britain did fight two protracted campaigns, against communists in Malaya and the Mau Mau in Kenya, to retain her control of those areas in the 1950s, but in both cases, the battles were fought to allow regimes more acceptable to the British government to develop and to eventually be granted independence. Harold Macmillan clearly indicated that independence would be granted to most colonies in his 'Wind of Change' speech in 1960. Following this, almost all Britain's remaining colonies were made independent in the next 20 years. Britain did face one more serious challenge in this period, however, in 1965, when the white settlers of Southern Rhodesia, the largest non-native population outside South Africa, led by Ian Smith, announced an illegal unilateral declaration of independence (UDI) to prevent majority rule by the black population. Harold Wilson intervened personally to try to resolve the crisis, meeting Smith on a British battleship. UDI led to a guerrilla war between blacks and whites which only ended in 1979, when the new Conservative Foreign Secretary, Lord Carrington brokered a cease-fire and free, one person, one vote elections in the Lancaster House Agreement. In the subsequent election, Robert Mugabe, leader of the largest black guerrilla force, became the first Prime Minister of an independent Zimbabwe.

 The outbreak of the Cold War

All that the Red Army needed in order to reach the North Sea was boots.

Denis Healey

The alliance with the USSR during the Second World War had never been very easy. Stalin had resented the slowness of the USA and Britain to invade France, and the West were deeply suspicious of the USSR's control of the Eastern European countries they occupied after 1944.

Attlee and Bevin had no ideological attachment to Stalin and Molotov and the Russians believed that in Britain 'the class face of power remained the same'. By 1946 Bevin was considering a Western strategy to stall both communist and Russian influence and sympathised with Churchill's famous '**Iron Curtain**' speech, commenting himself, 'Stalin, Molotov, they are evil men'. His Cabinet colleagues disagreed with such an anti-Soviet approach, but Attlee supported Bevin. Bevin also proposed that Britain should have their own atomic bomb ('we've got to have a bloody Union Jack flying on top of it') to allow them to have a foreign policy separate from the USA. As Attlee said 'If we had decided not to have it, we would have put ourselves entirely in the hands of the Americans'. However, by the time Britain did test a nuclear device, in 1952, events had already made British defence dependent on the USA.

Britain attempted to involve the USA in the defence of Europe by threatening to withdraw troops from Greece and Turkey, both of which were undergoing Russian-backed communist uprisings.

Table 8.2: Chronology of decolonisation, 1947–83

Imperial colony or mandated territory	Independent title (if different)	Date of independence
India	India[1]	1947
India	Pakistan[2]	1947
Ceylon	Sri Lanka (after 1972)	1948
Palestine	Israel	1948
Gold Coast	Ghana	1957
Malaya	Malaysia[3]	1957
Cyprus		1960
Nigeria		1960
Sierra Leone		1961
Tanganyika	Tanzania	1961
Jamaica		1962
Trinidad and Tobago		1962
Uganda		1962
Kenya		1963
N. Rhodesia	Zambia	1963
Malta		1964
Nyasaland	Malawi	1964
The Gambia		1965
S. Rhodesia[4]		1965
Barbados		1966
Basutoland	Lesotho	1966
Bechuanaland	Botswana	1966
British Guiana	Guyana	1966
Aden	S. Yemen	1967
Mauritius		1968
Swaziland		1968
Fiji		1970
The Bahamas		1973
Grenada		1974
Seychelles		1976
Dominica	The Dominican Rep.	1978
The Solomon Islands		1978
St Lucia		1979
St Vincent and Grenadines		1979
Antigua		1981
British Honduras	Belize	1981
Vanuatu		1981
St Kitts and Nevis		1983

1 Burma (now Myanmar) became independent of India in 1948.
2 Bangladesh became independent of Pakistan in 1971.
3 Singapore became independent of Malaysia in 1965.
4 S. Rhodesia made Unilateral Declaration of Independence in 1965. Became formally independent as Zimbabwe in 1079.

Figure 8.1 The British Commonwealth, 1967

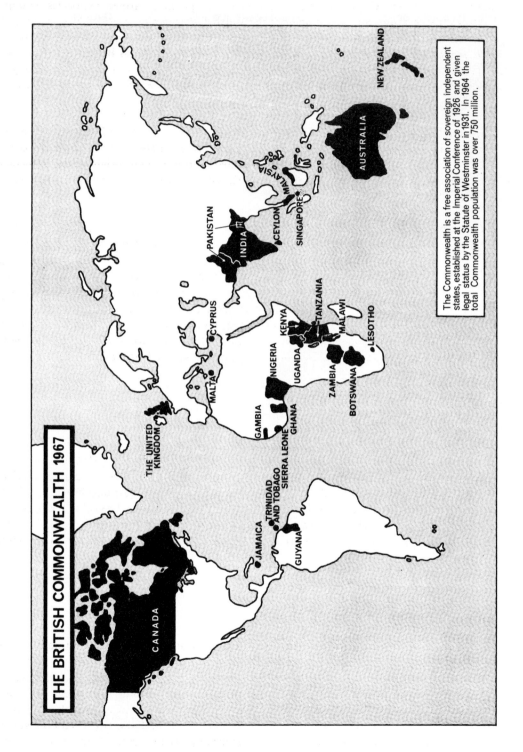

THE BRITISH COMMONWEALTH 1967

The Commonwealth is a free association of sovereign independent states, established at the Imperial Conference of 1926 and given legal status by the Statute of Westminster in 1931. In 1964 the total Commonwealth population was over 750 million.

In response, in 1947, the USA issued the Truman Doctrine 'it must be the policy of the US to support free peoples who are resisting attempted subjugation by armed minorities or outside pressures [i.e. communism]' and developed the Marshall Plan, which provided $12 billion for the economic recovery of Western Europe as a whole. As Britain was undergoing a serious economic crisis at the time, Marshall Aid 'was like a lifeline to a sinking man', as Bevin put it. The risings in Turkey and Greece were put down and Britain had successfully handed some of her great-power responsibilities to the USA, leaving herself freer to concentrate on controlling her restive Empire.

In Eastern Europe meanwhile, Britain and the USA were unable to prevent Bulgaria, Hungary and Romania being reduced to Soviet satellites. In February 1948, a Soviet-backed coup in Czechoslovakia led to the Brussels pact which united France, Britain, Belgium, the Netherlands and Luxembourg for defensive purposes. Bevin designed it as the first step towards a formal alliance with the USA.

The issue of Germany finally provoked the '**Cold War**'. Although they had little sympathy for the Germans, Labour realised the importance of stimulating economic recovery in the devastated regions of Central Europe and so called for Germany to be reunited. The USSR refused to give up control of her sector and then in 1948 cut off access to the western sectors of Berlin, which were inside the Russian zone. For a year the West flew in supplies and the 'Berlin airlift' managed to keep the city fed, watered and heated. US B-29s armed with atomic bombs were based in East Anglia and the USA formed the **North Atlantic Treaty Organisation** (NATO) with Western Europe and Canada. In this way Britain gained US commitment to the defence of Western Europe, despite the objections of the left, who disliked Britain's perceived subservience to the USA.

 ## The Korean war

After Mao's Communist revolution in China in 1949, the invasion of South Korea by the North was seen as part of the Communist global strategy of aggression. The USA felt they must act and British support was 'instantaneous and unqualified', although Attlee met Truman to make sure the war did not spill over into China or involve the use of nuclear weapons. In the conflict 686 British troops died and the North Koreans were expelled from South Korea. The rise in armaments spending produced the **balance of payments** crisis which itself forced the Labour Chancellor, Hugh Gaitskell to cut government spending, most controversially by introducing NHS prescription charges.

 ## The 'special relationship'

After Britain's support in the Korean War, the USA came to look on Britain as her firmest European ally. Eisenhower, who became President in 1953 and swiftly succeeded in carrying out his election pledge to end the Korean War, consulted closely with the new Conservative foreign minister, Anthony Eden over issues such as the French withdrawal from, and subsequent division of, Vietnam. Eisenhower also accepted Eden's suggestion that in exchange for allowing West Germany to rearm in order to contain Soviet hopes for expansion, she should join NATO and the Western European Union (WEU). As a result of this agreement, Britain based 50,000 troops in West Germany, but succeeded in securing more than 300,000 American troops there as well.

The only serious failure of the 'special relationship' came in the Suez Affair of 1956, when Britain attempted to act without consultation with any of the international bodies of which it was a member, such as the United Nations, NATO or the Commonwealth. Most seriously of all, she had attempted to pursue a dangerous policy, independent of the United States. Unforgivably in Eisenhower's eyes, Eden had also lost the West the moral high ground that it had gained over the USSR when the Russians had attempted to use force to control Hungary. With the media's attention focused on Egypt, the Russians chose to use the opportunity to send tanks back into Budapest. The response of the USA, to threaten Britain's economic stability until she backed down and withdrew her troops, demonstrated how little room for unilateral action Britain now had. Never again did Britain attempt such an action, and from this point on she remained a strong supporter of the USA in the **Cold War**. Macmillan worked hard to mend the relationship with USA after he became Prime Minister. He visited Eisenhower at Bermuda in March 1957 and reached agreements on joint targeting of nuclear weapons and managed to persuade the President to allow for the free exchange of nuclear weapons research. Luckily for Macmillan, the USA had been shocked by the launch of the Russian Sputnik satellite, and they were keen to co-operate. As a consequence Britain got access to American missile technology. In particular, Macmillan struck up an unlikely friendship with John F. Kennedy, President from 1961 until his assassination in 1963, which led to the Americans agreeing to allow Britain access to US Polaris technology. This certainly saved Macmillan much embarrassment after the cancellation of the British Blue Streak nuclear missile system, but it did not endear Macmillan to President de Gaulle of France, who resented the close Anglo-American relationship and used it as a key reason for rejecting Britain's application to join the European Economic Community in 1963.

When Labour took over in 1964, Wilson did not enjoy the same rapport with President Lyndon Johnson, Kennedy's replacement. Wilson was not an enthusiastic Cold Warrior, but he did want to try and maintain Britain's role east of Suez, which had the support of the Americans, who saw Britain as a useful ally in the Gulf and the Far East in holding back the spread of communist regimes. After the economic problems of 1966 and especially the **devaluation** of 1967 however, Wilson had to reverse this policy and withdraw as he now needed to concentrate on economic difficulties at home. He also earned Johnson's permanent ire when he refused to send British troops to help the Americans in Vietnam, despite the presence there of Australian forces. In 1965, following Johnson's unofficial declaration of war in the Gulf of Tonkin resolution, Wilson advised the US government not to get involved any further in the conflict. The American Secretary of State was furious and responded bitterly, 'If the Russians invade Sussex, don't expect us to come and help you'. In addition, Britain and USA began to disagree in their policy in the Middle East. In the 1967 and 1973 Arab-Israeli Wars, the USA was keen to support their ally, Israel, and to use British bases to send supplies to her. Britain, who favoured a much more balanced negotiated approach, largely because of her fears of disruption to Arab oil supplies, refused to allow the use of British bases. The USA increasingly began to pursue her policy in the Middle East without consulting Britain, even ordering her troops to a state of high nuclear alert in 1973, again without consultation with her Western allies. In the 1970s, as Britain disengaged from her commitments east of Suez, the special relationship became less important for both America and Britain, especially in a time of **détente** with the Soviet and Chinese communist regimes. With the success of her application to the EEC in 1973, Britain began to focus her chief defence priorities on Europe and to distance herself from US policy.

Britain's defence policy in a nuclear age

In terms of conventional forces, Britain found herself even more overstretched after the Second World War than she was before it. Not only were more troops needed in the restive parts of the Empire, but she had to maintain occupation forces in Trieste, Libya, Germany and Austria. The granting of independence to India in 1947 did not help Britain either, as she could no longer call on the Indian Army to help police other colonies in the Middle and Far East. Britain was forced to reintroduce conscription in 1946, only a year after abolishing it, and even then was not able to cope with the scale of the civil war in Palestine. It was therefore, not surprising that both the Chiefs of Staff and successive governments should look to nuclear weapons as offering a cheaper alternative in such a situation.

In 1946, the USA placed restrictions on the sharing of nuclear secrets, despite the role of British scientists in the 'Manhattan Project' which had developed the atom bombs used on Hiroshima and Nagasaki in 1945. Consequently, the British Cabinet decided, in secret, to order the production of a British atomic bomb. Britain exploded their first atomic bomb in the Pacific in October 1952. The Labour government also ordered the construction of a fleet of long range jet bombers – the Vulcan, the Victor and the Valiant ('the V-bombers') in order to be able to bomb the Soviet Union.

With the outbreak of the Korean War, Britain began to rearm even more rapidly, and, by 1954, when she began research on the hydrogen bomb she was spending as much on defence as she had spent during the Second World War. The purpose for all this expense was, however called into question by the failure of the British expeditionary force to secure the Suez Canal in 1956. As the new Prime Minister, Harold Macmillan wanted to concentrate on the economy at home, he appointed Duncan Sandys as Minister of Defence. Sandys won approval for his White Paper, 'Defence: Outline of Future Policy', which advocated a dramatic reduction in conventional forces, the ending of conscription and concentration on nuclear forces (Britain had just successfully tested its first hydrogen bomb). The only difficulty with this policy was that the delivery of British nuclear weapons depended on the V-bombers which became vulnerable to the improved Soviet air defence systems, which were demonstrated in 1960, when an American U-2 spy plane was shot down over the USSR. The Conservative government therefore embarked on the construction of a British missile delivery system called Blue Streak. In the meantime, Macmillan agreed that 60 American 'Thor' missiles would be stationed in Britain, but that they could only be launched with the consent of the British government. In gratitude, President Eisenhower allowed the resumption of co-operation between British and American scientists on nuclear technology. This renewed co-operation was fortunately timed for Britain as Macmillan's government was forced to scrap the Blue Streak, due to its expense and vulnerability to Soviet defences. Macmillan was able, first, to gain use of American Skybolt missiles which could be fired by the V-bombers, and then, when America cancelled Skybolt, to be provided with Polaris, submarine-launched missiles. Britain still had a viable nuclear defence force, but, by now, it was extremely questionable how independent that force was.

Despite support among the left wing of the Labour party for unilateral nuclear disarmament, the bulk of the party realised that, in her straitened circumstances, nuclear weapons allowed Britain to maintain a world role that she would otherwise lose. Even Aneurin Bevan, the champion of the Labour left in the 1950s, when he became shadow Colonial Secretary in 1956, argued that to scrap the bomb would be 'to send the British Foreign Secretary naked into the conference

Table 8.3 **Percentage of research and development budget spent on defence**

Country	1963–65	1966–70	1971–75	1976–79
Britain	34.5	25.6	28.9	29.3
USA	40.6	31.9	27.7	25.4
France	26.2	22.5	18.4	19.6
Japan	0.9	0.9	0.7	0.6

Table 8.4 **British defence spending as a percentage of gross national product**

1948	7.1	1959	6.4	1970	4.8
1949	6.5	1960	6.3	1971	4.8
1950	6.6	1961	6.3	1972	4.8
1951	7.9	1962	6.4	1973	4.7
1952	9.8	1963	6.2	1974	4.9
1953	9.7	1964	5.9	1975	4.9
1954	9.2	1965	5.9	1976	4.9
1955	7.9	1966	5.8	1977	4.8
1956	7.8	1967	5.9	1978	4.6
1957	6.9	1968	5.6		
1958	6.7	1969	4.9		

chamber'. When Wilson became Prime Minister in 1964, therefore, he cancelled only one of the five nuclear submarines that the Conservatives had ordered, stating that 'we cannot afford to relinquish our world role'. Eventually, financial strain meant that Britain had to scrap her aircraft carriers and cancel orders for American fighter bombers, and Wilson began to put more emphasis on Britain's role as part of NATO and as part of a common Western European defence policy.

With the admission to the EEC under Edward Heath, this policy continued (although Heath saved one of the aircraft carriers due to be scrapped), especially as the onset of the oil crisis in 1973 and the turmoil caused by the miners' strike eliminated any possibility of increased defence spending. When Labour came back to power in 1974, they pledged that Polaris would not be replaced when it was decommissioned in 1980 and gave maximum priority to Britain's role in NATO and the protection of the North Sea and the English Channel. It was only with Callaghan that the ongoing defence cuts which had begun with Sandys White Paper in 1957 were finally halted and in secret he agreed to the deployment of new cruise missiles in Britain, but it was the Thatcher government that actually publicly reversed the policy of defence cuts. She dramatically increased defence spending, employing the same argument that Gaitskell and Attlee had done in 1950: that Soviet aggression had to be challenged, thus bringing post-war defence policy almost completely full circle.

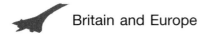 ## Britain and Europe

In an attempt to prevent another catastrophic European war, six countries of Europe (France, Belgium, the Netherlands, Italy, West Germany and Luxembourg) decided to make future conflict impossible by pooling their iron, steel and coal resources. The subsequent European Coal and Steel Community (ECSC), designed by the French Foreign Minister, Robert Schumann and founded in 1951 was the basis on which the European Economic Community (EEC) was founded in 1958, following the Treaty of Rome of 1957. Under the terms of the Treaty of Rome, regulations, monetary policies, agriculture and indirect taxes of the member states were harmonised. Britain, in particular Winston Churchill, had been an enthusiastic sponsor of European co-operation, but Britain was unsure about joining. Labour's Foreign Secretary, Bevin was pre-occupied with countering the menace of Russia and regarded the proposal for a Council of Europe as an unwelcome and distracting threat to Britain's independence. As he famously put it, 'if you open that Pandora's box, you never know what Trojan horses will jump out'. The fear of losing Britain's sovereignty (the control of domestic and foreign policy) was the main reason why Labour didn't participate in the ECSC, but Britain also felt closer ties with her wartime ally, USA, in the so-called 'special relationship'. Britain also had a considerable imperial role, especially in Africa, as well as economic links to the now independent Commonwealth countries. Britain therefore hesitated in 1955 when the negotiations for the formation of the EEC were held at Messina in Sicily and the European Community was founded without her.

By the early 1960s, it was acknowledged that this had been a mistake as Britain's inability to act as an independent world power was shown up in the humiliation of the Suez crisis. The members of the EEC, especially the French, doubted Britain's commitment to the ideals of the Treaty of Rome, however, especially as Britain had been behind the establishment of a less ambitious rival union, the European Free Trade Association (EFTA) in 1960. It was, therefore, no great surprise that Macmillan's application for membership was vetoed by de Gaulle of France in January 1963. Most British people did not see the failure to join as a serious set-back at the time, however, and resentment of de Gaulle's behaviour was relatively mild, as best expressed in the 1964 song *All Gall*, by Michael Flanders and Donald Swann, (to the tune of *Nick-Nack Paddy-wack*)

Figure 8.2
Wilson's failure to join the EEC, 1968

> . . . This old man, he played six,
> France and England they won't mix.
> 'Eyetie, Benelux, Germany and me,
> that's my market recipe . . .'
> . . . This old man, nine and ten
> he'll play nick 'till God knows when.
> Cognac, Armagnac, Burgundy and Beaune,
> This old man thinks he's Saint Joan!

During the 1960s both Conservative and Labour governments continued to pursue membership. In 1967 Wilson's government applied again, but De Gaulle refused again. De Gaulle was eventually forced to resign in 1969, and the subsequent EEC summit meeting at the Hague advocated further expansion of the community so Heath's new Conservative government of 1970 immediately renewed its application.

Figure 8.3 **Britain and Europe, 1945–72**

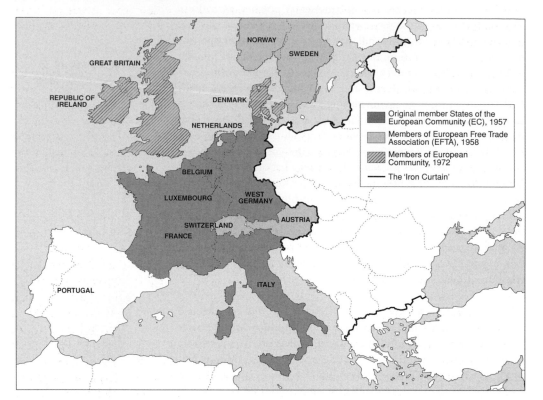

Britain's application was accepted by the other EEC members in 1971 and the Commons voted in favour of membership by a majority of 112. Heath signed the Treaty of Accession in January 1972. Parliament then had to legislate to bring British law into line with European law in the 1972 European Communities Act. Some Conservatives actively opposed this measure and it only passed with Labour support. Britain became a full member of the EEC on 1 January 1973 when Denmark and Ireland also joined.

Part 2: Essays

1. Foreign policy under Labour 1945–51 (OCR)

Was Bevin's foreign policy a sensible reaction to Britain's circumstances after the Second World War?

(90 marks)

Ernest Bevin's tenure at the Foreign Office between 1945 and 1950 has provoked a variety of responses from observers. Even before his death, the *Observer* newspaper called him a 'great' Foreign Secretary, and his biographer, Alan Bullock concluded his study by quoting Attlee that 'He [Bevin] was a great Englishman', adding 'there are no words which better sum up his career'.

Since the 1970s, however, historians have become more critical of his conduct of policy, believing that he attempted to continue Britain's traditional world role at a time when it was no longer economically realistic to do so. It is therefore best to assess Bevin's career in the context of Britain's post-world position.

Britain found herself, by 1945, deeply in debt, chiefly to the USA, with an overextended and often rebellious Empire and an economy exhausted by six years of continual war effort. Bevin's party had won power in a landslide election, promising the construction of an extensive welfare system at home, which placed further financial strain on her foreign policy. Consequently Britain rapidly demobilised, ending conscription in 1945 and reducing her armed forces to under one million men. Although some observers wondered whether these circumstances would lead to a more socialist and less imperial approach to foreign affairs, Bevin was soon to demonstrate his commitment to Britain's Great Power status.

When the USA decided to end collaboration with Britain on the development of atomic weapons in 1946, Bevin reacted angrily, asserting that Britain 'could not afford to acquiesce in an American monopoly of this new development'. After Hiroshima, it was clear that great power status depended upon possession of nuclear weapons, and for Britain, in particular, with her limited economic and military strength after the war, it would provide the means of ensuring her continued role on the world stage. In October 1946 Bevin therefore decided, 'we've got to have this thing over here, whatever it costs'. Although Britain's control of both India and Palestine was abandoned, Bevin was keen to support action to limit opposition elsewhere. In areas with wholly native populations, such as Gold Coast, he supported attempts to retain control through the inclusion of black leaders in the legislative process. But in colonies with substantial white settlement such as Kenya or with vital economic resources such as Malaya, military and police action was used against opponents. For Bevin, Britain's world role was based on her imperial and Commonwealth links and he had no intention of weakening any of these. During the war, Britain was alarmed by the intentions of the Soviets in Eastern Europe. Although Stalin had signed the Declaration of Liberated Europe at Yalta in February 1945, Poland and Romania had had communist regimes forced upon them. Neither Britain, France nor the USA had sufficient forces in Europe to attempt to intervene. By 1946, Britain was forced to reintroduce conscription. Bevin, therefore chose to draw closer to her European allies, signing the Brussels Treaty of mutual defence in March 1948 with France, Belgium and Holland.

Bevin was acutely aware, however, that none of the Western European countries had the resources to resist a full scale Soviet assault. He therefore chose to involve the USA, the only atomic power at that time, in the formation of European defence. First, in the case of Greece and Turkey, where Britain was supporting anti-communist forces, she announced that, due to the economic crisis in Britain in 1947, she would abandon her role. This forced the American President to issue the 'Truman doctrine', committing the USA to give $400 million to aid 'free people . . . resisting attempted subjugation'. Second, he seized on a speech by the US Secretary of State, George Marshall, suggesting that American help pay for economic reconstruction and organized a common response from Western Europe that resulted in $12 billion of aid, $3.2 billion for Britain. This played a huge role in helping the British economy to rebuild and the successful operation of the fledgling Welfare State. It also solved the majority of the food shortages in Europe and began effective reconstruction on the continent.

Finally, with the communist takeover in Czechoslovakia and then Stalin's aggressive response to the introduction of the Deutsche Mark into the Western zones of Berlin, as road links to the city were closed in 1948 , Bevin was able to present the USA with what seemed clear cases of attempted Soviet expansion. The USA therefore participated willingly in the subsequent 'air-lift' to keep Berlin supplied for the next 11 months. American B-29 atom-bomb carrying planes were allowed use of four airfields in East Anglia from July 1948. Most importantly of all for Britain's security, America and the Western allies formed the **North Atlantic Treaty Organisation** (NATO). Bevin now had the USA with its vast economic wealth and military arsenal committed to the defence of Western Europe for at least ten years.

With the USA taking a leading role in the defence of Europe, it was expected that a quid pro quo arrangement would apply, whereby Britain would assist America in containing the perceived threat of communist expansion, outside the continent. When South Korea appealed to the United Nations for assistance against an invasion by North Korea, Britain supported America in the Security Council in sending military aid. Britain sent over 10,000 ground and naval troops, the largest non-American force, and helped to drive the North Korean forces back.

It is therefore most accurate to see Bevin as successfully reducing Britain's commitments and involving the USA in the vital military and economic defence of Western Europe against the perceived expansionism of the Soviet Union, whilst at the same time managing to retain some degree of independence in Britain's defence and foreign policy. In the medium and long terms, of course, such an attempt to retain Britain's world role was to prove unfeasible, as the Suez crisis clearly demonstrated. Perhaps both judgements of Bevin have some truth in them and he proved too successful a foreign minister for a country with such shrunken resources.

2. Britain's defence policy in the 1960s and 1970s (AQA)

Read the following quote from *The Defence of the Realm: Britain in the Nuclear Age* by Michael Dockerill and then answer the questions which follow:

While Britain's defence planning has often been characterised by confusion and muddle, the changes that have taken place can be seen in hindsight as sensible adjustments to changing circumstances. Most of the crucial decisions which were taken were not sudden improvisations but were the product of much heart searching and careful consideration of the alternatives. Clearly, once the decision was made to grant independence to Britain's remaining colonial empire after 1958 and to downgrade Britain's role in the Middle East and the Gulf by 1966, the maintenance of a large garrison and intervention forces was no longer sensible.

a) **What was Britain's role in the Middle East and the Gulf before 1966?** (3 marks)
b) **Why did successive governments reduce defence spending after 1957?** (7 marks)
c) **Is it accurate to describe the government's defence policy after 1957 as 'sensible adjustments to changing circumstances'?** (15 marks)

a) After the failure of her attempt to reassert control of the Suez Canal in 1956, Britain still had a number of bases in the area. Aden was the most important of these and Britain had offered 'protection' to the tribes of southern Yemen in order to secure their hold on the area. Britain also had treaties, promising defence to the Arab sheikdoms around the Persian Gulf such as Bahrain, Kuwait and Qatar.

b) Britain's defence priorities had begun to shift with the publication of the White Paper on Defence by the Conservative defence minister, Duncan Sandys, in April 1957. Given the relatively fragile state of the economy which the Suez crisis had exposed, the Chiefs of Staff recommended reducing Britain's commitment to NATO by a third, and Sandys pointed out that spending 10 per cent of Britain's gross national income on defence was unsustainable and unrealistic. As the two major post-war military engagements in Malaya and Kenya came to an end and Macmillan was increasingly recognising the need to give independence to those colonies who sought it, attention could focus instead on confronting the Warsaw Pact in Europe.

Facing a nuclear power across the frontier in Germany, Britain could therefore concentrate on developing her independent nuclear deterrent and the means of delivering it. As a result, national service, in place since 1939, was phased out and funding given instead to missile delivery research. Unfortunately the proposed long range ballistic missile, Blue Streak proved even more expensive than anticipated and the project had to be abandoned in 1960, having already cost £65 million. Britain became dependent on purchasing American missile technology instead, first Thor air-to-ground missiles, then, following the cancellation of the Skybolt missile, the submarine-launched, Polaris system.

Britain's spending on land and sea forces actually increased after 1960, however, as her decolonisation process needed military assistance in Kuwait, Kenya, Tanzania, Malaysia and Uganda. This was only a temporary expedient, however, and when Wilson's Labour government came to power in 1964, they were determined to cut defence spending further. At first the Defence Secretary, Denis Healey, cut the budget from 6 per cent to 7 per cent of the GNP, but with the **balance of payments** crises of 1966 and 1967, Wilson had to abandon Britain's role 'East of Suez', ending the British presence in Aden and Malaysia. Although many leftwing Labour ministers welcomed this retreat from Empire, it clearly had been caused by economic, rather than ideological motives.

c) Macmillan, in carrying out his so-called foreign policy 'revolution' between 1957 and 1959, was clearly recognising the limitations of Britain's economic and strategic position following the Suez crisis of 1956. Although it is not clear that the failure in Egypt led directly to a shift in policy, Macmillan had clearly accepted that the British economy could not sustain massive defence spending after its weaknesses were exposed by America's financial sanctions. He therefore commissioned Sandys' White Paper and helped force it through in the face of bitter opposition from the service chiefs. In many ways, this review of defence allocation was long overdue, as Britain's extensive conventional armed forces were increasingly redundant in the **Cold War**, dominated by nuclear confrontation. On the other hand, it did still accept that Britain would continue to maintain its existing military commitments outside Europe. It was only with the emergencies in Cyprus, East Africa and the Gulf States that Britain found that it no longer had the manpower or the funds to honour its commitments to its former colonies and to NATO in Germany, and was forced, reluctantly, to abandon its role East of Suez and concentrate on Europe instead.

Britain was also forced to accept limitations on its nuclear defences. As Soviet anti-aircraft technology improved, as spectacularly demonstrated in the U-2 incident in 1960, British nuclear bombers became obsolete. Macmillan managed to patch up relations with Eisenhower after Suez, in order to secure the use of Skybolt air-to-ground missiles to extend the bombers' operational life, after Britain had found the cost of developing their own inter-continental ballistic missile, Blue Streak, too expensive to bear. The new President, Kennedy had, however, scrapped Skybolt, forcing Macmillan to threaten to pull Britain out of NATO, if a replacement was not forthcoming. When Kennedy met Macmillan at Nassau in 1961, the American President insisted that Polaris ought to be controlled by NATO, but Macmillan managed to persuade him to allow Britain unilateral control, 'where supreme national interests are at stake', thus retaining at least an element of independence to Britain's nuclear deterrent.

Therefore, although attempting to maintain Britain's role East of Suez, on the part of both Macmillan and Wilson was not especially realistic, in light of the state of the British economy and the cuts imposed by Sandys' White Paper and Healey's review in 1965, Britain's approach to defence was essentially pragmatic. Britain went from a defence strategy based on expensive and outmoded Second World War technology and a large conscripted army to one dependent on the latest weapons systems and a small, highly skilled armed force. As a result, Britain was one of the most well-defended states by the late 1970s. The cost of this was the abandonment of her greater world role, but given Britain's economic conditions, that seems to have been a very sensible decision, given that the priorities of the voters in that democratic state clearly now lay elsewhere.

3. Britain and Europe (EDEXCEL)

a)   **Explain why Britain did not join the EEC in 1957.**   **(30 marks)**
b)   **Why was Britain unable to became a member of the EEC until 1973?**   **(30 marks)**

(Total: 60 marks)

a)   Britain had participated in all the major international agreements after the Second World War, such as the founding of the United Nations, NATO and the Council of Europe, but they did not want to join the European Coal and Steel Community (ECSC) which was established by six states (France, West Germany, Italy, Holland, Belgium and Luxembourg) in 1951.

Britain rejected the requests of Jean Monnet and Konrad Adenauer, to join Robert Schumann's scheme, largely because the British Foreign Secretary of the time, Ernest Bevin, was convinced that the scheme was not in Britain's interests. As the political representatives of organised labour, the Labour Party was concerned that a policy that required the pooling of coal and steel resources would prove unpopular with the trade unions and would nullify the benefits that it was hoped would result from nationalising these two areas. The Schumann plan required the participating countries to give up some aspects of their sovereignty, and, although Britain was certainly interested in European integration, she was not prepared to go this far. Since the signing of the NATO agreement, Bevin, as well as his Labour and Conservative successors tended to regard the USA as a more important economic and strategic ally. There was much doubt over how much the European Community could achieve in a Europe still recovering from the devastation of a World War and with half of Europe (and a third of Germany) inaccessible behind the **Iron Curtain**. With her own economic difficulties, Britain was reluctant to risk joining an organisation that might prove a major financial burden to her. Britain was therefore prepared to approve the creation of the ECSC, in order to speed reconstruction in Europe, but not to participate in it herself, especially as Schumann himself was not keen to involve Britain. By the time talks were held at Messina in 1955, which led to the creation of the European Economic Community (EEC), Britain had been drawn into closer co-operation with Europe. Fear of the intentions of the Warsaw Pact countries had drawn Britain's defence policy closer to Western Europe. The 1955 Paris Accords created the Western European Union (including West Germany) and committed Britain to keeping 50,000 troops on mainland Western Europe for 50 years. However, this changing military attitude was not matched by a change in Britain's economic strategy. Britain's achievement in winning the war continued to mask the true state of Britain's economic condition and her future role in the world. Mainland Europe's experience of occupation and liberation was felt by most British politicians and voters to have created entirely different economic conditions there and what was best for the rest of Europe was not necessarily best for Britain. Second, the British Empire and Commonwealth still had prior claims on Britain's economic, political and even emotional attention, and it was certainly not intended in 1955 that there should be as rapid a decolonisation programme as subsequently occurred. Therefore, Britain only sent observers to the Messina negotiations, with the consequence that, when the Treaty of Rome was signed in 1957, Britain was not among the signatories.

b) Britain's reaction to the Treaty of Rome had been first to try to negotiate a European Free Trade agreement, but this was rejected by the six founder members, led by the new President of France, General de Gaulle. Britain then established the European Free Trade Association (EFTA) as a rival group to the EEC with Austria, Denmark, Norway, Portugal, Sweden and Switzerland. By 1961, however, Britain realised that she had to join the EEC. Britain was rapidly withdrawing from her Empire and reducing her defence spending, and she looked enviously at the rapid rate of economic growth that 'the six' were enjoying. The Suez crisis had revealed the limitations of the 'special relationship' with the USA and Britain had found it necessary to accelerate decolonisation, which was rapidly producing a Commonwealth which was as much a liability as it was an asset. Macmillan therefore saw membership of the EEC as a means of developing Britain's interests at a time when other avenues were proving disappointing. When his government formally applied for membership, however, de Gaulle argued that Britain's links with EFTA and the Commonwealth proved they were not serious in doing so. He was also concerned that if Britain joined the EEC they would be, as the French Agricultural minister put it, 'two cocks in the henhouse'. De Gaulle therefore vetoed the British application in 1963.

Despite some reservations on the left wing of his party, Labour's Prime Minister, Harold Wilson, realised the economic necessity of joining the EEC and renewed Britain's application in 1967. He was, however, unable to persuade the other five members that Britain's membership was so important that they should risk France withdrawing and support his application. De Gaulle, stated, quite accurately, that little had changed since 1961. By now, however, the other members of the EEC were getting annoyed by de Gaulle's dictatorial approach, and when a domestic crisis in France forced his resignation in 1969, they invited Britain to re-apply. Wilson was reluctant however, as the other members insisted on a large financial contribution to the EEC's **Common Agricultural Policy** (CAP). It was therefore left to Edward Heath, a committed pro-European, to apply for entry for a third time. The new French President, Georges Pompidou and Heath held talks and agreed that Britain's contribution to the CAP should be fixed at a later date. Consequently, Britain's application was accepted and Britain signed up to the Treaty of Rome and joined the EEC on January 1, 1973.

4. The end of Empire (OCR)

When did Britain accept the need for decolonisation after 1945?   (Total: 90 marks)

In South East Asia, the British colonies had been overrun with surprising ease by the supposedly inferior troops of another Asian state, Japan. Although the bulk of colonial forces had stayed impressively loyal to the British authorities, the blow to Britain's prestige of the loss of Malaya, Hong Kong, Borneo, Burma and most of all, Singapore was considerable, as was the fact that when the Japanese surrendered in August 1945, most of the these territories were still in Japanese hands. Although the British reimposed their rule, the USA forced the Dutch to grant independence to their colonies, giving those ruled again by the British and French, an example to aspire towards. Although the granting of self-government to India, Pakistan, Burma and Ceylon in 1947 was a key moment in the retreat from Empire, it was not Labour's intention that this should lead inevitably to the granting of independence for all her colonies, at least not in the short term. After all, the white-dominated **Dominion** territories had been granted self-government during the nineteenth century, while the Empire had grown to its peak. The Labour government recognised that Britain now lacked the military and financial power to enforce their rule over a people which seemed unwilling to co-operate with it. In addition, the people of Britain seemed unwilling to spend the lives of their troops and their resources on maintaining an Empire, when domestic reconstruction and the nascent **Welfare State** were requiring large contributions from primary taxation.

However, once India had gained her independence, other nationalists began to increase their demands, hoping for a similar result. Even in Africa, there were nationalist riots in the Gold Coast in 1948, which led to the granting of a new constitution, with an African majority on the legislative council, in 1950. This was, however, designed to win the support of the moderate Western-educated nationalist leaders and thus avoid violent confrontation, rather than to pave the way towards immediate independence.

In colonial territories where British rule was violently challenged, she fought to protect her interests. In Malaya, a state of emergency was declared after the assassination of the High Commissioner, Henry Gurney, by the Malaya Communist Party. Britain fought a protracted guerrilla war. In order to retain the support of the more moderate Malay population, she had to allow majority elections for the Legislative Assembly, but Britain ensured her economic and security interests were guaranteed. In Kenya, Britain fought a war against the Mau Mau, a violent form of nationalism among the majority Kikuyu tribe, which was aimed as much against other Africans and 'loyalist' Kikuyu as white settlers and British rule. A further war was fought against Greek nationalists in Cyprus. In all these and other areas where large-scale opposition to British rule was found, Britain's policy was not that of continued monopolistic rule by Whitehall, but an attempt to preserve British influence, preferably through some direct control, but essentially through compromise with moderate, pro-Western native politicians, to whom self-government would eventually be handed, but not for at least a decade.

After the Suez crisis of 1956, Prime Minister Macmillan at first attempted to continue with a hardline policy towards the nationalist forces attempting to speed the pace towards independence in Britain's colonies. In Kenya, the number of troops sent to crush the Mau Mau rising was increased and more troops were sent to Cyprus. Having won the 1959 election however, he was able to take a more realistic approach to Britain's problems. With continuing economic weakness at home and the threat of Soviet communism to confront in Europe, Macmillan knew that Britain lacked the military strength to control an Empire that no longer wanted such close association with the 'motherland'. During the Suez crisis, the USA had clearly indicated that they would not allow Britain to pursue an independent policy towards its colonies where it conflicted with American interests. Additionally, after Belgium's withdrawal from the Congo in 1960, the number of countries in Africa calling for independence had dramatically increased. Faced with a number of possible colonial wars such as the French were still fighting in Algeria, Macmillan decided it would be better to keep on good terms with the colonies by granting independence and then inviting them to join the Commonwealth, as had been successfully achieved with Malaysia, Sudan and Ghana. As Iain MacLeod, Macmillan's Colonial Secretary put it, 'we could not possibly have held by force our territories in Africa'. Finally, Macmillan had decided that Britain's future prosperity required admission to the European Economic Community, and that the colonies were more of an economic burden than an asset. It would be better to do as the USA did and to exercise influence over the former colonies by economic means, a policy described as 'neo-colonialism'. Therefore Macmillan and Macleod chose to grant independence to those colonies who demanded it, and between 1959 and 1964 Nigeria, Tanzania, Malawi, Zambia, Kenya and Jamaica all became independent. Despite the intentions of Harold Wilson, under Labour, the continued economic difficulties of Britain, meant that Britain's role 'East of Suez' was gradually abandoned, and in a revealing case of her reduced strength, she was unable to prevent the white settlers of Southern Rhodesia from breaking away from Britain's drive towards majority rule and declaring herself unilaterally independent. By the mid-1970s all that remained of the British Empire were a few small island properties and a number of strategically or economically important bases, such as the Falkland Islands, Hong Kong and Gibraltar. In less than 20 years, the largest Empire in the world had been swiftly abandoned, largely, but not exclusively because of the economic and social priorities of the 'mother-country'.

Additional essay questions

1. Foreign policy under Labour 1945–51 (AQA)

Read the following source and then answer the questions which follow.

It was Bevin, above all, who saw to it that the Foreign Office view of Britain's place in the world prevailed. The result was that unlike her economic rivals, apart from USA, the British economy has had to service a world role that in the end it just could not sustain.

From *Britain and the Cold War* by Peter J. Taylor, 1990

a) **What is meant by 'the Foreign Office view of Britain's place in the world' in the context of post-war international relations?** **(3 marks)**
b) **Explain why the British economy was unable to support Britain's attempts to fully maintain a world role between 1945 and 1951.** **(7 marks)**
c) **Explain why and in what ways British Foreign Policy changed between 1945 and 1951.** **(15 marks)**

2. Britain's defence policy in the 1960s and 1970s (EDEXCEL)

a) **Analyse the reasons why Britain signed the Nassau agreement with the United States in 1962.** **(30 marks)**
b) **Did Britain have any alternative but to announce the end of her commitments 'East of Suez' in 1968?** **(30 marks)**

(Total: 60 marks)

Essay plan

a)   In 1962, Macmillan signed the Nassau agreement with President Kennedy, under which the USA agreed to sell the submarine-based Polaris missile system under favourable terms. A necessary conclusion to the 1950s which had seen greater US and British co-operation on nuclear weapons, but a failure by Britain to produce an independent delivery system.

After successfully testing its own atomic bomb in 1952 and its own H-bomb in 1957, Britain had an independent nuclear weapons capacity. This was necessary as the US McMahon Act of 1946 had ended collaboration with Britain on atomic research. The problem for Britain was how to successfully threaten to deliver its atomic and hydrogen weapons.

Britain developed the V- force – long range nuclear bombers, such as the Vulcan and Valiant and Victor bombers. The bombers became increasingly vulnerable to Soviet anti-aircraft missiles however and the proposed Avro-730 supersonic bombers were cancelled as part of the reduction of defence spending carried out by Duncan Sandys.

Macmillan met with Eisenhower and secured the deployment of 60 Thor intermediate ballistic missiles in Britain –not an independent force, as it required US as well as British authorisation to launch, but this was intended as a short-term solution to the delivery problem. Britain also secured an agreement on US-British co-operation on atomic defence.

Britain aimed to produce the Blue Streak missile, but the costs proved too much as the economy faltered in 1960. Blue Streak had been found to be vulnerable to Soviet defence missiles and its storage in land silos made it vulnerable to first strikes by enemy forces.

In 1960, Macmillan went back to Eisenhower, and secured the Skybolt missile system which would be launched by the V-bombers. Macmillan also got a guarantee that in an emergency, the navy could use the submarine-based Polaris system, and Macmillan offered the US the use of a base in Scotland.

In 1961, however, President Kennedy cancelled Skybolt, and at Nassau Macmillan was forced to threaten Kennedy with Britain's withdrawal from NATO in order to win the right to use Polaris independently from the USA and NATO.

Conclusion – Britain's 'independent' nuclear deterrant was now wholly dependent on US delivery systems, leading de Gaulle to oppose Britain's application to join the EEC in 1962, as he felt Britain was too closely linked to the US. That Britain jeopardised their application in this way demonstrates how desperate they were to have access to Polaris technology.

b)   By 1964, when Labour came to power, Britain had gradually been withdrawing from her Imperial role for seven years, but Wilson recognised the strategic advantages of maintaining Britain's role east of Suez. It was felt, the greatest threat to Britain's interests from communist and nationalist forces were in Africa and Asia and so the bases at Aden and Singapore were to be maintained. Britain was encouraged by the USA as part of global anti-communist policy.

*After the economic problems of 1966 and especially the **devaluation** of 1967 however, Wilson had to reverse this policy and withdraw as he now needed to concentrate on economic difficulties at home. The cost of the maintenance of the bases was too high.*

*Political cost – concerns of voters – no longer as interested in the preservation of Britain's position abroad – more concerned with the growing unemployment, the waves of strikes, such as the damaging seamen's strike in 1966, and the legal reforms that created the **permissive society** – Britain becoming more insular.*

Internal problems in colonies – Bahrain, Kuwait; threats to British bases – Aden (from Yemen) and Singapore (from Indonesia).

Cost of nuclear arms race – 1966 defence review saw need to reduce proportion of spending on defence – Aden to be evacuated within a year. With 1967 devaluation crisis, Aden was immediately evacuated, and British presence in Singapore and Malaysia to be halved by 1971 and removed by mid-1970s.

Continued economic problems of 1968 led to announcement of withdrawal East of Suez to be organised by 1971. There was an alternative – Arab states had offered to help fund continued British presence in Aden and US had promised economic support for pound in exchange for Britain retaining its bases. Wilson had chosen to be seen to be concentrating on domestic issues and not to risk further entanglement which could prove expensive in the longer term.

 ## 3. Britain and Europe (OCR)

To what extent did Britain's failure to sign the Treaty of Rome lead to her subsequent failure to join until 1973?   (90 marks)

4. The end of Empire (EDEXCEL)

a) **Describe the reasons which led to the end of British rule in India.**   (30 marks)
b) **Why was Britain unwilling to grant independence to any other colony until 1957?**   (30 marks)

    (Total: 60 marks)

Essay plan

a)   India had been promised self-rule in return for her help in the war and had been moving towards increasing autonomy as a result of the 1919 and 1935 Government of India Acts. The nationalist Indian Congress Party had won most of the provincial elections of 1937 and was demanding further moves towards British withdrawal.

During the Second World War, Indian forces were vital to defending the Empire, especially after the fall of France, but the Congress ministers had resigned when the viceroy declared war on India's behalf, without consulting any Indian politicians. With the Japanese advances in spring 1942, India became exposed to attack and this, as well as the economic costs of war caused the British administration to become less popular. Congress called for Britain to 'quit India' in 1942, forcing Britain to arrest many of its leaders. Instead the Muslim League led by Jinnah, co-operated with the government, thus making Muslim demands for a separate homeland in the independent India more likely.

*The decisive factor in Indian independence was Labour's commitment to granting India independence after winning the election after the war. The USA was critical of British rule and India was proving an economic liability, especially with the costs of the **Cold War**, domestic reconstruction and the new **Welfare State**. Britain chose to rationalise the empire by retaining the areas that had economic potential and would not challenge British rule. Britain hurried the pace of independence, setting the date of June 1948 for withdrawal, regardless of whether the Congress and Muslim League could find a compromise to keep India whole.*

Jinnah would not accept a strong central government and Nehru, the Congress leader, would not accept an Indian federation, and would only accept partition if it took place by August 1947. In this way Pakistan and India were created, at the cost of 250,000 deaths in the communal violence that followed.

b)   Britain wished to capitalise on its remaining Imperial possessions after granting independence to India, quitting Palestine and reducing aid to anti-communists in Greece and Turkey. It needed a stronger 'sterling area' to build up dollar reserves to prevent the financial collapse which threatened Britain between 1945 and 1948. Sales of raw materials from the colonies such as rubber from Malaya and cocoa from the Gold Coast brought dollars into the area and Britain could buy the dollars in exchange for sterling that the colonies could only spend on British goods. Britain therefore wished to fully exploit the remaining colonial possession, not allow them any independence while they remained useful.

*The colonial office recruited 4,000 more staff between 1945 and 1948 in order to help develop the remaining colonies. A Colonial Development Corporation was set up in 1948 to increase colonial production and thus help the colonies' (and in turn Britain's) **balance of payments**. The largest development scheme, the East African Groundnut Scheme ended in failure, but the development of oil fields in Kuwait and other Gulf states significantly helped Britain's **balance of payments**.*

Britain therefore fought against nationalist movements which used violence in strategically important areas such as Aden, Cyprus and Kenya, while attempting to create native groups sympathetic to Britain, to which Britain could safely begin the gradual handing over of power, as happened in the Gold Coast with Nkrumah – which explains why the Gold Coast became the first African colony to gain independence in 1957.

*Britain also wished to hold onto her colonies to prevent the spread of communism. In Malaya, Britain fought a war against Chinese communist rebels from 1948. By this stage, the **Cold War** had begun and Britain received aid in this struggle from the USA. Similarly, Britain received help from the CIA in overthrowing the Iranian government of Mossadeq and in maintaining the British bases at Suez and Aden.*

The humiliating failure of the Suez campaign, which forced Britain to withdraw from Egypt undoubtedly made Britain realise that she would not be able to afford to continue to fight nationalists, either economically or politically. Equally, Britain's share of trade with its Empire was declining, while that with the USA and Europe was expanding – the Empire was proving a costly liability that Britain could no longer afford.

Part 3: Sources

 ### 1. The Suez crisis (OCR)

Source A: Cabinet minutes on the Suez crisis, 27 July 1956

The Cabinet –

1. Agreed that Her Majesty's Government should seek to secure, by the use of force if necessary, the reversal of the decision of the Egyptian Government to nationalise the Suez Canal Company
2. Invited the Prime Minister to inform Commonwealth High Commissioners in London of this decision later that day
3. Invited the Prime Minister to send a personal message to the President of the United States asking him to send a representative to London to discuss the situation with representatives of the United Kingdom and France.

Source B: The Sèvres Protocol, October 1956

The results of the conversations which took place at Sèvres from 22–24 October between the representatives of the Governments of the United Kingdom, the State of Israel and of France are the following:

1. The Israeli forces launch in the evening of 29 October 1956 a large scale attack on the Egyptian forces with the aim of reaching the [Suez] Canal Zone the following day.

2. On being appraised of these events, the British and French governments during the day of 30 October respectively and simultaneously make two appeals to the Egyptian government and the Israeli government on the following lines:

    A. To the Egyptian government:
       a) halt all acts of war
       b) withdraw all its troops ten miles from the Canal
       c) accept temporary occupation of key positions on the Canal by the Anglo-French forces to guarantee freedom of passage through the Canal by vessels of all nations until a final settlement.

    B. To the Israeli government
       a) halt all acts of war
       b) withdraw its troops ten miles to the east of the Canal.

In addition, the Israeli Government will be notified that the French and the British Governments have demanded of the Egyptian Government to accept the temporary occupation of key positions along the Canal by Anglo-French forces.

Source C: From a telephone call from President Eisenhower to Prime Minister Anthony Eden, 31 October, 1956

Is that you, Anthony? Well, this is President Eisenhower and I can only presume that you've gone out of your mind.

Source D: From the Official Soviet Note to the British Government, 5 November, 1956

We [the Soviet government] are fully determined to crush the aggressors and restore peace in the Middle East through the use of force. We hope at this critical moment you will display due prudence and draw the corresponding conclusions from this.

Source E: From *The People's Peace* by K.O. Morgan

Over the next four weeks, a shabby and humiliating retreat took place. The American government . . . directed the full flow of its fury on the British UN delegates and ministers. Under US pressure, Britain had to concede the principle of withdrawal in favour of a United Nations force . . . even though no guarantees of a clearance of the Canal had been secured. It was, recorded [Sir Pierson] Dixon, a 'disaster'. The Canal itself, whose freedom of navigation was the ostensible purpose of the Anglo-French-Israeli collusion, was now totally blocked, with Egyptian sunk blockships obstructing shipping of any kind.

QUESTIONS WITH WORKED ANSWERS

a) **Consult sources A and B. How far did the Cabinet decision justify the signing of the Sèvres protocol?** (10 marks)

b) **Consult source D. In what ways did the Soviet Note make a British withdrawal more likely?** (25 marks)

c) **Consult sources C and E. Account for the strength of the US anger at British actions in October 1956.** (25 marks)

d) **Consult all the sources and use your own knowledge. What were the consequences of the Suez crisis for Britain?** (60 marks)

ANSWERS

a) The Cabinet meeting of 27 July in source A agreed that Britain had to seek to overturn the proposed Egyptian nationalisation of the Suez Canal 'by the use of force if necessary'. The agreement signed at Sèvres in October demonstrates that this was used as justification for Eden to arrange a joint attack on Egypt by France, Britain and Israel, as a result of which Egypt will have 'to accept the temporary occupation of key positions along the Canal by Anglo-French forces.'

On the other hand the Sèvres Protocol involves co-operation with Israeli forces, which had not been part of the original Cabinet discussion. The agreement therefore involves the Egyptians accepting the Israeli occupation of the Sinai desert to within ten miles of the Suez Canal. This had not been agreed by the Cabinet and the Sèvres agreement was kept secret from the US government, in contradiction to the third part of the Cabinet's resolution of 27 July.

b) The Soviet Note issued in November makes it very clear that the Soviet Union is well aware that the Israeli attack on Egypt has been organised with the co-operation of the British government and that they are therefore warning the British that the Soviet Union will 'crush the aggressors ... through the use of force'. As the Soviet Union was armed with atomic weapons by 1956, this was a very serious threat and one which the Soviets were careful to send to Eisenhower as well as Eden. In fact, the threat to international stability in the Middle East worried the US administration hugely, and the note may well have contributed to Eisenhower's determination to see British and French troops withdraw as soon as possible.

One might regard this note as posturing by the Soviet Union, however, as it was unlikely that they would become directly involved in the crisis, as they were pre-occupied with the Hungarian rising at the time and the atomic capacity of the Warsaw Pact was very limited, compared with that of NATO at the time. Far more serious for Eden and the Cabinet was the reaction of the British media and public and the attitude of President Eisenhower.

c) The anger displayed by the US President in his opening conversation with Eden following the air attacks on Egyptian airfields, largely resulted from the fact that Eisenhower and his administration felt that the actions of the British, French and the Israelis had allowed the Soviets the opportunity to reassert their control over Hungary by sending tanks into Budapest, whilst public attention was focused on Suez. It had seemed, by the end of October, that the Soviet Politburo would authorise a full withdrawal of troops from Hungary, which would have been a major victory for the US administration, especially the Secretary of States, John Foster Dulles. With the attack on Cairo having begun, that policy now lay in tatters.

In addition, the US administration had been trying its best to mend relations with the Arab world, still angered by US support for the fledgling state of Israel which they were fundamentally opposed to. The USA, increasingly dependent on the Arab world for oil supplies as her economy continued to grow, was horrified that two Western powers, Britain and France, the USA's closest allies, should be jeopardising this rapprochement by their clumsy action against a man, President Nasser, widely regarded as a hero in the Arab world. In particular they feared that Nasser would now approach the Soviet Union for assistance and thus give the Russian leaders a valuable ally in the Middle East.

d) Despite popular perceptions, the Suez disaster did not lead to either a major British review of foreign policy or an immediate withdrawal from possessions east of Egypt. Instead, there was a gradual acceptance that Britain would have to concentrate on the defence of Europe in future, but the USA was unwilling for her to leave a power vacuum for Communist states to fill, by withdrawing precipitously. This was not surprising, as the new Prime Minister after Eden's inevitable resignation was his former Chancellor, Harold Macmillan, one of the keenest supporters of the Suez campaign. It was not until after the 1959 general election was won that Macmillan's government, perhaps driven by the implications of the defence cuts introduced by Duncan Sandys in 1957, embarked on a policy 'revolution' that saw Britain substantially withdrawing from Empire in the following decade. The humiliation that Britain received at Nasser's hands must have encouraged many nationalists in Africa to push for independence, however. As Britain was no longer in a strong economic position to resist, following the US pressure on sterling, it could be said that, at least indirectly, the Suez crisis contributed to the process of decolonisation in Africa.

Some Arab states, such as Saudi Arabia and Syria did break off diplomatic relations with Britain, but the pro-British Persian Gulf states such as Jordan and Kuwait did not react, yet they survived, due to the despatch of British troops in 1958 and 1961 respectively. The most serious reaction was in Iraq, where the pro-British King and his Prime Minister were murdered after coming under huge pressure from other Arab countries to change their policies. On the whole, however, Nasser's ambitions in the Middle East as a whole made little progress until his death in 1970. When Wilson chose to announce Britain's withdrawal from 'East of Suez' in 1968, it was due to the condition of the British economy rather than pressure from Arab nationalists. Suez and the fall of Eden was 'no end of a lesson' for Britain as she was revealed as being almost completely dependent on the consent of the USA in the exercising of her foreign policy. Yet, despite humiliating exchanges such as that in source C, Anglo-American relations actually improved. This was largely because Macmillan took over at 10 Downing Street having first won the approval of the Americans. In 1957 he met Eisenhower in Bermuda and organised the free sharing of nuclear secrets between the USA and Britain in exchange for allowing US Thor missiles to be based in Britain. Britain's mended relationship was clearly dependent on Britain accepting a subservient role in foreign affairs and making her defence provisions dependent on the good will of the administration in Washington. There were two costs to this policy of 'special nuclear relationship', which can be seen as an indirect consequence of Suez. First, the basing of US nuclear missiles in Britain led to the establishment of the **Campaign for Nuclear Disarmament**, a hugely popular peace movement, and second, and more seriously, it caused the French to seriously doubt Britain's commitment to the EEC when they formally applied for membership in 1962. The Suez crisis may only have contributed to Britain's decision to decolonise, but it also led to Britain's isolation in Europe, as she felt obliged to draw closer to the USA.

2. Britain and the European Community (AQA)

Read the extracts below and then answer the question which follows:

Source A: From a speech by Winston Churchill in Zurich, 1946

The first step in the recreation of the European family must be a partnership between France and Germany. In this way only can France recover the moral leadership of Europe. France and Germany must take the lead together. Great Britain, the British Commonwealth of nations, mighty America, and I trust the Soviet Union, must be the friends and sponsors of the new Europe and must champion its right to live and shine.

Source B: From a Cabinet committee memorandum on joining the EEC, July 1960

Question: If it is going to succeed, is it desirable that the United Kingdom should be associated with it [the EEC] so that we can influence its policies?
Answer: Yes. If the Community succeeds in becoming a really effective political and economic force, it will become the dominating influence in Europe and the only Western bloc approaching in influence the big Two – the USSR, and the United States. The influence of the United Kingdom

in Europe, if left outside, will correspondingly decrease. Though we may hope to retain something of a special position *vis-à-vis* the United States, the latter will inevitably tend to attach more and more weight to the views and interests of the Six.

Source C: Chancellor of the Exchequer, Heathcote Amery on joining the EEC, July 1960

The Chancellor said that his personal conclusion was that we should be ready to join the Community if we could do so without substantially impairing our relations with the Commonwealth. We might seek to persuade other Commonwealth countries to relinquish some of their special advantages in the United Kingdom market in order to enable us either to accept membership of the Community on special terms or to enter into some form of association with it. But we should not press that persuasion to a point where it threatened the Commonwealth relationship . . . We should try to carry our partners in the EFTA with us.

Source D: From President De Gaulle's Press Conference, 1963 after vetoing Britain's application to join the EEC

Britain applied to join the Common Market after refusing to participate earlier, creating a Free Trade Association . . . She is insular, maritime, linked to distant countries, essentially industrial and commercial and with slight agricultural interest. The whole question is whether Britain can place herself 'inside a tariff which is genuinely common', renounce all Commonwealth preference, give up agricultural privileges, and . . . regard her EFTA engagements as 'null and void'.

QUESTIONS WITH WORKED ANSWERS

a) **Study source B. Explain the meaning of the phrase, 'the Six'.** (3 marks)

b) **Study sources B and C. How far do these two documents reveal that Britain's commitment to joining the EEC was largely based on self-interest?** (7 marks)

c) **Refer to all four sources and use your own knowledge. 'There was a powerful logic to De Gaulle's doubts concerning British sincerity'. Explain how Britain's behaviour towards Europe between 1950 and 1963 led to the rejection of her first application to join the EEC.** (15 marks)

---

a) 'The Six' refers to the countries who originally signed the Treaty of Rome in 1957 and therefore became the first European Economic Community. They were West Germany, France, Holland, Belgium, Luxemburg and Italy.

b) In source B, the Cabinet Committee in 1960 wants to join the EEC as the 'influence of the United Kingdom in Europe, if left outside, will . . . decrease', and sees the EEC as becoming 'the dominating influence in Europe'. At the same time the government hopes to retain its 'special' relationship with USA. Britain is therefore attempting to reverse her decline in world status by adding membership of the EEC to her existing assets, rather than seeking to join the organisation because she supports its principles.

Similarly, in source C, the chancellor, Heathcote Amery, argues that British membership of the EEC, should also not jeopardise Britain's existing strategic and economic advantages. Amery believes that Britain 'should be ready to join the Community if we could do so without substantially impairing our relations with the Commonwealth', although he is quite prepared to sacrifice something of the relationship with the Commonwealth as the price of membership or 'some form of association' with the EEC. The government's self-interest in their application is made clear when Amery rules out membership of the EEC if it 'threatened the Commonwealth relationship . . .' and he even believes that Britain could retain a relationship with the EFTA countries, despite the fact that it was a rival organisation to the EEC.

c) In source D, President de Gaulle states that he will not allow Britain to join the EEC unless she 'renounce[d] all Commonwealth preference . . . and . . . regard her EFTA engagements as "null and void" ', in other words to make her commitment to the EEC explicit in her actions. As the Chancellor, Heathcote Amery stated in source C, prior to Britain's application in 1962, 'we should be ready to join the Community if we could do so without substantially impairing our relations with the Commonwealth'. Here the British government is making it clear that they are not prepared to 'renounce all Commonwealth preference'. Heathcote Amery goes on to state that 'we should try to carry our partners in the EFTA with us', which may mean that he wishes to see Britain as members of two rival economic groups, something that de Gaulle would not allow, as, to his mind, Britain must 'regard her EFTA engagements as "null and void"'. De Gaulle also justifies his rejection of the British application by stating that 'Britain refus[ed] to participate earlier, creating a Free Trade Association . . .' Britain had not intended to become a member of the European Community, when it was first established as the European Coal and Steel Community in 1950, preferring to act as one of its 'friends and sponsors', as Churchill states in source A. When it seemed after 1957 that the EEC may act as a serious trade rival to Britain in Europe, Britain helped to establish the European Free Trade Association, with other European non-members of the EEC. As this was therefore a direct rival for trade with the EEC, it is unsurprising that de Gaulle mentions this to support his doubts for British commitment to the Community.

De Gaulle accuses Britain of being 'insular, maritime, linked to distant countries'. The reference to distant countries might be taken as another reference to the Commonwealth, but it more likely that he was referring to Britain's perceived 'special position *vis-à-vis* the United States', as the Cabinet refer to it in Source B. Britain had recently purchased the Polaris submarine-launched nuclear missile system from America, making her in many ways dependent on the USA for defence and de Gaulle feared that Britain would therefore act as 'the Trojan horse' of American influence in the EEC. In particular, de Gaulle feared that Britain would continue to serve as USA's main route for the dumping of cheap crops, thus undercutting the European, and in particular the French farmer.

De Gaulle's criticism that Britain was 'essentially industrial and commercial and with slight agricultural interest' was also of some importance, as the fundamental nature of the EEC, as De Gaulle saw it, was to protect the agriculture of Europe, through the **Common Agricultural Policy**. As the industrial needs of the Community were largely being fulfilled by West Germany, de Gaulle saw the membership of another large industrial nation to the EEC as potentially threatening the CAP and the overall priorities of the Community. It is certainly true that the CAP did prove to be one of Britain's biggest worries both during and after subsequent applications for membership.

In conclusion therefore, although it reflects a rather narrow definition of the scope of the EEC, given de Gaulle's priorities, it must be said that he had good reason to doubt Britain's commitment to the EEC as it stood then, and to fear the consequences of Britain's entry to the EEC, at least as it suited the French. Of course the French were also keen that they should not lose, what

Churchill described as 'the moral leadership of Europe' to the British. That Britain had been so clumsy in her approaches to the EEC, in publicly refusing to relinquish other associations, merely made it easier for de Gaulle to justify his veto. It has also led to suspicions that Britain may not have been particularly keen to join, and may have welcomed de Gaulle's veto as a convenient excuse.

3. Decolonisation (EDEXCEL)

Read the following quote and then answer questions (a) to (c) which follow:

Source 1. From Harold Macmillan's speech to the South African Houses of Parliament, 3 February 1960

In the twentieth century and especially since the end of the war, the processes which gave birth to the nation states of Europe have been repeated all over the world. We have seen the awakening of national consciousness in peoples who have for centuries lived in dependence upon some other power. Fifteen years ago this movement spread through Asia. Many countries there of different races and civilisations pressed their claim to an independent national life. Today the same thing is happening in Africa and the most striking of all the impressions I have formed since I left London a month ago is of the strength of this African national consciousness. In different places it takes different forms, but it is happening everywhere. The wind of change is blowing through this continent and, whether we like it or not, this growth of national consciousness is a political fact. We must all accept it as a fact, and our national policies must take account of it.

QUESTIONS WITHOUT WORKED ANSWERS

a) **Explain the sentence 'Fifteen years ago this movement spread through Asia'.** (10 marks)

b) **Was Macmillan's acceptance of the growth of Africa national consciousness purely the result of his trip to Africa between 1959 and 1960?** (14 marks)

c) **What were the consequences of this speech for the speed of African decolonisation?** (36 marks)

(Total: 60 marks)

---

4. Britain and USA 1945–51 (OCR)

Source A: From the minutes of a Cabinet Meeting of ministers on the construction of a British atomic weapon, February 1947

The Foreign Secretary [Ernest Bevin] said that in his view that we should press on with the study of all aspects of atomic energy. We could not afford to acquiesce in an American monopoly of this new development.

Source B: From a memorandum to the Cabinet by Ernest Bevin, March 1948

Having in mind Soviet tactics from Yalta onwards, we should decide what common arrangements can be made and what consultations should be entered into to prevent Soviet tactics succeeding on an even wider basis than hitherto and to halt any further expansion of Soviet dictatorship. . . In this connection we cannot limit ourselves to Europe. We must bring in the Commonwealth and the Americas, and eventually every country outside the Soviet group.

Source C: From the government committee's report on the need for Marshall Aid, October 1947

We are setting out to develop our colonial and Commonwealth resources but this must be a long term matter. In time we can expect to develop sources of supply within the Empire of goods we must now buy for dollars, so that some relief from the problem of the dollar deficit in the future can be expected. Equally our own agricultural programme will in time save us dollars. But none of these will relieve the immediate dollar problem . . . the answer then must clearly be that we need assistance from the United States, and we need that assistance in 1948 if not sooner.

Source D: Chiefs of Staff Report on defence policy, June 1950

The British Commonwealth and the Continental Powers, whether individually or collectively, cannot fight Russia except in alliance with the United States . . . Today it makes no sense to think in terms of British strategy or Western European strategy as something individual and independent. Full collaboration with the United States in policy and method is vital.

QUESTIONS WITHOUT WORKED ANSWERS

a) **Study source B. Explain the reference in source B to 'Yalta'.** (10 marks)

b) **Study sources A and B. Compare Bevin's position on co-operation with the United States in these two sources.** (25 marks)

c) **Consult sources C and D. How useful are these two sources to the historian seeking to explain British foreign policy in the early years of the Cold War?** (25 marks)

d) **Use all the sources and your own knowledge. To what extent did Bevin and the British government have no choice but to become a junior partner to the USA in the Cold War?** (60 marks)

(Total: 120 marks)

Part 4: Historical skills

Working with others – British decolonisation 1945–79

The scale of British decolonisation is vast, involving dozens of countries, hundred of politicians and campaigners and millions of inhabitants. It is therefore a perfect opportunity to create a whole class of investigation in which small groups or pairs of students investigate a number of areas.

As there are a large number of colonies that could be investigated (see Table 8.2 on p. 287), and the number of students carrying out this project may be limited, the following list could be used to focus students on the most important and revealing examples of decolonisation. The examples are, in the author's opinion, in declining order of importance for the student of the period to understand the factors that led to the end of the British Empire:

1. India
2. Malaysia
3. Kenya
4. Ghana (Gold Coast)
5. Palestine
6. Southern Rhodesia
7. Nigeria
8. Cyprus

For each of the colonies or areas, you should consider the following issues:

1. How long had an organised political opposition to British rule existed in the colony?
2. Where did the opposition come from? (Remember that there may have been a number of groups all demanding slightly different degrees of autonomy, some of which co-operated from time to time. Also there might have been opposition to direct British rule from white settlers as well as native groups).
3. What forms did opposition to British rule take? (i.e. demonstrations, direct actions such as tax boycotts, formation of parties, terrorist action, guerrilla warfare, etc.).
4. Did Britain attempt to resist these moves to independence? If so by what methods (i.e. imprisonment of opposition leaders, restrictions on native peoples, use of military force, intervention by British armed forces).
5. Was the whole area granted independence, or just particular regions?
6. What were Britain's motives for granting independence? (This will, of course, be a matter of debate among historians – attempt to find what motives the majority of the historians cited below agree on).
7. Were there any limits to the autonomy of the former colony after independence was granted?
8. Did the former colony become and remain a member of the British Commonwealth?
9. Was the granting of independence done purely on the particular circumstances of that country or as part of a wider programme of decolonisation in that area?
10. What consequences did the granting of independence have on other colonies in the area or on the British Empire as a whole?

TEXTS YOU MIGHT CONSULT INCLUDE:

Brown, Judith and Louis, W.R. (eds), (1999) *The Oxford History of the British Empire: The Twentieth Century*, Oxford: OUP.

Chamberlain M.E. (1998) *The Longman Companion to European Decolonization in the Twentieth Century*, London: Longman.

Chamberlain, M.E. (2000) *Decolonization: The Fall of the European Empires* 2nd ed., Oxford: Blackwell.

Gallagher, John and Seal, Anil (2002) *The Decline, Revival and Fall of the British Empire*, Cambridge: CUP.

Holland, R.F. (1985) *European Decolonisation 1918–1981*, Basingstoke: Macmillan.

James, Lawrence (1995) *The Rise and Fall of the British Empire*, Time Warner Books UK.

McIntyre, W. David (1999) *British Decolonization, 1946–1997: When, Why, and How did the British Empire Fall?*, New York: St. Martin's Press.

Porter, Bernard (1996) *The Lion's Share* 3rd ed., London: Longman.

Chapter 9

Social and Economic Change, 1945–1979

This chapter covers the huge changes that took place in British society in the thirty years after the Second World War. It was a period in which traditional attitudes towards women, the media and young people were challenged. It also saw the fastest rate of non-white immigration to Britain and saw the rise of racism as a political force in Britain for the first time since the days of the British Union of Fascists (BUF). By the mid-1970s many people felt that British society was in serious crisis. Yet it was also the period in which the standard of living in Britain rose at the fastest rate it ever has. There has been much puzzlement among historians about how this was possible at a time when the British economy appeared to be declining in comparison with other industrialised nations.

 ## Historical background

The economy 1945–79
The oil crisis of 1973
Industrial relations
The rise of consumerism
Social change in the 1960s and 1970s

   a) censorship
   b) the permissive age?
   c) legal reform
      a) death penalty
      b) abortion
      c) divorce
      d) homosexuality and the age of consent

The status of women since 1945
Immigration since 1945
Race relations
Youth culture and modern media

 ## Essays

1. The economy
2. Social improvement

3. The position of women in Britain since 1945
4. Immigration and race relations
5. Consumerism and youth culture

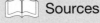 ## Sources

1. Immigration since 1960
2. The position of women in Britain since 1945
3. Industrial relations in the 1970s
4. The emergence of youth culture in the 1960s

 ## Historical skills

1. Analysis of statistics about the performance of the British economy through the use of spreadsheets

Chronology

1946	Report of Royal Commission on Equal Pay
	Cinema attendance in Britain peaks at 1.6 billion visits a year
1947	Sterling Crisis
1948	National Health Service established
	British Nationality Act
1951	Festival of Britain
1953	Coronation of Elizabeth II
1955	Launch of commercial television
1956	*Rock around the Clock* released
1958	Race riots in Notting Hill
1960	Penguin books tried for obscenity for publishing *Lady Chatterley's Lover*
1961	*Private Eye* launched
1962	Commonwealth Immigration Act
1963	The start of 'Beatlemania'
1965	Abolition of Death Penalty
	1st *Race Relations Act*
1966	Financial crisis
1967	Legalisation of abortion and homosexuality
	Devaluation of pound
1968	Kenyan Asian immigration leads to second Commonwealth Immigration Act
	Enoch Powell's 'Rivers of blood' speech
	2nd Race Relations Act – Race Relations Board set up
	Abolition of theatre censorship
	Creation of British Leyland
1969	Reform of Divorce law
1970	Equal Pay Act
1971	Immigration Act
	Industrial Relations Act
1974	Miners' strike
1975	Sex Discrimination Act – Equal Opportunities Commission set up
1976	Race Relations Act – Commission for Racial Equality set up
	IMF crisis
1977	Queen's Silver Jubilee
	'God Save the Queen' by the Sex Pistols is the best-selling single in Jubilee week
1978	Unemployment rises above one million for first time since 1945
1978/9	The 'winter of discontent' – a series of public sector strikes

Part 1: Historical background

The economy 1945–79

As Table 9.1 below shows, in the second half of the twentieth century, Britain was moving from a manufacturing economy to a service economy. This transition was by no means smooth and involved the decline of large-scale production in the north of England, Scotland and South Wales and its replacement by financial and other services, mainly located in the south-east of England and the Midlands, a trend which had begun during the 1920s and 1930s and had been only interrupted by the war.

In such a time of change, although Britain's rate of economic growth was much faster than at any other time in Britain's industrial history, it was not as fast as that of other major industrial countries.

Table 9.1 **Proportions of work-force in different sectors, 1951–81**

	Primary*	Production**	Services
1951	8.9	43.6	47.4
1961	6.6	44.3	48.7
1966	5.4	44.0	50.3
1971	4.3	42.9	52.8
1976	3.3	39.5	57.2
1981	3.2	35.3	61.5

* Primary = agriculture, forestry, fishing, mining, quarrying, oil and gas extraction/processing.
** Production = manufacturing, gas, water, electricity, construction.

A good example of the failure of the British economy in the years after 1945 is the motor vehicle industry. It expanded rapidly after 1945 (comprising 7.5 per cent of Britain's manufacturing output in 1966), as the after-effects of the war allowed British and US firms to dominate until the mid-1950s. As competitors in Europe and the Far East emerged however, Britain failed to remain competitive. In 1973 it was revealed that British factories needed 67–132 per cent more labour to produce identical vehicles.

Two of Britain's oldest car manufacturers, Morris and Austin merged in 1952 to form the British Motor Corporation (BMC). BMC specialised in small cars, such as the Morris Minor and the Mini where profit margins were low and the company faced competition from US manufacturers such as Ford, General Motors (who bought the British brand Vauxhall) and Chrysler producing their cars in Britain. To combat the large European and American producers, the Labour government in 1968 attempted to create a 'national champion' by merging Leyland trucks (owner of Standard-Triumph), BMC and Rover cars to form British Leyland (BL). Although this created the world's fifth largest car-maker, supplying 40 per cent of British cars, it meant there were 48 different plants, a massive model range, and very unwieldy management. The company, dependent on the sale of small cars, was not helped by market changes in the late 1960s as sales of smaller cars for private buyers declined relative to fleet sales of larger cars, especially Ford's Escort and Cortina. The lack of demand both at home and abroad for Leyland's products, meant that little finance was available for model development. British Leyland's first new models, the Marina and Allegro were poorly designed and, unsurprisingly, not successes. Labour nationalised BL in 1975 and endorsed a new investment programme, but labour unrest at an efficiency-driven 44 per cent cut in work-force, further hindered development. As BL's market share declined and Thatcher's Conservative government were unwilling to invest further, the company was forced into co-production with the Japanese firm, Honda, in 1979. In 1988, BL, now re-named Rover, was sold cheaply to British Aerospace and then even more cheaply to the German manufacturer, BMW, in 1994, by which time Rover only supplied 13 per cent of British cars. BMW, who only wanted the company for the profitable Land Rover and Mini brands, announced their plans to sell or close Rover in 1999 and the company was sold for a mere £10 in 2000. The only positive development in recent history of the car industry has been the establishment of Japanese car-makers (Nissan, Honda and Toyota) and of their European production bases in the UK, attracted by government aid and a cheap, highly skilled workforce.

The decline of the British vehicle industry was due to:

- Government interference, introducing car tax and raising of Hire Purchase terms at times when the British car economy actually needed stimulating.
- Regional policies taking factories to unsuitable sites, in order to ensure employment and the favourable response of the electorate.
- Trade union power, controlling the pace of work and initiating strikes.
- Inadequate management who secured only low levels of investment, failed to recognise market limitations, and failed to rationalise production and marketing.

By contrast, some parts of British manufacturing performed well after the war, such as the computer industry. The first computer and the first commercially available computer were both British, but British firms lacked the resources and domestic market for long-term viability. The American computer firm, IBM, received military contracts worth £350 million from the US government during the 1950s. In the same period, British government sponsorship was only worth £12 million. Wilson's government created Independent Computers Limited (ICL). ICL performed relatively successfully in the 1970s and 1980s, but lacked the funds needed for research and development in order to compete with American companies. It was therefore logical for the company to enter into partnership with Fujitsu, the 2nd largest computer producer in 1990.

The failure to achieve sufficient growth in the post-war years was not demonstrated by British service industries, however. In the case of the retailing industry, business swiftly took advantage of the abolition of resale price maintenance in the 1950s and 1960s, which paved the way for rapid expansion of more efficient parts of distributive trades. This resulted in the dominance of large retailing companies:

1961   100 retailers had 21 per cent of total sales
1980   12 retailers had 21 per cent of total sales

Some sections of retailing had always been dominated by large businesses such as footwear, men's clothing and furniture, but after the 1960s there was a dramatic growth in the size and number of off-licences and most particularly, supermarkets. The largest private firms, Sainsbury, Tesco, Asda and Safeway soon had huge shares of the profitable food market, pushing out the co-operative movement.

Table 9.2 **Comparative annual percentage growth rates, 1960–79**

Country	Percentage growth
Britain	1.9
USA	2.8
Germany	3.4
Japan	5.8
France	4.1

This was mainly because:

a) Larger retailers were able to secure large economies of scale (forcing small retailers to form purchasing organisations such as Spar, VG)
b) With increased car ownership supermarkets were able to move from high rent town centres to lower-rent, peripheral, suburban locations with good parking facilities, which enabled the establishment of much bigger stores with could supply thousands of products.
c) Large retail chains were able to exploit changes in labour market. They devised working practices to suit the use of a largely female, unskilled and part-time work force which was easier to manage and cheaper to employ.
d) Retailing, in contrast to car manufacture appeared to be well managed. Retail companies invested heavily in training programmes and facilities, which resulted in good performance in the management of stocks, distribution, purchasing and marketing.

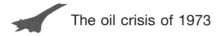 The oil crisis of 1973

Britain's economy, especially her manufacturing sector was, therefore, quite fragile by the early 1970s. In 1973, war broke out between Israel and her Arab neighbours. Israel, with support from the West, won the war. In retaliation the Arab countries chose to use their control of important oil-fields to hit back at the West. The Arab members of the Organisation of Petroleum Exporting Countries (OPEC) reduced the amount of oil reaching the West and persuaded OPEC to dramatically increase the price of the fuel which most of the industrialised world depended on. A barrel of oil had cost $2 in 1972, but by 1980, this had risen to $35. The whole of the West suffered severe inflation by this dramatic increase, but it hurt Britain particularly badly, as her economy was not strong enough to be able to offset the effects of the financial shock. Within a year, Britain's **balance of payments** deficit had reached one billion pounds, the value of sterling had fallen to $1.57 and inflation had soared to 16 per cent. By a remarkable coincidence, however, Britain discovered oil beneath the North Sea and by 1980, Britain was actually a net exporter of oil and an important member of OPEC herself. This was one reason why the British economy was able to recover so swiftly from the major recession of 1979–83.

 Industrial relations

In light of the figures shown in Table 9.3, some economic historians have explained Britain's relatively poor economic performance in the post-war years by blaming the power of the trade unions and the poor labour relations, especially in the manufacturing industries. This led, so the argument runs, to over-manning, low productivity and damagingly high wage settlements.

While it is certainly true that relations between workers and employers were particularly poor in the 1960s and 1970s, it is, however, unreasonable to suggest that the trade unions caused the poor state of the economy, as they were simply reacting, albeit rather unrealistically, to the decline in their industries. The trade unions viewed their role as protecting their members' interests by keeping wages up as long as they could and limiting the number of redundancies as the manufacturing industries contracted. Most of the time this was done amicably through negotiation, but occasionally, when the trade unions or the workers felt badly treated, relations would break down and result in strikes or 'go-slows'.

Table 9.3 **Number of strikes, 1949–79**

Year	Strikes	Year	Strikes	Year	Strikes	Year	Strikes
1949	1,426	1957	2,859	1965	2,354	1973	2,873
1950	1,339	1958	2,629	1966	1,937	1974	2,922
1951	1,719	1959	2,093	1967	2,116	1975	2,282
1952	1,714	1960	2,832	1968	2,378	1976	2,016
1953	1,746	1961	2,686	1969	3,116	1977	2,627
1954	1,989	1962	2,449	1970	3,906	1978	2,349
1955	2,419	1963	2,068	1971	2,228	1979	4,583
1956	2,648	1964	2,524	1972	2,497		

The largely right-wing media in Britain tended to present the strikes as unreasonable, confrontational and violent (much as they had done during the general strike in 1926). Even the Labour Prime Minister, Harold Wilson and his Employment Secretary, Barbara Castle, were convinced that the wave of strikes were a cause of Britain's difficulties, rather than a symptom of the structural changes she was undergoing. In 1969, they attempted to limit the power of the unions by restricting their legal right to call strikes, a strategy they announced in a White Paper called 'In Place of Strife'. Given the fact that the trade union movement provided the bulk of the Labour Party's funds, this was bound to prove a difficult course of action. When senior Labour figures such as James Callaghan and Roy Jenkins refused to support the policy, Wilson was forced to back down. The Conservatives under Edward Heath in 1971 did introduce similar restrictions to those proposed by Labour, but were faced with mass union action which resulted in the political crisis of 1973–74 and the declaration by Heath of a three-day week. Given this history, in the late 1970s, the Conservative Party led by Mrs Thatcher, successfully persuaded the electorate that the unions were the main source of Britain's economic decline, using the public service strikes of the so-called **'winter of discontent'** of 1978–79 as the final proof. When in power, Mrs Thatcher was to ruthlessly pursue a policy of limiting the power of the unions, whom she branded 'the enemy within'.

 The rise of consumerism

Despite the problems in the British economy, the post-war years saw a long and sustained rise in living standards for all social groups in Britain. Seebohm Rowntree in his third and final survey of York in 1950 found that absolute poverty had declined to under 3 per cent of the population, largely as a result of the **Welfare State** set up by Attlee's government and sustained by the Conservatives. Wages continuously rose and with the unemployment very low until the 1960s, people were able to afford many labour-saving and home entertainment consumer products for the first time. Cheaper 'package' holidays allowed people to travel abroad for their annual holidays Only two million holidays were taken abroad in 1951, but by 1978, it had reached nine million. The total number of holidays taken by British people rose from 27 million in 1951 to 49 million by 1974. As Harold Macmillan put it, when he became Prime Minister in 1957, 'Let's be frank about it: most of our people have never had it so good'. The symbol of this new power of the consumer was the private car. Sales increased from 1.5 million in 1945 to 5.5 million in 1960. Even more important in fuelling the consumer boom, however, was the increase in house purchases with loans, in the form of mortgages, readily available from banks and building societies. Once houses were bought, as well as needing to be equipped with the latest consumer products, such as washing machines and televisions, they could be improved with central heating, carpeting, and decoration. In 1970, houses were, on average, 5°C warmer than they were in 1950.

Table 9.4 **Ownership of consumer durables in percentages of houses**

Item	1955	1975
Television	35	96
Washing machine	18	70
Fridge	8	85
Vacuum cleaner	51	90
Telephone	19	52
Central heating	5	47

Table 9.5 **Types of housing tenure, 1939–77**

	Council tenants	Private tenants	Owner-occupiers	Others
1939	14.0	46.0	31.1	9.0
1966	25.7	22.5	46.7	5.1
1977	32.0	9.0	54.0	5.0

There was a social cost for all of this, however, as average working hours increased between 1946 and 1955, to 48.7 hours per week, as successive Chancellors and business leaders attempted to revive the British economy. These then fell to 43 hours a week in the following 20 years until 1975. Working hours for men in Britain were still the longest in the European Community, however, with the female hours the shortest.

On the other hand, with the economy growing so slowly, the rate of increase of wages was not realistic and led to the decline of the value of the currency as prices went up as quickly as wages. The purchases of this consumer boom did not help the British economy either, as the British manufacturing sector was not able to satisfy the demands for new products and imports flooded into the country, thus making it even more difficult for the British producers to grow and become more competitive.

Not everyone shared in the new prosperity however, especially in the 1960s and 1970s as unemployment grew and inflation reduced the value of savings. In a striking example of just how important television had become as a potential agent for social change, the screening of *Cathy Come Home* on the BBC in 1966, showed up the persistence of acute poverty in Britain. The main character, a young woman, is forced from progressively poorer lodgings to a hostel and then onto the streets, having her children taken from her. Such cases were all too common, as the newly established charity for the homeless, Shelter, soon discovered.

Table 9.6 **Income distribution, 1949–74**

	1949	1954	1964	1974
Top 10%	27.1	25.3	25.9	23.2
Next 40%	46.4	48.4	48.9	49.8
Bottom 50%	26.5	26.3	25.2	27.0

Table 9.7 **Unemployment in Britain, 1949–79**

Year	1,000s	Year	1,000s	Year	1,000s	Year	1,000s
1949	413	1957	383	1965	376	1973	785
1950	404	1958	536	1966	564	1974	628
1951	367	1959	621	1967	603	1975	1,152
1952	468	1960	461	1968	631	1976	1,440
1953	452	1961	419	1969	595	1977	1,567
1954	387	1962	566	1970	628	1978	1,608
1955	298	1963	878	1971	868	1979	1,464
1956	297	1964	501	1972	929		

Social change in the 1960s and 1970s

a) CENSORSHIP

Before the 1960s, books with explicit depictions of sex were banned from sale in Britain, even if they were of literary merit. The most famous banned works of literature were James Joyce's *Ulysses* and D.H. Lawrence's *Lady Chatterley's Lover*. After a shopkeeper in London received a prison sentence for stocking Lawrence's book in 1955, the publisher of Lawrence's work, Penguin Books, decided to print an uncensored version of *Lady Chatterley's Lover* in 1959 as the *Obscene Publications Act* of that year permitted literary merit as a suitable defence against criminal charges. Hearing that they had printed 200,000 copies, the Director of Public Prosecutions brought a case against Penguin Books for obscenity. In the famous trial at the Old Bailey in 1960, Lawrence's work was defended by literary experts and even a bishop. The chief prosecutor also ruined his case when he asked the largely working class jury, 'is it a book that you would even wish your wife or your servants to read?'. The jury found Penguin Books not guilty of obscenity and it became a bestseller, along with *Ulysses* which was published and sold in Britain without prosecution. Soon, other much more explicit titles such as *Last Exit to Brooklyn* and *The Tropic of Cancer* were being published.

In cinema, the British Board of Film Certification (BBFC) which had practised some of the severest film censorship in the world, realised the need to moderate its views in light of changing attitudes towards the depiction of sex and violence on screen as early as 1958. The new secretary of the BBFC, John Trevelyan, allowed the film *Room at the Top* with its themes of sexual conquest and strong language to pass almost uncut (albeit with an 'X' certificate, which meant it could only be seen by over-18s). A scene in which abortion was discussed in *Saturday Night and Sunday Morning*, in 1959, was also allowed, demonstrating that official tolerance for such realistic films of working-class, provincial life (often known as 'kitchen-sink' dramas) had arrived.

By 1968, theatre censorship was finally abolished and cinema censorship became even more relaxed in its depiction of violence, in films such as *If . . .* and *A Clockwork Orange* and sex in films such as *Emmanuelle* and *Last Tango in Paris*. By the late 1970s, however, attitudes had begun to harden once again and Britain's censorship laws did not relax any further, remaining some of the harshest in Europe. In particular, local councils still had the power to ban films and plays being shown in their local cinemas and theatres and this resulted in the *cause célèbre* of *Monty Python's Life of Brian* (1980), a spoof biblical epic, being banned in one half of the country, but not the other.

b) THE PERMISSIVE AGE?

Many historians have considered carefully whether the 1960s, with the explosion of pop music and the creation of an influential youth culture, did actually significantly change Britain as much as contemporaries believed. The attention given to the music of the Beatles and the Rolling Stones and their bohemian lifestyles, seem to suggest that 'a permissive age' had begun where drug-taking was wide-spread and sexual restraint was no longer practised in clothing styles as well as in personal relations, and the 'mini-skirt' gave way to the 'micro-skirt'. But the media's focus on celebrity lifestyles and the behaviour of the young and rich in London tended to distort the true extent of change, as the section above on censorship has already discussed. Contraception had certainly existed for most of the twentieth century, but the coming of the contraceptive pill to Britain in the 1960s, certainly allowed much more opportunity for sexual freedom. This oral contraceptive was not widely available, however, until local authorities set up family planning clinics in 1967 which could offer 'the pill' for those who applied and it became available on the NHS in the mid-1970s. As a result of the pill, the risk of unwanted pregnancy, especially among working-class women significantly declined. Sex could therefore be practised more casually if one chose, and more couples co-habited, before or instead of marrying. Whether this really amounted to a significant growth in casual sex is unclear, as there is very little way of verifying the anecdotal evidence that is often cited as proof. What is clear, is that, as a result, the age at first marriage increased while the incidence of marriage declined with more children being born outside marriage. Perhaps it is best to conclude that the opportunity for more sexual experimentation now existed, but in more traditional communities outside bigger cities, there were no changes in sexual behaviour until such behaviour was no longer regarded as deviant or dangerous.

The expression of a new generation seemed most clear in the protest movements of the 1960s. As well as the feminist movement, the late 1950s and 1960s were marked by a strong youth interest in peace campaigns. The **Campaign for Nuclear Disarmament** (CND) had some limited influence over Labour politicians, while the anti-Vietnam War protests of the 1960s clearly helped to persuade the government to stay out of America's war. Most of these protests were peaceful, until 1968, when an attempted invasion of the American Embassy in London led to violent clashes between police and demonstrators in what became known as the 'battle of Grosvenor Square'. This event, inspired by American protests, was the start of a wave of student activism, especially in London, which also followed the US lead, with demands for more democracy in Universities, the ending of military research and the expulsion of those connected to the racist and repressive regime in South Africa. Unlike in America, this was a very limited and short-lived wave, and calm and authority was soon restored to Britain's campuses. Clearly, British students were more concerned with improving their employment opportunities, especially as the British economy began to seriously decline in the late 1960s.

These protests, hardly significant when compared to the campus riots in the USA and the 'even-ements' of Paris in 1968, were largely the result of a dramatic expansion in higher education, offering wider opportunities for many, and the basis for radical protest for the few. Older universities grew and a large number of new universities (often called 'redbricks'), polytechnics and colleges of higher education, were established in the ten years after the Robbins Report proposed expansion in 1963. The Prime Minister of the later 1960s, Harold Wilson, strongly supported this attempt to create a more technocratic society, even personally helping to set up a university for home study, called the Open University, but the beneficiaries were largely the children of the middle classes, as still only 5 per cent of the over-18s went on to any form of higher education.

Religion, at least traditional organised religion, is commonly thought to have lost much of its influence over British people in this era. However, even before the changes in thinking that occurred in the late 1950s and throughout the 1960s, only 10 per cent of the population were regular church-goers. During this period, attendances at Roman Catholic churches actually increased, partly due to the continuing growth in the Irish communities who came to build Britain's motorway network, and partly due to the unprecedented reforms in church practice, usually referred to as 'Vatican II'. The Church of England continued its slow and steady decline in the numbers of communicants from the Edwardian Age, falling from 10 per cent of the population in 1940 to around 7 per cent in the late 1960s. Its services were still in great demand for baptisms, weddings and funerals, even by those who would not otherwise enter a church – a state of affairs common since the seventeenth century. One religious group in particular did see a dramatic decline in attendances – the Nonconformist sects, most notably Baptists and Methodists.

Chapels, which had been numerous in Britain's cities, swiftly became disused and were pulled down or converted to other use, even bingo halls. On the other hand, new sects and non-Christian religions saw a dramatic increase in popularity, especially in the 1960s when they became fashionable, such as when the Beatles visited Hindu gurus such as Maharishi Mahesh Yogi.

c) LEGAL REFORM

a) The death penalty

Roy Jenkins, the Labour Home Secretary between 1965 and 1967 was perhaps the single most influential politician of the twentieth century in promoting legal reform of social issues. Reform of the criminal justice system took up much of his time, in particular, after much debate, the use of hanging for criminal offences. There had been a series of executions in the late 1950s and early 1960s, culminating in that of James Hanratty for the 'A6 murders' in 1962, which provoked much disquiet, due to limited evidence. Despite public polls showing clear support for the retention of the death penalty, the law abolishing hanging for all crimes except treason was passed in 1965. Despite notorious cases in the late 1960s such as those of the 'Moors Murderers' Brady and Hindley, and the Kray brothers, no serious attempt has been made since to re-introduce the policy.

b) Abortion

David Steel, a young Liberal MP, was encouraged by Jenkins to introduce a bill to legalise abortion on wider grounds than had previously existed. Feature films such as *Alfie* and *A Taste of Honey* and the BBC adaptation of Nell Dunn's *Up the Junction* had exposed the prevalence and danger of unsupervised, illegal, 'back-street abortions' and prepared the public for such reform. The subsequent Abortion Act of 1967 allowed termination of a pregnancy if two doctors agreed that continuing the pregnancy would damage the physical or mental health of the woman or existing children, or that the child would be born with serious abnormalities. The issue divided society between those outraged at the 'legal murder' of unborn children (especially the Catholic community) and those who supported 'a woman's right to choose' (most notably feminist groups).

Table 9,8 **NHS abortions**

1961	2,300*
1967	9,700
1968	22,332
1975	106,648
1980	128,600

* In addition approximately 10,000 private abortions and possibly as many as 100,000 'back street abortions'.

c) Homosexuality and the age of consent

Another backbencher, Leo Abse, pressured Jenkins to review the laws on homosexuality. The Sexual Offences Act of 1967, saw the decriminalisation of male homosexuality between 'consenting adults' in private. Female homosexuality had never been illegal in Britain. The age of consent for sexual acts was lowered in Britain to 16, but intriguingly, was fixed at 21 for homosexual acts. It would be quite wrong to suggest that homosexuality suddenly became more acceptable, however. In most communities outside London, it remained a furtive and largely shameful practice until the 1990s, with violence and abuse for most who lived openly 'gay' lives.

d) Divorce

In 1951 a Royal Commission on Divorce had been appointed due to a rise in divorce from 1.6 per cent in 1937 to 7.1 per cent in 1950. At this stage, divorce was only achievable if one side could be proved to be responsible for the breakdown of marriage, through ill-treatment or adultery.

The Commission's Report said that over-hasty marriage in wartime and the introduction of 'legal aid' in 1949 caused a temporary rise in the number of divorces. The Report also reiterated women's

Table 9.9 **Divorce in England and Wales, 1951–81**

	1951	**1961**	**1971**	**1981**
No. of divorces	28,767	25,394	74,437	145,713
No. of people divorcing (per 1,000 married couples)	2.6	2.1	6	11.9

traditional duties as wives and mothers and attacked the 'tendency to take the duties and respon-sibilities of marriage less seriously'. As a result marriage guidance counsellors were to be created rather than reform of the divorce laws.

During the 1950s and 1960s, however, medical, religious and popular writers stressed the import-ance of personal commitment and love (and sex) in marriage, but opened the way for people to argue that all these were achievable without marriage and that marriage without love was logi-cally meaningless. Although, one female Labour MP opposed the bill on the grounds that it was a 'Casanova's Charter', the 1969 Divorce Act, made no-blame divorces after a five-year separation period possible. With changing attitudes towards the position of women and gradually more open sexual behaviour, divorce rates began to rise and these reached a peak in 1985, with nearly half of all marriages ending in divorce.

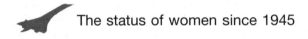 ## The status of women since 1945

The women's struggle for political rights had been largely achieved by 1945 and can be measured by the legislation passed: women were granted the right to vote in local elections in 1888; in 1918 women over 30 were granted the right to vote; and in 1929 women over 21 were granted the right to vote.

While the concentration of women's campaigns in the 1940s and 1950s was on the achievement of equal pay and equitable treatment by employers, by the 1960s, a more radical feminism arose. Inspired by the writings of intellectuals such as Kate Millet and Germaine Greer, this loose asso-ciation of a number of feminist groups is often referred to as the Women's Liberation Movement (WLM or 'women's lib') and was largely modelled on similar feminist groups in the USA. The first WLM workshops were held in Oxford in 1970 where they demanded increased wages for low paid women and wages for housewives. Unlike the more traditional feminist groups such as the Fawcett Society and female trade unionists, these new feminists concentrated on sexual issues, such as control over reproduction, access to divorce and abortion, gay rights and violence against women and were less concerned with work and training. Often criticising the effectiveness of legis-lation, these feminists attempted to change the public's perception of women, by criticising sexism in institutions, the media and in behaviour. Some went as far as to challenge traditional female roles in society, accusing the typical family structure as oppressive, through slogans like 'Y be a wife?' and 'a woman needs a man like a fish needs a bicycle'.

Such feminists tended to be young, articulate, often college educated. They were inspired by expec-tations of equal opportunities fostered at higher education institutions, which were followed by early marriage and child bearing. The conflict between their expectations and the social role they were subsequently expected to fill, made many such women eager to challenge the position of women in British society. One commentator described the process of become actively involved in

Table 9.10 **Part-time and full-time female employment in Britain, 1951–81 (in 1,000s)**

	Full-time	Part-time	All	% part-time
1951	5,752	754	6,506	11.6
1961	5,351	1,892	7,243	26.1
1971	5,467	2,757	8,224	33.5
1981	5,321	4,141	9,462	43.8

the feminist movement as the 'personal became political'. The first national women's liberation demonstration took place in London in 1971, and the following year the feminist magazine *Spare Rib* and the publisher *Virago* were established. With the failure of the Equal Pay Act of 1970 to correct unequal treatment of women at the workplace, the Labour government of 1974–19, convinced by many of the feminists' demands, chose instead to introduce wider measures to end sex discrimination. The 1975 Sex Discrimination Act established the Commission for Equal Opportunities, and outlawed two types of discrimination: direct discrimination, where a woman (or a man) was judged to have been treated less favourably than a man (or woman) would have been treated; and indirect discrimination, where a condition or requirement is imposed on a group that does not appear to have anything to do with gender, but where more of one sex can comply with it than the other. For example, the upper age limit of 28 for recruitment to the Executive Officer grade of Civil Service was outlawed as it indirectly discriminated against women as a large number of women took time out from work in their twenties for child-bearing. A further significant reform was the 1977 Employment Protection Act which gave women the right to six weeks' paid maternity leave, and, more importantly, the opportunity of returning to their job, for up to 29 weeks after the birth.

In some ways the Women's Liberation Movement should be seen as part of an assault on authority by student movements in the later 1960s and 1970s. It became increasingly separated from this wider movement when it became clear that for many men in the student movement personal moral freedom meant self-indulgent and self-regarding sexual adventure and experiment which left women with the consequences.

Feminism became associated instead with campaigns for individual rights ('a woman's right to choose') and tended to ignore the problem that in any framework of individual rights, the most powerful groups in society tend to benefit. As a result, in the period, power tended to remain in male hands, despite increased female self-perception and personal equality within the home.

 Immigration since 1945

1945–79 was a very important period in immigration to Britain, but both contemporaries and historians have tended to make a number of assumptions when studying this period. First, the focus has tended to be on non-white immigrants, mainly Asians and Afro-Caribbeans. Before 1971, the largest immigrant community was actually southern Irish – 957, 830 of whom were mainly employed in the post-war reconstruction of cities and the building of the motorway network. A large Polish community of over 100,000 developed in Britain after 1939, many of whom refused to return to Poland after the war, once it fell under communist control. For similar reasons Estonians, Lithuanians and Latvians remained in Britain after 1945, along with Belgians, Germans and Italians. Since 1945, war and internal unrest has led to many Hong Kong Chinese, Cypriots, Czechs, Hungarians, Chileans, Vietnamese, Africans and Sri Lankans settling in Britain.

Table 9.11 **Migration to and from Britain, 1900–79**

Years	Emigration (from Britain)	Immigration (into Britain)
1900–09	4,404,000	2,287,000
1910–19	3,526,000	2,224,000
1920–29	3,960,000	2,590,000
1930–39	2,273,000	2,361,000
1940–49	590,000	240,000
1950–59	1,327,000	676,000
1960–69	1,916,000	1,243,000
1970–79	2,554,000	1,900,000
Total	20,550,000	13,521,000

It is also forgotten that Britain has always been a destination for immigrants. Britain had a historic tradition of welcoming immigrants in the nineteenth century but most of these groups were small. At the time of the 1971 census, only 6.6 per cent of the population were immigrants or refugees. The traditional tolerance for accepting refugees was first seriously questioned by political leaders in the 1900s in the 'aliens scare' of 1900–05 which resulted in the *Aliens Act* of 1905 which first restricted immigration.

Finally, as Table 9.11 shows, Britain has, in fact, been a net exporter of people throughout the twentieth century. In particular, Britons have migrated to the USA, Canada and Australia and more recently to South East Asia and the Middle East.

Figure 9.1 **Distribution of the non-white population of Great Britain as a percentage of the total population, 1989**

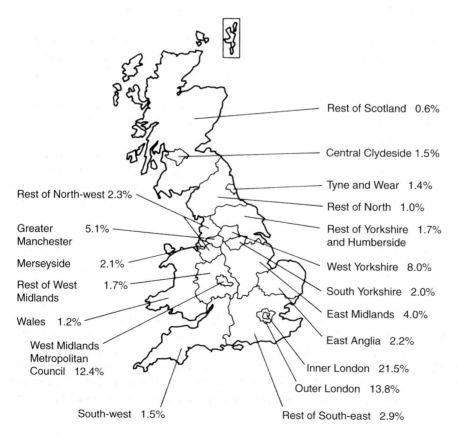

After 1945 the size of the black population certainly grew, but the majority of immigrants remained white and they were also invited to come to Britain to fill the employment shortage after the war. The black population in 1945 was mainly involved in the shipping trade, so the new communities tended to be concentrated around East London, Bristol, Liverpool, Cardiff, Glasgow and Manchester at first. By the 1970s the Pakistani community was involved in the textile trade in the North-west and the Midlands. Asian groups in the Midlands were involved in engineering and foundry trades. Afro-Caribbean workers predominated in the public sector as nurses and in public transport. The Chinese community, traditionally associated with laundries became more involved in restaurants and high technology industry. During the 1960s and 1970s as Britain abandoned her colonies, the breakdown of government in some areas, wars between neighbouring countries, and the persecution of minorities, especially Asian businessmen in Africa, led to a new movement of political refugees who sought sanctuary in Britain. By 1979, a black and Asian community was found in all major conurbations in Britain.

 Race relations

The Race Relations Acts of 1965, 1968 and 1976 increasingly strictly outlawed discrimination on grounds of race, colour, culture or national origin. The coming of the immigrants from the Commonwealth provoked Enoch Powell, a member of the Conservative Shadow Cabinet, to make a speech to West Midlands Conservatives in Birmingham in 1968, shortly before the introduction of the second Race Relations Bill, which was designed to reduce racial discrimination. The intention of his speech to whip up popular anger is clear from the following passage.

A week or two ago I fell into conversation with a constituent, a middle-aged, quite ordinary working man employed in one of our nationalised industries. After a sentence or two about the weather, he suddenly said: 'If I had the money to go, I wouldn't stay in this country.' I made some deprecatory remark, to the effect that even this government wouldn't last forever, but he took no notice and continued: 'I have three children, all of them been through grammar school and two of them married now, with family. I shan't be satisfied till I have seen them all settled overseas. In this country in 15 or 20 years time the black man will have the whip-hand over the white man.

I can already hear the chorus of execration. How dare I say such a horrible thing? How dare I stir up trouble and inflame feelings by repeating such a conversation. The answer is that I do not have the right not to do so. Here is a decent, ordinary, fellow-Englishman, who in broad daylight in my own town says to me, his MP, that this country will not be worth living in for his children. I simply do not have the right to shrug my shoulders and think about something else.

Later in the speech, Powell prophesied Britain torn apart by racial violence: 'As I look ahead, I am filled with foreboding. Like the Roman, I seem to see "the River Tiber foaming with much blood".'

The so-called 'Rivers of Blood' speech, led to Powell's immediate dismissal from the Conservative Shadow Cabinet, but a Gallup poll revealed that around 75 per cent of the country was in sympathy with his views. Support for Powell often came from working-class groups who lived closest to non-white communities, most famously the London dockers who marched to Parliament in support of Powell, chanting, 'knock, knock, we want Enoch!'. The immediate consequence for race relations was a dramatic increase in racial attacks against non-white residents in 1969 and 1970.

Between 1977 and 1979, with the country suffering the social consequences of high unemployment, right-wing groups were able to blame the economic conditions of Britain on the non-white population. The National Front, a loose association of various hard-line nationalist and racist groups, openly advocated 'repatriation', the forcible deportation of Asians and Afro-Caribbeans. They saw their membership triple and won third place in by-elections in Stechford (in East London) and Ladywood (in Birmingham)

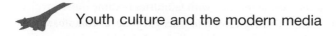 ## Youth culture and the modern media

The rise of rock 'n' roll in the 1950s was part of:

1) a growing impact of US culture on British life
2) the 'discovery' of the teenager
3) the development of new recording and other technologies
4) the shift of distribution of political power.

For many, including the popular press, the arrival of rock 'n' roll in Britain announced by the film soundtrack *Rock Around the Clock* by Bill Haley and the Comets in 1956. This was the first opportunity to see the new music increasingly popular in the USA, associated with Little Richard, Jerry Lee Lewis and Elvis Presley. British rock acts such as Cliff Richard and Tommy Steele emerged, who in turn influenced Lennon and McCartney, and Keith Richards and Mick Jagger. At this stage, 'America' represented ideas and values, a particular idea of freedom (and affluence) which the young found attractive.

There was consequently a fear among broadcasters of the 'americanisation' of British (often just English) culture, with the BBC acting as 'the front line of defence' against it. British artists were played on the BBC in preference to US singers. 'Skiffle', played by such as Lonnie Donegan, was acceptable, rock 'n' roll wasn't. Records were deemed 'unsuitable for broadcasting'. Failing to satisfy the new teenage market led to the emergence of rivals to the BBC, first Radio Luxembourg, ITV and later 'pirate' radio.

In the 1950s, young people became an important economic market. They had money of their own due to parents' increasing wealth and their growing social and economic independence. But the idea of the 'teenager' with a distinct identity was a marketing strategy with rock 'n' roll as a key consumer product around which the market was constructed.

This new music inspired fearful reaction from the establishment; parents, church, police, magistrates and politicians. As one clergyman expressed it, 'Rock'n'roll is a revival of devil dancing . . . the same sort of thing that is done in black magic ritual'. Parliament attempted to ban certain records. The establishment also disliked the new consumer behaviour. These consumers had no responsibilities, did not need to save, but lived for the moment by making leisure – not work – their target – they challenged conventional values of the use of money and work. The left saw youth pursuit of pleasure as eroding their political consciousness, the right as eroding their moral and religious commitments.

The British record industry managed to control and profit from the new fashion – only two new companies emerged (Pye and Phillips) to challenge the existing majors (such as EMI, Decca) who simply integrated new styles into existing structures of production, promotion and programming.

There was no revolution in the music industry and the most famous counter-culture labels, such as the Beatles' own Apple Records, soon crumbled in the face of aggressive, well-targeted marketing and publicity from the existing commercial companies. Even the central element of popular music, the 'Top Ten', was an adaptation of the old 'hit parade' and was designed to ensure the rapid obsolescence of pop music. Only when young entrepreneurs started exploiting their knowledge of and contacts within the popular music world did the first serious rival to the older companies emerge in the shape of Richard Branson's Virgin label.

The symbolic meaning of the 1960s as a time of liberation and changing moral climate, much exaggerated by the media, in itself influenced people's thinking and actions. Despite claims for rock 'n' roll as a vanguard of the cultural and social changes of the 1960s, it was an economic arrangement whereby a product (records and stars) found a market (fans).

The early part of the decade saw a flourishing of indigenous British culture: the Shadows, the Beatles, the Rolling Stones, and Billy Fury were signed to major record labels and found a new market in the USA. Liverpool and London, both exposed to black urban rhythm and blues music, were the unquestioned centres of this new music culture. Liverpool produced the artists (as did art schools in London – Pete Townsend, Eric Clapton, Keith Richards) and London marketed this success.

The myth of the 1960s is most typified by the Beatles. Inspired by the vocal style of Tamla Motown, given identity as artists by art school, they were aided by producer George Martin at EMI, and cleverly managed and repackaged by Brian Epstein (the manager of a record retail business) who cultivated the group's image and style, with distinctive haircuts and collarless suits.

When the Beatles received MBEs in 1965, it was less a tribute to their musical ability, than to their economic success, (as by then the British record industry turned over £100 million a year) and their appeal to potential young voters. The new music had become accepted as largely harmless and it was possible for the Prime Minister, Harold Wilson to pose for pictures at a charity event with the Beatles, without risking any criticism of his morality.

In the mid-1960s consumerism became linked to self-expression. One could now purchase a life style. Images and products were defined by personalities such as Barbara Halinuki (Biba), Mary Quant, Jean Shrimpton and Twiggy, David Bailey and Terence Donovan. Carnaby Street in London embodied the new fashion, shops such as Lord John and Chelsea Girl produced cheap copies of new fashion for the lower classes with which to ape their idols and proclaim their refusal to conform.

By the later 1960s, a genuine counter-culture had begun to develop, again much influenced by developments in USA. 'Underground' media, magazines such as *Oz, International Times*, and *Rolling Stone* began to emerge. This 'hippy' sub-culture, inspired by freely available drugs, especially LSD, with radical political programmes – the student movement, the anti-Vietnam campaign, the environmental movement and closely linked to the women's movement – was actually very small and elitist, but pioneered sounds and artistic approaches copied by marketing companies. Record companies formed 'alternative' labels, EMI founded Harvest, Polydor, Vertigo. In Britain, the influence of the counter-culture was most clearly seen in the cinema. Richard Lester moved from the Beatles' *A Hard Day's Night*, to a parody of British war movies in *How I Won the War*. Lindsay Anderson mocked the entire class system in, *If . . .* and *Oh, Lucky Man*.

Figure 9.2 **The Sex Pistols outside Buckingham Palace**

By the late 1960s rock was mainstream. Broadsheet newspapers printed reviews of pop music alongside classical concerts. Radio One was launched in 1968 by the BBC and BBC2 showed the *Old Grey Whistle Test*. After 1970, pop music increasingly fragmented into niche markets as it chased sales – 'glam rock', reggae, teeny-bop, progressive rock, folk-rock. Despite its greater claims, punk, launched in 1976 as a counter-blast to over-inflated rock egos soon became another marketing strategy. Manager Malcolm McLaren was, if anything, more visible than the Sex Pistols themselves and punk sold magazines, fashion and lifestyle. Punk courted notoriety, and the Sex Pistols were egged on to swear on national television, as in a circus act. By late 1977 one could literally buy rebellion off the shelf by purchasing the Sex Pistols' 'God Save the Queen' single at the time of the monarch's Silver Jubilee. Capitalism had finally managed to market even anarchy.

Part 2: Essays

1. The economy (OCR)

'Despite the occasional short term boom, the real story was one of continuous decline'.
To what extent and for what reasons did the economy suffer 'decline' between 1945 and 1979?

(90 marks)

Since 1951, the British economy grew on average more rapidly than at any time in its industrial history. Between 1948 and 1973, although growth fluctuated, falling most seriously in the recession of 1957–58, the British economy never actually failed to grow in any single year. After 1973, the British economy's performance was a lot less positive. There was a serious recession in 1974–75, in which the economy actually contracted, before achieving a fragile recovery between 1976 and 1979.

Although the British economy did enjoy a 'golden age' between 1948 and 1973, every other developed country experienced faster growth during these boom years. Britain saw its share of manufactured exports fall from over 25 per cent in 1950 to only 9 per cent by 1979. Perhaps, most worryingly, Britain was not even competing successfully on the domestic market either. Imports especially of consumer durables increased from £2.4 billion in 1948 to £54 billion by 1979. This which left Britain with a series of serious **balance of payments** crises in 1958, 1966–67 and, most serious of all, due the effects of the oil **blockade**, 1974–76. On all these occasions this sparked increases in inflation and in the case of the latter two, led to requests for loans to the **International Monetary Fund** (IMF).

After 1945, the Labour and Conservative governments operated a policy that guaranteed a high and sustained level of employment. Unemployment was not fully eliminated, but it remained consistently low until the mid-1960s. As in the 1930s, unemployment tended to be concentrated in regions dependent on single industries and long-term unemployment was rare and mostly the preserve of older men. By the late 1960s, however, Britain's economic difficulties, particularly in the manufacturing sector, caused unemployment to rise. The effect of the oil crisis of 1973 was to worsen an already worsening picture and in 1975, unemployment passed one million for the first time since 1940. By 1978, one and half million workers were unemployed, with few new jobs being created. Britain had moved into a period of high unemployment caused by the structural changes to the economy and exacerbated by the new concentration on fighting inflation in place of tackling joblessness.

Britain's relatively poor economic performance after the war has been the subject of limitless historical debate, but the over-concentration on the small, volatile, domestic market, especially after the Conservatives won the 1951 election and ended **austerity** and Cripps' relentless drive for exports, appears crucial. Concentrating on this small market meant that unit costs were high, profits were small and there was, consequently, insufficient accumulation of capital for investment and modernisation of industry. Concentrating on producing goods at competitive prices for the export market would have lead to a more positive **balance of payments**, sufficient to ease the effects of the periodic global slow-downs in demand. Factories would have been able to work at fuller capacities and thus higher levels of skilled employment would have been sustained, leading to a higher level of national income.

On the other hand British industry ought to have been able to cope with volatile domestic demand, for Japan's economy was equally small. But in Germany and Japan, the 'reconstruction growth' after 1945 sometimes led to over-production which had to be exported, often quite cheaply. In Britain, by contrast, home production was frequently out-stripped by domestic demand, which inevitably caused a rush of imports and **balance of payments** crises. Such a crisis would force the government to put up interest rates and curb spending, resulting in a staccato pattern of economic growth, usually referred to as 'stop-go'.

In order for the economy to grow as a whole in the post-war period, manufacturing was vital, as it promoted transport and distribution and service industries. British products were uncompetitive however, in terms of price, due to the persistent over-value of sterling, but also in delivery dates, reliability, design and quality. What is often described as Britain's 'supply-side' difficulties were caused by a number of structural problems in the manufacturing industries. First was the relatively poor qualifications and low quality of British management, which resulted in insufficient attention to research and development and poor training of staff. This in turn, helped to create an adverse climate of labour relations in which trade unions refused to co-operate in improving efficiency. The large-scale membership of the unions and relative immunity from legal control gave them great power and so over-manning was not corrected and inefficient firms remained in business. Further, the London stock exchange and the British banking system inadequately monitored company performance and failed to give long-term support to newer businesses, concentrating instead on maximising swift profits for share-holders, thus further limiting the ability of companies to modernise and expand.

The result, which observers called the 'British disease' was the growing penetration of imports, and the lack of success of British exports. Imports of electrical goods increased dramatically in 1970s, especially in the form of domestic appliances and audio equipment. In the case of the vehicles and textiles industries, this happened without compensating export gains. Perhaps most seriously of all, the one area of manufacturing that Britain had a strong tradition of success in, shipbuilding, saw an equally steep decline in exports. As Britain proved unable to compete in manufacturing, her economy gradually turned towards the service industries to provide growth and employment. This process took a long period however, and was still underway in the mid 1970s.

Britain was therefore in a very weak position when she faced two new burdens after 1973. First, and most seriously, the impact of the huge rise in oil prices by the OPEC countries and second, the costs of restructuring Britain's legal and administrative systems to comply with the terms of admission to the EEC, which also included a substantial annual budget contribution. It would therefore be an exaggeration to consider that the British economy was in a terminal condition by 1978, as the growth of the service industries was bound to eventually provide new opportunities for investment and employment and the two short-term cash crises of the mid-1970s would be alleviated as the British economy, aided by the revenue from North Sea oil and gas, adjusted to accommodate them.

2. Social improvement (OCR)

'Britain enjoyed a period of unprecedented social advance and rising living standards between 1945 and 1973'. How far do you agree with this statement?

(90 marks)

After the achievements of the post-war Labour governments, Britain had for the first time an effective welfare provision. With the work of Bevan and subsequently Macmillan, she enjoyed far better housing than had existed before. The impact of Butler's Education Act, especially when enforced by Ellen Wilkinson, led to wider educational opportunities for the intellectually able of the lower middle and working classes. This in turn, led to a need for a larger higher education system in the 1960s, including a more flexible mode of learning as was introduced by the Open University, under the patronage of Harold Wilson himself.

Real wages continued to rise throughout the period, despite the relatively poor performance of the British economy, and the majority of the population found work easily, as unemployment remained below one million until the early 1970s. Women's wages continued to lag behind men's, but, as more women went out to work, the overall size of household budgets increased. Credit became increasingly easily available, allowing consumers to afford products that would have previously taken them years to save for. Cars became affordable, and most importantly of all, home ownership, rather than rental, increased dramatically. By 1977, spending on consumer durables was up 1,000 per cent on 1948, and consumption of food was up 30 per cent. This, despite a drop in the proportion of income spent on food, as well as alcohol, tobacco, clothing and footwear. This is not to say that poverty did not still exist, especially among the disabled and the elderly, but the living standards of even these groups were relatively good compared to their positions in pre-war society.

In particular, the health of the nation improved dramatically after 1948. The number of children dying before their fifth birthday had been 55 per 1000 in 1938, but by 1981 this had fallen to 15. Largely as a result of this fall, most of which was caused by programmes of vaccination and the preponderance of hospital as opposed to home births, life expectancy rates increased. Male life expectancy was 66 in 1950 and increased to 70 by 1979. Female figures were similarly impressive, from 71 in 1950 to 75 in 1979.

Immediately after the war, the introduction of high levels of direct taxation, only previously seen in wartime, created greater equality in terms of income. In 1949, the top 10 per cent of earners in the country accounted for 33.2 per cent for the nation's domestic income, but by 1976, the top 10 per cent had only 26 per cent.

The trend towards greater equality had been evident since the reforms of the Liberal government before the First World War, but it seemed to be accelerated by the actions of the post-war governments, especially in the maintenance of high levels of employment, which allowed workers, especially skilled workers to charge a premium for their labour, and in the continued expansion of the **Welfare State**. Family allowances and widows' pensions had particularly contributed to the elimination of many of the problems of the 1930s. Rowntree in his third survey of poverty in York in 1950, estimated that the effects of these changes had been to reduce the proportion of the population living in poverty from 18 per cent in 1936 to 1.6 per cent by 1950. As both the political parties accepted the need to maintain direct taxes at high levels, the Conservative Home Secretary, R.A. Butler was able to claim in 1959, that 'the people are divided not so much between the 'haves' and the 'have-nots' as between the 'haves' and the 'have-mores'. Some, like the left-wing campaigner, Frank Field, believed that this was an admission that while much poverty had been abolished, substantial inequality still existed. As he wrote, 'the age old inequalities remained. The position of the poor improved. But so, too did that of the rich'. The elimination of mass poverty served only to expose less common experiences of deprivation, such as those endured by children, the disabled and the infirm elderly. Elderly people living on National Assistance, in particular, had a very poor standard of living, and those who chose not to claim due to memories of the Poor Relief Board of the 1930s lived in dire poverty.

There were, of course, important attempts to legislate to eliminate inequality in two areas, those of race and gender. The introduction of the Sex Discrimination Act of 1975 and the third Race Relations Act of 1976 made it illegal to discriminate against people on the basis of their sex, race or culture, thus allowing, in theory if not always in practice, the opening of opportunities to all. Similarly, in the 1960s, legal reform had removed the need for homosexuals to conceal their sexual preferences, but to say that this period saw a widespread acceptance of gay lifestyles, would be far too optimistic and most homosexuals continued to live in fear of social rejection if not violent attack.

By the late 1970s, however, as the numbers of unemployed again began to exceed one million, Britain began to follow a pattern of inequality similar to that in the 1930s, with those in work enjoying increasing standards of prosperity and purchasing power, while those out of work were only maintained at a basic standard, which meant particular hardship for the children of unemployed families. Although Britain had become a more equal society by the later 1970s, particularly with the increases in direct taxation and indirect taxes on luxury goods enforced by Denis Healey in 1975, there was growing resentment from those paying the taxes against those receiving state payments. A European survey in 1976 found that 43 per cent of UK residents believed that poverty was caused by laziness and lack of will power and that welfare cheating and fraud was widespread. This was to have a political reaction as the Labour government of 1974–79 reintroduced means tests for supplementary benefits which discouraged as many as 35 per cent of the eligible elderly from claiming. In this way, inequality was beginning to be inadvertently re-introduced by politicians forced to respond to tax-payers who had come to regard the poor as a burden.

3. The position of women in Britain since 1945 (EDEXCEL)

a) **To what extent had women achieved equal rights of pay by 1979?**   **(30 marks)**
b) **Did the social reforms of the 1960s and 1970s improve the position
    of women in British society?**   **(30 marks)**

                                                                       (Total: 60 marks)

a)   The first attempt to introduce equal pay was for teachers in 1944 as part of Butler's Education Bill. The clause was removed at Churchill's insistence, however, as he believed the morale of male soldiers would suffer if this was passed. Such was the protest caused by this that the coalition government were forced to set up a Royal Commission into the issue. The Commission reported in 1946, once Labour were in power. They acknowledged the problem lay in defining what was 'equal work'. At the time, work was mainly divided by gender with male jobs (such as manual work) paid more than female work (in manufacturing and service industries). The Commission also pointed out that the question of 'equal pay for equal work' was also a middle-class issue, as pay rates differentiated by gender only existed in the civil service, local government and teaching. There was equal pay for equal work in university teaching, the BBC, architecture, medicine and among MPs, but in these areas, female employees were few. Finally, the Commission identified the problem of the marriage bar, whereby female workers were sacked on getting married. This was only formally imposed in the civil service, but was often informally exercised in teaching and the private sector. The Commission's report had favoured equal pay for women, but had expressed concerns as to whether the economy could afford it. On these grounds, equal pay was largely opposed by employers, who claimed that men got higher wages as they were more efficient, more flexible, more ambitious, took less time off work, were physically stronger, had a longer commitment to a career (and were therefore worth training), needed higher pay to support a family and could manage other men. There was however, no evidence to support these views.

The Trade Union Congress (TUC) demanded equal pay for equal work, but insisted that the choice of working hours was a woman's prerogative. They demanded that women should be given more training and blamed low female wages on employer exploitation. They didn't want legislation to achieve all this, preferring to operate through union pressure and collective bargaining. Legislation to enforce equal pay was only supported by women's groups such as the London and National

Society for Women's Service, the National Council of Women and the Fabian's Women's Group. In their campaign in the 1960s and 1970s, they had the support of medical experts, who believed that higher pay for women was necessary in order to improve women's poorer standards of health. They reported that menstruation, the menopause and gynaecological disorders, had, in contrast to male employers' beliefs, little effect on the work of most women.

There appeared to be no hurry to address the problem from politicians, despite a majority of women voting Labour in 1945 and the economic need to keep women in work as they left to start families and as wartime nurseries closed. The numbers of women returning to work after having had children began to increase in the 1940s, largely part-time, and largely to afford their own houses and the range of new consumer products that were available as **austerity** came to an end. The only protest about equal pay in the 1950s was in 1952 in the civil service, with the result that equal pay was introduced there in 1955.

As the 1950s continued, however, feminist thinking began to transform popular attitudes, most notably in Myrdal and Klein's *Women's Two Roles: Home and Work*, de Beauvoir's *The Second Sex* and Lessing's *The Golden Notebooks*. As a result, the 1960s saw the emergence of feminist organisations such as the Six Point Group and the Fawcett Society who wanted equal opportunities, equal pay, equal taxation, and better treatment for unmarried mothers. They encouraged women to join trade unions, which resulted in a series of strikes for equal pay, such as the Dagenham women machinists strike in 1968, and put pressure on trade unions and the Labour Party to campaign for legislation.

With the recognition that membership of the EEC would mean granting equal pay for women, the Confederation of British Industry and the TUC began negotiations on equal pay, but these broke down in 1970, which forced politicians to introduce legislation. The Equal Pay Act, which ensured equal pay for the same or similar work was pushed through Parliament with incredible swiftness by the Labour Minister of Labour, Barbara Castle, before the 1970 general election. The legislation was only voluntary in order to soothe Conservative misgivings, but it had some, albeit small effect. When Labour returned to office, they began drafting legislation which led to the 1975 Sex Discrimination Act (SDA) and a compulsory Equal Pay Act. Despite the achievement of the SDA in outlawing inequalities of pay, the Act only covered discrimination to do with appointment, promotion, dismissal, redundancy, access to training, education and credit, though. Requirements of 'decency', 'privacy' or 'authentic male characteristics' were still acceptable to necessitate the employment of a man. Discrimination in social security, tax and pension rights were not covered. Actually defining the 'worth of work' remained problematic until 1983 when the Act was amended to fit EEC regulations to reward 'work of comparable value'.

b)   Divorce was made easier in the 1969 Divorce Act, as blame was no longer apportioned and divorce could be granted after five year's separation. The level of divorce rose rapidly, reaching a peak in 1985. More women co-habited and more children were born outside marriage. The same attitude of allowing more personal choice was evident in the 1967 Abortion Reform Bill. Although the Act did not allow for 'abortion on demand' the decision to allow abortion on the grounds of a risk to the health of the mother, did permit a much wider access to abortion than before. Significantly, it allowed the medical profession rather than politicians and other social agencies control over the decision making process. Abortions increased to 169,362 in 1973, with no significant decrease thereafter, despite easier access to divorce. The reforms of divorce and abortion law certainly allowed women a greater degree of choice over their lives and consequently enhanced their personal freedom. On the other hand though, control over abortion remained in (mainly) male doctors' hands, while divorce often left women with a reduced standard of living as their ability to command a premium salary was clearly not fulfilled by the late 1970s.

The Sex Discrimination Act of 1975 led to a series of high profile cases such as those against the Civil Service in 1977 or Cammell Laird in 1983 in which female employees managed successfully to have discriminatory practices over-turned. These have been the exceptions however. In 1984, for example, out of 380 cases of sex discrimination brought to industrial tribunals, only 63 were upheld. In fact, the position of women in the workplace remained difficult. Women were still largely expected to take the bulk of responsibility for bringing up their children and to carry out the bulk of everyday tasks in most households, which are both unpaid occupations. They still encountered informal discriminatory practice at work, whereby they either encountered 'glass ceilings' preventing any further career advance, or failed to be offered the 'golden pathway' of the necessary information and encouragement to promotion.

4. Immigration and race relations (OCR)

How and why did British governments attempt to limit immigration to Britain between 1945 and 1979?

(Total: 90 marks)

After the war, displaced persons camps in Europe encouraged workers to come to Britain to help with reconstruction. In the West Indies, traditional imperial loyalties were called on to supply nurses and public transport workers in the new **Welfare State**. In the 1948 British Nationality Act, freedom of entry to Britain was granted to citizens of all independent Commonwealth countries. As a consequence the converted troopship *Empire Windrush* arrived in Britain from Jamaica in 1948, with hundreds of young men and families seeking work. At first the immigrants were welcomed and the continuing labour shortage meant that employers extended their recruitment to the Indian sub-continent by the 1950s.

The new arrivals were not always made welcome by their hosts, however. Most dramatically, there were anti-black riots in Liverpool (1948), Deptford and Birmingham (1949) and Camden Town (1954), but more commonly, the growing black community was discriminated against in housing, employment opportunities and welfare. Tension between black and white communities was worst in the poorer areas of Britain's cities, where existing shortages of affordable housing were made worse by the increased competition caused by the new arrivals. This eventually caused widespread unrest in 1958 in Notting Hill and Nottingham. Although the white ringleaders of the riots were jailed, many, including Notting Hill's Labour MP called for the government to introduce legislation quickly 'to end the tremendous influx of coloured people from the Commonwealth'. A *Daily Express* poll in 1958 found that 79.1 per cent of the population favoured immigration controls.

Therefore in 1962 the Commonwealth Immigration Act was passed by Macmillan despite opposition from Labour. All those seeking to enter the UK from the Commonwealth or colonies after 1 July 1962 needed either a job to come to, to possess special skills in short supply or to belong to a special group (such as veterans). The measure was therefore purposely designed to restrict the entry of unskilled black workers. The threat of the Act actually stimulated a 'beat-the-ban' rush. Of the half million black and Asian immigrants to enter Britain between 1945 and 1962, a quarter of a million came between 1960 and 1962.

Labour's attitude towards immigration was challenged in 1964 when Patrick Gordon Walker (the shadow Foreign Secretary) was defeated in Smethwick by Peter Griffiths, whose supporters used openly racist attacks on Labour. The reaction of Labour's Richard Crossman was typical of many in the new government: 'Immigration can be the greatest potential vote-loser for the Labour party if we are seen to be permitting a flood of immigrants to come in'. Therefore, once in office, Labour produced a White Paper in 1965, 'Immigration from the Commonwealth', which actually enforced tightened regulation of the 1962 act.

In 1968, the newly independent Kenya expelled large numbers of its Asian population. Refused a return to India, they turned to Britain for sanctuary, as British passport holders. Fearing the political consequences of allowing the Kenyan Asians to enter Britain, Labour hurriedly passed the second Commonwealth Immigration Act of March 1968, restrictions were placed on those who had secured passports overseas. The rate of immigration was strictly controlled to 5,000 per year. Promises of rights given to Asian British passport holders at the time of Kenyan independence were not honoured, leading one politician to describe the Act as 'one of the most immoral pieces of legislation to have emerged from any British parliament'.

In the midst of the crisis, the Conservative MP for Wolverhampton, Enoch Powell, made a notorious speech in Birmingham, warning of the dire consequences of allowing large numbers of immigrants to come to Britain. The Conservative leader, Edward Heath, immediately sacked Powell, but it seemed to signal that the Conservatives would be even harder on immigration than Labour, especially when it was revealed that 327 of 412 Conservative Constituency Associations wanted all 'coloured' immigration stopped immediately. In the 1970 general election there was a crucial swing to the Conservatives among the white working class, especially in the West Midlands. The Conservatives duly introduced an Immigration Act in 1971, under which unrestricted primary immigration became dependent upon proof of connection with the UK through blood, descent, settlement or due to citizenship. Without these qualifications, immigrants became subject to deportation (although this was not applied to Irish citizens). Workers coming to Britain from the Commonwealth became, in effect 'guest-workers', with no rights to bring their families or to settle in Britain. Britain was still prepared to make exceptions on humanitarian grounds, though. In 1972, Idi Amin's Ugandan regime expropriated and expelled its Asian citizens. Powell vociferously opposed their reception in Britain, but he was bravely opposed and defeated by the Home Secretary, Robert Carr at the Conservative Party Conference. Consequently, the Conservative government decided to accept the majority (29,000) of the Ugandan Asians and Powell resigned from the Conservative party in disgust.

Why and with what consequences did governments legislate to improve race relations between 1945 and 1979?

(Total: 90 marks)

While the governments of the 1960s and 1970s deliberately legislated to make it harder for non-white immigrants to enter this country, ironically, they also legislated to try to reduce discrimination towards non-whites. Popular opposition to now-settled immigrants had long been a feature in British society, but it had mainly come from outside the highest political circles. It tended to take the form of public speeches, published material and differential treatment. Collective violence, as the reaction to the British Union of Fascists in the 1930s had demonstrated was quite rare in Britain.

Events like the Notting Hill riots of 1958 were notable largely for their rarity. Far more common in the 1950s was the refusal of employers (even nationalised companies such as British Railways) to employ or promote non-whites and the refusal of landlords to rent property to non-whites (the sign 'no dogs, no coloureds' was often seen in boarding house windows. Inspired by the Civil Rights movement in the USA, however, campaigners began to expose and protest against these levels of discrimination.

The Labour Home Secretary of Wilson's first government, Roy Jenkins, was sufficiently convinced by campaigners that the media hostility towards non-white immigrants and the potential for ugly political exploitation of the issue, as seen at Smethwick in the 1964 election warranted action. The first Race Relations Act was introduced in 1965 which made it illegal to discriminate in public places or on public transport. The Act, although a significant first step was clearly limited, as the two most important areas of discrimination, employment and housing, were omitted and the new Race Relations Board (RRB), which the Act established, had little power.

In 1967, the publication of Racial Discrimination in England revealed the persistence of prejudice. The report's authors used white and black actors to test for racial discrimination when applying for jobs, accommodation and insurance. They found that 45 per cent of West Indians, 34 per cent of Pakistanis, 35 per cent of Indians, 6 per cent of Cypriots claimed personal experience of discrimination. The position was worst in housing with discrimination from councils, building societies, landlords.

Stung by the limited effects of the first Act, Labour passed the second Race Relations Act in 1968, making it illegal to discriminate in employment, housing and provision of commercial or other services. The RRB was now given the power to investigate and initiate proceedings into cases of racial discrimination.

When Labour returned to power in 1974, the effectiveness of the legislation had still been found wanting, so in 1976, the third Race Relations Act was passed. Indirect discrimination was outlawed, and individuals were given the right to take cases of personal discrimination to court or industrial tribunal. The RRB was replaced by the Commission for Racial Equality to assist those who believed that they had encountered racial discrimination and to combat discrimination. The Conservative shadow cabinet did not oppose the Act. The new Conservative leader, Margaret Thatcher personally opposed it, but after a threatened rebellion by liberal Tories, she was forced to back down. Forty-three Conservatives still voted against the Act, though. The police and the army were exempt from the Act however, as it might damage morale in both services. Unfortunately this led to serious problems, especially in the police, where some officers used 'sus' (suspicion) laws to harass non-whites and many took crimes against non-whites less seriously than those against whites. This caused social tensions throughout the rest of the decade and was only forcefully addressed in the 1990s following the murder of Stephen Lawrence, a black student.

5. Consumerism and youth culture (AQA)

'The great social revolution of the past fifteen years may not be the one which redivided wealth amongst adults in the Welfare State, but the one that has given teenagers economic power' (Colin MacInnes, 1958).

a) **Explain the reference to the Welfare State.** (3 marks)
b) **Why had teenagers gained economic power by the late 1950s?** (7 marks)
c) **Did the discovery of the teenager amount to a 'great social revolution'?** (15 marks)

a) The **Welfare State** as established by the Labour government immediately after the Second World War had as its priority the improvement of the standard of living of the poorest groups in society which would be financed by higher levels of direct taxation on the wealthy. It was based on the principle of providing the best possible social services for everybody, regardless of income.

b) Those children born in, or shortly after the war, amounted to a 'baby boom' and by the time they were in their teens in the late 1950s and early 1960s, they were a significant proportion of the population. In the 1950s, young people became an important economic market. They had money of their own due to parents' increasing wealth as well as growing social and economic independence. But the idea of the 'teenager' with a distinct identity was a marketing strategy with rock 'n' roll as a key consumer product around which the market was constructed. Producers soon began to aim goods at this new group, who had more money to spend on transistor radios, records and clothes than the previous generation due to the economic prosperity of the country and who had no commitments yet such as children or house payments. Teenagers also had more free time as working hours decreased and they were able to adopt a lifestyle which revolved around coffee bars, youth clubs and record shops.

c) During and after the second world war, economic conditions had allowed young people more freedom than ever before. Gangs of working class youths were not new, neither was the adoption of a distinct identity. Spivs, Teddy Boys and other less well known characters were a feature of the 1940s and 1950s. Most of these sub-cultures were frowned upon by authority, though, and such behaviour tended to end when a young man was called up to National Service. The 'discovery of the teenager' in the later 1950s and early 1960s, was in many ways the realisation by commercial companies of the new buying power of those young people not old enough to be at work or married. As a result, the latent rebellion of adolescents was given full indulgence and encouragement by business. With the ending of National Service in 1960, the new 'teenagers' were freer than before to spend their money (or their parents' money) on the new records and clothes that were being especially produced to appeal to them. Working-class youths were just as likely to steal, fight and drink, but they would no longer get in to trouble for how they danced or how they dressed.

Youth culture was, therefore, most obviously defined by its music and its dress. The influence of rock 'n' roll music from America through imported records and films such as those of Elvis Presley, and, most famously, *Rock Around the Clock*, led to British rock musicians emerging. While early figures such as Cliff Richard and Joe Brown attempted to retain elements of more traditional popular music, it was the Liverpool group, the Beatles, who came to symbolise and deeply influence the nature of youth culture in the 1960s. Under the management of Brian Epstein, a Liverpool record shop owner, the group was carefully packaged with distinctive clothes and hair and exaggerated stage personas added to the unquestionable genius of their song writing and music playing skills.

The influence and importance of the 'social revolution' of the teenager that MacInnes refers to in the quote given, was largely due to the way in which various media chose to depict the emergence of a youth culture. Feature films such as *Alfie* and television with its youth programmes such as *Ready, Steady, Go!*, proved popular with the new audiences wanting to watch films and programmes that talked of 'their' lives and experiences, rather than those of their parents. Unsurprisingly, given the importance of the music to defining youth identity, the radio became associated with this. As rock wasn't played by the BBC, a number of transmitters were placed on ships moored off the coast and 'pirate' stations, such as Radio Caroline, became hugely popular. Eventually, in 1968, the BBC bowed to public demands and launched 'Radio 1'. By the end of the 1960s, any visit to the shops and clubs of the high street, any watching of television or films or listening to the radio, would demonstrate just how much popular tastes had been altered by the assault of 'youth culture'.

By the later 1960s, however, the teenager had become associated with political rebellion as well as social non-conformity. The 1960s had seen significant social change and legal reform in Britain, and many young people now wished to see the removal of the traditional social and moral restraints in the country. The 'youth movement' was made up of many different strands, including anti-nuclear campaigners, supporters of what later became known as women's liberation and student protesters who wanted more control over their academic studies and who particularly attacked the US policy in Vietnam at that time. In some ways it began a label for the automatic rebellious stance of many young adults that had always been part of British life. This more polit-ically active aspect of youth, was the product of widening access to higher education, and was therefore a largely middle-class affair. But it must be remembered that youth culture, originally of working class origins, in particular rock music did much to give these groups a sense of sepa-rate identity and a desire to challenge authority where it was felt to be outmoded or pernicious. In light of this, and considering that teenage groups existed long before the 1950s, it is therefore more accurate to describe the discovery of 'teenagers' economic power' as a cultural rather than a social revolution.

Additional essay titles

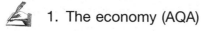 ### 1. The economy (AQA)

Read the following source and then answer the questions which follow.

By the end of the 1970s, new broad strategies were being advocated for reversing Britain's economic and industrial decline. Great stress was placed upon the need to emulate certain features of the Japanese, West German and French economies.

> Adapted from 'The Economic Record' by M.W. Kirby in *Britain since 1945*, edited by Terry Gourvish and Alan O'Day

a) **Using the source and your own knowledge, comment on 'Britain's economic and industrial decline' in the context of the period between 1945 and 1979.** **(3 marks)**

b) **Explain why Britain's share of world trade decreased between 1945 and 1979.** **(7 marks)**

c) **Explain why and in what ways British economic growth was slower than that of its main European rivals.** **(15 marks)**

2. Social improvement (EDEXCEL)

a) **In what ways did the legal reforms passed by the Labour government of 1964–70 transform British society?** **(30 marks)**

b) **Why did the standard of living improve for most people in Britain between 1945 and 1979?** **(30 marks)**

(Total: 60 marks)

Essay plan

a) •   *Death penalty – abolished for criminal offences in 1965*
    •   *Divorce made easier by Divorce Reform Act 1969*
    •   *Abortion legalised in 1967*
    •   *Homosexuality legalised in 1967*
    •   *Censorship abolished in theatre in 1968*

Significant changes to the law, but reflected changes already taking place in society especially in London, rather than changing society from above. Increased prosperity and access to education encouraged questioning of moral attitudes – government was responding to change laws open to abuse and which people were largely avoiding.

b) *Economic factors*

•   *Lack of war – after the end of the Korean War more money available to spend on welfare – governments repeated cuts of defence expenditure until 1979 to fund low level of unemployment and a Welfare State.*
•   *Full employment, at least until the early 1960s, ensured that all shared in the benefits of unprecedented economic growth. Trade unions used the shortage of labour to ensure high pay and good conditions (safety, holidays). More women worked, especially in retailing and offices – allowed more spending on luxuries such as cars and holidays*
•   *Redistributive taxation – ensured that even those at the bottom of society rose above the poverty line.*
•   *Consumer goods – competition from abroad made these more widely available and cheaper – time-consuming activities such as cleaning, washing clothes and cooking made far quicker and less tiring.*
•   *Food imports – made food and drink cheaper and therefore a lower proportion of income spent on this.*
•   *Credit available – to fund purchases for all – interest rates low until 1970s.*

Ultimately economic growth created rising living standards – at the end of the period, after 1973, the boom came to an end and Britain was in a poor position to cope – hence sudden and shocking halt in what had been thought of as a permanent improvement of living standards.

3. The position of women in Britain since 1945 (OCR)

Assess the contribution of feminist groups in achieving equality for women between 1945 and 1976.   **(90 marks)**

Essay Plan

Feminism – different groups – political pressure groups such as Fawcett Society, intellectual groups and the popular Womens' Liberation Movement. Four basic demands – by 1960s –

equal pay, equal education and job opportunities, free contraception and abortion on demand and 24-hour nurseries. None of these fully achieved by 1979.

However, although full equality was not achieved:

- *Feminism, with its high profile events drew media attention to the issues they campaigned for.*
- *Intellectual groups such as 'Spare Rib' promoted feminist ideas at the new universities set up in the 1960s – influenced future generations.*
- *Limited appeal to working women – perhaps greatest weakness of feminist movement.*
- *Campaigns for equality of pay – culminating in the Ford machinists strike at Dagenham in 1968.*
- *Equal Pay Act 1970 – equal remuneration for men and women for work of equal value – discretionary until 1975 – had little effect – role of Barbara Castle in ensuring the act was passed before Labour lost office.*
- *Little enforcement of the act and little enthusiasm for legislation under Heath. Sex Discrimination Act (SDA) therefore made discrimination on the grounds of sex unlawful in employment, education and training and the provision of housing, goods, facilities and services. Discriminatory advertisements were also made illegal. An Equal Opportunities Commission was set up to enforce this. Based on the experience of problems with the Race Relations Acts of 1965 and 1968.*

Ultimately politicians chose to implement acts such as equal pay and SDA for political advantage – policies limited to suit their agendas – women were not hugely influential in Parliament – notable exception of Barbara Castle. Most women MPs more determined to prove themselves in other areas, like Margaret Thatcher.

4. Immigration and race relations (EDEXCEL)

a) **Explain why the immigration of non-whites to Britain became so politically controversial between 1945 and 1979.** **(30 marks)**

b) **Describe the nature of race relations in Britain in the 1960s and 1970s.** **(30 marks)**

(Total: 60 marks)

5. Consumerism and youth culture (OCR)

Identify and explain any *three* factors which led to the development of a culture of mass consumption in Britain between 1945 and 1979?

(Total: 90 marks)

Part 3: Sources

📖 1. Immigration after 1960 (AQA)

Study the following source material and then answer the questions which follow.

Source A: From *The Diaries of a Cabinet Minister* by Richard Crossman, 1965

Ever since the Smethwick election it has been quite clear that immigration can be the greatest vote loser for the Labour Party if one seems to be permitting a flood of immigrants to come in and blight the central area of our cities . . . Immigration is the hottest potato in politics at the moment!

Source B: Table 9.12 **Perceived positions of the political parties on control of immigration, 1946–70: Which party is most likely to keep immigrants out? (responses in %). Poll by Daily Telegraph**

Responses	1964	1966	1969	1970
Conservative	26	26	50	57
Labour	19	13	6	4
No difference	41	53	36	33
Don't know	14	8	8	6

Source C: From a speech by Enoch Powell, 20 April, 1968

We must be mad, literally mad, as a nation to be permitting the annual inflow of some 50,000 dependants who are for the most part the material of the future growth of the immigrant-descended population. It is like watching a nation busily engaged in heaping up its own funeral pyre.

QUESTIONS WITH WORKED ANSWERS

a) **Study source A. Using your own knowledge, explain briefly what Crossman meant by his reference to 'the Smethwick election'.** (3 marks)

b) **Study source B. With reference to your own knowledge, explain the changes in opinion during the 1960s as described in source B.** (7 marks)

c) **Consult sources A, B and C and use your own knowledge. 'The exploitation of racism could reap political dividends'. How far does this statement explain the policies of the two main political parties towards immigration and race relations in the 1960s?** (15 marks)

---

a) Crossman is referring to the 1964 general election result of the Smethwick seat in the West Midlands, where a Conservative candidate managed to defeat the Labour shadow Foreign Secretary, Patrick Gordon Walker by using a crude racist campaign which threatened an influx of non-white immigrants to the area if Labour won.

b) According to source B, in 1964, only 7 per cent more of those polled believed that the Conservatives were more likely than Labour to keep immigrants out, with 41 per cent believing that there was no difference between the parties. With the introduction of Labour's White Paper in 1965, Immigration from the Commonwealth which actually tightened the implementation of the Conservatives' 1962 Commonwealth Immigration Act, the impression of difference between the parties appeared to lessen and by 1966 it was felt by a majority of the population (53 per cent) that there was no difference in the efficacy of either party's immigration policy. With the speech by Enoch Powell, a member of the shadow Cabinet, in April 1968, which was violently critical of continued immigration in its tone and language, the public perception of the party's position appears to alter. Possibly alarmed by the admission of Asians deported from Kenya and by the introduction of liberal race relations legislation, Labour was only seen to be more likely to keep immigrants out by 6 per cent of those polled in 1969. The Conservatives, despite the immediate dismissal of Powell by the party leader, Edward Heath, were now clearly more closely associated with anti-immigration policies, as was reflected by their polling of 50 per cent. The continued activity of Powell and the clear support he enjoyed among many in his party, and the reluctance of Heath to discipline him further meant that, by 1970, the year of the general election, that figure had risen to 57 per cent and many Labour ministers subsequently attributed their surprise defeat in that election to the race and immigration issue.

c) In 1960, following a series of race disturbances which culminated in serious riots in Nottingham and Notting Hill in 1958, the Conservative government, that had previously encouraged immigration of both skilled and unskilled blacks and Asians to Britain, introduced plans for restrictions on immigration from other countries in the British Commonwealth. This resulted in the 1962 Commonwealth Immigration Act.

This act was vigorously opposed by the then Labour leader, Hugh Gaitskell. After his unexpected death in 1962, many expected the same approach from his successor, Harold Wilson. Wilson made a point of describing Peter Griffiths, a Conservative who defeated the Labour shadow Foreign Secretary in the Smethwick constituency in the 1964 election with the use of racist slogans as 'a political leper'. But, as Richard Crossman acknowledged in his diaries, quoted in source A, the loss of a seemingly safe seat as a result of the issue of immigration had made it 'the hottest potato in politics at the moment!', and in the privacy of his diary, he confessed his fear that 'if one seems to be permitting a flood of immigrants to come in and blight the central area of our cities' it could be 'the greatest vote loser for the Labour Party', a feeling that was clearly shared by many members of the Cabinet, all too aware that, following the election, Labour only had a majority of four. Labour therefore chose to tighten the operation of the 1962 Immigration Act, to such an extent that, according to source B, by 1966, a majority of those polled saw no difference between the parties in the operation of immigration control. In 1966 the general election saw Conservative candidates much less easily able to use immigration to gain political advantage and this may have contributed to the majority which Labour won that year.

The Labour government, while certainly seeking to prove themselves as determined to limit immigration as the Conservatives, did feel that there was a need to legislate to reduce racial discrimination against those now living in Britain. In 1968, the second Race Relations Act was passed, which demonstrated that, with rate of immigration slowed, politicians could begin to handle racial issues in a more responsible fashion. While the bill was being prepared however, the first senior politician to openly use race, as well as immigration, to attack both the government and his own party's leadership, emerged. Enoch Powell, in a speech in Birmingham in 1968, painted an apocalyptic picture of race relations in Britain, prophesising 'rivers of blood' in the future and passing on hearsay stories of anti-social behaviour by immigrants. It is still unclear what his motives were, whether he was naively passing on the racist views of a minority of his constituents in Wolverhampton, whether he was seeking to destabilise the Conservative leader Edward Heath, whether he sought to halt the race relations legislation, or whether he wished to prevent Britain accepting any of the immigrants recently deported from Kenya. In his speech Powell claimed to be motivated purely by a concern for Britain's future, but the timing and extreme language of the speech, suggest otherwise. As it was, he failed in his immediate aims. He was sacked from the shadow Cabinet and never held office again. The Race Relations Act was passed and Heath survived the crisis to win the 1970 general election. While certainly, the issue of immigration was also one of race, as the restrictions placed on black and Asian immigration from Commonwealth countries were not imposed on immigrants from the Republic of Ireland, politicians, including Powell, argued that they were merely speaking up for their constituents. As Crossman put it in his diary, immigration became a crucial electoral issue and in a period when no single party dominated, it was unsurprising that all politicians were forced to confront prejudice and fear from their electorate. That some politicians sought to gain advantage from that was equally unsurprising. It could be said, that like Peter Griffith, they stirred up racial tensions for electoral gain, but Powell and many others on both sides of the House of Commons, defended their opposition to immigration by claiming that they were simply passing on the views of their constituents as their representatives in Westminster. Others claimed that if the issue of immigration was not openly discussed by the main political parties, it would encourage dissatisfied voters to turn to extreme right-wing parties such as the National Front. It is therefore very difficult to generalise as to the motives of those politicians who raised the issue of immigration in Parliament, but one can record, perhaps ironically, that the man most often accused of exploiting racism, Enoch Powell, was dismissed from the shadow Cabinet and eventually driven out of the Conservative Party, because of his stance on this issue. The man who sacked him, Edward Heath, became Prime Minister. Clearly in some cases, the exploitation of race by politicians did not always reap rewards.

2. The position of women since 1945 (OCR)

Read the sources below and then answer the question which follows.

Source A: From an article in *The Guardian*, by Christopher Driver, 1966

Contemporary men and women who share education and jobs are coming to like living in each other's pockets, not to speak of borrowing each other's fashions. It's hardly surprising if some of them also find it companionable, if advisedly complicated, to dwell temporarily in each other's beds. It is part of the strain involved in the reinterpretation of marriage and the redrawing of the human life-span though which we are living. There is no room for jealousy in this process because there is no room for ownership.

Source B: From *Britain's Married Women Workers* by Viola Klein, 1957

The outstanding impression gained from this survey is that women's lives, today as much as ever, are dominated by their role – actual or expected – as wives and mothers . . . there is no trace of feminist egalitarianism . . . not even is it implicitly assumed that women have the 'right to work' . . .

Men appear on the whole to be less conservative than they are usually assumed to be . . . the majority of women seem to get moral support from their husbands in their decision to take a job . . . the idea of marriage as a partnership is widely accepted today.

Source C: A defaced billboard advertisement for a car, 1974

Caption: If this car was a woman, you'd pinch its bottom.
Graffiti: If this woman was a car, she'd run you down!

Source D: Table 9.13 **Numbers of female part-time workers, 1951–81**

1951	779,000
1961	1,851,000
1971	2,757,000
1981	3,781,000

Source E: From *Women and Families* by E. Roberts, 1995

In a period when the taxation system, the Health Service, the **Welfare State**, the unions and many other institutions had concentrated on diminishing the inequalities between social classes, little was consciously done to attack the inequalities between genders. [Working class women] were not interested in the women's movement which was becoming more vocal and active . . ., but which still seemed to be confined to intellectual circles. Very few, by 1970, had asserted their rights and had developed a career or taken and kept a job with prospects of advancement, responsibility and promotion.

QUESTIONS WITH WORKED ANSWERS

a) **Study source A. From this source and your own knowledge, explain why the position of some women in marriage was changing.** (10 marks)

b) **Study source C. How useful is source C in explaining changing attitudes towards womens' position in society in post-war Britain?** (25 marks)

c) **Study sources A and B. Explain the reasons why sources A and B differ in their views of women's position in marriage.** (25 marks)

d) **Study all the sources. Using all the sources and your own knowledge, explain whether the position of women of all classes in Britain significantly changed between 1945 and 1979.** (60 marks)

(Total: 120 marks)

---

a) Source A suggests that men and women are increasingly experiencing the same educational and employment opportunities and are therefore engaged in 'the reinterpretation of marriage'. No longer does the husband regard his relationship with his wife as one of 'ownership', but rather marriage is increasingly 'companionable'. Distinct gender roles and behaviour are being dissolved and pre-marital sex and cohabitation are becoming more common.

b) Although source C is merely the action of one unknown person, protesting against sexist attitudes towards women routinely employed by the advertising industry in post-war Britain, the language of both the caption and the graffiti itself reveal much about changing attitudes towards women in the 1960s and 1970s. The caption itself accepts that it was appropriate and expected that one might pinch a woman's bottom if one found her attractive, at least among those who worked in both the higher levels of the motor industry and advertising, who were almost exclusively male in this period. The graffiti, written to be clearly read, is designed to undermine the effectiveness of the advert and to force those reading it to question such sexist attitudes. It also displays something of the aggressive and violent attitude of many of those protesting against what they felt to be discriminatory attitudes in public, by threatening to 'run you down'. Although, not particularly reliable as an indication of the scale and aims of the feminist movement, the defacing of a large sign, on a town street, gives quite a good indication of the nature of the movement. The protester who defaced this poster was attempting to challenge what was felt to be ingrained prejudice against women in society in a fashion that all members of society would notice outside academic and political circles. The similarity to the pre-1914 campaign of the suffragettes is striking.

c) Source A views the role of women in marriage as significantly changing, as women are no longer regarded as objects to be owned by their husbands and marriage becomes a partnership between two people. This source, written by a journalist of the progressive newspaper, the *Manchester Guardian*, refuses to take a moralising position on these changes, and the changing attitudes towards sex outside marriage that accompany them. The journalist sees the changes as 'the redrawing of the human life-span though which we are living'. The journalist does not suggest that all marriages are changing in these ways, only new marriages among 'contemporary men and women who share education and jobs'.

Source B, by contrast, sees women still occupying a distinct and inferior role in marriage. She comments that 'there is no trace of feminist egalitarianism' among married women. Women have not accepted that they 'have the "right to work" . . .'. The most revealing aspect of this comparison is that both sources A and B agree that the attitude of men was changing towards their wives, suggesting that, in theory at least, it was men, not women, who were most influenced by demands for 'egalitarianism'.

One can only reconcile these differences by suggesting that the journalist who wrote source A may have taken the experiences of those educated young women of his or her acquaintance and attempted to apply this more broadly, whereas the social investigator, Viola Klein, in source B, has, it is assumed, interviewed a broader spectrum of men and women in order to reach her conclusions. Source A is also written some nine years after source B and the challenging of separate gender roles had received much more popular attention in that time, which may have served to make women as egalitarian as their husbands, at least in the organisation of their marriages.

d) Source E suggests, that while middle-class women, who had access to higher education in far greater numbers than ever before in the 1960s and 1970s, had begun to challenge ideas of conventional gender roles, for working-class women little had changed since 1945. Roberts comments that 'very few, by 1970, had asserted their rights and had developed a career or taken and kept a job with prospects of advancement, responsibility and promotion'.

At first sight, source A seems far more optimistic about changing attitudes for both men and women, stating that marriages are becoming more open because 'there is no room for ownership'.

On the other hand however, the author's reference to 'contemporary men and women who share education and jobs' does lead one to assume that he is referring to the educated middle class, and that the attitudes he describes are not shared by working-class men and women.

Although source B questions how far women feel that they have a 'right to work' and suggests that traditional female roles 'as wives and mothers' still serve to keep women in a submissive role in the home, the author does recognise that, while the behaviour and attitude of women may not have altered, that of married men has dramatically altered, as 'men appear on the whole to be less conservative than they are usually assumed to be . . .' with women receiving 'moral support from their husbands in their decision to take a job . . .'. It might be worth noting as a word of caution though, that women only receive 'moral support' in this decision, not necessarily support with child care and housework. For whatever reason though, women clearly were taking jobs outside the home as source D shows that the number of women in part-time jobs had increased nearly five fold between 1951 and 1981. As the bulk of these jobs were unskilled, particularly in retailing, these figures are not enough in themselves to challenge source E's statement that 'a career or . . . a job with prospects of advancement, responsibility and promotion' was still not available to most women.

Perhaps it would be safest to conclude that, among the young at least, media images of women challenging stereotypical behaviour in news reporting and in fiction and occasional direct action, such as the slogan in source C, were serving to change attitudes of men and women, at least in their personal lives, as source A describes. Certainly, by 1979, it is unlikely that another survey, such as that carried out by Viola Klein, would have found such submissive views from so many women. Although Roberts finds little opportunity for optimism in the work place, her study concludes in 1970, and there are some grounds to believe that the employment opportunities for women did improve in the following decade, especially with the passing of the Sex Discrimination Act in 1975 and the establishment of the Equal Opportunities Commission. On the other hand however, all the available evidence seems to show that women had not begun to challenge male domination of more senior employment positions. 70 per cent of office staff and 99 per cent of typists were women in 1979, but only 14 per cent were office managers. Egalitarianism as a principle was enshrined in law and certainly espoused by the majority of Britons in 1979. Unfortunately, it was still actually practised extremely infrequently in the workplace and the home, as even those few women in relatively well-paid managerial jobs were still found to be putting their families first and sacrificing their careers for those of their husbands.

📖 3. Industrial relations in the 1970s (EDEXCEL)

Source 1: See Table 9.14.

Table 9.14 **Industrial disputes in the United Kingdom, 1970–79**

Year	Number of stoppages	Number of working days lost (in 1,000s)
1970	3,906	10,980
1971	2,228	13,551
1972	2,497	23,909
1973	2,873	7,197
1974	2,922	14,750
1975	2,282	6,012
1976	2,016	3,284
1977	2,703	10,142
1978	2,471	9,405
1979	2,080	29,474

Source 2: Minutes of the Conservative Shadow Cabinet weekend meeting at Selsdon Park Hotel, February 1970

Edward Heath: If we had trained men in the right places we would not have trade union monopoly. Employers will be prepared to spend if they know chaps won't strike. Never talked about this in public, perhaps we ought to. Point of industrial relations change is to redress the balance between employees and employer. Up to 1939 the balance was on the side of the employer. After 1945 the balance was on the side of the unions and it is still on the side of the unions.

Source 3: Adapted from the TUC General Council's Report, 1974

To meet the government's fears, the following assurance was put to the government on the afternoon of January 9:

The General Council accepts that there is a distinctive and exceptional situation in the mining industry. If the government are prepared to give an assurance that they will make possible a settlement between the miners and the National Coal Board, other unions will not use this as an argument in negotiations in their own settlements.

The Prime Minister [Edward Heath] told the TUC representatives at a meeting on January 21 that the government was unable to respond to this initiative. The General Council said that the government had missed a major opportunity to get Britain back to work on a full-time basis.

Source 4: From the Conservative Party election manifesto, February 1974

The action taken by the National Union of Mineworkers has already caused great damage and threatens even greater damage for the future. It must be the aim of any responsible Government to reach a settlement of this dispute at the earliest possible moment. The choice before the Government, and now the choice before the country, is clear. On the one hand it would be possible to accept the NUM's terms for a settlement. The country must realise what the consequences of this would be. It would mean accepting the abuse of industrial power to gain a privileged position. It would undermine the position of moderate trade union leaders. It would make it certain that similar strikes occurred at frequent intervals in the future. It would destroy our chances of containing inflation.

Source 5: From *Trade Unions, Government and the Economy* by Chris Wrigley

While it has been repeatedly asserted since 1945 that strikes are very damaging to the British economy, it is difficult to come up with the figures which show that they have had a major impact on the whole economy (as opposed to the particular industries affected). Obviously in most cases it would have been better for output if strikes had not occurred ... But the reality is that there was a 'silent majority' not involved in industrial stoppages at all. A Department of Employment survey of the years 1971–73 found that in the manufacturing industry an average of 98 per cent of establishments were free of stoppages.

QUESTIONS WITHOUT WORKED ANSWERS

a) **Study source 1. What does source 1 reveal about the extent of industrial unrest in Britain in the 1970s?** (6 marks)

b) **Use your own knowledge. Use your own knowledge to explain the importance of Heath's attitude at the Selsdon Park hotel meeting in 1970 (source 2) for the future stability of his government.** (10 marks)

c) **Study sources 2 and 4. How far does a study of sources 2 and 4 offer support for the view that the Conservatives had decided that unions were 'the enemy within' long before Mrs Thatcher became Prime Minister?** (10 marks)

d) **Study sources 1 and 3. How useful are these two sources to an historian studying the power of the trade unions in Britain in the post-war years?** (10 marks)

e) **Study sources 4 and 5 and use your own knowledge. Explain why the power of the trade unions was felt to be damaging the British economy in the 1970s. Explain your answer, using these two sources and your own knowledge.** (24 marks)

(Total: 60 marks)

4. The emergence of youth culture in the 1960s (EDEXCEL)

Read the source below and then answer the questions which follow.

Source 1: From *Shout! The True Story of the Beatles* by Phillip Norman

While Britain listened to Adam Faith and 'Pop', Liverpool listened to Rhythm and Blues. The Cunard Yanks were bringing over new records by a new young black performer still confined by his own country to the low indecent level of negro 'race' music. His name was Chuck Berry . . . His songs broke like anthems on the young of a northern city still gripped by the Victorian age, which had had no truck with black people since the slave hulks set sail from Liverpool bay. All over Merseyside each Saturday night, in ballrooms, town halls, Co-op halls, even swimming baths and ice skating rinks, there were amateur R&B groups playing Chuck Berry songs, Little Richard songs, Fats Domino and B.B. King songs.

QUESTIONS WITHOUT WORKED ANSWERS

a) **Explain why Liverpool became the centre of youth culture in Britain in the early 1960s.** (10 marks)

b) **How important was the example of America in influencing the fashions and politics of youth in Britain in the 1960s?** (14 marks)

c) 'The rejection by the middle class youth culture of bourgeois affluence had not extended to a rejection of long playing records and record players'. Discuss how far you agree with this view of youth culture in Britain in the 1960s.

(36 marks)

(Total: 60 marks)

Part 4: Historical skills

1. Analysis of statistics using spreadsheets

Use of ICT – creating a spreadsheet to detect trends in British economic performance between 1948 and 1979.

These materials are intended to be used as flexibly as possible. They can be used in an ICT suite with a whole class, or for individual study. Students could be supplied with a given set of data or they could use one or more files, depending on the task they have been set.

Table 9.15 **Imports of goods and services, 1948–79 (in £ millions)**

1948	2,407	1959	4,834	1970	11,053
1949	2,669	1960	5,499	1971	12,095
1950	3,046	1961	5,459	1972	13,658
1951	4,299	1962	5,554	1973	18,840
1952	3,899	1963	5,971	1974	27,007
1953	3,798	1964	6,798	1975	28,655
1954	3,922	1965	6,925	1976	36,483
1955	4,439	1966	7,215	1977	42,262
1956	4,510	1967	7,814	1978	45,234
1957	4,731	1968	9,329	1979	54,165
1958	4,535	1969	9,886		

Table 9.16 **Exports of goods and services, 1948–79 (in £ millions)**

1948	2,191	1959	4,836	1970	11,489
1949	2,489	1960	5,134	1971	12,890
1950	2,988	1961	5,366	1972	13,587
1951	3,639	1962	5,500	1973	17,027
1952	3,750	1963	5,852	1974	22,831
1953	3,677	1964	6,183	1975	26,803
1954	3,827	1965	6,596	1976	35,018
1955	4,166	1966	7,148	1977	43,210
1956	4,586	1967	7,370	1978	47,379
1957	4,823	1968	8,962	1979	51,804
1958	4,688	1969	10,064		

Table 9.17 **Unemployment rate, 1948–79 (%)**

Year	Rate	Year	Rate	Year	Rate
1948	1.8	1959	2.3	1970	2.7
1949	1.6	1960	1.7	1971	3.5
1950	1.6	1961	1.6	1972	3.8
1951	1.3	1962	2.1	1973	2.7
1952	2.2	1963	2.6	1974	2.6
1953	1.8	1964	1.7	1975	4.2
1954	1.5	1965	1.5	1976	5.7
1955	1.2	1966	1.6	1977	6.2
1956	1.3	1967	2.5	1978	6.1
1957	1.6	1968	2.5	1979	5.7
1958	2.2	1969	2.5		

Table 9.18 **Retail price index (January 1974 = 100)**

Year	Index	Year	Index	Year	Index
1948	33.3	1959	49.2	1970	73.1
1949	34.4	1960	49.8	1971	80.0
1950	35.1	1961	51.2	1972	85.7
1951	38.7	1962	53.0	1973	93.5
1952	40.5	1963	54.0	1974	108.5
1953	41.5	1964	55.8	1975	134.8
1954	42.3	1965	58.4	1976	157.1
1955	43.7	1966	60.7	1977	182.0
1956	45.8	1967	62.3	1978	197.1
1957	47.3	1968	65.2	1979	223.5
1958	48.7	1969	68.7		

This is an overall estimate of how much products in the shops cost. Looking at the difference between one year and the next will give you the annual rate of inflation.

Table 9.19 **Gross domestic product, 1948–79 (at 1995 market prices in £millions)**

Year	GDP	Year	GDP	Year	GDP
1948	224,486	1959	296,958	1970	416,793
1949	232,340	1960	312,850	1971	425,404
1950	239,480	1961	320,636	1972	440,444
1951	246,108	1962	324,608	1973	472,701
1952	247,168	1963	339,893	1974	464,842
1953	256,712	1964	358,498	1975	461,605
1954	267,730	1965	367,501	1976	474,508
1955	275,997	1966	374,597	1977	485,673
1956	278,707	1967	383,186	1978	502,201
1957	283,589	1968	398,858	1979	516,083
1958	284,625	1969	407,101		

This figure reflects how much money the country is actually spending in a year. It is made up of consumers' expenditure, government expenditure, investment, and the overall balance of payments. It is therefore a good indicator of the nation's wealth. As inflation makes the actual figures from different years useless for comparison, in this case they have been adjusted to reflect what each year's GDP figure would be worth in 1995.

Note the figures in Tables 9.15–9.19 begin in 1948, the first normal peacetime year, and the first year in which the Central Statistical Office (now the Office for National Statistics) began publication of these figures.

HOW DID THE BRITISH ECONOMY PERFORM BETWEEN 1948 AND 1979?

Between 1948 and 1979, Britain suffered a period of unprecedented economic growth and affluence, yet its economic performance was poor compared to the rest of the industrialised world.

Using spreadsheets to examine Britain's economic performance, it is possible to answer a number of questions, which can help to explain this paradox.

WHAT WAS THE PATTERN OF BRITAIN'S TRADE 1948–1979?

Your aim here is to get an idea of the overall pattern of trade across the period

- Open your spreadsheet package
- Input the statistics from Tables 9.15 and 9.16
- Graph the imports and exports together

Now answer the questions below:

1. What happened to British trade (imports and exports) between 1948 and 1967?
2. What was the total value of (a) imports and (b) exports for the period 1948–67?
3. What happened to British trade (imports and exports) between 1968 and 1979?
4. What was the total value of (a) imports and (b) exports for the period 1968–79?

HOW STRONG WAS THE BRITISH ECONOMY 1948–79?

- Now input the figures for unemployment from Table 9.17
- Graph these against the import/export figures
- Input the figures for the retail price index (RPI) and gross domestic product (GDP) from Tables 9.18 and 9.19
- Graph these next to each other

Now answer the following questions:

1. What appears to be the relationship between unemployment and the balance of trade between 1948 and 1967?
2. Does this relationship appear to change after 1968? If so, how?
3. What appears to be the relationship between RPI (a measure of inflation) and the GDP (a measure of national wealth)?
4. Does the rate of inflation appear to seriously affect the nation's overall wealth?

WHAT WAS THE CONDITION OF THE BRITISH ECONOMY IN 1979?

Consider the trends in all of these economic indicators and from them, consider how the British economy would have continued to perform after 1979 if Mrs Thatcher had not seriously altered British economic policy.

1. Which statistics seem to indicate that the British economy was in serious difficulty by 1979?
2. Which statistics indicate that in 1979 the British economy was already recovering from the slump between 1973 and 1976?

Research this issue further – are there other economic figures which suggest that the British economy was already in a state of recovery?

In particular, look for figures illustrating the growth of the following sectors of the economy:

a) Electrical engineering
b) Vehicles
c) Chemicals
d) Financial services
e) Retail

These are all sectors of the economy which would be important in Britain's economic well-being after 1979. In addition look at figures comparing the British economy with that of other countries, especially those on productivity. The following texts will provide you with the figures you need:

Booth, A. (1995) *British Economic Development since 1945*, Manchester: MUP.
Cairncross, A. (1995) *The British Economy since 1945* (2nd edn), Oxford: Blackwell.
Glynn, S. and Booth, A. (1996) *Modern Britain: an economic and social history*, London: Routledge.
Middleton, R. (2000) *The British Economy since 1945*, Basingstoke: Macmillan.
Office for National Statistics (1979) *Annual Abstract of Statistics*, London: HMSO.
Office for National Statistics (1979) *Social Trends no 9*, London: HMSO.
Pollard, S. (1997) *The International Economy since 1945*, London: Routledge.

Chapter 10

Towards the Millennium, 1979–2000

This chapter covers the final years of the twentieth century and attempts to analyse the political, social and economic developments of modern British society. The period is one dominated by the Thatcher era, as even the last decade, when she was no longer Prime Minister, saw Britain coping with her legacy. Mrs Thatcher once claimed that she wanted to change everything about Britain, and it is certainly true that her unmatched period of premiership was the most influential since that of Attlee. Whether or not she created a new political consensus to replace the previous one, is a matter of ongoing public and academic debate. Certainly, the Britain of 2000 was a very different place, to that of only 20 years earlier.

 ## Historical background

'Thatcherism'
Thatcher's first term in office,
    1979–83
The Falklands War and Mrs Thatcher's
    1983 election victory
'High Thatcherism' 1983–88
Mrs Thatcher's foreign policy
Thatcher in retreat 1988–90
The legacy of Thatcherism
John Major and the 1992 election
The strange death of Tory England,
    1992–97
The Labour Party in opposition
    1979–97
Northern Ireland since 1979
The economy since 1979
Immigration and race since 1979
The position of women since 1979
The decline of women since 1979
The decline of the traditional family
The role of the media
'An asteroid hitting the planet' –
    the 1997 election
Tony Blair, 'New Labour' and
    pre-millennial Britain

 ## Essays

1. The Thatcher governments 1979–90
2. Foreign policy under Thatcher
3. Labour in opposition 1983–97
4. New Labour in government
    1997–2001
5. Britain and the European Union
    1979–2000
6. Social and economic history since
    1979

Sources

1. The impact of the Falklands War
2. 'Thatcherism'
3. The fall of Thatcher
4. The European Union and the
    Conservative Party

Historical skills

1. Attempts to improve students'
    understanding of the influence of
    the media, by analysing the attitude
    of the media towards race and
    immigration in the last 20 years of
    the twentieth century.

Chronology

1979	Conservatives win general election – Thatcher Prime Minister
1980	Callaghan resigns as Labour leader, replaced by Foot
	Unemployment rises above two million for first time since 1938
1981	British Nationality Act
	Secondary picketing outlawed
	'Gang of Four' breaks from Labour to form Social Democratic Party (SDP)
	Rioting in London, Liverpool, Bristol, Leeds and Manchester
1982	Falklands War
	Unemployment exceeds three million
1983	Conservatives win general election
	Foot resigns as Labour leader, replaced by Kinnock
1984	Miners' strike begins
	Re-privatisation of British Telecom
	Britain agrees to hand Hong Kong to China in 1997
1985	Anglo-Irish Agreement
	Kinnock attacks Militant Tendency group
	Mikhail Gorbachev becomes leader of Soviet Union
1986	Re-privatisation of British Gas
	Britain agrees to the Single European Act
1987	Thatcher's visit to Moscow
	Conservatives win general election
1988	Baker's Education Act introduces a 'National Curriculum' for Schools
	Immigration Act
	Thatcher's Bruges speech
1989	Poll tax introduced in Scotland
	Collapse of communist regimes in Eastern Europe
1990	Poll Tax introduced in England and Wales – riots ensue
	Thatcher resigns as Prime Minister, replaced by Major
1991	The Gulf War against Iraq
	Collapse of Soviet Union – war breaks out in the Balkans
1992	Conservatives win general election
	Kinnock resigns as Labour leader, replaced by Smith
	Britain signs Maastricht Treaty on closer European integration
	'Black Wednesday' – Britain forced out of the Exchange Rate Mechanism – the pound is devalued
1993	Downing Street Declaration on Northern Ireland
1994	Smith dies, Blair becomes Labour leader
1995	Clause IV of Labour Party constitution re-written
	Dayton Agreement on peace in former Yugoslavia
1996	Re-privatisation of railways

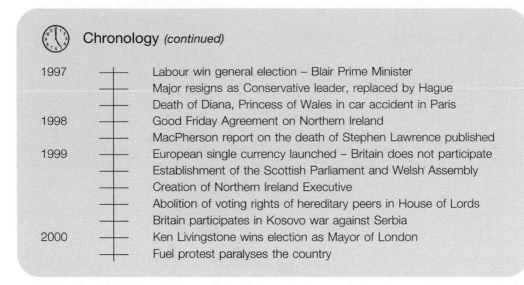

Chronology *(continued)*

1997	Labour win general election – Blair Prime Minister
	Major resigns as Conservative leader, replaced by Hague
	Death of Diana, Princess of Wales in car accident in Paris
1998	Good Friday Agreement on Northern Ireland
	MacPherson report on the death of Stephen Lawrence published
1999	European single currency launched – Britain does not participate
	Establishment of the Scottish Parliament and Welsh Assembly
	Creation of Northern Ireland Executive
	Abolition of voting rights of hereditary peers in House of Lords
	Britain participates in Kosovo war against Serbia
2000	Ken Livingstone wins election as Mayor of London
	Fuel protest paralyses the country

Part 1: Historical background

 ## 'Thatcherism'

Mrs Thatcher may have sounded like many other post-war Prime Ministers when she stood outside 10 Downing Street following her election and quoted the consensual prayer of St Francis of Assisi – 'where there is discord, may we bring harmony', but in reality her attitude was quite different to almost all her predecessors since 1945. Her attitude towards the 'consensus politics' was clear:

To me consensus seems to be: the process of abandoning all beliefs, principles, values and policies in search of something in which no one believes, but to which no one objects; the process of avoiding the very issues that have to be solved, merely because you cannot get agreement on the way ahead. What great cause would have been fought and won under the banner 'I stand for consensus'?

With the perceived failure of 'consensus politics' in the 1970s and the abandonment of Keynesian economics by Denis Healey, Mrs Thatcher, after being persuaded by colleagues such as Keith Joseph, decided to adopt a policy of '**monetarism**' as soon as politically advisable. This policy meant that instead of increasing government spending, the state needed to reduce public expenditure and thereby restrict the amount of money in circulation. As a result, her governments had a number of key aims. These included the following:

1) In order to operate a monetarist policy, the government would no longer subsidise unprofitable industries.
2) Welfare expenditure would be reduced by only providing benefit to those in genuine need.
3) Taxes on business and on personal income would be cut, so that people could spend more and businesses could expand further.
4) Companies and public utilities (such as gas, water, telephones and electricity) currently owned by the state would be privatised.

Table 10.1 *General election results, 1979–97*

	Conservative		Liberal		Labour	
	% vote	No. of seats	% vote	No. of seats	% vote	No. of seats
1979	43.9	339	13.8	11	36.9	269
			(SDP-Lib Alliance)			
1983	42.4	397	25.4	23	27.6	209
			(SDP-Lib Alliance)			
1987	42.2	376	22.6	22	30.8	229
1992	42.3	336	18.3	20	35.2	271
1997	30.7	165	16.8	46	43.2	418

Thatcher also felt that certain institutions, especially the trade unions, were exploiting Britain's troubles for their own benefit and so she sought to bring more accountability into the unions and public services (whose unions were the most troublesome). Her concern at maintaining the sovereignty of Parliament, as she saw it, was also demonstrated in her aims towards Europe:

1) Trade unions would be made more democratic and thereby more responsive to the wishes of their members.
2) Local government, hospitals and schools would be made more accountable to those who used these services.
3) The rights of the British Parliament to control Britain's affairs would be upheld in the face of EEC demands for greater power.

In Foreign Affairs, three particular problems confronted Mrs Thatcher – the **Cold War**, Northern Ireland and the remnants of Britain's Empire. As her premiership continued however, a fourth problem came to dominate her thinking, the nature of Britain's relationship with the European Union, of which Britain had only been a member for six years. Her aims were as follows:

1) Britain would remain in the EEC, but attempt to reform it from within, and attempt to reduce Britain's annual contribution.
2) Britain would continue to reduce its direct involvement in ruling former colonies, but would still protect the rights of British citizens living abroad.
3) America would be supported as it attempted to confront Communist expansion and Britain would continue to press for human rights reform in Communist controlled countries.
4) British and Irish governments must co-operate to defeat the terrorism plaguing Northern Ireland.

 Thatcher's first term in office 1979–83

The government's first crisis was, in fact, a foreign issue. The ongoing war in Southern Rhodesia between the white rebels who had announced UDI in 1965 and the black nationalists caused huge embarrassment to Britain, the former colonial ruler. Mrs Thatcher tried to persuade both sides to accept the moderate black bishop, Abel Muzorewa, as an interim leader until elections were held, but the leader of the black independence fighters, Robert Mugabe, refused to agree. Mrs Thatcher had to agree to let her Foreign Secretary, Lord Carrington arrange a meeting between both sides at Lancaster House in London. Here, the inevitability of Mugabe's claim to leadership became clear and a peaceful transition to majority rule, with elections that Mugabe duly won, was achieved.

Unlike this diplomatic success, Mrs Thatcher was aware that her economic policies might spark widespread protest, and she took care to secure large pay awards for the police and army. And, despite her long-term monetarist intentions, she agreed to the Clegg recommendations for pay awards for public sector workers, to keep happy those who gave her a narrow victory. The result was actually increased government spending and inflation of 22 per cent by spring 1980. **Monetarism** was not yet being implemented.

Mrs Thatcher's Chancellor, Geoffrey Howe's first budget raised indirect taxes (most importantly Value Added Tax – VAT) from 8 per cent to 15 per cent, but he cut the top rate of direct (income) tax from 83 per cent to 60 per cent and the standard rate from 33 per cent to 30 per cent. This shift from direct to indirect tax was designed 'to boost incentives' by allowing the successful high earners to keep more of their income. Interest rates were raised to 14 per cent and these later reached 17 per cent, rewarding those with large savings, but hurting people with debts.

In their attempt to curb the powers of the trade unions, the 1980 *Employment Act* made secondary picketing illegal but didn't make ballots compulsory or ban sympathetic strikes. Thatcher carefully arranged leaks to the press from her private office, so that she conveyed her annoyance with James Prior, the Employment Secretary.

After the first year, which Thatcher's guru, Sir Keith Joseph called 'the lost year', the attack on government spending began in 1980. Mrs Thatcher and her government were prepared to risk worsening the current economic slump in order to reduce inflation for the longer term benefit of the economy. Exacerbated by the government's policies, manufacturing production, which was already declining, fell by 14 per cent in just one year, 1980–81, and gross national product (GNP) fell by 3.2 per cent. Unemployment rose to 2.7 million, the highest since the Depression in the 1930s.

All in all, Britain lost 25 per cent of her manufacturing capacity between 1979 and 1981 with the old manufacturing areas in the North and Wales the hardest hit. As a result, the country became increasingly dependent on the service economy (insurance, banking, advertising and retail). Luckily for the government, North Sea oil and gas supplies increased by 70 per cent and helped to save the country from bankruptcy. On the other hand, productivity increased among those still in work and inflation did finally come down to under 10 per cent in 1982, although this was partly due to the high value of the pound and increased unemployment levels.

Despite the government's intentions, though, public expenditure continued to rise, reaching 44.5 per cent of the gross domestic product (GDP) by 1982, largely as a result of the huge increases in number of those receiving unemployment benefit. Although direct taxes fell, the overall tax burden rose from 34 per cent of GDP in 1978–79, to 40 per cent of GDP in 1982/83. Faced with mounting criticism from the moderates in her cabinet, Mrs Thatcher demonstrated her determination to continue with the government's policy, to which she claimed 'There is no alternative'. Moderates (or as she termed them, '**wets**') such as Norman St John Stevas and Ian Gilmour were sacked, and right wingers like John Nott and Leon Brittan promoted. Mrs Thatcher knew that the Conservative party would not yet accept a Cabinet made up of what were increasingly being referred to in the press as 'Thatcherites', so Francis Pym, Michael Heseltine and James Prior remained. Instead,

Thatcher increasingly avoided informing her Cabinet of the government's economic policy. The 1981 budget, which brought in further deflationary tactics at the height of the recession was only revealed to Cabinet on budget day. Economic policy was being determined by Treasury ministers and advisers such as Alan Walters. Eventually, Mrs Thatcher went further and James Prior was moved to administer Northern Ireland and replaced by the Thatcherite, Norman Tebbit, and the equally loyal Nigel Lawson was made Energy Secretary.

The social consequences of the economic 'recession' were seen in waves of riots across inner-city London, Liverpool, Manchester, Leeds and Bristol in summer 1981, which the government blamed on the lawlessness and the lack of personal responsibility of the rioters. Mrs Thatcher's opinion poll ratings were now the lowest in history. Fortunately for her Labour had appointed Michael Foot as party leader following Callaghan's resignation in 1980 and he had been unable to prevent a party split caused by the increased influence of the left wing of the party. Four senior, moderate Labour leaders, including the former Foreign Secretary, David Owen and the former Chancellor, Roy Jenkins, had left the Labour Party with several important followers to form the Social Democratic Party (SDP). There was no sign yet that the Tory Party was prepared to replace Mrs Thatcher, but they were anxious that the government's fortunes should improve in time for the next election.

The Falklands War and Mrs Thatcher's 1983 election victory

In 1982, Thatcher's fortunes were dramatically reversed by the conflict with Argentina that broke out over the Falkland Islands in the South Atlantic. The islands, close to Argentina, were a British possession, inhabited by British citizens. Argentina had laid claim to them as 'las Malvinas' for many years and had been negotiating with Britain to administer the islands, while they remained British. The military dictatorship of General Galtieri was becoming increasingly unpopular in Argentina however, and so he ordered an invasion force of 4,000 troops to seize the islands in April. Mrs Thatcher immediately ordered that a military taskforce should re-take the islands, brushing aside calls to involve the United Nations in a negotiated settlement.

Once the taskforce arrived, a 200 mile exclusion zone was placed around the islands, and military exchanges began in which three British ships and the Argentine cruiser, *Belgrano*, was sunk. British troops then landed on the Falklands in May and the islands were recaptured in June. Two hundred and fifty-five British and 665 Argentine soldiers were killed, but Mrs Thatcher's forceful actions seemed vindicated, and she was fêted by the right-wing press for having restored Britain's prestige abroad after long years of decline and retreat.

Mrs Thatcher, eager to take political advantage of her sudden popularity called an election for spring 1983. She was also conscious that the economy was beginning to show signs of recovery and that none of her opponents, Labour, SDP and Liberal, had managed to prevent the anti-Conservative vote from being fragmented between them. Mrs Thatcher had also introduced a policy which managed to combine her economic priorities with political popularity, when she introduced the compulsory sale of council houses to tenants. Working-class groups who had not traditionally supported the Conservatives were grateful for this opportunity to buy their own homes, especially as the sales were fixed at prices below the houses' market value. Mrs Thatcher's party won 397 seats, while the Labour Party held onto 209 seats. The Liberal party only won 17 seats, while the SDP only managed 6 seats.

Mrs Thatcher's victory was only tarnished in one minor fashion. A civil servant at the Ministry of Defence, Clive Ponting, leaked information to a Labour MP, revealing that the Argentine cruiser, *Belgrano*, had been sailing away from the British fleet when it was ordered to be sunk, and that the decision to attack was taken by the War Cabinet, not the British submarine captain, as Mrs Thatcher had previously claimed. This was a minor embarrassment, but it troubled the Defence Minister, Michael Heseltine enough to put Ponting on trial for breaching the Official Secrets Act, and thus giving the issue even more publicity, especially when the jury unanimously found Ponting not guilty, despite him confessing to having leaked the documents.

'High Thatcherism' 1983–88

By January 1983, inflation had fallen to 5.4 per cent, the lowest level since 1970. Despite the continuing high level of unemployment, which didn't reach its peak until 1985, when 3,200,000 people were out of work, Mrs Thatcher now felt able to turn her attention to the nationalised industries and those groups she termed the 'enemies within', most particularly the unions.

Privatisation was the sale of publicly owned assets, such as gas and electricity, coal and telecommunications. These nationalised industries were widely seen as inefficient and uncompetitive, giving consumers no choice over where to get their basic household services. Selling shares in these businesses would, the Conservatives stated, make services cheaper as well as raise millions of much needed capital. To make the process popular, share prices were fixed attractively low and every attempt was made to advertise the quick and easy profits available to all. In the case of the **privatisation** of British Gas, the initial share floatation was over-subscribed five fold.

Table 10.2 **Privatisation of industries**

Year	Major industries privatised	Total revenue from privatisation (millions of £)
1979	British Petroleum	290
1980	—	n/a
1981	British Aerospace	373
1982	Amersham International (medical research group)	455
1983	—	1,139
1984	British Telecom Jaguar Cars	2,050
1985	—	2,706
1986	British Gas	4,458
1987	British Airways Rolls Royce British Airports Authority	5,140
1988	British Steel	7,069
1989	10 regional water boards	4,226
1990	12 regional electricity companies	5,346
1991	—	7,923
1992	—	7,962

The Conservatives concealed the main political motive for the policy, however. The revenue saved from the government purse and generated by the share sales was largely spent in funding tax cuts in the elections of 1987 and 1992. Some Conservatives spoke out against the policy, such as Harold Macmillan who deplored what he saw as 'selling off the family silver', but they were very much in the minority, and in the short term, the policy was highly successful and contributed to Mrs Thatcher's historic third electoral victory in 1987. On the other hand, only a minority of the population (albeit a large one) participated in these sales. The number of private share-holders did increase from 3 million in 1979 to 11 million by 1990, but this was a long way from Mrs Thatcher's vision of a 'share-owning democracy'. The policy was also soon tarnished. First, by the stock market crash of October 1987, which wiped out many of the initial gains, and second, by the high wages that new directors of the privatised industries paid themselves, while they sacked scores of workers. These accusations of 'sleaze' also affected Tory ministers, such as Norman Tebbit and Norman Fowler, who managed to find themselves lucrative positions on the boards of the privatised companies they had helped to de-nationalise.

The most important test of strength for Mrs Thatcher's second government was the year-long miners' strike from 1984 to 1985. Thatcher's choice of Ian MacGregor as chairman of the National Coal Board (NCB) in September 1983 helped to provoke a strike, in the knowledge that the government had built up coal reserves in preparation for a long stoppage. The government's tactics in calling for a ballot of the miners before recognising the legality of the strike was a clever move, as the Nottinghamshire miners who were reluctant to strike, had felt pressured by the extremists in the National Union of Mineworkers (NUM), and eventually broke away to found the Union of Democratic Mineworkers (UDM). After violent confrontations with the police, and the killing of a taxi-driver taking strike-breakers to work, the miners were eventually forced back to work and the government was then free to pursue its policy of closing unprofitable pits and preparing the industry for **privatisation**. Similarly, the power of the newspaper print unions was crushed after violent confrontations with the police at the new newspaper offices in Wapping.

The only serious crisis in the whole of Mrs Thatcher's second term in office came over the relatively minor issue of the British Westland helicopter company in 1986. The Defence Secretary, Michael Heseltine wanted to see the company go into partnership with European companies, while the Industry Minister, Leon Brittan wanted a deal with the large US company, Sikorski. Heseltine, already annoyed by Thatcher's unwillingness to allow debate in Cabinet, resigned when he found that confidential material had been leaked to the press to discredit his position. Thatcher was able to blame the leak on Brittan, who also resigned, but doubts were raised over her involvement in the affair and she earned the enmity of Heseltine, who began to act as leader of the opposition to Thatcher from the Conservative back benches.

 Mrs Thatcher's foreign policy

As a convinced opponent of communism, Mrs Thatcher was an unquestioning Cold Warrior. She found a staunch ally in Ronald Reagan, US President after 1981, and it was not by accident that he first described the Soviet Union as an 'Evil Empire' when addressing the Houses of Parliament in 1982. Mrs Thatcher promised that 'Britain and America will stand side by side' and willingly purchased the new Trident missiles, as secretly agreed by the previous Labour government, seeing them as vital protection against the new Soviet SS-20 missiles. This prompted a revival in the **Campaign for Nuclear Disarmament**, especially focused at the American Airbase at Greenham Common, but Mrs Thatcher was unrepentant.

The restoration of the 'special relationship' was only jeopardised when Reagan forgot, on two occasions, to consult sufficiently with Britain. The first was when Reagan announced the Strategic Defence Initiative (SDI) research project (popularly known as 'Star Wars') in 1983, which would create an anti-missile shield over USA, but not Western Europe. The second was when Reagan ordered an invasion of Grenada to overthrow a marxist regime also in 1983, ignoring the fact that Grenada was a member of the British Commonwealth. The disagreement did not last long, however, as was shown in 1986, when Britain allowed USA use of her airbases to launch attacks on Libya.

Thatcher's staunch anti-communism did not prevent her from supporting communist leaders when they attempted to move away from confrontation with the West and to liberalise their regimes. In particular, Mrs Thatcher was swift to praise the Russian leader after 1985, Mikhail Gorbachev, as 'a man I can do business with'. She encouraged Reagan to negotiate with him and this led in part to the dramatic breakthrough in arms reductions talks at Reykjavik in 1986. To emphasise her support for his efforts in modernising the Soviet system itself, Mrs Thatcher paid a visit to Moscow. The sight of Mrs Thatcher being warmly received by the ordinary people of Moscow seemed to indicate that the **Cold War** was over, and carefully stage managed prior to the 1987 election, it significantly contributed to her sustained popularity.

Mrs Thatcher's dealings with Europe were similarly direct. She was deeply suspicious of the bureaucracy of the EEC and determined to minimise Britain's contribution to the Community when the British economy was in recession. Her tactics, putting British interests above those of Europe, and refusing to back down, alienated the other European leaders, but proved highly popular at home. Typical of her approach was her statement in July 1979 that she would not 'play Sister bountiful to the Community while my own electorate are being asked to forego improvements in the fields of health, education, welfare and the rest'. To her credit, these tactics had some success in the short term as Britain received a rebate of £1,570 million on her contribution to the EEC in 1980. In the long term, her approach began to make the other European leaders distrust her and exclude her from important policy making, leaving Britain on the fringes of European affairs.

Mrs Thatcher was thus forced to respond to European initiatives as they arose. She agreed to the Single European Act of 1986, as it liberalised trade in the community, but she kept Britain out of the **Exchange Rate Mechanism** (ERM) for as long as she could, regardless of the economic dangers, as she feared it as a major step towards the loss of British economic sovereignty. Her worries about a more federal Europe came to the fore in 1988, when she made a speech in Bruges, largely for domestic consumption, in which she challenged the vision of the then President of the European Commission, Jacques Delors: 'We have not rolled back the frontiers of the state in Britain, only to have them reimposed at European level, with a European superstate exercising a new dominance from Brussels'.

This speech, more than any other statement, began the 'civil war' over Europe within the Conservative party. It was this approach which led to Geoffrey Howe's resignation and her own eventual resignation after a back-bench revolt. And it was the battle between the 'euro-sceptics' who agreed with the Bruges speech and the 'euro-enthusiasts' who repudiated it, which was to ruin John Major's government after 1992.

Like the USA, Thatcher seemed entirely unprepared for the dramatic events of 1989 as the communist regimes of Eastern Europe collapsed and the Soviet Union failed to intervene. Demonstrating her lack of sympathy with European politicians, she actually attempted to impede the attempts of East and West Germany to reunite, fearing the impact of a larger, stronger Germany on the European **balance of power**. She demonstrated her prejudices when commenting to a young foreign policy adviser as she watched the collapse of the Berlin Wall in November 1989:

You know, there are things that people of your generation and mine ought never to forget. We've been through the war and we know perfectly well what the Germans are like and what dictators can do and how national character basically doesn't change.

For her attempts to delay German unification during 1990, she earned the hostility of the West German Chancellor, Helmut Kohl, who made it clear that he would welcome an alternative British leader to Mrs Thatcher.

 ## Thatcher in retreat 1988–90

After her spectacular third victory in which the Tories again received a majority of over 100 seats, Mrs Thatcher seemed secure. The much anticipated 'economic miracle', seemed finally to have arrived, as Britain saw steady economic growth after 1982, and in 1989, unemployment finally fell below two million. However, this boom led to an increase in consumer spending, which, following the decline in manufacturing, was mainly on imports. The 'yuppie' lifestyle of conspicuous consumption, therefore led to a poor **balance of payments** and rising inflation (reaching 8 per cent in 1989). In order to control this, the then Chancellor, Nigel Lawson, was forced to use his only remaining financial weapon, a rise in interest rates, to control this. As this made mortgages more expensive for the new house-owning voters, the consequences were political unpopularity. At this crucial moment, Mrs Thatcher's political sure-footedness suddenly deserted her in her attempts to bring the finances of local governments (which were often Labour-run) under central government control. She wanted a change to the inequitable system of paying for local government services, called rates, as these were set by local councils, and were, in a number of Labour controlled councils, deliberately high for the owners of large houses and low for the poorer citizens. Mrs Thatcher therefore favoured an alternative, the 'community charge' which was fixed by central government where all paid the same amount. No doubt she was prepared, even happy, to face opposition from local governments, but when the scheme was applied in Scotland as a test in 1989, it provoked massive popular anger and mass non-payment, with the charge being branded the '**poll tax**', an allusion to the medieval system of charging all taxpayers the same, whether rich or poor, which had led to the Peasants' Revolt in 1389. In a quite unbelievable case of putting doctrine above political sense, Mrs Thatcher overrode the concerns of her Cabinet and insisted on the system being introduced to the whole of Britain in 1990. Within days of the decision being announced, demonstrations were held across the country, culminating in a massive riot in Trafalgar Square, shown live on television in which 400 police officers were injured, and only luck prevented any fatalities. Of course, it would have still been possible for Mrs Thatcher to have survived, as she had a huge parliamentary majority, and the support of the bulk of her party on the issue.

At this moment, however, the tensions over Mrs Thatcher's increasingly personal approach to leadership came to the surface. In particular, dissatisfaction with her policy towards Europe, which had been causing unrest since her speech in Bruges in 1988, finally spilled out. Mrs Thatcher declared at a meeting of the European Council in Rome that she would veto any future treaty on economic monetary union, accusing the other heads of government of living in 'cloud-cuckoo land'. When she made the following outburst in Parliament on 30 October 1990, events happened swiftly.

I do not want the Commission to increase its powers at the expense of the House [of Commons] . . . Mr Delors said . . . that he wanted the European Parliament to be the democratic body of the Community, he wanted the Commission to be the Executive, and he wanted the Council of Ministers to be the Senate. No, no, no!

First, Geoffrey Howe, her deputy and former Foreign Secretary resigned. Although being criticised by Howe had been described as 'being savaged by a dead sheep' by Denis Healey, he gave a passionate denunciation of Mrs Thatcher's attitude to Europe in his resignation speech.

People throughout Europe see our Prime Minister finger-wagging, hear her passionate, 'No, no, no!' much more than the content of carefully worded formal texts. The task has become futile . . . of trying to pretend there was a common policy when every step forward risked being subverted by some casual comment or impulsive answer . . . That is why I have resigned.

Seizing this opportunity, Michael Heseltine, who had been awaiting his opportunity since resigning from the Cabinet over the Westland Affair in 1986, immediately challenged Mrs Thatcher for the leadership of the Conservative Party, without which she would be unable to continue as Prime Minister. Mrs Thatcher won the first ballot, but she failed to win sufficient votes to prevent a second ballot, with 152 of her own party voting against her. At this point, her Cabinet colleagues refused to back her and forced her to resign. She gave her personal support to her Chancellor, John Major, and there was sufficient distrust of Heseltine for Major to win.

The legacy of Thatcherism

Despite losing office in 1990 and retreating to the House of Lords, in British politics of the 1990s, the legacy of **Thatcherism** was clearly evident. Her aggressive response to all those who challenged her was particularly copied by Tony Blair who ill-advisedly took a belligerent approach to the fuel-tax protestors in 2000 but more successfully advocated Britain's contribution to the war against Serbia over the treatment of Kosovo Albanians in 1999. Most seriously for Britain, the consequences of under-resourcing of various elements of the infrastructure under Mrs Thatcher became apparent as the inadequacies in the rail network, state education, the health service, social security and even flood defences were laid bare in the 1990s. Such was the strength of the new consensus that Mrs Thatcher had created, however, that both Major and Blair's government continued to rely on indirect taxation, as Mrs Thatcher had made the reduction in income tax an accepted government priority. Mrs Thatcher's last years clearly helped to create a growing distrust of the European project especially among the popular media, which the right wing of the Conservative Party continued to encourage throughout the 1990s. Mrs Thatcher's attacks on certain professional groups led to a lack of affluence among traditionally comfortable groups such as teachers, local government ministers, health workers and social workers. Her reluctance to allow any state interference in the power of the employer and her reduction of the reach of social security seemed to threaten the creation of an underclass of casually employed, badly housed and poorly educated workers.

In political terms, though, the greatest legacy of her years in power and those of her immediate successor appeared to have been the apathy and contempt of many towards the political process in Britain and towards politicians in particular. The need for alternative approaches to political life in Britain appeared pressing, but John Major at least, was unable to offer a distinct alternative to the Thatcherite approach.

John Major and the 1992 election

John Major had only been a member of the Cabinet since 1987, and although he had served as Home Secretary, Foreign Secretary and Chancellor, he not held any of these positions for long. As he put it, when he entered 10 Downing Street for the first time, at the very young age of 47, 'Well, who'd have thought it?' Major was keen to try to put his stamp on the government before calling an election, which was due in 18 months. He followed a much more conciliatory approach than his predecessor, both in Cabinet and in the country, calling for 'a classless society' and swiftly dropping the hated **poll tax**. He led Britain calmly during the short-lived 'Operation Desert Storm', a US-led coalition to expel Iraqi forces from occupying the small neighbouring state of Kuwait. He also managed to (temporarily) paper over the divisions in the Conservative Party over Europe, by signing up to the **Maastricht Treaty** on greater integration (which pleased the pro-Europeans) while achieving an opt-out for Britain from joining the **European Monetary Union** (EMU) and from a **Social Chapter** of fairly mild common welfare policies (which pleased the Thatcherite anti-Europeans). When the election came, many people were prepared to give Major the opportunity of a full term of office, not convinced that Labour offered a viable alternative government.

The influence of the tabloid press was, for once, as crucial as they usually claimed. The following front page of the most popular newspaper in Britain, the *Sun*, on election day, carefully attacked the weakest point of Labour's challenge, the credibility of their leader, Neil Kinnock:

> IF KINNOCK WINS TODAY
> WILL THE LAST PERSON TO
> LEAVE BRITAIN PLEASE
> TURN OUT THE LIGHTS
> You know our views on the subject but
> we don't want to influence you in your
> final judgement on who will be Prime
> Minister.
> But if it's a bald bloke with wispy red
> hair and two K's in his surname, we'll
> see you at the airport.
> Goodnight and thank you for every-
> thing.

As subsequent research has revealed, there was an 8 per cent swing to Major among *Sun* readers in the three months before the election. Although it might be going too far to agree that 'IT'S THE SUN WOT WON IT' (as it claimed two days later), its influence was clearly significant. Perhaps even more significant was Labour's shadow budget, which revealed that taxes would have to rise to pay for improvements to public services. At a time of recession, many voters genuinely feared the consequences of such increases and still associated Labour with the 'tax and spend' approach of the 1960s and 1970s. Conservative posters warning of 'Labour's tax bombshell' made sure the message, albeit crudely exaggerated, was not ignored.

The 'strange death of Tory England' 1992–97

By 1992, politics had returned to the state they had been before the heady days of 'high' **Thatcherism**. John Major, a largely unknown Conservative leader, like Thatcher in 1979, was given his chance over a Labour party which still appeared spend-thrift and internally divided. Major's party in 1992 gained only three seats less than Thatcher had done in her first election in 1979 and also saw Labour pegged at a distance of around 65–70 seats behind. The great difference this time was in the continued strength of the nationalists and the liberals, who reduced his overall majority to 21, less than half the majority that had protected Mrs Thatcher during her tumultuous first term of office. If Major wanted an untroubled full five years of premiership he needed the loyalty of his party and economic calm. He got neither.

Almost unquestionably the most damaging incident of Major's premiership was 'Black Wednesday', 16 September 1992, when the government, having spent billions of pounds in trying to prevent it, was forced to suspend sterling from the **Exchange Rate Mechanism** (ERM). This affair, or more particularly the incompetent handling of it by Major's chancellor, Norman Lamont, lost the Tories their reputation for financial competence. Although it was less than six months into a new parliament, it cast a pall over the next five years, which the Conservative Party was unable to remove.

Following this humiliation, it was announced by the government that 31 out of 50 coal pits were to be closed in preparation for **privatisation** . Such harsh treatment of the miners, shortly followed by the chaos caused by the **privatisation** of the railways and well-publicised failures in the first privatised prison, led many to question the advisability of extending the role of the private sector much further. The institution of an 'internal market' in the National Health Service led some to fear creeping **privatisation** here, in the one part of the public sector that most people felt some respect for.

In a desperate attempt to regain the political initiative, Major announced a policy of 'Back to Basics', reasserting high standards of moral behaviour from politicians, following accusations of ministerial involvement in improper arms sales to Iraq. This backfired spectacularly as newspapers competed to reveal ever more lurid stories of ministerial sexual misbehaviour and financial 'sleaze', culminating in the 'cash for questions' scandal, when Conservatives were found to have asked parliamentary questions in return for money and gifts. In all, 17 Conservative ministers were forced to resign during Major's premiership. Although Major was never personally involved in the scandals and moved swiftly to set up a permanent committee to investigate future impropriety, it seemed that the long years of Conservative rule had encouraged some of its members to ignore the standards expected of public servants.

The Major government's mismanagement was perhaps most strikingly in evidence in the BSE crisis, when it was revealed that the cheap production techniques employed in beef farming had led to an outbreak of 'mad cow disease', more properly known as BSE. Challenged on whether the disease could be transmitted to humans, the government vigorously denied this, with one minister publicly feeding a beefburger to his daughter to demonstrate their safety. After it was revealed that the disease could in fact be transmitted to humans, European Union countries banned British beef from being imported. Although British officials moved swiftly to try to eradicate the disease, the public asked searching questions about food standards, which revealed alarming information about pork, chicken and lamb production. The government, keen to try to deflect criticism, as it had been under Mrs Thatcher that food safety standards had been relaxed, announced a policy of non-cooperation with the European Union, which seemed an unhelpful gesture when faced with a possible epidemic of unknown proportions.

If the ERM crisis was the most important factor in damaging the reputation of the Conservative Party, the issue of Europe was the most important in damaging Major's personal standing. The Conservative Party was torn apart by division over Europe between 1992 and 1997. Major claimed that he successfully negotiated a compromise position for Britain at the Maastricht negotiations in 1992, by securing an 'opt-out' for Britain from both the moves towards European and Monetary Union (EMU) and the **Social Chapter** which guaranteed modest standards of protection for workers. For the Thatcherites on the right of the party, agreeing to any aspects of the treaty was not acceptable and they began to organise against Major. After they failed to stop the **Maastricht Treaty** being accepted by Parliament by one vote, Major felt strong enough to expel eight of the 'Euro-rebels' from the party, but the criticisms of his leadership did not stop. Eventually, in 1995, he was forced to take the unprecedented step of resigning as leader of the Conservative Party and immediately standing for re-election, in order to force his opponents, to 'put up or shut up'. To his horror, a member of his own cabinet, John Redwood, the Welsh secretary, announced his nomination and there were rumours of other ministers, in particular, Michael Portillo, the Defence Secretary, preparing to run if the first vote was inconclusive, as it had been in 1990. Major won fairly comfortably on the first vote, but the impression of a scheming Cabinet lacking a firm leader remained. Major was forced to take a more hard-line towards Europe to keep his back-benchers happy, but this attempt to woo the 'euro-sceptics' was thwarted when the maverick right-wing businessman, Sir James Goldsmith, founded a new political party, the Referendum Party, in time for the 1997 election, which called for a national vote on Britain's membership of the EU. In one last humiliation for the Prime Minister, George Gardiner, one of Major's own MPs defected to the Referendum Party weeks before the election. The party approached the election as divided and demoralised as it had done in 1906, when the issue had been **Tariff Reform**, and Major suffered a similar fate as Balfour had done then. Unlike Balfour, however, Major had the good sense to resign as swiftly as he could after the election.

 ## The Labour Party in opposition 1979–97

In opposition, the party which had managed to stay together when in government, largely due to the astute work of its leaders, began to split apart, as it had done between 1951 and 1964. Callaghan resigned as leader in 1980, and the Parliamentary Labour Party (PLP) elected Michael Foot as a compromise between the right-wing candidate, Denis Healey and the left-wing candidate, Tony Benn. However, the party quickly began to polarise under Foot's weak leadership.

The Labour Party was comprised of a number of institutions in 1979 – the leadership, the shadow Cabinet, the National Executive Committee (NEC), the Conference and the larger unions. Traditionally the right of the party controlled all the key institutions and thereby the parliamentary leadership. In the late 1970s, however, the left-wing of the party gained a majority on the NEC. This group, largely made up of Labour activists, then supported Tony Benn's campaign to make Labour MPs more accountable to rank and file via mandatory reselection of sitting MPs and the election of the leader and deputy leader by an electoral college made up of: trade unions – 40 per cent; PLP – 30 per cent; Constituency parties – 30 per cent.

This was adopted by a special party conference in 1981. The day after the conference four prominent former Labour ministers, Roy Jenkins, Shirley Williams, David Owen and William Rogers, issued the 'Limehouse Declaration' which led to the establishment of the Social Democratic Party (SDP), which 17 other Labour MPs joined during the year.

But the right-wing of the Labour Party resisted both the challenge from these rebels and the attempted coup by the left, led by the deputy party leader Denis Healey, Roy Hattersley and the centre-right unions. Healey warned that left-wing extremists were attempting to take over the party and the new rules for selection of MPs meant that some constituencies 'were easy prey to penetration and capture by a handful of conspirators who knew what they wanted'.

The collapse of Keynesian economics after 1976 had led the party to adopt a far more radical programme and the Labour manifesto of 1983 was the most left-wing in history. It promised tax raises for rich, import duties, unilateral nuclear disarmament, leaving the European Union, repeal of Conservative limits on trade unions and increased subsidies for housing, health and education. It was described by one critic in the party as the 'longest suicide note in history' as it paid little attention to the profound changes in political economy that were taking place at home and abroad. The public's dissatisfaction with such policies was clear in the scale of Labour's defeat in 1983. Labour won 209 seats, but with only 28 per cent of vote, only 2 per cent above the 'alliance' of the SDP and Liberals. This was the lowest proportion of the vote that Labour had won since 1900 when the party was founded. Most notably, Tony Benn lost his seat. After the electoral disaster in 1983, Michael Foot resigned and was replaced by Neil Kinnock, a left-winger, but a far more pragmatic politician than Foot. The Labour Party has been accurately described at this point as 'demoralised, deeply polarised and virtually ungovernable'. Kinnock realised the need for the party to regain its credibility with the voters by cultivating a more modern image. The Labour Party, like the Conservatives, needed to be cohesive and well managed, and to adopt more moderate policies. Shortly after becoming leader, policies such as the guarantee of full employment, the pledge to re-nationalise industry and opposition to membership of the European Union and council house sales were abandoned, but non-nuclear defence policy was retained. Labour's spending pledges were cut back. Many of these policies were opposed by the extra-parliamentary party, and it was clear that the activists needed to be controlled by the collective parliamentary leadership, if the party was to be re-electable again.

Kinnock faced a serious difficulty in handling the 1984–85 miners' strike and the dispute over rate controls, but the collapse of the rate-capping campaign and the miners' strike severely damaged the left and extra-parliamentary approach. Most importantly for Kinnock this led to a split between the 'soft left' (particularly David Blunkett, Michael Meacher, Gordon Brown and Bryan Gould) and the 'hard left' (Tony Benn, Eric Heffer and Dennis Skinner). This gave Kinnock the opportunity to modernise the party in the following ways:

a) Centralisation, in particular the increased strength and importance of Leader's Office.

Another disaster like the 1983 manifesto was to be avoided by the establishment of a Policy Review Group composed of shadow Cabinet members. A Campaign Strategy Committee was set up, answerable directly to Kinnock, co-ordinated by the Campaigns and Communications Directorate (from 1985 , this was led by Peter Mandelson). The NEC was given the power to choose by-election candidates. A new disciplinary system was introduced to crack down on the Trotskyist 'Militant' group, which had infiltrated the party.

b) Direct Membership enfranchisement.

There was a gradual introduction of the principle of One Member One Vote (OMOV) rather than bloc-votes, as individual Labour Party members tended to be less radical than activists. This tactic was first used to purge the hard left from the NEC (Tony Benn finally lost his seat in 1993) to be replaced by members of shadow Cabinet.

After the election in 1987, when Labour was again defeated, but most importantly managed to beat off the challenge of the SDP-Liberal alliance's strongest campaign since the war, three new courses of action were introduced:

1. There was a wider franchise for selection and re-selection of candidates – to prevent extremism.
2. The shadow Cabinet and the PLP were given greater power over the NEC and Party Conference.
3. There was a wide-ranging policy review to improve Labour's chances of returning to office in 1990s.

This policy review was endorsed in 1989. As a result the most overt socialist policies were dropped and the free workings of the market were accepted by Labour. Instead, education and skills, research and development, the use of technology, partnership between government and industry ('business where appropriate, government where necessary') were stressed. The party emerged from the 1980s united, as extremists such as 'Militant' had been expelled, but it was still a long way from being trusted by the public, as the shock result in 1992 demonstrated.

After that unexpected defeat, Kinnock resigned, to be replaced by his Shadow Chancellor, John Smith. Smith proceeded to extend the principle of OMOV to almost every aspect of policy making and senior appointment, fighting against last-ditch defence of the bloc-vote by the more radical unions. That he succeeded said much for his ability and genuine popular appeal, especially as the Major government quickly lost direction after 1992. After his triumph, Smith led the party into the European Parliament elections and won 62 of the 84 seats (against the Conservatives' 18). It was therefore, as a likely future Prime Minister that his loss was felt when he suddenly and unexpectedly died in May 1994.

Many now expected Smith's own shadow Chancellor, Gordon Brown, to emerge as the new leader, but Brown chose instead to support the candidature of the shadow Home Secretary, Tony Blair, who had created an impressive reputation in Parliament since 1992. Blair was a young, public-school-educated lawyer, and therefore far more likely to appeal to the vital middle-class voters of South and Central England. What no one quite expected was the ambition and energy with which Blair, with Brown as his economics guru, Peter Mandelson as his communications director and the reassuringly working-class John Prescott as his deputy, set about 'modernising' the party to ensure that Labour did not lose a fifth election in a row. He and Mandelson effectively re-branded the party as 'New Labour' and significantly succeeded where Gaitskell had failed. At a special conference in 1995, the party agreed to re-write its famously socialist **Clause IV** of the constitution, which committed it to **nationalisation**. In its place was a vague, far more liberal statement:

. . . in which power, wealth and opportunity are in the hands of the many, not the few, where the rights we enjoy reflect the duties we owe, and where we live together, freely, in a spirit of solidarity, tolerance, and respect.

The need for free working of the market, first recognised by the 1989 policy review, was now extended in the new constitution which hoped for 'the enterprise of the market and the vigour of competition . . . joined with the forces of partnership and co-operation'. Blair spoke of 'a third way' between socialism and capitalism. It was fairly nebulous, but it seemed to offer the potential of a future government prepared to intervene to eliminate inequality and dire poverty, yet happy to allow the industrious and successful to operate freely and to enjoy the rewards for their hard work.

It was of course, ultimately unclear how much the success of New Labour was due to its policy reforms and how much to the perceived incompetence of the Major Conservative government.

Northern Ireland since 1979

1979 saw some of the worst terrorist violence both within Northern Ireland and on mainland Britain. First, Airey Neave, one of Mrs Thatcher's closest aides was murdered in the House of Commons car park shortly before the election by the radical Irish National Liberation Army (INLA). Then the last **viceroy** of India, the Queen's cousin, Lord Mountbatten, was murdered by the INLA while on holiday in the Irish Republic later in the year. Then the Provisional IRA killed 18 members of the Parachute regiment (whom they blamed for the **'Bloody Sunday'** killings of 1972) in a bomb attack at Warrenpoint, close to the Irish border.

Mrs Thatcher was determined not to give in to the terrorists, even when Republican prisoners in jail in Northern Ireland went on hunger strike. One of them, Bobby Sands, was elected as MP for Fermanagh and South Tyrone, before starving himself to death along with nine others. Attempts by the British government to find a common policy with the government of the Irish Republic foundered as political power in the Republic shifted between those willing and unwilling to co-operate.

The need for a breakthrough was underlined in 1984, when the Provisional IRA attempted to murder the British Cabinet, during the Conservative Party conference at Brighton by bombing the hotel in which they were staying. Mrs Thatcher was incredibly lucky not to be hurt, but her close colleague, Norman Tebbit, was badly injured and five people were killed. In 1985, therefore, with the moderate Garret Fitzgerald as Prime Minister of the Irish Republic, Mrs Thatcher was able to sign the Hillsborough Anglo-Irish Agreement. This created an Inter-Governmental Conference of Irish and British ministers to discuss problems in Northern Ireland and to expedite security arrangements. This was a major breakthrough, as it was the first time that the Irish Republic's government had recognised the existence of Northern Ireland, as the country's original constitution of 1937 called for a united Ireland.

The political violence did not stop, however, and Provisional IRA bombs killed 11 civilians at a Remembrance Day service at Enniskillen in 1987 and 11 army musicians in Kent in 1989. The violence was increasingly ostracising the Provisionals, though, and, under Gerry Adams' leadership, Sinn Fein advocated a political campaign instead, which saw them winning 40 per cent of the nationalist vote, sufficient to have a claim for participation in any future Irish policy. The violence of the Provisional IRA was finally shown to be counter-productive by the outrage on all political sides when a bomb was exploded in Warrington, Lancashire in 1993, and two schoolboys were killed.

To his credit, in the midst of party scandal and internal division, Major had bravely managed to open negotiations with Northern Irish republicans and the Irish government which culminated in the Downing Street Declaration of December 1993. In this, Major and the Irish Prime Minister, Albert Reynolds, stated that any political settlement in Northern Ireland should be based on 'the right of self-determination' of the people of both South and North and could lead to 'a united Ireland, if that is their will'. As a consequence, the Provisional IRA declared a ceasefire in August 1994, giving their support to the peace process. Unfortunately for Major, his parliamentary majority was fast disappearing, leaving him dependent on the support of the Ulster Unionists, who were unenthusiastic about the Downing Street Declaration and who insisted on the IRA giving up their weapons before allowing their political wing, Sinn Fein into talks on Northern Ireland's future. The IRA lost patience in 1996 and bombed Canary Wharf and Manchester City Centre. It would take the general election of 1997 to move the peace process on again.

After the general election victory for Labour, the Provisional IRA announced a second ceasefire in July 1997, which held for the rest of the Parliament. Tony Blair and his new Northern Irish Secretary, Mo Mowlem, moved swiftly to involve all parties, even the paramilitaries, in a new agreement, signed on Good Friday 1998. This created a Northern Irish Assembly, a Council of all Ireland and a Power-Sharing Executive and was supported by the people of both north and south Ireland in a subsequent referendum. A Northern Ireland Executive was finally created and contained members of Sinn Fein. Blair had to accept the release of paramilitary prisoners as the price for the deal, and the level of criminality in Northern Ireland increased as a consequence. In the worst case, a breakaway republican faction, the 'Real IRA' killed 29 people in Omagh with a car bomb in August 1998, the worst single killing since 1969. Decommissioning of paramilitary weapons also proceeded very slowly, causing many to fear that now they had gained political power, the paramilitaries would not give up their guns. But dramatic progress had been achieved in the 1990s, especially in contrast to the previous two decades.

 The economy since 1979

The British economy plunged into recession in 1979, which was worsened by the implementation of harsh monetarist policies, designed to limit the money supply and lower inflation. The consequence was the elimination of about 25 per cent of Britain's manufacturing sector in the following three years, as British businesses lost government investment and contracts. Only the profits from North Sea oil prevented Britain from becoming bankrupt in this period. The economy began to recover in 1983 and grew steadily for the rest of the decade, but this was largely due to the growth of the service sector. Conservative ministers claimed that the 'economic miracle had arrived' and productivity levels at last began to rise, as the persistent fear of unemployment and the decline in protection offered by trade unions, enabled employers to sack workers and demand more of their remaining staff. Manufacturing output increased by less than 2 per cent per year, however, and the consumer boom of the late 1980s saw another influx of imported goods. Inflation increased again at the end of the decade and a further recession began in 1990 and although not as deep, was the most tenacious and long-lasting since the 'slump' of 1929–32. In this recession, service industries were affected as badly as manufacturing, and unlike 1979–82, the South East of England was not spared the consequences of high unemployment and suddenly falling house prices, which left many with mortgages they could not afford, on houses worth less than the loans.

The recession, after much searching for the 'green shoots of recovery', finally ended in 1994 and there was another boom which lasted until the end of the century. On this occasion, inflation

Table 10.3 **Proportion of the workforce in different sectors of the economy, 1981–91**

	Primary*	Production**	Services
1981	3.2	35.3	61.5
1986	2.6	30.6	66.8
1991	1.9	26.9	71.2
1996	1.5	22.8	75.7

* Primary = Agriculture, forestry, fishing, mining, quarrying, oil and gas extraction/processing.
** Production = Manufacturing, gas, water, electricity, construction.

Table 10.4 **Distribution of UK overseas trade in 1999 (in %)**

	Exports	Imports
Western Europe	60.4	60.4
North America	13.9	14.8
Rest of world	25.7	24.8

Table 10.5 **Share of income by levels of wealth**

Year	Top 20%	Top 40%	Bottom 40%	Bottom 20%
1979	43	70	12	2
1985	47	74	10	3
1992	50	76	8	2
1996	52	78	7	2

Table 10.6 **Households with less than 60 per cent of average household income**

1981	12%
1986	15%
1991	21%
1998	17%

Table 10.7 **Consumer durables ownership (in %)**

	1981	1992	1999
Television	97	98	98
Telephone	75	88	96
Freezer	49	83	93
Washing machine	78	87	92
Video recorder	–	68	85
Microwave	–	55	79
CD player	–	27	68
Tumble drier	23	48	52
Home computer	–	21	34
Dishwasher	4	14	24

remained low, however, and unemployment eventually fell to under one million for the first time since the mid-1970s. For the first time, British economic growth matched or exceeded that of its competitors. The economy remained dependent on the service sector and manufacturing continued to decline though, albeit more slowly than in the 1980s. To support ailing British manufacturers, the Conservative government encouraged foreign investment to such an extent that, by 1995, 25 per cent of British manufacturing output was owned by non-British citizens, employing 16 per cent of the population. The Labour government of Tony Blair, with Gordon Brown as Chancellor, continued to pursue the same economic priorities as their Conservative predecessors, focusing on the need to keep inflation as low as possible and even sticking to the Conservatives' own spending limits for two years. Unlike their predecessors, however, Labour attempted to address the major obstacle to the recovery of Britain's manufacturing base, by investing in education to support the needs of business and encouraging schools to develop more of the basic and vocational skills needed by British business.

Immigration and race since 1979

In 1978, while still leader of the opposition, Mrs Thatcher made clear her sympathy with those who called for tougher immigration controls:

People are really rather afraid that this country might be swamped by people with a different culture and you know, the British character has done so much for democracy, for law and done so much throughout the world, that if there is any fear that it might be swamped, people are going to react, and be hostile to them coming in. So if you want good race relations, you have got to allay people's fears on numbers.

Mrs Thatcher's statement was criticised by many, including Edward Heath. One journalist said, 'if you talk and behave as though black men were some kind of virus that must be kept out of

Table 10.8 *Population by ethnic group, 1999*

Ethnic group	Thousands	% of population
Black – Caribbean	485	0.9
Black – African	365	0.7
Black – other (non mixed)	108	0.2
Black – mixed	192	0.3
Indian	942	1.7
Pakistani	591	1.0
Bangladeshi	257	0.5
Chinese	159	0.3
Other – Asian (non-mixed)	191	0.3
Other – non-mixed	165	0.3
Other – mixed	248	0.5
All ethnic minority groups	3,702	6.5
White	53,090	93.5
Total	56,807	100

Table 10.9 *Unemployment rates by ethnic origin*

Year	White	Afro-Caribbean	Indian	Bangladeshi/Pakistani
1979	5	10	6	11
1990	7	13	10	20
1998	6	15	9	20

the body politic, then it is the shabbiest hypocrisy to preach racial harmony at the same time'. In the 1979 general election there were substantial swings to Conservatives in North and East London and the West Midlands, where the immigrant communities were largest, and the racist National Front vote collapsed.

The new Conservative government introduced a new British Nationality Act in 1981, which included a 'primary purpose rule' which required British citizens to prove that fiancées or spouses seeking to move to Britain were not engaged or married for purposes of settlement. Restrictions were also placed on elderly immigrants and students from overseas. In essence, the concept of 'citizenship' devised in the Nationality Act of 1948 was replaced by much narrower definition. A further Immigration Act in 1988 meant that Commonwealth citizens had to prove that they could maintain and accommodate their families. The entry of second wives was forbidden and over-staying a temporary visa became a criminal offence. Airlines and shipping companies had to pay a fine of £1,000 per person if they were brought in illegally thus passing the responsibility for preventing immigration onto private businesses at the point of departure, rather than the Home Office authorities at the point of arrival. Even after the crackdown on human rights in China after the Tiananmen Square massacre in 1989, Britain refused to admit all but a very highly qualified minority of Hong Kong Chinese and began repatriating the Vietnamese from Hong Kong.

At the end of the century, immigration remained a politically sensitive subject, with the media focussing on 'bogus' asylum seekers and economic migrants and the New Labour government building detention centres for refugees and issuing them supermarket vouchers instead of cash benefits. There was clearly a racial element to this, as differing attitudes were displayed towards white Zimbabweans and Slovakians both of whom were fleeing persecution in their own countries.

Race relations, too, proved a very difficult area for the new administration. Despite the repeal of the 'sus' laws which allowed the police to stop and search any they suspected of intending to commit crimes, which disproportionately targeted black men, relations between the police and black communities remained poor. Perceptions of racism on the part of the police contributed, in part, to a number of the riots that disfigured Britain in the 1980s:

1980   St Paul's (Bristol)
1981   Brixton, Southall (London), Toxteth (Liverpool) Harehills (Leeds), Moss Side (Manchester) and Handsworth (Birmingham)
1985   Broadwater Farm – where a police officer was stabbed to death by a mob

Despite the passage of the Race Relations Act in 1976, racist treatment was still evident among employers, especially during the early 1980s recession, and among local government, most notably in the case of Liverpool City Council in the allocation of housing. Most publicly of all, racism was still evident in sport, despite the achievement of athletes such as Daley Thompson and footballers such as John Barnes of Liverpool.

It would be quite wrong, however, to see the period as entirely negative. There were individuals who demonstrated it was possible to be black and successful. The first Black and Asian MPs Bernie Grant, Diane Abbott, Keith Vaz (Labour) and Nirj Deva (Conservative) challenged racism in law and public life. There were an impressively large number of successful Black and Asian businessmen such as Shami Ahmed (the owner of the Joe Bloggs clothing firm), and Mohammed Sarwar, the first Muslim MP.

The need for further understanding of different cultures to that of Western, Christian, European, led to a drive among academics, such as the History Workshop, to focus on the values and

Figure 10.1 **The Commonwealth in 1998**

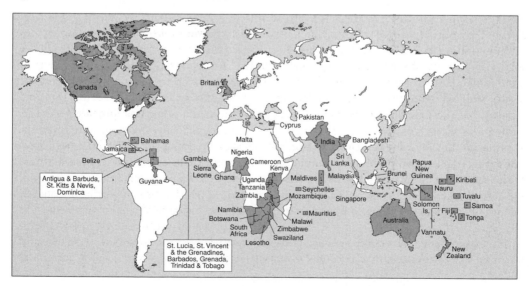

Figure 10.2 **Murder suspects at the Stephen Lawrence enquiry**

contribution of other peoples. By the end of the century, schools were directed to study the history, religion and culture of a wider range of the world's population than ever before. Perhaps most importantly of all for the attitude of future generations, the Black presence in the media, undoubt-edly helped to create a more tolerant attitude, as news readers such as Trevor MacDonald, comedians such as Lenny Henry, writers such as Meera Syal and cooks such as Madhur Jaffrey became well-loved household names.

Attitudes still remained ambiguous by the end of the century, though. For many Whites British tolerance did not extend to allowing inter-marriage or to living next door to a black family. Attitudes towards traditional practices such as arranged marriages were still hostile, even in the media, and the rise of fundamental regimes in the Middle East resulted in fear and distrust of Islam. Non-white communities were still only accepted in urban areas in particular parts of the country and this could result in the development of separate White and Black areas developing in a town or city, where those from different backgrounds were abused or even physically harmed.

In particular, the murder of the black student Stephen Lawrence in 1993 did cause a re-evaluation of racism in Britain, especially in the police force. That the police failed to secure a conviction despite overwhelming evidence against a number of suspects, led to a formal apology by the Metropolitan Police Force and the setting up of the MacPherson inquiry which found evidence of 'institutional racism' in the police in Britain. This accepted the need for police to be brought under the jurisdiction of the Race Relations Act. By the end of the century though, there was still massive under representation of the Black community in the criminal justice systems, in particular in the police, the probation service, magistrates and prison officers.

The position of women since 1979

After the dramatic challenges to the position of women in the 1960s and 1970s and the legal removal of obstacles to their equality, direct discrimination against women had largely been eliminated. Attitudes in the media proved much more stubborn. Advertisements continued to show women as largely confined to the home, and progressively younger female viewers were still encouraged to define themselves by activities such as shopping or applying make-up.

The extent of equality for women was now largely decided within the household. When children were born, women still had to juggle the commitments of work and home, and this task was made far more difficult by the limited numbers of state nurseries. For many women, a choice had to be made between staying at home with children or working, only to give the bulk of one salary to the private nursery where the child was placed. It was a lucky mother who could count on help from her own family to alleviate some of this burden. Even when children went to school, parents struggled in order to match the working day with the shorter school day. The media presented a positive image and encouraged women that 'having it all' – both a successful career and a family, was possible, even desirable, but failed to explain how this was practically achievable for those on more modest incomes. As the expectations for leisure and personal comforts grew, most families needed two salaries to satisfy these, but the consequence was that children could increasingly be seen as a burden and parents could spend little time with them.

A survey from 1989 concluded that, at the executive level of industry at least, men remained in control:

There are some companies which require their managers to have a non-employed wife, so that she is available for entertaining and can give him the domestic support necessary to ensure his total dedication to the firm. The assumption, of course, is that *all* managers *must* be male. Social rituals of work, trade union activities and so forth reflect male timetabling and interests and priorities. All over the world, men give orders, women obey. The patriarch may have lost his seat in the drawing room, he is still comfortably lodged in the office or behind the boardroom table.

Gendered Jobs and Social Inequality by Harriet Bradley

Perhaps the most striking step forward for women in this period was the decision of the General Synod of the Church of England to allow women to become priests in 1993. Although this caused much anger on the part of conservative Christians and even some high-profile conversions to the Catholic Church, the vast bulk of the population, Christian or agnostic, saw it as a long overdue step. Women were permitted to serve in the front-line armed forces in the same decade.

Returning to politics as an indicator of women's status, the 1997 election saw a record number of female candidates, with 120 becoming MPs, 100 of whom were Labour. It was noticeable, however, that the senior governmental positions in the new Labour government were still held by men.

Table 10.10 **Women in the labour force (by age)**

Year	16–24	25–44	45–54	55–59	60–64	65 +	Total
1971	2.3	3.5	2.1	0.9	0.5	0.3	10.0
1981	2.7	4.6	2.1	0.9	0.4	0.2	10.9
1991	2.6	6.1	2.4	0.8	0.3	0.2	12.4
1997	2.0	6.4	2.9	0.8	0.4	0.2	12.7

Table 10.11 **The decline of the traditional family**

Year	No. of marriages
1987	397,937
1992	356,013
1997	310,218

Table 10.12 **Divorce rates, England and Wales**

	1987	1992	1997
No. of divorces	151,007	160,385	146,689
No. of people divorcing (per 1,000 married couples)	12.7	13.7	13.0

Table 10.13 **Birth occurrence inside and outside marriage**

Year	Inside marriage	Outside marriage
1981	640,000	91,000
1986	597,000	158,000
1991	556,000	236,000
1996	473,000	260,000

 Role of the media

The media had undoubtedly grown in importance after the end of the Second World War, as literacy rates increased and the rise in the standards of living made newspapers, books and magazines more affordable, as well as bringing radio, television and eventually computer networks into more homes. By the 1980s, the press, still the most influential and most openly partisan part of the media was controlled by four great press barons, four of whom were Conservative supporters.

The most important of these was Rupert Murdoch, the owner of News International, who by 1989, not only controlled the *Sun* and *The Times*, but was the major share-holder in Sky TV, the first satellite TV station, which provided additional channels on payment of a subscription. So popular was this new service and so wealthy was Murdoch, that he was able to buy the rights to show sporting fixtures, especially football, which had previously been shown by the BBC or ITV.

Table 10.14 **Main daily national newspapers in Britain in 1999**

Newspaper title	Current chairman of owners	Ideological sympathy	Market share
Tabloids			
Sun	Rupert Murdoch	Nationalist	29%
Daily Mirror	Victor Blanc	Labour	18%
Daily Mail	Lord Rothermere	Conservative	18%
Daily Express	Lord Hollick	Conservative	9%
Daily Star	Lord Hollick	Conservative	4%
Broadsheets			
Daily Telegraph	Conrad Black	Conservative	8%
The Times	Rupert Murdoch	Conservative	6%
Guardian	Bob Gavron	Labour	3%
Financial Times	Lord Blakenham	Pro-European	3%
Independent	Tony O'Reilly	Labour	2%

Table 10.15 *Reading of national newspapers by gender (in %)*

Newspaper	Males			Females		
	1981	1991	1999	1981	1991	1999
Sun	31	25	24	23	19	17
Daily Mirror	27	20	15	22	15	12
Daily Mail	13	10	12	11	9	12
Daily Express	6	8	6	13	8	5
Daily Telegraph	9	6	6	7	5	5
Daily Star	13	8	5	8	4	2
The Times	3	3	5	2	2	3
Guardian	4	3	3	2	2	2
Independent	–	3	2	–	2	1
Financial Times	2	2	2	1	1	1
Any national daily newspaper	76	66	60	68	57	51

No other satellite service could rival this and it was only with the advent of digital television at the end of the century that any serious rival subscription services emerged. By that stage, Murdoch had moved to take control of film companies and newspapers in the USA, and had developed an international influence to rival prime ministers and presidents, which, to borrow Stanley Baldwin's phrase, gave him unprecedented 'power without responsibility'.

Perhaps the clearest indication of the power of the modern popular press was their ability to shatter the status of the Royal Family. The media had willingly publicised the 'fairy-tale' marriage of the Prince of Wales to Lady Diana Spencer in 1981, largely as an escape from the desperate economic condition of the country. When it became clear that the marriage was in difficulty, the media refused to turn a blind eye as they had done with the future Edward VIII's relationship with Mrs Simpson, or Princess Margaret's affair with an airforce officer in the 1950s.

By 1993, both the Prince of Wales and his estranged wife had confessed to adultery in the media, after lurid tales of royal sexual misconduct had filled the pages of even the 'quality' broadsheet papers. By the time of the death of the Princess of Wales in a car accident in 1997, despite accusations of culpability, the press felt able to lecture the Queen on how to react to this event, and effectively stage managed a bizarre funeral ceremony which combined high Anglican ceremony with pop songs and mass public participation. It was telling that the Royal Family consulted the Prime Minister's office on how to respond and took care thereafter to cultivate a more 'media-friendly' approach, which seemed to be the price for their continued existence.

'An asteroid hitting the planet' – the 1997 election

The 1997 election seemed in many ways, a foregone conclusion, given the rock-bottom reputation of the Conservative government and the personal popularity of Tony Blair. On the other hand, memories of Major defying the opinion polls in 1992 to snatch victory from Neil Kinnock, continued to give heart to the Tories. In the event, Blair was careful to take no risks at all during the election campaign, forcing the Conservatives to use more and more clumsy tactics to try to scare voters as to his intentions (most laughably in the childish 'New Labour, New Danger' posters, showing Blair with 'demon eyes'!).

The night of the election was perhaps the greatest political entertainment since the fall of Thatcher as viewers watched senior Conservative ministers losing their seats (Malcolm Rifkind, the Foreign Secretary, Michael Portillo, the Defence Secretary, Norman Lamont, the ex-Chancellor), traditional Tory seats turning to Labour (even Mrs Thatcher's old seat, Finchley was lost) and the Labour majority exceeding that of even 1945. Labour finished with 419 seats and the Tories were reduced to 165, their worst result since 1832, as even the Liberal Democrats enjoyed the Tory's misfortunes, winning 46 seats and bringing them back to a level of political significance they had not enjoyed since Lloyd George's last great campaign in 1929. John Major immediately resigned as Tory leader and the party demonstrated that their deep divisions over Europe were still not settled as the euro-sceptic William Hague, who had only held the most junior position in Cabinet, the Welsh Office, for two years, beat the euro-enthusiast, Kenneth Clarke, who, as Chancellor, had succeeded in reviving the economy after the recession of the early 1990s. This time, the newspapers owned by the media tycoon, Rupert Murdoch, such as the *Sun*, and the *Evening Standard* had supported Tony Blair. Clearly though, media support alone was not enough to account for Labour's victory, as the Conservatives still had the support of the *Daily Mail*, the *Daily Telegraph* and the *Daily Express*.

The scale of the swing to Labour immediately caused commentators to ponder which historical antecedent the May 1997 result resembled. That of 1945 which led to a sea-change in the priorities and practices of government, or that of 1951 which saw a victorious party continue to implement the most significant and most popular policies of their predecessors, thereby creating a new consensus in British politics?

Tony Blair, 'New Labour' and pre-millennial Britain

At the age of 44, Tony Blair, son of a Conservative local councillor, became the youngest British prime minister of the twentieth century. Perhaps the single most radical achievement of Blair's first government was the introduction of national assemblies for Scotland, Wales and Northern Ireland. Referendums were held in Scotland and Wales, but unlike 1979, they required a simple majority 'yes'. The Scots were asked if they wished to have a Scottish Parliament (to which 74 per cent voted 'yes') and if it was to have the power to determine income tax levels (to which 63.5 per cent voted 'yes'). As a result the Scottish Parliament with 129 MSPs was established at Holyrood. The Welsh were only able to vote on whether to have an Assembly, and it was only approved on the narrowest of margins, by 50.3 per cent against 49.7 per cent. The Welsh Assembly was to have 60 members and was located in Cardiff, while its new headquarters in the 'Tiger Bay' area of the city was constructed. The government also proposed and passed a bill removing the hereditary peers from the House of Lords in 2000, apart from a temporary reprieve for a rump of 92. This measure, completely altering the composition of one of the three key elements of the legislature, and the one part of Parliament with the longest pedigree, might have got the attention it deserved had Labour been able to come up with an alternative means of staffing an upper chamber. Their proposal of a Royal Commission seemed to suggest to many observers, that Labour knew what it didn't want in the Lords, but was unable to decide what it did.

There was discussion of altering the electoral system for the Commons as well, largely under pressure from the Liberal Democrats, who, like every third party in British politics saw distinct advantages for themselves in a system of proportional representation. Here, Tony Blair gave another commission, under the former Chancellor, Lord Jenkins, the opportunity to suggest alternatives. The ones that were proposed were ingenious and they did lead to the use of proportional

Figure 10.3 **Labour election poster for 2001 election**

representation in the European Parliament elections of 1999. Sadly for the proponents of reform, the Tories came off best in these, winning seven more seats than Labour, thereby losing any governmental enthusiasm for reform. The replacement of Paddy Ashdown, who had built a good working relationship with Blair, by the less co-operative Charles Kennedy as Liberal Democrat leader in 1999, didn't help either. Ultimately, however, the proposals ran into the usual problem with electoral reform. That, in order to pass, they must be approved by those who won power under the old system, and who have nothing to gain, but much to lose, especially, when, like Labour they held such a substantial majority of seats, which was not reflected in a similar majority of votes. With the Conservatives under Hague failing to make any headway in improving their abysmal approval ratings, there seemed little incentive to change. The example of the introduction of a directly-elected mayor for London seemed to confirm such doubts. The Labour candidate, the former health minister, Frank Dobson, was humiliatingly defeated by the former leader of the Greater London Council (GLC), Ken Livingstone, who had been ejected from the party for standing against the official candidate.

In economic terms, Labour was determined to demonstrate their new 'business-friendly' approach, aware of how a lack of confidence in previous Labour governments among financiers had damaged them in the past. The fact that, for once, Labour was not faced with an immediate financial crisis helped enormously. The new Chancellor, Gordon Brown was open in his willingness to stick to Conservative spending plans for the first two years, and promised not to raise income tax before the next election. Labour's acceptance of monetarist priorities for the economy, which they had reluctantly introduced in 1976, seemed confirmed, when the government effectively handed control of the setting of interest rates over to the Bank of England, almost as soon as they entered office. Labour followed Mrs Thatcher's economic policy with a tight control kept on spending, with the emphasis on keeping inflation low, even if that meant high interest rates, dwindling exports and rising unemployment.

On Europe, Blair was able, supported by a united party to pursue a more positive policy. He did have to take into account the widespread anti-European feeling especially among younger people though, which had been fostered by a continued diet of anti-Brussels messages in the bulk of the popular press since the late 1980s. Blair enthusiastically signed up to the Amsterdam Treaty, which

Figure 10.4 **New Year's Eve party at the Millennium Dome, 1999**

stimulated further European integration and hastily scrapped Major's opt-out to the Social Chapter of the **Maastricht Treaty**. He refused however, after much pressure from the tabloid newspapers, to join the single European currency (unimaginatively named the 'Euro') when it was launched in January 1999, preferring instead to wait until the economic conditions were right for Britain. This was a fairly obvious attempt to avoid making a risky economic decision until the public could be convinced of it. There was little danger of Labour joining before the next election, but they were not so ideologically opposed to the idea that they ruled out joining for ten years, as William Hague's Conservatives did.

By 1999, the difficulties of the health service, especially in winter, required a substantial increase in expenditure, as the government were released from their self-imposed two-year straitjacket. Education, the issue that Blair had stressed more than any other also needed investment. When it came, it provoked even more controversy. Schools were 'encouraged' to adopt prescriptive, centrally directed curricula for English and Maths, while the proposed expansion of higher education was to be funded by charging the wealthier students (or rather their families) tuition fees. Luckily for Labour, The Conservatives' continuing obsession with Europe prevented there being too much serious analysis of their performance, but clearly the methods of the Labour Party had changed, even if they claimed to have the same priorities as ever.

Table 10.16 **British views on joining the single European currency, 1999 (%)**

Would vote yes to joining a single currency	30
Would vote no	54
Don't know/would not vote	16

Part 2: Essays

1. The Thatcher governments 1979–90 (EDEXCEL)

a)   **How important was the Falklands War to Mrs Thatcher's popularity?**   **(30 marks)**
b)   **How far did Mrs Thatcher's domestic policies succeed in her aim to
     'change everything' between 1979 and 1990?**   **(30 marks)**

(Total: 60 marks)

a)   Many have argued that Mrs Thatcher's handling of the Falklands conflict in 1982, helped her to stay in office for so long. It is certainly true that her government was deeply unpopular before the conflict, but on the other hand, she did have a major ally in the British press, who, by and large, supported Mrs Thatcher's policies. Most of all, the *Sun*, the most read paper in Britain, consistently stayed loyal to Thatcher's monetarist approach, even when unemployment topped three million in 1982. Once the Falklands conflict began, the press took every opportunity of contrasting Thatcher's patriotic defence of Britain's interests with the calls for negotiation from the opposition parties. Once the election of 1983 was over, however, the Falklands swiftly faded from the political agenda, and Thatcher found herself facing the Westland crisis in 1986, the most serious threat to her government before 1990.

The sale of shares from privatised utilities, at absurdly low prices certainly helped, but there were not enough people in this new 'share-owning democracy' to explain the continued success of Thatcher's governments. Far more important than the re-privatisation policy was the sale of council houses. Councils were forced, many against their will, to allow tenants to buy their council houses, at prices fixed by central government to be very attractive. This policy allowed a large swathe of the working classes, many of whose families had been consistent Labour voters, to become property owners. The consequence of this, in widening Mrs Thatcher's appeal to traditionally non-conservative groups, was important in explaining why Mrs Thatcher's popularity was so long-lived.

It is very easy to overlook the significance of Mrs Thatcher's foreign policy outside the Falklands. Britain had only been a member of the EEC since 1973, and there was much popular dislike of the community, which, it was felt, largely served continental, rather than British interests. Mrs Thatcher's successful re-negotiation of Britain's contribution to the EEC, certainly boosted her image as a powerful and forceful patriot, and she reinforced this by her dogged resistance to any institutional changes that she felt did not suit Britain. Second, her refusal to concede to Irish Republican terrorists, which resulted in a bomb being detonated at the hotel in which she was staying during the 1984 Conservative Party Conference, won her much admiration. Perhaps most important though, was Thatcher's robust response to communist Russia. Mrs Thatcher's cultivation of her reputation as the 'Iron Lady', was particularly well received in Britain as she supported President Reagan's uncompromising stand against perceived communist threats in the early 1980s, and then helped to secure the startlingly swift end to the **Cold War** in her dealings with premier Gorbachev, the man, who, she famously said, she 'could do business with'. It is frequently forgotten by historians that Mrs Thatcher's visit to Moscow in 1987, when she was cheered by crowds on a walkabout, was a public relations triumph, deliberately arranged before the election, which Labour was completely unable to match.

b)   After winning the general election of 1979 with an overall majority of 43 seats, Mrs Thatcher embarked on fulfilling her pre-election pledge to 'change everything'. Thatcher felt that the root of Britain's continuing social and economic problems was the intrusion of the state into the economy and the consequent creation of dependent welfare culture, where initiative and enterprise were stifled. She sought to privatise nationalised industries and to promote a more competitive spirit in Britain's economy, while limiting benefit to those who genuinely needed it. She was quite prepared to confront those who opposed these policies, such as trade unionist and local government leaders, and she welcomed the opportunity to defeat the groups that she later labelled 'the enemy within'.

Her priority was the economic recovery of Britain, which was to be achieved by 'rolling back' the influence and power of the state. The economy seemed to perform well after the recession of 1979–82, but Britain's manufacturing industry never recovered from the recession and Britain's economy became increasingly dependent on service industries, which were very susceptible to trade fluctuations, as demonstrated in the slump of the early 1990s. As for reducing the intrusion of the state however, Thatcher seemed to have failed in many ways. Government spending amounted to 43.2 per cent of gross domestic product in 1980, but five years after her resignation as Prime Minister, it was still 42.5 per cent. As the Conservative government faced so much opposition to its policies from Labour-controlled local governments, Thatcher's governments actually centralised more and more powers in Westminster and of course, helped to contribute to her downfall when she insisted on the unpopular replacement of rates by the community charge or '**poll tax**'.

Mrs Thatcher's more targeted policies did show much more success, however. As she intended, the unions were emasculated and their membership fell by 10 per cent between 1981 and 1991. The number of strikes fell in tandem with this. Her policy of **privatisation** was clearly a major change in the operation of the economy with all the nationalised utilities, with the exception of the railways, being floated on the stock market. In particular, Mrs Thatcher's governments did encourage many more people to buy stocks and shares than previously and she oversaw a dramatic shift in housing from the council to the private sectors, as the *Housing Act* of 1980 enabled tenants to buy their homes at considerable discounts. Although Britain was by no means a 'share-owning democracy' by 1990, it had gone a very long way towards becoming a 'property owning' one.

Perhaps, despite the specific failures of Thatcher's programme, she did succeed in radically changing the priorities and principles of government in Britain. No longer was it the government's job to ensure work for all as far as possible. No longer would the government attempt to shore up ailing British manufacturers. No longer would governments act to alleviate poverty as directly as they had done between 1945 and 1979. Now the priority was to encourage wealth creation and to reward those who succeeded. The most needy would still be helped, but any state provision had to be justified, targeted and accountable by those who used it. By 1990, British politics was almost completely transformed and the Labour Party was already well on the way to accepting this change. The British people, on the other hand, were never fully convinced of the need for the more radical of the Thatcherite changes, and this limited acceptance of her agenda ultimately cost Mrs Thatcher the premiership, and cost the Conservatives their position as the natural party of government, as New Labour ensured that they more carefully reflected the public's wishes, rather than ideological commitments, in their policies. That they had to absorb many of the changes of the 1980s, in order to do so though, perhaps reflects just how much had changed under Mrs Thatcher.

2. Foreign policy under Thatcher (OCR)

Assess the success of Mrs Thatcher's Foreign and Defence Policy.   **(90 marks)**

As a result of her NATO commitments and Britain's purchase of the Trident submarine-launched nuclear missile system, in 1979 Britain was spending a greater proportion of her GDP on defence than any other European country. In order to afford this, a Defence Review entitled *The Way Forward* proposed a 25 per cent cut in the Navy's surface fleet. This included the decommissioning of *HMS Endurance*, the South Atlantic ice-breaker which protected the Falkland Islands. This move was interpreted by the faltering Argentinian dictatorship led by General Galtieri as an indication that Britain was no longer prepared to fight to keep the Falklands which the Argentinians claimed as 'las Malvinas'. Despite clear indications that Argentina was preparing an invasion fleet, the British government did nothing and on 1 April 1982, the small garrison of British marines were overwhelmed by a huge invasion force. Despite having clearly failed to protect the Falklands, Mrs Thatcher ordered the preparation of a naval task force immediately, brushing aside all suggestions of negotiation from the USA, the UN and her Cabinet colleagues. The Islands were recovered after a pitched battle outside the capital, Port Stanley and the loss of six ships and over 200 men. Mrs Thatcher's Foreign Secretary, Lord Carrington resigned due to the embarrassing circumstances of the islands' capture, but Mrs Thatcher was able to escape blame due to her firm resolve in pursuing a military victory. She went as far as to claim that the Falklands victory marked the end of Britain's post-war decline and with the support of the press dramatically increased her popularity, contributing significantly to the Conservatives' stunning election victory in 1983.

Mrs Thatcher's principled stand over the Falklands was not repeated in the case of other dependent territories, most notably Hong Kong. The 99 year lease from China on which the area had been purchased was due to expire in 1997, but many feared the consequences of handing the territory back to the communists. At first Britain attempted to renew the lease, but in 1984, was forced to accept that it should be handed back. China did agree to allow Hong Kong some autonomy over its affairs for a further 50 years. Doubts over the colony's future were revived in 1989, however, when a massive pro-democracy movement in Beijing was bloodily dispersed by government troops in June 1989. Despite Mrs Thatcher's much vaunted anti-communist credentials, she did nothing to attempt to re-negotiate the 1984 agreement. Those anti-communist attitudes led Mrs Thatcher to place great store in close relations with the USA, especially when Ronald Reagan was president. Although the USA had not supplied troops for Britain in the Falklands conflict, and had advised Britain against taking military action, Reagan had helped to keep other regional powers neutral and had offered military and intelligence support, albeit grudgingly. The relationship was not always so friendly however, most notably in October 1983, when Reagan ordered the invasion of the Caribbean island of Grenada to oust a pro-communist regime. Reagan ignored the fact that Grenada was a member of the Commonwealth and failed to consult or even inform Britain of the attack. In a similar demonstration of the USA's unsentimental interpretation of the 'special relationship', Reagan happily signed away Western Europe's nuclear defences at the Reykjavik and Washington summits with the Russian leader Gorbachev, without considering Mrs Thatcher's views. Britain was expected to provide services for the USA, such as bases for the bombing of the headquarters of the Libyan leader, Colonel Gaddafi in 1986 and she had to bear the consequent increase in terrorist activity which culminated in the destruction of a Pan Am airliner over the Scottish town of Lockerbie in 1988. By the end of the decade, however, relations had been so successfully restored that, when Saddam Hussein of Iraq invaded his small oil-rich neighbour, Kuwait, Britain contributed 35,00 troops to the US led coalition that went on to drive the Iraqis out in operation 'Desert Storm' in 1991.

While Mrs Thatcher's initial relations with the USSR in the aftermath of the Soviet invasion of Afghanistan were certainly hostile, attempting to persuade British athletes to boycott the 1980 Moscow Olympics in protest, she did play a role in the rapprochement that took place in the middle of the decade. While still 'heir apparent' to the General Secretary of the Soviet Communist Party in 1984, Mikhail Gorbachev visited Britain and his promise of *glasnost* (openness) in the Soviet system encouraged Mrs Thatcher into declaring that he was 'a communist I can do business with'. This in turn encouraged Reagan to re-open arms control negotiations with the USSR which began the road to Reykjavik. Mrs Thatcher was always keen to continue to encourage the new Soviet leader, even visiting Moscow in February 1987 as a gesture of good will. Certainly, no British leader before or possibly even since, had such a high standing in the eyes of the Russian people, where the nickname 'the Iron Lady' had more than a hint of respect.

Ultimately, however, Britain remained a peripheral player in the end-game of the **Cold War**. In order to control the massive expenditure on nuclear weapons that the **Cold War** had necessitated, the Russian leadership needed to negotiate directly with the chief Western nuclear power, USA. Although Mrs Thatcher was occasionally consulted by Reagan, and did much to convince him that Gorbachev was a man worth trusting, the break-through in negotiations to reduce arms came after face-to-face discussions between Gorbachev and Reagan at Reykjavik in October 1986 and Washington in December 1987. Mrs Thatcher in fact attempted to slow the dramatic pace of the agreements as she feared that the removal of all nuclear arms in Europe would leave Western Europe dangerously exposed to the threat of conventional Warsaw Pact forces. Her failure to retain tactical and battlefield nuclear weapons in Europe showed again how dependent on the USA Britain's own nuclear deterrent was.

Although Mrs Thatcher's robust approach to her European neighbours certainly proved popular at home with working-class voters who were ambivalent about the European project from the start, it has to said that she brought Britain's relations with Europe to a low unmatched since the days of de Gaulle. Her confrontational attitude in the negotiations over Britain's budgetary contributions led European leaders to christen her 'Lady de Gaulle'. In particular, under Mrs Thatcher, Britain's relations with Germany deteriorated. Despite a pressing economic need to cut defence spending, Thatcher refused to reduce the size of the British army on the Rhine in the early 1980s. The relationship reached its nadir in 1990 when she attempted to use her influence to stem the pace of German reunification following the fall of the Berlin wall in the previous November.

In conclusion therefore, it is possible to say that as an exercise in public relations and electioneering, Mrs Thatcher's foreign and defence policy was an outstanding success, as it played a part in her victories in 1983 and 1987. In terms of strategy, however, she left Britain closely linked to a superpower, that, while condescending, had little compunction in ignoring Britain's interests where it suited her to do so. Due to this closeness to the USA and her arrogant attitudes towards the non-English speaking European, she was distrusted by the European powers with whom so much of her trade now depended, and it was up to her successor, John Major, to try to mend relations at the Maastricht summit in 1991.

3. Labour in opposition 1983–97 (EDEXCEL)

a) **Describe the 'fundamental changes' that the Labour Party experienced in its policies and leadership between 1983 and 1997?** **(30 marks)**

b) **Why did New Labour win such a dramatic victory in the 1997 general election?** **(30 marks)**

(Total: 60 marks)

a) The Labour Party, committed to public ownership of means of production, distribution and exchange in **Clause IV** of its constitution since 1918, transformed its image, structure and policy between 1983 and 1997, in order to re-position itself on the new centre ground of British politics largely defined by Margaret Thatcher. This process was supported by a number of organisational changes which gave greater authority to the leader and by a mastery of modern media-focused campaigning.

Despite its formal commitment to socialism, Labour's practical policies were always influenced by the more pragmatic views of Fabians, trade unions and Christian socialists. After the defeat at the hands of Mrs Thatcher in 1979, however, the former Labour minister, Tony Benn led a grass-roots movement towards a more radical socialist agenda. The Labour government of 1974–79 was criticised by the 'Bennites' of the party for its use of pay restraint, welfare cuts and the acceptance of mass unemployment. The left-wing solution to this was restoration of full employment and improved public services and their influence was strengthened by the election of the weak Michael Foot as Labour leader, following Callaghan's resignation and the decision of a group of right-wing Labour leaders to leave the party and form the SDP.

The impression of party division, compared to Thatcher's leadership during the Falklands War and a mismanaged election campaign in 1983, resulted in a serious fall in voter confidence in Labour's 'fitness to govern'. With a manifesto full of apparently unrealistic and ideologically motivated policies such as withdrawal from the EEC and unilateral nuclear disarmament, the disastrous election result, which saw Labour winning only 2 per cent more of the vote than the Liberal/SDP alliance, was no surprise to political observers. Foot immediately resigned and Neil Kinnock, a former left-winger took over, intent on making Labour electable once more. He first attacked the power base of the 'Bennite' or hard left, Labour's National Executive Committee and oversaw the expulsion of 'Militant', a group of revolutionary Trotskyites who had infiltrated the party. Having done this, he concentrated on modernising the image of the party to the voter in time for the 1987 election. He knew he had little chance of winning with the economy and the world situation favouring Thatcher's government, and concentrated on defeating the SDP/Liberal alliance. In this he succeeded, winning ten more seats than in 1987 and eight per cent more of the vote than the Alliance.

Kinnock now set about modernising the party's policies, dropping the commitments to re-nationalisation of the privatised utilities and unilateral nuclear disarmament and demonstrating a new-found enthusiasm for Europe. As Mrs Thatcher became increasingly unpopular after 1987, it seemed as if Labour's opportunity had come. The astute replacement of their leader with the classless John Major in 1990, however, meant that the Conservatives were able to mount a very effective campaign in 1992, with the enthusiastic backing of the majority of the print media. The Labour Party failed to win power, largely due to fears of Kinnock's suitability as Prime Minister and Labour's taxation plans, which seemed threatening to voters at a time of economic recession.

Kinnock, realising he could take the party no further, stepped down and his shadow Chancellor, John Smith became the new leader. Smith decided to remove the trade unions' block vote for selection of candidates and Party Conference decisions and introduced a more democratic principle of 'one member, one vote' (OMOV). In this way the relationship between the trade unions and the Labour Party became based more on individual membership and voluntary participation, than on the influence of the leaders of large unions. Having succeeded in this important step, Smith died unexpectedly in 1994. The young, media-aware Tony Blair was overwhelmingly elected as his successor and he proceeded to introduce more populist, right-wing policies on law and order and education. On **Clause IV**, Blair managed to persuade the party to accept a new, more modern definition. Instead of a commitment to state control, it now declared that the party sought 'to create a community in which power, wealth and opportunity were in the hands of the many, not the few' and where rights enjoyed by individuals were reflected in the duties owed by them to the community. His '**New Labour**' talked of 'partnership' between public and private sector, 'fairness' in taxation and social security and 'democracy' in health and education. Labour's policies prior to the 1997 election, although far less interventionist than ever before, still retained some of the Party's traditional interests, promising to use the tax and social security systems for some redistribution of income and wealth from the better off to the poor and pledging higher spending on the NHS, pensions, education, and social security. The introduction of the minimum wage and increased workers' rights were also promised. Elected assemblies for Scotland and Wales, subject to referenda and reform of the House of Lords signalled the party's commitment to political radicalism in contrast to their relative economic conservatism. Blair asserted that **New Labour** had not abandoned its commitment to social justice, but it had balanced that with a recognition of new economic and political realities in Britain and the wider world.

b) John Major's government had been unexpectedly re-elected in 1992, but with a much reduced majority. It had almost immediately lost credibility in the humiliating, embarrassing and unsuccessful attempt to keep the pound in the European **Exchange Rate Mechanism**. Coming at the same time as a second serious recession under the Conservatives, Major saw his party lose its reputation for financial competence that could not be salvaged as it lost £6 billion in a day, despite the sustained economic recovery after 1992. It has to be said, however, that many of those lower middle-class voters who could not bring themselves to vote Labour in 1992, suffered ongoing problems from the collapse of the housing market and job insecurity, so the political benefits of the recovery were extremely limited for Major.

The government also proved itself prone to the most embarrassing lapses, attempting to insist on high moral values shortly before a record number of ministerial infidelities were exposed and a series of inquiries found frequent, if relatively minor, examples of corruption among Conservative ministers and MPs. Perhaps most damagingly for the government and the Conservative Party's reputation, the party endlessly feuded over the level of Britain's involvement in the European Union. Major seemed helpless to stop the in-fighting and was seen to shift policy against his will to attempt to keep the party united in the run up to the 1997 election. While his government was certainly unlucky, it must also go down as one of the most incompetent administrations of the twentieth century, squandering the chance of a lasting peace in Northern Ireland, for example, for the sake of an electoral alliance with the Ulster Unionists.

After 18 years in government, there was clearly the desire for a political change, but, as in 1992, the response of the Labour Party to this opportunity was crucial. After the wave of sympathy that followed the untimely death of John Smith in 1994, the new leader, Tony Blair, threw himself into modernising the party to make it electable once again. Re-launched as 'New Labour', the party showed itself willing to accept economic and social changes such as **privatisation** introduced by the Conservatives in the 1980s, in a fashion reminiscent of earlier Conservative willingness to accept post-war Labour changes. First, the party issued a pledge not to raise income tax rates for five years after being elected, largely to prevent a repeat of their unexpected defeat in 1992. The Labour shadow Chancellor, Gordon Brown, went even further, promising to abide by the Conservative government's spending plans for the first two years of Labour government. The party re-affirmed its commitment to help the poorest in society, but promised to do so through a widening of opportunity rather than a forcible redistribution of wealth.

By 1997, however, constant Conservative in-fighting and relentless media criticism meant that John Major's party had become so unpopular that it was unclear whether Blair's revisionism was really necessary. The Labour election campaign focused instead exclusively on the failures of the Conservatives and Blair's personal image as a young, charismatic family man who could be trusted with the country's future. Some traditional Conservative-supporting newspapers such as Rupert Murdoch's the *Sun* threw their weight behind Blair, such was their exasperation with Major's government. In the general election, his party won 419 seats – a majority of 179 (but with only 43 per cent of the vote). The Conservatives dropped to 31 per cent, 165 seats and were entirely eliminated from Wales and Scotland, where their opposition to any degree of **devolution**, which Labour had always supported, hurt them dearly. As one commentator at the time put it, the political transformation of Britain was so great, it resembled 'an asteroid hitting the earth'. But it was a prime example of the maxim that oppositions do not win elections, governments lose them, and the Major government had lost this one in spectacular fashion.

4. 'New Labour' in government 1997–2001 (OCR)

Assess the similarities between New Labour and Thatcherism during Tony Blair's first term as Prime Minister, 1997–2001.

(Total: 90 marks)

On Tony Blair taking office in 1997, Mrs Thatcher famously declared that her legacy was 'safe in his hands'. It is clear that the Labour Party, transformed into New Labour since 1994, had substantially changed, but is it an exaggeration to describe Blair's first term in office as essentially **Thatcherism** in another guise?

In many respects, the economic approach of New Labour was similar to Thatcher in sharing the belief in the entrepreneurial ideal and remaining critical of traditional elites. There was the same belief in widening opportunity rather than redistributing rewards. In policies as well, the two approaches seemed similar, with the Chancellor, Gordon Brown, favouring the continued private ownership of utilities and, in some cases, such as Air Traffic Control and the Bank of England, taking the Conservatives' policies further. The increased casualisation of the labour force, which had become more popularly accepted in the late 1990s as the growing economy meant a dramatic fall in unemployment, was not challenged either.

Blair also used many of the same political methods as Mrs Thatcher. He felt something of an outsider in his party like she had done and therefore disliked parliamentary or even Cabinet government. Prime Minister's question time was reduced to one session a week instead of two, and the full Cabinet met infrequently. As with Mrs Thatcher, Blair governed with a hand-chosen circle of advisers, and would risk political injury to keep them in important positions. His insistence on giving Peter Mandelson a second Cabinet post after he was forced to resign as Trade and Industry Secretary in 1998, could be compared with Mrs Thatcher's insistence in 1989 on retaining Alan Walters as her financial adviser, even if it meant the resignation of her Chancellor, Nigel Lawson. Prime Ministers in both the 1980s and the late 1990s were quite prepared to use the media as a political weapon against opponents to their wishes. The power of Alastair Campbell, Blair's Press Officer mirrored that of Bernard Ingham, Mrs Thatcher's formidable spokesman.

Leaving aside general economic policy and the fondness for political in-fighting, however, there are clear distinctions between the two political approaches. Blair favoured a policy of 'new consensus' rather than the confrontational stance of Thatcher, with her rhetoric of attacking 'enemies within'. Blair's political approach was possibly best described as a 'Christian democracy', inclusive, well-intentioned and essentially charitable. Within a framework of creating equality of opportunity, Blair, in his first term, demonstrated a willingness to continue to use state funding for health, education and housing. He was also prepared to use the power of the state to alleviate employment, with the 'New Deal' for the jobless, and poverty with the introduction of the first national minimum wage in 1999. Although Blair certainly shared the Thatcherite belief in the dominance of the marketplace and the need for global **free trade**, unlike Thatcher, he was more willing to work with Europe in order to achieve this, signing up to the Social Chapter of the **Maastricht Treaty** and integrating European human rights legislation into British law. Blair even privately favoured eventual European monetary union, although he was a wise enough politician to promise only to do so when it suited Britain's economic interests, for fear of provoking the virulently anti-European tabloid press in Britain.

The most distinct difference between New Labour and **Thatcherism** was over the issue of political reform, however. Mrs Thatcher's government centralised political power in Whitehall, whereas New Labour spent much of its first term decentralising. Successful referenda led to the establishment of national assemblies in Northern Ireland and Wales and a Parliament in Scotland for the first time since 1707. London was granted its first elected mayor, and proposals for a *Freedom of Information Act*, were considered. In the most radical reform of the House of Lords in the modern age, Blair's government did what even Lloyd George and Asquith had not, and removed the majority of hereditary peers from the House of Lords. There were limits to the process, however. The possibility of proportional representation, much discussed before the election, faltered, perhaps not surprisingly given Labour's huge victory under the 'first past the post' system. Blair himself, showed a reluctance to accept the consequent loss of central government influence, as he tried to ensure some control over the new assemblies and the London Mayor by promoting his own candidates. The fall of Alun Michael in Wales and the election of Ken Livingstone in London, brought home the diminished power of the central executive. After these experiences, the process of reform slowed and the debate on the future composition of the House of Lords proceeded at a snail's pace.

The validity of any comparison between New Labour and **Thatcherism**, ultimately depends on whether one chooses to compare New Labour with the 'high **Thatcherism**' that was frequently proclaimed by the Conservatives' leader and her spokesmen. These policies, anti-Europe, anti-local government, centralist and low-tax, only became Conservative policy with the advent of her loyal disciple, William Hague as leader in 1997, and clearly were not shared by New Labour, or by Shaun Woodward, a Conservative MP who defected to Labour in 1999. On the other hand, the reality of Mrs Thatcher's 11 years of office was quite different from the ideological rigour that she later claimed, with its compromises and half-completed changes. In a sense that gulf between reality and presentation of policy to the media (or 'spin' as it became known in the late 1990s) seemed to be the most enduring element of Thatcher's years in office. New Labour, in its first term in office went out of its way to appeal to all groups in British political life. It therefore had to pose as the ally of business, but at the same time attempt to introduce genuinely redistributive economic policies to alleviate the growing gulf between rich and poor. That it managed to virtually retain its huge majority in the 2001 election was proof that, as with Mrs Thatcher in 1983, it had, temporarily at least, managed to create a new consensus, that ostracised an opposition that had become too radical, at least in the public's eyes.

Account for the continued popularity of New Labour in its first term in office. (OCR)

(Total: 90 marks)

During his first period as Prime Minister, Tony Blair proved himself quite an effective national leader. After capturing the public mood on the untimely death of Diana, Princess of Wales, to such an extent that even the Queen sought his advice, Blair responded effectively to the Kosovo crisis in 1999. He wisely chose to involve President Clinton of America in the coalition to stop Serbian aggression against ethnic Albanians in the area, and helped to retain faith in an air campaign to drive the Serbians out, even when civilians, including Chinese diplomats were killed. Unlike his ambitious Foreign Secretary, Robin Cook, Blair did not pretend to guarantee an 'ethical foreign policy', knowing that such a policy was almost impossible in international relations, but his government's work in Kosovo, which led to the fall of the Serbian dictator, Slobodan Milošović, and its role in helping to reduce third world debt and the global use of landmines, seemed in marked contrast to the unscrupulous behaviour of previous Conservative ministers, one of whom, Jonathan Aitken, was jailed for perjury in 1999.

It is difficult to detect much overt enthusiasm for the New Labour government. The resignation of Peter Mandelson, Blair's Minister for Trade and Industry, over a loan from a the wealthy Paymaster General, Geoffrey Robinson, in December 1998, was just the first in a number of financial scandals, most of which concerned Labour Party donations from industrialists, keen to curry favour with the new regime. It was quite easy to see how government policy might be affected by such links, and Blair found the accusation of 'sleaze' with which he'd taunted the Conservatives, coming back to haunt him. There was much frustration over the slow pace of welfare reforms, which was largely due to the chancellor, Gordon Brown's decision to assure the financial markets of his 'prudence', unlike his Labour predecessors, by sticking to the Conservatives' own spending plans for the first two years of the government. There were breakthroughs, such as substantial increases in state pensions and the introduction of a minimum wage, but there was no increase in direct taxation to increase state welfare and the job security offered by the Social Chapter of the **Maastricht treaty** proved to be fairly feeble. Blair and Brown continued to assure the public that, once the debts they inherited from the Tories were paid off, funding for hospitals and schools would be more forthcoming, and the public seemed prepared to give them time to do so. Only once did Blair seem to lose his impressive rapport with the British people, when in September 2000, a bizarre alliance of protestors, angry at the rising cost of fuel, attempted a **blockade** of oil refineries in order to force the government to reduce fuel tax. Blair was aggressive in his initial response, condemning any illegal blockades but he failed to appreciate how unpopular high fuel prices were. The government waited for the campaign to peter out, as popular anger turned against the protestors and they then slightly reduced the fuel tax for those groups worst hit. Luckily for the government, the global price of oil, which had actually caused the high prices at the pumps, came down and a later attempt to restart the protest was an embarrassing flop. Blair had that most important of political allies, luck, to thank for his government's survival.

Perhaps the crucial factor in the continued popularity of New Labour was in its handling of opposition. In a fashion similar to the consensual 'Big Tent' politics of Clinton's Democrats in the USA, Blair attempted to draw elements from the other parties into cooperation with the government. A joint government committee was established with members of the Liberal Democrats, including their leader, Paddy Ashdown, participating in debate on constitutional reform. A campaign group, 'Britain in Europe', set up to promote the case for British involvement in the EU, had the former Conservative ministers, Kenneth Clarke and Michael Heseltine on its platforms, alongside Labour Cabinet ministers. In a way very similar to Mrs Thatcher's good fortune in having Michael Foot as the leader of the opposition for the bulk of her first term in 10 Downing Street, Blair found himself confronting William Hague, chosen by the Conservatives as reassuringly anti-Europe, and even younger than Blair. Hague was a highly skilled parliamentary debater, but his public appeal was very limited, having only briefly served as Welsh secretary under Major, and allowing himself to appear in a number of clumsy publicity events designed to appeal to a younger, more ethnically diverse electorate but which only made him look ridiculous. As with Labour in the early 1980s, the Conservative Party continued to fight among themselves after their defeat, with the divisions over Europe becoming ever more bitter and more public. Hague, relatively inexperienced, made the same mistake as Foot and began to move his party in the direction demanded by his party activists, ignoring the fact that the Conservative Party, with an average membership age of over 60, was no longer representative of mainstream opinion in Britain. With his obsessive pursuit of the European issue and promises of further tax reductions under a future Conservative government, Hague distanced his party from the popular concerns over education, the health service and crime. Labour failed to live up to their pre-election promises on all these issues, yet Hague and his shadow Cabinet refused to capitalise on these opportunities. Although many people grew impatient with the slow pace of improvement under Blair, they knew that there was no alternative solution to their concerns available from the Conservative Party, rather, a return to Thatcherite dogma which had proved to be of limited utility in these areas. It was therefore not a ringing endorsement of the government, but a continued rejection of the Conservatives, when Labour achieved a similar electoral landslide in the 2001 election to that of 1997.

5. Britain and the European Union 1979–2000 (EDEXCEL)

a) **How has Britain been affected by membership of the European Union?**   **(30 marks)**
b) **Why has British membership of the European Union caused so much controversy since 1973?**   **(30 marks)**

(Total: 60 marks)

a) Since joining the EEC in 1973, Britain now had a huge bureaucratic network of relations with the European Union; with the institutions in Brussels, Strasbourg and Luxembourg; with other member governments and within Whitehall itself.

Negotiation and implementation of policy took much government time, for example, three quarters of the Department of Agriculture's time was spent on negotiation and enforcement of the **Common Agricultural Policy** (CAP) in Britain. The departments responsible for trade and industry, the environment, transport, education and employment were also kept busy with European directives and regulations. Even the British Treasury and Home Office were affected in this way.

There was a similar impact on Parliament since 1973. This was emphasised most by 'euro-sceptics' of all parties as the most serious consequence of the decision to join the EEC in 1971. As was made clear in the acrimonious debates on the **Maastricht Treaty** in 1992–93, many MPs, regardless of their party affiliations, feared that national parliaments would be reduced to the role of County Councils, under the overall rule of the institutions of the European Union. MPs came to realise that they could exercise little control over European decisions, they could only affect the implementation of policy. On the other hand, governments had always been able to carry out foreign policies and to conclude treaties without parliamentary approval, as Her Majesty's Government acted on behalf of the crown not Parliament.

Before 1973, Parliament had supreme jurisdiction over British national laws, but it now had to share this with the European Parliament and it had no control over issues of direct European law such as the **Common Agricultural Policy**. Since the Single European Act of 1986, member states could not always veto proposals in the Council of Ministers, but the European Parliament could block or amend legislation, so the European Parliament's power increased, much to the concern of British MPs.

British political parties at the end of the twentieth century needed therefore to conduct politics at local, national and European levels. The EU also influenced pressure groups in Britain. Farmers' groups lobbied the European Commission and Parliament via their European organisations because the key decisions (such as on BSE, farm prices and levies) which affected their livelihood were taken at a European level. A similar attitude began to develop among manufacturers and industrialists as the Single European Market grew and among financiers as the Single European Currency (the 'Euro') was introduced. Local government bodies could look to Europe for financial assistance and political support, in particular the European Social and Regional Funds. Nationalists in Scotland, Wales and Northern Ireland all hoped for support for their claims for independence in European political circles.

The position of the media and consequent public opinion was affected by British membership, either over single issues (such as BSE or fishing) or political in-fighting (such as withdrawal of the Tory whip to euro-rebels in 1994/95). At most other times though, Europe continued to take second place to national or local pre-occupations. A distinct gulf in attitude towards Europe was evident in the younger generations after 1973. The better educated and wealthier, who travelled to Europe on business and pleasure much more freely, took the EU for granted and saw themselves as 'Europeans' as much as English, Welsh, Scottish or Northern Irish. The less wealthy young British were far more influenced by the nationalist popular press and became increasingly suspicious and resentful, largely at the bidding of the older generation. This group clearly still needed a good deal of persuading, especially over the most contentious issue at the end of the century, the introduction of the European single currency.

b)   Edward Heath's application for membership of the EEC in 1971, had split both the Conservative and Labour parties and it had only passed the Commons debate with cross-party support. When Wilson regained power in 1974, he cleverly avoided worsening the divisions over Europe in his own party by calling a national referendum on Britain's continued membership. When this took place in 1975, the British people voted two to one in favour of membership. Unfortunately for Labour, the event did not settle the animosity in the party, and the most prominent pro-European Labour leader, Roy Jenkins, eventually left Labour to form the SDP.

Since then, British membership has not been seriously in doubt. But there have been long battles by the British government (especially during Mrs Thatcher's first administration) to improve the terms of membership with regard to the **Common Agricultural Policy** (CAP) and Britain's net contribution to the European budget (or as Thatcher put it 'it's my money and I want it back'). Although her combative approach was largely for domestic consumption and annoyed her European partners, by the mid-1980s most of these issues were resolved and Mrs Thatcher willingly agreed to the 1986 Single European Act (SEA).

Things changed in the late 1980s, however. The new President of the Commission, Jacques Delors, proposed a Social Charter for minimum standards of education, employment and social security. Mrs Thatcher disliked this proposed intrusion of the state into the economy and was also alarmed by Delors' plan for Economic and Monetary Union. She famously vetoed her Cabinet's demand for membership of the **Exchange Rate Mechanism** (ERM) and proceeded to attack what she perceived as the attempt to build 'a European superstate' in a speech in Bruges in 1988. The Cabinet finally forced her into joining the ERM in 1990, but Mrs Thatcher's opposition to greater European economic and political integration, eventually prompted the resignation of her own deputy, Geoffrey Howe and thereafter forced Mrs Thatcher's resignation. Although John Major, the new Prime Minister accepted the need to 'deepen' economic and political integration at the 1992 **Maastricht Treaty**, he tried to keep the Thatcherite 'euro-sceptics' happy by negotiating an opt-out for Britain on the **Social Chapter**. Unfortunately, Britain had entered the ERM too late and the pound was consequently over valued. After spending £6 billion in a day trying to shore it up, Britain was forced to drop out of the ERM in September 1992 and devalue the pound. After this, and encouraged by Mrs Thatcher and ambitious rivals for the Conservative leadership, the party's 'euro-sceptics' grew in number and demonstrated that they were prepared to sabotage their own government rather than accept increasing European unity. Faced with such a serious backbench rebellion, John Major attempted to 'lance the boil' by resigning as leader of the party, in order to force his critics to confront him. This brave move was undermined however, when the eventual challenger came from within his own cabinet, John Redwood. Having regained the leadership, but having clearly lost the support of many of his party members, Major now swung in the opposite direction and the Conservative party as a whole became more hostile to Europe, eventually withdrawing all co-operation with Europe over the ban on British beef in the wake of the BSE scandal.

Labour meanwhile became more Euro-enthusiastic, partly as a means of distancing themselves from the Tories and partly to pose as a responsible party of business (as the bulk of British business took place with members of the EU). In 1997, the new Labour government signed the Treaty of Amsterdam, which decreased the areas that one member could exercise a veto over. In keeping with popular, especially tabloid, hostility towards Europe, Labour announced they were opposed to the concept of a European superstate and preferred a Europe of independent nation states choosing to co-operate for common good. Labour signed up to the **Social Chapter** and agreed to join the single currency if economic conditions suited Britain and if British people agreed to it in a referendum. This was opposed by the Conservatives, who were now led by a 'euro-sceptic', William Hague, who refused to join the single currency for at least ten years.

6. Social and economic history since 1979 (AQA)

Read this extract from *The State We're In* (1995) by Will Hutton and answer the questions which follow:

We live in a new world of us and them. The sense of belonging to a successful national project has all but disappeared. Average living standards may have risen but have not generated a sense of well-being; if anything there is more discontent because the gains have been spread so unevenly and are felt to be so evanescent*. The country is increasingly divided against itself, with an arrogant officer class apparently indifferent to the other ranks it commands. This privileged class is favoured with education, jobs, housing and pensions. At the other end of the scale more and more people discover they are the new working poor, or live off the state in semi-poverty. Their paths out of this situation are closing down as the world in which they are trapped becomes meaner, harder and more corrupting. In between there are growing numbers of people who are insecure, fearful for their jobs in an age of permanent 'downsizing', 'cost-cutting', and 'casualisation' and ever more worried about their ability to maintain a decent standard of living.

a) Explain the phrase 'casualisation'. **(3 marks)**
b) In what ways did a two-tier system of 'education, jobs, housing and pensions' exist in the 1990s? **(7 marks)**
c) To what extent has Britain become a more divided society since 1979? **(15 marks)**

a) 'Casualisation' refers to the greater freedom with which employers could hire and fire staff in the 1980s and 1990s, once the powers of trade unions were reduced and employment law was altered. Staff could be employed only for as long as they were needed and in some cases, could be called into work and paid for short periods before being sent home again.

b) The phrase 'two-tier' implies that there are different levels of experience in the provision of services, with the rich entitled to better quality services than the mass of the population. In education, of course, a two (or in some areas three) tier system was embodied in the state system in the 1944 Education Act which used the 11-plus exam to identify the more able and to provide them with better equipped 'grammar schools'. With the introduction of comprehensive schools under Labour in the 1960s, this system was largely abolished. Many middle-class parents refused to send their children to these new schools, however, and used their higher incomes to send them to fee-paying independent schools. Under Thatcher's and Major's governments, parents were given the freedom to choose which state school to send their children to and this resulted in over-demand for the better schools, which became semi-independent or 'grant maintained' and consequently introduced admission criteria to select the best pupils. Wealthier parents, able to afford more books and extra schooling for their children usually benefited, while the less wealthy were forced to accept places at schools where bullying, peer pressure or bad teaching were more common and made the chances of success in future life much reduced.

After the recession of the early 1980s, unemployment became extremely uneven. The North of England saw unemployment above the national average for the whole of the 1980s and 1990s, and particular areas such as Sunderland saw an even higher rate than the rest of the region. Particular

---

*evanescent = quickly fading

groups were more likely to find themselves excluded from the world of work, such as young black men who experienced unemployment rates twice those of young whites. In paid employment, the opportunities for the less well educated shrank in the last decade of the century. Manufacturing and manual jobs became increasingly hard to find and consequently poorly paid, whereas salaries for professionals such as lawyers, accountants and managers increased dramatically. Those in the public sector saw a much more ambivalent picture however, as despite the high levels of qualifications necessary for teachers, nurses, doctors and local government officers, their salary levels did not keep pace with their contemporaries employed in the private sector.

In the 1980s and the later 1990s, the value of private houses increased rapidly in South East England and the Midlands. As a result, many young people and those on lower incomes in these areas were not able to afford to buy a home and were forced to rent property instead. As private rents were also quite high, they spent a significant proportion of their income on housing and were unable to save enough to afford a deposit for a private house. Local authorities were forced by central government to sell council houses to those able to buy them at very generous prices. Those unable to do so, found themselves in properties which the local authorities were unable to afford to maintain, as they were forbidden by the government from spending the money earned from sales in this way. As only the very poorest remained in council property, these became notorious in the 1980s and 1990s for social problems such as alcoholism, drug-taking, violence, theft and prostitution, which forced out those who could afford to move and created 'sink-estates' for the rest.

Those with occupational pensions, which were tax-exempt up to a certain point, provided either by insurers or companies enjoyed a comfortable period of retirement. Part-time, temporary (in other words a large proportion of female workers) and self-employed workers, as well as the jobless of course, did not enjoy such privileges and were likely to be dependent on the state pension. This was linked to the level of inflation under the Labour government of 1974–79, but this link was broken under Mrs Thatcher's first government and was not restored by the end of century, by which time the standard of living of those whose sole income it was, had seriously declined.

c) Following the intensification of a redistributive approach to taxation, particularly under Harold Wilson's Labour governments, by 1977 the top 20 per cent of the richest people in Britain owned 43 per cent of the nation's income, in salaries or property, while the bottom 40 per cent owned 14 per cent. When Mrs Thatcher changed this by offering substantial tax cuts for the rich in her first government, the closing of the gap between rich and poor which had been evident since 1945, was suddenly and dramatically reversed. By 1985, the top 20 per cent now owned 47 per cent of GNP, and this increased to 50 per cent by 1992, while the bottom 40 per cent's share fell to 10 per cent by 1985 and to 8 per cent by 1992. As the rich were able to invest their extra incomes in the booming stock market, and to see the value of their privately owned property increase, those without capital were unable to exploit these opportunities.

The very poorest proportion of the population had had their incomes improved by state pensions and benefits in the post-war period, but under the Conservative governments of 1979–97 these were cut either directly, or failed to keep up with inflation. The result was that while the poorest 20 per cent of Britain had only a 4 per cent share of the nation's income in 1977, this had fallen to 2 per cent by 1992. In 1968 five million households had an income less than the national average wage, by 1992 this had increased to 11 million. This was not due to large scale reductions in social security programmes, but to a cumulative loss of entitlement to payments during the 1980s. Benefit rights for 16 and 17 year olds were withdrawn and means-testing reduced the 'universality' of benefits, particularly for the unemployed, where receipt of benefits became dependent on proving that one is 'actively seeking work' and compulsory participation in training programmes. The programme for public housing was largely abandoned as Mrs Thatcher's government encouraged those who could to buy their houses, while those who could not were left in rotting accommodation or, at worst, homeless.

One group in particular, students in higher education, saw their incomes plummet. First, during the 1980s, students became no longer eligible for unemployment benefit during their vacations and then the grant, given to the poorest students to enable them to study, was frozen. In the 1990s, the grant was gradually reduced, while students were encouraged to take out loans at low interest rates to pay for their time at college. The Labour government of 1997 refused to reverse this policy, and actually further worsened students' economic position by introducing tuition fees of up to £1,000 per year, from which only those from the very poorest backgrounds were completely exempt. By the end of the century, students were among the poorest 10 per cent of the nation's social groups.

The increased extent of division in Britain since 1979 was evident in other ways apart from just wealth. Job security clearly declined among the less wealthy, as the power of trade unions was cut in the 1980s, and Labour was forced to side with business interests for the sake of electoral respectability. Shorter contracts were offered to encourage workers to work harder and even 'zero-hours' contracts were introduced where workers were called in, only when work was available. Companies took advantage of new technologies and cheaper work forces in less developed countries to cut large numbers of workers and middle managers.

Britain may have been the fourth strongest economy in the world by the end of the century, but it was clear that the benefits of the economic recovery of the mid-1980s and 1990s was enjoyed more fully by those who were already the highest earners in the country. While the relative wealth of almost all groups increased to some extent, for the less wealthy, job insecurity, longer hours and a shortened and possibly impoverished retirement have been the price of their modest improvements.

Additional essay questions

1. Europe (OCR)

Did Tony Blair's European policies between 1997 and 2001 demonstrate a significant change to those of Margaret Thatcher and John Major?

(Total: 90 marks)

2. Mrs Thatcher's governments (EDEXCEL)

a) **Describe the causes of the Miners' Strike of 1984–85.** **(30 marks)**

b) **Why was Margaret Thatcher able to achieve considerable reduction of the power of Trade Unions between 1979 and 1990?** **(30 marks)**

(Total: 60 marks)

Essay plan

a)   Mining industry – dangerous, poorly paid, but increasingly unprofitable and relatively over-staffed due to power of national Union of Miners (NUM).

Thatcherite policies – restriction of union rights. Deliberate exposure of industry to international competition to force efficiency – meant job losses and closure of unprofitable industries. Desire to destroy power of unions, especially that of miners, blamed for fall of Conservative government in 1974. Militancy of miners' union, especially Arthur Scargill. Worried by the introduction of compulsory balloting and ban on secondary picketing. Willing to use threat of power cuts as in 1972 and 1974 to force government to reverse policy. The government's tactics in calling for a ballot of the miners before recognising the legality of the strike – Nottinghamshire miners reluctant to strike.

Scargill saw himself as only effective means of reversing government's economic policy after defeat of radical Labour programme in 1983. Provocation by the government – no longer dependent on coal, they had built up reserves. Ian MacGregor appointed chairman of the National Coal Board (NCB) in September 1983 – pursued policy of closing pits and sacking workers to provoke a confrontation. Metropolitan police drafted in to break pickets as less sympathetic to miners' cause.

b)   Electors' dissatisfaction with union power – outcome of 1970, 1974 and 1979 elections had been affected by union activity. Unions blamed by influential media for poor performance of British economy in 1960s and 1970s. Memories of power cuts in 1972 and 1974 kept alive by both Labour and Conservative election campaigns in 1979.

Winter of discontent 1978–79 – actions of public sector unions had caused huge public anger – support for restrictions on unions. Public sector workers unlikely to strike again following quite generous pay settlement in 1979. Support of her party – although divided on economic policy, following the defeat in 1974 on 'who governs Britain' – desire for revenge on unions united Mrs Thatcher's Cabinet 1979–1983.

Mistakes by unions, especially miners – rash strike in 1984 allowed Thatcher to paint unions as violent and irresponsible. Issue of ballots before strikes allowed Thatcher to appear as moderate and Scargill as dangerous. Lack of influence of Labour party – divided over the SDP split, nuclear disarmament and the infiltration of 'militant'. Poorly lead until 1983 – then preoccupied by internal reform. Labour had lowest number of MPs since 1945 in the 1983–87 Parliament – unable to prevent reform.

Period of economic recession 1979–83 – manufacturing industry worst hit where the militant unions were strongest. In period of recession, unions weak – all time low number of strikes, fall in union subscription and membership. Ideal opportunity for union reform. When economy recovered – more dependent on service industries where unions were weaker – Thatcher could claim that recovery came because trade union power had been broken – Britain more competitive.

3. The decline of the Conservatives (OCR)

Why did the Conservative Party become so divided after 1992? (Total: 90 marks)

4. Foreign policy (OCR)

Why did the Anglo-Irish Agreement of 1985 fail to lead to peace in Northern Ireland?
(Total: 90 marks)

5. The Labour Party in opposition (OCR)

Why was the Labour Party in opposition from 1979 to 1997? (Total: 90 marks)

Explain how the election of Neil Kinnock as leader in 1983 affected the Labour Party. (Total: 90 marks)

6. Tony Blair as Prime Minister (AQA)

Read the following source and then answer the questions which follow.

The key components of New Labour's project are modernisation of the Welfare State and modernisation of the constitution. Socialism is left far behind. New Labour is a coalition of the centre with both radical and conservative elements, but it is still unclear whether the radical or the conservative elements will gain the upper hand. Both are represented in the Government and there is likely to be increasing conflict between them. The trade unions are still an element in this coalition but are much reduced in influence, and their role is likely to diminish still further.

Adapted from After the Watershed *by Andrew Gamble, 1998*

a) **Using the source and your own knowledge, comment on the 'modernisation of the constitution' in the context of Blair's Labour government from 1997–2001.** (3 marks)

b) **Explain why the trade unions were 'much reduced in influence' in the New Labour government.** (7 marks)

c) **Explain why and in what ways there was conflict within the Labour government of 1997–2001.** (15 marks)

7. The economy since 1979 (EDEXCEL)

a) **Describe the performance of the British economy under Margaret Thatcher's and John Major's governments.** (30 marks)

b) **How important was government policy in the performance of the British economy between 1979 and 2000?** (30 marks)

(Total: 60 marks)

Essay plan

a)   *Britain undergoing structural decline by 1970s, due to failures in manufacturing and primary production. Post-1973 cyclical decline made the first years of Mrs Thatcher's government the worst economic performance of any post-war government – low growth, unemployment and low productivity – bankruptcy only avoided by North Sea oil and gas income.*

- *Decline of manufacturing, especially in early 1980s – northern England, South Wales and Scotland worst affected. Britain's relative decline continued.*
- *Steady economic growth after 1982, and in 1989, unemployment finally fell below two million – rise of service industries, especially financial. Manufacturing output increased by less than 2 per cent per year.*
- *Crash in 1989–1992 – South East. This was a cyclical recession however, and not as serious as that of 1979–83. Revival after 1993 – due to deregulated labour market – inflation remained low, unemployment fell to under one million.*
- *British economic growth matched or exceeded that of its competitors. The economy dependent on the service sector – manufacturing continued to decline.*

b)   *Traditional view – boom of 1980s largely due to government reforms allowing businesses more freedom. Thatcher's 'sado-monetarism' in early 1980s high interest rates and high level of pound (due to North Sea oil) to curb inflation – made effects of recession worst – two million manufacturing jobs lost in 1980s.*

- *By 1983 harshest monetarist targets abandoned.*
- *Improvement in the economy after 1983, largely due to global economic recovery, government action in reducing business taxes gave incentive to compete.*
- *Stoking of pre-1987 election boom due to reduction in interest rates, sale of shares in privatised utilities – this boom led to an increase in consumer spending, which, following the decline in manufacturing, was mainly on imports – led to a poor **balance of payments** and rising inflation (reaching 8 per cent in 1989).*
- *Stock market crash of October 1987. Rise in interest rates, post-election collapse. ERM membership after 1989 made British goods over-priced and put pressure on the pound – led to 1992 crash – loss of £6 billion. Government de-regulation led to a boom of mid 1990s – but one in which the workers did not share as they had done in 1953–73.*
- *To support ailing British manufacturers, the Conservative government encouraged foreign investment to such an extent that, by 1995, 25 per cent of British manufacturing output was owned by non-British citizens, employing 16 per cent of the population.*
- *New Labour continued business-friendly politics – inflation kept as low as possible – sticking to the Conservatives' own spending limits for two years. Labour – invested in education and training to help rebuild Britain' manufacturing base.*

Summary – striking similarity between performance of British economy and world economic trends – with a free market policy and little state intervention, British economy at mercy of global trends.

Part 3: Sources

📖 1. The impact of the Falklands War (EDEXCEL)

Study sources 1–5 below and then answer the questions (a) to (e) which follow:

Source 1. From Hugo Young, *One of Us*, 1994, writing about the causes of the Falklands War

The war to reclaim the Falklands from Argentinian occupation was the result of a great failure in the conduct of government: arguably the most disastrous lapse by any British government since 1945. Precipitated by Argentina's aggression, it was provoked by Britain's negligence.

Source 2. From a speech by Mrs Thatcher on victory in the Falklands, July 1982

We have ceased to be a nation in retreat. We have instead a new-found confidence, born in the economic battles at home and tested and found true 8,000 miles away.

Source 3. From the *Financial Times*, December 1982

In December 1981, just 12 months ago, the MORI polls suggested that only 25 per cent of the electorate were satisfied with the way Mrs Thatcher was doing her job as Prime Minister and only 18 per cent were satisfied with the way the Government was running the country. It is true that there was some improvement in the ratings before the Argentine invasion, but nothing like the leap that occurred in May and June. In the latter month satisfaction with the Prime Minister rose to 59 per cent and with the Government to 51 per cent. Only Mrs Thatcher's handling of the crisis can explain that.

What of the consequences so far? Apart from the Tory recovery in the polls, the most obvious is that Mrs Thatcher immensely increased her authority in the party ... It is Mrs Thatcher's Cabinet now, and Mrs Thatcher's party.

Source 4. A cartoon from the *Sun*, June 1983 (see Figure 10.5)

Figure 10.5 **Front page of the Sun, election day 1983**

Source 5. From Eric J. Evans *Thatcher and Thatcherism*, 1997 writing about Mrs Thatcher's wartime leadership

Thatcher had to take immediate decisions and sell them to a British audience. She did so quite brilliantly, emphasizing the moral dimension. British military intervention was right; not to intervene would be cowardly; Britons would never be slaves . . . In her view she was faced with a crisis and dealt with it by invoking British patriotism. She knew in her bones that she was right, but was equally aware of the immense political value of success . . . In the Falklands War, her leadership gave the British people a success which most of them rejoiced at, while raising the country's stock internationally.

QUESTIONS WITH WORKED ANSWERS

a)   Study source 2. What evidence in this source suggests that Mrs Thatcher used victory in the Falklands to justify her approach to politics? **(6 marks)**

b)   Use your own knowledge. Use your own knowledge to explain what 'great failure in the conduct of government ' (Source 1) led to the invasion of the Falkland Islands by Argentina. **(10 marks)**

c)   Study sources 4 and 5. How far do these sources agree on Mrs Thatcher's wartime leadership? **(10 marks)**

d)   Study sources 3 and 4. How useful are these two sources to an historian examining the impact of the Falklands War on Mrs Thatcher's popularity? **(10 marks)**

e)   Study sources 3 and 5 and use your own knowledge. Do you agree with the view that Mrs Thatcher's leadership was only fully accepted by the Conservative party after the success of the Falklands campaign? Explain your answer using these two sources and your own knowledge. **(24 marks)**

(Total: 60 marks)

ANSWERS

a)   Mrs Thatcher believed that her style of government, combative and confrontational, as well her policies both at home and abroad, were capable of reversing the decline of what she described in source 2 as 'a nation in retreat'. She therefore links Britain's military victory in the Falklands, '8,000 miles away' with the 'economic battles at home', implying that the struggle against inflation and uncompetitive industrial practice was being won as well and that in these two areas her government has transformed Britain's global standing.

b)   Defence cuts, carried out by successive Labour and Conservative governments in the 1960s and 1970s had given the impression to the Argentinian government that Britain was no longer willing or able to defend the Falkland Islands to which Argentina lay claim. The actions of Mrs Thatcher's government convinced the Argentinian dictatorship of this when the ice-breaker ship, the Endurance, was removed from the area and the aircraft carrier responsible for defending the islands was scrapped. In negotiations with the Argentinian government in 1981, Britain failed to demonstrate a clear commitment to the Falklands. She was clearly wanting to give the Argentinians hope that they would be able to make progress in their claim to the islands, in order to prevent their government resorting to military action. In fact, this had the opposite effect. When Argentinian forces invaded the islands on 2 April, the small Royal Marine detachment was unable to prevent their capture. The Foreign Secretary, Lord Carrington, despite no personal fault, resigned as a matter of principle after such a government failure.

c)   The cartoon in source 4 shows Mrs Thatcher as Britannia, the embodiment of Britain. It shows the way in which Mrs Thatcher in the period following the Falklands conflict appeared to epitomise the characteristics that the nationalistic press thought of as typically British, courageous, undefeatable and proud. It shows that, by 1983, her leadership and the Falklands victory had become inextricably linked, and that the belief in a renewed Britain that had found its confidence in a successful war, could be channelled to suit the electoral needs of an astute politician. Of course, Mrs Thatcher, as the first woman Prime Minister of Britain, could be depicted by cartoonists as a symbolic character such as Britannia in much the same way as she was compared to famous British warrior queens such as Boudicca or Elizabeth I. The image is also a reflection of the combative imagery that she habitually employed, even when speaking about domestic affairs, with language such 'the battle of ideas' and most famously, the 'enemy within'.

Source 5 explains the reasons for this popularity, stating that Mrs Thatcher convinced the British people of the need for military intervention and 'did so quite brilliantly'. Her argument that 'not to intervene would be cowardly' evoked memories of Neville Chamberlain's failure at Munich and associated her with the Churchillian tradition of strong British leaders. The evocative phrase from 'Rule Britannia' that 'Britons would never be slaves' was never used explicitly by Mrs Thatcher, but her refusal to abandon the Falkland Islanders and her decision to send a Royal Naval taskforce to recapture the dependency, allowed her to revive a strongly historical sense of British patriotism that had, after the retreat from Empire, not been heard for many years. Therefore to portray Mrs Thatcher as Britannia was, in many ways a very suitable visual shorthand for the type of public reaction that her handling of the Falklands campaign evoked.

d)   Source 3, from the largely politically neutral *Financial Times*, offers a dramatic interpretation of the impact of the Falklands War on Mrs Thatcher's popularity, suggesting that she went from an approval rating of 25 per cent in December 1981 to one of 59 per cent in only six months. This gives the historian an impression of the impact of the successful Falklands war on the political equilibrium. It also gives the historian some indication of why Mrs Thatcher was able to remain in control of the Conservative Party for so long, despite the misgivings of many in her party towards her economic policy in general and her attitude towards the European Union in particular. Although, in light of subsequent events, it was an exaggeration to claim that 'it is Mrs Thatcher's Cabinet now, and Mrs Thatcher's party', such was the increase in popular approval for Mrs Thatcher herself in the Falklands conflict, that no one was able to seriously challenge her leadership for eight years and then only as a result of a major recession and a number of political blunders. That a cartoon such as that in source 4 should be drawn of a politician who had, only months before, received the lowest approval ratings for a sitting Prime Minister since records began, seems in many ways extraordinary. But, the *Sun*, in common with many other right-wing newspapers had fully supported Mrs Thatcher's unpopular deflationary economic policies, even when unemployment was rampant and thousands of manufacturing businesses were folding. As it was owned by an Australian businessman, Rupert Murdoch, the *Sun* supported

Thatcher's policies such as the restriction of unions' right to strike, a lowering of top-level income tax, and the decrease of government regulation of business. The cartoon in source 4 can therefore be seen as a welcome opportunity for the newspaper to unashamedly praise a Prime Minister for a policy popular with the *Sun*'s working class readership, as a respite from having to act as an apologist for the government's policies for the previous two years.

e) Mrs Thatcher had not enjoyed the full backing of the Conservative Party following her sensational defeat of Edward Heath in 1975 for the leadership of the Party. Her position had been so weak, that she had been forced, unwillingly, to offer important Cabinet positions to many of those whose political and most significantly whose economic views she abhorred. In particular, James Prior, Francis Pym, Ian Gilmour and Lord Carrington held consensual views, often described as 'one-nation Conservatism', yet all were given senior Cabinet positions. At no time, between 1979 and 1983, did Mrs Thatcher's Cabinet have a majority for **monetarism** and the economic policies of her Chancellor, Geoffrey Howe, did much to upset this group, whom Mrs Thatcher christened 'wets'. They did not openly rebel, however, as they felt they owed loyalty to their leader at a difficult time, when the government was under enormous pressure.

With the victory in the Falklands, however, Mrs Thatcher became increasingly confident that she could dispense with the services of those she saw as 'moaning minnies'. Lord Carrington had resigned as a result of the invasion, and Prior and Pym were sacked shortly after the 1983 election campaign. In their place, men such as Norman Tebbit, Nigel Lawson and Leon Brittan, who Mrs Thatcher could confidently assert were 'one of us', were appointed. As the 1980s progressed the social composition of the Conservative Party itself began to alter as the number of Tory MPs educated at Oxbridge declined, while the number of those from provincial universities grew. Fewer senior professionals such as bankers became Conservative MPs, but many more accountants, estate agents. solicitors and car dealers did. The party was, by 1990, at both grass-roots level and at Westminster, a far more middle-class party, far more in tune with Mrs Thatcher's political principles.

One might argue however, that the victory in the Falklands made it impossible for those Conservatives who did not share her views to consider rebelling with the party likely to face a general election in the next year. However, once the Falkland issue had faded from the headlines, Mrs Thatcher continued to face opposition from within her party during the next Parliament, most notably from Michael Heseltine over the Westland Helicopters issue. Heseltine, in common with other dissatisfied Tories, knew that in the midst of an economic boom he stood no chance of ousting Thatcher and so waited until after the 1987 election when the economy began to slip into recession. Then, in 1990, after the disaster of the **poll tax**, he challenged Thatcher for the party leadership. Mrs Thatcher was so confident that she had the support of her party that her leadership campaign was poorly run, and she was astonished when she failed to win on the first ballot, with 152 of her party voting against her. It is therefore possible to conjecture, that while the Falklands victory was fresh in people's minds, and the economic boom continued, the Conservative party was happy to accept her leadership, but once the circumstances became less propitious, the parliamentary party at least was quite prepared to abandon her. Therefore one can seriously question if the Conservative party at Westminster ever fully accepted Mrs Thatcher's leadership.

2. 'Thatcherism' (OCR)

Source A: From Mrs Thatcher's speech to the Church of Scotland General Assembly, 21 May 1988

Regarding the creation of wealth:
Nevertheless, the Tenth Commandment – 'Thou shalt not covet' – recognizes that making money and owning things could become selfish activities. But it is not the creation of wealth that is wrong, but love of money for its own sake. The spiritual dimension comes in deciding what one does with the wealth.

Source B: From an interview with Mrs Thatcher in *Woman's Own*, 3 October 1987

I think we've been through a period where too many people have been given to understand that if they have a problem, it's the government's job to cope with it. 'I have a problem, I'll get a grant'. 'I'm homeless, the government must house me'. They're casting their problem on society. And, you know, there is no such thing as society. There are individual men and women, and there are families. And no government can do anything except through people, and people must look to themselves first. It's our duty to look after ourselves and then, also to look after our neighbour. People have got the entitlements too much in mind, without the obligations. There's no such thing as entitlement, unless someone has first met an obligation.

Source C: From *The Downing Street Years* by Margaret Thatcher

What I learned in Grantham ensured that abstract criticisms I would hear of capitalism came up against the reality of my own experience: I was thus innoculated against the conventional economic wisdom of postwar Britain.

Source D: Mrs Thatcher on socialism

In the end, Churchill was right. Whether socialism needed a 'Gestapo' as it did in Eastern Europe and the Soviet Union, or just those banal and bureaucratic instruments of coercion, confiscation, taxation, nationalization and oppressive regulation employed in the West, ultimately depended only on the degree of socialism desired. In diminishing economic freedom, the socialists had embarked on a course which, if pursued to its ultimate destination, would mean the extinction of all freedom.

QUESTIONS WITH WORKED ANSWERS

a) **Study source A. From this source and your own knowledge, explain why Mrs Thatcher was keen to stress that 'it is not the creation of wealth that is wrong' (line 4).** (10 marks)

b) **Study source B. How completely does this source reveal Mrs Thatcher's political beliefs?** (25 marks)

c) **Study sources C and D. Compare the justifications given for Mrs Thatcher's economic principles as shown in these sources.** (25 marks)

> **d)** Study all the sources. Using all the sources and your own knowledge, explain how far you agree with the view that 'Mrs Thatcher's sheer stamina, her persistence and belief in her own rightness made her a most unusual, perhaps unique, Prime Minister'. **(60 marks)**
>
> **(Total: 120 marks)**

ANSWERS

a) As Mrs Thatcher had, by 1988, pursued an economic policy which favoured entrepreneurial capitalism and had encouraged the pursuit of profit by the reduction of income tax and business tax, she was keen to argue that 'it is not the creation of wealth that is wrong' in this justification of her economic policies to the Scottish clergy. Mrs Thatcher was well aware of the opposition that her economic policies had generated within the Christian churches of Great Britain and was keen to explain her view that the generation of wealth was not immoral in itself, rather 'love of money for its own sake'.

b) Mrs Thatcher rejected the post-war political consensus that held that it was the responsibility of the state to care for its citizens 'from the cradle to the grave', believing that individuals should make their own provision for health care, pensions and housing. As she said in source B, 'people must look to themselves first', which would allow the government to commit less of its money to the **Welfare State**. Mrs Thatcher believed in the role of the state being reduced more widely than this even, so that people would be encouraged to work hard and becomes entrepreneurs, rather than adopting the attitudes of a dependency culture, which she believed the pre-1979 **Welfare State** had encouraged. She explained in source A 'too many people have been given to understand that if they have a problem, it's the government's job to cope with it'. In this way she was revealing her iconoclastic attitude towards the accepted role of government that led to resentment from what she dismissed as 'the establishment'; civil servants, clergymen, the BBC and even members of her own party.

The source does not clearly enunciate all of the ideas of **Thatcherism**, however, as she does not attempt to explain the macro-economic monetarist policies that her governments pursued to bring inflation under control, nor does she dwell on the British nationalism that led her to confront the European Union at this time. However, one might read much of her populist approach and intelligent use of the media into the choice of publication for this important statement of her beliefs, a popular women's magazine, that would be read by working- or lower-middle-class housewives and women workers.

c) In source C, Mrs Thatcher states that 'abstract criticisms ... of capitalism came up against the reality of my own [childhood] experience in Grantham', meaning that her day to day experience, working in her father's grocery shop taught her the value of hard work, thrift and personal responsibility and the need for competition to produce economic success. She implies that she contrasted this with the failure of state-run industry and welfare provision in 'postwar Britain', where the 'conventional economic wisdom' of Keynesian economics held that one could manage demand and thus prevent unemployment. In source D, however, she refers to a famous broadcast by Churchill during the 1945 election in which he claimed that any form of socialism would have to rely on some type of 'Gestapo' or secret police, in order to achieve its ends. The comment helped to defeat the Conservatives in 1945, but Mrs Thatcher sees that it does have some truth. Unlike source C, where she justifies her belief in free market economics from her personal experiences, in source D, she argues that any form of state-intervention in the economy will inevitably lead to the restriction of political and civil liberties.

d) Mrs Thatcher's stamina as Prime Minister was legendary. She apparently survived on three or four hours' sleep a night and was able to debate effectively for long periods at international conferences and in Parliament. Her belief in her rightness was clear as well, as in her pronouncement that 'there is no alternative' when she faced criticism for her harsh economic policies in the early 1980s. After the Falkland Islands were invaded by Argentina in 1982, she was informed by her Cabinet colleagues and her foreign allies that only negotiation could resolve the crisis. She knew that the nation would support military action if it was in defence of the rights of the Falkland islanders and immediately ordered the formation of a taskforce to liberate the islands.

In some ways her belief in her own rightness contributed to her downfall. She gradually excluded all but those who shared her opinions from government, eventually even sacking two of her most loyal lieutenants, Nigel Lawson and Geoffrey Howe when they began to question her increasingly impatient attitude towards the European Union. Most seriously of all, in the eyes of the public, her attempt to replace the system of rates with a 'community charge' (soon nicknamed the **poll tax**) proved a disaster. No minister dared to question this project even when it led to widespread non-payment in Scotland, where it was introduced first in 1989. The wave of public anger and Mrs Thatcher refusal to admit a mistake led to Michael Heseltine's challenge for the party leadership and her subsequent fall from power.

The **poll tax** affair was in many ways a negative example of the final quality described in the question, persistence, with the Falklands war a positive one. On the issue of her economic policy, however, despite her boast in 1980 that 'the lady's not for turning', one begins to encounter evidence that she was not always as persistent as she was in specific incidents like these. After the battle to control the money supply between 1980 and 1982 had seen inflation fall to 5.4 per cent, monetary policy became a lot less rigorous. Exchange controls were abandoned and restrictions on consumer credit were relaxed. After the 1983 election was won, fiscal targets were loosened and inflation began to rise as the government began to deliberately encourage an economic boom, keeping interest rates deliberately low. By 1990 inflation had exceeded 10 per cent and the economy was heading for a serious recession. Despite her protestations of a strict monetarist approach, Mrs Thatcher had actually stimulated the economy for political benefits and had not persisted with her avowed economic intentions. Her most clear persistence was in the pursuit of political advantage, and once a policy no longer brought that, it was swiftly discarded. The result was that as a politician she was uniquely successful, winning all three of the general elections she fought. As a Prime Minister, she managed to sustain her position for an unusually long time, mainly as a result of the divisions among her political opponents. But ultimately, her refusal to listen to the views of others forced her party to depose her before it was prepared to face the judgement of a disillusioned electorate.

3. The fall of Thatcher (EDEXCEL)

Study Source 1 below and then answer questions (a) to (c) which follow:

Source 1. From *Thatcher and Thatcherism* by Eric Evans, published 1997

[Geoffrey Howe's] resignation speech was as action packed as anything in his political life. It contained a cogent recantation of monetarist policy, which he himself had implemented as Chancellor a decade earlier, and the accusation that Thatcher's dithering about entering the ERM had caused the recent damaging increase in inflation. He also included a withering denunciation of the prime minister's 'nightmare image' of a European Community stalked by malevolent anti-democrats who wanted to destroy national sovereignty . . . His final sentence was dynamite: 'The time has come for others to consider their own response to the tragic conflict of loyalties with which I have myself wrestled for perhaps too long'. Michael Heseltine had been presented, gift wrapped, with just the opportunity he said he could not foresee, but for which the last four years of his life had been a preparation.

QUESTIONS WITHOUT WORKED ANSWERS

a) Why, according to Eric Evans, did Geoffrey Howe's resignation lead to the fall of Margaret Thatcher as Prime Minister? (10 marks)

b) What was the most important factor in causing Mrs Thatcher's downfall, the poll tax or Europe? (14 marks)

c) Mrs Thatcher, writing in her memoirs, said of her dismissal, 'it was betrayal, with a smile on its face'. How far do the events of November 1990 support her view? (36 marks)

(Total: 60 marks)

---

4. The European Union and the Conservative Party (AQA)

Source A. From Mrs Thatcher's speech at Bruges, 1988

We have not rolled back the frontiers of the state in Britain only to have them reimposed at a European level, with a European superstate exercising a new dominance from Brussels.

Source B. John Major's view of the European Union, 1991

My aims for Britain in the [European] Community can be simply stated. I want us to be where we belong. At the very heart of Europe. Working with our partners in building the future . . . Europe is made up of nation states: their vitality and diversity are sources of strength.

Source C. George Gardiner, a Conservative MP on his opposition to the EU

Given all the history of the Conservative Party standing up for Queen and constitution and so on, I do not think that an instinctive Conservative would ever have considered the possibility of joining a European Single Currency and putting us in on the fast track really to a European super-state.

QUESTIONS WITHOUT WORKED ANSWERS

a) Study source A. With reference to your own knowledge, explain Mrs Thatcher's reference to 'a European super-state' in the context of Britain's relationship with the European Union. (3 marks)

b) Study source B. With reference to your own knowledge, explain how useful source B is as evidence about the attitude of the Conservative party towards the European Union. (7 marks)

c) Refer to sources A, B and C and use your own knowledge. 'Mrs Thatcher helped to create the Eurosceptic monster and it has divided and defeated the Tory party'. Explain why you agree or disagree with this statement.

(15 marks)

(Total: 25 marks)

Part 4: Historical skills

Media awareness

Race and the media

Read the following quotes:

To be a black resident of this country is to be subject to a continuous assault on your identity and integrity. Your presence in this country is signalled to you as being unreal since the news media refuse to see you as a citizen, but as an immigrant . . . The possible arrival of more people with a similar background to yourself is reported in the press in the language of natural disasters as 'a flood' or 'a tidal wave'. A continuous assumption implicit in much of the news programming is that, in various ways, you and your kind are an unwanted burden, a black parasite on a white society . . . These aspects of news have made it difficult for black citizens of this country to feel accepted and settled here. Indeed, it is more accurate to say that they are tolerated.

From Charles Husband *White Media and Black Britain – a critical look at the role of the media in race relations today* (1975)

The main way in which black people are treated in newspapers is as a social problem. Black people are portrayed as constituting a threat to white British society, first through their immigration to this country and then, when settled here, as posing a law and order problem. This is done in a number of ways: through dramatic presentation of stories involving banner headlines and prominent positioning, provocative or damning quotations and statements from people portrayed as authoritative figures, popular stereotypes, repetition of unreliable stories, and the creation and manipulation of popular fears.

From P. Gordon and D. Rosenberg, *Daily Racism* (1989)

Violence doubles that by whites, Yard reveal
BLACK CRIME:
THE ALARMING FIGURES

Scotland Yard revealed for the first time yesterday the extent of black crime in London and immediately started political controversy. The figures were broken down from statistics showing an increase in 1981 of 34 per cent in cases of 'robbery' and other violent 'thefts' in the capital. Out of 18,763 crimes in that category, the assailants were described as 'coloured', according to the Yard, in 10,398 cases – or 55.42 per cent of the total.

From the *Daily Mail*, 11 March 1982

Over the 200 years up to 1945, Britain became so settled in internal peace that many came to believe that respect for the person and property of fellow citizens was something which existed naturally in all but a few. A glance at less fortunate countries might have reminded us that such respect scarcely exists unless law is above the power of tribe, or money, or the gun. But we did not look; we let in people from the countries we did not look at, and only now do we begin to see the result. Many young West Indians in Britain, and by a connected process, growing numbers of young whites, have no sense that the nation in which they live is part of them. So its citizens become to them mere objects of violent exploitation.

From the *Daily Telegraph*, 11 March 1982

Britain is being swamped by a tide of illegal immigrants so desperate for a job that they will work for a pittance in our restaurants, cafes and nightclubs. Immigration officers are being overwhelmed by work. Last year, 2,191 'illegals' were nabbed and sent back home. But there are tens of thousands more, slaving behind bars, cleaning hotel rooms and working in kitchens. And when officers swoop on an establishment, they often find huge numbers of illegal workers being employed . . .

Illegals sneak in by:

- *Deceiving* immigration officers when they are quizzed at airports.
- *Disappearing* after their entry visas run out.
- *Forging* work permits and other documents.
- *Running* away from immigration detention centres.

From the *Sun*, 2 February 1989

Scores of gypsies from the Czech Republic and Slovakia have been put into bed-and-breakfast and guest houses on the Kent coast after arriving in Dover at the weekend in the hope of being granted asylum here.

Gwynn Prosser, Labour MP for Dover, will today meet Mike O'Brien, the immigration minister, to request assistance. A warning by Roger Gale, the Conservative MP for Thanet North, that 3,000 more gypsies were on their way was condemned as scaremongering by Mr O'Brien yesterday. However, Mr O'Brien acknowledged that further arrivals were inevitable until word filtered back to Slovakia and the Czech Republic that Britain was not a soft option. Some gypsies report having seen a television programme at home which said that the British welfare system would support them.

The influx of gypsies began several months ago, but until Friday was just a trickle, comprising about sixty families in total. Of the weekend's arrivals, thirty-six people were immediately deported and twenty-eight left voluntarily. Twenty-two others, mainly heads of families, were detained by immigration authorities. 'Our resources are being drained quite rapidly' said Terry Birkett, leader of Dover District Council. 'Kent cannot bear the full burden of these people'

From the *Independent*, 20 October 1997

The public hugely overestimates the number of asylum seekers in the UK, according to a poll to mark the start of the United Nations' Refugee Week. It found that most people questioned believe Britain takes in nearly a quarter of the world's asylum seekers, when the true figure is less than 2 per cent. Young people were even less well-informed, with those aged 15 to 18 believing the UK takes in 31 per cent of the world's refugees. The research was commissioned by a number of refugee organisations including Amnesty International, the Refugee Council, Refugee Action and the United Nations High Commissioner for Refugees.

They blamed the media for misleading the public with inaccurate and often highly emotive reporting, using words such as 'tide', 'swamping' and 'hordes'. Nick Hardwick, chief executive of the Refugee Council, said: 'Much of the media inflames the asylum debate with emotive and vitriolic language.

The public is clearly not being given the facts about refugees . . . at least some of this misunderstanding must come from the media focus on people trying to reach our shores, rather than reporting the whole spectrum of the refugee experience'.

From *BBC News Online*, 17 June 2002

Table 10.17 **Accepted applications for settlement in Britain by region of origin (in 1,000s)**

	1976	1981	1986	1991	1998
Europe	9.5	6.6	5.2	5.6	7.6
America	7.7	6.3	6.4	7.2	10.8
Asia	34.6	30.0	22.8	25.2	30.1
Africa	8.6	4.1	4.1	9.6	16.1
Other	20.4	12.0	9.2	6.3	5.2
Total	80.7	59.1	47.8	53.9	69.8

Using the extracts above and your own research, prepare a talk for the class on the changing depiction of race in the media between 1979 and 2000.

Chapter 11

Conclusion: End of the Period Survey

This chapter offers a synoptic assessment of the development of Britain across the whole century.

Since the beginning of the century the population of Britain increased by over 50 per cent, though the rate of growth varied during the century and from region to region. For example, while the population of England increased by 62 per cent from 1901 from 1998, that of Scotland only increased by 14 per cent. The fastest rate of growth was seen in the first two decades of the century and in the 1960s, due to the high birth rate in these decades. The birth rate remained fairly consistent throughout the century, with 632,000 deaths in 1901 and 661,000 in 1998.

In 1900, British society was largely based on the nuclear family. Birth and death rates were high. Marriage was usually postponed until the mid-20s to allow couples to save for their own home. Divorce was extremely uncommon. A relatively large proportion of the population remained unmarried and therefore infertile as illegitimate births were very rare. After the First World War, the birth rate began to fall, but marriage became, if anything, increasingly popular, with couples marrying earlier. It was only after the Second World War that cohabitation, single motherhood, separation and divorce began to increase from a very low level. These modes of social behaviour grew relentlessly through the second half of the century, and by 2000, Britain had the highest levels of divorce, cohabitation, and illegitimate births in Europe.

More people lived in Britain at the end of the twentieth century than at any other time in history. The population in 1998 was 59.2 million, the eighteenth largest in the world.

As Table 11.2 shows, life expectancy has increased at a speed unparalleled in any other period of British history. For women, life expectancy at birth has increased by 30 years across the century. This is partly due to the rapid improvements in personal wealth since the early 1930s, but mostly due to the availability of free healthcare after 1948 and the reduction in the average number of

Table 11.1 **Population of the United Kingdom, 1901–98 in thousands**

	1901	1931	1961	1991	1998
England	30,515	37,359	43,561	48,208	49,495
Wales	2,013	2,593	2,635	2,891	2,933
Scotland	4,472	4,843	5,184	5,107	5,120
N. Ireland	1,237	1,243	1,427	1,601	1,689
United Kingdom	38,237	46,038	52,807	57,808	59,237

Table 11.2 **Life expectancy, 1901–2000**

	1901		1931		1961		2000	
	male	female	male	female	male	female	male	female
At birth	45.5	49.0	58.4	62.5	67.9	73.8	74.5	79.9
At age 1	53.6	55.8	62.1	65.1	68.6	74.2	74.0	79.3
At age 10	50.4	52.7	55.6	58.6	60.0	65.6	65.2	70.5
At age 20	41.7	44.1	46.7	49.6	50.4	55.7	55.4	60.6
At age 40	26.1	28.3	29.5	32.4	31.5	36.5	36.2	41.0
At age 60	13.3	14.6	14.4	16.4	15.0	19.0	18.7	22.7
At age 80	4.9	5.3	4.9	5.4	5.2	6.3	7.0	8.8

pregnancies in a woman's life. For many people, however, the cost of living longer has been a period of sustained poverty and deprivation, for those who did not save sufficiently to pay for their retirements, and longer periods of infirmity and ill-health which are relieved but prolonged by modern medicine.

Despite recent increases, the hours of paid employment have been considerably shortened, and the demands of domestic chores lightened by mechanical appliances. On the other hand, the domestic chores that do exist are still allocated on traditional gender lines in most households. In 2000, women did 260 minutes of unpaid work each day, with men only doing 172. Crime, traffic congestion and atmospheric pollution are all negative experiences that have risen across the century, but gender equality at work, racial and sexual tolerance, leisure time, freedom of movement and perhaps most significantly, educational opportunity have all increased. I myself come from a family who were definitely working class in 1900, with a grandfather who was selling newspapers on the streets at 12 years of age. My mother and father both left school to work at 14 in the 1930s, but following my father's promotion, they were able to buy their own home in the suburbs in the 1950s. Their first child, my elder sister, went to a 'redbrick' University in the 1960s and gained a senior professional position that enabled her to retire in her mid 50s.

In the second half of the century, the lives of women have significantly altered as they moved from domesticity to participation in the workforce. Economic changes have led to much greater opportunities for women both in education and paid employment. These have been made possible by the development of household technologies taken for granted in the twenty-first century, such as refrigeration, automatic washing machines and convenience foods, but which enabled women to escape from the restricting demands of running a household.

In terms of political developments, the great change in the century was the achievement of the vote for women, and the creation of universal suffrage that it brought. The growth of the working-class Labour party, in the place of the Liberals, once they won over the financial support of the trade unions and took advantage of the Liberals' failings in the First World War, was also a major change, although the Labour Party have emerged at the end of the century far more like Campbell-Bannerman's 'New Liberals' than anything that Keir Hardie would recognise. The political party that dominated the twentieth century, the Conservatives, did so until 1964, largely by adapting their ideals effectively to the needs and wishes of the people. After that, the traditionally benevolent upper-class Tory party leadership was gradually replaced by a more middle-class, more entrepreneurial type of politician. When Mrs Thatcher became leader, she announced a cultural revolution in her conversion to monetarist policies and, although she was not always rigorous in carrying out her beliefs, she imbued the Conservatives with an ideology. Like the Labour Party in the 1950s and the early 1980s however, that ideology eventually caused the internal dissension that brought down the party and which showed no sign of abating by 2000.

The reduction in the power of the Lords in 1912, then again in 1947 and finally the removal of hereditary peers' right to vote in the Lords in 1999, saw a confirmation of the nineteenth-century rise of the dominance of the Commons. As power became more centralised as the collectivist pattern of government grew until the 1960s, this was reflected in mass participation in elections, especially in the 1950s. With Mrs Thatcher and then Tony Blair's impatience with Parliament, the growth in power of the EU and the distractions of youth culture, by the end of the century the

Table 11.3 **Women as a percentage of those in higher education**

Year	%
1929	28
1959	25
1989	40
1999	48

Table 11.4 *Trade union membership, 1900–93*

Year	Trade Union members (in thousands)	% of workforce in TUs
1900	353	6
1911	1,502	13
1921	3,973	22
1938	5,842	30
1951	9,289	44
1961	9,897	43
1970	11,179	48
1974	11,756	50
1981	12,947	44
1993	7,762	36
1998	7,807	30

Table 11.5 *Unemployment in Britain, 1900–98*

Year	% of population
1900	2.8
1910	5.8
1922	10.8
1931	16.4
1937	10.1
1951	1.3
1964	1.7
1973	2.0
1979	4.7
1986	12.3
1989	7.9
1992	13.3
1998	6.2

people's enthusiasm for voting had cooled. Politicians were so concerned that less than two out three British citizens could be bothered to vote, they actually introduced the subject of 'citizenship' to the school curriculum, to encourage children to take greater interest in their political responsibilities. It was a stark admission of how far politicians had alienated their own electorate.

Possibly the greatest area of change in the twentieth century which affected the life of every individual in Britain was that of communications. As personal wealth increased, a society which had depended upon the public transport network of railways, trams and buses was transformed into a society which had access to personal motorised transport. Between 1940 and 1975 cars became common and a modern road network was constructed. After 1975, with the increase of oil prices, motoring became less cheap, but the growth of personal motoring was now unstoppable and the century ended with grave concerns for the environmental and health consequences of mass car-ownership. Similarly from an age when newspapers were the main form of information technology, the century witnessed the growth of radio, television, the telephone network and ultimately the computer-based internet.

There are some changes that provoke argument as to whether or not they illustrate improvement or decline. Chances for social mobility have definitely increased, but the distribution of wealth, after equalising in the years after 1945, has begun to widen in the last two decades of the century. Perhaps the best summary of the century was in the conclusion to the veteran sociologist A.H. Halsey's essay on 'A Hundred Years of Social Change', printed in the Office for National Statistics' publication *Social Trends* (2000 edition):

It has been an exciting century of progress and barbarism throughout the world, with paradoxical movements towards both a longer and fuller life and towards unprecedented genocide and slaughter, towards democracy and towards dictatorship. For the aristocrat perhaps a century of dispossession, culminating in the last days of the century in the removal of the right of hereditary peers to vote in the House of Lords. For the old and the ill, perhaps a rather more comfortable hundred years. For the homeless and dispossessed, a time of persistent degradation, accentuated by surrounding opulence. For women, the young and the fit and ordinary citizens perhaps the greatest century in the world history of humankind.

Next steps: from AS to A2

The purpose of this book has been to prepare for essays and examinations at AS rather than A2, which has a different approach. But some of the topics studied and all of the historical skills acquired at AS lead naturally and logically to the next conceptual stage represented by A2. This includes two approaches which are rooted in AS but grow beyond it. One is Historical Interpretation, with an emphasis on historiography or the study of different historical viewpoints. The other is a Synoptic Study of a period of about 100 years. These are common to all the Examination Boards.

AS to A2: Historical Interpretation

An example of the approach to Historical Interpretation at A2 can be seen in the OCR Specifications for the paper entitled *Historical Investigations*.

Investigations are built around topics of current interests to historians and the specific aim is to develop an understanding of how the past has been interpreted and represented, and how historical research generates controversies over interpretation. Candidates are expected to understand the principal arguments surrounding their chosen topic and to be able to offer their own explanations and interpretations.

One dimension of this has already been extensively covered. All AS students are familiar with at least one historical issue which is inherently controversial. They know how to interpret this issue in response to a specific question about it, making selective and creative use of the factual material relating to the topic.

The AS approach to Historical Interpretation

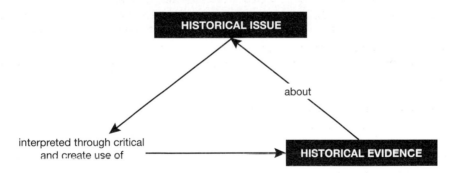

This has been the whole point of answering questions which begin with '*Why* . . . ?', '*How far* . . . ?', '*To what extent* . . . ?', '*Assess the reasons for* . . .' and many others. Use has been made of evidence from the period (factual knowledge) to consider possible reasons, to explain how these fit together, and to weigh up which are the most valid.

This is the starting point for the A2 approach, which adds the extra dimension of assessing other *views* which have been put forward by different historians and groups of historians (who are part of 'schools of thought'). At A2 students have to be aware of the *real* controversy behind the issue as well as the *possible* interpretations which will have occurred to them at AS. Historiography is therefore added to History. But the whole process still has to take account of the historical evidence. Historiography does not replace History – it provides additional perspectives and further opportunities for creative and original thought.

The A2 approach to Historical Interpretation

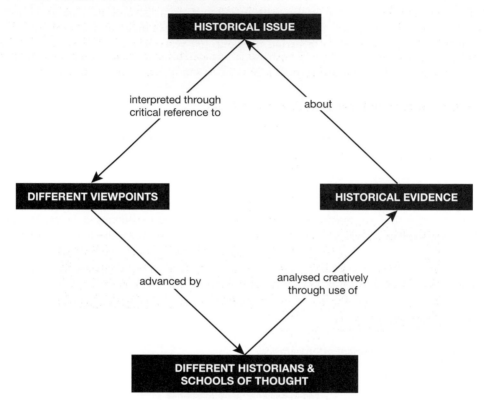

To give a practical example, an AS task might involve assessing the reasons for the success of the Liberals in tackling social reform between 1906 and 1914. At A2 the emphasis would be more on explaining why there is a major controversy about the decline of the Liberals and assessing the reasons given for the introduction of social reforms.

AS to A2: Synoptic Study

'Synoptic' in the context of A2 History has two possible meanings. The first is the connection *between* some of the different topics covered at AS and A2 to create a broader perspective on another paper; this is required by some Specifications but not by others. The second is an approach *within* an A2 paper (whether or not it involves areas previously studied) which requires an analysis of the broad sweep of change over a period of approximately 100 years. The OCR Specifications, for example, refer to the Synoptic Study as *Themes in History*, which:

develop understanding of connections between different elements of the subject. They draw together knowledge, understanding and the values of diverse issues centred on Key Themes. The topics are based on Key Themes covering an extended period of approximately a hundred years with an emphasis on continuity and change within the topic. The emphasis is on developing a broad overview of the period studied. They are historical perspectives modules, so concern is centred on links and comparison between different aspects of the topics studied.

As with the Historical Interpretation, the skills developed at AS lead to those needed at A2. This time, the change concerns the way in which perspectives are viewed. At AS the approach was to analyse a specific topic in a broad sweep (for example, the reasons for the victory of Labour in the 1945 general election). At A2 the perspective is considerably extended, but the topic becomes much more selective. The contrasting approaches can be seen as an open pair of scissors.

The A2 Synoptic approach and how it compares to AS

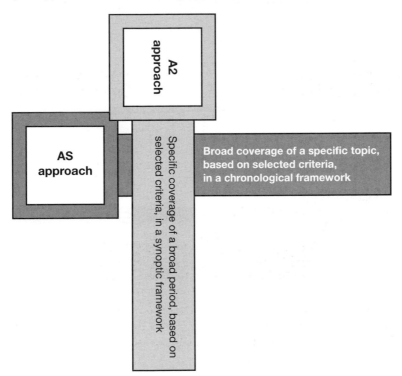

A typical A2 topic would cover Britain 1895–1951 or Britain 1929–98. Coverage at A2 is based on 'themes', some of which cover the whole period; an example of 'theme' might be the development of the Welfare State in Britain 1895–1951. It also takes in comparisons – possibly between individuals and certainly between periods, for example between Lloyd George in the First World War and Churchill in the Second World War. This is an extension of AS-style questions based on the instructions '*Compare and contrast . . .*'. At A2, however, the range of coverage is so extensive that careful selection has to be made of criteria for discussion. Again, this will not be entirely new, since one of the AS styles of question requires the student to '*Identify and explain three reasons for . . .*'. At A2 this is extended to identifying the subject matter itself. Finally, A2 coverage of this subject matter is less likely to be chronological than at AS: different periods are considered quickly and without necessarily looking at the connecting phases. Even this, however, will not be completely unexpected, since any AS essay depending strictly on chronology always runs the risk of narrative.

The Synoptic Study is so complex that it really needs a specific example of how it works and how it builds on the AS approach. Here are the stages by which an answer to a typical A2 question might be built up.

Which was the most successful British war leader in the twentieth century, Lloyd George or Churchill?

1. The first preparatory stage is to identify the issues involved and then to distinguish between Lloyd George's and Churchill's leadership. This is one of the simpler AS skills.

A2 essay (1) identifying the periods for coverage

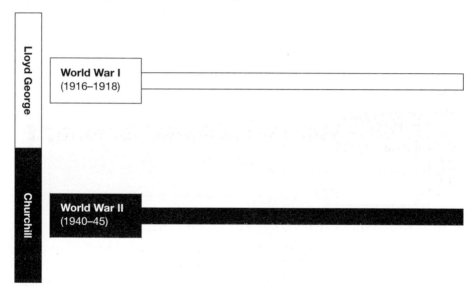

2. The second stage is to select three or four key criteria for assessing the success of these two war leaders. These should be distinctive and examples should be drawn – overall – from the full time span 1916–18 and 1940–45. Again, this approach is reasonably familiar to AS students used to choosing criteria. See diagram facing page (top).

In terms of technique – if not of content – this could still be an AS essay. Many students would tend to use the criteria by working *chronologically* through the two war leaders' periods' in charge. What would convert this into a full A2 approach is a direct comparison between them, acting as the basic structure of the essay. Although this may sound complex, it is actually using a skill already acquired at AS – but notching it up to a more demanding A2 approach. See diagram facing page (bottom).

The transition from AS to A2 is therefore entirely logical. In a sense, it represents the two main dimensions of History twofold – the study of the past and an enquiry into methods used for that study.

A2 essay (2) identifying criteria for analysis

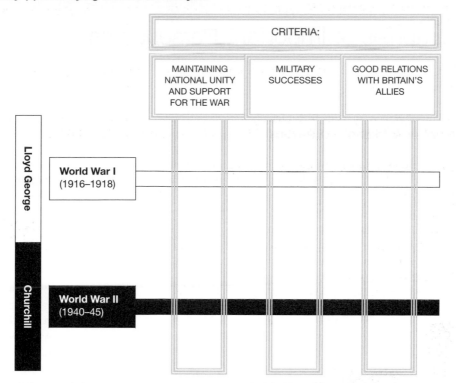

A2 essay (3) making comparisons through the whole period, using the criteria

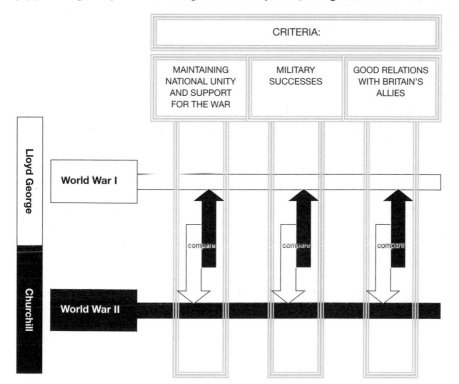

Biographies of Important Personalities

Christopher Addison, 1869–1951

Christopher Addison was a professor of anatomy and Liberal MP from 1910. He was brought into Lloyd George's Cabinet in 1917 as Minister for Reconstruction and was the first Minister of Health. His proposals for a programme of post-war state house building were devastated by the 'Geddes Axe' in 1921 and he resigned in protest. He lost his seat in 1922 and joined the Labour Party in protest against the Liberals' lack of reforming zeal. He became a peer in 1937 and helped to navigate many of the Attlee government's reforms through the Lords, before his death in 1951.

Maxwell Aitken (Lord Beaverbrook), 1879–1964

Maxwell Aitken was born in Canada and emigrated to Britain in 1910, becoming a Conservative MP that year with the encouragement of his fellow Canadian, Andrew Bonar Law. As a newspaper proprietor, he played a role in replacing Asquith with Lloyd George in 1916. He used his successful 'tabloid' paper, the *Daily Express*, to depose Lloyd George in 1922 and then to demand that Baldwin support tariff reform after the Conservative defeat in 1929. He became a close ally of Churchill in the 1930s and Churchill appointed him as Minister of Aircraft Production in May 1940, helping to produce enough fighters to win the battle of Britain. He remained in the government for the rest of the war, but his influence waned after he quarrelled with Bevin. He concentrated on building up his newspaper empire until his death in 1964.

H.H. Asquith, 1852–1928

Herbert Henry Asquith was born in Yorkshire in 1852 and after becoming a lawyer, was elected as a Liberal MP in 1886. Gladstone made him his Home Secretary in 1892, and then Campbell-Bannerman appointed him as Chancellor of the Exchequer in 1906. He succeeded Campbell-Bannerman as Prime Minister in 1908 and worked closely with Lloyd George, his Chancellor of the Exchequer, to introduce a series of reforms including the *Old Age Pensions Act* (1908) and the *National Insurance Act* (1911). In the constitutional crisis over funding these measures, Asquith successfully overcame the opposition from the House of Lords and succeeded in limiting their powers of veto.

Although several leading members of the government favoured granting women the vote, Asquith opposed the measure and faced personal attack from the suffragettes. He took an equally stern attitude towards those opposing Home Rule in Ireland, refusing to allow any concessions for the counties of Ulster and pushing the Unionists towards open rebellion.

After the outbreak of the First World War, Asquith was accused of failing to prosecute the war vigorously enough and in May 1915 he was forced to form a coalition government. His abilities as a war leader continued to be questioned as the war went badly, especially by the Conservatives and the right-wing press. In December 1916 Lloyd George agreed to collaborate with the Conservatives in the Cabinet and removed Asquith from power. This split the Liberal Party and those who stayed loyal to Asquith were devastated in the 1918 election. Asquith lost his seat in 1918 and only regained one in 1923, by which time Lloyd George had been deposed by the Conservatives. Asquith insisted on remaining leader of the Liberals however and the continued rivalry between him and Lloyd George made a Liberal government impossible and Labour were given their chance instead. Asquith finally retired to the Lords as the Earl of Oxford in 1925 and died in 1928.

Clement Attlee, 1883–1967

Clement Attlee was born in Putney in 1883 and developed an interest in social problems while doing voluntary work at a boy's club in Stepney. He served in Gallipoli, Mesopotamia and on the Western Front reaching the rank of major. After the war he joined the Labour Party and in 1919 was elected Mayor of Stepney. He became a Labour MP in 1922 and a minister in 1929. Like most ministers, Attlee refused to serve in the National Government formed by MacDonald in 1931 and he was one of few Labour MPs to retain his seat in the 1931 general election and became deputy leader of the party under George Lansbury almost by default.

When Lansbury retired in 1935 Attlee became the new leader of the Labour Party and began to speak out against the National Government's policy of appeasement. In 1940 Attlee joined the coalition government headed by Winston Churchill. He was effectively deputy Prime Minister although this post was not created until 1942.

In the 1945 general election Attlee lead the Labour Party to an unexpected victory at the polls and during his six years in office he carried through a vigorous programme of reform. The coal-mines, civil aviation, cable and wireless services, gas, electricity, railways, road transport and iron and steel were nationalised. The National Health Service was introduced and independence was granted to India (1947).

After Labour was narrowly defeated in the 1951 general election, Attlee led the Labour Party until resigning in 1955. He was granted a peerage and died in 1967.

Stanley Baldwin, 1867–1947

Stanley Baldwin was the son of an industrialist and joined the family iron and steel business before entering Parliament in 1906. He served in Lloyd George's Cabinet and in October 1922 helped to organise the plot that ousted Lloyd George as Prime Minister of the coalition government. The new Prime Minister, Bonar Law, appointed Stanley Baldwin Chancellor of the Exchequer in October 1922 and he negotiated a loan from the USA on terms that disgusted Bonar Law. But, when ill-health forced Bonar Law to resign in May 1923, Baldwin became the new Prime Minister. He immediately announced his intention to introduce taxes on imports to boost the British economy, which proved sufficiently unpopular for the Conservatives to lose their majority in the 1923 general election, but which re-united the Conservatives who had remained divided since October 1922. After the Conservative victory in 1924, Baldwin successfully faced down the threat of industrial action by the miners by granting a subsidy to the industry to keep up wages. When the subsidy was exhausted, he had prepared the government to face the general strike which broke out in 1926. Baldwin offered to act as an honest broker between the owners and the miners and the TUC trusted him sufficiently to end the strike after only nine days. In 1927, however, Baldwin's Government passed the *Trade Disputes and Trade Union Act* which made all sympathetic strikes illegal. This seeming breach of faith and the high levels of unemployment led to his defeat in the 1929 general election after which he faced criticism from the right-wing media. He joined the National Government in August 1931, becoming President of the Council until he replaced MacDonald as Prime Minister in June 1935.

Baldwin was criticised for his policy of non-intervention in the Spanish Civil War and his reluctance to rearm against the growing threat from Adolf Hitler and Nazi Germany but he was praised for his handling of the abdication crisis in 1936. He resigned from office following the successful coronation celebrations of George VI in May 1937. He was granted the title Earl Baldwin of Bewdley, but was bitterly attacked during the war for his failure to prepare Britain and stop Hitler earlier. He died on 14 December 1947.

Arthur Balfour, 1848–1930

Arthur Balfour was born in Scotland in 1848. He entered the House of Commons in 1874 and in 1885, his uncle, the Marquess of Salisbury appointed him Secretary for Scotland and then in 1887 Secretary for Ireland. Although he was successful in restoring some calm to the country, his willingness to use force caused him to be nicknamed 'Bloody Balfour'. He went on to become leader of the House of Commons in 1892 and regained this post in 1895.

Balfour replaced his uncle as Prime Minister in 1902, but he inherited a difficult situation. The victory in the Boer War had been tarnished by revelations of mistreatment of women and children and at home his attempts to reform licensing laws and education caused much anger. In particular, his inability to settle the argument within the Conservative Party between those in favour of tariff reform and those in favour of free trade split the Party and made him appear weak. Balfour resigned in 1905 and in the general election of 1906, Balfour's Conservatives suffered their worst defeat since 1832.

Balfour remained leader of the Conservative Party until he lost two further elections in 1910 and failed to prevent the powers of the lords from being curbed in 1911, when he was replaced by Andrew Bonar Law. Balfour returned to government in 1915 when Asquith invited him to join the coalition government as First Lord of the Admiralty to replace Winston Churchill. Lloyd George made him Foreign Secretary the following year and in 1917 he issued the 'Balfour Declaration' which promised a national home for the Jews in Palestine. Balfour left Lloyd George's government in 1919 but Baldwin appointed him Lord President of the Council in 1925. Balfour died a year after losing office, in 1930.

Tony Benn, 1925–

After serving in the Second World War, Tony Benn became a Labour MP in 1950, but was barred from Parliament in 1961 when he inherited his father's title, Viscount Stansgate. He successfully fought to renounce his peerage and was re-elected as an MP. He became postmaster-general under Wilson in 1964, before being appointed minister of technology, where he championed the production of Concorde. As industry secretary in 1974 and then Minister for Energy, he emerged as the leader of the left wing of the Labour Party and after the 1979 defeat attempted to change the party's structure to give the party activists more influence. In 1981 he stood for the party leadership, which he lost and then the deputy leadership, for which he was narrowly defeated by Denis Healey. He was criticised for encouraging the party to shift leftwards and cause the SDP defections and the party's loss of electoral credibility in the 1980s. He lost his seat in the 1983 general election and was marginalised under Neil Kinnock's leadership, eventually retiring from politics in 2001.

Aneurin Bevan, 1897–1960

Aneurin Bevan, the son of a miner, was born in Tredegar in Wales in 1897. At the age of thirteen Aneurin left school and began working in the mines. He joined the Independent Labour Party and became a union activist. The owners of the mine where he worked tried to sack him, but he took his case to a tribunal and won his job back. He went on to study at the Central Labour College in London, but the mine-owners refused to employ him when he returned to Wales. He became a miners' union official and helped to organise the relief of the miners during the strike that followed the collapse of the General Strike in 1926. He entered local politics and then won a seat in Parliament at the 1929 general election. He was a critic of the 1929–31 Labour government's moderate policies and, retaining his seat in 1931, he became one of Labour's leading critics of the National Government, speaking out against the Means Test in particular.

Bevan supported the creation of a European Popular Front between socialists and communists to resist fascism, and he was briefly expelled from the Labour Party for this policy in 1939. When war broke out, he demanded that Churchill should replace Chamberlain and used his position as editor of the *Tribune* to criticise the government's lack of decisive action. When Churchill became Prime Minister, he referred to Bevan as 'the Minister of Disease'. Bevan saw the war as an ideal opportunity to build a better society and he criticised Churchill for his failure to swiftly implement the findings of the 1942 **Beveridge Report**.

After Labour's victory in 1945, Attlee appointed Bevan as Minister of Health. He oversaw the passage of the 1946 *National Insurance Act* which extended the 1911 act to all workers. He fought a long battle with the doctors' associations to establish a National Health Service in 1948, which provided all people in Britain with free medical, dental and opthalmic services for the first time.

Bevan served for a short period as Minister of Labour in 1951 but resigned when the Chancellor of the Exchequer, Hugh Gaitskell announced prescription charges for medicines, spectacles and false teeth. After Labour lost the 1951 general election, Bevan became an outspoken critic of Attlee's style of opposition. In 1956, however, he agreed to serve the new leader, Hugh Gaitskell, as shadow Foreign Secretary and shocked his supporters by refusing to support unilateral nuclear disarmament. Bevan became deputy leader of the Labour Party in 1959, but he developed cancer and died the following year.

William Beveridge, 1879–1963

William Beveridge, the eldest son of a judge was born in India in 1879 and became a lawyer after leaving university. Beveridge became the country's leading authority on unemployment insurance and joined the Board of Trade in 1909 and helped Churchill organise a national system of labour exchanges. He continued to advise the government before and during the First World War and was knighted for his services. In 1919 he left the civil service to become director of the London School of Economics (LSE). In 1940, Ernest Bevin invited him back into government to review the social security system. The Beveridge Report on Social Insurance and Allied Services was published in December 1942 and recommended a free health system and benefits in exchange for national insurance contributions. A second Beveridge Report in 1944 recommended an economic policy to eliminate unemployment. In 1944, Beveridge was elected as a Liberal MP, but he ironically lost his seat in the 1945 general election which brought to power a Labour government determined to implement the recommendations of his report. Beveridge was created a life peer and continued to represent the Liberals in the Lords and died in 1963.

Ernest Bevin, 1881–1951

Ernest Bevin was born in Somerset in 1881 and after only two years education, he became a farm labourer. After moving to Bristol and becoming a van driver, he joined the Dockers' Union and became an official and joined the Labour Party, unsuccessfully standing for election in 1918.

In 1921, when 32 unions formed the Transport and General Workers Union (TGWU), Bevin was elected general secretary, which he remained for the next nineteen years. He was also a member of the General Council of the Trade Union Congress (TUC) between 1925 and 1940, where he attempted to prevent and then swiftly end the General Strike of 1926. He also spoke decisively against George Lansbury's leadership of the Labour Party in 1935.

In May 1940 Winston Churchill invited Bevin to become Minister of Labour in his coalition government and Bevin won a seat in the House of Commons. He played a huge role in Britain's war effort, successfully mobilising the population for victory.

When Labour won the 1945 general election, Attlee appointed Bevin as Foreign Secretary, and Bevin remained unswervingly loyal to Attlee throughout the turbulent post-war Labour government. Bevin, a strong anti-communist, helped to negotiate the Marshall Plan and the setting up of NATO, tying Britain closely to the USA, while developing a British nuclear deterrent. He was forced to resign in March 1951 due to poor health and died the following month.

Tony Blair, 1953–

Tony Blair was born in Edinburgh in 1953 before becoming a barrister and then entering parliament as a Labour MP in 1983. In 1992, he was appointed shadow Secretary of State for Home Affairs, where he effectively attacked the Conservatives' failures on crime prevention. He was elected leader of the Labour Party in July, 1994, following the unexpected death of John Smith. He swiftly rebranded the party as 'New Labour' dropping any remaining vestiges of socialism and rephrasing the iconic Clause IV of the constitution. His positive, youthful image contrasted with that of the Conservatives, tired after 18 years in office and he achieved an enormous landslide for Labour in 1997, winning their largest majority. He played a central role in the new government, especially in foreign affairs, signing the Good Friday Agreement with the Northern Irish parties and leading Britain in the Kosovon war against Serbia. His partnership with Gordon Brown, his Chancellor of the Exchequer, brought stability to a government otherwise rocked by resignations and undergoing considerable constitutional change. In the face of a Conservative shift to the right on issues such as Europe and tax, he was able to hold the centre ground and achieve an almost identical landslide victory in the 2001 general election.

Andrew Bonar Law, 1858–1923

Andrew Bonar Law was born in Canada in 1858 and moved to Scotland to work in the family's ironwork business at the age of sixteen. Bonar Law became a Conservative MP in 1900 and then Secretary of the Board of Trade in 1902, before losing his seat in the 1906 general election. Re-elected later in 1906, he became leader of the Conservative Party in 1911 when Balfour resigned. He proved a much more aggressive leader, encouraging the Ulster Unionists to break the law and resort to violence to resist the implementation of Home Rule. When Asquith was forced to create a coalition government in 1915, Bonar Law became a member of the War Committee. He then encouraged Lloyd George to oust Asquith and was rewarded with the post of Chancellor of the Exchequer in 1916. He continued to support Lloyd George after the war until he retired due to ill health in 1921. He returned to convince the majority of the Conservative party to remove their support from Lloyd George at the Carlton Club meeting in 1922, he was reappointed Conservative leader and in this way became Prime Minister. He only served for eight months before his poor health led to his second retirement in May 1923 and he died later that year.

R.A. (Richard Austen) Butler, 1902–82

R.A. Butler, the son of a civil servant, was born in India in 1902. He joined the Conservative Party at university and became an MP in 1929. After holding junior posts in the National Governments, Churchill appointed him Minister of Education in 1941. In 1944 Butler's *Education Act* organised the three tier system of secondary education, based on the 11-plus exam and raised the school-leaving age to 15.

Butler encouraged the Conservatives to accept the **Welfare State** set up by Labour after 1945, and he continued to fund it generously as Chancellor of the Exchequer between 1951 and 1955. When Eden was forced to resign following the Suez crisis, many expected Butler to become Prime Minister, but the Conservatives chose Macmillan instead. Butler became Home Secretary and was appointed deputy Prime Minister. When Macmillan resigned in 1963, Butler was again passed over, this time for Alec Douglas Home. Butler became Foreign Secretary, and accepted a peerage rather than attempt to gain the leadership for a third time. He died in 1982.

James Callaghan, 1912–

James Callaghan was born in Wales in 1912 and worked as a tax officer. After serving in the navy, he joined the Labour Party and won a seat in 1945. He became Chancellor of the Exchequer in 1964 under Harold Wilson and increased the higher levels of taxation. His economic policy was jeopardised by the financial crisis of 1966–67 and he was forced to devalue the pound in 1967. He resigned as chancellor and was appointed Home Secretary. He refused to support Wilson when he tried to limit Trade Union powers in 1969 and opposed British entry into the EEC. He became Foreign Secretary in 1974 and replaced Wilson as Prime Minister in 1976. He faced a shrinking parliamentary majority, rising inflation and industrial disputes, yet managed to remain in power for three years. In 1979, however, his pact with the unions to limit pay demands collapsed during the 'winter of discontent' and his government lost a vote of no-confidence. Labour lost the 1979 election and Callaghan resigned as leader in the following year.

Henry Campbell-Bannerman, 1836–1908

Henry Campbell-Bannerman, the son of a Scottish businessman, was born in 1836. He was elected as a Liberal MP in 1868 and held ministerial positions under Gladstone and Rosebery. He opposed the Boer War and was seen as a reformer when he became leader of the Liberal Party. He became Prime Minister in 1905 when Balfour resigned and shrewdly called an immediate general election which he won with a landslide. He made his first priority in government the restoration of trade union rights and the protection of children. He was prevented from passing other legislation by the Conservative veto in the House of Lords however, and was forced to resign by ill health in 1908, dying only seven days later.

Austen Chamberlain, 1863–1937

Austen Chamberlain, the eldest son of Joseph Chamberlain, and the half-brother of Neville Chamberlain, was born in 1863. He was elected as a Liberal Unionist in 1892 and, like his father served in a Conservative Cabinet, becoming Chancellor of the Exchequer in 1903. He joined Lloyd George's cabinet in 1916 and remained a minister after the war. In 1921, when Bonar Law retired, he became leader of the Conservative Party. At the Carlton Club meeting in 1922, he spoke in favour of supporting Lloyd George, but his party voted against him and he resigned as leader and refused to serve under Bonar Law and Baldwin between 1922 and 1923. Following the 1924 election, he accepted the post of Foreign Secretary and helped to negotiate the Locarno treaty of 1925 that led to improved relations in Europe for the rest of the decade. Despite joining the National Government in 1931, Chamberlain chose not to stand in the election that year. He died in 1937.

Joseph Chamberlain, 1836–1914

Joseph Chamberlain, the son of a shopkeeper, was born in London in 1836. He became a successful businessman in Birmingham, joined the Liberal Party and was elected a councillor in 1868. Becoming mayor in 1873, he led a comprehensive improvement of gas, water and housing services in the town. He entered Parliament in 1876 and Gladstone appointed him President of the Board of Trade in 1880. He soon developed a reputation as a radical, demanding land redistribution and taxation of the rich. In 1885, frustrated by Gladstone's refusal to step down as Liberal leader and his sudden adoption of Home Rule for Ireland, he resigned and led a group of Liberal Unionists into opposition. Gladstone's government fell and Chamberlain signed a compact with the Conservatives. He eventually joined Salisbury's government in 1895 and served as Colonial Secretary, where he was largely responsible for the outbreak of the Boer War.

In 1903, he resigned to announce a campaign for an Imperial Trade Federation, usually referred to as tariff reform. The issue split the Conservatives and led to their defeat in the 1906 election. Chamberlain suffered a serious stroke that left him half-paralysed after the election and played no further part in politics until his death in 1914.

Neville Chamberlain, 1869–1940

Neville Chamberlain, the son of Joseph Chamberlain, and the half-brother of Austen Chamberlain, was born in 1869. He spent seven years managing his father's plantation in the Bahamas, before going into business and local politics in Birmingham. After an unsuccessful period in charge of manpower allocation during the First World War, he was elected as a Conservative MP and became Minister of Health under Baldwin (1924–29). Here he built a reputation as a social reformer, finally abolishing the Poor Law and organising a boom in house building. He served as Chancellor of the Exchequer in the National Governments of 1931–37, keeping interest rates low and concentrating on orthodox financial solutions. He became Prime Minister when Baldwin resigned and found his premiership dominated by foreign affairs in which he lacked experience. He felt he could reach a compromise with Hitler and took the policy of appeasement to its logical conclusion at Munich when he agreed to the transfer of the Sudetenland to Germany in 1938. He was thus bitterly disappointed when Hitler marched into Prague in 1939 and abandoned appeasement, guaranteeing the sovereignty of Hitler's next target, Poland. He reluctantly led Britain into the Second World War, but was a poor war leader. Following the disastrous Norway campaign in 1940, he was unable to create a coalition with the Liberals and Labour and was forced to resign as Prime Minister. He stayed in the Cabinet until ill health caused him to resign later in the year. He died in November 1940.

Winston Churchill, 1874–1965

Winston Churchill, the son of a Conservative politician and an American heiress, was born in Blenheim Palace, in 1874. He became a soldier and took part in the Sudan campaign of 1898 before working as a war correspondent. During the Boer War he was taken prisoner but became an overnight celebrity when he escaped. He was elected as a Conservative MP in 1900, but frustrated by the lack of progress on social reform, he joined the Liberal Party in 1904, becoming a junior minister in 1906. When Asquith promoted Lloyd George in 1908, Churchill replaced him as President of the Board of Trade, where he implemented many reforms, most notably the establishment of employment exchanges.

Churchill became Home Secretary in 1910, but despite his work on prison reform, became notorious for sending soldiers to maintain order during a Welsh miners' strike. He became First Lord of the Admiralty in October 1911 where he helped modernise the navy. His determination to help the war effort led to the disaster at Gallipoli in 1915 though and he rejoined the army and saw action on the Western Front. Lloyd George brought Churchill back as Minister of Munitions in 1917, before making him War Minister in 1919.

Churchill lost his seat in the 1922 election and, worried by the rise of the Labour Party, rejoined the Conservatives and won a seat in 1924. Baldwin then appointed Churchill as Chancellor of the Exchequer and as Chancellor he returned Britain to the gold standard and took a tough approach to the general strike, editing the government news sheet, the *British Gazette*. Increasingly opposed to the growing independence of India, he was seen as an extremist by 1931 and was not invited to join the Cabinet of the National Government and entered his 'Wilderness Years' as he later called them.

His warnings about the threat of Fascism and Nazism were therefore ignored by a government intent on appeasement, but, by 1938, he appeared to be vindicated. Neville Chamberlain bowed to popular pressure and made Churchill First Lord of the Admiralty when war broke out and he was chosen as Chamberlain's successor when Chamberlain lost the support of a large part of his party in May 1940. Churchill became Prime Minister at the age of 66 on the same day that the Germans launched their invasion of Western Europe. He formed a coalition government, placing the leaders of the Labour and Liberal Parties in key positions. His impassioned leadership helped to give Britain the resolve to keep fighting Germany alone after the fall of France and a series of further military disasters. He gladly welcomed the USSR as an ally after the German invasion in 1941 and was able to bring the USA into the war in Europe as well as that against Japan in Asia, forming a strong relationship with President Roosevelt. He was unable to prevent Britain becoming the junior member of the 'big three' at Tehran and Yalta, however. At home, although he promised to implement the Beveridge Report, his reluctance to do so swiftly caused many to question the desirability of his leadership after the war and he led the Conservatives to a crushing defeat in 1945. Although out of office, he continued to comment on world events and contributed to the outbreak of the Cold War in 1946, when he described the 'Iron Curtain' that was descending across Europe. He won the election of 1951 and, despite poor health and old age, he remained Prime Minister until 1955, when he finally allowed Eden to succeed him. He remained an MP until the age of 90, and retired in 1964, dying the following January. Such was his prestige that he was given a state funeral, despite being a commoner. He was also a skilled writer, and his six volumes, *The Second World War*, led to him being awarded the Nobel Prize for Literature.

Michael Collins, 1890–1922

Michael Collins, the son of a farmer, was born in Southern Ireland and took part in the 1916 Easter rising, escaping execution by chance. He became minister for finance in the provisional Irish Dail set up in 1918, but became famous as the leader of the Irish republican forces launching guerrilla attacks on the British. He reluctantly participated in the negotiations with the British government that led to the Anglo-Irish Treaty of 1921, which set up the Irish Free State. He became Ireland's first Prime Minister when de Valera denounced the Treaty, but during the Civil War between the Treaty's supporters and opponents, he was killed at an ambush in County Cork, aged only 32.

Richard Stafford Cripps, 1889–1952

Richard Stafford Cripps was born in London in 1889. Although a pacifist, he served with the Red Cross on the Western Front in the First World War, before becoming a successful and wealthy lawyer. After joining the Labour Party he won a seat at a by-election in 1931 and shifted to the left of the party, supporting a Popular Front of socialist and communist parties in Europe. He and Aneurin Bevan were expelled from the party in 1939 for their views.

A leading critic of the government's efforts in the Second World War, he was a surprising choice as a member of Churchill's War Cabinet, but fell out with the Prime Minister and was sent as ambassador to the USSR. Attlee appointed him Minister of Trade in 1945 and then promoted him to Chancellor of the Exchequer in 1947, following Dalton's resignation. A teetotaller and vegetarian, he became popularly associated with austerity, as he kept taxes and spending high and froze wages to try to control inflation and push for exports. He resigned due to ill health in 1950 and died in 1952.

Eamon de Valera, 1882–1975

Eamon de Valera was born in New York to Irish and Spanish parents, but was educated and worked as a schoolteacher in Ireland before commanding a battalion in the 1916 Easter Rising. He was spared execution following his capture due to his American nationality and following his release from internment, became leader of Sinn Fein. After escaping from Lincoln jail where he had been interned in 1918, he fled to the USA to raise funds for the Dail. He was appointed provisional President of the Dail government, but refused to support the 1921 Anglo-Irish Treaty and led his supporters in the Irish Civil War. After losing the war, he left Sinn Fein and founded Fianna Fail. In 1932 he became Prime Minister of Ireland and helped to establish the Republic of Eire in 1937. He kept Ireland neutral in the Second World War, which caused much British anger, and lost office in 1948. He was Prime Minister twice again in the 1950s and became President in 1959, remaining in this position until his retirement in 1973, by which time he was 90.

Anthony Eden, 1897–1977

Anthony Eden, served on the Western Front in the First World War and was elected as an MP for the Conservative Party in 1923. He held junior offices until Stanley Baldwin became Prime Minister in 1935 and he appointed Eden as his Foreign Secretary. Eden disagreed with Neville Chamberlain over appeasement and in 1938 he resigned from office. When Winston Churchill took over from Chamberlain in 1940, however, Eden was reappointed as Foreign Secretary. After the Labour Party victory in the 1945 general election, Eden became deputy leader of the opposition and in 1951 he became Foreign Secretary for the third time. He finally succeeded Winston Churchill as Prime Minister in April, 1955. In November 1956, Eden ordered British troops to occupy the Suez Canal after a deal with the Israeli government at Sèvres. His action was condemned by the United Nations and criticised by President Eisenhower, and as a result, Britain was forced to withdraw her troops from Egypt. After a nervous collapse, Eden resigned on 9 January 1957. He died in 1977.

Michael Foot, 1913–

Michael Foot, the son of a Liberal MP, was a supporter of Aneurin Bevan, and became an MP in 1945, before taking over Bevan's seat after the deputy Labour leader's death in 1960. He unsuccessfully challenged for the Labour leadership in 1976, but served Callaghan well, mediating with the unions and the Liberals. He won the leadership contest in 1980, but his intellectual leadership was ineffective in controlling the disputatious party and was no match for Margaret Thatcher and her loyal tabloid press. He led Labour to its worst post-war defeat in 1983 and resigned immediately afterwards.

Hugh Gaitskell, 1906–1963

Gaitskell joined the Labour Party during the General Strike of 1926. He held junior posts under Churchill and Attlee before being appointed Chancellor of the Exchequer in 1950 to replace the ailing Stafford Cripps. His policy to introduce NHS charges to balance increases in defence spending as a consequence of the Korean War caused a split in the Labour Party. He won the leadership of the party after Attlee resigned in 1955 and distinguished himself in his opposition to the Suez crisis. Having lost the 1959 election, he attempted unsuccessfully to persuade the party to drop Clause IV of the Party's constitution, but managed to prevent the party from adopted a policy of unilateral nuclear disarmament. He died unexpectedly in 1963 and is widely regarded as the best Prime Minister Britain never had.

Edward Grey, 1862–1933

Edward Grey was a member of a Liberal family and became an MP in his twenties. He was appointed Foreign Secretary in 1905 and remained in post for 11 years. He brought Britain closer to France, following the 'entente cordiale' in opposition to Germany. His secret military agreements with the French were criticised by some of his own Liberal colleagues and he supported Britain's declaration of war against the Central Powers in August 1914. He regarded the war as a personal failure, however, and championed the establishment of the League of Nations after the war, whilst becoming a distinguished naturalist in the inter-war years.

Arthur Griffith, 1871–1922

Arthur Griffith was born in Dublin and became a Nationalist, supporting the establishment of a republic. He founded and became president of Sinn Fein in 1903, and was imprisoned in 1916, despite playing no part in the Easter Rising. He became vice-president of the provisional republic in 1918 and effectively ran southern Ireland in de Valera's absence. He was a member of the Irish delegation which negotiated the Anglo-Irish Treaty in December 1921, and became the first president of the Free State when de Valera refused to support the treaty. He died in August 1922, just as the Irish Civil War was breaking out.

William Hague, 1961–

William Hague was born in Rotherham, Yorkshire in 1961. He was educated at his local comprehensive school, and made a dramatic speech at the Conservative Party conference in 1976 at the age of 15, before winning a place at Oxford. He became a Conservative MP in 1989 and held junior office until 1995 when he became Welsh secretary to replace John Redwood. After the Conservative defeat in 1997 he successfully campaigned for the party leadership, defeating Kenneth Clarke in the final vote. His period as leader was marked by the party shifting further to a right-wing agenda on Europe and social policy. His undoubted excellence as a Commons debater masked a failure to address matters of public concern and he paid for his pre-occupation with issues designed to appeal to Conservative activists, when he only managed to improve on the 1997 Conservative result by one seat in 2001. He immediately resigned as Conservative leader.

Douglas Haig, 1868–1928

Douglas Haig, the son of a Scottish distiller, was born in 1868. He joined the army in 1885, serving under Kitchener in the Sudan and the Boer War. After helping Haldane to reform the army between 1906 and 1909, he commanded part of the British Expeditionary Force under Sir John French. He became Commander-in-chief of the BEF in December 1915. He was much distrusted and disliked by Lloyd George who despaired of his willingness to sacrifice huge numbers of men for limited territorial gains at the battles of the Somme, Arras and Passchendaele. He did finally achieve a breakthrough in August 1918 at Amiens and led the BEF to victory. After the war he initiated the 'Haig fund', with its distinctive 'Poppy Day' appeal. He died, already a figure of great controversy, in 1928.

Richard Haldane, 1856–1928

Richard Haldane became a Liberal MP in 1879, but failed to reach senior office until 1905 when he was appointed War Secretary, a post he held for seven years. He undertook major reforms of the army, creating a proper general staff, a British Expeditionary Force and a Territorial Army, all of which served Britain well in the First World War. Unfairly dismissed as Lord Chancellor in 1915 and accused of pro-German sympathies, he left the Liberal Party and joined the Labour Party, serving as the first Labour Chancellor of the Exchequer in 1924.

Maurice Hankey, 1877–1963

After serving in the Marines, Maurice Hankey became a civil servant. During the First World War he created the Cabinet secretariat system and helped establish the smaller War Cabinet under Lloyd George. He remained Cabinet secretary until 1938 and was a valuable servant of Churchill's War Cabinet as well.

Walter Hannington, 1896–1966

Walter Hannington was born in London in 1896 and, after training as a toolmaker, became an active trade union shop steward during the First World War. He helped establish the Communist Party of Great Britain in 1920, but is most remembered for setting up the radical National Unemployed Workers' Movement (NUWM) in 1921. He organised demonstrations and hunger marches throughout the inter-war years and was frequently sent to prison for these activities. During and after the Second World War he returned to traditional trade union activity with the Amalgamated Engineering Union which he had earlier helped to establish. He died in 1966.

Denis Healey, 1917–

After seeing service in the army in the Second World War, Denis Healey joined the Labour Party and became an MP in 1952. He was Wilson's defence secretary between 1964 and 1970 and cut back substantially on Britain's overseas commitments and defence spending. He was appointed as Chancellor of the Exchequer by Wilson in 1974 and remained in this post until the 1979 general election. His determination to end Keynesian economics at the Treasury brought him into conflict with the trade unions and led to Britain's dramatic request for an IMF loan in 1976 when the value of the pound collapsed. He was unable to prevent the public sector strikes of the 'winter of discontent' of 1978–79 which helped to bring down Callaghan's government. In opposition, he challenged for the Labour Party leadership in 1980, but was defeated by Michael Foot, but managed to narrowly defeat Tony Benn's attempt to capture the deputy leadership. He tried to limit the party's leftward shift and, although he resigned as deputy leader in 1983 after the landslide defeat for Labour, he was retained in the shadow Cabinet and played a role in Neil Kinnock's struggles to purge extremists from the Party.

Edward Heath, 1916–

Edward Heath, a grammar school boy and organ scholar, entered politics in 1950 and became Minister of Labour in 1960 and was in charge of Britain's first application to join the European Community.

Heath became the first elected leader of the Conservative Party while in opposition in 1965, and defeated Wilson to become prime minister in 1970. In 1971, Britain signed the Treaty of Accession, joining the European Community and Britain became a member of the EEC in January 1973. His government was marred by serious industrial unrest, culminating in a miners' strike that left the country on a three-day week with limited electricity supplies. He was defeated in both the general elections of 1974, and after losing the second, he was challenged and defeated by Margaret Thatcher, his former education secretary. He was critical of Thatcher's policies especially her stand against full participation in the European Community, throughout the whole of her premiership.

Arthur Henderson, 1863–1935

Arthur Henderson was a trade union official who became a Labour MP in 1906. He was elected to replace Ramsay MacDonald as party leader in 1914 following MacDonald's opposition to the war and served as Minister for Labour under Lloyd George, acting as Labour's representative in the War Cabinet. He resigned from the War Cabinet when Lloyd George ordered him not to attend the Stockholm socialist peace conference in 1917. He led Labour out of the coalition government in 1918 and helped to draw up the party's constitution of that year and reorganise its structure. He was Home Secretary under MacDonald in 1924 and then Foreign Secretary between 1929 and 1931. He opposed the cuts in unemployment benefit that brought the second Labour government down and became Labour leader again following MacDonald's establishment of the National Government. He lost his seat in the 1931 general election and turned his attention to world affairs, attempting to persuade the powers to continue with disarmament until his death in 1935.

Michael Heseltine, 1933–

Michael Heseltine, was born in Swansea in 1933 and, after making a fortune in publishing, became a Conservative MP in 1966. Although not a committed right-wing Conservative, he served under Margaret Thatcher as Environment Secretary and then as Defence Minister. He dramatically resigned from the Cabinet in 1986 over the Westland affair. He remained on the backbenches until 1990 when he took the opportunity of Geoffrey Howe's resignation speech to challenge Mrs Thatcher for the Conservative leadership. He won enough votes to force Mrs Thatcher to resign, but was defeated by John Major on the second ballot. He became Major's chief supporter in the troubled Conservative government of 1992–97, using his influence to return Major as party leader when he was challenged by John Redwood in 1995. He received the post of deputy Prime Minister in return. He would have been an ideal choice for Major's replacement, following the 1997 election disaster, but his ill health led him to retire from politics and to leave the Conservative Party divided between euro-sceptics and euro-enthusiasts.

Roy Jenkins, 1920–2003

Roy Jenkins, the son of a Welsh miner and Labour MP, was born in 1920 and became a Labour MP himself in 1920. He served as Home Secretary under Wilson between 1965 and 1967, where he steered a number of liberal social measures through Parliament, such as the legalisation of abortion. He became Chancellor of the Exchequer in 1967 and managed to produce a trade and revenue surplus. He became Home Secretary again in 1974 and is credited for the *Equal Opportunities Act* of 1975 and the third *Race Relations Act* of 1976.

When Callaghan became leader, he left Parliament to become Britain's first President of the European Commission. After leaving this post in 1981, he helped to found a new centre party, the Social Democratic Party, in protest to the leftward swing of Labour under Michael Foot. He was instrumental in creating an alliance with the Liberals in 1983 and helping to merge the two parties in 1988. He was appointed by Tony Blair in 1997 to investigate and report on the possibilities for electoral reform. His ideas led to the European elections of 1999 being decided on the basis of proportional representation. He was also a distinguished historian, having written acclaimed biographies of Asquith, Gladstone, Baldwin and Churchill.

John Maynard Keynes, 1883–1946

John Maynard Keynes, son of a Cambridge economist, worked at the Treasury during the First World War, but resigned in protest at the scale of reparations imposed on Germany at the Paris Peace Conference in 1919 and wrote a critical book, *The Economic Consequences of the Peace* (1919). During the 1920s, he produced radical ideas for tackling mass unemployment through state intervention and deficit financing, which influenced Lloyd George's 1929 election campaign and Mosley's memorandum of 1930. He explained his ideas in *The General Theory of Employment, Interest and Money* (1936) and in the Second World War returned to the Treasury as an adviser, where he helped to promote Beveridge's ideas for a Welfare State. After the war, with a Labour government keen to introduce his economic policies of full employment, central economic management and high taxation, he was sent to the USA to negotiate a loan. He succeeded, but died in 1946, shortly after his return to Britain. His economic ideas, 'Keynesianism', continued to influence governments' economic policies until the 1970s.

Neil Kinnock, 1942–

Neil Kinnock was born in Wales in 1942 and after working as a teacher and trade unionist, he became a Labour MP in 1970. After junior office under Wilson and Callaghan, he became party leader following Michael Foot's resignation in 1983. Facing electoral decline, Kinnock reformed the party, expelling the Militant Tendency after a bitter internal battle and discarding many unpopular policies such as unilateral nuclear disarmament. He improved Labour's electoral performance in 1987, seeing off the threat of the SDP/Liberal Alliance. He went on to further improve Labour's media profile and to strengthen the position of the leader, but he unexpectedly lost the 1992 general election. He resigned as leader and took on the post of senior commissioner in the European Union in 1995, becoming Vice-President of the Commission in 1999.

George Lansbury, 1859–1940

George Lansbury, the son of a railway contractor, was born in Suffolk, in 1859. Lansbury started work in an office at the age of eleven and later emigrated to Australia, but was forced to return to Britain. He joined the Liberal Party, but became disillusioned by the party's lack of interest in social questions and joined the Social Democratic Federation instead in 1892. He unsuccessfully contested seats in the 1895 and 1900 general election and then joined the Independent Labour Party in 1903. He finally won a seat in 1910 and spoke out in favour of women's suffrage, even resigning and recontesting his seat (which he lost) on the issue of female suffrage in 1912. He was imprisoned for making speeches in favour of arrested suffragettes and went on hunger strike, being released under the so-called Cat and Mouse Act.

Unable to regain a seat in the nationalistic fervour during and immediately after the First World War, he went into local politics and became Mayor of Poplar. Here he used his powers to increase the money spent on poor relief, but was judged to be acting illegally and was again imprisoned for his views. He was re-elected to Parliament in 1922 and became Labour Party chairman in 1928. He served in MacDonald's second Labour government, but refused to support the decision to cut unemployment benefits in 1931. When MacDonald formed the National Government, Arthur Henderson became Labour leader, but lost his seat in the 1931 general election. Lansbury was chosen to replace him. He was a strong opponent of rearmament and refused to support any form of military action, even against fascism and even when sanctioned by the League of Nations. The Labour Party, led by Ernest Bevin turned against him for this high-minded standpoint and he was forced to resign. He continued to work for peace, even meeting Hitler on the brink of the Second World War, but failed. He died in May 1940.

David Lloyd George, 1863–1945

David Lloyd George was born in Manchester on 17 January 1863. His father, a schoolmaster, died a year after he was born and his mother took her two children to Llanystumdwy in Wales. Lloyd George became a solicitor in 1879 and joined the local Liberal Party and served on the local council. He won a by-election for the Liberals in 1890, demanding religious equality in Wales, land reform and fairer taxes. As a committed Non-conformist he opposed the Boer War and the 1902 Education Act and spoke out on Welsh issues. Campbell-Bannerman made him President of the Board of Trade in 1906 and he was promoted to Chancellor of the Exchequer in 1908 when Asquith became Prime Minister.

He proved to be a radical appointment, introducing old age pensions and increasing direct taxation to pay for this. In the face of Conservative opposition, he used his skills as a speaker to amass support for his policies and helped to win the two elections in 1910 for the Liberals, which paved the way for the reduction in the power of the House of Lords. Lloyd George then introduced the National Insurance Act to provide medical care and unemployment benefit for British working men.

Lloyd George remained a controversial figure even after this. In 1912, Lloyd George was accused of corruption using government information to profit from share-buying in the Marconi Company. Although he personally supported women's suffrage, he did little, while in office, to help the cause which led to suffragettes burning down his new house. After his objections to the Boer War, he told Asquith that he would resign if Britain declared war during the summer crisis in 1914, but the Prime Minister persuaded him to stay on.

During the war, he made the achievement of victory his chief priority and was made Minister of Munitions in 1915. When the Conservatives and some Liberals questioned Asquith's suitability as war leader, Lloyd George persuaded them to support him and forced Asquith's resignation in December 1916, thus splitting the Liberal Party. As Prime Minister he tried unsuccessfully to limit the freedom of action of the front-line generals, but did manage to introduce convoy tactics to defend vital British shipping. He helped to keep the war effort going and gained much of the credit for Britain's ultimate victory, which he used to ensure victory for his coalition of Liberals and Conservatives in the general election of 1918. Lloyd George led the British delegation at the Versailles Peace Conference in 1919 and helped to prevent Germany being too harshly treated by the French. His coalition government proved very unstable however. A post-war economic slump frustrated most of his plans for reform and he found himself dealing with the Anglo-Irish war of 1918–21. With rumours of political corruption spreading, when he seemed to risk a war with Turkey at Chanak in 1922, most of the Conservative majority in his government refused to serve him and he was forced to resign as Prime Minister. He was frustrated by Asquith's refusal to allow him to lead the reunited Liberals until 1925 and by then found himself in charge of a shrinking party short of funds. His attempt to revitalise the party in 1929 by adopting a Keynesian economic policy was shattered by the 1931 creation of the National Government which he refused to join, although most of his party did. In September 1936 he visited Hitler in Germany and although quite impressed by him, continued to oppose the National Government's policy of appeasement. He spoke in 1940 in the Norway debate, helping to bring down Chamberlain and died in March, 1945.

Ramsay MacDonald, 1866–1937

James Ramsay MacDonald, the illegitimate son of a maidservant, was born in Lossiemouth, Scotland, in 1866. He moved to London in 1886 and worked as a clerk and joined the Fabian Society before joining the Independent Labour Party in 1894. He was defeated in the 1895 general election, but he met and married the wealthy Margaret Gladstone, and her fortune allowed him to devote more of his time to politics than most socialists could afford.

When the Labour Representation Committee was established in February 1900, MacDonald was chosen as the secretary as he did not need to be paid. He won a seat in the Commons in 1906 and retained his position as secretary in the newly established Labour Party. In 1910 he became leader of the Labour Party. MacDonald was a pacifist and refused to support Britain's involvement in the First World War, but the majority of the party disagreed and so he resigned as leader and Arthur Henderson replaced him. MacDonald lost his seat in 1918 but was re-elected in 1922 and was re-appointed as party leader. In the 1923 general election the Labour Party won enough seats to form a minority government and so MacDonald became Prime Minister as well as Foreign Secretary for eight months. Despite the limited success of this approach, MacDonald refused to support the 1926 General Strike and formed another minority government in 1929 when Labour became the largest party in the Commons. Faced with the economic depression and a financial crisis in 1931, MacDonald was unable to prevent the party splitting over whether to cut unemployment benefits. He went to Buckingham Palace to resign but was persuaded by the King to remain as Prime Minister and set up a National Government. When he did so, only three other Labour ministers supported him and they were all expelled from the Labour Party. In October 1931, MacDonald called an election and the Labour Party was reduced to 46 MPs. MacDonald, was finally Prime Minister of a majority government, but not a Labour one. His ability to influence events and policy was curtailed by the Conservatives and he was eventually eased from power in 1935. He lost his seat in the 1935 election, only regaining another the following year. He died on a cruise in the Atlantic in November, 1937.

Harold Macmillan, 1894–1986

Harold Macmillan, the grandson of Daniel Macmillan, the publisher, was born in 1894. He served on the Western Front in the First World War where he was wounded three times. In 1924 he became a Conservative MP. Unlike many Conservatives at the time, Macmillan was convinced that social reform was needed and that appeasement was wrong. In 1940, Churchill made him a junior minister, and he used his position to campaign to help establish the Tory Reform Group, whose members supported the implementation of the Beveridge Report. In 1951 he became Minister of Housing and achieved his target of 300,000 new houses a year. He was then appointed Minister of Defence in 1954, Foreign Secretary in 1955 and Chancellor of the Exchequer in 1956.

Although partly responsible for the disastrous Suez campaign, Macmillan emerged as the preferred choice as Eden's replacement of both the US government and the Conservative Party and became Prime Minister in 1957. He successfully increased the Conservatives' majority in the 1959 general election and at first the country enjoyed an economic boom, but this was short lived. He also rebuilt Britain's relationship with the USA and sought unsuccessfully to join the European Economic Community. He also began the rapid second phase of British decolonisation, which he announced in his famous 'wind of change' speech in 1960. His government was soon rocked by poor economic results and the Profumo scandal. In October 1963 Macmillan was forced, by ill-health, to resign from office and he was replaced by Sir Alec Douglas-Home. He died in 1986.

John Major, 1943–

Son of a circus performer, and born in Brixton, John Major was a bank executive until 1979. He entered Parliament as a Conservative in 1983 and became Foreign Secretary in 1989 until he took over from Nigel Lawson as Chancellor, later that year. He supported Mrs Thatcher in the contest for the Conservative leadership in 1990, and was able to defeat Michael Heseltine and Douglas Hurd on the second ballot and thus emerge as Prime Minister in November 1990. Despite the poor state of the economy, Major used his classless background and promises of low taxes to narrowly win the 1992 general election. Shortly afterwards, however, sterling was ejected from the European Exchange Rate Mechanism in the Autumn of 1992 and his government never recovered from this debacle. His 'Back to Basics' campaign for greater moral integrity ended in disaster following various sexual and financial wrong doings by several of his ministers. The Conservative Party was divided over the issue of Europe and Major was reduced to resigning as party leader to challenge his critics. The continued privatisation programme of the railways, schools, hospitals and prisons was badly managed and by 1997 Major had lost what support he had enjoyed at the beginning of his premiership. In the general election of that year, he led the Conservatives to their worst defeat since 1832.

Bernard Montgomery, 1887–1976

Bernard Montgomery, the son of a bishop, was born in 1887 and joined the army in 1908. He was wounded on the Western Front in 1914, but was promoted to the rank of general by 1918.

In the Second World War he commanded a division of the British Expeditionary Force in France, and was given command of the eighth army in North Africa in 1942. He was largely responsible for turning the tide of the desert war against Rommel at the battle of El Alamein in October 1942. He continued to command the eighth army when they invaded Sicily and Italy until he was appointed to command the Allied landings in Normandy on D-Day, June 1944. After this success, he was promoted to Field Marshal and led the British army through France, Belgium and Holland, his only failure being the attempt to capture the bridge at Arnhem using paratroop forces. He accepted the surrender of the German forces in the west at Lüneberg Heath in May 1945. After the war he became chief of the imperial general staff and then deputy supreme commander of NATO in Europe. He died in 1976.

Oswald Mosley, 1896–1980

Oswald Mosley was born in 1896. Educated at Sandhurst he fought on the Western Front during the First World War and was invalided out of the war after a plane crash in 1916. Mosley became the youngest MP in the House of Commons in 1918, but he left the Conservative Party and won his seat as an Independent in 1922, before joining the Labour Party.

Mosley was appointed Chancellor of the Duchy of Lancaster in Labour's second government in 1929, and in 1930 Mosley proposed a programme of government intervention to stimulate the economy and reduce the growing numbers of the unemployed. The Labour cabinet rejected these proposals and Mosley resigned from office.

In 1931 Mosley founded the New Party, but it won no seats in the general election that year. In January 1932 Mosley travelled to Italy and met Mussolini and was impressed by the achievements of fascism. When he returned to England he disbanded the New Party and formed the British Union of Fascists (BUF), also known as the 'blackshirts'. The BUF was originally anti-communist and argued for a programme of economic revival similar to the one Mosely had demanded in 1930. By 1934 Mosley was encouraging the BUF to become more anti-semitic and organised provocative marches through Jewish districts in London which led to riots. With the coming of war in 1939, support for the BUF dwindled and in 1940 Oswald Mosley was interned under wartime regulations. In 1947 Mosley formed the Union Movement which advocated British integration in Europe and an end to Commonwealth immigration. Mosley was unsuccessful in his two attempts to enter Parliament. He died in 1980.

Louis Mountbatten, 1900–1979

Louis Mountbatten, son of Louis, Prince of Battenberg and uncle of Queen Elizabeth II's husband, Prince Phillip, was born in 1900 and served in the navy in both the world wars. He became Supreme Allied commander in South East Asia in 1943, organising the defence of Burma and he accepted the surrender of the Japanese forces in Singapore in 1945. He became the last viceroy of India in 1947 and implemented the independence and partition of India and Pakistan. He then became the first Governor-General of India, before returning to the navy as First Sea Lord in 1955 and then Chief of the Defence Staff in 1959. He was assassinated by the Irish National Liberation Army (INLA) while on holiday in Ireland in 1979.

George Orwell (Eric Blair), 1903–50

Eric Blair was born in Bengal, India, in 1903, but was educated in England at Eton. He joined the Indian Imperial Police in Burma in 1922 but resigned when he saw the reality of British imperialism.

Back in England, he adopted the pseudonym, George Orwell and began writing. His novels, articles and books were well received and in 1936 he was commissioned to produce a documentary account of unemployment in the north of England. *The Road to Wigan Pier* established Orwell as one of Britain's leading writers.

Orwell went to Spain in December 1936 to report on the Spanish Civil War, but decided to join the fight against Franco's Nationalists. He was injured and then found himself wanted by the communists during a power struggle among the Republicans, but he was able to escape to France. He wrote about his experiences in *Homage to Catalonia* (1938).

In August 1941 Orwell began work for the BBC, writing scripts for a weekly news commentary on the war. He also wrote for the *Observer* newspaper and *Tribune*, a socialist journal. His next book, *Animal Farm* (1945), influenced by his experiences in Spain was a satire of the Russian communist revolution and upset many on the left. His final novel, written while seriously ill, was a parable on political tyranny in the modern world. *Nineteen Eighty-Four* (1949) had a tremendous impact on politics, language and literature and is regarded as one of the most important books of the century. Orwell died in 1950.

Emmeline Pankhurst, 1858–1928

Emmeline Pankhurst, was born in Manchester in 1858. In 1878, she married a lawyer, Richard Pankhurst, a socialist, and an advocate of women's suffrage. They had four children: Christabel, Sylvia, Frank and Adela and in 1889 they helped form the pressure group, the Women's Franchise League.

In 1895 Emmeline became a Poor Law Guardian and she was shocked to discover how badly poor women were treated and it convinced her that the right to vote was the only way these problems would be solved for women. Richard stood for election to Parliament as a member of the Independent Labour Party, but died in 1898 before he succeeded.

Disillusioned with existing women's political organisations, Emmeline founded the Women's Social and Political Union (WSPU) in 1903. In order to achieve publicity for the cause she began to advocate increasingly confrontational tactics. She moved to London in 1907 and over the next seven years she was repeatedly arrested and imprisoned and used hunger strikes to force the authorities to release her.

When England declared war on Germany in 1914, the WSPU agreed a truce with the government and Mrs Pankhurst threw herself into campaigns to demand that women be allowed to replace men who had left the factories for the front. In 1917 Emmeline and Christabel formed the Women's Party, after Sylvia had been expelled from the WSPU for setting up a working-class organisation for women in East London. The Women's Party became increasingly right-wing, demanding the abolition of trade unions.

After the war, Emmeline joined the Conservative Party, and, much to Sylvia's horror, was adopted as one of their candidates in the East End of London. Mrs Pankhurst died in 1928 before she was able to contest an election.

J.B. Priestley, 1894–1984

John Boynton Priestley was born in Bradford, West Yorkshire in 1894. He served and was injured on the Western Front in the First World War, before studying history at Cambridge. He then became a writer, producing very popular novels such as *The Good Companions, Angel Pavement* and more serious plays like *Time and the Conways, When We Are Married* and *An Inspector Calls*. He also began exploring the divisions in British society in the 1930s, most famously in *English Journey* (1934), an account of his travels through England. During the Second World War Priestley wrote and presented *Postscripts*, which followed the BBC nine o'clock news on Sunday evenings. His talks between June and October 1940, which were outspoken in their criticisms of the governments of the 1930s, were hugely popular with around 40 per cent of the adult population in Britain tuning in. His support for radical social reform was controversial, however, and the BBC chose to end *Postscripts*. Instead in 1941, Priestley helped to set up the socialist Common Wealth Party. After the war Priestley continued to write, and his criticism of Bevan's decision to renounce his support for unilateral nuclear disarmament in 1957 led to the formation of CND (the Campaign for Nuclear Disarmament). J.B. Priestley died in 1984.

Bertrand Russell, 1872–1970

Bertrand Russell, the grandson of the Prime Minister, Lord John Russell, was a gifted mathematician, whose study, *Principia Mathematica* (1910–13), was received as an academic masterpiece. He lost his Cambridge lectureship, due to his opposition to the First World War and his outspoken support for conscientious objectors, and was imprisoned for sedition in 1918. He returned to academic life after the war and became a philosopher, publishing many highly regarded books, such as *History of Western Philosophy* (1948) and winning the Nobel Prize for literature in 1950. Late in life he became an outspoken opponent of nuclear armaments and helped to found the Campaign for Nuclear Disarmament (CND) in 1958. He was again imprisoned for his actions as the first CND president in 1961 and continued to play an active role in public life until he died in 1970 at the age of 98.

Lord Salisbury (Robert Cecil), 1830–1902

Robert Cecil, son of the second Marquis of Salisbury, was born at Hatfield House in 1830 and was educated at Eton and Oxford. He was elected as Conservative MP for Stamford in 1853 and played an important role in the defeat of the Parliamentary Reform Bill proposed by Gladstone in 1866.

In 1868 Robert Cecil succeeded his father as the third Marquis of Salisbury and in 1874 he became Secretary for India under Disraeli. Four years later he became Foreign Secretary.

After Disraeli's death, in 1881, Salisbury became leader of the Conservative Party and became Prime Minister as well as Foreign Secretary in 1885. He held these two offices again between 1886 and 1892 and between 1895 and 1900. In 1900, he retired as Foreign Secretary, while remaining Prime Minister and finally retired from politics in 1902, after ensuring that his nephew Balfour succeeded him. Although an active Foreign Secretary, largely responsible for the policy of 'splendid isolation', he was reluctant to introduce social reforms at home and fearful of the growth of democracy, which threatened the power of the aristocracy. He died later in 1902.

John Smith, 1938–94

John Smith became a lawyer in Edinburgh before he became a Labour MP. A moderate socialist, he supported Neil Kinnock in his campaign to purge the Labour Party of extremism and was appointed shadow Chancellor in 1989. His 'shadow budget' during the 1992 general election campaign, with its implications of higher taxes, is regarded as one of the chief reasons for Labour's narrow defeat, yet he was swiftly elected leader following Kinnock's resignation. He continued Kinnock's work in reforming the party, applying the democratic principle of 'one member, one vote' to all policy issues and the selection of parliamentary candidates, thus removing the bloc voting power of the trades unions. He was seen as a principled and compassionate politician and his sudden death in 1994 genuinely shocked a nation that was increasingly despairing of the Conservative government of John Major.

Philip Snowden, 1864–1937

Philip Snowden, the son of a weaver, was born in West Yorkshire in 1864. Snowden joined the Keighley Liberal Club, before joining the local branch of the Independent Labour Party (ILP) and becoming one of their most celebrated speakers. Snowden was elected as Labour MP for Blackburn in 1906. He lost his seat in 1918 for opposing Britain's involvement in the First World War, but he was re-elected in 1922.

In the first Labour government in January 1924, Snowden became Chancellor of the Exchequer and he reduced taxes on various commodities, but was criticised by members of the Labour Party for not introducing any socialist measures. Snowden returned as Chancellor of the Exchequer in the Labour government of 1929 when he was faced with the world economic depression. An orthodox economist, Snowden's main concern was to produce a balanced budget. As Britain faced a financial crisis in 1931, Snowden suggested that the government should reduce unemployment benefit. This split the party and caused the government to fall. When MacDonald formed a National Government with Conservative and Liberal support, Snowden remained as Chancellor and now introduced the measures that had been rejected by the previous Labour Cabinet. Snowden, along with MacDonald, was expelled from the Labour Party. After the 1931 election, in which he bitterly attacked the policies of his former colleagues, Snowden resigned as Chancellor and took a peerage. He died in 1937.

David Steel, 1938–

David Steel, the son of a Scottish churchman, became Britain's youngest MP when he was elected as a Liberal in 1965. He immediately made a name for himself introducing the measure to legalise abortion in 1967 and he became leader of the Liberal Party in 1976, when he took over from the disgraced Jeremy Thorpe. He agreed the Lib–Lab pact with Callaghan that kept Labour in power after 1977 and then led the Liberals into the Alliance with the Social Democratic Party in 1981. He helped to arrange the merger between the two parties to create the Liberal Democrats in 1988. He campaigned for Scottish devolution throughout his career and in 1999 was elected as an MSP and became the first presiding officer (speaker) of the Scottish Parliament.

Marie Stopes, 1880–1958

Marie Stopes trained as a botanist and worked as a lecturer at Manchester University. In 1918, she published *Married Love* on sexual relationships and *Wise Parenthood* on birth control, both previously taboo subjects. She opened Britain's first birth control clinic in London in 1921 and founded the National Birth Control Association in 1931, which later became the Family Planning Association in 1939. She died in 1958, her work having significantly contributed to an unheralded revolution in social attitudes towards sex and contraception.

Margaret Thatcher, 1925–

Margaret Thatcher was born in Grantham in 1925. Her father was a grocer and a leading local politician. She studied chemistry at Somerville College, Oxford, but then became a barrister, concentrating on tax law. She married Dennis Thatcher, a millionaire, before being elected to the House of Commons in 1953 as a Conservative. She held several ministerial appointments including Education Minister (1970–74), but came to despair of Heath's willingness to abandon strict economic principles. Surprisingly defeating Heath to be elected leader of her party in 1975, she became Britain's first female Prime Minister in 1979. Known as a strong leader and an astute Parliamentary tactician, she knew how to handle disagreement, no matter from which bench it issued. In 1982 she ordered British troops to the Falkland Islands to retake them from Argentina. She took a strong stand against the trade unions during the miner's strike (1984–85), and moved Britain toward privatisation, selling the public utilities to business interests. She also introduced 'rate capping' which effectively took control of expenditures out of the hands of city councils, part of her policies aimed at reducing the influence of local governments. In 1989, she introduced the community charge or 'poll tax'. In 1990, her Cabinet was divided over issues including the European Community which forced her resignation. In 1992, she entered the House of Lords, created Baroness Thatcher of Kesteven. Her memoir of her time as Britain's longest serving twentieth-century Prime Minister, *The Downing Street Years*, was published in 1993.

H.G. Wells, 1866–1946

Herbert George Wells was born in Kent and worked as an apprentice draper before studying science. He became a member of the Fabian society in 1903 and served briefly as minister of information during the First World War and championed the League of Nations after the war. He is most famous for his science fiction novels such as *The Time Machine* (1895), *The Invisible Man* (1897) and *The War of the Worlds* (1898), the last of which is a barely disguised satire on empire-building. His later novels, such as *Love and Mr Lewisham* (1900), *Kipps* (1905), *Ann Veronica* (1909) and *The History of Mr Polly* (1910) are fascinating insights into the world of lower-middle-class Edwardian society and politics.

Ellen Wilkinson, 1891–1947

Ellen Wilkinson joined the Independent Labour Party in 1912 and became an active trade unionist during the First World War. She joined the Communist Party in 1920, but rejoined the Labour Party in 1924, becoming an MP that year. As MP for Jarrow, she led the Jarrow March to London in 1936 and publicised her constituency's plight in her book, *The Town that was Murdered* (1939). After serving as a junior minister during the war, she became Minister of Education under Attlee, implementing the ambitious 1944 Education Act. Such were the efforts she undertook in recruiting and training teachers, organising the building and equipping of schools in order to achieve the raising of the school leaving age to 15, that it is widely believed that her death in 1947 was due to over-work.

Harold Wilson, 1916–95

Wilson was born in Huddersfield, West Yorkshire, in 1916. He attended his local grammar school and then at Oxford he trained as an economist. He was a civil servant during the Second World War and entered Parliament in 1945 and became president of the Board of Trade (1947–51). Wilson, with Bevan, resigned in protest against Gaitskell's cuts in social services. He become Labour Party leader and opposition leader in 1963 following Gaitskell's unexpected death. Under his leadership, the Labour Party narrowly won the 1964 election and he became Prime Minister, going on to increase Labour's majority in the 1966 election. Although his government passed many important social reforms, its economic record was poor and relations with the trade unions deteriorated. He lost the 1970 election to Edward Heath, but won twice in 1974 and became Prime Minister for the second time. His ministry was hindered by economic problems and his party was divided over the issue of Britain's admission to the European Community. Although only 60 in 1976, he was exhausted by the task of keeping his party together and he resigned and was knighted. He became Lord Wilson of Rievaulx in 1983 and died in 1995.

Edward VII, 1841–1910

Edward VII was born in 1841, the eldest son of Queen Victoria. He married Princess Alexandra of Denmark in 1863, who bore him three sons and three daughters. He became king in 1901 and died on 6 May 1910, after a series of heart attacks.

George V, 1865–1936

George V was born in 1865, the second son of Edward VII and Alexandra. He married Mary of Teck in 1893, who bore him four sons and one daughter. He became king in 1910 and died the year after his silver jubilee after a series of attacks of bronchitis, on 20 January 1936.

Edward VIII, 1894–1972

Edward VIII was born in 1894, the eldest son of George V and Mary of Teck. He married an American divorcee, Wallis Simpson, abdicating the throne after reigning for eleven months in 1936 and never being crowned. The couple failed to produce children and Edward died in 1972.

George VI, 1895–1952

George VI was born in 1895, the second son of George V and Mary of Teck. George married Lady Elizabeth Bowes-Lyon in 1923, who bore him two daughters, Elizabeth and Margaret. He unexpectedly became king in 1936, following his elder brother's abdication. Unlike his brother, he remained in London throughout the war, recovering much of the lost prestige of the monarchy. He died from cancer on 6 February 1952.

Elizabeth II, 1926–

Elizabeth II was born in 1926, the eldest daughter of George VI and Elizabeth Bowes-Lyon. She married Philip Mountbatten in 1947 and they had four children: Charles, Prince of Wales, Anne, Andrew and Edward. Elizabeth became Queen in 1952 and she reigned for the rest of the century, becoming the keystone of the post-imperial Commonwealth, but watching the dignity of the monarchy diminish due to the intrusion of the media and the unwise marriages of her three eldest children.

Glossary of Key Terms

abdication crisis   In 1936, shortly after becoming King, Edward VIII announced his intention to marry Mrs Wallis Simpson, an American divorcee. As head of the Church of England, which did not allow divorce at this time, Edward alienated his own government and was advised by the Prime Minister, Stanley Baldwin to abdicate in favour of his brother. He did so in December 1936, after reigning for only 325 days.

Aden crisis   The British protectorate of Aden in the Middle East, a valuable military base, had become a target for Arab nationalists in the early 1960s. British forces clashed with insurgents from the Yemen and local protestors and 57 troops were killed. After a United Nations mission, the British withdrew in 1967 and Aden became the People's Republic of South Yemen.

Agadir crisis   During anti-French riots in Morocco in 1911, the German Kaiser's government sent a gunboat, the 'Panther' to the Moroccan port of Agadir to try to force the French to give compensation for having taken control of the area. The French received strong backing from the British government in resisting this aggressive act, and it encouraged the entente powers to prepare for a possible future war with Germany.

Amritsar massacre   In 1919, following a series of disturbances, Brigadier General Dyer ordered his troops to open fire on a crowd of demonstrators who refused to disperse. 379 men, women and children were killed. After an official enquiry, Dyer was forced to resign and the event helped to discredit British rule in India.

appeasement   British foreign policy designed to avoid risk of war by achieving a compromise. Between 1936 and 1939 the British and French governments sought to appease Hitler's Germany by acquiescing to his demands over the remilitarisation of the Rhineland, the *Anschluss* with Austria and the German claim to the Sudetenland in Czechoslovakia. The policy was abandoned in Spring 1939, following the German invasion of Czechoslovakia, and Poland was given guarantees of independence which led to Britain declaring war on Germany in September 1939.

armistice   An agreement to ceasefire, the term is used to describe the end of the First World War at 11.00 a.m. on 11 November 1918.

austerity   The years immediately following the end of the Second World War are often called the 'age of austerity', as Britain's poor economic position made shortages worse, with bread rationed for the first time. When a severe winter in 1946–47 struck, Britain's coal stocks were exhausted and power cuts took place. The policy is associated with the Chancellor of the Exchequer between 1947 and 1950, Stafford Cripps, who warned that Britain must 'export or die'.

balance of payments   Also known as the Trade Balance, the balance of payments is an economic indicator, produced by deducting the annual costs of imported products and services from the revenue generated by exports. A positive result is described as a trade surplus and brings valuable revenue to the government. In the post-1945 British economy negative results, or trade deficits were far more common.

balance of power   British foreign policy aimed at preventing one continental power from dominating Europe. Britain went to war in 1914 and 1939 partly due to a desire to prevent Germany upsetting the balance of power in Europe.

Bevanite   A supporter of Aneurin Bevan in his struggle in the 1950s to move the Labour Party towards the left, especially on the policies of nuclear disarmament and further nationalisation.

Beveridge Report   A government report on Social Insurance and Allied Services by Sir William Beveridge, published in 1942, which became the blueprint for the post-war Welfare State. The report suggested three basic conditions for governments to enforce: a compulsory system of National Insurance leading to uniform benefits for the sick, the elderly, the unemployed and children and mothers; a comprehensive and free provision of medical service; a high and stable level of employment. The differing attitudes of the political parties towards implementing the Beveridge Report became one of the decisive factors in Labour's victory in the 1945 general election.

'Black and Tans'   Hurriedly recruited from ex-servicemen and named after their improvised uniforms , the 'Black and Tans' were additional forces sent to Ireland to crush the nationalist resistance after 1918. They soon became notorious for their violent tactics and helped to finally discredit British rule in the south of Ireland.

Blackshirts   Members of the British Union of Fascists, founded by Sir Oswald Mosley in 1932, so called, due to their paramilitary clothing, based on Italian fascism.

Blitz   Following their defeat in the Battle of Britain, the German airforce turned to attacking industrial and civilian targets in Britain, launching nightly raids on most major cities between September 1940 and May 1941. British morale failed to collapse, however, and the worst of the Blitz ended when the German forces invaded the USSR in June 1941.

Blitzkrieg   'Lightning war': the type of tactics employed by the German army between 1940 and 1942, which relied on surprise and swift motorised advance and brought the Germans their initial victories in Europe and North Africa.

blockade   As it had the strongest navy in the world in the early twentieth century, Britain used a blockade in the First World War, restricting the imports to Germany and her allies and isolating her diplomatically and financially. This policy severely weakened Germany's ability to fight and contributed to the eventual allied victory. German blockade tactics, using submarines (known as U-boats), caused shortages in Britain but failed to seriously damage her ability to fight. The Germans repeated the tactic in the Second World War, and it threatened Britain far more, given her isolation in Europe, but improved tactics and technology allowed Britain to survive.

'Bloody Sunday'   On 30 January 1972, an unauthorised civil rights demonstration in Derry in Northern Ireland was stopped by the British army. British troops claimed to have been fired on and killed 14 demonstrators. The ensuing government enquiry excused the British soldiers from blame, but the nationalists refused to accept its findings. A further enquiry into the event was launched by Tony Blair's government in 1998.

Campaign for Nuclear Disarmament (CND)   The Campaign for Nuclear Disarmament originated after a protest march to Aldermaston nuclear base in 1958. It grew in influence in the Labour Party, until, in 1983, the party included a policy of nuclear disarmament in its manifesto. The disastrous showing of the party in that year effectively ended the group's political influence, though it continued to garner much important support until the end of the Cold War.

Clause IV   The fourth clause of the Labour Party's constitution, written in 1918, committed the party to ensuring, 'the common ownership of the means of production, distribution and exchange' and, in effect, committed the party to a comprehensive policy of nationalisation. Hugh Gaitskell attempted to re-write it in the 1950s, but was defeated by the Party Conference. After Neil Kinnock's acceptance of Mrs Thatcher's programme of privatisation in the 1980s, the policy was a dead letter and was eventually re-written in less precise terms by Tony Blair as a symbolic re-launch of Labour as 'New Labour' in 1995.

Cold War   Period of tension between the communist countries dominated by the Soviet Union and the West that began in the mid-1940s and which continued in varying degrees of intensity until the fall of the communist regimes of Eastern Europe in 1989. It was marked by an arms race between the two blocs, a series of international summits, the intervention by both sides in the internal affairs of many nations across the world and one limited military confrontation in Korea between 1950 and 1953.

collectivism   Policies aimed to promote social equality and for the benefit of all are described as 'collectivist'. The term is often used to describe government social reforms of the early and mid-twentieth century.

Common Agricultural Policy (CAP)   A long-standing policy of the European Community which guarantees prices for agricultural produce, but which is seen as a subsidy for inefficient farmers (particularly the French) which keeps prices high and prevents fair competition from outside Europe.

'coupon election' of 1918   In the election of December 1918, swiftly called after the armistice, the coalition government of Conservatives and Liberals were able to secure victory by issuing an endorsement signed by Lloyd George (known as 'the coupon') to loyal candidates in opposition to rebel Liberals, Conservatives and the Labour Party.

Détente   The decline in tension in the confrontation between the NATO powers and the countries of the Warsaw Pact that followed the Cuban Missile Crisis of 1962 and which lasted until 1979.

devaluation   The decision to reduce the value of a currency against other currencies. This can help stimulate an economy by making exports abroad cheaper and thereby more competitive. The pound (called sterling on the international finance market) was effectively devalued during both the world wars, as well as in the financial crisis of 1931, when the gold standard was abandoned. In the years since 1945, Labour governments were forced to devalue the pound in 1948 and 1967, damaging their reputation for financial competence. The Conservatives also had to effectively devalue the British currency in 1992, when Britain was forced out of the Exchange Rate Mechanism (ERM).

devolution   The process whereby the nations of the United Kingdom are allowed to elect their own regional assemblies with political powers. The Stormont parliament in Northern Ireland was the longest lasting example of devolution in the twentieth century, lasting from 1921 until 1972. During the 1970s, Scotland and Wales demanded some degree of autonomy and referendums were held in both regions in March 1979, but in both cases the vote in favour of devolution failed to reach the required level. The Labour government of Tony Blair reintroduced the process of devolution, and in 1999, a majority of voters supported the establishment of regional assemblies in Scotland, Wales and Northern Ireland, leading to the fulfillment of devolution at the end of the century.

dilution   During the First World War, under the Treasury Agreement of 1915, trade unions allowed complex skilled tasks to be broken down into simpler stages or 'diluted', so that women and unskilled workers could help boost production of war materials. Dilution was still unpopular however and women workers suffered victimisation and the issue caused strikes, especially in the shipbuilding industry.

disestablishment   The separation of Church and state, in Britain, the ending of state support for the Anglican Church. The Church in Ireland had already been disestablished by 1900, and the Church in Wales was disestablished in 1920. The Church in England continued to be officially supported by the state, until the end of the century, despite calls for it to be disestablished as Britain became more multi-cultural.

Dominion   A member of the British Empire with control of their internal affairs, such as New Zealand, South Africa, Canada and Australia. After the 1931 Statute of Westminster, they had complete legal and diplomatic independence, although the British monarch remained head of state.

Eire   Name given independent southern Ireland from 1937 to 1948, while it was a Dominion within the British Commonwealth.

'entente cordiale'   From the French meaning 'cordial understanding', it describes Britain's relationship with France before, during and after the First World War. It was initiated by Edward VII in 1904 in the face of German aggression. It formed the basis of the Anglo-French alliance that lasted until France's defeat in 1940. The French, British and Russian forces in the First World War were often called the 'entente powers'.

European Monetary Union (EMU)   The economic policy of the European Union, which attempts to align the values of the various member countries' currencies and then replace them with a common, single currency. This policy became reality with the launch of the 'euro' currency in 1999, but Britain refused to participate.

eurosceptic   Term used to describe an opponent of greater European unity. Usually used to describe those Conservative MPs who objected to John Major signing the Maastricht Treaty in 1991 and who undermined his leadership in the following Parliament.

Exchange Rate Mechanism (ERM)   The first stage towards European Monetary Union, the ERM attempted to align the various currencies of the EU members from 1979. Britain refused to participate until 1989, when she joined, much against Mrs Thatcher's wishes. Britain's membership only lasted until 1992, when the over-valuation of the pound caused a financial crisis and Britain was forced to pull out of the ERM, after spending £4 billion in a day in an effort to stay in. This hardened British attitudes against the EMU process.

Fabian Society   Socialist intellectual group founded in 1884. Early members included George Bernard Shaw and Beatrice and Sidney Webb. The society helped to found the Labour Party and became a research and pressure group within the party.

fourteen points   The war aims of US President Woodrow Wilson, published in January 1918, which formed the basis for the armistice of November 1918, and which included the aim of national self-determination – the right of peoples of similar racial characteristics to live in separate nations.

free trade   The teaching of Adam Smith and David Ricardo which held that the state should not interfere in economic policy. Also called 'laissez faire' or free market economics, it was traditional British policy in 1900 until challenged by Joseph Chamberlain in 1903 and abandoned during the First World War. It was reintroduced as a part of Thatcherism and is an important element of 'globalisation' (q.v.).

Gaitskellite   A supporter of Hugh Gaitskell, the Labour leader from 1955 to 1962 who resisted Bevan's attempts to move the Labour Party towards the left, especially on the policies of nuclear disarmament and further nationalisation.

'Gang of Four'   David Owen, Roy Jenkins, Shirley Williams and William Rodgers. These four former Labour ministers left the Labour Party in 1981 in protest to the leftward shift of the Party, and founded the Social Democratic Party

globalisation   The economic principle of the late 1990s, which saw the relocation of manufacturing and some basic services to less developed countries, to save costs, and saw the emergence of a world market, using modern transport and communications systems such as the internet.

gold standard   If a country's currency has a fixed value against gold, it is described as being on the gold standard. Britain's gold standard led to the pound sterling becoming the common international unit of exchange until 1914, when the economic disruption caused by the war led Britain to abandon its standard. In an attempt to recapture pre-war prosperity, Winston Churchill returned Britain to the Gold Standard in 1925, but this actually worsened the effects of the depression of 1919–31 and stimulated a financial crisis in 1931 that finally forced Britain to abandon the gold standard.

Great Depression   The period of economic recession which produced unprecedented unemployment which followed the collapse of the US economy in the Wall Street Crash of 1929. Although the British economy began to recover by 1933, certain parts of the economy, such as staple industries, were still depressed until 1939.

Home Rule   The policy of granting some degree of self-government to Ireland, which would include an Irish Parliament, which won the support of the Liberal leader, William Gladstone in 1885. Home Rule Bills were introduced in 1886, 1893 and 1914, but none reached the statute book.

hunger marches   During the Great Depression (q.v.), the Communist National Unemployed Workers' movement (NUWM) organised mass marches of unemployed men to London to demand government action. These took places throughout the inter-war years, but the best known example was that from the shipbuilding town of Jarrow in 1936.

Independent Labour Party (ILP)   Founded in 1893, this group of socialists helped to form the Labour Representation Committee in 1900. They maintained a separate organisation, however, as their aim of common ownership of industry was not always supported by the Labour Party. Led by James Maxton after the First World War, their influence on the party was not great and they were absorbed into the main Party following Maxton's death in 1946 and the nationalisation programme of the Attlee government.

International Monetary Fund (IMF)   A central fund of capital created in 1947 to prevent countries suffering serious balance of payments (q.v.) problems from having to cut basic social services. The Labour government of 1976 negotiated a £4 billion loan in 1976, but was forced to drastically cut public expenditure, thus preparing the ground for the confrontation with public sector unions in the 'winter of discontent' (q.v.).

iron curtain   Phrase used by Winston Churchill in 1946 to describe the frontier between capitalist and Soviet dominated countries in Europe and which was used for this purpose for the rest of the Cold War (q.v.)

Keynesianism   The economic policy favoured by British governments from the Second World War until the mid-1970s. These involved the government attempting to stimulate the economy by increasing benefits and wages to encourage consumption, as well as intervening in the economy to produce what was needed both at home and for export, and thus avoiding crippling depressions such as that of 1929–33. Keynesian economics were first abandoned by the Labour chancellor, Denis Healey in 1976, in the face of serious inflation, rising unemployment and a sterling crisis, but the full implementation of the alternative, monetarism (q.v.) did not take place until Mrs Thatcher's first government of 1979–83.

Liberal Unionists   The group of Liberals who opposed Gladstone's policy of Home Rule (q.v.). led by Joseph Chamberlain and who had accepted government office under Lord Salisbury in 1895 in what was properly termed a 'unionist' government. They were divided over Chamberlain's call for tariff reform (q.v.) and were eventually absorbed into the Conservative Party in 1912.

Lib–Lab pact (1977)   When the majority of James Callaghan's Labour government fell to one in 1977, the Liberals promised to support Labour in a vote of 'no-confidence' forced by the Conservatives, in exchange for a veto over proposed legislation. The removal of the pact by the Liberals in 1978, helped to bring down the Labour government and bring Mrs Thatcher to power.

Loyalist   A member of the Protestant community of Northern Ireland, who favoured the province's continued position within the United Kingdom. Loyalist groups included democratic politicians as well as paramilitaries, both of whom provoked the 'troubles' by their treatment of the Catholic minority in the province.

Maastricht Treaty   An agreement on greater European integration signed in December 1991, which provoked huge rifts in the Conservative government of John Major for the following six years. Major achieved an opt-out of the proposed single currency (European Monetary Union) and the Social Chapter, which attempted to regulate working conditions and wages, but even so, the government was so divided that it was only able to ratify the treaty in Parliament by one vote.

When Labour under Tony Blair entered power, they signed up to the Social Chapter, but not to the EMU.

mandated territories   Known as 'mandates' these were former German or Turkish colonies administered by Britain and France on behalf of the League of Nations. Britain's mandates included Palestine.

monetarism   The economic policy first introduced under Labour in 1976, but fully implemented by Mrs Thatcher's first government. The policy was designed to prevent inflation damaging economic performance by limiting the amount of money in circulation. Governments could do this by cutting expenditure and raising borrowing rates and introducing a free market, instead of interfering in economic policy.

nationalisation   Taking an industry into public (in other words government) ownership with or without compensation to the previous private owners. The Labour Party was committed to nationalisation, under Clause IV of its constitution and nationalised a number of utilities in its first majority government of 1945–51. The policy was reversed by the process of privatisation (q.v.) under Margaret Thatcher's second government (1983–87).

Nationalist   Members of the Northern Ireland community who favour a united Ireland. They include both democratic politicians and paramilitary extremists who attacked the Ulster police and the British army forces based in Northern Ireland

New Liberalism   The social reforming approach of the Liberal governments of 1905–15, which contrasted with the laissez-faire attitude of the nineteenth century Liberal Party. It is seen either as a genuine desire to improve living conditions or as a last-ditch attempt to counter the rise of the socialist Labour party.

'New Labour'   The attempt by Tony Blair to distance the Labour Party from its previous, unpopular policies following his election as leader of the party in 1994. Blair's successful ditching of Clause IV of the constitution was the first symbolic step towards creating a party which advocated a far less socialist economic policy than its predecessors. The scale of the 1997 general election victory was seen as a vindication for this dramatic policy change.

Non-Conformist   A member of a non-Anglican Protestant church, such as Methodism, Baptism or Congregationalism. They opposed the influence of the Anglican church over issues such as education.

North Atlantic Treaty Organisation (NATO)   Alliance formed in 1949 between Western European countries and the USA to defend Europe against further Soviet expansion. The collapse of the Soviet Union in 1991 did not lead to its demise, however and it remained a powerful force, especially in its intervention against Serbia in the Kosovo conflict of 1999.

permissive society   The relaxation of traditional moral authority in the 1960s, marked by the reforms of the censorship, abortion and divorce laws, the decriminalisation of homosexuality and the ending of the death penalty.

poll tax   The local government tax, properly known as the 'community charge' introduced into Scotland in 1989 and into the rest of Britain in 1990, which obliged all over 18s to pay the same rate of tax, regardless of income. This provoked mass non-payment, the worst rioting for eight years and, in part, the fall of Margaret Thatcher as Prime Minister.

privatisation   In effect, reversing the policy of nationalisation. This was carried out by the Conservative governments after 1979, when shares were sold in previously publicly owned corporations, such as British Gas and British Telecom. It also involved the contracting out of services previously offered by public authorities, such as hospital cleaning and the provision of school meals, and the opening up of services to competition, to prevent inefficiency and reduce government expenditure.

Profumo affair   Political scandal of 1963 that ended the career of the Conservative War Minister, John Profumo and seriously damaged the government of Harold Macmillan. Profumo denied having an affair with a prostitute called Christine Keeler, who had also had a relationship with a Russian diplomat and was backed by the Prime Minister. When it emerged that Profumo had lied he was forced to resign.

protectionism   The economic system of protecting domestic industries by imposing taxes on imports, the opposite of 'free trade' (q.v.). Joseph Chamberlain championed 'imperial protection' in 1903, but import duties on foreign goods were not imposed until 1932.

Raj   Meaning literally 'rule', this refers to the period of direct British sovereignty over India from 1858 to 1947.

Social Chapter   Section of the Maastricht Treaty of the European Union of 1991 that John Major's British government refused to accept and from which they negotiated an 'opt-out' as it appeared to prescribe conditions for employees in contradiction of the Conservative ideology of the free market. It was accepted by Tony Blair's Labour government in 1997.

splendid isolation   Description of the mode of foreign policy most associated with Lord Salisbury, who attempted to keep Britain free from international commitments, especially those which might drag Britain into a European war. It was abandoned after Salisbury resigned as Prime Minister and Britain signed an alliance with Japan in 1902.

Suffragette   A nickname for a supporter of the Women's Social and Political Union (WSPU) which supported militant action such as damage to property and illegal demonstrations in order to win the right to vote in general elections for women.

Suffragist   A nickname for a supporter of the National Union of Women's Suffrage Societies (NUWSS) which supported constitutional methods of protest in order to extend the right to vote to include all adults, including women.

'sweated' labour   Workers in trades such as sewing, flower-making and box-making, usually female, children or immigrants who were severely underpaid for their work and worked in poor conditions. After investigation, the Liberal government of Herbert Asquith introduced the *Trade Boards Act* in 1909, which set minimum wages.

syndicalism   The idea that workers could overthrow capitalism through organised mass industrial action, rather than campaigning for improvements through individual trade unions. The ideas of syndicalism were thought to have been partly responsible for the wave of industrial unrest in the years before the First World War and the general strike of 1926.

Tariff Reform   Campaign for the introduction of import duties on goods produced outside the British Empire, led after 1903 by Joseph Chamberlain, former Colonial Secretary.

temperance movement   Movement to limit or ban the sale of alcohol, often championed by non-conformist religious groups. Temperance campaigners were influential in the Liberal Party in the early years of the twentieth century.

Thatcherism   The policies associated with Margaret Thatcher, despite her lack of consistent support for these when in office. The term usually indicates economic policies of monetarism (q.v.), privatisation (q.v.) and support for the free market, but can also indicate a rigid moral attitude to law and order, opposition to the power of the European Union and a vigorous defence of British interests abroad. Those who supported her ideas, during and after her premiership, such as Michael Portillo and John Redwood, are referred to as 'Thatcherite'.

'Troubles'   Both the Anglo-Irish War of 1918–21 and the civil unrest and terrorism in Northern Ireland after 1968, in which conflict between loyalist (q.v.) and nationalist (q.v.) forces has lead to the involvement of British troops and terrorist attacks on the mainland of Britain.

Ulster   The area of north Ireland settled by Scottish Protestants in the seventeenth century, which was the centre for resistance to Home Rule. The Loyalist (q.v.) Protestants of Ulster armed themselves after the *Third Home Rule Bill* was introduced in 1912 and were eventually granted their own devolved parliament, but still within the United Kingdom, when Ireland was partitioned in 1921. Ulster's separate status was never accepted by the independent south and was the focus of terrorist activity. It also was the site of continued discrimination against Catholics. These two factors eventually led to the collapse of the Ulster parliament in 1972 and direct rule from London. In 1998, both Loyalists and Nationalists (q.v.) agreed to accept elections to a new devolved parliament, the Northern Ireland Assembly.

Unilateral Declaration of Independence (UDI)   In 1965, Ian Smith's white minority government of South Rhodesia declared independence from Britain to prevent power-sharing with the black majority. Britain refused to accept this and the United Nations condemned UDI as it led to a protracted civil war in the region. In 1980, Britain brokered an agreement at Lancaster House which led to free elections and the appointment of Robert Mugabe as Prime Minister.

viceroy   A ruler who has the authority of the monarch within a dependent country or colony of an Empire. The viceroy of India effectively ran this vast area, with little accountability to Parliament.

Welfare State   The system of comprehensive social welfare begun by the Liberal Government of Asquith between 1908 and 1914, which William Beveridge recommended should be extended ('from the cradle to the grave') during the Second World War. Under Attlee's Labour government, a true Welfare State with free health provision, welfare benefits for all, subsidised housing and free secondary schooling was created. The cost of supporting this system remained a contentious issue for the rest of the century, particularly under Margaret Thatcher and John Major's Conservative governments when it was perceived to be in danger from government reform.

'wet'   Term of abuse applied by Thatcherites to describe Conservatives who favoured a more traditional, mixed economic policy and who wished to preserve the Welfare State (q.v.) in its current form. When she began to introduce her monetarist economic policies after 1980, Thatcher removed those she viewed as 'wets', such as Ian Gilmour and James Prior, from positions where they could influence her economic policy.

'winter of discontent'   The months between October and April 1978–79, when the Labour government's wage restraint policy was undermined by a series of public sector strikes, often unofficial, which were made worse by a particularly harsh winter. The confrontation between unions and government was depicted by the Conservatives and their allies in the media as a crisis of governance and the anti-trade union feeling generated by it helped to defeat Callaghan's government in the 1979 general election. Memories of the 'winter of discontent' remained a potent propaganda weapon for the Conservatives throughout the 1980s.

Bibliography

Primary sources

The Institute for Contemporary British History (ICBH) helped in the publication of the following two volume collection of primary sources:

Butler, L. and Jones, H. (1994) *Britain in the Twentieth Century Vol 1 1900–1939*, London: Heinemann.
Butler, L. and Jones, H. (1995) *Britain in the Twentieth Century Vol 2 1939–1970*, London: Heinemann.

The Manchester University Press series, Documents in Contemporary History is also extremely useful:

Baylis, J. (1997) *Anglo-American Relations: the Enduring Alliance*, Manchester: MUP.
Booth, A. (1996) *British Economic Development since 1945*, Manchester: MUP.
Fielding, S. (1997) *The Labour Party since 1951*, Manchester: MUP.
Greenwood, S. (1996) *Britain and European Integration since the Second World War*, Manchester: MUP.
Jeffreys, K. (1996) *War and Reform: British Politics during the Second World War*, Manchester: MUP.
Jones, M. and Lowe, R. (2002) *From Beveridge to Blair: The First Fifty Years of Britain's Welfare State 1948–98*, Manchester: MUP.
Negrine, R. (1998) *Television and the Press since 1945*, Manchester: MUP.
Ovendale, R. (1996) *British Defence Policy since 1945*, Manchester: MUP.
Panikos, P. (1999) *The Impact of Immigration: a Documentary History of the Effects and Experiences of Immigrants in Britain since 1945*, Manchester: MUP.
Smith, H. (1996) *Britain in the Second World War: A Social History*, Manchester: MUP.
Wrigley, C. (1997) *British Trade Unions, 1945–1995*, Manchester: MUP.

The best source on the Second World War comes from the collection of the mass-observation records on the Blitz, edited by one its founders:

Harrisson, T. (1976) *Living through the Blitz*, London: Collins.

The following collection covers British foreign policy in the Middle East from the 1930s to 1968 as well as the Suez crisis itself:

Gorst, A. and Johnman, L. (1997) *The Suez Crisis*, London: Routledge.

Hodder's 'History at Source' series includes one very useful collection for this period:

Brendon, V. (1996) *The Edwardian Age (History at Source)*, London: Hodder.

Very useful are the Government's own published statistics and their annual summary of social trends, which comes with an invaluable commentary.

Office for National Statistics (1900–2000) *Annual Abstract of Statistics*, London: HMSO.
Office for National Statistics (1970–2000) *Social Trends*, London: HMSO.

The HMSO has also published a series of documents on controversial topics in recent British history called Uncovered Editions:

The Amritsar Massacre: General Dyer in the Punjab 1919
Bloody Sunday 1972: Lord Widgery's Report
The Boer War: Ladysmith and Mafeking 1899–1902
British Battles of World War I 1914–1915
Dealing with Adolf Hitler 1939
D-Day to VE Day: General Eisenhower's Report 1944–45
Defeat at Gallipoli: The Dardanelles Part 2 1915–16
The Irish Uprising, 1914–1921
Kitchener and Churchill – The Dardanelles, Part 1 1914–15
The Loss of the Titanic 1912
John Profumo and Christine Keeler 1963
Tragedy at Bethnal Green 1943
War 1914: Punishing the Serbs
War in the Falklands, 1982

Secondary sources

General

Clarke, P. (1996) *Hope and Glory: Britain 1900–1990*, London: Penguin.
Cook, C. and Stevenson, J. (1996) *The Longman Handbook of Modern British History*, London: Longman.
Glynn, A. and Booth, A. (1995) *Modern Britain: An Economic and Social History*, London: Routledge.
Gourvish, T. and O'Day, A. (eds) (1991) *Britain since 1945*, Basingstoke: Macmillan.
Irwin, J.L. (1994) *Modern Britain: an Introduction*, (3rd edn), London: Routledge.
Marwick, A. (2000) *A History of the Modern British Isles, 1914–1999: Circumstances, Events and Outcomes*, Oxford: Blackwell.
Morgan, K.O. (1990) *The People's Peace: British History 1945–1990*, Oxford: OUP.
Oakland, J. (2001) *Contemporary Britain*, London: Routledge.
Pearce, M. and Stewart, G. (2001) *British Political History, 1867–2001*, (3rd edn) London: Routledge.
Pugh, M. (1994) *State and Society: British Political and Social History 1870–1992*, London: Edward Arnold.
Taylor, A.J.P. (1965), *English History 1914–1945*, Oxford: OUP.
Tiratsoo, N. (ed.) (1998) *From Blitz to Blair*, London: Phoenix.

Politics (general)

Boyce, D.G. (1996) *The Irish Question and British Politics 1868–1996*, (2nd edn), Basingstoke: Macmillan.
Charmley, J. (1996) *A History of Conservative Politics,1900–1996*, Basingstoke: Macmillan.
Childs, D. (2000) *Britain since 1945: Progress and Decline*, (5th edn), London: Routledge.
Dorey, P. (1995) *British Politics since 1945*, Oxford: Blackwell.
Jeffreys, K. (1997) *The Labour Party since 1945*, Basingstoke: Macmillan.
Lee, S.J. (1996) *Aspects of British Political History 1914–1995*, London: Routledge.
Pelling, H. (1996) *A Short History of the Labour Party*, (11th edn), Basingstoke: Macmillan.
Phillips, G. (1992) *The Rise of the Labour Party 1893–1931*, London: Routledge.
Porter, B. (1994) *Britannia's Burden: the Political Evolution of Modern Britain, 1851–1990*, London: Edward Arnold.
Powell, D. (1998) *British Politics and the Labour Question 1868–1990*, Basingstoke: Macmillan.
Pugh, M. (1993) *The Making of Modern British Politics*, (2nd edn), Oxford: Blackwell.

Searle, G.R. (1992) *The Liberal Party: Triumph and Disintegration, 1886–1929*, Basingstoke: Macmillan.
Seldon, A. and Ball, S. (eds) (1994) *Conservative Century: the Conservative Party since 1900*, Oxford: OUP.
Sked, A. and Cook, C. (1993) *Post-War Britain: A Political History*, Harmondsworth: Penguin.
Spittles, B. (1995) *Britain since 1960*, Basingstoke: Macmillan.
Stevenson, J. (1993) *Third Party Politics since 1945: Liberals, Alliance and Liberal Democrats*, Oxford: Blackwell.
Thorpe, A. (1997) *A History of the British Labour Party*, Basingstoke: Macmillan.

Social welfare

Gladstone, D. (1999) *The Twentieth-Century Welfare State*, Basingstoke: Macmillan.
Glennerster, H. (1995) *British Social Policy since 1945*, Oxford: Blackwell.
Lowe, R. (1993) *The Welfare State in Britain since 1945*, Basingstoke: Macmillan.
Thane, P. (1996) *The Foundations of the Welfare State*, London: Longman.

The First World War

Constantine, S. (ed.) (1995) *Britain and the First World War*, London: Arnold.
De Groot, G. (1996) *Blighty*, London: Longman.
Marwick, A. (1991) *The Deluge*, (2nd edn) London: Palgrave.

1918–39

Constantine, S. (1991) *Lloyd George*, London: Routledge.
Laybourn, K. (1996) *The General Strike*, Manchester: MUP.
Riddell, N. (1999) *Labour in Crisis: The Second Labour Government, 1929–31*, Manchester: MUP.
Skidelsky, R. (1970) *Politicians and the Slump*, Harmondsworth: Penguin.
Stevenson, J. (1977) *The Slump: Society and Politics During the Depression*, London: Cape.

The Second World War

Addison, P. (1994) *The Road to 1945*, London: Pimlico.
Barnett, C. (1986) *The Audit of War*, London: Pan.
Calder, A. (1969) *The People's War*, London, Pimlico.
Calder, A. (1991) *The Myth of the Blitz*, London: Pimlico.
Fielding, S. (ed.) (1995) *'England arise!': The Labour Party and Popular Politics in 1940s Britain*, Manchester: MUP.
Lamb, R. (1993) *Churchill as War Leader: Right or Wrong*, London: Bloomsbury.

1945–79

Barnett, C. (1995) *The Lost Victory*, Basingstoke: Macmillan.
Hennessy, P. (1992) *Never Again: Britain 1945–51*, London: Hutchinson.
Hennessy, P. (2002) *Having It So Good: Britain 1951–1964*, London: Cape.
Pearce, R. (1994) *Attlee's Labour Governments, 1945–51* London: Routledge.

1979–2000

Evans, E. (1997) *Thatcher and Thatcherism*, London: Routledge.
Young, H. (1993) *One of Us: a Biography of Margaret Thatcher*, London: Pan.

Foreign policy

Bartlett, C.J. (1994) *British Foreign Policy in the Twentieth Century*, Basingstoke: Macmillan.
Brown, J.M. and Louis, W.R. (eds) (1999) *The Oxford History of the British Empire – Vol. 4: The Twentieth Century*, Oxford: OUP.
Carlton, D. (1988) *Britain and the Suez Crisis*, Oxford: Blackwell.
Darwin, J. (1991) *The End of the British Empire: the Historical Debate*, Oxford: Blackwell.
Dockrill, M.L. (1988) *British Defence since 1945*, Oxford: Basil Blackwell.
Fraser, T.G. (1999) *Ireland in Conflict, 1922–1998*, London: Routledge.
George, S. (1994) *An Awkward Partner: Britain in the European Community*, (2nd edn), Oxford: OUP.
Greenwood, S. (1999) *Britain and the Cold War, 1945–1991*, Basingstoke: Macmillan.
Henig, R. (1985) *The Origins of the Second World War 1933–1939*, London: Routledge.
Henig, R. (1995) *Versailles and After 1919–1933*, (2nd edn) London: Routledge.
Henig, R. (2001) *The Origins of the First World War*, (3rd ed), London: Routledge.
Kent, J. (1993) *British Imperial Strategy and the Origins of the Cold War*, Leicester, Leicester University Press.
Louis, W.R. and Owen, R. (1989) *Suez 1956: the Crisis and its Consequences*, Oxford: Clarendon.
McDonagh, F. (1998) *Neville Chamberlain, Appeasement and the British Road to War*, Manchester: MUP.
McIntyre, W.D. (1998) *British Decolonisation 1946–1997*, Basingstoke: Macmillan.
Ovendale, R. (1998) *Anglo-American Relations in the Twentieth Century*, Basingstoke: Macmillan.
Painter, D. (1999) *The Cold War*, London: Routledge.
Porter, B. (1996) *The Lion's Share: a Short History of British Imperialism, 1850–1995*, (3rd edn), London: Longman.
Young, H. (1998) *This Blessed Plot: Britain and Europe from Churchill to Blair*, Basingstoke: Macmillan.

Society

Aldgate, A. (1994) *Britain can take it: the British Cinema in the Second World War*, (2nd edn), Edinburgh : Edinburgh University Press.
Bourke, J. (1994) *Working Class Cultures in Britain 1860–1960*, London: Routledge.
Bruley, S. (2000) *Women's Century of Change*, Basingstoke: Macmillan.
Cannadine, D. (1992) *The Decline and Fall of the British Aristocracy*, Basingstoke: Macmillan.
Constantine, S. (1983) *Social Conditions in Britain 1918–1939*, London: Routledge.
Durham, M. (2000) *The Permissive Society*, Basingstoke: Macmillan.
Fowler, D. (2000) *Youth Culture in the Twentieth Century*, Basingstoke: Macmillan.
Goulbourne, H. (1998) *Race relations in Britain since 1945*, Basingstoke: Macmillan.
Harris, J. (1993) *Private Lives, Public Spirit: Britain 1870–1914*, London: Penguin.
Holmes, C. (1988) *John Bull's Island: Immigration and British Society 1871–1971*, Basingstoke: Macmillan.
Holt, R. (ed) (1990) *Sport and the Working Classes in Modern Britain*, Manchester: MUP.
Kirkham, P. and Thoms, D. (eds) (1995) *War culture: Social Change and Changing Experience in World War Two Britain*, London: Lawrence & Wishart.
Layton-Henry, Z. (1992) *The Politics of Immigration*, Oxford: Blackwell.
Lewis, J. (1992) *Women in Britain since 1945*, Oxford: Blackwell.
Marwick, A. (1991) *Culture in Britain since 1945*, Oxford: Blackwell.
Marwick, A. (1998) *British Society since 1945*, (3rd edn) London: Penguin.
Marwick, A. (1998) *The Sixties*, Oxford: Blackwell.

Obelkevich, J. and Catterall, P. (eds) (1994) *Understanding Post-War British Society*, London: Routledge.

Page, N. (1990) *The Thirties in Britain*, Basingstoke: Macmillan.

Pugh, M. (1992) *Women and Women's Movements in Britain 1914–1959*, Basingstoke: Macmillan.

Roberts, E. (1995) *Women and Families*, Oxford: Blackwell.

Seymour-Ure, B. (1991)*The British Press and Broadcasting since 1945*, Oxford: Blackwell.

Spencer, I. (1997) *British Immigration Policy since 1939*, London: Routledge.

Stevenson, J. (1990) *British Society 1914–1945*, London: Penguin.

Economics

Cairncross, A. (1995) *The British Economy since 1945*, (2nd edn), Oxford: Blackwell.

Middleton, R. (2000) *The British Economy since 1945: Engaging with the Debate*, Basingstoke: Macmillan.

Pollard, S. (1992) *The Development of the British Economy*, (4th edn), London: Arnold.

Pollard, S. (1997) *The International Economy since 1945*, London: Routledge.

Tranter, N.L. (1996) *British Population in the Twentieth Century*, Basingstoke: Macmillan.

Index